FROM JESUS TO PAUL

FROM JESUS TO PAUL

By Joseph Klausner

Translated from the Hebrew by
WILLIAM F. STINESPRING

BEACON PRESS   BOSTON

TRANSLATOR'S PREFACE

Jesus of Nazareth appeared in English in 1925. Written in modern Hebrew by the author of the present work, and translated into English by Dr. Herbert Danby, then Residentiary Canon of St. George's Cathedral Church, Jerusalem, now Regius Professor of Hebrew at Oxford University, *Jesus of Nazareth* marked a new departure in Jewish-Christian co-operative scholarship. As a Christian student of the ancient Hebrew language and literature, I was deeply interested in the fact that such a book could be written in modern Hebrew by a Jew, and then be translated into English by a Christian. It seemed to me that, in the interests of mutual understanding, more Christian scholars should study Jewish literature, and more Jewish scholars should study Christian literature—especially the respective literatures of the first several Christian centuries, when disagreement between the two faiths was so sharp. Such study, carried on in a strictly friendly and scientific spirit, should, I felt, do much to lay a foundation for better relations between Jews and Christians in the future. As outstanding examples, attention could be called to Hermann Strack and George Foot Moore, who were no mean Christian Talmudists, and to Claude G. Montefiore, that splendid Jewish interpreter of the New Testament. In pursuance of this plan, it seemed that Christian scholars should become better Hebraists; Canon Danby had certainly shown the way.

After a time, it was my happy privilege to go to Palestine on archaeological business and to stay for several years. I met both Dr. Klausner and Dr. Danby, and also worked at reading and speaking modern Hebrew. Hence the present undertaking.

A few words about method and viewpoint may be in order. The reader is asked to reread Danby's remarks at the beginning of *Jesus of Nazareth* about the problems of translating modern Hebrew into English, to save repetition here. This translation is not intended to be a model of English style; I only hope that it will be easily understood. In certain cases, I have kept some of the author's Semiticisms and other peculiarities of style in order to convey the flavor of the original.

In quotations the three periods indicate, as is usual in English, omitted words or phrases; elsewhere they are a device of the author's. In general, brackets indicate explanatory matter added by the translator, although there may be exceptions here and there, as when the author himself used brackets— which was infrequently. The bracketed bibliographies preceding certain chapters are of course the author's.

In presenting quotations from ancient sources, it has been necessary in nearly all cases to consult the original Hebrew, Aramaic, Greek, and Latin; and in many cases, it has been necessary, in order to preserve Klausner's line of reasoning, to translate directly from these sources instead of using available English translations. Nevertheless, such translations have been consulted. For the Old Testament, I have leaned most heavily on the version of the Jewish Publication Society of America; for the New Testament, on the American Standard Version; for the Apocrypha and Pseudepigrapha, on the edition of Charles; in the case of classical authors, on the Loeb Classical Library; of course, the other well-known translations have also been consulted. But my greatest debt in this regard is to the magnificent translations of the Talmud Babli and Midrash Rabbah recently issued by the Soncino Press under the editorship of Rabbi I. Epstein, Rabbi H. Freedman, and Mr. M. Simon. Without these and Danby's great translation of the Mishnah, my task would have been far more difficult.

In the transliteration of Hebrew into Latin characters, I have made little effort to be consistent, since consistency in this matter seems to be unattainable. Where there are more or less traditional spellings, as in the case of Biblical names, Talmudic tractates, and the like, I have used such spellings. In the case of modern Hebrew, I have tried somewhat to imitate present Palestinian pronunciation. In particular, I have often rendered spirant Kaph (sound of *ch* in German *Buch*) by *kh* to call attention to it, since this sound is so prominent in modern Hebrew speech.

I wish to acknowledge particular gratitude to President Julian Morgenstern of Hebrew Union College and President Louis Finkelstein of the Jewish Theological Seminary of America for aid in difficult matters of Jewish scholarship; and to Professor W. F. Albright of Johns Hopkins University for advice on archaeological and other matters. I am also greatly indebted to Mr. B. Netanyahu, who represented the author and made many valuable suggestions in the final revision of the manuscript. Last, but far from least, is my obligation to my wife, Mary A. Stinespring, who learned the rudiments of Hebrew for the specific purpose of serving as amanuensis, critic, and advisor in this particular undertaking.

W. F. STINESPRING

Durham, N. C.
December 17, 1942.

APOLOGY OF THE AUTHOR

Thirty-two years ago, in the year 1907, I began to concern myself with the writing of a book about "Jesus of Nazareth." I devoted fifteen years to this project, although there were many interruptions during that time. I soon came to the conclusion that this book needed a complement in the form of another book about the events, historical, religious, and intellectual, which occurred from the time of Jesus to the end of the days of Paul the Apostle. For Jesus alone does not explain the rise of Christianity as a new community. I came to the conclusion, after much research, that Jesus considered himself to be the Messiah, and that, by means of the repentance and the morality which he preached in Jewish cities, he expected to bring redemption to Israel; but it is clear to us now, that Jesus never intended to found a new religion and spread it among the Gentiles.

So, while collecting material on Jesus himself, I was also continually collecting for another book to be entitled *From Jesus to Paul*. I went through the Christian Church Fathers and writers, and also through everything which has been written in the last one hundred and fifty years about the beginning and growth of Christianity; and I repeatedly took notes on many scraps of paper, which were placed in one large envelope among the rest of my documents.

On the 17th of Ab, 5689 (end of August 1929), disturbances broke out against the Jews of Palestine, and on Saturday night before the 19th of Ab, my house in Talpioth, near Jerusalem, was attacked. The rioters took many valuable books, and also tore and scattered about in thorough fashion most of the manuscripts which they found in my house. Apparently they were seeking money beneath them or perhaps they found satisfaction in a deed of violence and destruction. Some of the manuscripts were found in the garden beside my house, and some were totally lost. For two months it was not possible to return to Talpioth for fear of fresh outbreaks, and also because of necessary repairs to the plundered houses. When I did return, among the documents which I never found was the envelope containing the material for the book *From Jesus to Paul*.

With my great sorrow only one who has lost a son who was his joy and hope through many years can sympathize.

However, I comforted myself with the thought that a day would come when I would again go over all the sources and restore the material to its former state.

But the day was not soon to come. At the Hebrew University in Jerusalem I was busy finishing another work: a history of modern Hebrew literature, which has nothing in common with the history of the Second Temple or with the growth of Christianity; and out of concern for my students I first published all three volumes of this literary "History." Also vital problems upon which depends the building of the National Home in Palestine obliged me to give them diligent care, for the simple reason that, if the Jews do not have a National Home in their own land, the Jewish nation will have no existence in the world, and then there will be neither a living Hebrew language nor modern Hebrew science and literature, and thus all our cultural labor will have been in vain.

Because of these and similar vicissitudes, I was not able to resume work on the book *From Jesus to Paul* until Nisan, 5694 (1934), after I had again gathered material during the years 5689–5694 (1929–1934). In the course of the last five years, with a few interruptions, I have finished the entire book, in spite of the fact that the last three and a half years have been years of tumults and riots in the land, during which it has been difficult to do meticulous scholarly work in peace and tranquillity of soul.

Obviously, it was not within my power to go over again all the copious material which I had accumulated during the course of thirty-two years for the book *From Jesus to Paul*, and which had been destroyed in the disturbances which I have mentioned. So I crave pardon in advance if there are in the present book certain defects from this cause.

Nevertheless, I hope that if I have not here drawn upon all material relevant to the subject I have drawn upon most of it. The important thing is that the new book sets before the reader the two great questions: How was Christianity separated from Judaism, and why did Judaism not accept the teaching of Paul as it likewise did not accept the teaching of Jesus? The book also proposes a solution to these questions which, it seems to me, is clear and trustworthy. In addition, the new book clarifies the nature of Judaism and of Christianity in general, and shows what is common to both of them and what divides them and distinguishes them from each other.

If the reader approaches the present book from this viewpoint, even though he does not find in it all he seeks, he will find in it a great part of what he cannot find, so it seems to me at least, in any other book concerning that great problem of the relations between Judaism and Christianity. For my particular viewpoint as a Jew upon these relations is different from that of the Christian investigators who have concerned themselves with primitive Christianity; and therefore my conclusions are necessarily different from theirs. The chief need in the investigation is to view the problem scientifically from all sides, because only by this method do we bring ourselves near the truth.

Jerusalem-Talpioth, Eve of the first of Nisan, 5694 [spring 1934]—Eve of Rosh ha-Shanah, 5700 [autumn 1939].

The late Joseph Klausner was known in the world of Jewish scholarship not only for his Biblical studies but also for his efforts to broaden the Hebrew language to meet modern needs. He was born in Lithuania in 1874 and received his Ph.D. degree from the University of Heidelberg. From 1904 to 1919, he held various academic positions in Odessa; in 1920 he went to Palestine, where he taught modern Hebrew Language and literature at the Hebrew University.

Dr. Klausner has written a number of books in Hebrew, notably *Jesus of Nazareth* and *From Jesus to Paul*.

CONTENTS

SIXTH BOOK

The Life and Work of Saul (Paul) of Tarsus
(C. 10–64 C.E.)

SEVENTH BOOK

The Teaching of Paul

JUDAISM OUTSIDE OF PALESTINE AT THE TIME OF THE RISE OF CHRISTIANITY

CHAPTER I

Jesus and Christianity

"Jesus was not a Christian, he was a Jew"—this short and incisive sentence of Julius Wellhausen [1] is a result of a hundred and fifty years of research. And this is also the principal conclusion of a Hebrew book of some hundreds of pages.[2]

Jesus called upon the Jews to repent and do good works in order that they might become fit for the Days of the Messiah. Elijah the prophet, herald of the Messiah, had already come, and he himself, Jesus, was the Messiah. He said plainly to his disciples: "There are some here of them that stand by, who shall in no wise taste of death, till they see the Kingdom of God come with power," [3] and ". . . verily I say unto you, Ye shall not have gone through the cities of Israel, till the Son of Man be come"; [4] also he said, "This generation shall not pass away, until all these things be accomplished." [5] There was only one condition necessary in order that the Kingdom of Heaven might come: to fulfill all that was written in the Law and the Prophets as the Pharisees demanded and even in greater measure than they demanded: "For I say unto you, that except your righteousness shall exceed the righteousness of the scribes and Pharisees, ye shall in no wise enter into the Kingdom of Heaven." [6] The meaning was that

[1] See J. Wellhausen, *Einleitung in die drei ersten Evangelien*, Berlin 1905, S. 113.

[2] Joseph Klausner, *Yeshu ha-Notsri*, 4th ed., newly enlarged and revised, Jerusalem 5693 [1933], xv+480 pp. [English edition entitled *Jesus of Nazareth*, translated by Herbert Danby, London and New York 1925, 434 pp.]

[3] Mark 9:1.
[4] Matt. 10:23.
[5] Mark 13:30.
[6] Matt. 5:20.

3

the ceremonial laws, the laws of relations between man and
God, cannot release man from carrying out the moral laws,
the laws of relations between men and their fellows: ". . .
these ye ought to have done, and not to have left the other
undone." [7] In spite of the opposition to this on the part of
manifold scholars for various reasons, one must assert the view
that Jesus saw himself sent, as Messiah, first of all and above
all, "to the lost sheep of the house of Israel," [8] and that he
conceived of his relationship to the "Gentiles" as did every
Jew of those days: the relationship of a son of the Chosen
People (for whom the names "son of Abraham" and "daughter of Abraham" were appellations of love just as they are
for the Talmud) [9] to an errant and inferior mankind.[10]

It is clear, then, that it did not even enter the mind of Jesus
to form a new religion and proclaim it outside the Jewish
nation. The Law and the Prophets—these were his faith and
his religion; the people of Israel—this was the people to whom
this religion had been given as an inheritance and who must
establish it in its fulness—in its two parts: the ceremonial and
the moral; as a result "the Days of the Messiah" and "the
Kingdom of Heaven" would come, and then also the rest of
the nations would be changed into worshippers of the One
God and fulfillers of his Law, that is to say, they would
become Jews.

By this two important questions are raised: *one*, How did
it happen that from this completely Jewish, prophetic
Pharisaic teaching there came forth a new religion?—and the
second, How was there formed by this thorough Jew a faith
which had such a particular appeal to pagans?——

[7] Matt. 23:23; Luke 11:42.

[8] Matt. 10:5, 6; 15:24.

[9] Compare Luke 19:9 and 13:16 with Hagigah 3a; Tosephta, *ibid.*, II 1;
Pesikta Rabbathi XV (edition of R. Meir Friedman, 74a).

[10] Mark 7:27; Matt. 6:7; 18:17 and other passages. And see B. H. Brans-
comb, *Jesus and the Law of Moses*, New York 1930; this author also recognizes, although with reservations, that Jesus was a Pharisee and had the
attitude of a Pharisee toward Gentiles.

The first question I have attempted to answer in my book *Jesus of Nazareth*.[11] In my opinion there were certain elements in the Judaism of Jesus that made it non-Judaism. When Jesus, for example, *overemphasized* that God was "*my* Father in heaven," he thereby brought it about that the disciples and their immediate followers found it possible, because of foreign influences in their environment, to take his words too literally and to make him only a little less than God, and finally—even to see in him the real Son of God. When Jesus, in his interpretation of prophetic-Pharisaic Jewish ethics, went to extremes and forbade *all* swearing and the administration of justice *in general, completely* disregarded marriage and property relations, and did not recognize *at all* the importance of bettering existing conditions, since "the present world" is nothing but a state of transition to the Days of the Messiah and "the world to come"—by overfilling the measure of Judaism he caused his disciples and those that came after them to make from it non-Judaism. Specialists in optics know that there is a way of increasing light whereby the light is turned to darkness. Quantitative exaggeration of a thing sometimes turns it into a new quality, as many drops of water turn a brook into a river and a river into a sea, or as exaggerated resoluteness becomes impertinence and excessive humility, servility.

But this is only one of the answers to the first question: because of the extremism of Jesus with regard to the relations between himself and deity and because of his extreme emphasis on ethics, his disciples were able to attach the new religion to a good authority—to Jesus, who gave, although unconsciously, a certain impetus toward a new religion. One reason like this is not sufficient. By an impetus alone a new religion is not formed and spread with the speed and to the extent that characterized Christianity. There is need for still other reasons and causes.

[11] See in particular pp. 416–56 of the 4th ed. [pp. 369–407 in Eng. ed.].

This is the case also with regard to the solution of the second question: the departure of the new religion from the community of Israel and its spread among the Gentiles. Also here there are reasons and causes outside of Jesus.

The rise of Christianity and its spread among pagans were brought about by three other fundamental causes: first, *the dispersion of the Jews outside of Palestine;* second, *the spiritual conditions among the Gentiles at that time;* and third, *the Hellenistic Jewish culture of the non-Palestinian Jews in those days.*

CHAPTER II

The Jewish Diaspora at the Time of the Rise of Christianity

The political, economic, and spiritual state of Jewry in Palestine in the time of the rise of Christianity has been dealt with in some detail by the writer of these lines in his book *Jesus of Nazareth*.[1] Jesus was a Palestinian, and only Palestinian, Jew; therefore a book concerned with him could be limited to a description of conditions in Palestine alone. Anything which had to do with the conditions of the Diaspora of Israel outside Palestine had nothing to do with him.

This is not the case in a book which deals with what happened after Jesus was crucified and what was done by Paul: here it is of particular importance to describe the life of the Diaspora of Israel in the years 30–70 C.E., as well as a little before and a little after that period.

1. From the days of the Assyrian and Babylonian captivities numerous Israelites had been living outside Palestine. Many of them, particularly those from the northern tribes of the Kingdom of Israel, had been scattered in various countries along with the Tyrians and Sidonians, who had more or less a common native land and language. There was not even complete cleavage in religion between them; many also in Israel were worshippers of Baal and Astarte.[2] The prophets from the First

[1] J. Klausner, *Yeshu ha-Notsri*, 4th ed., pp. 135–247 [Eng. ed., pp. 129–228].

[2] I have already remarked in another place (*Ha-Bayit ha-Sheni bi-Gedulato*, Tel-Aviv 1930, pp. 128, 129, 142) upon the surprising fact that the most flourishing period of Canaanite colonization, religion and commerce begins precisely at the time when the tribes of Dan, Naphtali, Asher,

Isaiah on all speak of a gathering of "the dispersed of Judah and Israel" from Egypt and Assyria, from Cush and Put [Ethiopia and Libya], and even from the isles of the sea (apparently, the Ionian islands); and a later prophet continued with this proclamation:

> For from the rising of the sun even unto the going
> down of the same
> My name is great among the nations;
> And in every place offerings are presented unto My
> name,
> Even pure oblations;
> For My name is great among the nations,
> Saith the Lord of hosts.[3]

It is evident that clear words like these indicate a large Israelite-Jewish dispersion, through which much conversion to Judaism was brought about in various countries.[4]

This scattering occurred not only because the kings of Assyria and Babylonia uprooted a certain part of the Israelites and Judeans from their land, but also because of a voluntary dispersion for the purpose of business and financial gain. If the Tyrians and Sidonians in early times spread over almost all the ancient world, so likewise the Israelites and Judeans, especially the northern tribes who lived in the midst of the Canaanites, were scattered in various lands from the days of Solomon and Jehoshaphat, when they began to concern themselves with sea trade; yet they were not scattered in great numbers, because the vast majority of them were peasants bound to the soil.[5] Despite this, the Jews were said "to lack connexion with the land"; the anti-Semitic scholars see in this

Issachar and Zebulon, and the half-tribe of Manasseh, settled among the Canaanites, near Phoenicia proper. These tribes almost became complete Canaanites, as we see from the book of Judges (1:27-33) and from the Blessing of Jacob (Gen. 49:13).

[3] Malachi 1:11.

[4] See below, in the next chapter.

[5] See L. Herzfeld, *Handelsgeschichte der Juden des Altertums*, 2 Aufl., Braunschweig 1894, SS. 50-61; 300-4.

a shortcoming of the Jews, while those absorbed in Jewish lore see in this signs of a more than ordinary spirituality. Moreover, it was not only the Jews who wandered from their own country, but also all the gifted nations, whether possessing or not possessing the power of conquest: the Canaanites, the Egyptians, the Syrians, and the Greeks too were scattered throughout the whole world in relatively early times.

In the days of the kings of Persia the Jews came as soldiers to Egypt and founded a special community in the city of Yeb (Elephantine), not far from Syene (Aswan), and built there an altar to the God of Israel; and of course they were at that time scattered in other provinces of the Persian Empire.[6] Artaxerxes III Ochus settled Jews in Hyrcania by the side of the Caspian Sea.[7] Many Jews were in Babylonia from the beginning of the Babylonian captivity on; there were Jews living in Arabia from the beginning of the period of the Second Temple. Alexander the Great settled Jews in Alexandria, Egypt, and possibly also in other provinces. During the wars of the Diadochi and the Epigoni, and especially after the conquest of Judea by Ptolemy I Soter (of the house of Lagus), from the year 320 on, the Jews were scattered by the conquering kings, and they also fled before the successive tumults and wars in Judea to various lands, including Asia Minor; and perhaps at that time they reached even Greece. Already Aristotle, who sojourned in Asia Minor in the years 348–345, met a Jew who was "a Grecian not only in his language, but in his soul also."[8] The increase of the Jews in Egypt and the tumults in Palestine in the days of Antiochus

[6] Esther 3:8.

[7] J. Klausner, *Historia Yisreelit*, I³, 170–1, 181–2.

[8] Josephus, *Against Apion* I 22 (§180), quoting Clearchus, a pupil of Aristotle. See on this E. Silberschlag, "The Earliest Record of the Jews in Asia Minor," *Journal of Biblical Literature*, LII, 1 (1933), 66–77. Silberschlag defends the fundamental authenticity of the report against all those who consider it a forgery or invention. Of contrary opinion is A. Tscherikower, *Ha-Yehudim ve-ha-Yevanim ba-Tequphah ha-Hellenistit*, Tel-Aviv 5691 [1931], p. 365.

Epiphanes and his successors brought it about that Onias IV [9] built, about the year 160, a sanctuary on the model of the Temple in Jerusalem, but smaller and somewhat different, in Lower Egypt in the city of Leontopolis in the district of "the City of the Sun" (עיר־ההרס—Heliopolis); and apparently he was supported in this great deed by the prophecy of Isaiah,[10] since it is difficult to date this passage after the decree of Antiochus; this verse in Isaiah, which has in the Hebrew text עיר־ההרס ("city of destruction"), is already translated in the Septuagint "city of righteousness" (πόλις ἀσεδέκ), which may be a reflexion both of the building of the temple and the choice of the site. This is the "House of Onias" which is mentioned in the Mishnah [11] and the Talmud.[12] And in the vicinity of this temple many Jews settled, until the whole district was called "the land of Onias," and the Jews who were in this "land" resisted the army of Mithradates, king of Pontus, who had gone to assist Julius Caesar, until Antipater the Idumean influenced them by means of a letter from Hyrcanus II to cease their opposition.[13]

Many Jews were found at a comparatively early time in Cyrenaica and all of northern Africa; these Jews reached there from Egypt. From Egypt and Greece they also reached Italy. They became an important community in Rome after the conquest of Pompey and the ransom of the captives from Judea or after Pompey and Julius Caesar of their own free will liberated the Jewish captives which Pompey had brought from Judea after his conquest.[14] In the period of the rise of Christianity the Jews reached even Gaul and Germany. They

[9] And not Onias III, son of Simon II, as in Josephus, *Jewish War* VII x 2, since Onias III was killed by Andronicus in Daphne near Antioch (II Macc. 4:34).

[10] Isaiah 19:18–21.   [11] Menahoth XIII 10.

[12] *Babli, ibid.* 109b; Megillah 10a (top).

[13] J. Klausner, *Historia Yisreelit*, II, 204 and 208.

[14] See on this in particular G. La Piana, "Foreign Groups in Rome during the First Centuries of the Empire," *Harvard Theological Review*, XX (1927), 341–93.

came also to the north shore of the Black Sea a short time after this period, and they may have reached there in earlier times—in the days of the Hasmoneans. At any rate, we have a Jewish-Greek inscription of the year 81 C.E. from the city of Panticapaeum—now Kerch—near the Cimmerian Bosporus.[15]

Indeed, not without reason did the earliest Jewish Sibyl sing about the year 140 B.C.E. with regard to Judea: "all the earth shall be filled with thee, and all the sea." [16]

And about the year 85 B.C.E. the Greek geographer Strabo says that the Jews "have already gotten into all cities; and it is hard to find a place in the habitable earth that hath not admitted this tribe of men, and is not possessed by them." These explicit words Josephus presents as a quotation from Strabo.[17] Josephus testifies on his own account that "there is no people upon the habitable earth [18] which have not some portion of us [the Jews] among them." [19]

The wide distribution of the Jews throughout the ancient world is described in more detail in the letter of Agrippa I to Gaius Caligula in the treatises of Philo:

It [Jerusalem] . . . is . . . the metropolis, not only of the one country of Judaea, but also of many, by reason of the colonies which it has sent out from time to time into the bordering districts of Egypt, Phoenicia, Syria in general, and especially that part of it which is called Coelo-Syria, and also with those more distant regions of Pamphylia, Cilicia, the greater part of Asia Minor as far as Bithynia, and the furthermost corners of Pontus. And in the same manner into Europe, into Thessaly, and Boeotia,

[15] The inscription of the year 41 C.E. from the city of Anapa is that of a Gentile influenced by Judaism. See A. A. Harkavy, *Ha-Yehudim u-Sephat ha-Slavim*, Vilna 5627 [1867] pp. 77–97; E. Schürer, "Die Juden im Bosporanischen Reich," *Sitzungsberichte der Berliner Akademie*, 1897, SS. 204–25.

[16] Sibylline Oracles III, 271.

[17] *Antiquities* XIV vii 2 (§ 115).

[18] See the Hebrew Ben-Sira 43:4, "the inhabited earth." I have remarked on this in my article "Ginze-ha-Lashon be-Sepher Ben-Sira," in the magazine *Sephatenu*, II (Berlin 5683 [1923]), pp. 33–4.

[19] *Jewish War* II xvi 4; *ibid.* VII iii 3.

and Macedonia, and Aetolia, and Attica, and Argos, and Corinth and all the most fertile and wealthiest districts of Peloponnesus. And not only are the continents full of Jewish colonies, but also all the most celebrated islands are so too; such as Euboea and Cyprus, and Crete.[20]

I say nothing of the countries beyond the Euphrates, for all of them, except a very small portion, and Babylon, and all the satrapies around, which have any advantages whatever of soil or climate, have Jews settled in them.[21]

2. Thus we see the Jews scattered and dispersed in almost the entire world which was then known to the Canaanites, the Greeks, and the Romans.[22] In various territories, great and small, far from Palestine and adjacent to it, the Jews were merchants, artisans, and petty or moderately high officials; sometimes they were high officials, and even commanders in the army of a state. The kings in the different countries would accord them political and religious privileges in order to win their affection; so that they, who did not demand rule for themselves in the lands where they sojourned, their eyes being fixed upon their religious center and the birthplace of their nation, would serve in the lands of their captivity as a shield against demands for freedom and insurrections on the part of the natives of the country. Thus they had, in many states,

[20] [In this note the author explains that the correct name of the island of Crete in Hebrew is קְרִיטָה and not כְּרֵתִים as some mistakenly call it. In his Hebrew translation from the Greek of Philo he uses the Biblical word כַּפְתּוֹר. Tr.]

[21] Philo Judaeus, *The Embassy to Gaius* XXXVI 281-2 [Eng. tr. by C. D. Yonge, Bohn Library, IV, 161].

[22] On the scattering of the Jews throughout the world and their political, economic and cultural status in the Diaspora see in particular A. Tscherikower, *Ha-Yehudim ve-ha-Yevanim ba-Tequphah ha-Hellenistit*, pp. 273-380; J. Klausner, *Historia Yisreelit*, II, 205-12; IV, 29-36; E. Schürer, *Geschichte des jüdischen Volkes im Zeitalter Jesu Christi*, III⁴, 1-188; A. Harnack, *Mission und Ausbreitung des Christentums*, Leipzig 1902, SS. 1-12; H. Dessau, *Geschichte der römischen Kaiserzeit*, II, 2, 729, Anm. 2; J. Juster, *Les Juifs dans l'Empire Romain*, I, 179-212; Ch. Guignebert, *Le monde juif vers le temps de Jésus*, Paris 1935, pp. 279-306 [Eng. ed., 211-37]; Foakes-Jackson and Lake, *The Beginnings of Christianity*, London 1920, I, 137-68.

complete or almost complete equality of rights.[23] Along with this they had special communities in the places where they had settled, with the privilege of having litigation among themselves settled in Jewish courts; in this manner the foreign government would recognize not only their religion but also their nationality and their religio-national rights.

Hence the Jews of the Dispersion were more or less autonomous with regard to their own affairs. They had in almost every city synagogues, in which they would gather on Sabbaths—and of course also on holidays and fast days—to read the Torah; the scholars and preachers would expound to them the reading for the week or deliver an ethico-religious sermon. Reading of the Torah in the synagogues was usually accompanied by an Aramaic or Greek translation, or they even read the Torah in Greek translation alone; in the Diaspora the sermon also was not in Hebrew but in Aramaic or Greek. Concerning the reading of the Torah and the sermons on Sabbaths in the Diaspora, we have an unintentional witness: "For Moses from generations of old hath in every city them that preach him, being read in the synagogues every Sabbath." [24] For Jews in the Diaspora it was necessary to translate the Torah into a foreign tongue as it was read, or else to read it to them directly from a translation. It was also necessary to preach to them in the language of the country, because these Jews spoke foreign tongues, and bore foreign names—sometimes even names compounded with the names of pagan deities—and followed foreign customs. And except for religious and moral beliefs and opinions, they were only slightly different from the dominant peoples. Even the inscriptions in synagogues and cemeteries—places of religio-national sanctity—were often not only in Aramaic but also in Greek and

[23] See what I have written against the idea that the Jews did not have equality of rights in Alexandria in my detailed examination of the book by A. Tscherikower mentioned in the preceding note (*Qiryat-Sepher*, IX [5692/3—1932/3], 163-4).

[24] Acts 15:21.

Latin, with a Hebrew addition or even without it. After all, these Jews of the Diaspora were uprooted, despite all their attachment to Jewish religion and all their loyalty to Palestine and to the Temple (so long as it was still existing).

Here there was no original cultural creativity and no pulsating life of a people dwelling upon its own historic soil. Even the one great man whom Hellenized Judaism brought forth, Philo of Alexandria, with all the originality of his literary productions, and with all his loyalty to his people, his religion, and their holy land, produced only an eclectic system in which Hellenism and Judaism lie together in confusion. An eclectic system like this could be acceptable to early Christianity, which also was a combination of Judaism and Hellenism and likewise was uprooted from its historic soil; but it was unacceptable to original Judaism.[25]

Undoubtedly, the majority of the Jews in the Diaspora were devoted to their religion, their people, and their ancestral land. They were organized, as has been said, into special communities, most of which had councils to supervise the affairs of the group. The idea that at the head of the great Jewish community of Alexandria there stood a leader who was called "Alabarch" is erroneous; the Arabarch (thus his title, not "Alabarch") was only an official in charge of the taxation of merchandise exported or imported by water; sometimes he was a Jew, as in the days of Philo. Naturally, he was rich and esteemed in the community but nothing more. At the head of the Jews of Alexandria, as also at the head of the Jews of Damascus, stood a "ruler of the people" (Ethnarch, ἐθνάρχης), who directed the Jewish community together with "magistrates" (Archons, ἄρχοντες), who were the judges of the group, and were in charge of the enforcement of laws, the payment of taxes, and the like. At the head of the synagogue stood a "ruler of the synagogue" (ἀρχισυνάγωγος)

[25] J. Klausner, *Philosophim ve-Hoge-De'ot*, I, 64–91 (Jerusalem 5694 [1934]).

or a "ruler of the elders" (γερουσιάρχης)—the elders of the synagogue apparently having in their hands decisions about specifically religious affairs. Thus the Jews of the Diaspora had the fundamentals of cultural autonomy.[26]

The Jews of the Diaspora kept the Sabbath and celebrated the feasts and the new moons (which were still at that time real festivals); they practiced circumcision even though they were living among uncircumcised Gentiles; most of them also guarded themselves against the forbidden foods, especially the flesh of swine; Juvenal mockingly says that they "see no difference between eating swine's flesh and the flesh of men."[27] They also maintained a strong attachment to Jerusalem and the Temple—the national and religious center of the whole people. Even the Jews of Egypt, who had the "House of Onias," would make the pilgrimage to Jerusalem; and the Jews of other countries were still more zealous in making this pilgrimage. Besides this, the Jews of all the world paid a half-shekel (two drachmae) to the Temple in Jerusalem every year. Philo, who praises highly the Temple in Jerusalem without even mentioning the "House of Onias," makes it known[28] that "practically in every city there are banking places for the holy money where people regularly come and give their offerings. And at stated times there are appointed to carry the sacred tribute envoys selected on their merits." In Nisibin and Nehardea there were central treasuries for the collection of these contributions from the Jews of Babylonia; these contributions reached such an amount that many thousands of Jews would accompany the sacred fund on its way to Jerusalem, out of fear of the ravages of the Parthians.[29] Again, about the year 70 B.C.E., Mithradates, King of Pontus,

[26] See for particulars Schürer, III⁴, 76-9, 132-4; Juster, I, 213-53, 409-89; II, 119-26, 153-82.

[27] Juvenal, Sat. VI 160; XIV 98.

[28] Philo, The Special Laws I: the Temple §78 [Eng. tr. by F. H. Colson, Loeb Classical Library, VII, 145].

[29] Antiquities XVIII ix 1 (§§ 312-3). See also Philo, The Embassy to Gaius 31 § 216.

took from the island of Cos 800 talents of silver which the Jews had collected from Ionia and Caria for the Temple.[30] The Roman governor of Asia Minor, Pomponius Flaccus,[30a] confiscated a hundred gold pounds (a great sum!) from the offerings which had been collected for the Temple in Apamea, Laodicea, Pergamum, and Adramyttium; when he was accused of this extortion, in which profanation of a holy thing was involved, Cicero defended him in his oration *Pro Flacco* delivered in the year 59 B.C.E. Also the Mishnah mentions the shekels "on behalf of Babylon, Media, and the regions afar off." [31] From these shekels the great treasure which was in Jerusalem (תְּרוּמַת־הַלִּשְׁכָּה, "oblation of the chamber"), had accumulated, especially since in place of the "half-shekel" the rich Jews would contribute "darics of gold." [32] This fund was used for the Daily Whole-offerings; for the display of the Shewbread and the preparation of the incense; for the wages of the women who wove curtains for the Temple; for the purchase of the garments of the High Priest, for the Red Heifer, and for the scapegoat; for the wages of the correctors of books (Holy Scriptures) and the wages for the Great Court. The remainder of the fund was used for the fortification of the wall of Jerusalem, for the strengthening of its towers, for the repairing of the conduits of water, and for the rest of the needs of the city. And still there was left a great surplus, which, according to the opinion of A. Schwarz, amounted every year to the sum of 23 silver talents.[33] From this annual surplus, there accumulated in the Temple a great treasure, which excited the cupidity of extortioners like

---

[30] *Antiquities* XIV vii 2 (§ 112), quoting Strabo.

[30a] [Klausner is here in error: Lucius Valerius Flaccus was governor of Asia Minor, in 62–61 B.C.; Lucius Pomponius Flaccus was governor of Syria, 32–35 A.D. Tr.]

[31] Shekalim III 4; Tosephta, *ibid.* II 3, 4.

[32] Tosephta, Shek. II 4.

[33] See A. Schwarz, "Die Schatzkammer des Tempels in Jerusalem," *Monatschrift für Geschichte und Wissenschaft des Judentums*, LXIII (1919), 234.

Heliodorus the Syrian and Crassus the Roman, who fell upon the Temple for violence and plunder.

In general, even apart from the Temple, there was a strong connexion between Palestine and the Diaspora. Once the Jewish commanders of the army of the kingdom of Egypt, Hilkiah and Hananiah, sons of the High Priest Onias, saved the kingdom of [Alexander] Jannaeus from the hands of Cleopatra, queen of Egypt.[34] I have already mentioned how, in response to a letter from Hyrcanus II, the High Priest and Leader of the People in Jerusalem, the Jews living near Pelusium and in "the land of Onias" put aside their loyalty to their Gentile king and allowed the army of the enemy to pass on to Egypt.[35]

The kings and leaders of Judea on their part regarded themselves as guardians of the Jews of the Diaspora, and they were concerned for the rights of citizenship, religion, and nationality of the Jews in all the Diaspora of Israel. Hyrcanus II sent a Jewish embassy to Rome carrying a shield of gold valued at 50,000 pieces of gold; he requested a renewal of the treaty between Judea and Rome which dated back to the days of Judas Maccabaeus—and his request was granted. Then he sent a second embassy which obtained from Julius Caesar and afterwards from Dolabella, the ally of Mark Antony, important decrees respecting exemptions for the Jews of the Diaspora in connexion with their religio-ethnic privileges and also their political rights as Roman citizens.[36] From these decrees we see that the Jews in Paros were allowed to assemble in their synagogues although the rest of the inhabitants were

[34] See J. Klausner, *Historia Yisreelit*, II, 125.
[35] See above p. 10 and *Historia Yisreelit*, II, 204.
[36] They are all collected together in *Antiquities* XIV x; XVI vi 2–7; XIX v 2, 3. See for particulars Juster, *op. cit.* I, 135–58. The apprehensions of H. Willrich, *Urkundenfälschung in der hellenistisch-jüdischen Literatur* (Berlin 1924), that these documents are mostly forgeries do not have sufficient foundation. See A. Tscherikower, *op. cit.*, p. 309. On the decree of Claudius (*Antiquities* XIX v 2) see J. Klausner, *Qiryat-Sepher*, IX, 163–4 against Tscherikower, *op. cit.*, pp. 399–407.

forbidden any sort of gatherings; that the Jews in Ephesus, in
Delos, and in other places were freed from military service so
that they would not be forced to profane the Sabbath or
defile themselves with forbidden foods;[37] that the Jews in
Ephesus, in Laodicea, in Miletus, and in Halicarnassus were
allowed to refrain from anything that would compel them to
profane the Sabbath and the other religious festivals.[38] In the
city of Sardis (the Sepharad of the Bible) the Jews were not
only permitted to serve their God without hindrance, but
also were given a plot upon which to build a synagogue.[39]
Also, a decree went forth from Augustus Caesar and Agrippa
his son-in-law, that the Jews were not to be summoned to
court on the Sabbath.[40] Again in the days of Hyrcanus II the
Jews were given the special privilege of being judged in
courts of their own according to the provisions of their own
law.[41] In Rome the government would distribute money,
bread, and oil to the poor of the city at a certain time in the
month; and it was decreed, that if this distribution fell upon
a Sabbath, the Jews were to be given their share on the next
day, the first day of the week; and in place of the "oil of
strangers," the prohibition of which the Jews were already
accustomed to, even in the Diaspora,[42] they were given
money.[43] So orthodox in their religion were even the Jews of
the Diaspora who were living in the great empire of Rome in
the days of the rise of Christianity!

3. In Babylonia, where there was an older and larger settle-
ment than in any other country, except perhaps Egypt, there

---

[37] *Antiquities* XIV x 12–4, 16, 18, 19.

[38] *Ibid*. XIV x 20, 21, 23, 25.   [40] *Ibid*. XVI vi 2, 4.

[39] *Ibid*. XIV x 24.   [41] *Ibid*. XIV x 17.

[42] In the decree of "Eighteen Things" [Shabb. I 5] which, according to
most scholars, was promulgated during the Great Revolt against the Romans
to strengthen the national spirit in the crisis, "They decreed with regard
to their [the Gentiles'] bread, wine, and oil" (see for particulars J. Klausner,
Historia Yisreelit, IV, 125–7); but apparently the Jews were wary of the
"oil of Gentiles" even before this.

[43] Philo, *The Embassy to Gaius* XXIII 158.

occurred at the end of the period of the Second Temple an important political event which bears credible witness to the cultural condition of one of the two greatest settlements of the Diaspora.

Two brothers, weavers of the city of Nehardea which is so well known from the Talmud, Hasinai [Asineus] and Hanilai [Anileus], were given a severe and humiliating punishment by the master of the shop where they worked. They fled to the environs of Nehardea and there gathered together a large band of malcontents, who began to attack towns and villages of the Gentiles and plunder them. They finally became so powerful that they dared to fight even with the army of the Parthians—and they conquered it! Artabanus II, king of Parthia, was at that time engaged in his wars against rebellious satraps; therefore, he found it expedient to make a treaty with the valiant brothers and to hand over to their control a whole province, in which they, doubtless, were to rule in the name of the king of Parthia, and bring him tribute.

This rule lasted fifteen years, until it broke down because of—*a Gentile woman!*

Hanilai saw the beautiful wife of one of the Parthian commanders, he fell in love with her, he killed her husband in combat and married her; and out of his great love for her he did not deprive her of her strange gods. Here was this Gentile woman worshipping her alien gods in the house of a Jewish ruler just as did the foreign women whom King Solomon married in his time! This offense of Hanilai aroused the anger of the people and the displeasure of his brother Hasinai, and a part of his army together with Hasinai poured forth their resentment in the presence of Hanilai and even warned him of punishment from heaven. This was the beginning of the end of Jewish control in the Babylonian province.[44] And from this it is to be seen how the Jews of Babylonia at that time

[44] See below, p. 22.

clung to Judaism, even Jews of little faith living by the sword, like the companions of Hasinai and Hanilai.[45]

4. Nevertheless, their separation from their native soil and the lack of a national language made the Jews of the Diaspora rootless and insecure in both their political and cultural relationships. Even with all the privileges which they had through the favor of the emperors of Rome and the kings of Parthia they were not saved from severe persecutions and fearful massacres. The pogroms in Alexandria in the days of Gaius Caligula were outstanding for cruelty.[46] And in the days of Tiberius Caesar came the first religious persecution by the Roman Empire. Tiberius disliked the Jews because he hated Judaism, which was different from all other religions and thought itself supreme above all of them. He praised Gaius Caesar [Caligula], his grandson, because he did not visit Judea on his journeys to the provinces of the East and thus was not compelled to sacrifice in the Temple at Jerusalem and hence honor it.[47] Sejanus, the counsellor of Tiberius, who had great influence with the emperor, strengthened him in his hate for the Jews. Quickly, with the advice of Sejanus, Tiberius found occasion to drive them out from Rome (and, some hold, from all Italy).

The Jewish proselyte Fulvia, wife of the noted senator Saturninus, sent gifts to Jerusalem by her teachers, the Jews who had introduced her to Judaism; but these Jews dishonored their mission and took the gifts for themselves. The thing became known to Tiberius Caesar and he made use of this opportunity. (The reason was that he was angry because the Jews had succeeded in catching in the net of their Law

---

[45] See I. A. Halevy, *Dorot ha-Rishonim*, part I, vol. III, pp. 122–32.
[46] See for particulars J. Klausner, *Historia Yisreelit*, III, 227–37; *idem*, "Rega' Gadol be-Hayye ha-Ummah," *Ha-Shiloah*, vol. 21, pp. 12–9; *idem*, *Ke-she-Ummah Nilhemet 'al Herutah*, 2nd ed. (Tel-Aviv 5699 [1939]), pp. 91–105.
[47] Suetonius, *Augustus* 39.

even the wife of a Roman senator; the embezzlement of the gifts was only an excuse.) Immediately he proposed to the Roman Senate to banish all Jews and all proselytes from Rome, and any who did not leave the city by a stated time or did not renounce Judaism by the same time were to be seized as slaves in perpetuity and sent away for forced labor. According to the witness of Josephus,[48] which is corroborated in substance by Tacitus,[49] except that the latter includes Egyptians with the Jews, 4000 Jews were banished to Sardinia, which was at that time a forsaken land indeed; and in addition many Jews were punished because they were not willing to fight on Sabbaths and holidays (19 c.e.). Only after the death of Sejanus, the persecutor of the Jews, did Tiberius annul the decree.

Even Claudius Caesar, who was not actually a hater of the Jews, sought to drive them out from Rome. At first he did not dare to do this for fear of stirring up a tumult in the city; but he forbade them to assemble in synagogues or to form themselves into groups.[50] However, according to the testimony of Suetonius, he also "banished from Rome the Jews who made a great tumult on account of Chrestus" (*Chresto impulsore*).[51] The Acts of the Apostles also knows about this expulsion from Rome.[52] It took place about the years 49–52 c.e., in the very days of the work of Paul the Apostle in Asia Minor. There is a division of opinion as to whether the "Chrestus" (and not "Christus") of Suetonius was Jesus of Nazareth ("Christus"—"the Messiah") or some Christian apostle or teacher,[53] as Graetz thinks.[54] An unknown Messiah who arose in Rome itself is not to be thought of at all! It is

---

[48] *Antiquities* XVIII iii 5 (§§ 81–4).
[49] Tacitus, *Annals* II 85.
[50] See Cassius Dio, LX 6; Orosius, VII 6, 15.
[51] Suetonius, *Claudius* 25.
[52] Acts 18:2.
[53] J. Klausner, *Yeshu ha-Notsri*, 4th ed., pp. 54–5 [Eng. ed., pp. 60–1].
[54] H. Graetz, *Geschichte der Juden*, III, 1⁵, 371, Anm. 4; III, 2⁵, 423, Anm. 3.

almost certain that Jesus was intended, since in the books and inscriptions of the Greeks and Romans "Chrestus" frequently appears in place of "Christus." [55] At any rate, shortly after the death of Agrippa I, new persecutions came upon the Jews in Rome and upon the proselytes likewise. In the course of about thirty years the Jews and proselytes were twice expelled from the city. And this was the Jewish community, important in numbers and in influence, about which Cicero some time before could speak not only with hate, but also with envy and with fear! [56]

5. Likewise, the great and powerful Jewish community in Babylonia, with all its great numbers, and with all its political and economic power, did not have the strength and the might of a people living on its own soil. After the Gentile wife of Hanilai had poisoned Hasinai because he had reprimanded her for her paganism in front of his brother her husband, internal strife arose within the army of the Jewish hero—and Mithradates, king of Parthia, conquered Hanilai. After the Babylonians had destroyed the remnant of Hanilai's force and had put him to death, they fell upon the Jews in Nehardea. Many of these Jews fled to Seleucia. There a thing happened that was typical of the Diaspora at all times:

In Seleucia, Syrians and Greeks were living side by side in more or less equal numbers; they were constantly striving for the political control of the city. But when the number of Jews in Seleucia was increased, they, speaking Aramaic and being Semites like the Syrians, tipped the scales against the Greeks to the advantage of the Syrians. It was like the case of the Jews in Galicia and the Czech country (Bohemia) before the Treaty of Versailles, who, since they spoke a German-Jewish dialect, tipped the scales to the side of the Germano-Austrians against the Poles and Czechs. Then "Midian

[55] Ed. Meyer, *Ursprung und Anfänge des Christentums*, III, 37–8.
[56] Cicero, *Pro Flacco* 28.

and Amalek made peace between them"—in order to oppress Israel.[56a] The ungrateful Syrians made peace with the Greeks, the enemies of Israel—and together they fell upon the Jews in Seleucia and wreaked slaughter and destruction upon them. According to Josephus,[57] 50,000 Jews were slaughtered at that time—all the Jews who had not been hidden away by their foreign friends (there were "good Gentiles" at that time, as in our own time). Many of them attempted to flee to Ctesiphon, winter capital of the kings of Parthia; but even there they were not safe from slaughter. Finally they were forced to return to Nehardea and to go from there to Nisibin, where Jews lived in great numbers and where there were many soldiers who were able to protect them.

Such was the political condition of the Jews at the end of the period of the Second Temple even in the most favorable of the countries of the Diaspora!———

6. In view of an unsafe political situation like this there was also no firm basis for economic life.

Avigdor [Victor] Tscherikower has judged rightly that "the Jewish Diaspora in the Hellenistic period was very far from the onesidedness of ghetto life in the Middle Ages." [58] Jews of the Diaspora were not engaged in business alone, or even in business for the most part, nor were so many of them government officials. There were among them common soldiers, army commanders, policemen, tax collectors, peasants, farm laborers, industrial laborers, merchants, money lenders, and so on; there is no foundation to the claim that ancient anti-Semitism grew out of business jealousy of the Jews or out of acts of trickery on the part of Jewish business men.[59] Nevertheless, Tscherikower is wrong when he thinks that

[56a] [The reference is to Judges 6:33. Tr.]

[57] *Antiquities* XVIII ix 9 (§ 376).

[58] A. Tscherikower, *Ha-Yehudim ve-ha-Yevanim ba-Tequphah ha-Hellenistit*, p. 350.

[59] *Ibid.*, pp. 340–53.

economic strata and ranks in the countries of the Diaspora were similar to those in Palestine. Correct is the statement that "there was not even one social rank which existed in Palestine that did not also exist in the Diaspora." [60] But the question is, whether the proportion of similar strata and ranks in the Diaspora was like that in Palestine. And to this question the answer is negative. Which is to say, that of course there were in the Diaspora Jewish tillers of the soil just as there were Jewish merchants in Palestine. But in Palestine the native tillers of the soil were a decisive majority and the merchants a comparatively small minority, just as in the rest of the countries and among the rest of the peoples of that time; whereas, among the Jews of the Diaspora, tillers of the soil were a minority—even though a comparatively large minority—and merchants were a majority or a much larger minority. Thus, even if Tscherikower [61] is right as against Herzfeld [62] that the Jews lived also in many villages and rural towns in Egypt and Asia Minor, in the final analysis great and powerful communities such as there were in Alexandria of Egypt, in the Syrian Antioch, in Babylonian Nehardea, and in other great cities like these, are a trustworthy witness to the fact that business took the first place among the Jews of the Diaspora, while tilling of the soil, and even industrial work, took among them only the second or third place.

Thus it becomes nearly certain that even by the end of the Second Temple there was an unnatural division into social strata and ranks among the Jews of the Diaspora; this grew out of the conditions of foreign life, through no fault of their own. From any standpoint, this was less natural than the situation in Palestine, even if it was much more natural than that of the Jewish ghetto of the Middle Ages.

The result of an unnatural division like this is rootlessness.

[60] *Ibid.*, p. 350. [61] *Ibid.*, p. 340.
[62] L. Herzfeld, *Handelsgeschichte der Juden des Altertums*, SS. 202–78.

There is in such a case no rootage in native soil such as there is for peasants indigenous to the land, whose fathers and grandfathers have been bound by a strong and tight bond to their own soil. And in any place where there is economic rootlessness there is no tradition which is strong and resistant to change. Hence, it was easy to pass from Judaism to Pauline Christianity in the Jewish congregations of the Diaspora, in spite of all the opposition which Paul met at the beginning in them.

7. Like the economic life thus also was the cultural life of the Diaspora.

To be sure, deliberate Hellenizing affected only a very few Jews. If the congregations were concerned about receiving privileges with regard to the keeping of the Sabbath, with regard to freedom from all civic festivals which were connected with pagan worship (λειτουργία), with regard to forbidden foods and even the "oil of strangers," if they sent money to Jerusalem and were obedient to the Leader of the People or to the king in Judea—all this indicates that the Israelite life in the congregations was decidedly loyal from a religio-national standpoint.

Naturally, many of the signs of assimilationism, such as change of names and change of languages, were only external, superficial and shallow; and many of the Greek customs, which the Jews took up in various lands, did not change radically the spirit of Judaism even in the Diaspora, since they touched only the surface of cultural life.[63] Nevertheless, there were also signs of a much deeper assimilationism.

Also, the fact that the Hasmoneans from the days of John Hyrcanus and afterward made use of two names—Jewish and Greek—was a bad sign. Mattathias ben Johanan, Judas Maccabaeus, Jonathan and Simon, sons of Mattathias—these

[63] A. Tscherikower, *Ha-Yehudim ve-ha-Yevanim*, pp. 354-64.

had no Greek names. The necessity of translating the Torah into Greek, the fact that the Jews in the Diaspora created a whole literature in the Greek language, the fact that the inscriptions upon the synagogues, the decisions of the congregations and the epitaphs on the tombstones were in Greek—all these were indubitable signs of an assimilationism deep enough to penetrate through the surface of things into the innermost religious and cultural life of individual and community.

In this connexion, we have an inscription of a "Jerusalemite" ('Ιεροσολυμίτης), who lived in the city of Iasos in Asia Minor and vowed a sum of 100 drachmae to the festival—of the god Dionysus! [64] And two Jews who considered it proper to give thanks to God because he had saved them from a storm at sea and from other dangers found no place in which to engrave their inscription of thanksgiving except—the temple of the god Pan! [65] There was a Jew by the name of Jacob ben Achilles who served as a guard in the temple of the Egyptian god Serapis at Oxyrhynchus; there was a Jew who swore by the name of the "Divine Caesar" and another Jew who made use of a seal upon which was engraved the image of Heracles.[66] Tiberius Alexander, son of the Jewish "Arabarch" Alexander Lysimachus and nephew of Philo, and thus from a noble and orthodox family in Judaism, forsook the religion of his fathers; and when he was made procurator of Judea (46–48 C.E.), he persecuted those zealous for national freedom with great cruelty like the rest of the Roman governors.[67] When he was appointed governor of Egypt, and further severe riots broke out against the Alexandrian Jews, apparently not without the knowledge of the governor, the apostate Jew acted cruelly toward his former brethren and

[64] See E. Schürer, *Geschichte d. jüd. Volkes*, III⁴, 16–7 (of course, not certainly a Jew; could this man have been a Gentile of Jerusalem?).

[65] See W. Dittenberger, *Orientis Graeci Inscriptiones Selectae*, I, 73–4.

[66] Tscherikower, *op. cit.*, p. 359.

[67] J. Klausner, *Historia Yisreelit*, IV, 4, 5.

gave permission to the savage Libyan soldiery "not only to murder the Jews, but also to plunder their possessions and to burn their houses." So the bloodthirsty soldiers set upon the houses of the Jews, murdering young and old, men and women, until "the whole place overflowed with blood and 50,000 dead bodies were piled up there." [68] Finally, Tiberius Alexander participated in the destruction of Judea and Jerusalem by Vespasian and Titus, his attitude throughout the war to everything that was done to his people being that of a complete stranger. [69]

Even worse was Antiochus the Apostate, also of an illustrious family, son of the head of the Jewish congregation in the Syrian Antioch. He slandered his father and his people with the charge that they wished to destroy Antioch with fire, and he advised that all the Jews of Antioch be forced to do as he did and bring sacrifices to idols; the results were riots and slaughter of the Jews. Moreover, he attempted, with aid from the forces of the Roman governor, to prohibit the keeping of the Sabbath in Antioch and its environs. When a great fire occurred in Antioch, this apostate laid the blame for the fire on his fellow-Jews. [70] Frightful examples like these *appear* to be mere isolated cases; historians take notice only of events and characters that stand out from the ordinary. But of course there were apostates like these in no small number. If two, who are known to us because they come upon the stage of history, could attain to such treachery and meanness in relation to their people, one may surmise how far assimilationism had gone among the Jews of the Diaspora in general.

There is no need to agree with the opinion of M. Friedländer who, in a large number of books, endeavors to prove that the Judaism of the Diaspora was much more "liberal"

[68] *Jewish War* II xviii 7, 8; see also Klausner, *op. cit.*, pp. 124-5.
[69] Klausner, *ibid.*, p. 184.   [70] *Ibid.*, p. 124.

than the Judaism of Palestine, and that all the "good" that came to the world of humanity came only from this Judaism of the Diaspora: the synagogue, Essenism, antinomianism (even this was "good," according to his opinion), and above all—"free" Christianity, which was immeasurably "superior" to a "petrified" Pharisaism that was "narrow" in "its zealous nationalism." [71] It is also hard to accept his opinion that in the Diaspora of Israel the Jews had two kinds of congregations: orthodox congregations and heretical congregations; and that it was the congregations of the "heretics" that produced antinomianism, which claimed the right to nullify the ritual commandments; and that Paul depended upon the antinomian heretical congregations in his war against the Torah and its commandments.[72] But there can be no doubt of the fact that there were many more "fickle" Jews in the Diaspora than in Palestine. These Jews, because of the influence of Greek philosophy, or by imitation of the Gentiles among whom they lived, would take a rather free attitude toward the paradoxical stories in the Torah and toward the various ceremonial laws of Judaism; and they would endeavor to find in the stories and laws hints for philosophical and ethical discussion, in order that they might not see the necessity of believing literally in the Biblical stories, and of observing the laws according to their plain intent. Philo of Alexandria fought against these "sons of Cain" who departed from the ways of the Jewish community on the pretext that the ceremonial laws are only a parable and that there is no necessity

[71] See the following books of M. Friedländer: *Zur Entstehungsgeschichte des Christentums*, Wien 1894; *Das Judentum in der vorchristlichen griechischen Welt*, 1897; *Der vorchristliche jüdische Gnosticismus*, 1898; *Der Antichrist*, 1902; *Geschichte der jüdischen Apologetik als Vorgeschichte des Christentums*, 1903; *Die Religiösen Bewegungen innerhalb des Judentums im Zeitalter Jesus*, 1905; *Synagoge und Kirche in ihren Anfängen*, 1908. On Friedländer see J. Klausner, *Yeshu ha-Notsri*, pp. 121–2 [Eng. tr. pp. 116–8].

[72] See especially the book of Friedländer last mentioned, *Synagoge und Kirche*, SS. 66, 72–6, 120.

for the one who understands the hidden idea behind them to obey them.[73] Likewise the "Wisdom of Solomon" contends against infidels like these.[74]

Of course, it can be answered that there are in all places and in every generation wicked and irreligious people who disrupt standards and leave behind a bad reputation; there were such irresponsible people also in Palestine. But in the Diaspora, with the double life of the Jews there, and with the unceasing pressure of the influence of the native peoples, this general evil necessarily took a more specific form. Jews who endeavored to be both Jews and Greeks; a Jew like Philo, for whom the Greek language was "our language"— even he calling Jews who did not speak Greek "barbarians"— a Jew to whom Plato was "holiest of the holy" just like Moses, and who called the stars any number of times by the name "visible gods"; [75] Jews who saw a necessity to apologize for the strangeness in their religion and in their customs, and to bring these up to the level of philosophical ideas (the "Letter of Aristeas," Aristobulus the Philosopher, Philo, Josephus during his Roman exile); Jews who, in order to glorify their nation and their religion and to prove the antiquity of both, found it necessary or proper to create a whole forged literature, according to which venerable figures among the Greek poets and authors recognized the importance of Judaism (Pseudo-Hecataeus, the Sibylline Oracles, the forged citations found in Josephus and the Christian Church Fathers) —Jews like these were not sound in their faith like the Jews of Palestine.

Thus the Jews of the Diaspora were prepared for the first compromise between Judaism and Hellenism as offered by

[73] See Philo, *On the Posterity of Cain* §§ 35–40; *On Penitence* §§ 180–6; *Life of Moses* I 6 (§ 31); *On the Migration of Abraham* §§ 80–94 (see also J. Klausner, *Philosophim ve-Hoge-De'ot*, I, 76).

[74] Wisdom of Solomon 2:7–18.

[75] J. Klausner, *Philosophim ve-Hoge-De'ot*, I, 65–6.

Aristobulus the Philosopher (whose existence is not to be doubted) and Philo and their associates. In like manner openings for Christianity were made by a second compromise, that between thorough Judaism and diluted Judaism. Even Stephen and Paul, Jews of the Diaspora, encountered violent opposition from the Jews of the Diaspora; and even the synagogues of the "foreign-speaking" persecuted them and plotted against their lives, as will be seen below; which is to say that even Jews of the Diaspora were for the most part Jews devoted to their religion and to their people. But among these Jews were found—much more than among the thorough Jews—those who had been plucked out and uprooted from the Jewish tradition, who did not live, and perhaps could not live, in the Diaspora a completely Jewish life surrounded by Torah and ceremonial laws. Therefore it was easy and convenient for them to accept a new Messianic faith, especially after it began to preach disregard of the ritual requirements and the opening of all the gates to idolaters. The thing was not done without a long and bitter struggle; but if it had not been for the state of affairs in the Diaspora, if it had not been for these half-assimilated people, the struggle would not have concluded with the complete victory of the "apostle of the Gentiles"—Saul-Paul of Tarsus.

The Proselytes and the "God-Fearers" at the End of the Period of the Second Temple

[A. S. Herschberg, "Tenu'at ha-Hitgayyerut bi-Tequphat Bayit Sheni" (*Ha-Tequphah*, XII, 129–43; XIII, 189–210); J. Klausner, *Ha-Ra'yon ha-Meshihi be-Yisrael*, 2nd ed., pp. 307–12, 333; *Historia Yisreelit*, II, 205–7; IV, 32–36; A. Z. Marcus, *Le-Toledot Dat Natseret*, part I, *Gerim*, Jerusalem 5697 (1937); A. Bertholet, *Die Stellung der Israeliten und der Juden zu den Fremden*, Berlin 1896; E. Schürer, *Geschichte*, III[4], 150–88; A. Harnack, *Mission und Ausbreitung des Christentums*, SS. 30–52; S. Bialoblocki, *Die Beziehungen des Judentums zu Proselyten und Proselytentum*, Berlin 1930; I. Levy, "Le Prosélytisme Juif" (*Révue des Etudes Juives*, LI (1906), 1–29—Hebrew translation in *Ha-Goren*, IX, 5–30); J. Juster, *Les Juifs dans l'Empire Romain*, I, 253–90; G. F. Moore, *Judaism in the First Century of the Christian Era*, I, 323–53; F. M. Derwacter, *Preparing the Way for Paul* (The Proselyte Movement in Later Judaism), New York 1930.]

1. That the Jews gathered proselytes under the wings of the Shekhinah at least from the days of the Babylonian captivity on—of this we have clear proofs from the Prophets [1] and from the Writings.[2] To be sure, in the book of Ruth there is no hint of the recognition of the validity of the Torah of Israel on the part of Ruth the Moabitess. She says to Naomi her mother-in-law, ". . . thy people shall be my people, and thy God my God," only out of love for her mother-in-law and unwillingness to be separated from her; nevertheless, Boaz blesses her thus:

May the Lord recompense thy work, and a full reward be given thee of the Lord God of Israel, under whose wings thou art come to take refuge.[3]

Likewise the statement (from the book of Esther), "And many from among the peoples of the land became Jews: for

[1] Isaiah 14:1, 2; 56:3–8.
[2] The entire book of Ruth, and Esther 8:17.   [3] Ruth 1:16; 2:11, 12.

the fear of the Jews was fallen upon them," [4] can be interpreted to mean that out of fear many of the peoples of the land pretended to be Jews, but were not actually converted. Nevertheless, it is clear that the Jews already had converts from the Gentiles before the days of the Hasmoneans.

The verse mentioned above [5] from the book of Malachi—

> For from the rising of the sun even unto the going
>   down of the same
> My name is great among the nations;
> And in every place offerings are presented unto My
>   name,
> Even pure oblations;
> For My name is great among the nations,
> Saith the Lord of hosts,

—this verse, clearly shows not only the great spread of the Jews in all the world near the close of prophecy, but, together with this, the increase of proselytes; a witness to this is the use of the words, "My name is great among the nations," two times by way of emphasis. One could not explain the great number of Jews in the Diaspora near the time of the destruction of the Second Temple without bringing into account a considerable addition of male and female proselytes.

This number reached, according to all estimates, to nearly three million (apart from the Jews in Palestine).[6] The debate is about the number of Jews in Palestine at that period: while Juster puts the figure up to five million,[7] Tscherikower [8] reckons only two and a half to three million, Derwacter [9] only one million (and a half-million non-Jews in all Palestine), and Harnack [10] only 700,000 by comparison with the number

---

[4] Esther 8:17.   [5] See above, p. 8.
[6] See Tscherikower, *op. cit.*, p. 300; Klausner, *Historia Yisreelit*, I, 209; Juster, *op. cit.*, I, 209–10; Harnack, *op. cit.*, S. 6; Derwacter, *op. cit.*, pp. 115–6.
[7] Juster, I, 210, note 2.   [8] *Op. cit.*, p. 300.
[9] *Op. cit.*, p. 115.   [10] *Op. cit.*, S. 6.

of inhabitants of Palestine in modern times—a comparison that is decidedly in error.[11] In any case, the number of Jews in Palestine alone was equal, more or less, to the number of all the rest of the Jews in all the lands of the Diaspora under Roman rule. The Jews of Palestine were a decided majority not only in their own country (according to my opinion, based on exact calculations the nature of which this is no place to explain, there lived in Palestine three million Jews, besides a half-million Syro-Canaanites, Greeks, Arabs, and Romans), but also in comparison with the number of Jews in any one country under Roman rule: in Egypt there were a million Jews; in Syria and Asia Minor a million and a half; and there were a million Jews in the countries of Europe (Greece, Gaul, Spain, and others) and in northern Africa (Cyrene, Carthage, etc.). And in Babylonia, which does not touch our interest here, there were also a million Jews.[12] If we do not count, then, the Jews of Babylonia (the majority of whom had not migrated to that country from Palestine, but were descendants of the captives who had been deported from Palestine in the days of Sennacherib and Nebuchadrezzar), they amounted to approximately three million Jews in Palestine in comparison with three and a half million Jews in all the "Roman Diaspora" (if it is possible to speak thus). It is evident that three million concentrated in one place, where they were a majority dominating the rest of the inhabitants, were an immeasurably greater power than the one million Jews among seven and a half million non-Jews in Egypt, for example; but three and a half million Jews constitute a great number when considered alone. It is hard to believe that all these millions of Jews had assembled themselves by emigration from little Palestine alone. One is forced to say that this great increase came also

[11] Juster, *loc. cit.*, has already discussed this.
[12] *Antiq.* XI v 2 (§ 133): the "ten tribes" beyond the Euphrates are "countless myriads whose number cannot be ascertained."

from the reception of male and female proselytes in large numbers.

Indeed, all the Jewish and Greek literature of that period is filled with statements about male and female proselytes from among the Gentiles. Josephus says: "The masses have long since shown a keen desire to adopt our religious observances, and there is not one city, Greek or barbarian, nor a single nation, to which our custom of abstaining from work on the seventh day has not spread, and where the fasts and the lighting of lamps and many of our prohibitions in the matter of food are not observed."[13] And when Josephus tells of the plundering of the treasures of the Temple by Crassus,[14] he says that the sources of the great amount of gold which Crassus found in the Temple were contributions which not only "Jews throughout the habitable earth" but also "God-fearers" in Asia and Europe were accustomed to contribute to the Temple in Jerusalem.[15] Concerning the increase of proselytes and "God-fearers" from among the Gentiles, Seneca [16] and Cassius Dio also bear witness.[17] Horace threatens that he and his associates will fall upon the hater of poetry, and "like the Jews, we will force you to come over to our numerous party."[18] The early section of the third Sibyl from the year 140 B.C.E. says that "the Jews were for all mortal men the guides to [the way of] life."[19] The Gospel according to Matthew puts into the mouth of Jesus these clear words: "Woe unto you, scribes and Pharisees, hypocrites! for ye compass sea and land to make one proselyte."[20] And

[13] *Against Apion* II 39 (§ 282).
[14] See on this J. Klausner, *Historia Yisreelit*, II, 202.
[15] *Antiq.* XIV vii 2 (§ 110).
[16] *Apud* Augustine, *Civitas Dei* IV 11.
[17] Cassius Dio, XXXVII 7.
[18] Horace, *Sat.* I 4 142; see also I 9 68–72.
[19] Sibylline Oracles III 195.
[20] Matt. 13:15. For no reason whatsoever Bialoblocki (*op. cit.*, S. 12) refuses to attribute to these plain and emphatic words "great historical importance"; the Evangelists would not have praised the Pharisees in strong terms like these, merely to blame them along with their praise.

in the prayer *Shemoneh Esreh*, in the Palestinian version which was found in the "Genizah" at Fusṭāṭ near Cairo, there is a special petition: "May Thy mercies be stirred over the righteous proselytes and give us a goodly reward with those who do Thy will; blessed be Thou, O Lord, support of the righteous." [21] In the Babylonian version, which is the accepted one among us, the Jews, to-day, it is said: "May Thy mercies be stirred over the righteous and over the pious and over the righteous proselytes and over the rest of Thy people, the house of Israel," etc. The Midrash says: "Every one who brings a proselyte near it is as though he created him." [22] And a whole chapter in the Midrash Rabbah speaks of the importance and desirability of the proselytes in words that are at the same time both forceful and tender. The Amora R. Abbahu says:

The verse *They that dwell under his shadow shall return*, etc. (Hos. xiv, 8), refers to the proselytes who come and take refuge in the shadow of the Holy One, blessed be He; *They shall keep themselves alive with corn* (*ib.*); that is, with Talmud; *And shall blossom as the vine* (*ib.*) in Haggadah. *The scent* [remembrance] *thereof shall be as the wine of Lebanon* (*ib.*): "The names [remembrance] of the proselytes," said the Holy One, blessed be He, "are as dear to me as the wine of libation which is poured out upon the altar." [23]

This is a late saying of an Amora. But there are in this wonderful chapter earlier and more ancient words. These, in my opinion, are found in another saying, accompanied by a parable:

[21] See this version, which was published by S. Schechter in *Jewish Quarterly Review*, X (1898), 654–9; also in G. Dalman, *Messianische Texte aus der nachkanonischen jüdischen Literatur*, Leipzig 1898 (Sonderabdruck aus *Die Worte Jesu*), S. 20.

[22] Genesis Rabbah LXXXIV 4 [Eng. tr. by H. Freedman, London 1939, p. 771].

[23] Numbers Rabbah VIII 1 [Eng. tr. by J. J. Slotki, London 1939, p. 202].

The Holy One, blessed be He, greatly loves the proselytes. To what may this be compared? To a king who had a flock which used to go out to the field and come in at even. So it was each day. Once a stag came in with the flock. He associated with the goats and grazed with them. When the flock came in to the fold he came in with them; when they went out to graze he went out with them. The king was told: "A certain stag has joined the flock and is grazing with them every day. He goes out with them and comes in with them." The king felt an affection for him. When he went out into the field the king gave orders: "Let him have good pasture, such as he likes; no man shall beat him; be careful with him!" When he came in with the flock also the king would tell them, "Give him to drink"; and he loved him very much. The servants said to him: "Sovereign! You possess so many he-goats, you possess so many lambs, you possess so many kids, and you never caution us about them; yet you give us instructions every day about this stag!" Said the king to them: "The flock have no choice; whether they want or not, it is their nature to graze in the field all day and to come in at even to sleep in the fold. The stags, however, sleep in the wilderness. It is not in their nature to come into places inhabited by man. Shall we then not account it as a merit to this one which has left behind the whole of the broad, vast wilderness, the abode of all the beasts, and has come to stay in the courtyard?" In like manner, ought we not to be grateful to the proselyte who has left behind him his family and his father's house, aye, has left behind his people and all the other peoples of the world and has chosen to come to us? Accordingly, He [the Holy One, blessed be He] has provided him with special protection, for He exhorted Israel that they shall be very careful in relation to the proselytes so as not to do them harm; and so indeed it says, *Love ye therefore the proselyte*, etc. (Deut. X, 19). *And a proselyte shalt thou not oppress* (Ex. XXIII, 9; *cf.* also Lev. XIX, 33 f.).[24]

This wonderful parable recalls in part the Gospel parable of the man who has a hundred sheep, and, when one of the sheep goes astray and then later is found again, "rejoiceth over it more than over the ninety and nine which have not

[24] *Ibid.* VIII 2 [Eng. tr. 204].

gone astray." [25] I think that this parable is ancient, notwith-standing the fact that its popular literary style in the Midrash makes it appear as though it is not so ancient. Indeed, without a sympathetic, and more than sympathetic, attitude toward the proselytes on the part of Israel, it would be impossible to explain the success of Judaism among the Gentiles. Josephus bears witness that in the city of Antioch, which became one of the first and most important Christian centers, the Jews "were constantly attracting to their religious ceremonies multitudes of Greeks, and these they had in some measure made a part of themselves" (that is, of the Jewish community).[26] Likewise he tells about Damascus, where Paul became a Christian, that when the pagan population decided to fall upon the Jews living among them at the beginning of the Jewish revolt against Rome (in the year 66–7 C.E.), they kept this decision hidden not only from their Jewish neighbors, but also from their own Greek wives, "all of whom, with few exceptions had been brought over to the Jewish religion," [27]—a passage that is important from any number of viewpoints for the history of Paul. Tacitus says that "the scum and outcasts of the rest of the peoples" were "forsaking the religion of their own lands and streaming in crowds to Jerusalem." [28] Of course, for this persecutor of Jews and hater of Christians, pagans who accept Judaism are nothing but "scum" of the human race and "outcasts" of the peoples; but the fact that pagans were "streaming in crowds to Jerusalem" after "forsaking the religion of their own lands" is not changed by this negative estimate of their deeds. Philo also confirms this fact.[29] Horace says that his friend in Rome was "one of many" (*unus multorum*) who observed the customs of the Jews.[30] At a later

---

[25] Matt. 18:12, 13; Luke 15:3–7. [26] *Jewish War* VII iii 3.
[27] *Ibid*. II xx 2. [28] See Tacitus, *Hist*. V 5.
[29] Philo, *The Special Laws* I: the Monarchy 51–3 [Eng. tr. by Colson, VII, 127–8]. *On the Virtues:* Patience § 179.
[30] Horace, *Sat*. I 9, 68–72.

time Juvenal [31] rages and sneers in words that are more specific and much more violent:

Some who have had a father who reveres the Sabbath, worship nothing but the clouds, and the divinity of the heavens, and see no difference between eating swine's flesh, from which their father abstained, and that of man; and in time they take to circumcision. Having been wont to flout the laws of Rome, they learn and practise and revere the Jewish law, and all that Moses committed to his secret tome, forbidding to point out the way to any not worshipping the same rites, and conducting none but the circumcised to the desired fountain.

The meaning is clear, it seems to me: there are those subject to Judaism who have not been circumcised; the father, who has not been circumcised and has still not renounced Roman laws altogether, yet keeps the Sabbath, believes in the God of the Heavens and refrains from forbidden foods, finally comes to the point of transmitting his faith to his son, who is circumcised, renounces Roman laws and becomes a complete Jew, not showing the way of faith and not giving to drink of its fountain to any except those who have dedicated themselves to the sacred practice of the Jewish religion. And it appears as though Juvenal took these stinging words of the satire from "an incident that happened"—from historic fact.

Josephus tells in detail and at length about the conversion of the kings of Adiabene.[32] A merchant from Judea, Hananiah [Ananias] by name, converted the queen, wife of Izates (or Zotos in the Midrash), son of Monobazus I and Helena his wife. Also Queen Helena, mother of Izates, was secretly converted by another Jew. The conversions, then, began with the women, who were inclined toward the sensitive ethics and

[31] Juvenal, *Sat*. XIV 96–104 [Eng. tr. by G. G. Ramsey, Loeb Classical Library, pp. 271–2].

[32] *Antiq*. XX ii–v (§§ 24–53). And see Klausner, *Historia Yisreelit*, IV, 32–6, where are given the Talmudic-Midrashic sources relevant to this matter. For the different versions see Bialoblocki, *op. cit.*, SS. 15–22.

emotional faith of Judaism; but the main thing was that they were not burdened with circumcision, and baptism alone was sufficient for them. This is also important for the understanding of the success of Paul, who spoke for the disregard of circumcision and for the sufficiency of baptism alone.

When it became known to Izates that his mother and his wife adhered to Judaism, he was ready to be circumcised; however, his mother restrained him from this, and even Hananiah [Ananias] argued that he should not do it, in these words: "It is possible to worship God even without being circumcised." Indeed, "to keep the tradition of the ancestors of the Jews—this is more important than circumcision" [33]— almost the exact words of Paul. But later there came to Adiabene a Jew from Galilee, Eleazar by name, who demanded of the king that he by all means be circumcised as required by the Law of Moses, which Izates had been reading.

Here we have the controversy about the necessity of circumcision for proselytes, which is already present in an old Baraitha in the Talmud, where two leading Tannaim contend: R. Joshua ben Hananiah thinks that a proselyte who "performed the prescribed ablution but had not been circumcised, behold he is a proper proselyte" (the opinion of this son of Hananiah is like that of the Hananiah in the preceding paragraph); but R. Eliezer ben Hyrcanus thinks that a proselyte who "was circumcised but had not performed the prescribed ritual ablution, behold he is a proper proselyte"; and only the Sages think that "he is not a proper proselyte, unless he has been circumcised and has also performed the prescribed ritual ablution." [34] This controversy, which is reflected in historical events recorded in the works of the Jew Josephus and of the Roman Juvenal, throws a clear light upon

[33] *Antiq.* XX ii 4 (§ 41).
[34] Yebamoth 46a [Eng. tr. by I. W. Slotki, London 1936]. See also Bialoblocki, *op. cit.*, SS. 17–9.

the controversy between Paul and Barnabas, on the one hand, and James, the brother of Jesus, and Simon Cephas-Peter, on the other hand. The main point of this controversy from the beginning was, whether to demand strict obedience to the law of circumcision of pagans who accepted Judaism in its Christian form, or whether baptism alone was sufficient;[35] only later was this controversy extended to all the rest of the ritual requirements of the Torah.

2. This brings us to another important controversial matter: to the problem of the "God-fearers" [or "Fearers of God" or "Worshippers of God" or the "God-fearing" as the phrase may be variously translated].

Josephus, when he speaks of the plundering of the treasures of the Temple by Crassus the Roman, mentions, as we saw above,[36] as contributors to the Temple, "all the Jews throughout the habitable earth, and *those that worshipped God*, nay, even those of Asia and Europe." [37] Of Poppaea (Sabina) the queen, wife of the emperor Nero, Josephus says that "she was a Worshipper of God." [38] Of Cornelius, "centurion of the band called the Italian," it is said [39] that he was a "devout man, and *one that feared God* with all his house." Paul turns at Antioch of Pisidia in the synagogue on the Sabbath to "Men

[35] Against S. Zeitlin (*Hebrew Union College Annual*, I [1924], 357–63) in whose opinion baptism of proselytes was later than the destruction of the Temple. See Klausner, *Yeshu ha-Notsri*, 4th ed., p. 272, note 5. We must add to what I have written there the words of the Talmud: "Whence does R. Joshua infer that the mothers performed ritual ablution [baptism]? —It is a logical conclusion, for, otherwise, whereby did they enter under the wings of the Shechinah!" (Yebamoth 46b [Eng. tr. by I. W. Slotki]). And why did not Zeitlin ask himself: If there was no baptism of proselytes before the destruction of the Temple, how did the numerous women before the Destruction (Queen Helena, the women of Damascus, and others) enter under the wings of the Shekhinah? By affirmation alone?

[36] See above, p. 16 f. [also p. 34, note 15].
[37] *Antiq.* XIV vii 2 (§ 110).
[38] *Ibid.* XX viii 11 (§ 195). Compare the *Life of Josephus* 3 (§ 16).
[39] Acts 10:2.

of Israel and *ye that fear God*"; [40] and he goes on to appeal to "Brethren, children of the stock of Abraham, and *those among you that fear God*." [41] In Philippi of Macedonia he finds, in the place of prayer, Lydia, a seller of purple from the city of Thyatira, a woman who "worshipped God." [42] And in Corinth, when Paul shakes himself free of the Jews who opposed him with all their might and says, "from henceforth I will go unto the Gentiles," he "went into the house of a certain man named Titus Justus, *one that worshipped God*, whose house joined hard to the synagogue." [43] Sometimes the phrase, "Fearers of God," is shortened and reduced to one word: at Thessalonica [44] Paul finds "of the *devout* Greeks a great multitude," obviously Greeks who were God-fearers; and in Athens "he reasoned in the synagogue with the Jews and the *devout* persons." [45] Here "devout" (σεβόμενοι) is a short form of "Fearers of God" (σεβόμενοι τὸν θεόν) to avoid the full repetition of a phrase made familiar even in its short form by much use, or to avoid profaning the name of Deity.

The phenomenon itself is natural and understandable. Between thorough Jews and thorough pagans there were necessarily to be found, standing in a middle position, some who accepted Judaism as a great and beautiful ideal, who observed a part of its customs, but who did not become complete Jews. They were like Naaman, captain of the host of Syria, in the Old Testament,[46] who knows that "there is no God in all the earth, but in Israel" and who "will henceforth offer neither burnt-offering nor sacrifice unto other gods but the Lord"; nevertheless, he continues "to bow down in the house of Rimmon" with his master, the king of Syria. Many of the Gentiles in the days of the Second Temple and for a certain time thereafter were in relatively the same position: in a formal

[40] Acts 13:16.
[41] Acts 13:26.
[42] Acts 16:14.
[43] Acts 18:7.
[44] Acts 17:4.
[45] Acts 17:17.
[46] II Kings 5:15, 17, 18.

way they remained within their own nations—Greeks, Romans, Syrians, and so on; but out of respect for monotheism
and the Torah of Israel (about which they knew from the
Septuagint) and out of admiration for beautiful Jewish customs (the lighting of the Sabbath light, the Sabbath rest, the
prudence with regard to the eating of blood, the abstention
from marriage with sisters, which was common in Greece,
and the like), they were drawing near to Judaism, visiting
the synagogues of Israel, reading the Scriptures in the Greek
translation, and observing various regulations which were not
too difficult. Complete Jews they were not; but they had departed from the ordinary pagan way of life. And it was easy
later to gather them in to Christianity—a mystery religion
close to the hearts of the "seekers after God" among the
Greeks; *first*, because there was in it a certain similarity to
the pagan mystery religions about which I shall speak later
on, and *second*, because Christianity was a religion of salvation, something about which the best among the sons of the
pagan world were deeply concerned in those days.

In the light of these facts it is difficult to agree with the
view of the scholar, A. Bertholet,[47] that there were not two
kinds of proselytes in Judaism: "God-fearer" is, in his opinion,
only a synonym for "proselyte"; that is why Paul in the
Pisidian Antioch addresses as "brethren" not only the "children of the stock of Abraham," but also "those among you
that fear God." That this is a weak proof is not hard to see.
Of course even "God-fearers" who were not complete Jews
were "brethren" to a man like Paul, who made things easy
for the pagans and endeavored to bring them over to his
own form of religion. It is also true that Judaism does not
recognize half-proselytes as real proselytes,[48] since "a proselyte who accepts all the words of Torah except one word, is

[47] Bertholet, *op. cit.*, SS. 331-4.
[48] Moore, *op. cit.*, I, 326-31.

not to be admitted." [49] But, "God-fearers" are not prose-lytes, nor even half-proselytes: [50] they are Gentiles, who have ceased to worship a foreign deity and are keeping some of the Jewish observances which they find agreeable. Thus we saw that Josephus calls Poppaea Sabina, wife of the emperor Nero, a "Worshipper of God," [51] although she was not a real proselyte. Likewise, the Midrash tells of "one of the Emperor's senators" in Rome, who was "a God-fearing man" and committed suicide in order to nullify a harsh decree against the Jews—then it transpired that he had been circum-cised a short time before his death; [52] hence he was "a God-fearing man" even before he was circumcised.

The centurion in Capernaum was a lover of the people of Israel and built a synagogue for the Jews; [53] yet he was not a proselyte, for if he had been, he would not have said to Jesus that Jesus should "not trouble himself" to come to his home because he was "not worthy" that Jesus should come under his roof, and also that he was not worthy to come to Jesus; likewise Jesus said: "I have not found so great faith, no, not in Israel" [implying that the centurion was not "in Israel"]. [54] Clearly, a real proselyte is in every way a part of Israel. The Ethiopian eunuch, guardian of the treasures of Candace, queen of Ethiopia, who was reading the book of Isaiah while he sat in his chariot, [55] even he was only a God-fearer before he was baptized as a (Christian) proselyte. Also Cornelius, the cen-turion in Caesarea, who was "a devout man, and one that feared God," was not a proselyte before he was baptized by Peter, [56] as is clearly seen from what Peter said in connexion

---

[49] Mekhilta de R. Simeon ben Yohai on Exodus 12:49 (ed. of D. Hoff-mann, p. 30); Siphra, Kedoshim VIII (ed. of I. H. Weiss, 91a).

[50] As even I called them by linguistic habit (Ha-Ra'yon ha-Meshihi be-Yisrael, p. 310).

[51] See above, p. 40.

[52] Deuteronomy Rabbah II 24 [tr. by J. Rabbinowitz, London 1939].

[53] Luke 7:5.   [54] Luke 7:6–9.

[55] Acts 8:27, 28.   [56] Acts 10:1–48.

with him, that "it is an unlawful thing for a man that is a Jew to join himself or come unto one of another nation; and yet unto me [Peter] hath God showed that I should not call any man common or unclean." [57] A real proselyte is not "one of another nation" and not "unclean."

But a still clearer proof, that we must distinguish between proselytes and God-fearers, is the Tannaitic saying, which is repeated in the more ancient Halakhic Midrashim and also in the Haggadic Midrashim:

> One shall say: "I am the Lord's" (Isa. 44.5), that is: "All of me is the Lord's and there is no admixture of sin in me." *And another shall call himself by the name of Jacob* (ibid.), these are the righteous proselytes. *And another shall subscribe with his hand unto the Lord* (ibid.), these are the repentant sinners. *And surname himself by the name of Israel* (ibid.), these are the God-fearing ones [literally, "Fearers of Heaven"].[58]

Therefore the God-fearers are different and are to be distinguished from the "righteous [or true] proselytes." To these "Fearers of Heaven" (and Heaven is a substitute name for God, as in the equations: "Kingdom of Heaven" equals Kingdom of the Almighty [Shaddai] or Kingdom of God; "Name of Heaven" equals "Name of God"), who are differentiated

[57] Acts 10:10, 28.

[58] Mekhilta, Mishpatim, Tractate Nezikin XVIII [Eng. tr. by J. Z. Lauterbach, Philadelphia 1935, III, 141]; Numbers Rabbah VIII 2; and in a different version—Aboth de R. Nathan, Recension A, XXXVI (ed. of Schechter, 54a); Seder Eliyahu Rabbah XVIII (ed. of Friedmann, p. 105). See also Aboth de R. Nathan, Recension B, XVIII, p. 40. In the Midrash Tehillim, cxviii. 11, there is [added] in various recensions the statement, "the God-fearers are the proselytes"; but see the edition of Buber, p. 482, and "Notes and Corrections," p. 242, for the claim that there is no such addition. And in Leviticus Rabbah III 2 we read: "'Ye that fear the Lord,' said R. Joshua ben Levi, means those that fear heaven [i.e., it bears its literal meaning]. R. Ishmael [Samuel?] bar Nahman said: It means the righteous proselytes" [Eng. tr. by J. Israelstam, London 1939]. R. Ishmael bar Nahman was a late Amora, and in his time it was possible to think that God-fearers were true proselytes. Nevertheless, in this difference of opinion between two Amoraim the distinction between "Fearers of Heaven" and "true proselytes" is brought out.

from the "righteous proselytes," were justifiably applied these words of the verse: ". . . and surname himself by the name of Israel";[59] for they were not genuine Jews, but only "called themselves by the name of Israel"—they approached in principle the religio-ethical views of Israel without really accepting all the requirements which are laid upon a real proselyte.

"The proselytes"—true proselytes (גריהצדק)—"are like Israel";[60] but God-fearers are not like Israel, either from their own standpoint or from that of Israel. However, they were beloved of Israel and Israel was beloved of them. They were beloved of Israel because, in the eyes of the Jews, they were among those "near the way of truth"; and Israel was beloved of them because in its faith and in its Torah they found good solid elemental principles, the like of which they did not find in the pagan faiths.

3. Nevertheless, the God-fearers, and even the true proselytes, did not always remain loyal to the people of Israel to the end.

Josephus says plainly:

Many of them [the Greeks] have come over to our laws, and some of them have continued in their observance, although others of them had not courage enough to persevere, and so departed from them again.[61]

Likewise the Talmud expresses trepidation, lest the proselyte return to his original evil way:

It has been taught: R. Eliezer the Great said: "Why did the Torah warn against a proselyte in thirty-six, or as others say, in forty-six places? Because he has a strong inclination to evil."[62]

Rabbah bar Samuel—though he was an Amora, and not a

<hr />

[59] Isaiah 44:5.
[61] *Against Apion* II 10 (§ 123).

[60] Numbers Rabbah VIII 2.
[62] Baba Metzi'a 59b.

Tanna—speaks of "a proselyte who had reverted to his previous errors." [63] In the Mishnah we read:

If a proselyte and a gentile inherited jointly from their father
who was a gentile, the proselyte may say to the other, "Do thou
take what pertains to idolatry [the idols] and I will take the
money," or "Do thou take the wine [of libation] and I will take
the produce"; but after the property has come into the possession
of the proselyte it is forbidden to him [to make any such pro-
posal].[64]

The purpose of the decree is "lest he [the proselyte] return
to his evil ways." [65] Indeed there is in the Talmud a story
about a proselyte who was an astrologer who in fact did
"return to his original evil way." [66] There is also in the Talmud a justifiable fear of the "false proselyte," [67] who is the
reverse of the "true proselyte" and not a "settler-proselyte"
(*ger toshab*), the latter being nothing except a Gentile living
in Palestine. According to R. Meir, it is sufficient for the
"settler-proselyte" to undertake in the presence of three Associates (*Haberim*) not to worship idols; or, according to the
Sages, he must take upon himself the seven precepts of the
sons of Noah; and there is also a strange opinion ("still others
maintain") that a "settler-proselyte" is "a proselyte who eats
of animals not ritually slaughtered, *i.e.*, he undertook to observe all the precepts mentioned in the Torah apart from the
prohibition of [eating the flesh of] animals not ritually
slaughtered"; but a halakhah agrees with the Sages. And in

---

[63] Gittin 45b. The saying, which Bialoblocki (*op. cit.*, p. 23) presents
from Horayoth 13a, is not concerned with the apprehension lest the proselyte return to his former state; it is said only that the proselyte "was not
brought up with us in holiness."

[64] Demai VI 10; Tosephta, *ibid.* VI 13 (here we find the word *tselamim*;
the words *elile-kokhabim* in the Mishnah or *abodah zarah* in the Gemara
[see the next note] do not occur except under duress of the censor).

[65] Kiddushin 17b; Abodah Zarah 64a (and there it is said "lest he return
to his corruption" [*qilqul*] instead of his "previous error" [*sor*]).

[66] *Yerushalmi*, Abodah Zarah II 2 (41a).

[67] *Ibid.*, Baba Metzi'a V 7 (10c, middle).

the opinion of all he "is like a Gentile in every other respect"; and in the opinion of R. Johanan, "a *ger toshab* who allows twelve months to pass without becoming circumcised is to be regarded as a heretic among idolaters!" [68]

Even for the true proselytes it was difficult to adapt themselves to the religion of Israel, which has so many strict requirements. The Talmud is replete with complaints about proselytes who are not well-versed in the ceremonial laws and who "hold the deeds of their fathers in their hands" [continue in the way of their fathers]. For example, the Tanna, R. Judah (ben Il'ai), declares unclean "all blood-stains that come from Rekem" [a place outside of Palestine] "since they are proselytes there and liable to err." [69] There is apprehension lest the proselyte turn away from his proselytism and "then betroth the daughter of an Israelite," in which case he is regarded as a "non-conforming Israelite." [70] It is said in the Talmud: "Evil comes upon those who receive proselytes." [71] And a Baraitha says that "the proselytes delay [the coming of] the Messiah." [72] R. Jose mocks the proselytes and says that in the Days of the Messiah they will be frightened because of "the battle of Gog and Magog" and will give up the observance of the ceremonial laws; [73] and R. Eliezer ben Hyrcanus says that all Gentiles will become "self-made proselytes in the time to come." [74] Finally must be mentioned the saying which although attributed to a later Amora, R. Helbo, was accepted by the nation and repeated many times in the Talmud: "Prose-

[68] *Babli*, Abodah Zarah 64b and 65a. A "proselyte of the gate" is the same as a "settler-proselyte," in accordance with the Biblical passage "thy stranger [proselyte] that is within thy gates" [Ex. 20:10, Deut. 5:14]. See Bialoblocki, *op. cit.*, SS. 4–6, 31 (notes).

[69] Mishnah, Niddah VII 3.

[70] Yebamoth 47b.

[71] *Ibid*. 109b.

[72] Niddah 13b. See on this Klausner, *Ha-Ra'yon ha-Meshihi be-Yisrael*, 2nd ed., pp. 275–7, 307–10.

[73] Abodah Zarah 3b.

[74] *Ibid*. 24a.

lytes are as hard for Israel as a sore [סַפַּחַת], for it is written in Scripture *And they shall cleave* [like a sore, וְנִסְפְּחוּ] to the house of Jacob." [75] To be sure, all these are sayings which were delivered by Tannaim not earlier than the second century c.e. and by Amoraim not later than the fourth century c.e.; but in the presence of the clear and explicit testimony of Josephus, that there were among the proselytes "others of them [who] had not courage enough to persevere, and so departed from them [Jewish observances] again," [76] there can be no doubt of the fact that also in the first century c.e., that is to say, in the days of Paul, the situation was similar. [77]

If among the proselytes many were returning to their paganism, among the God-fearers how many more! It is easy to understand that these "hangers-on," who had not within them the strength to shake off paganism completely and to take upon themselves the yoke of the Torah and the cere-monial laws, could not stand the test in the hour of persecu-tion. The law of circumcision was hard for them; only the abstractly religious and ethical conceptions of Judaism found favor in their eyes—not the whole Judaistic order of life, which enfolds the true Israelite in every step of his feet and every deed of his hands from the cradle to the grave. There-fore, it is not to be wondered at, when a man like Paul came and nullified in their presence the ritual laws and was satisfied with baptism alone without circumcision, and gave them a faith in one God with mystical conceptions of a Messianism saving and redeeming by the blood of atonement along with an Israelite ethic, that this new half-Jewish, half-pagan faith was taken to the pagan heart which was covered by only a

[75] Yebamoth 47b and 109b; Kiddushin 70b; Niddah 13b; Isa. 14:1.
[76] See above, p. 45.
[77] Already at the beginning of the second century Judah "son of prose-lytes" informs the government of the words of R. Simeon ben Yohai against Roman rule and causes the latter to flee lest he be killed by the government (Shabbath 33b).

light wrapping of abstract Judaism even before the coming of Paul.

Paul and his Christianity were built out of the ruins of the uprooted Judaism of the Diaspora; but even more than by the Jews of the Diaspora, Paul's Christianity was accepted by a great part of the proselytes—"true proselytes" and "false proselytes"—and especially by those God-fearers who were not proselytes, nor half-proselytes, but Gentiles attracted by certain abstract principles of Judaism which could easily be exchanged for the mystical principles of Pauline Christianity.

These were the basic human foundations upon which Paul built his first Christian congregations—especially outside of Palestine. For in Palestine there were not so many uprooted Jews and even the proselytes had more "courage to persevere"; and uncircumcised God-fearers were relatively few there as compared with the Diaspora.

But Paul built the Christian Church also upon complete Gentiles—outright pagans, who accepted Christianity directly from him and from his apostolic associates and not through the medium of Judaism. Christianized Gentiles like these were not so numerous at the beginning of the missionary work of Paul; but they continued to increase little by little until they became a decisive majority in the whole Christian Church.

This was brought about by the general state of the Gentile world in that period, to the description of which I now turn.

Second Book

THE PAGAN WORLD AT THE TIME OF THE RISE OF CHRISTIANITY

CHAPTER I

The World Empire of Rome and the General Situation Within It

[See L. Friedländer, *Hayye ha-Romaim*, Vilna 5669 (translated from the German of: *Darstellungen aus der Sittengeschichte Roms*, BB. I–IV, 8. Aufl., Leipzig 1910); E. Renan, *Les Apôtres*, Paris 1866, pp. 304–45; Foakes-Jackson and Lake, *The Beginnings of Christianity*, Part I, Vol. I, pp. 169–262; Ed. Meyer, *Blüte und Niedergang des Hellenismus in Asien*, Berlin 1925; P. Wendland, *Die hellenistisch-römische Kultur in ihren Beziehungen zu Judentum und Christentum*, 2. und 3. Aufl., Tübingen 1912; G. Wissowa, *Religion und Kultus der Römer*, München 1912, SS. 60–102; K. Latte, *Die Religion der Römer und der Synkretismus der Kaiserzeit*, Tübingen 1927; J. Geffcken, *Der Ausgang des griechisch-römischen Heidentums*, Heidelberg 1920; R. Reitzenstein, *Die hellenistischen Mysterienreligionen*, 2 Aufl., Leipzig-Berlin 1920; J. Leipoldt, *Sterbende und auferstehende Götter*, Leipzig-Erlangen 1923; Reitzenstein-Schäder, *Studien zum Antiken Synkretismus aus Rom und Griechenland* (Studien der Bibliothek Warburg, herausg. von F. Saxl), Leipzig-Berlin 1926; R. Eisler, *Orphisch-dionysische Mysteriengedanken in der christlichen Antike* (Vorträge der Bibliothek Warburg, 1922–3, II. Teil), Leipzig-Berlin 1925; K. L. Schmidt, *Der Apostel Paulus und die antike Welt* (Vorträge der Bibliothek Warburg, 1924–5), Leipzig-Berlin 1927, SS. 38–64; G. Kittel, *Die Religiongeschichte und das Urchristentum*, Gütersloh 1933; H. Gressmann, *Die orientalischen Religionen im hellenistisch-römischen Zeitalter*, Berlin-Leipzig 1930; Th. Birt, *Aus dem Leben der Antike*, Leipzig 1918; E. Dujardin, *Le Dieu Jésus*, Paris 1927; Th. Ziélinski, *La Sibylle* (Christianisme, Cahiers publiés sous la direction de P. L. Couchoud, 4), Paris 1914; W. R. Halliday, *The Pagan Background of Early Christianity*, Liverpool 1925; S. J. Case, *The Social Origins of Christianity*, Chicago 1923; J. Carcopino, *La vie quotidienne à Rome à l'apogée de l'empire*, Paris 1939]

1. In order that a new faith may be received by an old world, three sets of conditions are necessary. They may seem to be decided contrasts or even opposites, but, as a matter of fact, they always appear in the old world both singly and in combination when the hour arrives to change and give way to a new world:

(a) external conditions conducive to the spread of the new truth upon which the new world is founded;

(b) a high degree of cultural development and a seeking after an ideal which makes the old world ready to receive new truth;

(c) a weakening of the old truth, forcing people to seek new truth.

In these three important factors positive and negative are before us at the same time; both are necessary for a new movement. Out of the negative alone a new movement does not grow, because in a state of absolute moral decay ears are not attentive to lofty new conceptions. Yet in a high state of cultural health there is no need for a new movement, because the old is still sufficiently strong and good. Man is by nature a conservative creature and as long as the time of the old has not completely run its course, he is not quick to accept the new. Thus always is the course of history, and thus it was also in the first century C.E. Without the aforesaid three factors one could not conceive of the rise of a new religion at all. And undoubtedly, these three essential conditions, in both their positive and negative aspects, were all present together in the pagan world at the very time of the rise of Pauline Christianity.

2. The Tannaitic creators of the Talmud were not great lovers of the Roman Empire, which they called the "kingdom of wickedness"; they continually recalled that it had "laid waste our country and burned down our holy Temple and exiled us among the nations"; nevertheless the famous Tanna, R. Judah ben Il'ai once said of the Romans: "How fine are the deeds of this nation!—they have repaired streets, they have built bridges, they have erected baths." But R. Simeon ben Yohai answered this and said: "Everything which they have improved they have improved only for the need of them-

selves: they have improved streets—to accommodate prostitutes; baths—to luxuriate in themselves; bridges—to take toll from them." [1] Both men were right.

The Romans founded a far-reaching empire which included almost the whole civilized world of that time—excluding Parthia, India, and China, which were even then already known; also excluding the more remote lands, which were not yet known at all. Had it not been for this far-reaching empire, it would have been impossible for Judaism to spread in all these countries; thus, Christianity would not have been able to become a world religion, and Paul would not have been able to preach his new beliefs and opinions in so many lands. If primitive Christianity had confined itself to Palestine alone, it would have remained a Jewish sect, and possibly would even have been completely assimilated into Judaism, as was the case with the rest of the Jewish sects (Sadducees, Essenes, Zealots, *etc.*) immediately after the second Destruction.

The Roman Empire brought about the unification and connexion of all its conquered lands by means of excellent roads and highways. One can say, without any exaggeration, that the Roman routes of travel by land and by sea, traces of which are to be found wherever the Roman soldier set his foot, were the best that even western Europe knew until the beginning of the nineteenth century—until the coming of the railway into the world.[2] By means of these Roman roads journeys were made easier and commerce between various lands and nations was facilitated. We have an inscription on the tomb of a merchant from Phrygia in which it is said that this merchant journeyed to Rome during his lifetime seventy-two times! [3]

---

[1] Shabbath 33b.
[2] Friedländer, *Hayye ha-Romaim* (Hebrew translation), pp. 377–459; Halliday, *op. cit.*, pp. 64–104; Th. Birt, *op. cit.*, SS. 48–82.
[3] See A. Harnack, *op. cit.*, S. 13, Anm. 2.

The broad, improved roads—each one was called "the king's highway"—were crowded with people, and therefore were comparatively safe. There was superior Roman policing against highwaymen plundering by land and pirates plundering by sea.[4] There were, on the way, stations for the changing of horses and carriages, and there were also hostels, inns, and lodging houses. Bridges were built in order to shorten the route at rivers and small streams, hills were leveled down, and valleys filled up, while gravel was spread upon the surface of the roads in order that the way might not become a morass on rainy days. The Roman commanders, and the local kings and rulers who were subject to them, would fight local marauders and brigands who were interfering with business caravans and the passage of merchandise.[5]

There were uniform laws, which, with certain changes, were promulgated in all the conquered provinces. There was a certain order in the Roman Empire at large which the local authorities were responsible for maintaining, and there was peace—even though it was only a relative peace (*pax romana*)—in the land during the time of the first emperors, when the work of Paul was being accomplished. A testimonial of this is the splendid "Poem of the Ages" (*Carmen Saeculorum*) from the time of Augustus Caesar—an ornate paean of joy suitable to conditions of wealth, prosperity, and peace.[5a] To this testifies among others the Church Father, Origen, in his forceful words about the state of peace among the peoples in the days of the first emperors, a condition which alone made possible

[4] Of course, even in Roman times piracy increased because of the need for slaves (see Ed. Meyer, *op. cit.*, S. 73). But also here it must be said that both sides of the proposition are true.

[5] Of such kind was, *e.g.*, the war of Herod against the wild Arabs and bandits of Transjordania (Bashan, Argob, and the Hauran), in which he attempted to make them tillers of the soil and by curbing them to make safe the commerce between Damascus, Acco, Joppa, and Alexandria (see on this Klausner, *Historia Yisreelit*, III, 41).

[5a] [Klausner here means Horace's *Carmen Saeculare* ("Hymn of the Age"), produced in 17 B.C. Tr.]

the spread of the teaching of Jesus.[6] Because of this the peoples came into close contact with one another and there began a mixing of peoples by means of which the nations received from each other not only all kinds of merchandise—the produce of different countries and the products of different nations—but also many different beliefs and opinions.

These exchanges, both commercial-economic and cultural-religious, were facilitated by the sharing of a universal language—the Greek language, the language of culture of that time. To be sure, in western Europe the Latin language was in common use and even in the East the Romans used Latin not a little; but Greek was also used in western Europe, and in the East—in Asia Minor, Syria, Palestine, Egypt, *etc.*—the Greek language was the official international language—somewhat like French until after the [first] World War. Thus it was possible for a person who was fairly well educated to carry on business relations or philosophical conversation in almost every place where he encountered educated people (the masses used their own native languages, but even among these were found persons who understood Greek more or less, when they heard it).

The numerous journeys of Paul by land and sea were not a very difficult, or even a very unusual, thing in those days; likewise his preaching in various lands. We find orators, teachers of philosophy, literature and rhetoric passing from Greece to Rome, from there to Alexandria, and from there to Antioch, and even reaching Bordeaux in France and Cadiz in Spain. Philosophers native to Syria and Asia Minor scattered themselves in all the lands conquered by the Romans and were disseminating their own ideas or the ideas of their teachers far and wide. Thus Paul followed a more or less beaten track. Although the content of his teaching was different, Paul's ways of disseminating his ideas were in their externals like those of

[6] See Origen, *Contra Celsum*, II 30.

rhetoricians and sophists; but Paul added to them the Jewish inwardness and emotion which is peculiar to a monotheistic faith zealous for its separate existence—such inwardness and emotion as the rhetoricians did not know, since in most cases they had in view material glory and pleasure. Even when they were serious about their own doctrines they were not much moved—and they influenced only the intellect of the hearer and not his heart and his soul and all the feelings in him.

3. When we read the Latin literature of the time, the moral condition of all peoples in general and the Roman people in particular appears to us rotten to the core. The pursuit of gain had reached the utmost limit. For the sake of preferment at the imperial court even the great men among the Romans were ready for any folly or baseness. Family life had been ruined; most wives lightly betrayed their husbands, so naturally the men were even worse. Servants were treated like animals. The relationship of the patrons to their clients was base in the extreme. High in the Roman government were freedmen, corrupt women, and shameless concubines.[7]

Renan has pointed out that it is necessary to take the words of the Roman satirists *cum grano salis*.[8] And indeed it is impossible for even the fairest critics to be completely objective. Even the prophets of Israel exaggerated overmuch in describing the evils in their nation. When Jeremiah says that there is not to be found in the streets and broad places of Jerusalem even one man doing justice and seeking truth,[9] one should see in these words of his only an exaggeration justified by the anguish of heart and distress of soul of the prophet who is grieving because his own "idealistic demand" is not being realized in fact.

[7] See on all this the whole of Friedländer, *op. cit.*; Birt, *op. cit.*, SS. 1–47; 189–234.

[8] See Renan, *op. cit.*, pp. 306–10 (the factual material in this book is obsolete, but the book itself is still thought provoking).

[9] Jeremiah 5:1.

Furthermore, the fearful pictures of the degradation of moral standards in the days of the first emperors come from the pens of men who knew best the highest levels of the society of the Roman Empire; within the middle classes, of course, there were preserved the good old standards from which conservative people, zealous for their ancestral morality, were not quick to depart. Even in the top ranks there were at that time clean and moral people—or at least people who preached a pure morality—such as Vergil, Tibullus, Pliny the Younger, Quintilian, Tacitus, Seneca, Epictetus, Plutarch, *et al.* All this proves that it was not a leaderless generation even in a moral sense; there were in it many "saints among the Gentiles." If it had not been so, if the generation of Paul had been completely sunk in the morass of the pursuit of pleasures and the love of gain, no impression would have been made upon it by apostles of faiths in which morality was fundamental. Judaism and Christianity were able to influence that generation because the generation was ready for such influences both from the negative side—because in it the degradation of moral standards was great—and from the positive side—because there was in it a great longing for the building up of standards for clean moral living.

This positive side is to be recognized first of all in the philosophical thought of the Greeks and the Romans of that time.

CHAPTER II

Pagan Philosophical Thought in the Generation of Paul

[See on this: Zeller-Nestle, *Grundriss der Geschichte der griechischen Philosophie*, 12. Aufl., Leipzig 1910, SS. 246–342; P. Wendland, *Die hellenistisch-römische Kultur*, 1912, SS. 41–96; Gilbert Murray, *Five Stages of Greek Religion*, 2nd ed., Oxford 1930, pp. 103–207; C. Toussaint, *L'Hellénisme et l'Apôtre Paul*, Paris 1921, pp. 140–66; Th. Ziélinski, *Soperniki Khristianstva*, St. Petersburg, 1907.]

1. On the most cultured people of the generation of Paul and the generations near to him in time, the teaching of the Stoa or Stoicism had more influence than the other philosophical doctrines.

Stoicism taught a lofty ethical doctrine which, to be sure, did not have in it any of the ethico-religious warmth of soul which was completely at home in Judaism and Christianity; but there was in it something of the exaltation and loftiness of philosophical ethic reflected on a religious background. The principal representatives of Stoicism in the generation of Paul and in the generations close to him were Posidonius,[1] Seneca,[2] and Epictetus.[3] Therefore, I think it would be proper

---

[1] See for details about him the basic book of I. Heinemann, *Posidonios' Metaphysische Schriften*, Band I–II, Breslau 1921–1928; and in brief E. Bréhier, *Histoire de la philosophie*, Paris 1931, I, 2, 401–7; Ed. Schwartz, *Charakterköpfe*, 2. Aufl., SS. 89–98.

[2] On the relation of Seneca to Posidonius see Heinemann, I, 159–203. On the similarities between Seneca and Judaism see A. Kaminka, "Ha-Musar she-be-Siphre Seneca ve-ha-Musar ha-Yehudi" (in the monthly *Mozenayim*, IV [5695–1935], 46–51), and his notes to his Hebrew translations from the works of Seneca (see in the bibliography of the writings of Kaminka in the Jubilee volume dedicated to him, Vienna 5697, these items: 163, 165, 168, 210, 254, 276, 285, 289, 292, 295, 298, 309, 315, 317–20, 329–33, 347; to all this are now to be added his translations of *De Vita Beata* (*Gilyonot*,

to give the essence of the ideas of these three, rather than to discuss Stoicism in general. The first of these belongs to the "Middle Stoa" and the two others to the "New Stoa." (The "Middle Stoa" and the "New Stoa" are distinguished from the "Old Stoa" by the fact that these two tended toward the practical, and put less emphasis on the rule of reason alone.)

Posidonius, Seneca, and Epictetus taught in the very time of Paul, or a little before him, or a little after him. Seneca was born about 4 B.C.E. and died 65 C.E. He thus was almost an exact contemporary of Paul. He composed his philosophical works in the form of letters during the years 50–60 C.E., in the very time when Paul was writing his own "Epistles." Posidonius lived about 135–50 B.C.E.; his period of literary creativity was 90–60 B.C.E. Epictetus lived about 50–130 C.E.; hence his literary period was about 100–130 C.E., approximately forty years after the work of Paul.

The ideas in the writings of these three are so similar to the ideas of Christianity that the story arose of a meeting between Paul and Seneca in Rome, as a result of which there appeared an imaginary exchange of letters between the Stoic philosopher and the Christian apostle. As regards Epictetus, two scholars, a German and a Hollander, have claimed that he was influenced by the New Testament.[4] This claim has been refuted by clear and sufficient evidence.[5] The idea that Epictetus influenced Paul is, of course, impossible, since the teach-

---

VI, 381–403) and De Otio (ibid., VII, 34–41). See also his article "Yehudah ve-Yavan be-Darkhe ha-Melitsah ve-ha-Musar," Keneset, IV (5699), 345–64.

[3] See the three books of A. Bonhöffer, Epiktet und die Stoa (Stuttgart 1890), Die Ethik des Stoikers Epiktet (Stuttgart 1894), and Epiktet und das Neue Testament (Giessen 1911); also G. H. Gilbert, Greek Thought in the New Testament (New York 1928).

[4] See Th. Zahn, Der Stoiker Epiktet und sein Verhältniss zum Christentum, 2. Aufl. (Erlangen u. Leipzig 1895); K. Kuiper, Epictetus en de Christelijke Moraal (Amsterdam 1906).

[5] See Bonhöffer, Epiktet und das Neue Testament.

ing career of Epictetus began decades after Paul, as has been said, and the publication of his teaching by his pupil Arrian did not take place before 130 c.e. But the possibilities of supposing an exchange of letters between Paul and one Stoic, who was his contemporary, and of suspecting that another Stoic was influenced by the Epistles of Paul—these possibilities alone show how close the world-view of the Stoa, especially the Middle and New Stoa, was to that of Christianity. And since we know the profound influence of Stoicism, especially after the time of Panaetius (died c. 110 b.c.e.), the teacher of Posidonius, upon all the thinkers who lived in the Hellenistic-Roman world of culture, we can make use of the Stoic doctrines of these three philosophers as examples of the beliefs and opinions which prepared the ancient Gentile world to meet Christianity. On the other hand, we can also see in these doctrines a reflexion of the cultural world in which Paul lived and worked, by which he was influenced, and from which he received an impetus.

2. First of all, we shall try to describe the world view of Posidonius of Apamaea.

He was born about the year 135 b.c.e. After much travel in distant lands, he came in the year 86 with a delegation to Rome, and afterward conducted a Stoic school in Rhodes. There Cicero received instruction from him in the year 78, and Pompey visited the two of them there a number of times. Apparently, he was again in Rome in the year 51, and died soon after (c. 50 b.c.e.).

While Panaetius, his teacher, denied the existence of many gods, Posidonius believed in only one God; more correctly, he believed in a single godhead, in which he saw "a rational spirit of fire, which is without shape or form, but is able to change itself at will and to become at one with all creation," and which is "remote from the sensual eye and to be perceived only by the spirit." Zeus-Jupiter is in his eyes "not he who holds in his hand the bolts of lightning," but "the director and guardian of the universe, the soul and spirit [breath] of the world." [6] The popular gods are for him nothing but human beings who, having been strongly filled with the spirit of a holy "daimon" (a word midway between *holy spirit* and *conscience*, according to our ideas) and having increased the cultural possessions of mankind, have become gods—"beneficent gods" (θεοὶ εὐεϱγέται). The monotheism of Posidonius is not complete, for there is in it an inclination toward materialistic pantheism (see below); but his view of the godhead comes near to "the way of truth."

The same may be said with regard to his idea of the soul. Posidonius taught: "Our bodies are not ourselves; if I speak to *you*, I do not mean your body." The spirit and the soul are the "Ego" of man. And the soul and the godhead are from one source, of one essence: the soul is "a part of God from above," as the Hebrew would express it. Posidonius says: "God dwells in our hearts; he is beside us, round about us, within us." [7] In a certain sense man and the godhead are an undivided unity: "We are members of a great body." Accordingly, "between us and the godhead there is no difference except that reason fills us in part but it, completely." Nevertheless the soul has also a material essence: it has a real existence in the material world.

Man seeks after God and this search for God is an evidence of man's divine nature. Only the body, which is a prison and a tomb of the soul (according to the view of Plato), prevents the soul at times from lifting itself up to a vision of the godhead: "The high and holy soul, which has been sent to us

[6] In the language of Seneca "rector custosque universi, animus et spiritus mundi" (*Questiones Naturales* II 45). [English translation by John Clarke entitled *Physical Science in the Time of Nero* (London 1910), p. 91.]

[7] See also Seneca, *Epist.* XLI 1 [tr. by R. H. Gummere, Loeb Classical Library].

from above in order that we may have a vision of the godhead near at hand, dwells in us, yet remains bound together with its divine source"; and only when the spirit is completely separated from the body, do there come the ecstatic states, in which the spirit is prepared for the gift of prophecy.

With this conception of the godhead and the soul the ethics of Posidonius is connected.

The divine nature of the soul cannot be the source of moral evil and therefore Posidonius taught, like the "Old Stoa" before him, that "everything comes from the will of Zeus except what the wicked do"; that all the good which is in the world is the doing of God, and that the wickedness of men is responsible for all the evil. We are reminded of the opinion of the prophets of Israel: "Out of the mouth of the Most High cometh there not evil," [8] and "Thine own wickedness shall correct thee, and thy backslidings shall reprove thee"; [9] similar to this is the opinion of the men of the Talmud: "Everything is in the hands of God except the fear of God." [10]

And the life of the soul is eternal, since it is a part of the eternal life of the godhead. But the life of this world is only a small and fragmentary part of the eternal life of the soul; thus there is no value to all the things which man needs and wants in this brief and changing life. Therefore Panaetius, the teacher of Posidonius, already taught that man must live in accordance with nature, that is to say, in accordance with the conditions of life which are given us by nature (τὸ ζῆν κατὰ τὰς δεδομένας ἡμῖν ἐκ φύσεως ἀφορμάς). [11] And Posidonius added to this that nature had already taught us the right way by the fact that she "elevated our gaze towards the sky," while "she placed gold and silver beneath our feet," in the bosom of the earth. [12] Following in the footsteps of Panaetius, his teacher,

---

[8] Lamentations 3:38.   [9] Jeremiah 2:19.   [10] Berakoth 33b.
[11] See Clement of Alexandria, *Stromateis* II 29, 4.
[12] See Seneca, *Epistolae* XCIV 56-75.

he puts greatness of soul (μεγαλοψυχία) at the foundation of all human ethics in place of the "courage" (ἀνδρεία), which the Greeks valued so highly, the Romans receiving it from them in the form of *virtus* (ἀνήρ—*vir*), which became a general name for good character or right conduct.

There is a love of self in man, who is attracted by his own essence; but this essence is necessarily that of "a reasoning being"; "for man is dear to himself [only] in respect of that wherein he is a man." [13]

The ritual commandments (of the pagans) are to be obeyed because the people need them; but they have no essential value. Just as the Second (Third?) Isaiah gave us the great divine saying: "Heaven is My throne, and the earth is My footstool: what manner of house will ye build unto Me? and what place shall be My rest?" [14]—so taught also Posidonius that only the whole world is the true sanctuary of the godhead and not the temples and sanctuaries made by the hands of men.[15]

The essential thing is moral living, founded upon right conduct. For evil done to men is sin against the godhead. And all human beings are equal: men and women, Greeks and barbarians, freemen and slaves. No man is a slave by nature. Every man is born a freeman. Panaetius, teacher of Posidonius, created the concept of Humanity.[16] In opposition to the doctrine of Aristotle (τοῦτο φύσει καὶ βάρβαρον καὶ δοῦλον), the Stoics taught that there is no difference between barbarians and Greeks. Again, according to the teaching of Eratosthenes

[13] In Latin, "Ea enim parte sibi carus est homo qua homo est" (Seneca, *Epist.* CXXI 14). See on this Heinemann, *op. cit.*, I, 81.

[14] Isaiah 46:1.

[15] See Heinemann, *op. cit.*, I, 119, 122, 124-5. It is worth while to note that, when Titus threatened to destroy the Temple in Jerusalem, during the war between the Jews and the Romans, the leaders of the revolt answered that "the world was a better temple for God than this one [which was about to be destroyed]," *Jewish War* V xii 2; see Klausner, *Historia Yisreelit*, IV, 205, and note 1.

[16] See R. Reitzenstein, *Wesen und Werden der Humanität* (Strassburg 1907).

and Isocrates, the peoples are divided into barbarians and Greeks according to their culture, not according to their race or their origin. Men are different from each other according to their abilities and their knowledge, and the wiser must rule; but there are no peoples designed to rule, and no peoples designed for slavery. Also virtue is open to all, to both men and gods. This is the Stoic universalism, which prepared the way for the equality of all nations and the equality of slaves and freemen in Christianity as a religion. This Stoic universalism was developed by both Panaetius and Posidonius but it is worth noting that this same Panaetius thought it proper (πρέπον) that each man should recognize his own nationality and should not make himself ridiculous by pretending to be a Greek.[17] And Posidonius, his pupil, when he speaks about the cultures of the various peoples, knows how to distinguish between them and rejoices over the diversity in the world of men.

In general, nothing is dearer to Posidonius than culture—the culture of mankind in all its ramifications. The wonders of nature are revealed to us by the development of human knowledge, and the source of knowledge is wisdom. Therefore dear to us is knowledge, the fruit of wisdom, and dear to us is culture, the fruit of knowledge. And the Stoic culture is that within which and by means of which human morality is formed. It is possible to say categorically that the concept of culture in its very essence was created by the Stoics in general and Posidonius in particular. There is nothing which is more hateful to Posidonius than lack of culture or "barbarism," which is to him not the condition of a foreign people but the condition of the absence of culture.

But Posidonius knows also the other side of the coin of culture: the spiritual decline, the moral degeneration, which come on the heels of luxury, the fruit of culture. Culture leads

[17] Heinemann, I, 35.

to excesses in eating, drinking, and the niceties of life; and excesses lead to tumults and wars, which in turn bring destruction upon the nations; not only that, but men make use for evil purposes of arts, crafts, and discoveries of science.[18] Thus they made use of the discoveries of Archimedes for the production of the precious metals; yet these led to fearful wars, as did also the discovery of iron. It is as if Posidonius had seen from the beginning that knowledge would increase bombs and mines and airplanes and all sorts of deadly missiles. Culture is revealed in all its glory in the works of the poets, whose poetry is really "philosophy in metaphor, bound by meter and expressed in a mythological manner." But, except for a few, most of the poets pursue glory which gives them riches, and they do not educate the people but they corrupt them by filling their minds with idle tales and harmful superstitions. Even Homer did much harm in that he attributed human natures to the gods instead of attributing divine natures to men; most of the other poets did more harm than he. Likewise, the artists made use of art for an undesirable purpose and all their fervor was only to increase luxuries unprofitable from the standpoint of moral development. In science—especially in philology—and even in philosophy the learned men pile up great heaps of superfluous words (*supervacua literarum suppelex* [19]) and overdo the "word-play of the philosophers" (*ludus literarius philosophorum*).[20] This is the *decline* (διαστροφή) which follows the *rise* during the course of generations. Posidonius does not believe that the decline will be ended by the rotation of world periods, which are continually revolving, going through changes, and returning to their former states after the cycle of all possible kinds of separations

[18] These views are also to be seen in the Hebrew literature of the time. See, *e.g.*, *The Book of Enoch* (Ethiopic) 65:7, 8; 69:9–11, *etc.* Cf. Klausner, *Ha-Bayit ha-Sheni bi-Gedulato* (Tel-Aviv 5690), pp. 116–7.

[19] See Seneca, *Epistolae* LXXXVIII 36.

[20] *Ibid.* LXXI 6. And see Heinemann, I, 102–3.

and combinations is completed, as the "Old Stoics" and in particular the Cynics believed. Neither will the decline end in the time when a divine being shall make peace and establish brotherhood and friendship between lion and herd, as Vergil believed and set forth in his famous "Fourth Eclogue." The moral decline will end only by means of the moral purification of the individual, of every single personality, a purification which shall stir up the divinity in man to overcome the animal and the beast in him.[21]

3. Seneca is a disciple of the teaching of Posidonius, but he is also a disciple of the teaching of Chrysippus, who with Zeno his teacher (from the city of Citium in the island of Cyprus) founded Stoicism. Seneca lived in the days of the great Roman rulers, and his most important work was done in the days of the Emperor Nero—days in which the life of any famous man was in constant danger, and days in which the animal in man was revealed in all its terror. Therefore Seneca emphasizes more than the Stoics before him the moral as well as the intellectual weakness of man, and the old view that the body is the prison of the soul, which alone is holy and eternal.[22] Hence man must accustom himself to look upon death not as an evil and a misfortune, but as the law of nature.[23] For death is a gain, since the day of death is "the birthday of the eternal" (*natalis aeterni*): by means of death we fly back to our source and origin.[24] For, "We walk about in darkness and in half-light, and we desire to return to the full light, to the heavens, from which we came forth." [25] It is possible to attain this state by means of "the old precept" (*vetus praeceptum*): "to follow God" (*deum sequere*).[26] This

[21] See Heinemann, I, 107–8.
[22] *To Helvia on Consolation* XI 7.   [23] *Ibid.* XIII 2, 3.
[24] *To Marcia on Consolation* XXIII.   [25] See *Epistolae* LXXIX 11, 12.
[26] *On the Happy Life* XV 5. According to A. Kaminka (*Gilyonot*, VI, 392, note 29) the "old precept" (law) was that of Plato.

"old precept" is essentially the same as that of Judaism, "to cleave to the standards of the Holy One, blessed be He." [27] These divine standards are good and upright deeds: "Do you wish to be acceptable to God? Then be good; to serve him is to imitate him; it is not to employ sacrifices but to have a righteous and upright attitude"; [28] "for human life rests upon beneficence and harmony" (*Beneficiis enim humana vita constat et concordia*). [29] Hence "man is a sacred thing to man" (*homo sacra res homini*). [30]

Therefore, it is necessary to love men, even the sinful ones:

No man of sense will hate the erring; otherwise he will hate himself. Let him reflect how many times he offends against morality, how many of his acts stand in need of pardon; then he will be angry with himself also. For no just judge will pronounce one sort of judgment in his own case and a different one in the case of others. No one will be found, I say, who is able to acquit himself, and any man who calls himself innocent is thinking more of witnesses than conscience. How much more human to manifest toward wrong-doers a kind and fatherly spirit, not hunting them down but calling them back! [31]

In another place there breaks forth from the heart of Seneca the cry "All of us have sinned!" (*peccavimus omnes*). [32] Therefore we are not to repay evil with evil, but to pardon and to forget. [33] And if the wise man receives a blow on the cheek, he will do what Cato the Roman did:

[27] Ketuboth 111b.

[28] See Bréhier, *op. cit.*, I, 2, 426.

[29] *On Anger* I v 3.

[30] *On Benefits* III xviii; *Epist.* XXXI and XLVII.

[31] *On Anger* I xiv 2, 3 [tr. by J. W. Basore (Loeb Class. Lib.), I, 143].

[32] *On Mercy* I vi 3. Dr. Kaminka, the translator of the works of Seneca into Hebrew, mentions in the note to *On Anger* I xiv 2, 3, the saying of Beruriah, wife of R. Meir, and a saying from *Hovot ha-Levavot*. But it would be more fitting to mention here the splendid and more ancient saying of Ben-Sira: "Do not reproach a man who repents of sin; remember that all of us are guilty" (Ben-Sira 8:5).

[33] *On Anger* II xxxii.

He did not flare up, he did not avenge the wrong, he did not even forgive it, but he said that no wrong had been done (*factam negavit*). He showed finer spirit in not acknowledging it than if he had pardoned it.[34]

This is true greatness of soul: love of virtue, amiability, goodness of heart. For whoever is not good is not great:

A man will either be good or else not great, because greatness of soul, as I conceive it, is a thing unshakable, sound to the core, uniform and strong from top to bottom—something that cannot exist in evil natures. Evil men may be terrible, turbulent, and destructive, but greatness they will never have, for its support and stay is goodness (*bonitas*).[35]

Here we have the essential idea of the splendid saying in the Wisdom of Solomon:

> For wisdom cannot enter a deceitful soul,
> Or live in a body in debt to sin.[36]

Of Seneca's work called *De Beneficiis* did one scholar truly say: "This is indeed the finest work produced by antiquity on the subject of the love of man, that is to say, the duty of mutual help."[37] About this work Seneca himself says that in it he is "sanctifying the fellowship of the human race" (*societas generis humani sancit*).[38] Thus there is sanctity in human life; and this sanctity can be revealed as the perfect good by good deeds: "Virtue without a deed is an imperfect good" (*imperfectum bonum est virtus sine actu*).[39] In deeds the fundamental thing is the intention and not the deed itself:

[34] *On Firmness* (*De Constantia*) XIV 3 [tr. by Basore (Loeb Class. Lib.), I, 91].
[35] *On Anger* I xx 6, 7.
[36] Wisdom of Solomon 1:4 [Goodspeed].
[37] Birt, *op. cit.*, S. 182.
[38] See *On Benefits* I ii; IV xviii 2, 3; *On Tranquillity of Soul* II 9 and IV 5.
[39] *On Leisure* (*De Otio*) VI 2, 3.

If a man lies with his wife as if she were another man's wife, he will be an adulterer, though she will not be an adulteress. Some one gave me poison, but the poison lost its efficacy by being mixed with food; the man, by giving the poison, became guilty of a crime, even if he did me no injury. A man is no less a murderer because his blow was foiled, intercepted by the victim's dress.[40]

For only "two things which are the most beautiful of all accompany us everywhere we go: universal Nature and our own virtue" (*natura communis et propria virtus*).[41] We have here "the starry heavens above me and the moral strength within me," which filled the soul of Kant. No other earthly things have any real value. With an un-Stoic bitterness Seneca speaks about luxuries and about the rich who indulge in them:

Curses of gods and goddesses upon the wretches whose luxury overleaps the bounds of an empire that already stirs too much envy! They want game that is caught beyond the Phasis to supply their pretentious kitchens, and from the Parthians, from whom Rome has not yet got vengeance, they do not blush to get—birds! From every quarter they gather together every known and unknown thing to tickle a fastidious palate; the food which their stomachs, weakened by indulgence, can scarcely retain is fetched from farthest ocean; they vomit that they may eat, they eat that they may vomit (*vomunt ut edant, edunt ut vomant*).[42]

He also castigates those women who defile their faces with paint and cosmetics, who wear clothes only to reveal better their nakedness, who conceal their pregnancy as though it were an unseemly burden, and destroy "the hope of children" in their bodies, that is to say, they bring about artificial miscarriages.[43] He also denounces the rich as being pleasing on the outside and ugly inside, like the walls of their houses which are decorated superficially with thin plaster that easily

[40] *On Firmness* VII 4 [tr. by Basore (Loeb. Class. Lib.), I, 69–71].
[41] *To Helvia on Consolation* VIII 2, 3 [tr. by Basore].
[42] *Ibid.* x 2, 3.   [43] *Ibid.* XVI 3, 4.

falls away.[44] He asks the question, "Is the financial state fundamental and not the state of the soul?" Evidently, "Man will
not feel poverty as long as he holds himself within the bounds
of natural living; but if he goes beyond them he will be
pursued by poverty even though he has unbounded wealth." [45]

For only "the mind gives riches to man." [46] And a sound
mind is one "holding to the ways of Nature." [47] "The happy
life, therefore, is a life that is in harmony with its own
nature," [48] and "the happy man is he who allows reason to fix
the value of every condition of existence." [49] Man must do
what his nature requires him to do, since it is his own truth;
"for no man can be said to be happy if he has been thrust
outside the pale of truth." [50]

The sound, strong, and good mind does not fear anything
—not even pain and humiliation. For pain hardens and
strengthens a man: "Virtue without an adversary grows
weak" (*marcet sine adversario virtus*). Only in a storm is the
captain of a ship truly recognized; therefore we must seek
after a storm.[51] We must seek after blows as the struggling
athlete seeks after them.[52] We saw above that not even death
is to be feared, since death is a law of Nature by which the
soul, freed from the prison of the body, returns to the heavens
whence it came.[53]

The good must be done for its own sake, that is, for the
sake of the good, without ulterior motive or hope for pleasure,
since "virtue is its own reward." [54] At times pleasure is attached to the doing of good, yet the good is not to be done
for the sake of the pleasure that comes from it: "As in a
ploughed field, which has been broken up for planting, some

[44] *On Providence* VI. See Birt, *op. cit.*, S. 262.
[45] *To Helvia on Consolation* X 9 and XI 4.
[46] *Ibid.* XI 5.
[47] *On the Happy Life* III.
[48] *Loc. cit.*
[49] *Ibid.* VI.
[50] *Ibid.* V.
[51] *On Providence* IV.
[52] See *Epistolae* LXXVIII 16.
[53] See above, p. 68.
[54] *On the Happy Life* IX.

flowers will spring up here and there, yet it was not for these poor little plants, although they may please the eye, that so much toil was expended." [55]

To humble oneself before God is freedom.[56] To be obedient to God, to receive everything in love and without complaint, and not to be agitated even "if evil springs forth from good" —this is "to pattern after God" (*deum effingere*).[57] The man who orders his life thus is freed from suffering. For, apart from death, only one thing frees us from the pains, humiliations, and wounds of living: "the precepts of wisdom" (*praecepta sapientiae*); or as we would say to-day, science and philosophy. "They will comfort you, they will cheer you; if in earnest they gain entrance to your mind, nevermore will sorrow enter there, nevermore anxiety, nevermore the useless distress of futile suffering." [58] For, "he who has advanced toward the higher realm and has lifted himself to higher levels drags a loosened chain; he is not yet free, but still is as good as free." [59] Wisdom makes us free. But wisdom must be modest and moral. Seneca said:

I am not a "wise man," nor . . . shall I ever be. And so require not from me that I should be equal to the best, but that I should be better than the wicked. It is enough for me if every day I reduce the number of my vices, and blame my mistakes. I have not attained to perfect health, nor indeed shall I attain it.[60]

He said also: "Indeed, no man can be good without the help of God. Can one rise superior to fortune unless God helps him to rise?" [61] Here we have a religious ethic, which reminds us of charming verses in the Psalms and of pious sayings in the Talmud.[62] For, like a true Stoic, Seneca connects

[55] *Loc. cit.*
[56] *Ibid.* XV.
[57] *Ibid.* XV and XVI.
[58] *To Helvia on Consolation* XVII 4, 5.
[59] *On the Happy Life* XVII.
[60] *Ibid.* XVI.
[61] See *Epistolae* XLI 2.
[62] Is not Seneca's "help of God" like the "help of Heaven" in the Talmud (Baba Bathra 55a)?

wisdom with faith in the highest sense. This wisdom, which gives clear ideas and lofty conceptions of the great world, of Nature with all its wonders, from the lowliest creatures to the most exalted phenomena of which the divine intellect of man can conceive—this wisdom also enables man to enjoy "the noblest spectacle of things divine (*pulcherrimum divinorum spectaculum*), and, mindful of its own immortality, it proceeds to all that has been and will ever be throughout the ages of all time." [63]

A world-view like this is still not Christianity. In the ideas of Seneca there is a pantheism that is in a certain sense pagan; and the ethic of Seneca, unlike the Jewish-Christian ethic, is not bound with an unbreakable bond to religion—to faith in God and the world to come. In this ethic there is lacking the Jewish depth of emotion and the contrition of Christian morality.

Over against this, there is in the world-view of Seneca a positivistic morality and a negative attitude toward the crude idolatry of the period. It was not without reason that the story was told about the exchange of letters beween Seneca, the philosopher, and Paul, the apostle. For, on the one hand, the world-view of Seneca aroused the opposition of Christianity because of its pagan characteristics and its secular philosophical coloring and, on the other hand, it prepared the way for Christianity by its profound morality and its inchoate monotheistic tendencies.

4. Much more nearly related to Christianity than Seneca was the Stoic philosopher Epictetus, from Hierapolis in Phrygia, who was born about the year 60 c.e. In his youth he was a slave and, as such, he came to Rome in the time of the Emperor Nero. He learned philosophy from the Stoic, Mu-

[63] *To Helvia on Consolation* XX (end).

sonius Rufus. Having gained his freedom, he lived as a freed-man in Rome until the year 94 C.E., when he was driven out of Rome with the rest of the philosophers by the Emperor Domitian. Then Epictetus went to the city of Nicopolis in the province of Epirus and there he taught philosophy in his own school. His pupil Flavius Arrianus (Arrian) took down the main points of his sayings and published them around the time of the death of his teacher, about the year 130, in two treatises: *Discourses* (Διατριβαί) and the *Manual* (Ἐγχειρίδιον).

Epictetus concerned himself mainly with ethics, with which he joined his doctrine of God. According to his teaching, God is a merciful father, who takes care of mankind and has set the world in order by intelligence; and the spirit of man is divine by reason of its own nature. This spirit longs for freedom. And human freedom is possible since we have entirely in our own hands one thing: good will. This will we can direct according to reason: according to correct, logical ideas; and then we shall not fall into sin, and lusts will not rule over us, nor will misfortunes and humiliations move us. And since all men are equal in relation to deity, since all of them are, in the language of the Talmud, "sons of God" (בנים למקום), all men are also equal among themselves and there is no difference between a slave and a master. This is the religious side of the Stoic philosophy of Epictetus, which brings him near to Judaism and to Christianity. But more than either of these he emphasizes the divinity of man in general, and the bearing of cruel treatment in a spirit of love.

Out of the divine nature of man comes forth the demand of Epictetus that man shall desire to have all his deeds directed toward the divine ordering of the world in such a manner that he and the Deity and Nature shall be an undivided unity. And man is able to attain this desire even in complete solitude, away from state and society, since he carries God within him, in his inmost soul. By means of moral strength and confidence man is able to improve his character and to win victory over himself from day to day; thus he will be able to celebrate a holiday every day. But, even though man can become virtuous, it is forbidden to him to be the supreme judge of the wicked. It is forbidden to man to rebuke and to curse other men even though sin provokes grievous complaints, since the worst sins come from lack of understanding. Socrates truly taught that understanding has been put into the mind of man in order that he may reject the evil and choose the good.

True beauty is not found in external adornment, but is achieved by the virtuous deeds of men. And the deeds of men are not to be judged according to their external appearance, but according to the intention and purpose in them. On these grounds, Epictetus, like ancient Judaism and primitive Christianity, forbids the oath, which is only an external confirmation of an actual fact.

When misfortunes come to the wise man, or he finds himself in the greatest distress, he must see in this a call from above (κλῆσις) to the philosopher to prove by his quiet conduct and his submission to the inevitable the truth of the fundamentals of his teaching; this is an honor which God gives him. But if there is no other escape from his situation except baseness of soul and improper actions, the wise man finds before him an "open gate"—to death: he deliberately commits suicide—not from despair but from understanding that death is better than a life of baseness. For verily man has a moral purpose (τέλος) in life, and this is obedience to Nature or to God—which for Epictetus are one. This obedience makes him superior to all misfortunes and humiliations—even to slavery. For slavery does not really exist at all: "One man is not master of another man," cries Epictetus (ἄνθρωπος ἀνθρώπου κύριος οὐκ ἔστιν).[64] Every man has "communion in

[64] See *Discourses* I xxix 60 [tr. by W. A. Oldfather (Loeb Class. Lib.)].

the society of God" (κοινωνεῖν τῷ θεῷ τῆς συναναστροφῆς).[65]
He turns to man and says to him:

But you are a being of primary importance; you are a fragment
of God; you have within you a part of Him. Why, then, are you
ignorant of your own kinship? Why do you not know the source
from which you have sprung? Will you not bear in mind, whenever you eat, who you are that eat, and whom you are nourishing? . . . that you are nourishing God . . .

the God who is within you, of whom your soul is a part. And
he adds: "It is within yourself that you bear Him, and do not
perceive that you are defiling Him with impure thoughts and
filthy actions." [66] Impure thoughts and improper actions are
to be included under the term "error," and error comes only
from a lack of understanding of the true good; for when a
man commits an error while intending to do good to himself,
he only causes harm to himself; thus "Every error involves a
contradiction" (πᾶν ἁμάρτημα μάχην περιέχει),[67] that is, every
error has in it internal contradiction and conflicting tendencies. Only in virtue is there harmony and tranquillity. Epictetus speaks contemptuously about those foolish people who,
if loss of material possessions or bodily misfortunes come upon
them, become excited and complain and sob, calling themselves "miserable, paltry man" (ἀνθρωπάριον) and talking about
their "wretched, paltry flesh" (σαρκίδια).[68] For wretched indeed is the body, and the source of all misfortune to the one
for whom there is nothing better than the flesh,[69] who does
not recognize the divine soul and spirit within him. Therefore there is no need to mourn over the destruction of the
body of man, that is to say, over his death; "pity" (ἔλεος) is
only a bad sign of attachment to earthly life; and a great prin-

[65] *Ibid.* I ix 5.
[66] *Ibid.* II viii 12–4. See Bonhöffer, *Epiktet und das Neue Testament*,
SS. 58–9.
[67] *Discourses* II xxvi 1.
[68] *Ibid.* I iii 5.
[69] *Ibid.* I iii 6.

ciple with Epictetus is: "No good man mourns" (οὐδεὶς ἀγαθὸς πενθεῖ).[70] For, as we have already seen, even death is not the greatest of all misfortunes.

The wise man is always a freeman even if he is technically a slave. Philosophic judgment—this it is "which lifts up the neck of those who have become abject, which makes them look with level eyes into the face of the rich, and the faces of tyrants."[71] For only judgment is mine:

Property is not mine; kinsmen, members of my household, friends, reputation, familiar places, converse with men—all these are not my own. "What, then, *is* yours? Power to deal with external impressions." He showed me that I possess this beyond all hindrance and constraint; no one can hamper me; no one can force me to deal with them otherwise than as I will.[72]

With this power I am a freeman, and every man born of woman is a freeman. There is no difference, then, between a manservant and his master or between maidservant and mistress. All are equal. Since judgment is a part of God above, all men are sons of God. Therefore we must love all men. Since every man is a son of God, that is, he has in his mind and in his spirit a divine spark, he must strive for nearness to God. This is not to be attained except by purity of mind, and whoever has a mind that is pure and cleaves to God—such a one will not rage against the Deity even if misfortunes come upon him, but "will give thanks for all things to God"; such a one can truly be called "pious."[73]

Of course, between Epictetus, on the one hand, and Judaism and Christianity, on the other hand, there are fundamental differences;[74] hence one cannot say that Epictetus was influ-

---

[70] *Ibid*. II xiii 17; II xvii 26; IV vi 1.   [71] *Ibid*. III xxvi 35, 36.
[72] *Ibid*. III xxiv 68.   [73] *Ibid*. IV vii 9.
[74] These differences, together with similarities and parallels in Christianity and the doctrines of Epictetus, are presented clearly and in detail by Bonhöffer, *op. cit.*, SS. 339–90.

enced by Christianity, nor even that Christianity was influenced by Epictetus specifically. Nevertheless, it would seem that there is enough in the preceding short and imperfect sketch to make it apparent that Adolf Bonhöffer was right when he said: "Among all the various types of philosophic world-view which the Greek world put forth, not one is as near to Christianity as the Stoic type." [75]

But it must be noted that not even the Stoic philosophy gave complete satisfaction to the deeply religious spirits of the days of Paul; so they sought reorientation in a new faith. The pagan multitudes were certainly not able to find satisfaction in an abstract philosophic doctrine, which was very lofty, but lacked religious mysteries, a living God, a God who fashions and creates, who leads and oversees, who deals out rewards and punishments, who relieves from burdens, who dies and returns to life, who redeems and revives all those who cleave to him. Yet there can be no doubt of two facts: *First*, Stoicism in general—not any one Stoic in particular—influenced Paul and those that came after him. This influence cannot be restricted to this or that Stoic doctrine, nor to this or that point of view, nor to this or that phrase of a certain Stoic, but rather it came from the *general spirit* of the philosophical system. A similar example is the book of Ecclesiastes or Koheleth in the Bible. There is not to be found in this book this or that philosophical system, yet the Greek philosophic spirit in general hovers over all of it as an influence which is indefinite yet is not to be disregarded. Hence the story about the relations between Paul and Seneca, and hence the hypothesis that Epictetus was influenced by the New Testament. *Second*, it is an established fact that there is a close relationship of ideas between the Stoics, on the one hand, and the Sages of Israel and the early Christians, on the other, in spite of all the important differences between them. Examples are

[75] See Bonhöffer, *op. cit.*, S. 72, Anm. 1.

the evaluation of spirit and soul above matter and the body, the extreme ethics, the excessive importance which they attached to the world to come, *etc*.[76] This close relationship of ideas made easy the preaching of Christianity among educated Gentiles.

The Greek and Roman philosophers of the first century c.e. saw in both Judaism and Christianity "a faith of folly" (*superstitio*), and they opposed the spread of both with all their might. Yet they did not have a completely negative attitude toward the gods of their own people; they would remove the repellent features of pagan mythology by means of allegorical interpretation, and they would advise their pupils to honor the gods in order not to arouse the strong displeasure on the part of the masses of the people. Yet they did not recognize that they themselves by their ethical systems and their religious views were unintentionally preparing the best of the pagan world to meet Christianity. Likewise Paul did not recognize that he made his Christianity acceptable to the minds of the best people of the pagan world by means of an unconscious and unintentional absorption of pagan ideas into his Christian monotheism.

5. But, in the ancient world, there held sway one philosophical system which from the beginning had a tendency to destroy all faith from the foundation to the corbels.

The founder of this system gained a reputation in Hebrew literature; the personal name of Epicurus became a common

[76] Against A. Kaminka in his article "Ha-Musar she-be-Siphre Seneca ve-ha-Musar ha-Yehudi" (*Mozenayim*, IV, 50–1), according to whom "in content, in ideas" there is no difference between Stoic ethics and Jewish ethics; there is only "*a great historic difference* (the emphasis is Kaminka's) in the desire to carry out ethical and divinely-inspired ideas." However, this "great historic difference" cannot explain why the pagan world accepted only the faith coming from Judaism, and not the "divinely-inspired" Stoic ethic. For Paul and his associates could have taken the attitude toward the Stoic ethic that it was "actually practicable" and not merely "theoretically practicable."

noun and a standing epithet for any disbeliever in fundamentals and any religious heretic or scoffer at the ceremonial laws, so that in the Talmudic literature of the earlier period the plural number, *Epiqoresim*, came into use, and later the abstract noun, *Epiqoresut* ("heresy," "skepticism"), was formed.[77] Some suppose that even the verb PQR (in the Qal) and HPQIR (in the Hiph'il) and the verbal noun HPQR have a relationship to "Epiqoros" (the Hebrew spelling of Epicurus),[78] in spite of the fact that the Palestinian Talmud has in place of these forms BQR, HBQIR, and HBQR. And Rabbi David Kimhi explained the word *Biqqoret* in the Bible [79] in terms of the root PQR.[80] However that may be, the fact that the name of Epicurus became an epithet—even though not with entire justice—for any disbeliever or religious heretic or libertine—this fact shows that the system of Epicurus, like that of the Stoics, was widely current in the first centuries of the Christian era.[81] And we definitely find "the Epicurean and Stoic philosophers" side by side baiting Paul in Athens.[82]

But there is also a chronological difference between Stoicism and Epicureanism. The Stoa had three periods (Old, Middle, and New), each of which was different from the others. On the other hand, Epicureanism, which continued for at least 600 years (306 B.C.E. to 320 C.E.), did not develop much, changed very little, and certainly did not change funda-

[77] Mishnah, Aboth IV 14; Sanhedrin X 1; Tosephta, Sanhedrin XIII 5; Kiddushin 66b (Epicureanism). Even the Amoraim did not know the origin of the name, and they disagreed about its interpretation and meaning (Sanhedrin 99b). Sometimes the censor required the writing of *Epiqoros* in place of *Min* and *Epiqoresut* in place of *Minut*. Cf. "Foreign Epicure" (*Min*) and "Israelite Epicure" in Sanhedrin 38b. And see *Encyclopaedia Judaica*, VI, 686–8, s.v.

[78] For a contrary opinion see M. Jastrow, *Dictionary of the Targumim, the Talmud, etc.*, I, 104, s.v.

[79] Lev. 19:20.   [80] D. Kimhi, *Book of Roots*, art. BQR.

[81] Cicero says truly that the barbarian lands were receiving the teaching of Epicurus with enthusiasm (Cicero, *De Finibus* II 15).

[82] Acts 17:18.

mentally.[83] Therefore, I must give—contrary to what I did in connexion with Stoic philosophy—a sketch of the teaching of Epicurus himself (341–271 B.C.E.), and in addition, a sketch of the teaching of one of his followers of the first century B.C.E., Lucretius Carus (c. 95–50 B.C.E.), whose great poem "On the Nature of Things" (*De Rerum Natura*) clarifies many Epicurean views which are not known to us from any other source.[84]

Epicurus and his pupils consider sense-perception to be the source of all the conceptions and ideas of man. But alongside of sense-perception, Epicurus recognizes also "preconceptions" (προλήψεις), that is, the general conceptions which come from frequently repeated acts of vision. The world is for Epicurus a kind of mechanism, which man must know only insofar as is necessary to make use of it for a certain satisfaction and to recognize the good and the evil which is in it for man; beyond this man does not need to know or to investigate at all. And in order that he may know the world for this utilitarian purpose, it is sufficient for man to employ the natural intelligence which is in him and his own experience. For sense-perception and experience are not to be doubted, since they are clear, certain, and self-evident; if we doubt these two, we shall lack the possibility not only of knowledge, but even of action.

We can perceive the world only in this manner: all bodies come into being, according to the teaching of Democritus and Leucippus, by means of atoms (called "individual substances," Heb. עצמים פרדיים [Ar. *jauhar fard*], in the language of the medieval Jewish philosophers) and empty space. Some bodies are composed of close aggregates of atoms, and some

---

[83] See Zeller-Nestle, *op. cit.*, S. 278, Anm. 3.

[84] On the Epicurean system see *ibid.*, SS. 276–91; Bréhier, *op. cit.*, I, 2, 333–62; 407–11. Gilbert Murray, *op. cit.*, pp. 128–42, gives a picture of the system of Epicurus that is splendid, although somewhat marred by overidealization. A. Kaminka endeavors to show the good and bad sides of Epicurean doctrine in "Mishnat Epiqor" (*Mozenayim*, VII, 478–87).

of a combination of atoms between which are found larger or smaller spaces. Because of the different motions of the atoms, which draw near to one another, there being apparently in them, according to Epicurus, a certain rudimentary power of movement,[85] they intertwine and hook together, and collide and rebound from each other; thus they bring about powerful whirling motions, by which worlds without number are generated in different parts of the limitless, cosmic space; for "nothing comes from nothing, and nothing comes to an end in nothing." [86] These worlds are separated from each other by means of empty spaces, each one of which is called in Greek μετακόσμιον and in Latin *intermundium* ("space between worlds"). All these worlds came into being in time, and they have an existence only in time; a day will come when all of them will be destroyed, and they will return to a chaos of the atoms, even if they do not become completely non-existent. There exist in the teachings of Epicurus no Fashioner or Creator, no "purpose of a Director" and no "Lord of the Castle."

The soul of man is not fundamentally different from the soul of other living creatures. Both are made up of matter which is mobile but very thin; its real nature cannot be known, although it is the means by which sense-perception takes place. Thus the soul (*anima*) of man and other living creatures, which is composed only of matter and atoms, is lacking in reasoning power; but in man the soul is fused with the spirit [or mind] (*animus*), which is placed in the heart [Latin *pectus*, "breast"] of man while the soul is diffused throughout the body.[87] At the time of death, the atoms of the soul are

[85] See Gilbert Murray, *op. cit.*, p. 133.

[86] See Kaminka, *op. cit.*, pp. 482–3.

[87] So, at any rate, according to Lucretius, *De Rerum Natura* III 135 f. But there is also another tradition of Epicurus' view of the soul (see the note of Nestle to the remarks of Zeller, Zeller-Nestle, *op. cit.*, S. 284; see also Bréhier, *op. cit.*, I, 2, 352–3. [Klausner translates *animus* by רוּחַ, "spirit," but the translations of W. H. D. Rouse (Loeb Class. Lib.) and R. C. Trevelyan use "mind." Tr.]

scattered, since the atoms of the body have fallen apart from each other and are not able to recapture the atoms of the soul again. Therefore death is only a complete cessation, a complete stoppage of the existence of man. Man has no feeling or sensation at all after death. This tenet of Epicureanism frees man from the fear of Hades and of punishments in any other world except this present one. Also here, as in the question about the creation of the world, Epicurus is revealed to us as a disbeliever in the immortality of the soul (and, it is needless to say, in the resurrection of the dead, which the rest of the Greek philosophers likewise did not recognize), in the world to come, and in rewards and punishments such as the ancients, both Jewish and non-Jewish, had pictured to themselves.

Nevertheless, Epicurus is not "a disbeliever in the Ultimate," an atheist, in the strictest sense of the word. He does not deny the existence of the gods; for to him the fact that the belief in their existence is present in all nations and in all eras is a sign and a proof that the gods do exist in fact. Even the fantastic pictures which we have of the gods in our sleep, and even sometimes while awake, prove that the gods exist. These pictures come under the head of προλήψεις ("anticipations," "preconceptions"), mentioned above.[88] We are wrong, however, when we think that the gods concern themselves with the ordering of the world and with the affairs of mankind, watching over them, punishing evil and rewarding good; we are also wrong when we think that they reveal their will by means of visions and words of prophecy, and therefore that we must propitiate them with sacrifices and make prayers to them. All these ideas are only superstitions. The gods can be only perfect, unchanging, and completely happy; hence it is impossible that they should be concerned with the imperfect affairs of the wretched world and with the transitory and insignificant deeds of men; it is also impossible that they could

[88] See above, p. 82.

be influenced by sacrifices and prayers. There is not one phenomenon in nature or in life, the existence of which necessitates the interference of the gods or which cannot be explained by natural causes. The gods are of the nature of bodies of light, thinnest of the thin, who live in the space between the worlds, in the *intermundia* referred to above, without care and without activity. Recognition of this, according to Epicurus, gives to man comfort and happiness; by means of it he is freed from fear of the strong mysterious powers which rule over the fate of the world and of man. Complete freedom from "the yoke of religion"—this is what Epicurus gives to men, and therefore men should be very grateful to him, according to the opinion of his pupils.[89] But, according to the opinion of his opponents, this view of the gods as existing without activity, separated from the world and from men, and without any influence whatsoever upon either—this Epicurean view is not far from atheism. Cicero put it this way: "Epicurus . . . actually abolishes the gods, although professedly retaining them" (*Epicurus re tollit, oratione relinquit deos*).[90]

This view of the gods is connected with the ethics of Epicurus.

The Roman poet Ennius (died 169 B.C.E.) placed in the mouth of one of his heroes of tragedy the following words:

I have always said, and I shall always say, that the gods of heaven exist, but I believe that they have no care for what the race of man does. For if they had such care, it would be well with the good and ill with the wicked, which is not the case now.[91]

If there are no rewards and punishments, neither is there an idealistic ethical faith.

[89] See Lucretius, *De Rerum Natura* I 62–79.
[90] See Cicero, *De Natura Deorum* I 44 [tr. by H. Rackham (Loeb Class. Lib.), p. 121].
[91] See Foakes-Jackson and Lake, *op. cit.*, I, 1, 235.

Epicurean morality has become a synonym for looseness and depravity. But not rightly. Not only did Epicurus himself live a life of self-restraint and find satisfaction in little,[92] but also he taught that the wise man "with a little bread and water can vie in happiness with Zeus." [93] Nevertheless, in his ethical teaching, Epicurus is far from a religious idealistic morality.

"Desire" (πάθος) is the criterion of good and evil. Good is only what causes me pleasure, evil what causes me pain. Pleasure (ἡδονή) is everything. But pleasure is not good unless it brings to man true happiness. The main thing is not pleasure itself, but the removal of pain, the elimination of the unpleasant, and thus tranquillity of soul. Therefore mental pleasure and pain are immeasurably more important than physical, even when the former also come from certain conditions of the body. In the last analysis, the severest pains are not the most prolonged, and the most prolonged pains are not the severest. Thus Epicurus says on the one hand:

I know not how to conceive the good, apart from the pleasures of taste, sexual pleasures, the pleasures of sound and the pleasures of beautiful form.[94]

On the other hand he says:

When we say, then, that pleasure is the end and aim, we do not mean the pleasures of the prodigal or the pleasures of sensuality.[95]

And then he puts it still more clearly:

It is not an unbroken succession of drinking-bouts and of revelry, not sexual love, not the enjoyment of the fish and other delicacies of a luxurious table, which produce a pleasant life; it

[92] See G. Murray, op. cit., pp. 136–7.
[93] See Diogenes Laërtius, De Vita Philosophorum X 127.
[94] Ibid. X 6.
[95] See Bréhier, op. cit., I, 2, 356–7; Diog. Laër., op. cit. X 131.

is sober reasoning, searching out the grounds of every choice and avoidance, and banishing those beliefs through which the greatest tumults take possession of the soul.[96]

This freedom from passion (ἀταραξία), which is one with tranquillity of soul, is achieved by means of virtue, and it has value only if it brings about pleasure in the sense already explained. The Epicurean wise man does not remove himself from either physical or mental pleasure, and there is not in him the "lack of desire" (ἀπαθία) of the Stoic wise man; but even he does not attain his tranquillity of soul if he does not walk in the way of right and justice in such a manner that fear of punishment does not disturb his tranquillity of soul. Also here we see Epicurus preaching not an absolute and autonomous ethic, but an ethic sufficiently lofty in itself, yet conditioned by pleasure and pain or by tranquillity of soul and agitation of spirit. The main thing is not that man should bridle his desire and be satisfied with little, but that he should accustom himself to little from the beginning, in order that his tranquillity of soul be not disturbed.

Similar is Epicurus' doctrine of society. Here also he weighs the gain of participation in the life of the state against the loss. He does not reject social life and he loves people, yet in his opinion "it is better to do kindness than to receive kindness." The laws of the state must be obeyed in order that one may be saved from punishment and the fear of punishment; but from the function of an active participant in politics it is better to remove oneself—unless there are special reasons for fulfilling such a function—in order not to destroy one's spiritual repose. For the same reason Epicurus does not recognize the benefits of marriage and family life: they tend to take away spiritual repose. Over against this he favors friendship, in which there is spiritual pleasure, refreshment of soul, and peace of mind. The friendship (ἡ φιλία) of Epicurus and

[96] See Bréhier, op. cit., I, 2, 335.

his group turns out to be remarkably like that of the Pythagoreans. The wise man loves men, life, and their pleasures, yet he carefully avoids becoming enslaved to them lest they become for him absolute necessities which he cannot do without.

If pains are too great or distress too deep, Epicurus, like the Stoics, declares it right for a man to commit suicide; but Epicurus thinks that if man will take care to recognize that the severest pains are comparatively transitory and that the most prolonged pains are not so severe (see above), and if he will accustom himself to need little and thus preserve tranquillity of soul, man will not kill himself except in very rare instances.

6. In this doctrine of Epicurus there is, along with a certain spiritual and intellectual freedom of the kind one feels in the teaching of Spinoza, much skepticism, materialism, and relativism in all that concerns beliefs and opinions in general and morality in particular. Hence not without reason did our Sages give the name "Epicureanism" to any system of religious unbelief or relativistic ethics.

Lucretius Carus, pupil of the pupils of Epicurus, gave forceful poetic-philosophic expression to the Epicurean philosophy in both its positive and negative aspects in one profound and glorious philosophic poem, *De Rerum Natura* ("On the Nature of Things").[97]

Lucretius in his poem set up for himself one clear purpose. The poem is divided into six books, and begins by heaping praise upon Epicurus on the grounds that he brought peace

[97] A large part of this poem has been translated into Hebrew verse under the name *Teva' ha-Devarim* by Israel Rahl in his book *Shire-Romi*, Odessa 5627 [1867], pp. 33–71; and because pungent Epicurean ideas like these were not in accord with the spirit of the Hebrew readers of that time, the translator prepared an answer to the work he had translated, entitled "Know What You Should Answer" (*ibid.*, pp. 72–84).

to the world by proving that there is to be no fear of gods and evil spirits, no fear of fate, providence, and death, after he had shown that the laws of Nature are fixed, constant, and unchanging, and do not depend upon gods and spirits. The purpose of the poem is—the war against foolish beliefs, against "superstition," under which Lucretius included all irrational belief and opinion and all prejudice. The principal superstitions against which he fought are two: fear of the gods and fear of death. Against these two, which take away the spiritual repose and peace of man, he goes forth to war.

Religion in general brings much evil to the world. Thus out of religious superstition Iphigenia was sacrificed to the gods by her father in order that the ships might not stand still in the sea from lack of sufficient wind. And with strong resentment Lucretius cries:

> *Tantum religio potuit suadere malorum!*
> (So potent was Religion in persuading to evil deeds.)[97a]

Evil deeds like these arise, on the one hand, from the false belief that natural events are in the hands of the gods, and on the other hand, from the superstition that, even after death, man lives on, suffering torments in Hades or in the process of transmigration. In fact, these beliefs have no foundation. From nothing comes forth only nothing; never will a fig come forth from a vine. Nature has fixed and unchanging laws. It is impossible that spring flowers should blossom in the autumn, that wheat should ripen in the winter, and that the gathering of grapes should take place in the spring. It is impossible that man should be born not an infant, and that he should grow up as soon as he is born; likewise it is impossible that the earth could be productive without rains. It is impossible that man should cross the sea on foot, and that with his hands he should overturn mountains.

[97a] *De Rerum Natura* I 101 [tr. by Rouse (Loeb Class. Lib.)].

Everything is composed of atoms, and comes into existence in the midst of empty space. The atoms are infinite in number, and by means of ceaseless motions and countless combinations in limitless space and endless time they form eternal and indestructible substances. No power of the gods is to be seen in this. All being comes from being. And just as existence does not come from non-existence, likewise nothing is completely annihilated, but everything puts off one form and takes on another form according to laws which are established and constant forever. Thus there is not to be brought into the explanation of any of the things existing or coming into existence in the world, the power or the intervention or the influence of any god whatsoever. Nature is free and is not enslaved to those "proud lords"—the gods who in truth spend their days in repose and inactivity.

This is the general content of the first two books of *De Rerum Natura*.

In the third book Lucretius speaks about the nature of the soul.

The "soul" (*anima*) or the "intellect" (*mens*)—Lucretius identifies the two—are a part of the body like the eye, the hand, or the foot. The "soul" (*anima*) is associated with the "spirit" (*animus*). And just as the eye can be in pain without the whole body's being in pain, so can the soul suffer without the spirit's suffering also.[97b]

But the body and the soul are connected with each other by a strong bond. If the soul is disturbed by any great fear—

[97b] [This exposition of Lucretius may seem somewhat confused, but Lucretius himself at times confuses *anima*, *animus*, and *mens*. In *De Rerum Natura* III 94, he identifies *animus* and *mens*, whereas in III 421-4 he says that *animus* and *anima* are essentially the same. The strict identification of *anima* and *mens* is avoided by Lucretius. In III 140-3 the *anima* is diffused throughout the body, while the *animus-mens* is confined to the breast. Hence the *animus* is a part of the *anima* somewhat as the eye is a part of the body (III 147). See note 87 above on the question of the proper English term by which to translate *animus*. Tr.]

the face grows pale, the knees shake, the eyes grow dim, and the ears ring. Hence both the soul and the spirit are formed from matter, as is the body. The fact that it is sufficient to say to a man a word, which, it is self-evident, contains no material substance, in order that he may do actual deeds, proves that what we call soul, spirit, intellect, thought are also only matter; except that the matter of the soul is exceedingly fine and therefore the movement of thoughts is exceedingly swift. And as to the invisibility of the soul, it must be borne in mind that the wind, odors, and sounds, are also invisible, on account of the extreme thinness of their matter. Another proof that the soul is only exceedingly fine matter and nothing more is the fact that when a man dies and his soul flees from him, his body does not become any lighter than it was while the soul was still dwelling in the body; likewise if the flavor of wine has vanished or the sweet smell of ointment has been dissipated nothing at all is taken away from the weight of the wine or the oil.

The soul vanishes from the body like smoke and fog, and it never again has any existence in the world. The proof: while the child is weak and undeveloped in his body, his intellect also is weak and undeveloped; but when his body grows and becomes strong, his intellect also becomes stronger; and in the old age of man, when the body weakens and breaks down, the intellect also begins to disappear; so how then can we doubt that at the death of the body the soul also dies? When a part of the body is racked with pain, the soul is sad and depressed and is not in condition for any thought except the feeling of the pain; and when the body drinks much wine, the soul is disturbed and is in no condition for any proper thought. It is clear, therefore, that the soul is connected with the body and that it perishes along with it. If the eye is torn from the body, it will not see again; hence if the soul departs from the body, it will not again feel and think. The soul is

mortal just as the body is mortal. So what is there to fear
from death? And what are the terrors of Hades, by which
men are frightened?

And if they say to us that the atoms, of which my body
and my soul are composed, can or even must come together
once again after myriads of thousands of years in the same
union in which my spirit and my soul are now found[98]—I
say that there is no value in this, since I shall not remember
then, in the new union like the present one, what I was in the
life before, just as I do not now remember what I was when
I was being formed in the womb of my mother; in other
words, I shall be a stranger to myself. So why should we fear
death and tremble at the thought of Hades? It is impossible to
inflict torments after death on that which passes away and
ceases to exist! Truly, the soul is not immortal, but death itself
is immortal; Lucretius speaks of "mortal life" and "immortal
death" (*Mortalem vitam mors cum immortalis ademit*).[98a]
There is to be no sorrowing over this at all. If man recognizes
the true "nature of things," he will not be afraid of the gods
and of death, and he will find pleasure for his soul in knowledge—in knowing the truth of actual existence.

In the fourth book, Lucretius sets forth the views of Epicurus with regard to the "images," which all bodies throw off
from the surface of themselves. These images, reflexions of
the bodies, act upon the senses, and by means of these, upon
the mind; or they act directly upon the mind by means of
dreams or by means of visions during the waking hours. Thus
Lucretius explains belief in the continuation of the life of the
spirits of the dead. Really, there is no immortality of the soul
but only the appearance of such, and every semblance of
reality is caused by the images thrown off by the body while

---

[98] This ancient Greek idea of the "eternal cycle" was revived in our
time by Friedrich Nietzsche, who saw in it great comfort for transitory
mankind. But Lucretius had already removed this comfort.
[98a] *De Rerum Natura* III 868.

it was still in a state of material existence and could be perceived by human senses.

The most important book of *De Rerum Natura* is the fifth. In it Lucretius explains how the heavens, the earth, the sea, the sun, the moon, and the stars came into existence; what is the source of life on the earth; and how man has ascended from a state of savagery to a state of civilization. By means of these explanations, Lucretius seeks to prove that the world is not directed or guided by any divine power or divine act, and that there is not in the world anything of the divine or anything outside of the category of Nature:

> but because
> These primal atoms in such multitudes
> In so many ways through infinite past time
> Impelled by blows and moved by their own weight,
> Have been borne onward so incessantly,
> Uniting in every way and making trial
> Of every shape they could combine to form,
> Therefore it is that after wandering wide
> Through vast periods, attempting every kind
> Of union and of motion, they at last
> Collect into such groups as, suddenly
> Flocking together, oftentimes become
> The rudiments of mighty things, of earth
> Sea and sky and the race of living creatures.[99]

For the intervention of gods, for gods in the form of powers of Nature, and for an intelligent soul directing creation, there is here no need. Everything is explained by motion, combination, and fusion, which are natural processes only. And therefore there is no need of frequent bowing down and doing obeisance nor of repeated sacrifices before the gods, nor of "much blood of beasts." [100]

In the sixth and last book, Lucretius explains by completely

[99] *Ibid.* V 422–31 [tr. by Trevelyan].
[100] *Ibid.* V 1198–1202.

natural causes those strange and perplexing phenomena of
Nature, which appear the most difficult to understand and
therefore have attached to them the most superstition, such
as storms, volcanoes, earthquakes, and the like. Also these,
therefore, do not need to be explained in terms of divine
power, in terms of a mysterious power which is above Nature.

And thus we have in the Epicurean system, of which Lucretius is the enthusiastic and able exponent, almost complete
disbelief [101] with regard to the gods, the deification of the
powers of Nature, and divine providence. Also the Epicurean
ethic is completely devoid of any religious or idealistic foundations, and all of it becomes dependent on the convenience and
pleasure of the sensual feelings.[102]

Of course, the religious spirits of the days of the rise of
Christianity did not find satisfaction in Epicureanism. Indeed,
they did not find satisfaction even in Stoicism, which was
much more religious and ethical. Nevertheless, even Epicureanism fulfilled a certain function in the spread of Christianity. If Stoicism helped Christianity to prevail over paganism by its *positive* religio-ethical principles, then Epicureanism
(in the philosophical sense of this word) caused by means
of its *negative* principles the destruction and setting aside of
all paganism and of the relativistic ethics connected with it.
This was brought about by a deep and incisive skepticism,
which without any doubt influenced at least the educated
classes of the period and pushed them into the arms of Christianity, with its monotheistic religiousness and its exalted
Judaistic ethics, so closely connected with a strong and deep
faith in God and man alike.

[101] Not absolute denial. See T. R. Glover, *The Conflict of Religions in
the Early Roman Empire*, 3rd ed., London 1909, pp. 25–7.

[102] It was for this reason that Philo, like the Sages of the Talmud, opposed
"Epicurean disbelief" and spoke against it with vexation and contempt (see
M. Stein, *Philon ha-Alexandroni*, Warsaw 5697, pp. 76–7).

CHAPTER III

Religious Syncretism

[In addition to the books cited at the beginning of the two preceding chapters, I call attention to the following: F. Cumont, *Les religions orientales dans le paganisme romain*, 4-ème éd. Paris 1929: A. Loisy, *Les mystères païens et le mystère chrétien*, 2-ème éd., Paris 1930; C. Clemen, *Religionsgeschichtliche Erklärung des Neuen Testaments*, 2. Aufl., Giessen 1924; T. R. Glover, *The Conflict of Religions in the Early Roman Empire*, 3rd ed., London 1909; F. Legge, *Forerunners and Rivals of Christianity*, 2 vols., Cambridge 1915; W. R. Halliday, *The Pagan Background of Early Christianity*, Liverpool 1925; H. W. Willoughby, *Pagan Regeneration*, Chicago 1929; G. H. Box, *Early Christianity and Its Rivals*, London 1929 (a popular work); W. Schubart, *Die religiöse Haltung des frühen Hellenismus*, Leipzig 1937 (Der Alte Orient, XXV, 2); Ch. Guignebert, *Le Christianisme antique*, Paris 1926, pp. 84-106.]

1. Ancient Greek religion was, in its first period, the primitive, extending to about 560 B.C.E., a religion of nature. It deified powers and phenomena of nature, such as mountains, rivers, snakes, thunder, lightning, and the like, as did the religions of other primitive peoples.[1]

The second period begins with the rule of Pisistratus (560–527 B.C.E.), when the Homeric poems, product of the Greek islands, were disseminated in Hellas with the approval of the tyrant, and continues to the time of Alexander the Great (336–323). In this period, thanks to Homer and the great tragic poets on the one hand, and the great sculptors and painters on the other, the primitive gods became more human and thus more pleasant and romantic.[2] Yet this very change

[1] See in particular the important book of Gilbert Murray, *op. cit.*, pp. 15–55.

[2] *Ibid.*, pp. 59–101; see also on this period W. Nestle, *Griechische Religiosität vom Zeitalter des Perikles bis auf Aristoteles*, Berlin-Leipzig 1933 (Griechische Religiosität, II).

brought forth the problem of morals in religion. Mountain and river, serpent and lightning, are not responsible for their deeds, whether good or bad, while anthropomorphized gods do have moral responsibility for what they do.[3] Yet in the form in which the masses of the people in Greece believed in them and worshipped them—and it was the same in the popular religion of Rome—the Graeco-Roman religion became ritualistic and mechanical. The intention of the worshippers was to persuade the gods by means of sacrifices, prayers, and various religious practices to do the will of the worshippers. In particular, these gods became in this period gods of the city and the state; and Greek patriotism, ancient and deep, was closely associated with them.

But from the fifth century B.C.E. in Greece and from the second century B.C.E. in Rome, the educated people, who were gradually increasing in number, began to ask questions and raise difficulties about the nature of the gods and the destiny of man, and about rewards and punishments in life and after death. These questions and difficulties undermined the pagan religion. And in this educated group, which grew larger and larger, Christianity in the beginning of its growth was able to find its first admirers.

In the third century B.C.E., Euhemerus wrote a book called *Sacred History* (ἱερὰ ἀναγραφή), in which he sets forth in the form of a travelogue the "Acts" (πράξεις) of the gods Uranus, Cronus, and Zeus, as he had found these acts recorded on a column of gold in a temple of Zeus on one of the isles of the Indian Ocean.[4] These "Acts" seek to show that all three of these gods were at first only historic men, who after death attained the rank of gods because they had benefited humanity, although they had died like all men. Thus was the crown of divinity taken from the heads of the great gods led by Zeus; and all faith in divine powers which are above

---

[3] See Gilbert Murray, *op. cit.*, pp. 90–8.
[4] See Wendland, *op. cit.*, SS. 119–21.

nature was made out to be only imagination and popular fancy. This book of Euhemerus was translated from Greek into Latin by the early Roman tragic poet Ennius, who died in the year 169 B.C.E.

Also near the time of Euhemerus, there was composed an imaginary letter of Alexander the Great to his mother Olympias about the Egyptian religion, a letter in which the deities Osiris and Isis (who is identified with Demeter) are made out to be terrestrial rulers; even the god Dionysus here rules over the world like any great king.[5]

For, in the same period—the third period, which begins with Alexander the Great and comes to an end with Augustus Caesar (333 B.C.E.–14 C.E.)—there is recognizable in the ancient world a deliberate attempt to make religion rational, also human and popular (which in Latin are the same thing). The gods and goddesses became men and women of more than ordinary worth and power, and the immorality in their conduct was relieved by flashes of beauty in the mythological stories and by the splendor of great works of art.

But, in the last analysis, this was a religion only for the more superficial among educated persons. The more profound among them did not find satisfaction in it, and they turned to the mystery religions. There was in the sixth century B.C.E. in Greece a sect of the votaries of Orpheus,[6] who saw in ecstasy a means whereby man attains union with deity, since only the body of man is earthly, and if his soul is divine, then the body is only a prison for it; therefore it is possible by the purification from the filthiness of the body which comes through ecstasy to attain the complete union of man (that is, the soul of man) and God (*unio mystica*). The mysteries of Eleusis,[7] which were founded upon *the death and resurrection of a god*, offered hope to man that he also would not

[5] *Ibid.*, p. 121.
[6] See Willoughby, *op. cit.*, pp. 90–113; Legge, *op. cit.*, I, 121–48.
[7] See on them Willoughby, *op. cit.*, pp. 36–67; Loisy, *op. cit.*, pp. 51–82.

die with the death of the body, and that if he could be "sanctified" in these mysteries, he would rise again and live a
blessed life after death.

These mysteries spread not only in Greece, but in Rome
also, and they continued to exist until the fourth century C.E.
The leaders of Roman society became members and sought
sanctification in these mysteries. And these were not the only
mysteries; there was the secret worship of the Phoenician
Cabeiri from Samothrace, with which were connected the mysteries of Demeter and her daughter Persephone. There were
also the great orgiastic mysteries of Dionysus-Bacchus, which
in the year 186 B.C.E. already had in Rome a sect of devotees
numbering seven thousand men and women. Against this sect
the Roman Senate felt obliged to promulgate a harsh decree
because they saw in these mysteries acts of license and lawlessness.[8] In all these mysteries there were crude magical
beliefs and strange symbolic acts mixed with exalted ethical
views, all of which aimed to give satisfaction to the searching
and seeking spirit of man in the affairs of "what is above and
what is below." In the course of time all these beliefs took
away great numbers of educated people—not just isolated individuals—from the popular pagan religion and unintentionally brought them nearer primitive Christianity, which, although it had many mysteries and miracles, nevertheless kept
the ethical element in them more prominent, and was more
receptive to sound knowledge.

2. But with the conquest of the East by Pompey and Mark
Antony, there came into the states included within the world
empire of Rome the Orientals—people from Asia Minor,
Syria, Palestine, Babylon, Persia, Egypt and other such places.
And they penetrated into all branches of life, literature, and

[8] See Willoughby, *op. cit.*, p. 68–89; Loisy, *op. cit.*, pp. 25–43; Cumont,
op cit., pp. 195–204.

learning; they became merchants, soldiers, slaves, teachers, scribes, lawyers, astrologers, and philosophers. The East, which preserved an abundance of material and spiritual power while Greece experienced a general decline and Rome destroyed a great part of its sons by a long series of wars, kept on increasing its influence everywhere, and particularly in Rome.[9] Along with the rest of the Oriental influences there filtered into the Roman Empire also the great Oriental religions,[10] which, since the conquests of Alexander the Great, had burst forth from their old inclosures in their own lands and entered into the whirlpool of mixed Greek and Oriental life which we call "Hellenism." Thus begins that great religious movement which we call "religious syncretism," that is, the mixing of the various religions and the identification of various gods in various lands and nations.

Polytheists, idolaters, even the cultured among them in Greece and Rome, were tolerant of the gods of foreign peoples. Only the monotheists—from the time of the prophets on—did not acknowledge any other god except the one and only God. The prophet Jeremiah was able to say to the idolaters in their own Aramaic language: "The gods that have not made the heavens and the earth shall perish from the earth and from under these heavens."[11] Like Jephthah in his time,[12] no pagan in Greece or Rome, and needless to say, in the East, denied the existence of foreign gods, but only that these were *his* gods. The Greek people not only permitted foreigners living in Athens to establish there "associations" (θίασοι) or "meals in common" (ἔρανοι) in honor of their gods, but they allowed Greek men and women to participate in the "associations" or the "sacred meals" or "mutual-aid societies" con-

[9] See for particulars Cumont, *op. cit.*, pp. 1–9; G. La Piana, "Foreign Groups in Rome during the First Centuries of the Empire" (*Harvard Theological Review*, XX [1927], 276–81).

[10] And much earlier into Greece itself. See Nestle, *op. cit.*, SS. 28–32.

[11] Jeremiah 10:11.   [12] See Judges 11:24.

nected with the worship of foreign gods.[13] Not only that, but we find already in the time of Herodotus an identification of various gods from various nations and lands with the gods of Greece. Again, in the fifth century B.C.E., in Athens, the Phrygian goddess Cybele was identified with Rhea, mother of Zeus, the head of the gods, and she was thought to be "the Great Mother of the Gods." In the year 204 B.C.E. her cult-symbol (a stone) was brought to Rome, and in the days of the Caesars there was celebrated in her honor a great orgiastic festival in which Romans of all classes of the people participated.

In Athens, there were from a relatively early time worshippers of the Phoenician Adonis and Astarte (Aphrodite), and the Egyptian Amon and Isis. At a later time we find the worship of a god by the name of "Pantheos" ("god of all gods"), or the worship of the "Pantheon" ("assemblage of all the gods"). Even Isis alone is "Panthea," and we find applied to her a startling expression like this: "O thou one who art the all, goddess Isis" (*una quae es omnia dea Isis*).[14]

The more the peoples of the East and Asia Minor penetrated into Greece and Rome, the more their gods came in also. The gods of Gaul and Thrace came in as well, but in the main it was the gods of the East. Alexander the Great and his most important successors endeavored to commingle the gods of Greece with the gods of Persia, Egypt, and Syria. And merchants, people sold into slavery, captives, and soldiers from remote foreign service brought to Rome strange new gods, which became confused in the minds of their worshippers with the native gods. Thus the Canaanite Baal and the Egyptian Amon became synonymous with Zeus-Jupiter, the Canaanite Astarte and the Persian Anahita (Anaitis) were assimilated to the Greek Aphrodite, the Egyptian Isis to the earth-goddess Demeter-Ceres, and so on. Ptolemy I estab-

[13] La Piana, *op. cit.*, pp. 183–340.   [14] See Leipoldt, *op. cit.*, S. 17.

ו 7ו ס ס

lished in Egypt the worship of the god Sarapis (or Serapis), whom many think to be an artificial creation of the king aided by the Egyptian priest Manetho and Timotheus of Eleusis for a political purpose (the mingling of Egyptian and Greek religions in order to Hellenize Egypt).[15] At any rate, the Egyptians thought him to be Usus-Hapi or Osiris-Apis, that is, the bull Apis, who became Osiris. The Phoenician Eshmun was thought to be a great god of healing and was identified with Asclepius, Greek god of healing; many different peoples would come and seek from him healing and deliverance from their ills.[16] Somewhat later there came into Greece and Rome the cult of the Persian god Mithras, the apostle of the god of light in his war with the kingdom of darkness; this god, who became in large measure Hellenized, succeeded in acquiring for himself adherents in all classes of people in Greece and Rome, and by means of the Persian troops in the army of Rome reached Pannonia, Germania, and Britannia.[17]

Gradually art, on the one hand, and priests and scribes, on the other hand, began to identify great numbers of Oriental gods with great numbers of Greek and Roman gods. In vain did Augustus Caesar attempt to return to the ancestral religion, so that there actually arose in his time a religious romanticism, which took an attitude of esteem and adoration toward the old Roman faith. In vain did there come about near the same time a Hellenization of the Roman religion, which softened and beautified the Roman faith by contact with that marvellous esthetic feeling which characterized the Greek

[15] See Plutarch, *De Iside et Osiride* 28; Tacitus, *Historiae* IV 83-4; Willoughby, *op. cit.*, pp. 176-9; Cumont, *op. cit.*, pp. 69-75. And contrast Cumont, p. 232 with Isidore Levy, *Sarapis*, Paris 1913.

[16] See W. W. Baudissin, *Adonis und Eschmun*, Leipzig 1911.

[17] See F. Cumont, *Les mystères de Mithra*, 3-ème éd., Paris 1913; *Idem, Les religions orientales*, pp. 129-49; Willoughby, *op. cit.*, pp. 143-68; G. Kittel, *Die Religionsgeschichte und das Urchristentum*, S. 28; Loisy, *op. cit.*, pp. 157-98.

religion in its classical period. All this was of no avail. The mechanistic element, which was fundamental in the early Roman religion, and also the subservience of the later Hellenized and romanticized Roman religion to the needs of the Roman government, came near to taking out all the soul that was in it.

Thus the way was prepared for the mystery religions, which came particularly from Asia and Africa: from Syria, Phrygia, Persia, Egypt, and other countries. Without conscious purpose, without definite intention, the new gods were identified with the old native gods, whose veneration had been preserved by the persistence of ancestral tradition. Thus, for example, the Egyptian Isis was identified with Demeter, Hera, Aphrodite, Athena, Nemesis, and Tyche; the Phrygian Attis-Cybele with Rhea, mother of Zeus; the Egyptian Osiris with Dionysus, Attis, and Adonis; the Egyptian Serapis with Asclepius, Dionysus, Helius, Pluto, and even with Zeus; the Persian Ahura-Mazda with Zeus and Heracles; the Persian Anahita with Aphrodite and Artemis (Diana); likewise, the Persian Mithras was identified with Apollo and Helius (Sol). In various inscriptions we find complete confusion of all sorts of gods—religious syncretism in its most exaggerated form. For example, in an inscription of Antiochus king of Commagene (the ancient Qûmûaḥ [Assyrian Kummukhi], on the border between Syria and Parthia), Apollo, Mithras, and Helius are mentioned in one breath.[18] There is also an inscription dedicated at one and the same time to Zeus, Helius, and Serapis.[19] In this manner the clear and precise forms of most of the Oriental gods, and of most of the Graeco-Roman gods have been blurred. The high priest of Cybele carries on his forehead a medallion of Attis, and upon his hands a medallion of Zeus; the Baal of the city of Doliche in Syria (who was called *Jupiter Dolichenus*) is delineated as Zeus-Jupiter;

[18] See Dittenberger, *Orientis Graeci Inscriptiones Selectae*, I, nos. 383 ff.
[19] See *Corpus Inscriptionum Graecarum*, no. 4262.

above, over his head, is Nike, goddess of victory, together
with the head of Helius, god of the sun; and below, under his
feet, is the Egyptian Isis with the sistrum, and various other
divinities.[20] This is complete and thorough syncretism: gods
and goddesses of different nations and different religions with
their functions confused and dwelling side by side in peace
and quiet.[21] But there is no doubt that this mixing of religions
and divinities tended to diminish regard and true reverence
for them. All of them became weak and diluted, without any
clear or definite characteristics; and thus religious syncretism
helped Judaism, and Christianity after it, in showing pagans
all the futility of these gods and religions, and even in abolish-
ing them altogether.[22]

3. This is only one side of the influence of religious syncretism—the purely negative side. This side influenced pagans
to accept first Judaism and later Christianity. But religious
syncretism had also a positive influence—and in this case on
Christianity alone.

The Oriental gods most familiar in Greece and Rome were
dying and rising gods. Such was the Egyptian Osiris, such was
Adonis in Phoenicia, such was Attis in Phrygia. Likewise, the
Babylonian Baal-Bel-Marduk died and rose again; he was
arrested, he was sentenced, he was chastised, and together
with a malefactor he was sent away to death, while another
malefactor was freed. A woman cleansed away the blood
oozing from the heart of the god, which, it would appear, was
pierced by a spear or a javelin. Afterwards he was found in
a "mountain," that is, in the underworld, where he was being
watched over. A goddess had made a nest for him and was
caring for him. Finally Bel-Marduk came back alive and well
from the mountain (the underworld).[23]

[20] See Wendland, *op. cit.*, SS. 434–5; Kittel, *op. cit.*, SS. 34–5 (and illus-
trations); Cumont, *Les religions orientales*, pp. 104–7 (and illustration 7).
[21] See H. Dessau, *Geschichte der römischen Kaiserzeit*, II, 2, 803.
[22] See Wendland, *op. cit.*, S. 131.   [23] See Leipoldt, *op. cit.*, S. 9.

Osiris was slain by Set-Typhon (Baal Ṣaphon) his brother, who enclosed his body in a coffin—and the coffin was sunk in the Nile. Isis, wife of Osiris, found the coffin near the Phoenician city of Gebal (Byblos) and brought it back to Egypt; but there the coffin again fell into the hands of the brother, who cut the body of Osiris into fourteen (or sixteen) pieces and scattered them; but Isis found and gathered together all of them. Moreover, since he was the sun-god, it was impossible that Osiris should not be resurrected: for the sun expires every evening in the upper ocean—the firmament of heaven—and rises again every morning. The dead body of Osiris floated in the Nile and he returned to life, this being accomplished by a baptism in the waters of the Nile.[24]

The Phoenician Adonis was an extremely handsome youth, beloved of Astarte (Aphrodite, Venus). Once, when he went to hunt, a boar (or bear) from the forest dealt him a mortal wound. He died in the arms of his beloved Astarte, who was grief-stricken by his death. Serving to commemorate him were "gardens of Adonis," perforated dishes or flower-pots, in which were sown seeds that came to blossom quickly, but withered just as quickly.[25] These are the "pleasant plants" of the Bible, which "in the day of [their] planting" are made to grow, but do not last to the harvest: ". . . the harvest fleeth away in the day of grief and of desperate sorrow." [26] This Adonis is also the Babylonian Tammuz, "for whom the women weep," [27] like the weeping of Astarte, who mourned for her beloved Adonis.[28]

---

[24] See A. Moret, *La mise à mort du dieu en Egypte*, Paris 1928, pp. 14-9; Th. Ziélinski, *La Sibylle*, pp. 67-75; H. Gressmann, *Tod und Aufer-stehung des Osiris*, Leipzig 1923 (Der Alte Orient, XXIII, 3).

[25] See Klausner, "Niṭ'e Na'amanim" (memorial volume to A. Rabinowitz, Tel-Aviv 5684, pp. 10-4).

[26] Isaiah 17:10, 11.

[27] Ezekiel 8:14.

[28] Baudissin, *op. cit.*, SS. 430 ff.; Leipoldt, *op. cit.*, SS. 17-24; another story in Ziélinski, *op. cit.*, pp. 70-86.

The Phrygian Attis also died and rose to life again. He was a handsome shepherd, and Cybele, "the Great Mother of the Gods," fell in love with him. But he played her false and entered into a love affair with a nymph. In her rage Cybele killed the nymph. This affair brought Attis to the point of madness. He emasculated himself and died as a result. But he rose to life again. Cybele, who loved him, mourned for him and brought him back to life, as we see from the "Mysteries of Attis," handed down to us by the pagan who became a Christian, Firmicus Maternus (fourth century c.e.); and we have figures on coins, which portray the festival of the resurrection of Attis.[29]

Also the Greek Dionysus, who apparently originated in Thrace, but who in spreading widely through Asia Minor, Syria, Egypt, and Persia (Shushan) took on "a half-Oriental character,"[30] died and rose to life again. Orpheus, who has a close relationship to Dionysus, went down to Hades and returned thence; according to one story he was torn to pieces by mad and frenzied women or killed by the thunderbolt of Zeus.[31] In one of the poems of Callimachus of Cyrene and in one of a later poet who quotes the ancient Epimenides, we read that the Cretans[32] erected a building over a tomb in honor of even Zeus himself, as though he too had died; and the two poets reprimand the Cretans for this.[33]

The idea that a god can die and return to life was, therefore, in existence centuries before the rise of Christianity, and was widely current in the pagan world also in the very time of the rise of Christianity.

[29] See H. Graillot, Le culte de Cybèle, Paris 1912; Cumont, op. cit., pp. 43–68; Willoughby, op. cit., pp. 114–42; Loisy, op. cit., pp. 83–120.

[30] See Cumont, op. cit., p. 195–6.

[31] See Willoughby, op. cit., pp. 108–12.

[32] It is more likely that the island of Crete is represented in the Hebrew Bible by the word כפתור than by כרתים (see above, p. 12, note 20).

[33] See Leipoldt, op. cit., S. 4.

And this is not to be wondered at. In polytheistic my-thology the god is sometimes a man who became a god, and sometimes a god who became a man. The god Apollo, son of Zeus, became a man (servant of Admetus) in order to expiate a murder which he had committed. After he had served for some time, he went up to Olympus, and thereafter remained by the side of the glorious throne of Zeus. By contrast, Heracles the man, son of the god Zeus and the princess Alcmene, brought contentment and well-being to the world, and became a god by virtue of his great and good deeds.[34] And according to one story, Plato was the son of Perictione, who consorted with the god Apollo himself before her hus-band Ariston had any intimacy with her.[35] Thus Plato was, according to this story, a son of deity and at the same time born of a woman, very much like Jesus himself.

But the pagans knew not only a dying and rising *god*. A number of their religions promised resurrection, after a severely painful death, to the *man* who had attached himself to the god and had been sanctified by him.

According to the "Mysteries of Attis," handed down to us by Firmicus Maternus, whoever wishes to become a mystic votary (μύστης—initiate) to the dying and rising god Attis must go to his sanctuary, and there, within a dark cavern, be "slain," that is, be put down into the ground up to his neck. Then the assemblage sings songs of mourning over the victim in the darkness; suddenly the cavern is illuminated by a great light and the priest calls in a low voice:

> Take courage, initiates, the god has been saved;
> For you salvation will follow the pains.

[34] See Ziélinski, *op. cit.*, pp. 19–24.

[35] This story is adduced by Origen (who incorrectly calls the mother of Plato "Amphictione") in order to show the possibility of the belief that Jesus was the son of God, born of a virgin woman (see Origen, *Contra Celsum* I 37).

Thus the initiate, who has been a man, becomes the god Attis at the time of initiation, and like this god he himself suffers torments, is slain, and rises again. "He rises to everlasting life," as the inscriptions say (*in aeternum renatus*).[36]

Moreover, we have a certain amount of information that a god was sacrificed as a propitiation-offering for the people and their sins; yet this god rose again—surely, therefore, he was a god.[37]

Of course, there can be no toleration whatever of the idea that Jesus never existed and is only a concoction from these pagan stories about a god who was slain and rose again. The differences between the stories about the crucifixion and resurrection of Jesus and the stories of the pagans about the death and resurrection of their gods are so numerous and so great, the possibility of death by crucifixion, at the hands of the Roman procurator, for anyone who claimed to be Messiah was so near certainty, and belief in the resurrection of the dead was so widespread in Israel in the period of the Second Temple, that all three of these reasons force us to conclude that the fate of Jesus is not just a reflexion of the fate of the gods Osiris, Attis, Adonis, Mithras, and other such divinities.[38]

But, on the other hand, there can be no doubt that, had it not been for the general influence—however obscure and remote—of these pagan stories, a *Jewish Messiah* would never have become the *Christian Son of God*, who, in spite of his death on the cross, in spite of the fact that he became "the curse of God who was hanged," rose to life again in the vision of his followers and became not only Christ-Messiah, but also the only son of God the Father, a son who was begotten of

[36] See Willoughby, *op. cit.*, pp. 132–41; Cumont, *op. cit.*, pp. 64–8; Loisy, *op. cit.*, p. 104–12; Ziélinski, *op. cit.*, pp. 81–5.

[37] See E. Dujardin, *Le Dieu Jésus*, Paris 1927, pp. 81–214 (this book, in its main thesis, cannot bear critical examination).

[38] See Leipoldt, *op. cit.*, SS. 51–81.

the Holy Spirit, and rose to life again from the darkness of his tomb, and became like in all things to God the Father.—

4. There was another cause of this fundamental transformation of the Jewish Messiah at the hands of Christianity.

We have already seen above that a man could become a god or a son of a god or even be a son of a god while remaining a man. Heracles was a son of a god, though born of a woman, and he was raised to the rank of a god; Plato also was a son of a god, and was born of a woman, but he remained in the status of a man.

But the Orient—especially Egypt—was familiar with the deification of kings from the earliest times.[39] The Egyptian Pharaoh was the embodiment of the gods Amon, Re, and others; and the Greek kings of the house of Ptolemy, rulers of Egypt, received from the Egyptians adoration as divinities. The Persian king also demanded divine honor for himself, all who approached him being obliged to bow down and do obeisance before him as before divinity itself. Alexander the Great took over this practice from the Persians after his victory over Darius III; and when Alexander came to Egypt, he sought to have himself recognized as the son of Zeus-Amon, for the Greeks of the Ionian islands had paid him divine honor even before this. The Ptolemies were following in the footsteps, therefore, not only of the Pharaohs, ancient kings of Egypt, but also of the great Greek king, a part of whose empire they had inherited. Ptolemy II, Philadelphus, even in-

[39] See on this: E. Lohmeyer, *Christuskult und Kaiserzeit*, Tübingen 1919; L. M. Sweet, *Roman Emperor Worship*, Boston 1919; L. R. Taylor, *The Divinity of the Roman Emperor*, Middletown, Conn. 1931; J. Toutain, *Les cultes païens dans l'Empire Romain*, I (1911), 19–179; Wendland, *op. cit.*, SS. 123–7, 143, 146–52; Clemen, *op. cit.*, SS. 29–31; A. Deissmann, *Licht vom Osten*, 4. Aufl., Tübingen 1923, SS. 287–324; Toussaint, *op. cit.*, pp. 136–9; Willoughby, *op. cit.*, pp. 15–8; La Piana, *op. cit.*, pp. 282–5; M. P. Charlesworth, "Some Observations on Ruler-Cult," *Harvard Theological Review*, XXVIII (1935), 5–44; Schubart, *op. cit.*, SS. 15–9; Carcopino, *op. cit.*, p. 74.

troduced the worship of "the divine brother and sister" (θεοὶ ἀδελφοί): he and Arsinoë, his sister-wife were like Zeus and Hera, like Apollo and Artemis. The titles of the kings of the house of Ptolemy were titles appropriate to true divinities: Soter—"Savior," Euergetes—"Beneficent," and even Epiphanes—"the God made Manifest."

And like the Ptolemies, so also the Seleucids. One of them was Soter, and another Epiphanes. Seleucus I identified himself with Zeus the Victor (Nicanor); Antiochus I with Apollo the Savior (Soter); and the title of Antiochus II was simply "the God" (Theos). Also the title of Antiochus IV, the one who left such a painful memory in the history of Israel, was Epiphanes, because he was said to represent the embodiment of deity in the flesh. In a similar way Christianity later represented Jesus to itself. And from all these the Roman emperors inherited "apotheosis" or deification.

Here, in Rome, three elements intermingled and became one: (1) the native Roman religious worship of the *Lares Domestici* or *Lares Patrii*, which, when connected with the "genius" of the emperor, became the *Lares Augusti*; (2) the Oriental worship of kings; and (3) the Greek religious practices from the time of Alexander the Great on. Also the Gracchi and Marius, who saved Rome from the Teutons and Cimbri, received divine honor; and to the consul [praetor] Marius Gratidianus were erected pillar-images with lamps lighted and incense burning before the images. With regard to Julius Caesar, there is a difference of opinion among scholars as to whether divine honor was paid to him during his lifetime or only after his death.[40] At any rate, after the death of Julius Caesar, the Roman people in general believed

---

[40] See for particulars Charlesworth, *op. cit.*, pp. 22–6. But there is an inscription of the council of Ephesus from the year 48 B.C.E., in which Julius Caesar is already called "the god [who sprang] from Ares and Aphrodite, the manifestation [of deity on earth] and the readily accessible savior of human life" (Dittenberger, *Sylloge*, 3. Aufl., no. 760).

that Julius ascended to heaven and became a god; by a decision of the Senate in 42 B.C.E. Julius Caesar became "the Divine Julius" (*Divus Julius*). And Octavian, his relative and heir, began in the year 40 B.C.E. to call himself *Divi Filius*—"Son of the Divine"; in the year 27 B.C.E. he received the title *Augustus* or Σεβαστός—"the Holy," which exalted him above all mortal men and made him deity or almost deity. Both during his lifetime and after his death people were accustomed to swear by his divinity, his statue was a protection and asylum for those who fled to it, and all his family were considered to be a "divine house" (*domus divina*) as though he were a god equal in importance to Jupiter.[41] Even the philosopher Seneca rated Augustus Caesar as "one who was said to be born from gods and to be destined to give birth to gods."[42]

Tiberius Caesar, who succeeded him, did not demand deification for himself. But Gaius Caligula, who at first identified himself with the "heroes" who were elevated to the rank of divinity, such as Hercules (Heracles), later identified himself with actual gods, such as Mercury and Apollo; finally he called Jupiter Capitolinus, the highest god of Rome, "my brother."[43] All the peoples in the great Roman Empire built sanctuaries and altars in his honor, they made sacrifices to him, and they burnt incense to him, just as to actual deity— all the peoples, that is, except the Jews. So when the Jewish embassy from Alexandria told him that the Jews had offered sacrifices for him in their Temple at Jerusalem, he said: "All this may be true; you did sacrifice, but *to* another even if *for* me. What is the good of it if you did not sacrifice to *me*?"[44]

---

[41] See Charlesworth, *op. cit.*, pp. 29, 30; sometimes he was called "god" (θεός) and "savior" (σωτήρ) in one breath; and we have a papyrus in which someone swears by "Caesar, god from a god" (καίσαρ[α] θεὸν ἐκ θεοῦ), meaning that Augustus Caesar was the offspring of a god (see Deissmann, *op. cit.*, S. 292).

[42] See Seneca, *To Marcia on Consolation* XV 1.

[43] See Josephus, *Antiquities* XIX i 1 (§ 4).

[44] Philo, *The Embassy to Gaius* XLV.

Both Nero and Domitian demanded divine honor for themselves, and the Senate voted to deify them. When Nero returned from Greece, the Senators met him with the salutations: "Nero-Hercules!," "Nero-Apollo!"; and in accordance with a decree of the Senate, a statue of him was erected in the temple of "Mars Ultor" (the Avenger); and in the year 67 there was even a proposal to erect a special temple "to the Divine Nero" (*Divo Neroni*).[45]

Vespasian and his son Titus became "divine ones" only after death; but Domitian, son of the former and brother of the latter, demanded that his divinity be recognized during his lifetime; he sought to be called "Lord and God" (*Dominus et Deus*—in Greek κύριος Θεός, "Lord God," the very phrase used by the Christians![46] In the year 94 C.E. a soldier in Egypt swore by "Jupiter the greatest and best" and by the "genius of the most holy Caesar Domitian"; and there already existed the custom of pouring libations and burning incense before his image.[47]

M. P. Charlesworth [48] endeavors to prove that finally not even one of the Caesars succeeded in attaining the position of an actual deity; and as for the divine names with which the Caesars glorified themselves, they stood only for the sanctity of the State and the divinity of the Empire. It is possible that there is in this a partial truth. Nevertheless, the large number of inscriptions in which the Caesars are called "God," "son of God," and "Savior," the statues and monuments which were erected in their honor, the libations which were poured out before their statues, and the incense which was burned to them—all these proved that in Rome, as in both early and Ptolemaic Egypt, it was customary to deify the man who

---

[45] In one Greek inscription Nero is even called "the good god" (θεὸς ἀγαθός)! See Deissmann, *op. cit.*, SS. 293–4.

[46] Similarly, Nero was called "Nero the Lord" (Νέρων ὁ κύριος) and even "Nero Lord" without the article (Νέρων κύριος) exactly like χριστὸς κύριος!

[47] See Charlesworth, *op. cit.*, pp. 29, 32–5.

[48] *Ibid.*, pp. 4–42; see also Carcopino, *op. cit.*, p. 74.

became emperor. And although Vespasian became *Divus* (θεῖος) only after his death, his son Domitian was a "son of God," following the practice already started by Augustus Caesar in calling himself *Divi Filius* (θεοῦ υἱός).[49]

Is it possible to suppose that all these expressions, such as "Lord and God," "son of God," "he who makes God manifest," and "Savior," which were common in the East [50] and were also current in Rome, did not influence the titles by which Paul and his followers designated their Jewish Messiah? —especially after they found a certain precedent for this in Judaism, which calls God "our Father, who art in heaven" and "my heavenly Father," and says of the Messiah (according to the ancient interpretation): "Thou art My son, this day have I begotten thee." [51] Graeco-Roman influence here mingles with Jewish traditions and produces the special conception of Paul and his followers that Jesus the Messiah is a "son of God" (*Filius Dei*, θεοῦ υἱός and "Lord God" (*Dominus Deus*, θεὸς κύριος).

5. The strength of the new mystery religions, which came from Asia and Africa, lay in the fact that they satisfied a great spiritual need of that time.

Early pagan religion, especially that of the Greeks from the time of Pisistratus on, was a rationalistic faith, lacking mysteries, and at the same time was the religion of the state and the city. The early religion of the Romans was even more political, and was more concerned with the salvation of the community than with the spiritual well-being of the individual. But in the period with which we are concerned, this

[49] See Ziélinski, *Soperniki Khristianstva*, pp. 72–7.

[50] Matters reached such a state, that we have two inscriptions from Egypt in which human beings who are not kings are called θεὸς καὶ κύριος—"God and Lord" (Deissmann, *op. cit.*, S. 309, Anm. 7).

[51] See on this Klausner, *Yeshu ha-Notsri*, 4th ed., pp. 425–7 [Eng. ed., pp. 377–80].

communal religion was weakening. As in every period of social development in which community ties are gradually weakened and old established institutions and customs are losing their force, the individual now came to the fore and demanded spiritual satisfaction for himself.[52] In this romantic period of the ancient world, which fell in the days of the rise of Christianity, the individual began to seek the salvation of his soul. Salvation of the individual instead of salvation of the community was demanded of religion, and the individual was unconsciously dissociated from the state. The individual sought to be delivered from distress of both body and soul; therefore the god had to be above all a *savior* (σωτήρ), and the religion had to offer above all *salvation* (σωτηρία). The Oriental mystery religions promised the pagan individual this deliverance and salvation from his woes, and in particular from sin.

For these religions were those which promised to bridge the chasm between man and deity, to join man with God in complete union, so that man would be elevated to the rank of deity, becoming sinless like deity and immortal like deity. This state could be attained by means of ecstasy—the "sober intoxication," according to the felicitous expression of Philo, by means of which the priest or the "sanctified one" obtains a revelation of the divine Presence, a personal relationship to deity. But a relationship like this is also attained by means of a "sacred meal," in which the initiate eats "holy food" and it is as though he ate deity itself and thereby also became deity. "Sacred meals" like these are known to us as the chief element in the mysteries of Dionysus (Bacchus), Attis, Mithras, and Isis. By means of the eating of the holy foods and the drinking of holy potions which contain elements of

[52] In regard to the effect of the great changes in the political and social life of the Romans upon the old Roman religion, see the excellent treatment of Wilhelm Weber, *Der Prophet und sein Gott*, Leipzig 1925, SS. 31–48, 138–9. See also Carcopino, *op. cit.*, pp. 147–67.

divinity, man absorbs exalted and supernatural powers. These meals were partaken of in an "association"—the θίασος or ἔρανος mentioned above (*collegium* or *sodalitas* in Latin)—in which the members joined themselves together for the needs of burial (like our own "burial associations") and for religious worship, thus forming an association that was sacred, secret, and mystical. We have here a phenomenon which could not possibly have failed to influence the "Last Supper" of Jesus, which, in my opinion, was only the "Seder" meal of Passover, at which the Passover meat is eaten and the wine of the Four Cups is drunk;[53] but influenced by the "sacred meal" of the pagan mysteries, this Passover meal took on a new festive-mystical form. This was very different from its Jewish form, which is festive, but non-mystical.

In order to be received into the association, ablutions were required. We know this clearly with regard to the religions of Isis and Mithras at least. These ablutions had efficacy not only for physical cleanliness, but also for moral purity. In this regard the baptism of the pagan mysteries is similar to that of Judaism, which also from the days of the Prophet Ezekiel was connected with purity of soul:

> And I will sprinkle clean water upon you, and ye shall be clean: from all your filthiness and from all your idols, will I cleanse you. A new heart also will I give you, and a new spirit will I put within you; and I will take away the stony heart out of your flesh, and I will give you a heart of flesh.[54]

In the time of the Second Temple, baptism had great importance in the eyes of the Essenes; and in the reception of proselytes, baptism was customary along with circumcision. For female proselytes, to whom the law of circumcision did not apply (although there were people in the world who

---

[53] See for particulars Klausner, *op. cit.*, pp. 366–70 [Eng. ed., pp. 326–9].
[54] Ezekiel 36:25, 26. See I. Scheftelowitz, "Die Sündenvergebung durch Wasser," *Archiv für Religionswissenschaft*, XVII, 353 ff.

practised female circumcision as well as male), baptism was the sole religious act signifying the removal of pagan impurity.[55] Also here Christianity was able to combine the Jewish-Pharisaic-Essene view of the importance of baptism with the pagan-mystical view of baptism as affording purification and bringing about a new birth. Thus baptism assumed very great importance in Christianity—much greater than in Judaism.

Among the rites of the "marriage" of the Phrygian Cybele (and of the goddess Ma-Bellona) was an unusual one called the *taurobolium* or *criobolium*. In this rite a devotee of the goddess (in the particular form before us,[56] a priest or even a high priest) would enter a pit covered with perforated planks, while upon the planks was stationed a bull adorned with a band of gold. The breast of the bull was pierced with the consecrated spear, and the man in the pit would receive in his face and in his clothing the warm blood which flowed into the pit through the perforations; and the blood would wet his beard, his ears, his eyes, his nostrils, his lips, and even his tongue. It was as though he was purified and rose again to a new life, the life of a man who had become divine.[57] With regard to Attis, we have already seen above that the one consecrated to him goes, as it were, through all the experiences of the god himself, including his unusual death (or mutilation) and his resurrection.[58] And thus it was also in the mysteries of Osiris and Adonis.[59]

It is hard to doubt that these pagan practices, of which perhaps only a faint and far-away echo reached the first Chris-

---

[55] Against S. Zeitlin, *Hebrew Union College Annual*, I (1924), 357–63, who believes that baptism of Jewish proselytes was not instituted until after the Destruction, see Klausner, *op. cit.*, pp. 223–6 [Eng. ed., pp. 206–9], 270–2 [Eng., 245–7]. And see above, p. 37, n. 35.

[56] The particular form is that of Prudentius, *Peristephanon*, 1006–1050.

[57] Cumont, *op. cit.*, pp. 63–4; Loisy, *op. cit.*, pp. 112–20; Willoughby, *op. cit.*, pp. 129–32.

[58] See above, pp. 106–7.   [59] Wendland, *op. cit.*, S. 155.

tians from the pagans, influenced beliefs about the blood of
Jesus. This sacrificial gore at the beginning was only "the
blood of the covenant" of the Pentateuch [60] or "the blood of
the righteous" who are "the expiation of Israel" in the later
literature; [61] afterwards it was changed into a mystery, according to which the disciples "ate" the flesh and "drank" the
blood of Jesus, who thus gave the "ransom for many." [62]

The pagan world of that time, religious as well as political
and economic, was full of distress and perplexity. It longed
for the past, but felt that the past would never return. And
what there was in the present afforded no spiritual satisfaction.
The people thirsted for salvation from sin and death—but
the regular and accepted Graeco-Roman religion had no
savior-god and no redeemer from the grave. This religion was
rationalistic and limited to political and national affairs; it was
too this-worldly (if we may speak thus). Hence the pagan
world of the time of Paul was searching and seeking for new
paths in religion. In its distress it turned to the Orient (which
had anticipated Greece and Rome in its culture and religiousness by thousands of years, and had stored up from days of
old ancient wisdom and mystical religion),[63] expecting to find

[60] Exodus 24:5–11.

[61] "The righteous are seized [by death] for the [sins of the] generation"
(Shabbath 33b); "the death of the righteous affords atonement" (Mo'ed
Katan 28a). Compare the utterance of R. Ishmael, "The children of Israel,
may I be an atonement for them!" (Mishnah, Nega'im II 1), and especially
the forceful words of IV Maccabees 4:28, 29: "Be merciful to Thy people;
be content with the punishment which we [the righteous] bear on their
behalf; make my blood a purification for them and my life a ransom for
their life."

[62] See for particulars Klausner, *op. cit.*, pp. 368–70 [Eng. ed., pp. 327–9].

[63] G. La Piana, in his important study, *op. cit.*, pp. 321–7, explains the
tendencies toward universalism and individual salvation of the Oriental religions mainly on the grounds of their transplantation from their own native
soil as a result of the migration of their adherents throughout the Roman
Empire. I think that these tendencies were concealed within them in an
embryonic state even before their migration to foreign lands, and that these
tendencies are the result of a culture that was more ancient and more religious, that is to say, less rationalistic and more mystical.

there healing for its broken spirit and salvation for its despairing soul. Thus the way was opened for a Graeco-Roman-Oriental combination in religion and in ethics. This is the very religious syncretism upon which I have been elaborating. This syncretism prepared the way for Christianity; Christianity also came from the East and likewise became gradually a new combination—a compound of Judaism and Hellenism.

But Christianity sprang up at the beginning in the midst of a people who had an Oriental religion which was syncretistic to only a small degree. To be sure, even Judaism absorbed Babylonian-Persian elements—the belief in angels as embodying the highest spiritual personalities, the belief in demons and evil spirits, the belief in Satan and Asmodaeus. Also, from the book of Koheleth (Ecclesiastes) on we recognize in Judaism influences superficial and profound, direct and indirect, of the thought and culture and language of the Greeks. But in the *fundamental* matters of religion, Judaism did not yield in its essential quality even so much as the breadth of a hair. Therefore, even though it had penetrated into the pagan world and received from that world many male and female proselytes, it was impossible for that world to assimilate it—impossible for entire nations and countries to accept it.

Christianity, daughter of Judaism, with its exaggeration of Judaism which was turned into non-Judaism,[64] with its extreme ethics, product of its expectation of the immediate advent of the Days of the Messiah who had already come and redeemed with his blood his own people or at least those who believed in him (the salvation of all mankind was not explicit in the earliest Christianity), with its mystery of the Messiah's resurrection after he had tasted of a disgraceful death on the cross—on all these points, Christianity was more pliant than Judaism, its mother from whom it was brought forth; it was closer to the religious syncretism of the times, and closer to

[64] For a detailed exposition of this statement, see Klausner, *op. cit.*, pp. 416–42 [Eng. ed., pp. 369–97]. Also, see above, p. 5.

pagan hearts, being a religion which had as its chief element the savior from sin and the redeemer from death. And when it was influenced consciously and unconsciously by the paganism which surrounded it on every side, when it accepted freely all sorts of pagan beliefs and opinions, and even became a universalistic religion and a soteriological faith (a faith that seeks salvation for the individual), and particularly when it became a syncretistic faith—then it was in a position to take the place of syncretistic paganism. For this paganism was inferior to Christianity on three counts: *first*, there remained in it vestiges of the weird beliefs and savage practices of its earlier period; *second*, it had a compromising relationship with all sorts of strange beliefs and customs which was fatal to any sincere or profound religion; *third*, it did not give sufficient place to the ethical element.[65]

Here we have the solution to the enigma of the great and relatively swift success of Paul. He *consciously* opposed paganism and brought over the pagans to Judaism in the new Christian form which he had created; but he was *unconsciously* influenced by paganism and took over from it most of its sacred practices (sacraments) insofar as he could find for them a precedent in Judaism; or, he unintentionally colored Jewish customs with a pagan-mystery color. He also took over from the pagan mystery religions and from pagan philosophical-religious thought a part of their terminology. For example, the antithesis between πνεῦμα ("spirit") and ψυχή ("soul"), and between the "spiritual" or "heavenly" man (πνευματικός, οὐράνιος ἄνθρωπος) and the "natural" or "earthly" man (ψυχικός, ἐπίγειος ἄνθρωπος); the distinction between the "heavenly body" and the "earthly body," and the yearning for this "heavenly body"; the insistence that human nature becomes twofold in a time of ecstasy; and the like.[66] All these things were common to Paul and to the mystery cults of the pagan religions of salvation; but Paul introduced into them a new spirit and a new meaning, partly Jewish and partly original with himself.

The secret of his success is that he made use in large measure of those weapons which a paganism anxious for the salvation of the individual placed in his hands; and he added to them the ethical demands, the ways of salvation, and the irreconcilability with other religions which Judaism gave him. For Christianity inherited from Judaism, if not self-sufficiency, at least resoluteness and zeal in all those parts of Judaism which Christianity could not reject without being completely swallowed up by paganism. And abundant resoluteness and zeal not resulting from blindness of eyes but from inner conviction, confident and indivisible, are primary necessities for victory.

Truly, the great Jewish heritage which Christianity brought with it from Jerusalem, from Palestinian Judaism, from Jesus and his first disciples, was the proper earnest of victory.[67] But Christianity also brought with it, after a brief period of its existence, a heritage from Alexandria in Egypt, from Hellenistic Judaism; and it was this which enabled it to bridge the gulf between Judaism and paganism.

To this heritage I now pass.

[66] See Wendland, *op. cit.*, S. 156.

[67] A more or less satisfactory idea of Palestinian Jewish thought in the time of Jesus and Paul is to be obtained from my book *Historia Yisreelit*, II, 89–118, 152–80; III, 89–124; and in briefer compass from *Yeshu ha-Notsri*, 4th ed., pp. 208–47 [Eng. ed., pp. 193–228].

THIRD BOOK

HELLENISTIC JEWISH THOUGHT

CHAPTER I

The Wisdom of Solomon

In the period which we are studying, the intermingling of Judaism and Hellenism was already far advanced. This intermingling is revealed in three separate books, and in a series of books which are the spiritual product of a Hellenistic Jewish philosopher. The three separate books are the Wisdom of Solomon, Fourth Maccabees, and the Sibylline Oracles; the Hellenistic Jewish philosopher is Philo of Alexandria.

All these I have treated in detail in another place.[1] Here I will give only what there is to learn from these books in order to understand the rise of Christianity among the Jews after Jesus was crucified and its spread among the Gentiles in the days of Paul. I shall begin with the Wisdom of Solomon.

1. The current opinion with regard to the Wisdom of Solomon is that this book is made up of four different works, which were composed by different authors at different times:

[1] On the Wisdom of Solomon and IV Maccabees see for particulars: J. Klausner, *Historia Yisreelit*, IV, 39–50; the chapter on Philo in *Historia Yisreelit*, IV, 50–67 has been much expanded in my book *Philosophim ve-Hoge-De'ot*, I, 64–91; on the Sibylline Oracles see J. Klausner, *Ha-Ra'yon ha-Meshihi be-Yisrael*, 2nd ed. (Jerusalem 5687), pp. 230–40. All three of these books contain detailed bibliographies in various languages. Here I may add for the Wisdom of Solomon the book of B. Motzo, *Saggi di Storia e Letteratura Giudea-Ellenistia* (Firenze 1924), pp. 31–66; and for Philo, the important book of M. Stein, *Philon ha-Alexandroni* (Warsaw 5697). See also *Philon ha-Alexandroni, Kitve-Historia*, translation with introduction and notes, by M. Stein (Tel-Aviv 5697). With the Greek Baruch, the Slavonic Enoch, and the like, I do not deal here because parts of these pseudepigraphical books are too fantastic, and other parts are too difficult to date or are too full of late fabrications. In the Letter of Aristeas I do not find any essential material which Christianity could use for its propaganda.

(1) the "Book of Vision" (chaps. 1–5); (2) the "Book of Wisdom" (chaps. 6–9); (3) the "Book of Legend" (chaps. 10–12, 16–19); (4) the "Interpolation" or "Treatise against Idolatry" (chaps. 13–15). There is an opinion that the first part was written about 100 B.C.E., the second about 30–20 B.C.E., and the third, together with the "Interpolation," about 30–40 C.E. The second part was written in Greek by an Alexandrian Jew; but the first part was written in Hebrew by a Palestinian Jew; likewise the third part, according to the opinion of many.[2] With the ancient opinion that the Wisdom of Solomon was written by Philo (or by Philo and his associates in the embassy to Gaius), only one scholar, an Italian, agrees, so far as I know.[3] He offers proofs for his opinion, but his proofs are not compelling. This book, the Wisdom of Solomon, differs in the whole trend of its thought from the world-view of Philo; it is even difficult to find in it any Philonic influence, although it is concerned with matters similar to those with which Philo was concerned; for it really came forth before Philo.

I myself would propose—and this is not the place to offer proofs for my hypothesis—that the whole book was written by a Palestinian Jew, who had fled to Egypt at the time of the persecution of the Pharisees by Alexander Jannaeus (about 80 B.C.E.), and in Alexandria wrote all parts of his book in Greek at different times, during the years 70–50 B.C.E. This Palestinian Jew, who was permeated with the spirit of the Holy Scriptures in their original Hebrew form, as well as the teaching of the early Pharisees, was influenced in Alexandria by Greek doctrines also—particularly by Platonism and Stoicism. This explains why his book is so very different in spirit

[2] A contrary opinion is that of M. Stein in the introduction to his translation of the Wisdom of Solomon in the edition of the Apocrypha and Pseudepigrapha edited by Abraham Kahana (Tel-Aviv 5697), I, 2, pp. 463–71. See also *Philon ha-Alexandroni* by the same author, pp. 32–43.

[3] See B. Motzo, *Saggi, etc.*, pp. 31–66.

in its various parts, and why even its language in the later parts is more like original Greek than in the first and earlier part; also why the whole book is an amazing compound of Judaism and Hellenism—with the preponderance on the side of Judaism.[4]

For even his conception of Wisdom is compounded of what is said about it in the Hebrew books of Proverbs, Job, Koheleth, and Ben-Sira, and of the ideas of the Greek philosophers on the subject. Like a Jew he recalls at the beginning of the book that "Wisdom cannot enter a soul that devises evil, nor dwell in a body in bondage to sin"; [5] but like a Greek he goes on to say that "Wisdom is a benevolent spirit" (φιλάνθρωπον γὰρ πνεῦμα σοφία).[6]

After a short introduction, the author enters into debate with the skeptics of his day. Their philosophy can be summarized in the phrase "Eat and drink, for to-morrow we die." These wicked ones plead thus: Life is short, our days are like a passing shadow, there is no escape from death, therefore come, let us enjoy ourselves as long as we live! While we are young, let us delight in good wine, let us anoint our bodies with oil of myrrh, and "let no flower of the spring (ἄνθος ἔαρος) pass us by," for "this is our portion and this is our lot." [7] And if pleasure is the only value in life, why should we live righteously? Let us rob the righteous poor, let us show no consideration to widowhood, let us not honor old age; in other words, "Let our might be the law of right, for everything that is weak is to be deemed useless." [8] (This "Nietzschean" conception is already found in the ancient Sophists, Thrasymachus of Chalcedon and Callicles.) [9] Let us trip up

---

[4] That in spite of all the Greek intermixture in the Wisdom of Solomon "the basic attitude in it is in general Jewish" is also the opinion of Julius Guttmann, *Die Philosophie des Judentums* (München 1933), SS. 29–31.

[5] Wis. Sol. 1:4.   [6] Wis. Sol. 1:6.

[7] Wis. Sol. 2:7, 9.   [8] Wis. Sol. 2:11.

[9] See J. Klausner, *Philosophim ve-Hoge-De'ot*, I, 17.

the righteous person, for he is a nuisance to us: he is always reproving us, and we are in his eyes like "debased coinage" or "inferior mixed cloth" (κίβδηλος),[10] while he, the righteous, "boasts that God is his father." [11] In reality, the righteous man is not often fortunate at his end; so let us, who are wicked in his eyes, condemn him to death, and "if the righteous man is a son of God, He [God] will defend him and deliver him from the hands of his adversaries." [12]

The expressions "God is his father" and "the righteous man is a son of God" (υἱὸς Θεοῦ) are Jewish when taken in a spiritual sense.[13] We have in the Pentateuch, "You are the children of the Lord your God; [14] of King Solomon Nathan the prophet says in the name of the Lord, "I will be a father to him, and he shall be a son to Me." [15] Likewise we find in Ben-Sira, "And God will call you 'Son' "; [16] also, "I exalted the Lord (saying), 'Thou art my father'." [17] The Talmud knows the expression "sons of God"; [18] and the expressions "Our Father who art in heaven" and "My Father in heaven" are found in it times without number.[19] But in the pagan environment of the Judaism of the Diaspora, where deities had actual children (Horus was the son of Osiris), and where the Roman emperors bore the title *Divi Filius* ("son of the divine") [20]—in this pagan environment this expression had a special coloring even if used by a Jew. And Paul, who, as we shall see below, was almost certainly influenced by the Wis-

---

[10] M. Stein, in his Hebrew translation of and commentary on the Wisdom of Solomon, p. 477, translates this word *sige-keseph*, "dross of silver."
[11] Wis. Sol. 2:16.   [12] Wis. Sol. 2:18.
[13] Without good reason does Stein regard the second expression as "a later Christian elaboration."
[14] Deut. 14:1.   [15] II Sam. 7:14.
[16] Ben-Sira 4:10 (Heb.).   [17] Ben-Sira 51:10 (Heb.).
[18] Aboth III 3; Siphre Deut. § 308, ed. M. Friedmann 133 a and b.
[19] See J. Klausner, *Yeshu ha-Notsri*, 4th ed., pp. 425-6 [Eng. ed., pp. 377-8]; see also M. Stein in the commentary to his translation, *op. cit.*, pp. 476-7.
[20] See above, pp. 106-12.

dom of Solomon, materialized this conception in large measure —with definite results.

The author of the Wisdom of Solomon does not present this opinion about the bad state and lot of the righteous man as a proof of his unrighteousness, but in order to refute the opinion. The fact is that the righteous man is not to be judged according to his state and lot. "For God created man for incorruption, and made him the image of His own being." [21] The reason the righteous man goes to death like the wicked is because "by the envy of the devil death entered into the world"; [21a] "but the souls of the righteous are in the hands of God, and no torment shall touch them"; [22] or, as the Talmud says, "The righteous even in death are called 'living'." [23] The tribulations which come to the righteous man in life are only for testing him; like gold he is refined in the furnace, then God accepts him "like the sacrifice of a whole burnt-offering." [24] "In the time of their visitation" (day of death) the righteous "will shine, and will spread like sparks among stubble.[25] They shall judge nations and rule over peoples, and God shall reign over them forever." [26] Not so the ungodly, who despise the righteous and the wise; they and their seed after them shall be accursed. For "wretched is he who despises wisdom,[27] vain is their (the despisers') hope, unprofitable is their labor, and useless are their deeds." [28]

We have here purely Jewish ideas which are tinged with a light coloring of Stoic philosophy. These ideas are found

[21] Wis. Sol. 2:23.
[21a] Wis. Sol. 2:24.
[22] Wis. Sol. 3:1.
[23] Berakoth 18a.
[24] Wis. Sol. 3:6.
[25] Literally, "like sparks among reeds." Cf. Obadiah 18 and Mal. 3:19. M. Stein (*op. cit.*, p. 478) proposes that the Greek translator mistakenly read *ya'abru* ("will spread") for *yib'aru* ("will burn").
[26] Wis. Sol. 3:7, 8.
[27] Without good reason, Stein (pp. 478-9) thinks this half-verse a later addition.
[28] Wis. Sol. 3:9-11.

later, with certain changes, in the Epistles of Paul and in the other Epistles of the New Testament. They prepare a way to the answer to this question: If Jesus was Messiah and Son of God, why did not God his father save him from an unnatural and shameful death?——

One other ancient idea, rooted in the nation, was, as it were, an iniquitous stumbling-block for Christianity and for Jesus.

This ancient belief considered long life and numerous off-spring as a divine reward to the righteous and upright man, while a short life and childlessness were considered as signs of a wicked man ("Bloodthirsty and deceitful men shall not live out half their days"),[29] and as a punishment for heinous sins.[30] Thus thought the best men of the nation in earlier times. But in later times, when the individual stood out from the social group of tribe or nation, it was impossible not to see that upright and righteous persons—and perhaps they in particular—suffered grievous afflictions and died in their youth, and that among childless people, both men and women, there were righteous persons. The author of the Wisdom of Solomon contends against the old view, saying: "Happy is the barren woman who has not known the bed of harlotry; and happy is the childless man, even though a eunuch, who had obtained the fruit of good deeds instead of the fruit of the womb." [31] What if the wicked do have children, if the children are children of harlotry and iniquity? "Better is childlessness with virtue, for in virtue are immortality and [32] remembrance." [33] And when a righteous man dies in the prime of life, this does not prove that he was wicked: "For real old age is not mere length of time, and is not to be reckoned by the number of years; but understanding is gray hairs for men, and a blameless

[29] Ps. 55:23/24.
[30] Ps. 102:23/24 and 28/29; Ps. 127:3–5; Ps. 128:3, 4; and many other passages.
[31] Cf. Isa. 56:3–5.   [32] We should read καὶ μνήμη in place of ἐν μνήμη.
[33] Wis. Sol. 4:1.

life is ripe old age." [34] God takes the righteous man from among the wicked in order that he may not be corrupted by them.[35] In like manner, the Midrash argues with regard to the translation of Enoch: [36] because the soul of the righteous man found favor in the eyes of God, therefore God made haste to take it unto himself away from the world so filled with evil.[37] Then the author of the Wisdom of Solomon expresses this bold opinion: "A righteous man who has died will judge the wicked who are still living, and youth that has come quickly to maturity (will judge) the great age of the unrighteous man." [38] A day will come when the ungodly will perceive their own folly in thinking that the life of the righteous man is madness and his death a reproach, and then they will ask in amazement: "How was he (the righteous man) reckoned among the sons of God,[39] and his portion among the saints?" [40]

In words filled with wonderful poetic beauty, which reveals itself both in the fineness of the metaphors and word-pictures, and in the splendor of the parallelism of members characteristic of ancient Hebrew poetry, the author of the Wisdom of Solomon portrays the remorse of the ungodly over the worldly pleasures in which they indulged, but which could not fulfill their desires or satisfy their souls. Pleasure, along with riches and pride, fled like a shadow, like "a fleeting rumor," like a ship passing through the midst of the sea, its wake being obliterated by the waves;

Or as a bird flying through the air,
No sign of its course is found;
But the light wind, lashed by the stroke of her wings,
And pierced by the force of her flight,
Is traversed by the movement of (her) wings,

[34] Wis. Sol. 4:8, 9.   [35] Wis. Sol. 4:10, 11.
[36] Gen. Rabbah XXV 1, ed. Th. Albeck, p. 238 .
[37] Wis. Sol. 4:14.   [38] Wis. Sol. 4:16.
[39] See above, pp. 126–7.   [40] Wis. Sol. 5:5.

And then no sign of her passage is found therein;
Or as an arrow shot at a mark,
The air being cleft straightway closeth up into itself,
So that its path is not known.[41]

.   .   .

For the hope of the ungodly man is as chaff swept away by the
    wind,
And as thin hoar-frost scattered by the tempest;
And as smoke dispersed by the wind,
And it passeth as the remembrance of a guest who tarrieth but a
    day.[42]
But the righteous shall live for ever,
And from the Lord is their reward,
And the care of them is with the Most High.
Therefore shall they receive a glorious kingdom,
And a diadem of beauty from the hand of the Lord.[43]

That is to say, they shall obtain "The Kingdom of Heaven" in
the Days of the Messiah, and in the world to come "the righteous shall sit with their crowns on their heads and enjoy the
brightness of the Shekhinah." [44]

There is no need to emphasize how much Paul and his
associates were able to find here in the way of justification for
the life and death of Jesus and in the way of religious ideals
for early Christianity; for early Christianity was altogether
"not of this world," while the World to Come took in it a
more central place than it took in the Judaism of that time;
all this, of course, in spite of the fact that the author of the
Wisdom of Solomon had no idea whatever of preparing for
Jesus or for Christian beliefs and opinions.

2. In the second part of the Wisdom of Solomon (chapters
6-9) we have the personification of wisdom of a sort which is

[41] Wis. Sol. 5:9-12 (Oesterley).   [42] Wis. Sol. 5:14.
[43] Wis. Sol. 5:15, 16.
[44] Berakoth 17a and parallels (on the difference between "the Days of
the Messiah" and "the World to Come," see for particulars J. Klausner,
Ha-Ra'yon ha-Meshihi, 2nd ed., pp. 261-8).

already to be found in a similar form in the book of Proverbs.[45] Also here, in the Wisdom of Solomon, wisdom is a kind of personality antecedent to all creation, existing beside the deity and assisting him, as it were, in the creation of the world. But just as Plato knows two kinds of love personified in two Aphrodites, an earthly and vulgar love and a spiritual and heavenly love, so also wisdom is divided into two: *human wisdom*, which is able to exist in man together with unlovely traits and evil deeds, such as "morbid envy"; [46] and *divine wisdom*, which "cannot enter a soul that devises evil, nor dwell in a body in bondage to sin." [47] This divine wisdom is the source of all profound human knowledge: the knowledge of the constituent elements of the world and the laws of nature, the knowledge of astronomy and medicine, of plants, animals, men, and spirits—all this knowledge comes to mankind from the divine wisdom, which is "the artificer of all." [48] But in its most fundamental aspect, the divine wisdom is the source of truth and righteousness, of the knowledge of God and of the good; therefore, it is the choicest of human possessions.

Gradually, in this work, personified wisdom becomes the subject of a profound, and even mystical, philosophy. Wisdom is "the breath of the power of God," "an emanation from the glory of the Almighty," "a reflexion of the everlasting light." She has "a life of partnership with God"; she sits by him on his throne, she takes counsel with the Lord and selects his works—which works are to be brought to realization and which not, of those which have come before him in

---

[45] Proverbs, chs. 8 and 9.

[46] See Wis. Sol. 6:23.

[47] Wis. Sol. 1:4. Also see above, p. 125.

[48] Wis. Sol. 7:11-22. M. Stein (*op. cit.*, p. 487) supposes that the author of Wis. Sol. interpreted the word אָמוֹן in Prov. 8:30 [rendered "nursling" in the translation of the Jewish Publication Society of America] as "master workman" [which is the rendering of the American Standard Version].

thought. She was with God when he created the world; she knows what is good in his eyes and what is right according to his commandments.[49] For wisdom is a "spirit," an intelligent spirit, holy, refined, unique in kind, yet manifold; a spirit moving in everything, overseeing everything, penetrating into everything, beneficent, philanthropic, strong, without taint, without care, all-powerful, all-seeing, and permeating all beings that are intelligent, pure, and noble.[50] For the divine wisdom accomplishes everything, rules over everything, renews everything.[51] From generation to generation it passes into holy souls, thus making them friends of God and prophets.[52] It is she who was revealed in all the miracles performed for our fathers in Egypt and in the wilderness.[53]

Evidently, the author of the Wisdom of Solomon is inclined to see the great advantage of the Jewish divine wisdom over the Greek-Epicurean human wisdom, which permitted the enjoyment of all the delights of the flesh and proclaimed freedom for secular thought. Nevertheless, the author himself unconsciously went astray after "Greek wisdom"—although not after the Epicurean, but after the Platonic and Stoic, by making use of their ideas and phraseology. Thus, for example, he accepts the four cardinal virtues of Plato and the Stoa: wisdom, self-control, courage, and justice;[54] he thinks, like them, that the world was created "out of formless matter" (ἐξ ἀμόρφου ὕλης), *i.e.*, out of "primeval matter" (*homer hiyuli*), in the language of the later Jewish philosophers.[55] Also, for our author the body is an "earthly tabernacle"[56] for the mind; he says:

[49] Wis. Sol. 7:25, 26; 8:3, 4; 9:4, 9.   [50] Wis. Sol. 7:22, 23.
[51] Wis. Sol. 7:27; 8:1, 5.   [52] Wis. Sol. 7:27.
[53] See Wis. Sol., all of ch. 10.   [54] Wis. Sol. 8:7.
[55] Wis. Sol. 11:17.   [56] Wis. Sol. 9:15.

I was a well-favored child,
And a good soul fell to my lot;
Nay rather, because I was good,
I entered into an undefiled body.[57]

This means that the soul preceded the body and conditioned
the body's quality. All these are Platonic-Stoic ideas. And
once in our book, in the exposition of the Logos as related to
God, this expression is used: "Thine (God's) all-powerful
Logos" (ὁ παντοδύναμός σου λόγος);[58] such language is used also
of wisdom, and it reminds us of the *Logos* of Philo and of the
Maamar and *Mēmrā* of the Talmud and the Targums. Now,
if we take all words said about personified wisdom and about
the divinized Logos, and apply them to Jesus as Messiah and
Son of God, we shall inevitably reach the equation of Apollos
(who is considered to be the first to identify Jesus with the
Logos) and of Paul and of the Fourth Gospel: Jesus is the
Logos, just as he is also the personification of divine wisdom,
which is altogether different from human wisdom.

3. The third part of the Wisdom of Solomon (chapters
10–12 and 16–19) is historical in a certain sense, since it relates in detail the wonders of wisdom which were revealed
in the world and in the history of Israel from Adam up to
the entrance of Israel into the Holy Land. This part is not
so important for our purpose.[59]

There remains the "Interpolation" on idolatry (chapters
13–15). Here we have an amazing mixture. On the one hand,
there is an imitation of the trenchant satire of the great

[57] Wis. Sol. 8:19, 20.
[58] Wis. Sol. 18:15, 16. See also Wis. Sol. 9:1, 2 and 16:12. On these verses
in their relation to Philo, see B. Motzo, *op. cit.*, pp. 62–5.
[59] See on it J. Klausner, *Historia Yisreelit*, IV, 48; E. Stein, MGWJ,
LXXIII (1934), 558–75. On the matter of *lex talionis*, see also B. Jacob, *Auge
um Auge* (Berlin 1929), SS. 90–120.

prophet of consolation [60] against idols and their makers, and on the other hand, an imitation of the attitude of skepticism and negation with respect to idols such as is already to be found among the Stoics and Epicureans. The author (in my opinion a monotheist from Judea living in Alexandria, where learning abounded) was not able to reconcile himself to the fact that intelligent people like the Greeks worshipped wood and stone wrought by their own hands. Therefore, he produced for himself an ingenious explanation of this strange fact in the spirit of Euhemerus: A father, whose beloved son had died an untimely death, wished to assuage his grief; to this end he ordered an artisan to make him an image in the likeness of his son. This image, the sole reminder of his dead son, the father adored as a god, and after a time people came to regard it as an actual deity. And according to a decree of powerful rulers divine honor was given to such images.[61]

This explanation was not absorbed from the air. In the year 239/8 B.C.E., Ptolemy III decreed that his daughter, who had died in youth, should be deified.[62] There is also another explanation of this sort. A king was in a distant place and could not be honored face to face. An image in the form of a statue was made, and people honored this statue. Eventually they thought the statue to be a god. The artisan helped to bring this about, when, in his zeal to find favor in the eyes of the king, he made the likeness more excellent in beauty than the original; the people, being moved by the beauty of the image, began to adore this image as a divine thing, until finally they began to think the statue itself to be a deity.[63] This is not only a rationalistic-euhemeristic explanation, but also an esthetic explanation, influenced by the worship of beauty of the Greeks.

[60] Isa. 44:9–20.   [61] Wis. Sol. 14:15, 16.
[62] See W. Dittenberger, *Orientis Graeci Inscriptiones Selectae*, I, 56, 46–75. See also P. Wendland, *Hellen.-röm. Kultur*, S. 202.
[63] Wis. Sol. 14:17–21.

Worse than the image worship of the Greeks was the idolatry of the Egyptians, who made gods out of various beasts, insects, and reptiles. The greatest evil of idolatry is not the giving of divine honor to human beings in the form of wood and stone, or to animals and creeping things, but that which follows from it, such as murder and bloodshed, robbery and fraud, moral corruption, treachery, rebellion and tumult, perjury, persecution of the innocent, ingratitude, defilement of souls, sexual perversion (sodomy and bestiality), adultery, harlotry, and gluttony. Not so is the God of Israel, who is the God of ethical standards, and not so Israel his people, "the people [which is] the son of God." [64]

With these words we must compare the words of Paul about idolatry and its connexion with the corruption of moral standards [65]—and the similarity will amaze us. Of course, the possibility of an earlier source, shared both by the Wisdom of Solomon and the Epistle of Paul, is not to be ruled out; [66] but it is a more likely supposition that Paul was influenced by the Wisdom of Solomon. Nor is the great similarity of certain verses in the Wisdom of Solomon to certain passages in the Epistle to the Hebrews [67] by any means accidental. The late author of the Epistle to the Hebrews, wrongly attributed to Paul, certainly saw the Wisdom of Solomon and was influenced by it. Thus we see that the Wisdom of Solomon became a source of discussion, which "passed from the books of the Old Testament and of Greek philosophical investigation through the Jewish apologists into the Christian polemists (*i polemisti*)." [68]

[64] Wis. Sol. 14:22–6 and 18:13. With the phrase "the people [which is] the son of God" compare "You are the children of the Lord your God" and "sons of God," above p. 126.

[65] Epistle to the Romans 1:19–32.

[66] See E. Gärtner, *Komposition und Wortwahl des Buches der Weisheit* (Berlin 1912), SS. 90–6.

[67] *Cf.* Hebrews 1:3 and 4:12 with Wis. Sol. 7:22–6 and elsewhere.

[68] See B. Motzo, *op. cit.*, p. 41.

Truly therefore, the Wisdom of Solomon as a syncretistic book, a mixture of Judaism and Hellenism, had no equal for purposes of Christian propaganda, first, among the Hellenized Jews of the Diaspora, and afterward, also among the pagan "God-fearers," whose souls paganism did not satisfy, and hence who sought God in the middle path between polytheism and monotheism and between Greek mundane wisdom and Jewish divine wisdom. They finally found this "middle path"—in Pauline Christianity. . . .

CHAPTER II

Fourth Maccabees

Actually, the name "Maccabees" is not at all suitable to this book, inasmuch as it does not relate the history of the Maccabean rebellion or of the Hasmonean rule for their own sake; its author did not intend to write a historical book. This is a homiletic-philosophical book, whose real subject is "The Absolute Authority of Reason" (περὶ αυτοκράτορος λογισμοῦ). It is a synagogue sermon, which perhaps was written to be preached but was not delivered, or possibly was actually delivered in a synagogue.[1] Its purpose is to prove that Reason can triumph over all kinds of bodily torments. The author presents as evidence for this the cruel martyrdom of Eleazar, ninety years of age, who refused to eat swine's flesh even under compulsion, and of the mother and her seven sons, whom Antiochus Epiphanes afflicted with all kinds of tortures, yet of whom not even the youngest of the sons was heard to betray the faith of his fathers.[2] From the fact that these examples occur in it, the book was called Fourth Maccabees, and became one of the extracanonical books which were partially canonized by the Christian Church; and this church actually made the mother and the "Maccabean brethren" Christian saints. The tortures of Eleazar and of the mother and her sons are portrayed in our book to the last detail and with excessive realism; by this means the author desired to emphasize the great idea in the book—that there is no physi-

[1] See the too brief introduction to his translation of IV Macc. by A. Schorr in the Apocrypha and Pseudepigrapha ed. by A. Kahana, II, 1, pp. 258–9.

[2] As is related also in II Macc. 6:18–7:41 and in a number of Midrashim.

cal power in the world that can break down the spiritual strength whose source is in Reason—in firm and self-conscious human conviction.

Eusebius, Jerome, John of Damascus, *et al.*, attribute this book without good reason, to Josephus;[3] others attribute it to Philo—also without sufficient grounds. The writings of both Josephus and Philo are far from this book both in manner of presentation and in style. The book was written in Greek by an Alexandrian Jew, apparently in the time of the persecutions by Gaius Caligula (38–41 C.E.), that those being persecuted and tortured might be heartened by the great idea mentioned above—that Reason, the inner conviction for which the intellect is responsible, must and can triumph over all afflictions; faith and virtue are more powerful than anything, and by means of them an infirm old man, ninety years old, a weak woman, and tender children reached such moral grandeur that they could say "Death rather than transgression of the Law!"

This idea, in spite of the fact there is in it a Greek element and that it is one of the fundamental principles of the Stoic philosophy,[4] is essentially a Jewish conception. The "Reason" of the author is "God-fearing reason" (εὐσεβὴς λογισμός), that is to say, the conviction that the requirements of the Torah are more important than any decrees of the king, and that one must fulfill them completely under any and all circumstances. The influence of the Stoic philosophy and of the Greek reflective literature of the later Hellenistic period upon the author of this book is only general and superficial, showing itself mostly in phraseology current at that time and in the rhetorical style of the period. The majority of the beliefs and opinions of our author are thoroughly Jewish and were

[3] Eusebius, *Hist. Eccl.* III 10 6; Jerome, *De Viris Illustr.* ch. 13. On the rest, see E. Schürer, *Geschichte des jüd. Volkes*, III⁴, 525–7.

[4] See Julius Guttmann, *Die Philosophie des Judentums*, SS. 31–2.

current and regular in the Judaism of his time. But two of them deserve special consideration because they diverge in part from what was known and accepted in the Judaism of the Second Temple:

1. The resurrection of the dead of the author of IV Maccabees is not the resurrection of bodies and their restoration to earthly life, but is a blessed and everlasting life in heaven;[5] this is not a pure Jewish view, but is a Hellenistic Jewish view, which the Christians took over and connected with the belief in the resurrection of Jesus and his ascension to heaven.

2. The death of those slain for the sanctification of the name of God (martyrs) is a death of propitiation; it brings about atonement for the sins of the people. When the aged Eleazar is "already burnt to the bone and at the point of death," he lifts up his eyes to God and says:

Thou knowest, O God, that though I might have saved myself, I die in fiery torments for thy Law's sake. Be merciful to thy people and be content with our punishment on their behalf. Make my blood a purification for them and take my life as a ransom for their life.[6]

And the author himself says of the saints who died the death of martyrs in the time of the persecutions of Antiochus Epiphanes:

They became as it were a ransom for our nation's sin, and through the blood of these righteous ones and their propitiating death, the divine Providence preserved Israel which before was evilly treated (or, inclined to do evil).[7]

Of course, the idea of propitiatory sufferings is found, apart from the Second Isaiah, also in the Talmud: "The death of the righteous affords atonement";[8] "The righteous are seized [by death] for [the sins of] their generation";[9] and in the cus-

---

[5] IV Macc. 13:16; 15:2; 17:5; 18:23.　[6] IV Macc. 6:26-9.
[7] IV Macc. 17:21, 22.　[8] Mo'ed Katan 28a.
[9] Shabbath 33b.

tomary expression of R. Ishmael it was: "The sons of Israel
(or, the daughters of Israel)—may I be an atonement for
them!" [10] But in the Biblical literature, the Apocrypha, and
the Palestinian Pseudepigrapha this idea is not so frequent.
The Jews interpreted Isaiah, chapter 53—and thus we interpret it to this day—as applying to the nation Israel, which was
persecuted by the other peoples, and in that way he "bore
their pains and carried their sorrows" and "they were healed
by his stripes"; thus he, Israel, "bore the sin of many." This
is because in ancient Judaism the belief in propitiatory sufferings of the individual did not take a very great place:
"The soul that sinneth, it shall die," said the prophet. [11] But
Christianity from about the time of Paul on has applied Isaiah
53 to Jesus as a "ransom"; [12] Paul made this belief of IV Maccabees one of the foundation stones of his teaching. According to him, Jesus, with his blood, redeemed mankind from the
sin of the first man, becoming a propitiatory sacrifice for the
sin of the people, [13] although he himself was innocent of sin
and hence had no reason to suffer or to make expiation. In
this manner his sufferings on the cross became propitiatory
sufferings, first of all for those believing in him, and afterward—even for all of sinful mankind.

[10] Mish., Nega'im II 1 and elsewhere.
[11] Ezek. 18:4 and 20.
[12] Mark 14:24; Matt. 26:28.
[13] Paul made use of the word *hilastērion* of IV Macc. 17:22 in the very
same sense (Rom. 3:25), while in the LXX this word is the translation of
kapporet ("mercy-seat" or "ark-cover").

CHAPTER III

The Sibylline Oracles

[A bibliography on the Sibyllines is to be found in J. Klausner, *Ha-Ra-'yon ha-Meshihi be-Yisrael,* 2nd ed. (Jerusalem 5687), pp. 230–40. To this is to be added: Introduction to the translation of the Sibylline Oracles by Joseph Reider in the Apocrypha and Pseudepigrapha ed. by A. Kahana, II, 2, pp. 377–83; Th. Ziélinski, *La Sibylle* (Paris 1924), pp. 97–125. The great Hellenistic scholar Ziélinski follows the wrong line, in my opinion, when he says that "we find the real Old Testament of Christianity in the ancient classical faith," *i.e.* in the Graeco-Roman religion and not in the religion of Israel (see end of his book).]

The Sibyls were prophetesses of the Gentile nations. Oracles of the Sibyls were inherited by the Romans from the Greeks as early as the time of the Tarquins. Jews of Alexandria in Egypt or of Asia Minor composed for purposes of propaganda among pagans oracles with Jewish content and attributed them to the prophetesses of the Gentile nations in order to influence the people of those nations. Out of fifteen Sibylline Oracles which are mentioned in various books, only twelve have been preserved to us; we lack oracles Nine, Ten, and Fifteen. Almost all of them have a Jewish basis, but in the great majority there are so many Christian interpolations that they are no longer to be regarded as Jewish works. It is also worth noting that in some cases the Jewish Sibylline material is built upon the foundation of a pagan oracle.

Three of the Sibylline books are decidedly Jewish: Three, Four, and Five. With regard to book Eleven there is a difference of opinion, and some consider it also to be Christian; therefore I shall not make use of it here. In the rest of the books, the Christian element, either original or secondary, stands out in bold relief, and therefore they do not come into consideration in a description of Hellenistic Jewish thought.

The three Jewish Sibylline books, which perhaps contain minor Christian additions, are not from one source or from one time. The third book must be divided into two parts: lines 1–92 were written about 40–27 B.C.E.; but lines 97–829 were written as early as 140 B.C.E., approximately.[1] All of the fourth book belongs to about the year 80 C.E. (time of Domitian). Finally, nearly all of the fifth book comes from about 120–130 C.E. (time of Trajan and Hadrian), but it contains fragments from the years 70–80 C.E., that is, from the time of the fourth book.

The Sibylline books not only make "Jewish propaganda under a pagan guise," according to the expression of Emil Schürer, that is to say, they not only reprove the Gentiles because they believe in dumb idols, in images of wood and stone, like the Second Isaiah in his time, and like the author of the Wisdom of Solomon in the age which we are studying; but they also cry out against the immorality (particularly sodomy) of the pagans, and even of the Jews. They prophesy with regard to the Day of Judgment (or "the birth pangs of the Messiah"—the Messianic travail, the Messianic woe), which God shall bring upon the Gentiles with all the terrors and all the heavy punishments connected with this day; alongside of this they announce good tidings and mercy for Judea, and they call upon the Gentiles to turn away from their own gods and to join themselves to the house of Jacob in order that they may enjoy some of his blessings "in the end of days."

Here follows the principal contents of these three books, insofar as they concern our present undertaking:

---

[1] Otherwise is the opinion of J. Reider in the aforesaid Introduction, p. 379, *q.v.*

A. The Third Book

(INCLUDING THE FRAGMENTS, WHICH SERVE AS THE GENERAL INTRODUCTION OR "PROOEMIUM")

1. In forceful and trenchant language the Sibyl rebukes the idolaters—those who bow down to demons, to the shadows of human beings who have already gone down to Hades, to serpents, dogs, cats and crocodiles, to birds and creeping things and also to images made by the hand of man, and to heaps of stones in the streets (worship of Hermes). She turns to them and cries out: "Behold, your understanding has been taken from you! Do gods lick dishes and lap from pots?" (like the cat-gods of Egypt).[2] And she demands of the pagans that they forsake the darkness and step forth proudly to meet the light; that they worship nothing but the one and only God, he who "sends rain, winds, earthquakes, lightning, droughts, plagues, rainstorms, snowstorms, and ice"; he who is "lord of heaven and sovereign of earth"; who is "most exalted of all, who made the heavens, the sun, the stars and the moon—also the fruitful earth, the waves of the sea, the high mountains and the streams of ever-flowing springs," also reptiles and creatures that live in the water, varicolored birds on the wing, chirping and twittering; also the beasts who make their lairs in the secret places of the forests. Over all these he set as ruler man, to whom all other living creatures are subject. And who can comprehend and understand all these things except the One who made them?[3]

God is, therefore, unique in his capacity of fashioner and

[2] Fragments iii. 21–30 (in Eng. ed.) or Prooemium 60–9 (in Ger. ed.), as taken from Theophilus *ad Autolycum*, II 36. See Lanchester *apud* Charles, *Apocrypha and Pseudepigrapha of the OT*, II, 377–8 and Blass *apud* Kautzsch, *Apokryphen und Pseudepigraphen des AT*, II, 184–6. The Prooemium is lacking in the aforesaid translation of J. Reider, and in place of it stand the first 35 lines of Book III, which are lacking in the translation of Blass.

[3] Prooemium 31–55 (Fragments i. 26–iii. 16).

creator. He is also unique as Director—as righteous judge and the father of all morality. For he gives a good reward to the good, and punishes the wicked "with war and pestilence and tearful woes." [4] The Sibyl calls for repentance and the forsaking of all kinds of idolatry. Otherwise, sinners will inherit Gehenna and be burned with fire day after day forever and ever, while the righteous will inherit "the fertile garden of Paradise" (with its evergreen trees) and "will feast on sweet bread from the starry heavens." [5] This is compelling propaganda in favor of faith in the One God and against plurality of deities in all its forms.

So much for the Prooemium. We pass to the Jewish part of the third book proper.

The Sibyl turns with the cry of "Woe!" to the

bloodthirsty race, guileful, evil, impious: race of false men, double-tongued, crafty, adulterous, guileful in mind, in whose breasts evil is implanted, a raging frenzy: who grasp at plunder for themselves, shameless in spirit; for none that has wealth and possessions will give a share to another, but grievous wickedness shall be found among all mortals, and they will not keep faith, but many a woman that is a widow will give herself in secret love to men, and will not keep to the plumb-line of life in wedlock. [6]

Here the condemnation takes the form of prophecy—to be sure "prophecy after the event" (vaticinium post eventum). The Sibyl "prophesies" that after Rome conquers Egypt

then shall the great kingdom of the immortal king appear among men, and a holy king shall come who shall have rule over the whole earth for all ages of the course of time. Then shall implacable wrath fall upon the men of Latium: three men shall ravage Rome with pitiable affliction; and all men shall perish beneath their roof-tree, when the torrent of fire shall flow down from heaven. [7] Ah,

---

[4] Prooemium 56-8 (Frag. iii. 17-20).
[5] Prooemium 81-7 (Frag. iii. 43-9).
[6] Sib. Or. III 36-45.
[7] "A stream of fire" (Dan. 7:10; Hagigah 13b).

wretched me, when shall that day come, and the judgment of immortal God, the great king? [8]

Here we have, almost certainly, the Roman "triumvirate" and the great wars between Antony and Augustus. The proof: after an oracle of doom against the splendid Roman cities, which have been adorned with "temples and stadia (hippodromes), with market squares and images of gold, silver and stone," and upon which God will rain fire and brimstone "on the bitter day"—the Day of Judgment,[9] there comes another prophecy, in which are hints of that very period: "Now from the Sebasteni" (that is, from the Samaritans, whose city Herod rebuilt and called Sebaste) "shall come Beliar" (Belial)—the false Messiah, Satan the destroyer. The allusion is, in my opinion, to Herod, who built Sebaste in 27 B.C.E., four years after the fall of Antony and Cleopatra; Herod wished to be Messiah, and was recognized as such by a whole sect of "Herodians." The allusion is not to Simon Magus, mentioned in the Acts of the Apostles, as Schürer, Jülicher and Bousset believe, nor to Nero, as Charles would have it.[10] This Beliar will raise high mountains (really, will build lofty fortifications), will calm the waves of the sea, will make the blazing sun and the shining moon stand still; he will also raise the dead and perform many miracles.[11] Yet not moral perfection will he possess, but the power of leading astray. He will lead astray many men, both faithful and elect Hebrews, and other men also, who lack Torah and have never heard the word of God.

[8] Sib. Or. III 46–56.   [9] Sib. Or. III 57–62.
[10] See on all this J. Klausner, *Ha-Ra'yon, etc.*, pp. 230–2. On Herod as Messiah and the sect believing in his messiahship, see my *Yeshu*, 4th ed., pp. 181–3 [Eng. 170–2].

[11] If people believed Herod to be the Messiah, they could also attribute signs and wonders to him. When the Pharisees promised the eunuch Bagoas that the King-Messiah would restore to him the ability to beget children, Herod in anger slew Bagoas because he himself expected to become King-Messiah (see *Ant.* XVII ii end of 4, and what I have written on this in *Yeshu*, p. 182 [Eng. 170–1]).

But when the vengeance of the great God draws nigh, and he punishes Beliar with fire, consuming him and all the proud mortals who have put their trust in him——

then shall the (whole) world be ruled beneath a woman's hand, and she shall be obeyed in all things. And when a widow rules over the whole world, and gold and silver are cast into the everlasting sea, and the bronze and iron of short-lived men into the sea—then shall all the elements of the world be as one widowed (that is, the air will be forsaken by the birds, the sea by the fish, *etc.*) . . .[12] The heavens shall be rolled up like a scroll,[13] and the whole firmament shall fall upon the earth and into the sea, and a stream of liquid fire shall flow unceasingly and burn the land and the sea, the heavens shall melt, the days [time] and all creation shall cease to be . . . and there shall be no longer the shining luminaries in the firmament, nor shall there be any evening and morning, nor spring and autumn, nor summer and winter.[14] Then shall come forth the judgment of the great God in the great age [15] in which these things shall take place.[16]

Also here there is hardly any doubt that the woman in whose hand shall be sovereignty over the whole world, and the "widow" who shall rule everywhere is none other than Cleopatra in the time when she ruled the body and the spirit of Antony. We have before us, therefore, that troubled period of history which begins with Pompey and Julius Caesar and ends with the victory of Augustus over Antony and his being left as the sole ruler of Rome—the period during part of which Cleopatra is considered to have persuaded the enchanted Antony to make her ruler over the whole world; then Herod became king through the favor of Antony—and

[12] See Blass *apud* Kautzsch, *Apokryphen und Pseudepigraphen*, II, 186 f.

[13] *Cf.* "And the heavens shall be rolled together as a scroll" (Isa. 34:4).

[14] See Zech. 14:6–8; IV Ezra 7:33–43.

[15] A Stoic expression (*aiōn megas*), as noted J. Reider in his commentary, *op. cit.*, p. 386.

[16] Sib. Or. III 63–92.

Cleopatra fastened her eyes upon the kingdom of Herod also.[17]

Afterwards the Sibyl turns to the early history of mankind and combines the Tower of Babel and the confusion of tongues with the Greek theogony and cosmogony, thereby slyly intending to show that the gods and goddesses, with their hates and jealousies and their wars with one another, are nothing more than mere human beings—all this being in the spirit of Euhemerus.[18] This early (really, mythological) "history" leads the Sibyl to review the evolution of the kingdoms which had ruled in the world: Egypt, Assyria, the Medes and Persians, Ethiopia, the kingdom of Solomon and the kingdom of "the proud and profane Greeks," Macedon, and "many-headed" Rome, i.e., republican Rome, at the head of which stood no single ruler. Rome shall enslave the world and oppress all mortal men, shall extort gold, silver, and all precious things. But trouble shall come upon her, and along with the trouble there shall be gross immorality: "men with men shall have intercourse, and they will put boys for hire in houses of shame."[19] And Rome

shall stir up hatred, and guile of all kinds shall be found among them down to the seventh king's reign, the reign of a king of Egypt, a Greek by birth.

Then shall the people of the great God once more be strong, they who are to be the guides of life to all mankind.[20]

"The seventh king's reign," the reign of an Egyptian king of Greek origin, refers to none other than Ptolemy VII Physcon, who ruled together with his brother Ptolemy VI Philometor in the years 170–164 B.C.E., and by himself in the years 145–117. It was then, in the very years when Ptolemy Physcon began to rule alone, that "the people of the great God

[17] See on all this J. Klausner, *Historia*, II, 181–231; III, 1–35; *Ha-Ra'yon*, pp. 232–4.
[18] Sib. Or. III 97–158.   [19] Sib. Or. III 185–6.   [20] Sib. Or. III 191–5.

once more grew strong," so to speak: in 142, three years after Ptolemy Physcon became sole ruler in Egypt, Simon, son of Mattathias, proclaimed the complete freedom of Judea and stopped paying tribute to the Seleucids.[21] And in those great days for Israel there was an intensification of the effort to carry on propaganda among the Gentiles in the name of free and victorious Judaism. From that time "the people of the great God" had to be "the guides of life to all mankind."

For purposes of propaganda, the Sibyl prophesies calamity for all peoples. She pictures a kind of "birth pangs of the Messiah," which come first of all upon the Titans, and afterward upon the Greeks "over whom shall rule tyrants and lawless kings, proud and unholy, breakers of wedlock wholly evil; then shall men have no more rest from war."[22] The Egyptians, the Ethiopians, the Libyans, and all the peoples of Asia Minor shall suffer, but also "the godly men who dwell around the great temple of Solomon and are the offspring of righteous fathers."[23] Here follow words of praise and blessing for "the race of most righteous men," which comes from Ur of the Chaldees. They, sons of Abraham, of course are "ever given to wise counsel and good works." Unlike the wise men of the Greeks, they do not busy themselves with the study of the course of the sun and the moon, or of what is underneath the earth and in the depths of the sea. Unlike the Chaldean astrologers, they do not practise divination by means of the flight of birds, they do not practise magic and utter incantations, there is not among them any necromancer or sorcerer, and they do not gaze at the stars; for all these things lead men astray, and there is in them nothing but weariness of the flesh.

[21] In error writes J. Reider (*op. cit.*, p. 390): "The seventh king is Ptolemy VII Philometor, son of Cleopatra I, grandson of Antiochus III. The beginning of his reign fell in the year 182 B.C.E." Philometor was the Sixth and not the Seventh, and in his days (170–164) "the people of the great God" had not yet become strong enough to win complete freedom.
[22] Sib. Or.III 199–205.   [23] Sib. Or. III 213–5.

But the sons of "the race which springs from Ur of the Chaldees"—their thought is given to uprightness and goodness. There is in them no love of gain, which causes myriads of evils, war and famine without end. They do not give short weight in town or in country. They do not break in like thieves in the night, they do not plunder flocks of sheep and herds of cattle, and they do not remove landmarks. The rich among them do not oppress the poor and they do not deal harshly with the widow, but on the contrary they help with grain, wine, and oil. The rich always send a portion of the harvest to the poor and needy, in order to fulfill the commandment of the great God: "for the Lord of heaven made the earth to be possessed by all in common." [24]

Here the Sibyl relates the story about Moses, who was saved by Pharaoh's daughter, about "the people of twelve tribes," who came out of Egypt with a pillar of fire to light the way for them, and about the receiving of the Law on Mount Sinai. This Law must be revealed to all human beings, since the world was created for all of them, and in the hearts of all of them God planted faith and good understanding.[25]

These righteous people shall be happy in their land, and the earth will give them a hundred-fold from everything which they sow. But also upon them shall evil come to pass. They will be forced to leave their glorious temple and their holy soil and will be brought to the land of Assyria, while their wives and children will be enslaved, and all their possessions will be destroyed. Thus will the nation be scattered throughout all lands:

Every land shall be full of thee and every sea; and everyone shall be incensed at thy customs.[26]

[24] Sib. Or. III 218–47.
[25] Sib. Or. III 260–2. Without reason these lines are omitted in the English translation (Charles, *Apoc. and Pseudep.*, II, 383).
[26] Sib. Or. III 271–2.

All this will come upon you, she says, in effect, because you did not keep the commandments of the eternal God, the creator of all mankind, but worshipped the idols and images of mortal men. "For seven times ten years" (the seventy years of the Babylonian Captivity) shall your fruitful land be forsaken and your wonderful temple be desolate. But you shall again trust in your God, and he will send from heaven a king, who will judge every man in blood and fire (Cyrus, king of Persia); the race of "the royal seed" (the house of David) shall not fall, and again it shall build the sanctuary of God (Zerubbabel, of the house of David); and the kings of Persia shall give aid with gold and brass and iron because God will rouse them to do this by a dream of the night.[27]

And now come visions of evil: the Sibyl delivers a prophecy of doom against Babylon and Egypt, against the "land of Gog and Magog in the midst of the rivers of Ethiopia," against Libya, Asia Minor and Europe, and finally, against Rome, which, together with all Italy, shall be enslaved by Asia, and shall pay in tribute three times what she, Asia, paid to Rome. Then a happy contentment shall come upon Asia, and Europe shall be blissful. All their inhabitants shall be healthy, there shall be no tempests and hailstorms, and animal life shall abound on land and in the air. "Happy the man or the woman who lives to see that time." For from the starry heavens shall come to the sons of men justice and order, and along with these, tranquillity, love, confidence, and hospitality, while lawlessness, injustice, envy, anger and folly shall depart from them. Poverty shall be removed from mankind and in those days oppression, murder, strife, quarreling, and all evil shall vanish.[28]

The element of Jewish propaganda in these words stands out here in the boldest relief.

[27] Apparently an allusion to III Ezra (I Esdras), although no dream is found there.

[28] Sib. Or. III 303–80.

2. The Sibyl turns to the history of the time. She gives hints, apparently, about Antiochus Epiphanes and his young son, Antiochus Eupator, who was killed in his youth, and about Demetrius I and Alexander Balas and Tryphon, who were rivals of each other and fought with each other, committing oppression, murder, rapine, and every sort of abomination.[29] All this is said in order to show the complete villainy of the kings of the pagan peoples. Afterward come severe words against the greatest poet of the pagans—the blind Homer, who has clever ideas and beautiful verses, but relates many falsehoods and glorifies wars filled with bloodshed and warriors, at the side of whom he makes gods to stand, and thus leads astray emptyheaded mortals.[30]

There follows a long list of nations and lands which shall suffer woes and oppressions, defeat in war and slaughter and the heavy yoke of enslavement, in the nature of "the birth pangs of the Messiah." And not only the peoples mentioned in this list will God smite with a heavy blow, but also all the peoples who live on the face of the earth.[31]

The Sibyl prophesies that a barbarian host shall fall upon the Greeks and behead many select individuals, shall devastate and burn well-built houses; tender children and "deep-girdled women," who "had been going previously with tender feet," that is to say, who had not been accustomed to putting the soles of their feet on the ground, like those in the monitory passage in the Pentateuch,[32] they shall take to be slaves and carry away to a strange land, and there shall not be any one to bring them aid or to fight their battles. From before one of their enemies a hundred of them shall flee, and five of their enemies shall slay a whole regiment of them—like another

[29] Sib. Or. III 388–418. See on these kings Klausner, *Historia*, II, 9–55.
[30] Sib. Or. III 419–32.
[31] Sib. Or. III 512–9.
[32] *Cf.* Deut. 28:56: "The tender and delicate woman among you, who would not adventure to set the sole of her foot upon the ground for delicateness and tenderness. . . ."

monitory passage in the Pentateuch.[33] And the yoke of slavery shall be placed upon all Hellas. War and pestilence shall come upon all, "God will turn the vast heavens into brass, and drought will come upon all the earth, which itself will become iron"—again like a warning in the Pentateuch.[34] Then the Sibyl addresses to the chastened Hellas this severe admonition:

O Hellas, why trustest thou for leadership in mortal men, who cannot escape the end of death? Why dost thou offer vain gifts to the dead, and do sacrifice to idols? Who put this error in thy heart, to do these things and to forsake the face of the great God? Revere the name of the Father of all, and forget it not. A thousand years and five hundred more have passed since proud kings began to reign over Hellas, who led men in the first steps of evil, setting up many idols of dead gods, whereby ye were led to think vain thoughts. But when the wrath of the great God falls upon you, then shall ye know the face of the great God, and all souls of men, deeply wailing, holding up their hands to the broad heaven shall begin to call upon the great King as their helper, and to seek who shall save them from the great wrath.[35]

This is clear and forceful preaching that the Greeks should forsake their idols and serve the God of Israel, who is "the great God," "the Most High," "the great King."

And the Sibyl is confident that this great thing—the turning from paganism to Judaism—will surely come to pass.

After "an age of godless men" and after whatever God shall determine has come to pass, there shall arise "a race of righteous men" devoted to the counsel of the Most High, who will glorify the sanctuary of the great God with meal-offerings and with sacrifices from the first-born of sheep and with burnt-offerings of fat. The members of this race, "after they

---

[33] Cf. Lev. 26:7, 8 with Deut. 32:30.

[34] ". . . and I will make your heaven as iron, and your earth as brass" (Lev. 26:19); "And thy heaven that is over thy head shall be brass, and the earth that is under thee shall be iron" (Deut. 28:23).

[35] Sib. Or. III 545–61.

obtain the law of the Most High," shall live in righteousness, being happy and prosperous in town and in country. They themselves shall be prophets established by the Immortal (God) to bring great joy to all mankind. For to them alone the great God gave wise counsel, faith, and understanding hearts, that they should not follow after illusory values and works of gold, brass, silver, and ivory made by the hands of men, nor after images of dead gods made of wood and stone, nor after idols of clay smeared with vermilion in the likeness of animals—things worshipped by men lacking in understanding.

They lift up to heaven holy hands, rising early from their beds to hallow their hands with water, and they honour the immortal eternal Ruler alone, and after Him their father and mother; moreover above all men they are mindful to keep the bed undefiled; they have no unholy intercourse with boys, as do the Phoenicians, Egyptians, the Latins and wide Hellas and many nations besides, the Persians, Galatians and them of all Asia, transgressing the holy law of the immortal God, which He gave.[36]

Following this monotheistic propaganda comes another "prophecy after the event."

In Egypt "a young king" (or "a new king") shall come to the throne, "the seventh in succession during the rule of the Greeks" (Ptolemy Physcon). Then shall come from Asia (from the kingdom of the house of Seleucus) "a great king, a strong eagle" (Antiochus Epiphanes), who shall cover all the land with an army of footmen and horsemen, shall spread desolation everywhere, and bring down to ruin the kingdom of Egypt, and after plundering great treasures, shall depart by the way of the sea. Then [37] they (the Gentiles) shall bend the knee before "the great God, the king immortal," and all the

[36] Sib. Or. III 562–600.

[37] Apparently, after the Jews fighting Antiochus Epiphanes shall have been victorious.

idols made by the hands of men shall be thrown into the midst of the flame of fire.[38]

And then shall God give great joy to men; for the earth, the trees, and the full flocks of sheep shall give their proper fruit for men, wine and honey and white milk, and corn which is the best of all gifts to mortals.[39]

And along with the admonition to worship the one and only God and to offer sacrifices to him, "for He is God alone, and there is no other," the Sibyl demands also morality: "Honour righteousness and deal oppressively with no man; for this the Immortal commands to wretched mortals." [40]

Again there comes a fearful picture of "the birth pangs of the Messiah," part of which reminds us of Ezekiel 38 and 39, passages which portray the war of Gog and Magog in all its terrors.[41] After these terrors, God shall send "a king from the rising of the sun" (or "the East"), who "shall make all the earth cease from ruinous war, killing some, and with some making a sure agreement. Nor shall he do all this by his own counsel, but in obedience to the good ordinances of the great God." Then shall the temple (or the people) of the great God be loaded with "gold and silver and furnishings of purple, while the earth yields its increase and the sea abounds with all good things." [42] Here we have before us, *apparently*, the King-Messiah. But immediately after all this manifold good shall come, according to the Sibyl, new wars ("But again shall

[38] Apparently, the reference is to the mass conversion of various towns and districts in the days of the Hasmonean princes and kings, from the time of Simon son of Mattathias to the end of the days of Alexander Jannaeus.

[39] Sib. Or. III 601–23.

[40] Sib. Or. III 629–31.

[41] *Cf.* lines 649–51, "And then for many spaces of time in circling years (men shall gather and burn in their houses) [conjecture by Lanchester *apud* Charles, II, 390] targes and shields and javelins and divers kinds of weapons; nor shall wood be cut from the thicket to kindle fire," with the very similar picture in Ezek. 39:9, 10. See also lines 727–31.

[42] Sib. Or. III 652–60.

kings of the Gentiles make onset together against this land, bringing doom upon themselves"), and the war of Gog and Magog in particular.

It is difficult to believe that the Sibyl means to say that the war of Gog and Magog will come after the reign of the King-Messiah and after the Temple has been renewed and adorned. Also difficult is the statement that the King-Messiah will kill some of the Gentiles and make a treaty with others of them. And to suppose that the reference is to the Messiah son of Joseph is impossible, since there is here no mention of the death of the King-Messiah in the war.[42a] Is it not more natural to suppose, with Holtzmann,[43] that the reference is to a king of the Hasmonean house (but not specifically to Simon son of Mattathias, according to the opinion of Holtzmann) to whom the author of the Sibylline Oracles looked to come "from the rising of the sun," [44] after the great victories of Judas Maccabaeus and his brothers Jonathan and Simon, and to kill many and make a treaty with many, and to give prosperity and happiness to the people of Israel, as indeed Simon, the free and blessed ruler, had already begun to do? In like manner, the author of I Maccabees sees the time of the rule of Simon as the golden age of the people of Israel.[45] We, who know the end of the Hasmonean house, find it hard to picture to ourselves the great impression which the victories of the Maccabees made upon the Jews far and near, and especially upon the Jews of Egypt, who were at the same time both far and near—near in place but remote in viewpoint and outlook upon the world.

[42a] According to Jewish tradition, the real Messiah, son of David, is to be preceded by a Messiah son of Joseph, who will be killed in battle.

[43] H. Holtzmann, *Jahrbücher für deutsche Theologie* (1867), S. 395.

[44] On the expression ἀπ' ἠελίοιο (meaning "from the East" and not "from heaven"!) see Bousset-Gressmann, *Die Religion des Judentums im späthellenistischen Zeitalter*, 3. Aufl. (Tübingen 1926), SS. 225–6.

[45] See I Macc. 14:6–15. And on the importance of these lines see Klausner, *Historia*, II, 58–60.

Many have supposed [46] that the sole reason for conflict between the Pharisees and the rulers of the Hasmonean house was the fact that the latter thought themselves to be Messiahs. Even scribes like the author of the Testament of Levi (and others) held this opinion, while the Pharisees looked for the Messiah from the house of David only. So why is it impossible to suppose that the Sibyl also saw in one of the Hasmoneans who was destined to receive the kingdom (after Simon took the leadership, he and his sons after him had the heritage in perpetuity) the King-Messiah who would be both High Priest and great king, and would subjugate certain peoples and make a treaty with others just as Judas and his brothers had made a treaty with Rome?

3. The portrayal of the battle of the great God against the enemies of his people who have gathered to attack Jerusalem is one of the most striking in world literature. Unfortunately we are forced to render it here as simple prose.[47]

The kings of the Gentiles, having become envious of the happiness of God's people, shall each establish his throne round about the city [48] for the purpose of destroying "the temple of the great God" and "the choicest of men." Then shall God turn to all these evil-doing and evil-thinking Gentiles and call them to a judgment of nations, and "all of them shall perish by the hand of the Immortal." From the heavens shall fall fiery swords, and great torches shall be cast into the midst of the sons of men; the earth, mother of all things, shall be shaken in those days by the hand of the Immortal in anger, "the fishes of the sea and all the beasts of the earth and the

---

[46] See Klausner, *Historia*, II, 74, 128; also Charles, *Apoc. and Pseudep.*, II, 282–3, 289–90; V. Aptowitzer, *Parteipolitik der Hasmonäerzeit* (Wien 1927), SS. 85–116.

[47] The poetical Hebrew translation of Joshua Steinberg (supplement to *Ha-Asiph* 5647–1887, also published separately) is splendid for its lofty Biblical language, but is not sufficiently accurate.

[48] *Cf.* Jer. 1:15.

myriad tribes of birds, and every soul of man and every sea shall shudder before the face of the Immortal," and fear shall come upon all. "He (God) shall break asunder the craggy peaks of the mountains and the great hills," and the deep darkness (the abyss) shall be visible to all. The foggy clefts of the rocks in the high mountains shall be full of corpses, the rocks shall be drenched with blood, and every torrent shall fill the plain with it. The fortified walls of the enemy shall fall to earth because they did not acknowledge the ordinance and judgment of the great God, and in their folly rushed with spears against the Temple. God shall execute judgment upon all of them by war, by the sword, and by a flood of water; brimstone shall fall from the heavens, along with heavy hailstones; and death shall come upon their animals. Then shall they know the immortal God, who has done all these things. "Through the width of the earth shall sound the wailing and mourning of perishing men"; and all the barbarians [49] shall be bathed in blood. The very earth shall drink the blood of the perishing, and the beasts of prey shall be glutted with their flesh. [50]

After this terrifying picture comes the description of the bliss which shall come to "the sons of the great God." They shall dwell securely and peacefully around the Temple, rejoicing in the salvation of their God, who shall "protect them like a wall of flaming fire." "In town and country shall they live in peace"; for "not the evil hand of war, but the Immortal One is their protection." Then shall all the peoples,

[49] In the Greek text the word is ἄναυδοι, meaning "speechless," "dumb." The editions of Kautzsch, Charles, and Kahana emend to "streams," "shameless," and "unclean" respectively. In my opinion, there is no need to emend at all. The ἄναυδοι are speakers of foreign languages, barbarians, whom the ancients considered as lacking in intelligible speech, and even as dumb, since they could not understand their language. (Note also that the Slavs call all non-slavs "dumb.") Also here, as in many places, the reference is to the warning words, "a nation whose tongue thou shalt not understand" (Deut. 28:49).

[50] Sib. Or. III 660–97.

isles, and cities see how much the Immortal loves those men (the Jews). For all things work for them and come to their aid—the heavens, God's chariot (the sun), and the moon. And sweet music shall go forth from them in song thus:

O come, let us all bow to the ground to supplicate [51] the King immortal, the great and eternal God; let us pass in procession (or send gifts) [52] to His sanctuary, for He is Lord alone; and let us all pay heed to the law of God most high, which is the most just of all laws upon the earth. Verily, we have gone astray from the path of the Immortal, honoring in our foolishness the work of men's hands, even idols and graven images of men that perish.

Finally, again is pictured in the manner of Ezekiel 39, how they shall have firewood for seven years from the numerous weapons of the enemy, "and no wood shall be cut from the forest for burning in the fire." [53]

Here the picture of the war of Gog and Magog is mixed with the picture of the Days of the Messiah.

Then the Sibyl turns to Hellas and warns her that she must not oppress Israel (the Seleucid kingdom and its decrees). She must not stir up the leopard from its lair, lest evil befall her (the victorious Hasmonean house). Let Greece too serve the great God, that she may participate in the bliss which shall come after the great Day of Judgment. At that time, the earth, "the universal mother," shall yield to mortal men the choicest grain, wine, and oil; from the heavens shall come down a nectar of sweet honey, trees shall bear their fruit, there shall be fat sheep and oxen, and lambs from the sheep and kids from the goats; sweet fountains of white milk shall gush forth, the cities and the fertile fields shall be full of all good things, and there shall be no sword in the land and no noise of war; nor shall the deeply groaning earth again be shaken. Drought

[51] See Ps. 95:1-5.
[52] Contrast Charles, II, 391 with Kautzsch, II, 199.
[53] Sib. Or. III 702-31; and see above, p. 154, n. 41.

shall not again be upon the land, nor famine, nor hail to spoil the fruit, but a great peace shall be over all the earth; one king shall be friend to another to the end of days, and one law for all the earth shall the Immortal in the starry heavens establish for the sons of men. For he alone is God and there is none other.[54] So the Sibyl calls upon the idolaters to forsake their grievous and abominable sins: let them give up idolatry and serve the living God; let them shun adultery and unnatural lust; let them bring up their children and not slay them (as they were accustomed to do even in Greece to children who were weak or defective from birth); "for the Immortal will be wroth with him that sins in these things." [55]

Here the Sibyl unfolds a new picture of the "kingdom over all the sons of men" which God will raise up "forever and ever." Then shall offerings and incense from all the ends of the earth be brought to the house of the great God, and mankind shall have no other temple than this one which God appointed for the worship of his faithful ones. It alone shall be called the house of the great God.—Every plain, and the river valleys and the high mountains shall be good for pasture, and in those days the stormy waves of the sea shall become easy for the passage of ships. Only peace shall come upon the land of good men. The prophets of the great God shall put at rest the sword, for they themselves are the judges of mortal men and righteous kings. Also shall there be an abundance of righteousness among the sons of men. For this is the decision and the command of the great God.[56]

All this is in the spirit of certain parts of Isaiah.[57] And of course, it would have been impossible for the Sibyl without the picture of the King-Messiah as it is found in Isaiah 11. And when it is said of the Isaianic Messiah "for unto us a child is

---

[54] Sib. Or. III 732–60.
[56] Sib. Or. III 767–84.

[55] Sib. Or. III 762–6.
[57] See Isa. 2:2–5; 7:22; 30:26, *etc.*

born, unto us a son is given," [58] then the daughter of Jerusalem, the virgin daughter of Zion, is the one in whose midst
this child is born. Therefore the Sibyl enthusiastically says:

> Rejoice, O virgin, and be glad: for He that made heaven and
> earth hath given thee joy; and He shall dwell in thee, and thou
> shalt have everlasting light. The wolf and the lamb shall feed to-
> gether on the mountains, the leopard shall eat grass with the kid:
> the bear shall lie down with the herds of calves, and the devouring
> lion shall eat chaff at the stall as the ox, and little children shall
> lead them with a halter, for He shall make the wild beast harmless
> (lit. helpless) upon earth. And the babe shall lie down with the
> dragon and the asp, and shall suffer no hurt; for the hand of God
> shall be on them.[59]

Here we have before us almost word for word one of the
most glorious visions of Isaiah picturing the Days of the Messiah.[60] And even in the term "virgin" there is no necessity
whatever of seeing a Christian falsification.

But in order to know when the Days of the Messiah will
come, there is need of Messianic signs. So the Sibyl gives these
"unerring signs": When swords appear in the starry heavens
toward evening and toward morning; when clouds of dust
fall from the heavens over all the earth, and the rays of the
sun fail suddenly at high noon, and the light of the moon
returns and lights up the earth; when the rocks drip with drops
of blood; and when you shall see in the clouds a battle of footmen and horse like a hunt of wild beasts in thick fog—then
shall God, who dwells in the heavens, bring the end of days.
Accordingly, all must offer sacrifices to the great King.[61]

These are the signs of the Messiah which we find in the
Prophets, in the pseudepigraphical books, in the Gospels, in
Talmud and Midrash,[62] and even in the works of Josephus.[63]

---

[58] Isa. 9:6.   [59] Sib. Or. III 785-95.
[60] See Isa. 11:6-9.   [61] Sib. Or. III 796-807.
[62] For particulars, see Klausner, *Ha-Ra'yon*, index, items "Day of Yahweh," "Day of Judgment," "Birth pangs of the Messiah," and "Signs of
Heaven."
[63] *Jewish War* VI v 3. See also Tacitus, *Hist.*, V 31.

With this the Sibyl, that is, the author of the third book, concludes her prophecies, adding, however, at the end some words about herself: She is the Assyro-Babylonian Sibyl, who prophesies the fire which shall be kindled in Greece, and "reveals to mortals the mysteries of God"; but she shall be called "the shameless one of Erythrae," or "the mad deceiver" whose mother is Circe and her father Gnostos (or Agnostos—"the unknown"). But when everything which she prophesies is fulfilled, people will remember her and they will no longer call her mad, but a prophetess of the great God; God it is who revealed to her first things and last things—what has been and what will be. For she is the daughter-in-law of that man who was saved from the waters of the Flood in an ark of wood together with beasts and birds, and then refilled the earth again; that is, she is the daughter-in-law of Noah, and to her was made known first things and last things. Therefore, everything which proceeds from her mouth was told to her truly.[64] That is to say, she knows that the Gentiles will not believe her and will think her mad and a liar; but she really is the daughter-in-law of Noah of the days of the Flood, yet has foretold much of what actually took place thousands of years after her time; therefore, she is to be believed when she prophesies about what will take place in the distant future. And if the Gentiles believe her prophecies, they will follow her advice and accept the religion of the people who came forth from Ur of the Chaldees—they will join themselves with that people and revere its God, its temple, its land, and the holy people themselves.

The third book of the Sibylline Oracles is clearly a book of Jewish propaganda for the Gentiles—hence its great importance for the present work, and hence the unusual length of my presentation of its ideas. This propaganda is exceedingly shrewd, penetrating, and clever. Its cleverness is not

[64] Sib. Or. III 808–29.

that it knows how to cover its face with a pagan veil, as Schürer thinks, but that there is combined in it two parts, which always come in order one after the other: the sharp rebuke and the prophecy of doom, the revelations of the great iniquities attending the worship of idols made by men or the deification of dead persons, the sins of fornication and unnatural vice, and the like, and the threat of the universal Day of Judgment, on which the great God, the one and only God Most High, will judge all peoples with the sword and with fire and with brimstone. These strong condemnations, prophecies of doom, and fearful threats alternate with appealing and enchanting pictures of the Days of the Messiah, in which "an everlasting covenant of peace will be established between king and king" and in which there will be peace and contentment also among common men and even wild beasts, while the fertility of the soil will increase and all produce of the earth shall be multiplied sevenfold. And with the condemnation and the comfort are combined exhortations to serve the one and only God Most High, and praise for the people of Israel and their religion *in its ethical aspects, without any specific mention of the ceremonial laws.* This likewise was the preaching method of early Christianity in the days of Paul and his associates.

The Jewish Sibyl also excels in another way: she thoroughly understands the times. She does not limit herself to Judea and Egypt alone, but, like the prophets before her, whom she imitates in everything, she lifts her burden over all nations and all kingdoms which were known at that time. In all these excellencies of the Jewish Sibyl lies the secret of the influence of this Sibyl even upon pagans of high position; also from these considerations came the need to go into such detail here with regard to the third book of the Sibylline Oracles.

The pagan Roman poet who was the greatest of the Golden Age of Roman literature (the Augustan age), Vergil, describes in his Fourth Eclogue, written in the year 41/40 B.C.E., "the Age of Gold" of mankind which shall come after "the Age of Iron," after a time of devastation and ruin like that of "the birth pangs of the Messiah"; and indeed there can be hardly any doubt that the larger part of Vergil's glorious description is taken from the brilliant pictures of our Jewish Sibyl. For Vergil describes "the Age of Gold" as "the last age of Cumaeic verse" (*ultima Cumaei carminis aetas*)—and of course, in the city of Cumae in Italy there was a famous sibyl, to whom perhaps were attributed the oracles of the Jewish Sibyl who called herself "Assyro-Babylonian." [65] Thus it is not to be wondered at, that these oracles had such a great influence upon the best of the pagans. Except for the Hellenistic Jewish author of the third Sibylline book, no Jewish apocalyptist reached the twin heights of Jewish nationalism and universalism as they had already been reached by Isaiah, First and Second. Thus Isaiah became "a light to the Gentiles" by means of an Alexandrian Jew, who styled himself "Assyro-Babylonian Sibyl" and "daughter-in-law of Noah."

B. THE FOURTH BOOK

The fourth Sibylline book does not present much that is new. In it, the Sibyl returns to what is at the end of the third book. The Sibyl is not a lying oracular voice of Phoebus (Apollo), but she is "a prophetess of the great God, who is not fashioned by hands of men in the likeness of dumb idols graven in stone," and who is not to be sought in his temple with the aid of "an inanimate stone." He "cannot be seen on earth nor measured by mortal eyes" since he was "not fashioned by mortal hands." He it is who "sees all things together,

[65] On Vergil's Fourth Eclogue and its relation to the Sibyllines see Ed. Norden, *Die Geburt des Kindes* (Leipzig 1924); Wilhelm Weber, *Der Prophet und sein Gott, eine Studie zur Vierten Ekloge Vergils* (Leipzig 1925); Th. Ziélinski, *La Sibylle* (Paris 1924), pp. 121-5. For further bibliography see Bousset-Gressmann, *Relig. des Judentums im späthell. Zeit.*, S. 225.

yet himself is seen by no man." To him belong dark night
and the day, sun, moon and stars, the sea teeming with fish,
the earth, the rivers and the sources of unfailing fountains,
living creatures, the rains that nurture the produce of the
fields, and all the vines, olives and trees.[66] Then says the
Sibyl:

> Happy among men shall they be upon earth who love to bless
> the great God before taking food and drink, trusting in the ways
> of godliness: who shall turn away their eyes from every temple
> and all altars, vain structures of stones that cannot hear, defiled
> with the blood of living things and sacrifices of four-footed beasts;
> and will have an eye to the glory of the one God, doing no pre-
> sumptuous deeds of blood nor trafficking for thievish gain [67]—
> abominable are such works—having no base desires for strange
> women, nor for defilement with men, loathly and hateful.[68]

The Sibyl threatens idolaters with the Day of Judgment, on
which "God himself" will judge both the wicked and the
righteous; "then shall he send the ungodly into the fire beneath
the murky gloom," and then shall they know what evil they
have done; but the righteous will be left on the fruitful earth,
and God will give them "breath and life and grace." [69]

But all this will be fulfilled only in the tenth generation;
so now the Sibyl reveals what shall occur in the nine generations which shall precede the tenth generation. There is
not a nation or city in the ancient world against which she
does not "prophesy" woes and terrors ("prophecy after the
event" be it understood). Assyria, Media and Persia, Egypt
and Babylonia, Greece and Asia Minor, Sicily and Croton,
Carthage and Armenia, and even Bactra in India [Afghan-

---

[66] Sib. Or. IV 6–17.

[67] The reference is, apparently, to excessive usury.

[68] Sib. Or. IV 24–34. These last words are not found in one manuscript,
and the English translator (Charles, II, 394) considers them a gloss; but
there is no reason for this, since the Sibylline books emphasize the abominable sin of sodomy on every occasion.

[69] Sib. Or. IV 40–8.

istan]—upon all of these shall come the Day of Judgment with all the terrors of "the birth pangs of the Messiah." [70]

But "to Solyma (Jerusalem) too the evil blast of war shall come from Italy," and shall wreak havoc upon the temple of the great God when they (the natives of Jerusalem) forsake righteousness for folly.[71] Here follows a "prophecy" in the form of a veiled reference to the story about Nero current in ancient times (it was known also to the sages of the Talmud), that he neither was killed nor committed suicide, but fled to Parthia.[72] Then "a Roman chieftain" (Titus) shall come to Syria and burn with fire the temple of "Solyma" (Jerusalem), and at the same time he shall slay many people and lay waste "the great land of the Jews with its broad way." [73] Then shall a great calamity (earthquake) come upon Paphos, Salamis, Cyprus, and the lands of Italy, Syria (Antioch) and Caria. The Sibyl threatens that if the righteousness, faith, and justice of men disappear from the world, and if insolence grows great and evil deeds increase, and if to the righteous no man pays heed, and if men in their blindness and folly even destroy the righteous and rejoice in doing evil and make haste to spill blood—then they must know that God will no longer be great in mercy, but will gnash his teeth in rage and destroy the whole human race by means of a mighty conflagration.[74] So the Sibyl turns to "wretched mortals" and advises them not to stir up the wrath of the great God, but to forsake the sword and murders and deeds of evil, and to "wash your whole bodies in ever-running rivers" (no doubt the Jewish baptism of proselytes, not the Christian), and lifting

---

[70] Sib. Or. IV 49–114.   [71] Sib. Or. IV 115–8.

[72] Sib. Or. IV 119–24 and 138–9. Cf. Tacitus, *Hist.*, I 2 and II 8 with Ascension of Isaiah 4:2–4 and Gittin 56a (where it is said that Nero became a proselyte and R. Meir was descended from him).

[73] Sib. Or. IV 125–7.

[74] The "flood of fire." See on this Louis Ginzberg, in "*Ha-Goren*" of S. A. Horodezky, VIII, 35–51; R. Eisler, Ἰησοῦς βασιλεύς, etc. (Heidelberg 1929), II, 106–14.

up their hands to the heavens, to seek forgiveness for their former sins, and with praises to make propitiation for their fearful evils. If they repent thus, "God will relent and not destroy." [75] But if they do not turn from their iniquities and continue to sin "a fire shall come upon the whole world." And the "great sign" which shall precede "the birth pangs of the Messiah" shall be: swords and trumpets at the rising of the sun; all the world shall hear noises and a mighty blast; all the earth shall be burned up, and all the race of men shall perish, and all cities and even rivers and seas—everything shall burn with fire "until it becomes dust and ashes." [76]

We have here, besides the "flood of fire"—the *ekpyrōsis* of the Stoics—which I have already mentioned,[77] these Messianic signs: wars (swords), noises, the trumpet of the Messiah, and a mighty blast.[78]

Then shall occur the resurrection of the dead, whom God shall "restore again as they were before" (in their lifetime). Only then will come the Day of Judgment, on which "God himself" shall be the judge of the world. And all those who committed sin and wickedness shall be covered over by "a heap of dust and [engulfed within] dark Tartarus and the murky depths of Gehenna." But the righteous shall live again on the earth and God will give them "breath and life and grace" [79] and they will "behold the pleasant and delightful light of the sun." The fourth book of the Sibylline Oracles concludes with these enthusiastic words: "most blessed shall be he who lives to see that time!" [80]

The fourth book makes only a few important additions to what we learned in the third. In general spirit the two books are similar. Both offer admonitions against idolatry and all kinds of immorality; they deliver severe oracles of the terrible

[75] Sib. Or. IV 152–69.　　　　　　[76] Sib. Or. IV 170–7.
[77] See above, p. 165 and n. 74.
[78] See on these "signs" Klausner, *Ha-Ra'yon*, pp. 286, 304 and frequently.
[79] See above, p. 164.　　　　　　[80] Sib. Or. IV 179–91.

misery that comes as punishment for sins; they tell of "the birth pangs of the Messiah" and "Messianic signs," and finally of the consolations of the Days of the Messiah. All this is by way of exhortation to accept clean and ethical Judaism and forsake crude and obscene paganism, which reconciles itself to every sort of immorality.

C. The Fifth Book

1. As compared with the fourth book, the fifth book is greater in quantity and different in character. In the beginning it makes a veiled allusion to Romulus and Remus, the legendary founders of Rome—then suddenly it makes a big jump and passes on to the Roman Caesars, who are cryptically designated by means of numbers corresponding to the first letters of their names, from Julius Caesar to Hadrian, and perhaps even to Antoninus Pius.

Afterwards, the Sibyl prophesies evils against Egypt and against her more important cities and temples—evils which conclude with a prophecy of the Messiah (a "king sent from God"), who shall destroy "all the great kings and the best of men." "So shall justice be done upon men by the Immortal." [81]

After this prophecy against Egypt comes a severe oracle against all the rest of the countries of the East: Babylon and Persia, Pergamus and Lesbos, Smyrna and Bithynia, Syria and Phoenicia, Thessaly and all Greece. At this point comes a striking description of Nero without mention of his name, but with mention of all his misdeeds and shameful acts, such as his claiming descent from Zeus and Hera themselves on the grounds that he sang "songs sweeter than honey with a melodious voice," and his frightful murders, including that of his mother. To him the Sibyl attributes the overthrow of "the temple built by God" and the burning of "the inhabitants and the people who went up to it" (to the Temple on pilgrimage

[81] Sib. Or. V 52–101.

from other lands). That is to say, to him (Nero) are attributed
the deeds of Vespasian and Titus, because they were sent by
him and acted on his orders. Then the Sibyl adds; "When he
died [82] the whole creation was shaken, kings perished (Otho,
Galba, Vitellius), and those in whose hands the power remained (Vespasian and Titus) brought ruin on the great city
(Jerusalem) and the righteous people" (Israel).[83]

A prophecy of destruction comes in connexion with a
comet which appeared in the year 73 C.E.[84] This comet will
destroy Italy and Babylon—meaning, of course, Rome, which
is also called "Babylon" in the Revelation of John—and by
reason of Italy "many faithful saints of the Hebrews and the
people of truth have perished." Rome, "the unclean city of
the land of Latium" shall be blotted from memory [85] because
there have been within her sorcery,[86] harlotry, and unnatural
vice. Rome shall sit as a widow [87] on the bank of the river
Tiber, which shall ever shed tears over her because she did
not know the ways of God, and in her arrogance thought that
there was no one who could destroy her; but "the God who
lives forever" shall destroy her. The Jewish Sibyl, whose heart
burns within her over the destruction of Jerusalem by Rome,
just as burned the heart of the author of the Psalm "By the
Rivers of Babylon" over the destruction of Jerusalem by
Babylon, finishes her oracle of doom with a fearful curse:
"Abide thou alone,[88] O doer of evil, and seized by flaming fire
take up thine abode in the nether regions of lawless Hades!" [89]

Again an oracle of doom against Egypt and her cities,

---

[82] Thus we must read instead of "appeared"; see Charles, II, 400.
[83] Sib. Or. V 115-54.   [84] Pliny, *Hist. Nat.* II 25.
[85] Similar to the oblivion of Tyre (Isa. 23:15); note also desolate Babylon
(Isa. 13:19-22).
[86] Thus is φαρμακή to be translated here and not "Giftmischerei" as in
the translation of Blass *apud* Kautzsch, II, 209. *Cf.* Charles, II, 400.
[87] Like Jerusalem (Lam. 1:1, "How is she become as a widow!").
[88] "How doth the city sit *solitary*" (Lam. 1:1).
[89] Sib. Or. V 155-78.

against Barca and Libya (Africa), against Cyrene, and the Britons, and the Gauls, because the forces of the Gauls, and of the Britons too, it would seem, helped the Romans in the days of the Destruction "to do evil to the children of God" (the Jews). Even the Indians and the Ethiopians shall tremble with fear, because with a certain position of the planets shall come "a celestial conflagration on earth" (*ekpyrōsis*—flood of fire); and out of "the battle of the stars" [90] shall be brought forth "a new creation" [91]—the "new world" which shall come in the Days of the Messiah after "the birth pangs of the Messiah." [92]

Also to Corinth shall come days of distress and misfortune. "For upon all men bloodshed and terror are ordained by reason of the great city (Jerusalem) and the righteous people (Israel), which shall endure forever and be exalted by Providence." [93] Then, after an obscure section,[94] come words of consolation to "the godlike heavenly race of the blessed Jews, who dwell round about the city of God at the center (navel) of the world [95] and have surrounded themselves with a high wall as far as Joppa." They—the blessed Jews—"shall be exalted up to the dark clouds." They shall hear no more the trumpet of war, nor shall they anymore perish at the hands of their enemies; but on the contrary, they shall raise on a standard the tokens of their victory (over the wicked) in an age of uprightness.[96]

After a very evident Christian interpolation ("a man whose hands were fastened to the fruitful tree," that is, the Cross)

---

[90] See farther on, at the end of this book of the Sibylline Oracles, lines 512–31. A battle of this sort is also hinted at in the Ethiopic Enoch 10:9.

[91] Sib. Or. V 179–212.

[92] See Klausner, *Ha-Ra'yon*, pp. 215–6, 220–2, 239–40, and elsewhere.

[93] Sib. Or. V 214–27.   [94] Sib. Or. V 230–46.

[95] For Jerusalem as "the navel of the world," see the book of Jubilees 8:19; Eth. Enoch 26:1 (*cf.* Ezek. 38:12). See also *Jewish War* IV iv 3; Tanhuma ha-Qadum (A), ed. Buber, Kedoshim X 10 (III, 78).

[96] Sib. Or. V 247–55.

comes an oracle of consolation in which is prophesied the
great prosperity and bliss, both material and spiritual, which
shall come to the land of Judea in general and to Jerusalem
in particular. The Sibyl bestows upon the people of Judea
all kinds of endearing names: "child of God, full of riches,
only-beloved flower, pleasant light, noble protection, beloved
branch." And Jerusalem she calls, "beloved and beautiful Jewish city,[97] worshipped in song." The Sibyl speaks tenderly to
Judea, whose spirit shall no longer be vexed, for no longer
shall the unclean tread (impious foot) of the Greeks [98] pass
through its land in arrogance and with evil schemes; indeed,
their hearts shall turn toward your (Judea's) Law. Your re-
nowned sons shall encircle you with honor, and your table
(the altar) they shall honor with all kinds of sacrifices and with
prayers to your God. The righteous, who have endured misfortunes, shall have an allotment in life;[99] but the wicked, who
"have set their mouth in the heavens," [100] shall keep silence and
hide themselves until the world passes away (or is changed).[101]

Again comes a severe oracle of "a rain (flood) of fire," [102]
which shall lay waste the produce of the earth, and the ground
shall remain unploughed and unsown as long as mortals do not
acknowledge the God who is chief and first of all, eternal and

[97] In the edition of Charles, this is translated "well-favoured Judaea, fair
city"; but apparently here the translation of Kautzsch's edition is preferable.

[98] *Cf.* Isa. 52:1, Nahum 2:1.

[99] The Greek text is corrupt. The translator in ed. Charles (II, 402) con-
jectures the reading κάλων (cable of a ship) in place of καλόν (fair) and
translates "shall have a more ample and well-favoured *rope* of life"; the
Hebrew translator (II, 2, p. 426) follows him and translates: ". . . the
cord of their life shall be long and exceedingly well-favored." But it
appears to me that we have here a usage that is ill-adapted to Greek, being
influenced by the Hebrew word חבל, which has another meaning in the
Old Testament, *viz.* "lot," "portion": *cf.* "The *lines* [portions] are fallen
unto me in pleasant places (Ps. 16:6); "For the *portion* of the Lord is His
people (Deut. 32:9).

[100] See Ps. 73:9.

[101] Sib. Or. V 260–73.

[102] See above, p. 165 and n. 74.

immortal, and do not cease to worship dogs and vultures as do the Egyptians in their folly. But the Holy Land of the righteous shall blossom forth with everything, honey shall flow forth from the rock,[103] and milk from fountains; for they set their hope on the only Creator, the God exalted above all, and clung to him in great righteousness and steadfast faith.[104]

Then the Sibyl again delivers a severe oracle against Asia Minor in connexion with an earthquake which destroyed twelve cities in one night.[105] The provinces of Ionia, Caria and Lydia, and the cities of Sardis (Sepharad in the Bible), Laodicaea, Ephesus, Smyrna, Corcyra, Miletus, Lesbos, Tripolis and others shall be destroyed, and their temples with them, by means of thunder and lightning—a picture similar to "the birth pangs of the Messiah" in the Holy Scriptures and in the Palestinian Apocrypha and Pseudepigrapha. Then the Sibyl prays as follows:

Shew mercy, thou Father of all, upon the fertile and fruitful land, great Judaea, that we may behold thy judgments. For her thou didst know before others in thy grace, O God, that she might be known to all men as the land of thy favour, and that they should consider what privilege God has given her.[106]

Now the Sibyl turns to other lands and peoples: to Thrace and Hellespont, to Lydia and Galatia, to Pamphylia and Pisidia—all these are lands in which Paul worked. To Italy she cries out:

Thrice wretched Italy, thou shalt remain all desolate, unwept. A ravening beast in thy luxuriant land shall destroy thee.[107]

Then she prophesies days of darkness and gloom, when the light of the sun shall fail, the brightness of the moon shall be extinguished, the earth shall be covered with darkness and

---

[103] See Deut. 32:13; Ps. 81:17. [104] Sib. Or. V 274–85.
[105] See on this Tacitus, *Annals* II 47; Pliny, *Hist. Nat.* II 86.
[106] Sib. Or. V 328–32. [107] Sib. Or. V 342–3.

mist, and men shall be blind, while weeping and wailing prevail everywhere. All this will come about in order that mortals may know that God rules over all and oversees all from the heavens,[108] and thus no longer sacrifice "great bulls with gilded horns [109] to lifeless Hermes and gods of stone." Then must righteousness and wisdom and loveliness prevail among the righteous, in order that God may not destroy "the whole bloodstained race of men and their shameless offspring." So the Sibyl calls for love of the Creator who is our Father—the omniscient God who lives forever.[110]

2. Up to now the Sibyl has prophesied vague and general "woes" and "salvation." Now she connects the "Messianic birth pangs" and the Days of the Messiah with historical events, to which she gives clues that are sufficiently clear.

A new war shall come, which shall shake the ground like thunder in clear daylight and bring horrors upon the earth. The instigator of this will be "a matricide" (Nero), described here according to the belief mentioned above,[111] that he did not suffer execution or commit suicide but fled to one of the lands of the East. He shall conduct himself like the Antichrist ("the evil Armilus" in the later Haggadic literature). He shall subdue all and lay waste the entire earth, for he shall be more cunning than any man. But against him shall arise "from the West a great king of mankind:" [111a] blood shall flow like water, and fire shall rain upon men from the sky; blood and fire, rainstorms and hailstones, the darkness of night and misty gloom—all shall come and slay kings and the best of men. Then and only then shall come the Days of the Messiah.

Then shall the piteous ruin of war thus have an end; none shall any more make war with sword and steel and spear, for this shall

---

[108] Cf. Ps. 33:13, 14.   [109] Cf. Ps. 69:32.

[110] Sib. Or. V 344-60.   [111] See above, p. 165 and n. 72.

[111a] The English editions read here: There shall come "from the West a great war upon mankind." Tr.

be unlawful henceforth. And the people of wisdom, which was forsaken, shall have peace, having made trial of calamity, that thereafter they might have joy.[112]

All this is in accord with the Messianic promises of the prophets.[113]

Suddenly, the wrath of even this universalistic Alexandrian Jew (who is the Sibyl) breaks forth violently on account of the destruction of his metropolis (Jerusalem) and the burning of its holy Temple. Rome, he says, is full of matricides, paederasts, and houses of shame in which originally pure women are made into harlots; in this city are those who commit adultery with their mothers and with their daughters, kings who defile their mouths, and men who lie with beasts. So the Sibyl cries out to her: "Keep silence, thou city wretched and sinful! For no more in thee shall the virgins tend the sacred fire." That is to say, the Roman temple of the goddess Vesta shall be destroyed—the temple in which "the pure virgins"—the Vestals—kept the sacred fire which was never to be extinguished. (This temple was burned in 64 C.E. and again in 191 C.E.) The burning shall come as a punishment because by the hand of Rome was "the temple for the second time cast down, utterly destroyed with fire by unholy hands"—"the temple which was watched over by God, having been built by the consecrated hands of men who believed heart and soul that it would never be destroyed."[114] The burning of the temple of Vesta was, in the opinion of the Sibyl from the time of Hadrian, a punishment in advance (six years before the destruction of the Second Temple) for the burning of the Temple by the Roman army.[115]

---

[112] Sib. Or. V 361–85.
[113] See Z. Frankel, "Alexandrinische Messiashoffnungen," MGWJ, VIII (1859), 241–61, 285–308.
[114] See, e.g., Jewish War VI v 2 and 3.
[115] It is difficult to put forward the date of the fifth book of the Sibyllines to 191 C.E., and thus to say that the reference here is to the second burning of the temple of the Vestals in Rome.

Now follows a prophecy of doom against a king who shall die "as soon as he reaches the mainland [Italy] from the Eternal Land." [116] Then shall come "from the skies (or "from the expanses of Heaven") a blessed man holding in his hand a scepter bestowed upon him by God." He shall restore everything which enemies before his time took from "the upright people" (the Jews), and he shall destroy with fire the cities and dwellings of the wicked; but the city in which God took delight he shall make more brilliant than the stars, the sun, and the moon. He shall "set it like a precious jewel in the midst of the world," and build within it a glorious temple and "a great high tower reaching to the very clouds, visible to all men, that all the faithful and righteous may behold the majesty of the invisible God and praise his glory from the east and from the west." Then shall there be no more deeds of shame, such as harlotry, sodomy ("lawless lust for boys"), murder, and tumults; but there shall be emulation of righteousness among all (a wonderful vision—instead of the rule of force there shall be rivalry in righteousness in which all can participate!). It will be "the latter days of the saints" when God shall bring these things to pass—"the God who sends the thunder (not "the thundering Jupiter"!), the great Creator of the great Temple." [117]

At this point comes an oracle of woe upon Babylon in the hour when she is to be attacked by the Parthians. The Sibyl also prophesies concerning the fearful cataclysms of nature which shall come upon Italy and all Asia, Crete and Cyprus, Paphos and Salamis, Tyre and all Phoenicia. Also there shall

[116] J. Reider (ed. Kahana, II, 2, p. 430), suggests that the reference is to Titus, "whom the Jews fully expected to die immediately after he set foot in the land of Italy. Compare the stories about him in Tractate Gittin 55 ff." It seems to me that the reference is to Hadrian, in the beginning of whose reign the fifth book was written, and whose downfall was expected by the Jews as soon as he returned to Italy from his journeys (see Klausner, Ke-she-Ummah Nilhemet 'al Herutah, 2nd ed. [Tel-Aviv 5699], pp. 162-7).

[117] Sib. Or. V 414-33.

be a war in Egypt, "to which a king of Rome and rulers of the West shall put an end" (apparently, a reference to the "rulers" Pompey and Antony on the one hand, and to Augustus on the other).

Again shall come strange upheavals in nature, barbarians shall fall upon the Thracians, and men shall reach such a fearful extremity of hunger that they will eat their parents, while wild beasts devour out of their houses everything which is upon their tables, and birds (vultures) gorge themselves with men (the corpses of the slain). The ocean shall be filled with blood instead of water and shall be red with the blood of the men who shall fall in the war. Human beings shall become so scarce "that the number of men and the measure (proportion?) of women shall be known." The sun shall sink into the waters of the ocean in which it bathes, and shall not rise any more, "for he looked upon the unholy ways of many sinful men." Also the moon and the stars shall grow dark and again be hidden in gloom, while only good men who sang hymns to God shall have the guidance of God's light.[118] The pagan divinities of Egypt, Isis and Serapis, shall fall from their great estate, and "all those who sang hymns to God" shall know the utter insignificance of these divinities. One of their priests shall say:

"Come, let us set up in beauty the true temple of God; come, let us change the evil custom of our forefathers, through which in their foolishness they knew not that they were offering rites and processions to gods of stone and clay. Let us turn and sing praise to the immortal God, the Father, the Eternal, the ruler of all, the true God and King, the Father who holdeth our soul in life, the great God who lives for ever." And then shall there be in Egypt a great and holy temple, and the people whom God hath made shall bring sacrifices into it, and the immortal God shall grant them to dwell there.[119]

[118] Sib. Or. V 434-83.
[119] Cf. Isa. 43:21 and Ex. 15:16.

But days shall come when "the great temple of the land of Egypt" (the temple of Onias?) shall lie in ruins. Thereupon, God in his anger will destroy all the evil and sinful people and will no longer have pity on anyone in that land (Egypt), "because they kept not that which God had delivered to them." [120]

Finally comes "the battle of the stars," already mentioned above.[121] Here we have the whole circuit of constellations, which collide one with another and fight each other until in their clashing they fall to the earth,[122] and burn the whole earth—"the flood of fire" or *ekpyrōsis* known to us from the Stoics and the Midrash alike.

And with this the fifth book comes to a close.

In order to estimate the importance of the three Jewish Sibylline books for our present undertaking, it is necessary to keep in mind five fundamental considerations:

First, the ethical-monotheistic attitude; that is to say, the attention given to the sin of idolatry, on the one hand, and to the evils of adultery, unnatural vice and the shedding of blood, on the other. The Sibyl preaches against the moral evils connected with idolatry, such as the three things of which Judaism decreed: "It is better to be killed rather than transgress" in these (idolatry, incest, and the shedding of blood). The ceremonial laws are not emphasized; indeed, they are only hinted at. Early Christianity also, in the days of Paul, in its opposition to idolatry insisted only upon the requirements between man and man [and not those between man and God].

Second, outside of Egypt, from which the author (who dis-

---

[120] Sib. Or. V 484-511.   [121] See above, p. 169 and note 90.
[122] Sib. Or. V 512-31 (end of the book). Very similar to these lines is the lamentation for the night of the 9th of Ab: "Then for our sins was the Temple laid waste" (see on this and on its antiquity, Israel Davidson, *Otsar ha-Shirah ve-ha-Piyut*, I, 98, no. 2104).

guises himself as the Sibyl) comes, *the exhortation to conversion* is directed toward *Asia Minor* and *Rome*, that is to say, to precisely those two lands in which Paul, a native of one and a citizen of the other, carried on his work of preaching among the pagans. And the Sibylline Oracles undoubtedly helped Paul in his bold undertaking, since they prepared the way for him even if he did not actually make use of them.

Third, along with the exhortation to conversion, we find in the Sibylline Oracles *"prophecies of the last things"* (Jewish eschatology) in all their fullness: prophecies about "the birth pangs of Messiah" and "the signs of the Messiah," such as are known to us from the Old Testament, from the Pseudepigrapha, and from the Talmudic-Midrashic Haggadah; and prophecies about the Days of the Messiah, in which the Messiah takes an important place as "the sacred prince" and as "the king from the East," to whom has been appointed "the sublime kingdom of the Immortal King." And there can be no doubt of the fact that we have here the Jewish, and not the Christian or even the primitive Christian (Nazarene), conception of the Messiah. But undoubtedly, "the sacred prince" who is "the king from the East" must have been a preparation for "the Messiah not of this world" of Paul and his associates.

Fourth, all this *universalism*, which of course is already present in the prophets from Amos to Zechariah, the concern for foreign peoples, that even they shall recognize the true God and revere "the great land" (Judea), the holy city (Jerusalem), and "the holy people fashioned by God" (Israel)—all this universalism and all this great concern for foreign and pagan peoples, these are precisely the things in which Pauline Christianity takes an exclusive pride—but not rightly. Also in this it was anticipated by Judaism, even by Palestinian Judaism, and of course by Hellenistic Judaism all the more. The universalism and the proselytizing of early Christianity do not surpass at all the same tendencies in Hellenistic Judaism except in the matter of the open and deliberate setting aside of the ceremonial laws, such as we find in Pauline Christianity, but not in Hellenistic Judaism, for all its tolerance and all the lack of emphasis upon the ceremonial laws in its literary creations. It is for this reason that the Sibylline books are so important for our undertaking, and for this reason that so much space has been taken in the exposition of their contents.

Fifth and finally, *the mixing of Judaism and Hellenism*, which is the very essence of Christianity, appears first in Judaism. In spite of the dutiful attitude of the Sibylline books toward all the sacred traditions of Israel, in the last analysis these books are in one important respect far not only from the Old Testament and the Talmud-Midrash, but also from the Palestinian Apocrypha and Pseudepigrapha. For even in these latter the original Judaism is understood much better and emphasized much more. But in the Sibylline books we have a basic Greek influence, and if it is not felt so much in the contents, it is felt decidedly in the general tone of the oracles. The Sibyl imitates the Prophets and the Hagiographa (book of Daniel); yet not only is her language Greek, but also her general form and her manner of expression. But more important than this is the great value which the Sibyl unconsciously and unintentionally places upon pagan peoples and their poets and sages, even while she is taking an antagonistic attitude toward them. By contrast, original Palestinian Jewish literary creations were influenced much less by the Greek (or, more correctly, the Hellenized) spirit of the times, even when these creations were preserved only in Greek translation. Their tone is different, their style is different, their whole attitude toward the Gentiles is different. So in this respect also, the Sibylline Oracles anticipated early Christianity, particularly the Gentile Christianity founded by Paul.

CHAPTER IV

Philo Judaeus

[To Philo I have devoted a special and detailed investigation (of which the present chapter is only a revision with additions and corrections and omissions) in my book *Philosophim ve-Hoge-De'ot* (Tel-Aviv 5694), I, 64–91, and there is to be found all the literature with particular bearing on Philo known to me up to the year 1934. Now we must add to this literature the important book of Menahem Stein, *Philon ha-Alexandroni* (Warsaw 5697 [1937]), in which is to be found additional literature; and also *Philon ha-Alexandroni, Kitve-Historia* in the translation of M. Stein (Tel-Aviv 5697).]

1. Philo Judaeus or, as he has been called in Hebrew books from the time of *The Light of the Eyes* (*Meor 'Enayim*, 16th cent.) on, Jedidiah the Alexandrian, is the only Hellenistic Jewish philosopher and writer from whose works there have been left to us not only fragments (as, for example, from the works of Aristobulus), but even whole books, some of them great and some small in quantity, but all of them important in quality (Josephus *wrote* in Greek, but he was a Palestinian Jew in his origin and in his spirit). And Philo was a contemporary of both Jesus and Paul. In the year 40 C.E. he went to Rome on a mission for the Jews of Alexandria to Gaius Caligula, and in the book which he wrote about this mission he speaks of himself as being old. Apparently then, he was born about 20–15 B.C.E. and died about 45–50 C.E.

A whole series of Jewish and Christian scholars (Leopold Cohn, Bréhier, Schürer, and particularly Isaac Heinemann) have concluded, on the basis of manifold evidence, that Philo was more Greek than Jewish: and there are those who present numerous arguments (Menahem Stein) that Philo did not even know Hebrew. In opposition to these, I have attempted to

present proofs that everything which appears typically Greek
in the writings of Philo comes from only two causes: (1) because in the Judaism of his time there were not yet finished
and well worked out philosophical systems, and (2) because
he wrote about the concerns of Judaism in Greek and not in
Hebrew. As for the evidence that Philo did not know Hebrew, it is based upon his incorrect interpretation of certain
Biblical verses in an age when any sort of comparison of
letters or jingle of words was considered valid exegesis.[1] However, his broad Greek education, which he sought to combine
with Jewish learning, in which he was thoroughly steeped,
did make him unsettled, in spite of all his efforts to repair
the rent which had been created in his soul against his will
and without his recognition or acknowledgment of it. Therefore, his writings did not find acceptance within his people
Israel, to whom he was devoted heart and soul, but they
did find a response among the Christians, who sought and
found in them another compromise between Judaism and
paganism—with the emphasis on the side of paganism; yet
what Philo actually intended was a compromise between
Judaism and Hellenism—with the emphasis on Judaism.

This we shall learn in the course of the presentation of the
Philonic system—insofar as it is possible to piece together
from the scattered words of Philo a finished and complete
system.

For, as a matter of fact, Philo does not have a clear and
perfected philosophical system. He was influenced by various
philosophers and philosophical systems (Plato, the Pythagoreans, the Stoics, and others), and because of this it was im-

---

[1] See for particulars J. Klausner, *Philosophim*, I, 66–74. I am still not
convinced of the correctness of the opinion of M. Stein, in spite of his argument against me in his new book, *Philon ha-Alexandroni*, pp. 57–9. Moreover, from *Derashot la-Torah*, pt. I, sect. 7, it can only be concluded that
in a Greek book Philo used the LXX and based his interpretation on this
translation—and no more. And on p. 220, n. 1 contradicts the text.

possible for him to form a system unified and complete in itself. Nevertheless, one must not see in his beliefs and opinions a mere "eclectic system," without originality. Judaism, which he mingled and mixed into all these systems, profoundly affected these beliefs and opinions and made of them a creation which was in large measure original. Hence not justified are all those scholars who minimize his philosophic originality.[2]

2. At the foundation of his system lies the dualism of *deity* as complete and absolute spirituality, which is the active cause, and *matter*, which is an effect and a passive object. Man, too, is a mixture of matter and spirit. Matter is transitory and perishable, while spirit, as the "breath" and "radiation" of deity, is indestructible and immortal. The idea of deity is that of Judaism: unique, alone, eternal, unchangeable, unmixed (simple—ἁπλοῦς), free, and absolutely self-sufficient (αὐταρ-κέστατος ἑαυτῷ). It is more than "the idea of the good" of Plato.[3] Its essence cannot be described by means of specific definitions. Man is able to conclude from its revelations to the world only one thing—that it (deity) exists. The Hebrew appellation of deity, "Yahweh," "I Am," "I Am What I Am," inspires Philo to repeat time after time that deity is *being*, "that which is" or "that which is present" or "that which exists in fact." God is without attributes (ἄποιος), yet at the same time he is completeness itself, since he fills all and all is contained in him. Therefore Philo sometimes also calls God "Nature" (φύσις) or "the Father and Creator of all," or even "the universal mind" (ὁ τῶν ὅλων νοῦς).

But since God is perfect and infinite, and is not in any sense corporeal, how could he create the world as it is—a material world, which is troubled, imperfect, transitory, and perishable?

---

[2] See P. Wendland, *Die hellen.-röm. Kultur* (1912), SS. 206–7; Ed. Meyer, *Ursprung u. Anfänge des Christentums*, II, 366.

[3] See M. Stein, *Philon ha-Alex.*, pp. 196, 204.

To this philosophic question, which is essentially more Jewish than it is Platonic or Stoic, Philo adds another question, which is completely Jewish: In the world as it is there are good and evil; so how could God, who is absolutely good and perfect, form a world which contains evil, the essence of imperfection? To Plato deity was "the idea of the good," and hence the absolutely good; yet Plato did not exert himself overmuch with the question of evil in the existing world. For him evil was an offshoot of imperfect matter, having in a certain sense an independent existence. It was impossible for Philo *the Jew* to be satisfied with this explanation. Jewish monotheism is essentially ethico-religious, and its unique, living, and creative deity has a real relationship to man, to society, and to human history; hence for it evil is not a mere *phenomenon of nature*. Rather, Jewish monotheism concerns itself fundamentally with *the evil of human society*. Therefore, it seeks a more suitable solution to the question of the existence of evil.

Also, the question of contact between deity—pure spirituality—and impure matter is for a monotheistic Jew a more difficult question than it is for a Greek philosopher, whose monotheism is a theoretical principle of existence and not a principle of life (a "living God"—fashioner and creator, "the first and the last"—the God of society and the God of history). On this account, Philo was forced—like R. Solomon ben Gabirol after him—to come to the conclusion that there are mediators or intermediate causes between deity and the world, between absolute spirit and matter mixed with spirit. By means of these, then, there is formed a bridge or passageway from absolutely good deity to the corporeal world, where good and bad lie together in confusion.

These "mediators" or "intermediate causes" Philo found not so much in the Platonic "Ideas," which preceded all existence and include all existence; rather, he found them in the active causes that are nothing more than the active powers of nature, which the Stoics called Logoi Spermatikoi ("germinal principles"). Perhaps the angels of the Holy Scriptures provided Philo with the basis of his idea of the mediators; these angels are completely spiritual beings, and yet they are not deities but only beings who carry out the purposes of God, and thus are mediators between deity and the world of mankind. We must also take into consideration "Wisdom" in the book of Proverbs, and even more in the Wisdom of Solomon,[4] which, like "Torah" in the Midrash, is described as an idea antecedent to creation, according to which existing things have been created;[5] this is similar to "the pattern of the artificer" in the language of Philo, or "the plans and diagrams of the architect" in the language of the Midrash.[6]

But the "active causes" of Philo are not only antecedent or underlying forms, like the Ideas of Plato, but are also "intelligent powers" (νοητοὶ δυνάμεις), which are powers active within the actual world, like the Logoi Spermatikoi of the Stoics. These "active causes" penetrate into everything, animating and setting in order inert and unordered matter. This Stoic addition to the Platonic conception was for Philo a necessity growing out of his Judaism. *A power that was merely theoretical, not active in the world and in man, could not possibly satisfy the demands of ethical monotheism.*

The "mediating powers" of Philo have their existence (but not their work) outside of the world (as Plato taught), but not outside of deity. Philo expressly says that they are present only in the divine thought.[7] They are the "uncircumscribed

[4] See above, p. 131.

[5] See D. Neumark, *Toledot ha-ʿIqqarim be-Yisrael* (Odessa 5679–1919), II, 56–9; *idem, Toledot ha-Philosophia be-Yisrael* (New York 5681–1921), I, 28–33, 37–42.

[6] *Cf.* beginning of Gen. Rabbah with Philo, *De Mundi Opificio,* M. (=Mangey), I, 4; C.-W. (=Cohn-Wendland), I, 18–20 ("Creation of the World" in the Hebrew translation of J. Mann as edited by M. Schwabe, published by Junowitz [Jerusalem 5691], pp. 9, 10).

[7] See the passage from Philo referred to in the preceding note.

powers of God" (ἀπερίγραφοι δυνάμεις θεοῦ)—God also being uncircumscribed. But because, on the one hand, they are a part of deity, which includes them and operates by means of them, and, on the other hand, they come in contact with matter—for these reasons, Philo was *forced* to conceive them both as hypostases existing in their own right which have emanated from deity, and as powers included in deity as parts of its own essence. In no other way could Philo save himself from corporealism—either a corporealism of deity or a corporealism of the intelligent powers. Eduard Zeller has pointed out the internal contradiction in this reasoning, although Philo himself did not consciously recognize it.[8] But a contradiction like this is also presented by the Shekhinah of the Talmud and Midrash, where it too is at the same time a substance separate from deity and the essence of deity. In a certain sense the Spirit of God in the Pentateuch is a similar example. And at a later time we find a similar ambiguity in the concept of Will of R. Solomon ben Gabirol, who was, I have no doubt, influenced by Philo, even if we have not yet found out clearly by which way this influence came to him.[9]

The name Logoi for the intelligent powers comes to Philo from the Stoics. The Logoi are parts of that intelligence which is universal and antecedent to all existence; thus they are to a certain degree Ideas in the Platonic-Stoic sense, but they have also the Jewish connotations of the Wisdom, the Torah, or the Word by which the world was created. Serving as a center for all these Logoi-Ideas is the Highest Idea or "the Idea of Ideas," which is The Logos *par excellence* or the Word (*Mēmrā* in the Targum). If the individual Logoi are parts of the divine intelligence, then *The* Logos is the divine intelligence in the universal sense. In this respect there is a

[8] See E. Zeller, *Grundriss der Geschichte der griechischen Philosophie*, 12. Aufl., bearb. v. W. Nestle (Leipzig 1920), SS. 346–52.

[9] See Klausner, *Philosophim*, I, 137–42.

similarity between The Logos of Philo and "the world soul" or "the universal mind" of the Stoics. This Stoic "Logos" depends in turn upon the "Logos" of Heraclitus of Ephesus, who was the first to make use of this word as a philosophical term and for whom the Logos was an intelligent power which divides all existence into proper uses and functions (λόγος τομεύς).

But the Logos of Philo is different in a fundamental respect from that of Heraclitus and the Stoics. While for them the universal intelligence or "inspirited matter" (matter into which an animating breath has been blown) and deity are the same thing, and thus they reach pantheism as well as a certain materialism (even "inspirited matter" is matter)—by contrast Philo the Jew sees that for him deity is a separate entity (separate from the world) and not an included entity (included in the world). He also sees in the Logos a kind of "Idea of Ideas" in the manner of Plato, except that his (Philo's) Logos is separate from deity, yet at the same time included in it. The Logos is a hypostasis, which exists in its own right in relation to the world, but is only a partial entity in relation to deity, like "the intelligent powers," like the Talmudic "Shekhinah," and like the "Will" of Gabirol. Accordingly, two great students of Hellenism [10] have come to the conclusion that there is nothing in common except the name between the "Logos" of Philo and the "Word" of the Gospel of John (which depends on Philo) on the one hand, and the "Logos" of Heraclitus the Stoic and of Epictetus on the other hand. The Philonic "Logos" is an almost completely original creation, the fruit of Jewish thought and teaching based on the Scriptures (Midrash). These scholars are right, to my mind, even though a certain delimitation is necessary: namely, that the

[10] See Ed. Schwartz, "Aporien im Vierten Evangelium," *Nachrichten d. königl. Gesellsch. d. Wissensch. zu Göttingen*, Philol.-hist. Klasse, 1908, SS. 537 ff.; A. Bonhöffer, *Epiktet und das Neue Testament* (Giessen 1911), SS. 183–8.

Greek "Logos" influenced the form and tendency of the Philonic "Logos," but Philo found its general essence in original Judaism.[11] In the stories of creation in the Holy Scriptures occurs again and again the expression: "And God said, 'Let there be . . . !'—and there was . . . !" The Logos is, therefore, the power of creation included in deity, by means of which deity works. As spoken word and voice the Logos is not really material; but neither is it pure spirituality. It is a bridge and passageway from absolutely spiritual deity to the corporeal-spiritual world. The Logos is fashioner and creator without any material means whatsoever, being, as was said, only spoken word and voice; thus, in the ordering of creation the Logos mediates between the deity and the world. The Mishnah says, "By ten Sayings was the world created";[12] the Targum also makes use of this idea in "the Word (Mēmrā) of God." Philo only broadened and deepened this Jewish conception and gave it a Heraclitean-Platonic-Stoic coloring.

For in the Philonic "Logos" are included all the powers and all the acts of deity, and by means of the Logos they become a unity. The Logos is the representative and messenger of God, the interpreter or mediator (the "Paraclete" in the Gospel of John) [13] between God and the world, and it (or he) is also the tools of craftsmanship with which God formed the world (something like the Demiurge of Plato); but the Logos is likewise the high priest, who stands between God and men to intercede for the latter, also the Angel or

[11] So the matter appears to me, in spite of all the arguments of Leopold Cohn against Eduard Schwartz. See L. Cohn, "Die Lehre vom Logos bei Philo" (*Judaica*, Hermann Cohen Festschrift, Berlin 1912, SS. 303–31). Of course, the new coloring of the Logos, along with the Heraclitean name, is Greek; but the essence is Jewish (*Logos*, to be sure, could have also been a translation of *Maamar* or *Mēmrā*).

[12] Aboth V 1.

[13] On the difference between the "Paraclete" of Philo and that of the New Testament, see M. Stein, *Philon ha-Alex.*, pp. 224–6. The "Paracletes" in the Talmud are merely the precepts, repentance and good works (Mish. Aboth IV 11; Babli Shabb. 32a; Yer. Ta'anith beginning of I 1).

the Archangel, and is identical with the command of the Creator—all completely Jewish conceptions.[14] The Logos is neither created nor uncreated, since the concept "creation" is applicable only to things which are finite. For the most part, the Logos appears in the writings of Philo simply as "intelligence" or as the "thought" of deity. But sometimes Philo speaks of the Logos as of an individual substance (entity) distinct from deity, and he calls it "the first-born son of deity," "divine being" (θεός, in distinction from "God," ὁ θεός), or even "the second god." These are, to be sure, but metaphorical phrases, just as Philo calls the stars "visible gods." In the last analysis, for Philo, the complete and absolute monotheist, the Logos is nothing more than the messenger and minister of God, like the ministering angels, whom Philo also sometimes calls Logoi.

But Philo brought a great new conception to the interpretation of the Heraclitean-Stoic Logos—an entirely Jewish conception: deity is absolute spirituality to such a degree that it cannot have any immediate contact with the world of matter; therefore there is need of a mediating power, which is the radiation of deity and the individual hypostasis of one of its essential qualities. This Jewish concept, which was apparently anticipated by the "Maamar" and the "Shekhinah" of the Talmud and Midrash, provided a basis for the teaching of the Neoplatonists, for the conception of the "Will" as "the source of life" (*Fons Vitae*) and the first and most spiritual radiation of deity in the philosophy of R. Solomon ben Gabirol, for the conceptions of emanation and the "Original Man" (Adam Kadmon) of the Kabbalah, and even for the conception of the Messiah as "Word" and "heavenly man" in Chris-

[14] See what George Foot Moore has written about *Shekhinah*, *Mēmrā*, and *Mattatron*, "Intermediaries in Jewish Theology," *Harvard Theol. Rev.* XV (1922), 41–85; idem, *Judaism in the First Century of the Christian Era*, I, 437–8. On the difference between the Platonic and Stoic Logos, on the one hand, and the Logos of Philo, on the other, see also M. Stein, *Philon ha-Alex.*, pp. 210–1.

tianity and for the conception of "the world as will and idea" in the philosophy of Schopenhauer.[15] More important for our present concern is the fact that the Logos of Philo influenced *directly* the "Word" and the "Paraclete" [16] and the "heavenly man" of the Gospel according to John and of Paul. Little by little Christianity corporealized and coarsened this conception of the Philonic Logos and made of it the second person of the Trinity—the Son-God, the Man-God.

3. Very closely connected with the teaching about deity and divine powers is Philo's teaching about creation.

Since deity is absolutely perfect and good, it could not have created *ex nihilo* (and thus from its own substance) the world, which is imperfect and has evil in it. There was from eternity original matter, without form and attributes, without movement and life; from it God *formed* (not "created" being from non-being—ἔπλασεν and not ἐποίησεν!) the world through the mediation of the Logos ("Maamar" as the Talmud has it) [17] and of the "intelligent powers." Here there was only a fashioning of being from being and not a creation of being from non-being. This is the Platonic-Stoic view; [18] but Philo also found support for this in Judaism. According to the Pentateuch, when God created the heavens and the earth, chaos (*tohu* and *bohu*), darkness, and water were already in existence.[19] The Tannaim also looked upon the matter in this way:

[15] See Klausner, *Philosophim*, I, 140–1 and 166–8. Menahem Stein ("Hiddushe-Madda'," III, in the weekly *Badderekh*, 3rd yr. [1934], no. 22 [89]), finds in Philo's "Life of Moses" (II 127) these two stages of the Logos: the inner or immanental, in which it is a unity with God, and the external or transcendental in which it becomes a mediator between God and the world —exactly what R. Sol. ben Gabirol said of the Will.

[16] See above, p. 186, n. 13.

[17] See, *e.g.*, Gen. Rab. IV 3 and 4, ed. Albeck, p. 27; Aboth V 1; Megillah 21b.

[18] See on this Ed. Zeller, *Philosophie der Griechen*, II, 2⁴, 436.

[19] Gen. 1:2.

A certain philosopher asked R. Gamaliel, saying to him: 'Your God was indeed a great artist, but surely He found good materials which assisted Him?' 'What are they?' said he to him. '*Tohu, bohu,* darkness, water, wind (*ruah*), and the deep,' replied he.[20]

In like manner, R. Levi ben Gershon and many other Jewish thinkers before and after him considered the pre-existence of the world a doctrine not inimical to Judaism, on the basis of the first verses of Genesis.[21]

Furthermore, the directing of the world, like its formation, is accomplished through the mediation of the Logos and the "intelligent powers," and is nothing more than the continuation of creativity; for even the laws of nature are only a summing up of all divine acts.

The space of the world is filled with living beings or souls. The highest atmosphere or "ether"[22] is extremely thin, and, since it is near the heavens, is the dwelling place of angels and also of demons. The lower atmosphere, or "air" in the ordinary sense,[23] is less pure, and, since it is near the earth, the souls of men, which dwell within this lower air, are attracted by the sensate world, go down to earth, and enter into mortal bodies, although they themselves are immortal. Accordingly, the body is the bestial part of man, the source of all evil, the prison house of the soul, the dead corpse which drags the soul with it in life, and the coffin or tomb of the soul, which only after it is freed from the body begins to live an eternal life.

Nevertheless, there is also some value to the body. By means of its five senses man attains a knowledge of eternity; yet because of the senses "the heart of man devised evil from his youth." On this Philo refers to the words of Job: "Would

[20] Gen. Rab. I 9, ed. Albeck p. 8.
[21] See also M. Stein, *Philon ha-Alex.*, pp. 233–5.
[22] Greek *aither;* cf. '*athar*, Ezek. 8:11. Is it possible that this Greek word comes from the Canaanite-Hebrew?
[23] Greek *aer*, perhaps from Canaanite-Hebrew *or* (*ur*), "light," "fire."

that there were a pure one among the impure! There is not one." [24] But God breathed His spirit into the body, and He guides the body by means of intelligence, and this in turn makes possible perception and apprehension of the existing world. And the power of judgment, memory, and language are the principal powers of intelligence.

All this is basically Platonic. Yet even here the Jew in Philo comes to light. For Philo, unlike Plato and the Stoics, does not deem the body evil in itself, but evil only in comparison with the soul. Sense experience is not evil in itself; indeed, there is great good in it, namely, understanding of the world. It is evil only insofar as it brings about evil desires.

4. Likewise, the ethical teaching of Philo is decidedly Jewish. Here, of course, there are also many Stoic elements. Also for Philo the goal of morality is to be freed from the senses— from desires and external influences. Philo also has the four cardinal virtues: wisdom (φρόνησις), self-control (σωφροσύνη), courage (ἀνδρεία), and justice (δικαιοσύνη); also for him virtue is the only good; also for him the knowledge of truth and the doing of good are one, just as are one lack of knowledge and evil deeds (a wise man is good, a fool is evil)—according to the old distinction of Socrates, which passed on to the Stoics, who were pupils of his pupils; Philo also seeks, like the Stoics, "to live in conformity with Nature."

Nevertheless, the ethical teaching of Philo is *thoroughly Jewish*.

While the Stoics trust in the power of man—in his understanding and will, Philo thinks that man, in order to be free from the strong power of the senses, must have the help of God. Only God has planted morality in man, and it is the grace of God which gives man the power to be moral—a view which is the basis of the "doctrine of grace" in Christianity

[24] Job. 14:4; *De Mutatione Nominum* § 48 (6), M., I, 585; C.-W., III, 165.

from the days of Paul onward: man is justified not by his deeds but by the grace of God.[25] Therefore, man must adhere to the standards of the Holy One, blessed be He, and imitate his deeds—as is taught by the Talmud and by Plato alike. But Philo demands also of man himself, that he develop in himself the good by means of discernment. And since morality and discernment are one, Philo considers ethics the most important branch of philosophy.

The ethics which Philo preaches is the highest type of human morality of which Judaism can boast, since Philo bases his conclusions on the Torah, the Law of Moses.

When Moses, in speaking of Noah, "adds to the word 'man' the word 'righteous' and says 'righteous man,'" he means to teach that "whoever is not righteous is not a man."[26]

What is the ethical goal of Moses? Philo gives this answer:

This is what our most holy prophet through all his regulations especially desires to create, unanimity, neighbourliness, fellowship, reciprocity of feeling, whereby houses and cities and nations and countries and the whole human race may advance to supreme happiness.[27]

Philo is permeated with the idea that Israel is the chosen and peculiar people; but this deep nationalism is enclosed and held fast in a high and exalted universalism. In the opinion of Philo, there came forth from Abraham "a whole nation, and that the nation dearest of all to God, which, as I hold, has received the gift of priesthood and prophecy *on behalf of all mankind*."[28] And in another place, after he has described righteous men, Philo says:

[25] See M. Stein, *op. cit.*, pp. 140, 288.
[26] *De Abrahamo*, M., I, 6; C.-W., IV, 8.
[27] *De Virtutibus—de Caritate*, M., II, 395; C.-W., II, 119.
[28] *De Abrahamo*, M., I, 15; C.-W., I, 98.

one such nation [of righteous men] will stand above other nations, as the head, above the body, to be conspicuous on every side, *not for its own glory* but rather for the benefit of the beholders.[29]

Every man has in him something of the excellence of the righteous, since there is not a man in the world who does not have in him a divine spark:

Every man, in respect of his mind, is allied to the divine Reason, having come into being as a copy or fragment or ray of that blessed nature.[30]

In spite of this very idealistic viewpoint, Philo does not hold to a completely ascetic ethic. In his opinion, "Moses removed himself from the two extremes"—from the rigorous austerity of the Spartans and from the laxity of the Ionians and Sybarites:

He relaxed the overstrained and tightened the lax, and as on an instrument of music blended the very high and the very low at each end of the scale with the middle chord, thus producing a life of harmony and concord which none can blame.[31]

This moderate view of Philo (in spite of his opposition to the "golden mean"—μεσότης or μετριοπάθει—of Aristotle) [32] is like the moderate view in the sense of the avoidance of two extremes, as it is found in Judaism, and is not extreme in the manner of ascetic Christianity. Philo says, as Jesus also said,

[29] *De Praemiis et Poenis*, M., II, 426; C.-W., II, 114.
[30] *De Mundi Opificio*, M., I, 35; C.-W., I, 146.
[31] *De Specialibus Legibus—de Concupiscientia* § 102, M., II, 352; C.-W., V, 231.
[32] *Legum Allegoriae*, III, § 126, M., I, 113; C.-W., I, 141. Moses "loves in general not *metriopatheia* (moderated passion), but *apatheia* (lack of passion)." M. Stein (*op. cit.*, pp. 256-9, 263) emphasizes too much Philo's inclination to asceticism ("The natural thing with Philo is to despise all corporeality"). If this had been the case, Philo would not have been so opposed to the "spiritualists," and would not have emphasized that we must take into account the fact of creation and that we must remember that we live among human beings and not in a void—something to which Stein himself refers (pp. 130-1, 264-5).

that it is proper not to swear at all; [33] but not in the spirit of
Jesus he continues: since it is impossible in the life of society
to avoid swearing altogether, a man should postpone the oath
in the hope that he may not need to swear at all; but, if the
necessity should arise, let him swear only to the truth.[34] For,
in general, like a true Jew, Philo brings into consideration the
life of society and not the salvation of the soul of the individual alone. The worship of God, without the love of man
which reveals itself in social living, is only the half of true
piety; [35] yet "piety and holiness are possessions which we cannot obtain without the worship of God." [36]

Philo reaches the height of human morality—the love of
one's enemy, which Christians boast of as an innovation of
Jesus. Philo finds, and quite rightly, the love of one's enemy
already in the Law of Moses.[37] Philo concludes from the commandment "thou shalt not abhor an Egyptian": [38] "In spite of
all the wrongs which the Egyptians did to us, *love of man
must triumph in us over hate of the enemy*." [39] Love of man
extends itself to all mankind, even to *foreigners and enemies.*[40]
Since the Torah shows mercy even for animals, how could it
fail to show mercy for strangers, who are human beings? [41]
And Philo quotes the "Golden Rule" of ethics in its negative
form, as it is found in the book of Tobit [42] and in the sayings
of Hillel the Elder: [43] "It is commanded in the laws them-

[33] Matt. 5:34.

[34] *De Decalogo*, M., II, 194–5; C.-W., II, 84–5.

[35] *Ibid.*, M., II, 199; C.-W., II, 108–9.

[36] *De Sacrificio Abeli et Caini*, M., I, 108; C.-W., I, 37–8.

[37] G. H. Gilbert, *Greek Thought in the New Testament* (New York
1928), pp. 30, 31.

[38] Deut. 23:7/8.

[39] *De Virtutibus—de Caritate*, M., II, 393; C.-W., II, 106–7 [Although the
author encloses this sentence in quotation marks, it appears to be a para-
phrase rather than a direct quotation of Philo. Tr.]

[40] *Ibid.*, M., II, 394–5, 400, 402; C.-W., II, 116–20, 147, 160; *De Specialibus Legibus—de Septenario*, M. II, 294; C.-W., II, 167.

[41] *De Virtutibus—de Caritate*, M., II, 399; C.-W., II, 140–1.

[42] Tobit 4:15.

[43] Shabb. 31a.

selves that a man shall not do to his neighbor what he would not wish to have done to himself." [44]

But Philo, in his general ethical conception, reaches the highest degree of *humanitarianism*. His opinion of *the value of man*, upon which all human morality rests, is most exalted. In his eyes, the killing of a man is "subverting the laws and statutes of nature." [45] Indeed, murder is nothing less than sacrilege, since of all that is precious and important in the world there is nothing more sacred and godlike than man, "the glorious cast of a glorious image, shaped according to the pattern of the archetypal form of the Word." [46] Therefore, all those who have true knowledge of the one Father, "the Father of all" as Philo calls the deity over and over again, are to be regarded as "sons of God." [47] Only one holding a high conception of man and the value of man like Philo could have accepted without qualification the splendid saying of the Stoa: "No man is a slave by nature." [48] Even Aristotle, one of the three greatest among Greek philosophers, said: "The barbarian (one who is not a Greek) and the slave are alike by nature." [49] In fine, it is possible to say that the whole ethical teaching of Philo is expressed with the utmost clarity in this short sentence:

Among the vast number of particular truths and principles found therein (in the Torah), there stand out, so to speak, high above the others two main heads: one of duty to God as shown by

[44] Quoted from Philo by Eusebius, *Praeparatio Evangelica* VIII 7 6. See on this whole matter Klausner, *Yeshu*, p. 446, nn. 1 and 2 [Eng. ed., p. 397].

[45] *De Decalogo*, M. II, 202; C.-W., II, 132.

[46] *De Specialibus Legibus* III, M., II, 313; C.-W., V, 83.

[47] *De Confusione Linguarum* XXVIII 145, M., I, 426; C.-W., II, 256.

[48] *De Specialibus Legibus—de Septenario*, M., II, 283; C.-W., V, 60. M. Stein (*Philon ha-Alex.*, pp. 59, 60, n. 2) wrongly suspects me of wishing to take this saying from the Stoics and give it to Philo; I wished only to emphasize how much Philo approves of this idea. Stein himself makes this point in another place in his book (p. 268, n. 2).

[49] Aristotle, *Politica* II (II, 1252b).

piety and holiness, and one of duty to men as shown by love of
mankind and justice.[50]

Philo establishes not merely the logical foundations of
monotheistic ethics; he knows also the religious-emotional side
of Jewish morality. How fine and deep are, for example, these
two Philonic utterances:—"They who offer themselves offer
the highest of sacrifices"; [51] "God delights in altars on which
no fire is burned, but around which virtues dance." [52]

And what faith Philo has in the element of good in the soul
of man! For he says, "Assuredly there is in the soul of every
man, however undistinguished he may be, a detestation of
evil." [53]

This ethical teaching is Jewish—Jewish and not Greek, in
spite of the Stoic elements in it, because of its ties to a living
God and not only to a blind and abstract monistic principle
of being. For the highest reward of moral living is the exaltation of the self to heights upon which man sees God. And
man sees God by virtue of the fact that he is a part of God,
for only by means of God can God be perceived: "God is
his own brightness and is discerned through himself alone." [54]
Man can strengthen the divine part of his being by a stripping
off of the sensual. That is to say, by divesting himself of
desires, by living a pure life based on true knowledge (for
Philo, as for the Stoics, a pure life and true knowledge are
essentially the same), man attains elevation of soul, whereby
he can escape from his own nature and rise above himself:

For when the light of God shines, the human light sets; when
the divine light sets, the human dawns and rises. This is what regularly befalls the fellowship of the prophets. The mind is evicted

[50] De Specialibus Legibus—de Septenario II 63, M., II, 282; C.-W., V, 102.
[51] De Sacrif. III 270, M., I, 253; C.-W., V, 65.
[52] De Plantatione 108, M., I, 345; C.-W., II, 154.
[53] De Spec. Leg. III, M., II 312; C.-W., V, 170.
[54] De Praemiis et Poenis, M., II, 415; C.-W., V, 45.

at the arrival of the divine Spirit, but when that departs the mind returns to its tenancy.[55]

And when the human mind is evicted from us as the divine spirit enters in, when the human light sets and the divine light dawns and rises, there comes to man that intoxication of holy inspiration, an intoxication not of wine, which Philo calls by the wonderful name of "sober intoxication" (μέθη νηφάλιος).[56] This is *rapture* or *ecstasy* (ἔκστασις)—the state in which man's knowledge of himself is fused with the heavenly light which is shed from deity into the soul of man. Thus the spirit of God, coming down to dwell within man, actuates him just as the instrumentalist plays upon the strings of the lyre.[57] Only one who has achieved this state has attained the heights of pure spirituality and thus drawn near to deity. This "drawing near to God" is the greatest "good" which man can obtain in this world.

This view is thoroughly Hebraic:

> Whom have I in heaven but Thee?
> And there is none upon earth that I desire besides Thee.
> . . . .
> But it is good for me to draw near unto God.[58]

Thus did all Jewish mysticism, and in particular the Kabbalah, regard "rapture," and thus does the piety (Hasidism) of our time evaluate it. But early Christianity made of this "drawing near to God" of Philo a "mystic union" (*unio mystica*) with God, as we shall see below.[59]

---

[55] *Quis Rerum Divinarum Heres Sit*, M., I, 511; C.-W., III, 264–5.
[56] See on this Hans Levy, *Sobria Ebrietas* (Giessen 1929).
[57] *Quis Rerum Divinarum Heres Sit*, M., I, 482; C.-W., III, 68–9. Philo himself gives a marvellous description of illumination from above as the source of his creativity in *De Migratione Abrahami*, M., I, 441; C.-W., II, 275 (§§ 34–5).
[58] Ps. 73:25, 28.
[59] See on this also M. Stein, *op. cit.*, pp. 286–8 (particularly p. 288, n. 3).

5. But in his view of *the Messiah* Philo is completely Jewish. He sees in the Messiah not only a spiritual leader possessing spiritual attributes and ethical qualities, but also one who fights and conquers, who possesses, together with splendid qualities of soul, also bodily strength to an unusual degree.[60] Philo says:

For "there shall come forth a man," says the oracle,[61] and leading his host to war he will subdue great and populous nations, because God has sent to his aid the reinforcement which befits the godly, and that is dauntless courage of soul and all-powerful strength of body, either of which strikes fear into the enemy and the two if united are quite irresistible. Some of the enemy, he says, will be unworthy to be defeated by men. He promises to marshal against them to their shame and perdition, swarms of wasps to fight in the van of the godly, who will win not only a permanent and bloodless victory in the war but also a sovereignty which none can contest, bringing to its subjects (the saints or the righteous of the Days of the Messiah) the benefit which will accrue from the affection or fear or respect which they feel. For the conduct of their rulers shows three high qualities which contribute to make a government secure from subversion, namely dignity, strictness, benevolence, which produce the feelings mentioned above. For respect is created by dignity, fear by strictness, affection by benevolence, and these when blended harmoniously in the soul render subjects obedient to their rulers.[62]

Thus, with all the spirituality in Philo's Messianic picture—bloodless victory and obtaining submission by inculcating respect and doing benevolent deeds—there still remains in it a political and worldly side (war and conquest, rulers and subjects), and even violence and terror and bodily strength. This is a thoroughly Jewish (I might have said Judaistic) point of view, not purely Stoic and certainly not Christian. The

[60] M. Stein does not emphasize enough the political and secular side of Philo's Messianic idea (see *op. cit.*, pp. 271–2 and n. 4).

[61] See Num. 24:7 according to LXX.

[62] *De Praemiis et Poenis* 95–7, M., II, 423–4; C.-W., V, 357–8.

Messiah Jesus is not at all like the picture of the man "who leads his host to war and subdues great and populous nations." At this point Christianity was not able to borrow anything whatever from Philo.[63]

6. This historical fact is before us: Philo was thoroughly Jewish. In his writings there are many things which are much like what we find in Talmud and Midrash; he takes pride in the name of Israel; he makes the Greek philosophical systems subservient to Judaism; he preaches observance of the cere- monial laws, and is absolutely opposed to those "intellectuals" among the Jews of Alexandria who satisfied themselves merely with the allegorical interpretation or with the exalted ethical meaning of the ceremonial laws; [64] and finally, he expects a completely human Messiah, who shall conquer and rule over various lands and peoples, yet at the same time be endowed with great spiritual, intellectual, and moral attributes—that twofold aspect of the Messiah which we find standing out both in Old Testament Judaism and in Talmudic and later Judaism.

In spite of all this, there is before us still another clear his- torical fact. In spite of this Judaistic world view of Philo, Judaism does not accept him, but Christianity does accept him —this Christianity which set aside the ceremonial laws, made the Messiah a deity, and removed from its teaching Jewish national separateness and all the territorial and nationalistic aspirations contained in the Jewish Messianic conception. For this paradoxical fact there is only one explanation: Judaism rejected Philo and Christianity drew near to him precisely be-

[63] See Klausner, *Ha-Ra'yon*, p. 320. This opinion of mine is the exact opposite of what was found on Messianism in Philo by E. Bréhier, *Les idées philosophiques et religieuses de Philon d'Alexandrie*, 2-ème éd. (Paris 1925), pp. 5-7. See also on this P. Krüger, *Hellenismus und Judentum* (Leipzig 1908), S. 47; Franz Geiger, *Philo von Alexandrien als sozialer Denker* (Stutt- gart 1932), SS. 95, 106-9, 111-2, Anm. 6.

[64] *De Migr. Abrah.* 89-94, M., I, 450-1; C.-W., II, 285-6. See also on this Klausner, *Philosophim*, I, 75-7; Geiger, *op. cit.*, S. 8.

cause of the compromise which Philo made between Judaism and Hellenism.

Philo received both a Jewish and a Greek education. I have already said that I do not consider correct the view of the Jewish scholars Leopold Cohn and Isaac Heinemann on the one hand, and the Christian scholars Emil Schürer, Emil Bréhier and Travers Herford on the other hand, that Philo was more Greek than Jewish or that his training was more Greek than Jewish.[65] I think that in essential quality and interiority his Jewish background outweighed his Greek training, and only in quantity and in external aspects did his Greek training predominate over the Hebraic.[66] But in the last analysis Philo, the Jew of the Diaspora, was not completely a Jew like his contemporary Rabban Johanan ben Zakkai, for example; and in a certain sense not even like Josephus, the Palestinian Jew, who became a captive among the Gentiles, who was not a philosopher at all, who was incomparably inferior to Philo in depth and ethical outlook, and also wrote his books in the Greek language.

Like a Jew of the Diaspora, Philo is immersed in Greek culture. He calls the Greek language ἡ ἡμετέρα διάλεκτος ("*our* language"), and the Jews who do not speak Greek are considered by him, as by the pagan Greeks, to be "barbarians" (βάρβαροι). In Greek belletristic, scientific, and philosophic literature he is very well versed. He offers citations from Homer and Euripides, he knows Thucydides and Demosthenes, and the philosophers Parmenides, Empedocles, Zeno, and others; they are for him "men of God" like Moses "the man of God," and a "holy company" (*sacer coetus*).[67] In like manner he speaks of "the most sacred sect of the Pythag-

---

[65] See above, pp. 179–80. M. Stein, *op. cit.*, *passim*, insists upon Philo's ignorance of the Hebrew language, but emphasizes strongly the Jewish spirit in his views.

[66] Klausner, *op. cit.*, pp. 66–73.

[67] *De Providentia* II 48, according to the Latin translation of Aucher from the ancient Armenian translation.

oreans." [68] He calls Plato "the great" and "most holy" (ἱερώτατος).[69] Philo learned much from the Stoic, Posidonius of Rhodes.[70] And Philo is so influenced by Greek ways of expression that he, the thoroughly faithful and monotheistic Jew, any number of times calls the stars "visible gods" or "perceptible gods" or even "visible and perceptible gods"; [71] and he does not feel the contradiction between these pagan expressions and Jewish monotheism. Whoever unintentionally, or against his own will reaches such a point, has a division in his mind, and it is impossible for him to be entirely sound, impossible for him to be a thorough Jew.

And yet, however much Philo reveres Pythagoras and Plato, he reveres Moses more. Moses is for Philo the greatest man who ever was on earth. "He attained the very summit of philosophy, and . . . had been divinely instructed in the greater and most essential part of Nature's lore." [72] The whole Law of Moses consists of "words of God" (λόγια θεοῦ) [73] or "divine words" (θεῖα λόγια),[74] which are "oracles" (χρησμοί).[75] Philo, like the Sages of the Talmud, expounds even the small words such as *eth* (the sign of the accusative), *gam* ("also"), *akh* ("nothing but"), and *raq* ("only"), since there could not be a superfluous word in a holy book like the Law of Moses. If

---

[68] *Quod Omnis Probus Liber Sit*, M., II, 445; C.-R., VI, 1 (§ 2).

[69] *Ibid.*, M., II, 447; C.-R., VI, 4 (§ 13) *et passim*.

[70] See on this P. Wendland, *Die hellen.-röm. Kultur*, S. 207; and especially the two important books of I. Heinemann, *Poseidonius' metaphysische Schriften*, Band I–II (Breslau 1921–28) and *Philons griechische und jüdische Bildung* (Breslau 1932).

[71] *De Mundi Opificio*, M., I, 6; C.-W., I, 8 (§§ 27–8); *De Aeternitate Mundi*, M., II, 496; C.-R., VI, 95 (§ 73); *ibid.*, M., II, 501; C.-R., VI, 87 (§ 46); *ibid.*, M., II, 509; C.-W., VI, 107 (§ 112).

[72] *De Mundi Opificio*, M., I, 2; C.-W., I, 2 (§ 8).

[73] *De Decalogo*, M., I, 182–3; C.-W., IV, 272 (§ 16); *ibid.*, M., I, 188; C.-W., IV, 279 (§ 48).

[74] *De Vita Mosis* I 85, M., II, 94; C.-W., IV, 139; *De Specialibus Legibus* IV 50, M., II, 343; C.-W., V, 220.

[75] *De Vita Mosis* II (III), M., II, 163; C.-W., IV, 244 (§ 188); *De Cherubim*, M., I, 161; C.-W., I, 199 (§ 124).

מות יומת ("he shall surely be put to death") is written in the Pentateuch, of course the additional word מות ("surely") is to be given its own special interpretation. The prophets, and even the writers of the Hagiographa (we know for certain that Philo was familiar with Psalms, Proverbs, and Job) were possessed of the holy spirit, or more precisely, were "instruments of expression for deity" (θεσπέσιοι) [76] and "interpreters of God" (ἑρμηνεῖς θεοῦ).[77] By them the will of God was revealed and they were disciples or colleagues of Moses. The Holy Scriptures of the people Israel are the source of all wisdom, and from them even Heraclitus and Zeno, and of course Pythagoras and Plato also, derived their knowledge and their philosophy.

But, if the wise men of Greece are not equal in importance to Moses, the prophets, and the writers of the Hagiographa, in the last analysis they do approach them in importance. Moses is a holy of holies, but Plato likewise is "supremely sacred." The prophets are instruments of expression and interpreters of deity, but "the Pythagorean sect" also is "most sacred." Against his own will Philo attempted to bring about a compromise between Judaism and Hellenism. The wise men of Israel and the wise men of Greece—both had the same purpose. Moses and Plato said the same thing. Between the Holy Scriptures and the best of the Greek philosophical writings (excluding the philosophy of Epicurus, to which Philo was opposed, just as were the Sages of the Talmud and the Church Fathers) [78] there is no contradiction. Whatever appears in them to be mutually opposed is to be interpreted "according to the understanding" (πρὸς διάνοιαν), that is to say, by means

---

[76] De Migratione Abrahami M., I, 450; C.-W., II, 286 (§ 90); De Special. Leg.—de Circumcisione, M., II, 211; C.-W., V, 2 (§ 8); ibid.—de Sacrif., M., II, 259; C.-W., V, 75 (§ 314); and in any number of other passages.

[77] De Special. Leg.—de Monarchia, M., II, 222; C.-W., V, 16 (§ 65); De Praemiis et Poenis, M., II, 417; C.-W., V, 348 (§ 55).

[78] See above, p. 94 and n. 102.

of allegory, which although it does not nullify the plain meaning, the obvious sense (τὸ ῥητόν), in the last analysis does carry
the words of the Law beyond their plain meaning.

It was this very thing which original Judaism feared most.
It feared compromise, because all its advantage lay in its determined opposition to compromise. For what it claimed and
taught and believed was that its truth was unique in the world,
that its Torah was absolutely without parallel, and that its
ethics could not be equaled in any other nation. But Philo
comes and says that there is also truth in the books of the
pagans, that their philosophers are also saints and holy men,
that Greek morality is very lofty and comparable in its basic
principles to Jewish morality. A view like this necessarily
weakened the opposition between Judaism and paganism, although Philo did not intend it so, nor was he even conscious
of the fact. But there was no more dangerous thing to ancient
Judaism, surrounded by pagans, than the weakening of this
opposition. The instinct of self-preservation of the Jewish
nation and of the Jewish religion, which indeed are one and
the same thing, whispered to orthodox Judaism that it must
not admit this compromising doctrine into its house. There
was a great and deep-seated fear that, with the cessation of
opposition between Judaism and Hellenism, with the cessation
of the recognition of the uniqueness and peculiarity of the
Torah of Israel, also the Jews would cease to exist as a nation
and Judaism as a religion. And in very truth, Hellenistic Judaism, which did not sense this danger, did pass away and cease
to exist in the world. On the other hand, Palestinian and
Babylonian Judaism, which did sense it, rejected the Philonic
compromise—and has survived under the most difficult conditions until this day.

7. The very same reason which caused Judaism to reject
Philo and his compromise, caused Christianity to accept him

and his teaching, albeit, for the most part, in a changed and emasculated form.

For compromise between Judaism and Hellenism, between Israel and the pagans, is the foundation and basis of all Christianity—not the compromise of Jesus, but that of Paul and those who came after him. If it had not been for this compromise, the Gentiles would not have accepted a purely Jewish doctrine at all. Philo pointed the way to a compromise like this, although he certainly did not intend the result which followed in his time through the agency of his contemporary Paul. Philo wished, like Paul, to bring the Gentiles into Judaism as proselytes; but *first*, Philo was not prepared for any reduction of requirements. As we have seen,[79] he was not willing to yield in any way whatsoever in the matter of obedience to the ceremonial laws, in spite of the allegorical interpretation which he himself applied to them; on the other hand, Paul yielded to the Gentiles who believed in Jesus as Messiah on every requirement of the Law. And there is no doubt of the fact that the teaching of Paul would have aroused strong opposition on the part of Philo if he had had occasion, to encounter it. *Secondly*, Philo would not have agreed to any half-pagan additions to pure monotheistic Judaism, such as Paul made in his time, and Christianity after him still more; for in order to endear this mutilated and perverted Judaism to the pagans, Christianity introduced into it any number of Graeco-pagan elements.

Nevertheless, Christianity borrowed much from Philo.[80]

Above all, it borrowed the "Logos" as set forth by Philo.

Philo could not imagine as possible any immediate relationship between the corporeal world and deity, which is absolutely spiritual, so he elaborated on the Heraclitean-Stoic "Logos" in the spirit of the Hebraic-Talmudic "Maamar."

[79] See above, p. 198.
[80] See on this also M. Stein, *op. cit.*, pp. 306–7.

The Christians came along and said: Truly, the situation is impossible without a mediator between this crude and materialistic world and abstract deity, remote and hidden from mankind. This mediator is the Messiah (Christ), who is not a human savior of flesh and blood, endowed with both physical and spiritual attributes and bringing about both politico-territorial and ethico-spiritual salvation with the aid of God, who is the real savior; rather, the Messiah is the "Logos"— a heavenly being, the essence of deity in his real nature and a man only according as he is revealed in action; thus the Logos-Messiah is the "son of God" in a more concrete sense than these words bear in the Old Testament and in a less absolute sense than they bear in the later Trinity. But not far is the way from this "heavenly man" of Paul to the later God-man who is one of the three "members" of the half-pagan Trinity. . . .

The Christians borrowed another great thing from Philo— Biblical allegory.

Philo advocated as one process the understanding of Holy Scripture both according to its plain meaning and in a figurative sense. The Christians took metaphorical interpretation of Scripture, the Philonic allegory, and made use of it for two purposes. *First*, they were enabled by it to accept the Old Testament and to apply some of its words to Jesus; as a matter of fact, apart from the Old Testament, the New Testament had nothing upon which to rely for support. *Secondly*, they were able by means of the Philonic allegory to evade the obligatory character of the ritual requirements and to preach openly that there was no need to observe them, since the *intent* in them was the main thing, and not the act of observance. It is hard to exaggerate the importance of this matter. Not for nothing did the Christian Church preserve Philo's writings and even interpolate them in numerous places, while Judaism neglected or forgot his existence and hardly men-

tioned his name until the time of Azariah min ha-Adummim
[Azariah ben Moses dei Rossi, 1513–1578, author of *Meor
'Enayim*].

Christianity also borrowed many other things from Philo.
For example, the idea of *grace*,[81] any number of ethical opinions, and the like. But in general, it was the very compromise
between Judaism and Hellenism, as embodied in all the works
of Philo, which gave occasion and impetus to the rise of a
doctrine which was Judaism and Hellenism at one and the
same time, yet in a certain sense was neither Judaism nor
Hellenism, but a new kind of doctrine compounded of the
two, or more correctly, compounded of certain elements of
the two—in other words, Christianity as it developed in the
short time between the crucifixion of Jesus and the decisive
victory of Paul the Tarsian.

But before we can obtain an understanding of this short
period, we must examine the sources from which we draw
our knowledge of the time between Jesus and Paul and our
knowledge of Paul himself.

[81] See above, pp. 190–1.

Fourth Book

THE SOURCES

CHAPTER I

The Acts of the Apostles

[See on this: K. Weizsäcker, *Das apostolische Zeitalter*, 3. Aufl., 1901; K. Clemen, *Die Apostelgeschichte im Lichte der neueren textquellen und historisch-kritischen Forschungen*, 1905; A. Harnack, *Geschichte der altchristlichen Literatur*, II, 1, 1897; *idem*, *Lukas der Arzt*, 1906; *idem*, *Die Apostelgeschichte*, 1908; *idem*, *Neue Untersuchungen zur Apostelgeschichte und zur Abfassungszeit der synoptischen Evangelien*, 1911; Johannes Weiss, *Die Schriften des Neuen Testaments*, Band II, 2. Aufl., 1908; P. Wernle, *Die Anfänge unserer Religion*, 2. Aufl., 1902; P. Wendland, *Die hellenistisch-römische Kultur—die urchristlichen Literaturformen*, 2. Aufl., 1912, SS. 314–35 u. 342–67; H. von Soden, *Urchristliche Literaturgeschichte*, Berlin 1905, SS. 107–26; Eduard Meyer, *Ursprung und Anfänge des Christentums*, III, 3–206; A. Schweitzer, *Geschichte der paulinischen Forschung*, 2. Aufl. Tübingen 1933; E. Renan, *Les Apôtres*, Paris 1866 (Introduction); M. Goguel, *Les livres des Actes*, Paris 1922; A. Loisy, *Les Actes des Apôtres*, Paris 1920; Aimé Puech, *Historie de la littérature grecque chrétienne*, I (1928), 359–405; Foakes-Jackson and Lake, *The Beginnings of Christianity*, Part I, Vol. III, *The Acts of the Apostles*, London 1926; J. H. Ropes, *The Text of Acts*, London 1926; George A. Barton, *The Apostolic Age and the New Testament*, Philadelphia 1936, pp. 103–14; A. T. Robertson, *Luke the Historian in the Light of Research*, New York 1934; A. Omodeo, *Prolegomeni alla Storia dell' Età Apostolica*, Messina 1920, pp. 3–118.]

1. In the New Testament, the book immediately following the four Gospels is the *Acts of the Apostles* (in Greek *Praxeis Apostolōn*). It is mentioned first, as far as is known to us to-day, in the fragment of a list of sacred books which is called the Muratorian Fragment, from the end of the second century C.E.[1] In this fragment the book before us is called the Acts of *All* the Apostles, apparently in order to exclude apocryphal Acts of individual apostles, which were already numerous in those days and which included miracle stories without any historical value (for example, the Acts of Peter, Paul, John,

[1] See on this fragment H. Lietzmann, *Wie wurden die Bücher des Neuen Testaments Heilige Schrift?* (Tübingen 1907), SS. 52–63.

Andrew, Philip, Thomas, Matthew, and Barnabas, some of them—the Acts of Paul, John, and others—preserved to this day). From the year 200 C.E. onward we find that the Acts of the Apostles is considered sacred, that is to say, as a part of the "Canon." Irenaeus, Tertullian, the Syrian Canon, which did not yet accept a number of the "Epistles of the Apostles" [Catholic Epistles] which are in the present New Testament, and also did not number among the canonical writings the Revelation (Apocalypse) of John—all of them count the Acts of the Apostles among the sacred books. Only Clement of Alexandria, the contemporary of Irenaeus and Tertullian, who also knew the Acts of the Apostles, did not make use of it as a sacred book. But by Origen it was considered equal in importance to the Gospels.

It would appear, therefore, that as regards canonization, the Acts of the Apostles is less ancient than the Gospels and most of the Epistles of Paul. Up to the second half of the second Christian century the Acts of the Apostles had not yet been accepted by Christianity as had the earlier parts of the New Testament.

Therefore, it is not to be wondered at, that we have the Acts of the Apostles in two divergent versions. One version is that accepted in the present New Testament, being found in the great majority of manuscripts. But there is another version, which is found in Codex D, now at Cambridge (Codex Bezae or Codex Cantabrigiensis).[2] In this codex there are, to be sure, differences also in the Gospels, particularly in the Gospel according to Luke; but the differences in the Acts of the Apostles are more and greater.[3] These differences are

[2] On this codex see in detail A. Resch, *Agrapha*, 2. Aufl. (1906), SS. 338–52; and in brief Klausner, *Yeshu*, pp. 63–4 [Eng. ed., pp. 68–9].
[3] In the great work, Foakes-Jackson and Lake, *The Beginnings of Christianity*, I, 3, 2–270, these two versions, the "Alexandrian" and the "Cantabrigian," are presented in direct comparison, along with a critical apparatus and many important notes.

sometimes confirmed by a few Greek manuscripts and by the translations into Latin, Syriac (the Peshitta), and Coptic [4]—a fact which proves the antiquity of the readings of Codex D (about 150 C.E.). Nevertheless, the received text is the more important one.[5]

2. The Acts of the Apostles purports to relate what happened after the crucifixion of Jesus: how the dissemination of Christianity in Palestine began, and how it was spread throughout the Roman Empire of that time. At the very beginning of the story we see this clear purpose: the author relates that Jesus appeared to his disciples after he was crucified and told them that they should not leave Jerusalem; and when they asked him after they had again assembled themselves together in Jerusalem: "Lord, dost thou at this time restore the kingdom to Israel?"—he answered them:

It is not for you to know times or seasons, which the Father hath set within his own authority. But ye shall receive power, when the Holy Spirit is come upon you: and ye shall be my witnesses both *in Jerusalem, and in all Judaea and Samaria, and unto the uttermost part of the earth*.[6]

That is to say, the revelation of the Messiah as the king who shall restore the kingdom to Israel is a mystery with which the disciples are not permitted to concern themselves; what the disciples can and must do now is to propagate Christianity first in Jerusalem, then in all Judea and in Samaria, and afterwards even "unto the uttermost part of the earth," *i.e.* in the whole vast world empire of Rome. There is here a clear indication that shortly after the crucifixion the disciples of Jesus decided to give up the politico-national Messianic conception

[4] See for details on all these Foakes-Jackson and Lake, *op. cit.*, pp. 276–453.
[5] See Aimé Puech, *Histoire de la littérature grecque-chrétienne*, I, 403–5.
[6] Acts 1:4–8.

of the Jews, which involved a certain danger in the Roman
Empire on account of its revolutionary implications, and to
devote themselves solely to the propagation of the primitive
Christian Messianic idea, which was abstract, mystical, and
entirely spiritual—first in Palestine and afterwards in all the
world.

The Acts of the Apostles may be divided into three parts,
which correspond to three centers of activity in different
geographical areas: (1) chapters 1–7, relating the spread of
Christianity in Jerusalem and all Judea; (2) chapters 8–12—
its spread in Samaria and Syria; (3) chapters 13–28—its
spread in Asia Minor until it reached even Rome. The center
of Part I is Jerusalem, the center of Part II is Antioch in Syria,
and the center of Part III is Greece and Asia Minor, particularly the cities of Corinth and Ephesus, with a clear outlook in
the direction of Rome.

But there is another possibility of dividing the book, this
time into two parts: (1) chapters 1–12, in which the central
personality is Peter, and in which Paul treads his first steps;
and (2) chapters 13–28, in which Paul is the principal character, while Peter is made subordinate to him. There are, to
be sure, in both parts other apostles and saints, who take a
certain place, and sometimes even an important place—for
example, John, Philip, James the brother of Jesus, Stephen,
Barnabas, and others; but in the main Peter stands out in the
first part and Paul in the second. Moreover, it has been clearly
recognized that the whole story of the events in the Acts of
the Apostles is unfolded for just one purpose: to enhance the
reputation of Paul, who even in the first part has a great
importance, and in the second part obscures with his brilliance
all the apostles and saints, even Peter "the Rock" (Cephas).

The Acts of the Apostles, in spite of the fact that it is full
of signs and wonders everywhere, purports to be a historical
book. It wishes to relate and describe how the relatively large

primitive church developed out of the small nucleus of the twelve disciples.[7] Of course, there is no question here, in a religious book, of a desire for historical objectivity. *First*, this book, like all religious history, has, apart from the historical purpose, also another purpose: to influence religious opinion. It wishes to show how the grace of God protected the little band, how it was saved from all misfortunes, and how it continually grew until a weak little Jewish group in Jerusalem became a great and powerful Church Universal. Naturally, this would not have been possible without signs and wonders —marvels and miracles which the apostles themselves displayed, and many wonderful things which happened to them. —*Secondly*, the author, writing in the time when the Pauline point of view was close to complete victory, finds it proper to tone down the sharp conflicts of Peter *versus* Paul on the one hand, and of James the brother of Jesus *versus* Peter and Paul, on the other hand. He obscures the definite accomplishments of Barnabas, who without any doubt prepared the way for Paul in the matter of receiving the pagans into Christianity without circumcision and the rest of the ritual requirements. In general, the author shortens the earliest history of Christianity and lengthens everything having to do with Paul or Paulinism. Hence the excessive length of the story of Stephen, designed to show that the "protomartyr" of Christianity held "Pauline" views; hence also the sharp contrast to what is revealed in the Epistles of Paul with regard to the above matters.

With this is combined another obvious purpose: to show that everywhere the Jews persecuted the Christian apostles, flogged them, slandered them before the Roman authorities, and even stoned some of them to death. Thus did the Jews to

[7] Against the opinion of H. von Soden, *Urchristliche Literaturgeschichte* (Berlin 1905), SS. 119-20, according to whom the book is "not a historical work, but a defense of Christianity against the government, a defense enveloped in historical descriptions."

the Christians not only in Jerusalem but in the whole Diaspora of Israel, particularly in Asia Minor, and even in Rome. The author's hatred of Jews is strong—and at the same time it is as though he already despaired of them and it was not worth his while to fight with them in order to bring them back to the proper course. This is a hate leading to estrangement; no longer are the Jews "the people of God," the chosen people; the glorious promises which were given to the Jews by the prophets have passed to the new and youthful church, which is "the true Israel." Therefore, it is no longer worth while to attempt Christianization of the Jews. They are no longer capable of restoration; they are stiff-necked and insist in their rebelliousness that they will not recognize "the curse of God that was hanged" as Messiah and Savior. It is more proper to attempt the Christianization of the pagans. Hence the cautious tone with regard to the Roman Empire. In the persecutions of the apostles the Jews are more guilty than the Romans. The Roman officials Gallio, Felix, and Festus took a tolerant attitude toward Paul, and only the Jews sought his blood.

The Acts of the Apostles, therefore, flatters the Romans by pretending that their acts of cruelty in the provinces, known to us from the writings of Josephus, Philo, and others, were to be charged to the account of the Jews. This is not to be wondered at. At the earliest, the Acts of the Apostles *in its complete form* could not have been composed before 95–100 C.E. (see below). By that time the Second Temple was already destroyed, the conquered Jews had been sold into slavery and had become as dust to be trod upon, while the Romans stood at the height of their power; so naturally, the author of Acts seeks to find favor in the eyes of the mighty Romans in whose hands was the fate of the Christians, and not in the eyes of the Jews, who were weak in a *political* and *worldly* sense, particularly after they had offered strong opposition in a *religious* and *moral* sense not only to the Romans but also to the preachers of Christianity.

3. Undoubtedly, the Acts of the Apostles has but one author. Both the style and trend of thought bear witness to this. But this one author made use of different sources. We are forced to this conclusion on account of the repetitions and contradictions in the book.[8] Thus, for example, the apostles —with Peter at their head—are judged twice before the high priest and the Sanhedrin.[9] Twice Peter is confined in prison —and the angel of the Lord miraculously delivers him.[10] Apparently, these stories were combined by the author from two different sources. James is first mentioned twice without any explanation as to who he is and what is his importance among the disciples of Jesus, and even without the title "brother of the Lord."[11] This is an indication that the passages were taken from a source in which it had been previously mentioned who this James was and what his position among the "brethren."

Also the contradictions are not a few. For example, on the one hand, it is related in chapters 10 and 11 that Peter was the first to permit the reception of Christians from among the Gentiles, and that, when the apostles and "brethren" became angry at this, Peter defended himself on the ground that he had received permission for this in a heavenly vision; on the other hand, in chapter 15 all this is attributed to Paul and Barnabas, and it is against *them* that the "brethren" become angry, and they are forced to defend themselves before the "brethren" and to bring about some sort of compromise. In

---

[8] All these are listed and discussed briefly in P. Wendland, *Die hellen.-röm. Kultur*, SS. 314–35. See for details Ed. Schwartz, "Noten zur Apostelgeschichte" (*Nachrichten der Gesellschaft der Wissenschaften zu Göttingen*, 1907); J. Wellhausen, *Kritische Analyse der Apostelgeschichte* (Berlin 1914).

[9] *Cf.* Acts 4:5–21 with 5:26–40.

[10] *Cf.* Acts 5:18, 19 with 12:4–11.   [11] See Acts 12:17 and 15:13.

the same chapter Peter himself says, "*a good while ago* God made choice among us, that the Gentiles by *my* mouth should hear the word of the gospel, and believe"; [12] this is opposed to any number of statements that we know from the Epistles of Paul and even from the Acts of the Apostles itself. There are many other instances like this.

Clearly, contradictions and repetitions and inconsistencies like these can be, on the one hand, the result of a Paulinistic tendency, of which I have already hinted,[13] and on the other hand, the result of the different sources which the author used.

One source like this stands clearly revealed before us. It is found in four sections, varying in length, in which the author writes in the language of the characters themselves (first person plural): "*we* sought to go . . . , concluding that God had called *us*"; "but these had gone before *us* and were waiting for *us*," *etc.*; "*we* departed," *etc.*; "*we* went on board the ship," and so on.[14] These sections are called the "We-Journal" or "We-Source" (*Wirbericht* or *Wirquelle*). These sections are without any doubt the words of eyewitnesses, which the author of the Acts of the Apostles introduced into his book and combined with other sources which he had reworked according to his need and his purpose. Similar are the sections of the book of Ezra standing in the first person,[15] which the editor of the book of Ezra-Nehemiah-Chronicles introduced verbatim and in their own language into various reworked sources. Likewise here, in the book of Acts (the author of which perhaps imitated in this respect the book of Ezra), we have the We-Source amidst other sources which have been more or less reworked.

The sources are different in extent and in importance. Even the reader who is not an expert in textual criticism sees immediately that the sources of the first chapters of the Acts of the

[12] Acts 15:7.   [13] See above, p. 213.
[14] Acts 16:10–17; 20:5–15; 21:1–18; 27:1–28:16.   [15] Ezra 7:12–9:15.

Apostles are briefer and much more fragmentary than the sources of the remainder of the book; and in general, that everything which pertains to Paul or to Pauline tendency is related at great length (for example, the story of Stephen, the baptism of Cornelius). In the last twelve chapters of the book, from chapter 16 on (chapters in which the We-Source is found), and particularly from chapter 20 to the end, everything is related at length and in great detail, as though the author were an eyewitness of most of the events described and had learned very little by hearsay. Most scholars consider this to be the case only in the four sections of the We-Source,[16] in which the author uses the first person and the plural number; but it must be concluded that the words between the sections in chapters 20–28 (although some see in them differences recognizable by contrast to the sections in which "we" is explicitly used) also come from the We-Source, except that here there was no occasion to use the word "we." Thus it may be supposed that at least the last nine chapters of the Acts of the Apostles, from chapter 20 to the end of the book, belong to the We-Source.[17] Chapters 17–19 do not belong to this source, because Luke, who is almost universally agreed to be the author of the third Gospel and of its continuation, the Acts of the Apostles (see below), remained in Philippi and was not an eyewitness of what is related in these chapters. Since the We-Sections were put into the book without change of wording, being before us in the first person just as they came from the pen of the writer, it must be concluded that the author of these sections is the author of the entire Acts of the Apostles just as we now have it; but in the chapters preceding those of the We-Source he made use of other sources, which he reworked according to his own ideas.

[16] Acts 16:10–17; 20:5–15; 21:1–18; 27:1–28:16.
[17] See Ed. Meyer, *Ursprung und Anfänge des Christentums*, III, 3–36.

What were those sources? Were they written or oral?

It is difficult to believe that these sources were only oral sources. Of course, the very brief and general sections in the beginning of the book could be the record of what the author heard from aged primitive Christians, from Paul himself or his disciples and helpers, or even from more remote hearsay, passed from person to person. But even in the first part of the book, that is to say, in the first twelve chapters, there is so much information containing details and names, that it would have been difficult to obtain them by hearsay and to remember them so exactly unless the author had had a written source before him. Thus it is necessary to assume that also in the first chapters the author made use of written sources along with oral. What were these sources and who their author or authors we cannot know to-day; even to distinguish between the written and oral sources is very difficult. We can make only this generalization: the vague and general information may have come from oral sources, but the specific and detailed information almost certainly came from written sources.

Since the Acts of the Apostles, as would clearly appear from the two accordant "introductions," [18] is only the second part of the Gospel according to Luke, it is assumed that the author of the Third Gospel is also the author of the Acts of the Apostles. But is Luke, whose name is borne by the Gospel and to whom the Church attributed the Acts of the Apostles, really the author of the two books in the New Testament which are separated only by the Fourth Gospel?

But, first of all, who is this Luke?

4. Luke (Λουκᾶς), the familiar form of Lucius and not of Lucanus as was formerly thought,[19] is mentioned three times

[18] Luke 1:1–4; Acts 1:1–5.

[19] See A. Deissmann, *Licht vom Osten*, 4. Aufl. (Tübingen 1923), SS. 372–7; A. T. Robertson, *Luke the Historian in the Light of Research* (New York 1934), pp. 16–9.

in three epistles of Paul.[20] In the first of these three epistles he is called "Luke the beloved physician." In the second it is said, "Only Luke is with me." And in the third epistle Luke is counted among the "fellow-workers" of Paul along with Epaphras, Mark, Aristarchus, and Demas. Concerning his life and deeds we have late and contradictory reports. It is almost certain that he was in his origin not a Nazarene Jew but a Greek pagan who became a Christian under the influence of Paul or Barnabas, since Paul distinguishes between him and "the circumcision." [21] Even his Greek style in the two books attributed to him, the Third Gospel and the Acts of the Apostles, does not attest a Jewish origin. There are in them, to be sure, Hebrew and Aramaic idioms; but the Hebrew idioms come to him through the influence of the Septuagint, and the Aramaic may come from the fact that Luke made use of reports by Jewish Christians who spoke Aramaic or of a written Aramaic source. Even a Greek-born intellectual could have known Aramaic as a widespread language of his time or could have learned this language in the primitive Christian environment into which he entered at the time of his conversion.[22]

If Paul mentions Luke and calls him "the beloved physician," and if in Pauline sources which, although suspected, at any rate come from the disciples of Paul it is mentioned that "only" Luke remained with Paul and that he was one of Paul's "fellow-workers"—then there is no reason to oppose the opinion that Luke is the author of the We-Source. And since the special characteristics of Luke as a writer—the inclination to connect the affairs of Christianity with general historical

[20] Col. 4:14; II Tim. 4:11; Philemon 24.

[21] *Cf.* Col. 4:14 with 4:11. Against the argument that Lucius, Jason, and Sosipater are called "my kinsmen" in Rom. 16:21 and thus that Lucius (Luke) was also a Jew, see A. Deissmann, *op. cit.*, SS. 376–7.

[22] See on his style F. Dornseiff, "Lukas der Schriftsteller," ZNW, XXXV (1936), 129–43.

events, beauty of expression, and the like—are found not only in the We-Sections, but in the whole Acts of the Apostles; and since this book in content and purpose is only a sequel to the Gospel of Luke, as stated above—then we *do* have reason to suppose that Luke, being the author of the Third Gospel, is also the author of the whole Acts of the Apostles, and not merely of the We-Source which another writer combined with the Acts of the Apostles.[23]

But it is well to give attention to this fact: the We-Sections relate events in detail and at length; and there is in them so great a naturalness that one sees in them actual history, even if it is history tinged with a religious coloring. Not so the earlier chapters, particularly those before chapter 15, or even before chapter 13. In this first part of the Acts of the Apostles, there are long and detailed stories and speeches: for example, the story about the lame man whom Peter healed and the detailed speech of Peter, in chapter 3; the story of the stoning of Stephen and his great speech (6:8–8:2); the story of the conversion of Paul (9:1–30); the story about the baptism of Cornelius by Peter (chapter 10); the story of the imprisonment of Peter and his deliverance in the time of persecution by Herod Agrippa I (chapter 12). But alongside of these there are, particularly in chapters 1–5, any number of short and abbreviated sections, in which very important facts are

[23] This has been convincingly demonstrated by A. Harnack in his three books mentioned above (p. 209, bibliog.). Harnack found proofs in the book of Hobart, *The Medical Language of St. Luke* (1882), that the author of the Third Gospel and Acts was a physician by profession. But Cadbury, in *The Style and Literary Method of Luke* (1919), claims that the medical expressions which Hobart and Harnack found in Luke's writings are not typical of Luke alone, but are the linguistic usages of all educated writers of Greek at that time. And P. Wendland says: "Philo's knowledge on this subject goes much farther than that of our author, and yet Philo was not a physician" (*Hellen.-röm. Kultur*, S. 335). But even without the "medical" argument, it is possible to attribute the Third Gospel and Acts to Luke on the basis of the "introductions" and on the basis of the *general* similarity of style between the two books and between the different parts of Acts itself.

told in a few lines (for example, the speaking with tongues, 2:1–14; the communistic life, 2:44, 45 and 4:34–5:12; and so on). It is clear that in the first chapters of the Acts of the Apostles facts are related from which the author of this book was already far removed, knowing them not at first hand, but remotely from hearsay, or drawing them from impoverished sources; hence they are less detailed and the legendary element in them predominates over the historical. To be sure, the historical part of the Acts of the Apostles is not free of legend; but it cannot be concluded for this reason that an eyewitness could not have written this also. All ancient history in general, and religious history in particular, must have its miraculous deeds. Thus, for example, the pagan orator Aristides, of the second century C.E., described in all seriousness and innocence the miracles of which he *himself* had been the beneficiary; and these are no less amazing than those related in the Acts of the Apostles.[24]

As we see from clear words in Acts,[25] Luke joined Paul in the city of Alexandria Troas, which belonged to Pergamum as a part of the land of Mysia in the Roman province of Asia. From there he accompanied Paul to the city of Philippi in Macedonia. It would appear that Luke then remained in Philippi some years, and only joined Paul again at the time of Paul's last journey to Jerusalem and Rome. Therefore, Luke could have related at length in the chapters from 20:4 to the end of the book everything which he saw in the course of Paul's last journey, while in the chapters before this he related the events only in brief (the speeches he himself elaborated upon, according to the custom of the writers of that time). What he himself saw, perhaps he noted down in a travel-diary, such as distinguished travelers were accustomed to have kept by one of their companions. In like manner, a famous

[24] See Aimé Puech, *Histoire de la littérature grecque-chrétienne*, I, 388–9.
[25] *Cf.* Acts 2:5, 6 with 16:10–12.

Hellenist (Hermann Diels) has proposed that the *Anabasis* of Xenophon was composed on the basis of such a travel-diary.[26]

What Luke did not see for himself he could have heard from Paul or from the disciples of Paul, who were the companions of Luke also, since Luke was closely associated with Paul for five or six years (in Troas, in Philippi, on the way to Jerusalem, in Caesarea about two years, on the way from Jerusalem to Rome, and in Rome itself about two years). While with Paul in Caesarea he met Philip the Evangelist and his four daughters who prophesied,[27] and he could have heard from them much about the beginning of the Nazarene movement. In Rome he undoubtedly associated with John Mark, disciple of Peter and nephew [cousin] of Barnabas; [28] Mark could have told him everything that had happened to Peter his master and to Barnabas his uncle [cousin]. Luke saw also James the brother of Jesus in Jerusalem,[29] and even from him he could have heard something. All this was information by word of mouth. Yet this does not exclude the possibility that there may already have come into existence written accounts of the beginning of Christianity. If there were such accounts, they could have been in Hebrew or in Aramaic, both of which were spoken and written by the first generation of the disciples of Jesus—Galilean Jews who had seen Jesus and who spoke his language—and their own immediate disciples. Hence the Hebraisms and Aramaisms in chapters 1–15.[30]

But I incline more to oral sources; also by means of them it is possible to explain the Aramaisms in chapters 1–15: James the brother of Jesus, Philip the Evangelist, Barnabas, John Mark, and others—all of them spoke Aramaic; and in Aramaic

[26] See H. von Soden, *Urchristliche Literaturgeschichte*, S. 124.

[27] Acts 21:8.   [28] I Pet. 5:13.   [29] Acts 21:17, 18.

[30] On an Aramaic source specifically insists Torrey, *Composition and Date of Acts* (1916). A Hebrew source is proposed by Nestle, *Expositor* (1895), p. 238.

they related the events of the first years of the development of Christianity, while the numerous Hebraisms are the result of diligent reading of the Septuagint.

5. But there are those who propose that Luke used, besides these sources and his diary (and of course his memory also), two other sources: the Epistles of Paul and the works of Josephus.

A whole literature has been written on the question of the use of these two sources. Many scholars point to the contradictions between what is related in the Acts of the Apostles and what appears from the words of Paul in his Epistles. They point, for instance, to the differences between the vision on the road to Damascus as it is described in the Acts of the Apostles (9:1–30) and the same vision as Paul describes it in the Epistle to the Galatians (1:12–24). And in particular they point to the fact that Paul makes no mention whatever of the "Apostolic Council," and the compromise which was effected between the three "pillars" of the early Church (James, Peter, and John) on the one side, and Paul and Barnabas on the other, in the matter of the reception of Christians from among the Gentiles on condition that they refrain from idolatry, fornication, and the shedding of blood, also the eating of certain forbidden foods, such as the flesh of an animal that has been strangled.[31] Nothing of this is to be found anywhere in the Epistles of Paul, not even in those passages where he speaks of the dispute which he had with the Nazarenes about the observance of the ceremonial laws.[32]

These contradictions are real and are not to be set aside; but I do not think they prove that Luke did not see the principal Epistles of Paul. It cannot be imagined that the com-

[31] Cf. Acts 15:1–29 with 16:4 and 21:25. I shall discuss all this in detail below, in the chapter on the "Apostolic Council."

[32] See Gal. 2:1–10, 15, 16; 3:23–8; 5:1, 2; Rom. ch. 14; I Cor. ch. 8 and 10:18–33.

panion and favorite of Paul took no notice of Paul's most original and distinctive literary compositions. In my opinion, the contradictions between the Acts of the Apostles and the Epistles are to be explained in a simple manner: an ancient writer is not a meticulous modern scholar. The ancients for the most part did not have at hand their sources while they were writing, and they did not hesitate to make changes in the writings of other authors when the changes were not important in their own eyes or when the changes suited the general purpose of their own compositions. Luke heard orally what Paul had done in Jerusalem or he had written sources on this—but he did not investigate the veracity of the reports or of the sources by comparison with the Epistles of Paul. Likewise, Paul in his Epistles mentioned only what was important to him at the time; but the compromise on the matter of the ritual requirements, that the Christians from among the Gentiles were partly free from them and partly obliged to observe them—this, like any compromise, was a thing which a strong personality like Paul accepted only under compulsion and rather unwillingly; therefore, he did not mention it in his Epistles, which are the fervid expression of ideas very dear to him.

Likewise, the description of the "vision on the road to Damascus" must necessarily have been different from the pen of the one who experienced it and from the pen of a writer enthusiastic in his faith and possessed of a talent for description like Luke. On the contrary, one should be surprised at the multitude of things in Acts and in the Epistles that agree, and not at the distinctions and differences between them, which are decidedly natural, like the differences between the figure of Socrates in the Dialogues of Plato and in the Memorabilia of Xenophon. The same vision and event, when described by two writers differing in temperament and talents, even in our generation will necessarily be portrayed quite differently; in ancient times, when scholarly exactness was not customary at all, would it not be the case all the more? Indeed, the author of Acts himself speaks three times of the Damascus-road vision; [33] and in all three of them there are recognizable differences. Even if we say that the author of Acts drew information from three different sources—which is difficult to suppose in view of the many similarities in the three versions—we are still prone to ask why the author did not take the pains to make his three versions agree absolutely with each other. The answer is, necessarily, that the ancients were not so scrupulous and exact in details, and did not take pains to quote the words of others with the exactness of a modern scholar.

I think the same view correct with regard to Luke's use of the works of Josephus.

In the speech of Rabban Gamaliel at the time of the trial of Peter before the Sanhedrin in Jerusalem it is said:

> For before these days rose up Theudas, giving himself out to be somebody; [34] to whom a number of men, about four hundred, joined themselves; he was slain, and all, as many as obeyed him, were dispersed, and came to nought. *After this man* rose up Judas of Galilee in the days of the enrolment, and drew away some of the people after him: he also perished; and all, as many as obeyed him, were scattered abroad. [35]

This is in general the story which is found in the second work of Josephus, [36] which was not published before 94 C.E. But there are differences. *First*, according to Acts, Judas of Galilee arose some time after Theudas; but according to Josephus, Judas of Galilee preceded Theudas by a considerable period, since Theudas was active during the time that Cuspius Fadus was procurator in Judea (about 44–46 C.E.), while Judas of

---

[33] Acts 9:3–9; 21:6–11; 26:12–18.

[34] *I.e.*, an important personage; the speaker or author was not willing to give him the title of "Messiah" because of the sacredness of that title.

[35] Acts 5:36, 37.   [36] *Antiq.* XX v 1 (§§ 97–8).

Galilee was active in the time of the "enrolment" (census) of
Quirinius, a short time after the death of Herod.[37] *Secondly*,
Josephus speaks of a "great multitude" which Theudas "persuaded," and this does not agree with the number of "about
four hundred."

But if we suppose what I said, that Luke did not examine
the *Antiquities of the Jews* at the time when he wrote his own
account, but wrote it from memory, these two differences
will not be so decisive. Rightly does the distinguished scholar
Hermann Dessau say: "In my opinion, too much commotion
has been raised over a lapse of memory or a slip of the tongue
of the speaker or reporter, in the words 'After this man' in
verse 37" (Acts 5:37).[38] I have already attempted to make
clear in another place that Rabban Gamaliel did not say this;
but that Luke, who loved to create a general historical framework for Christian events, was the one who introduced these
two historical figures *parenthetically* into the speech of Rabban Gamaliel, just as a historian in our day would introduce
such items in parentheses or in a footnote.[39]

The second item which is found both in Acts and in a
work of Josephus is the death of Herod Agrippa I.[40] Now
here the similarity is much greater. Both of them mention the
"royal apparel," both of them speak of the sycophants who
hailed Agrippa as a god, and both of them speak of a disease
of the intestines ("he was eaten of worms and gave up the
ghost").

The third item shared by both of them has to do with the
time of the riots in the Temple against Paul, when the Roman
military tribune said to Paul:

[37] *Antiq.* XVII x 5 (§§ 271–2). Because of this difference, various scholars
have supposed that there were two rebels by the name of Theudas! (See
A. T. Robertson, *Luke the Historian*, pp. 169–71.)

[38] See H. Dessau, *Geschichte der römischen Kaiserzeit*, II, 2, 785.

[39] See for details Klausner, *Historia*, III, 251; IV, 3 and 4.

[40] *Antiq.* XIX viii 2 (§§ 343–50); Acts 12:21–23.

Art thou not then the Egyptian, who before these days stirred up to sedition and led out into the wilderness the four thousand men of the Assassins? [41]

About this "Egyptian prophet" Josephus speaks in his two principal works.[42] In the *Jewish War* it is said that "the Egyptian" gathered together 30,000 men; this, of course, does not agree with the number 4000 in Acts; but in the *Antiquities* it is said that of those who followed the "Egyptian" 400 men were slain and 200 taken alive,[43] and by a lapse of memory or a copyist's error this became 4000 men. There is still another possibility. Luke himself may have supposed that if 400 men were slain, then the number of those following the Egyptian must have been about 4000 men.

Finally, there is a fourth item, which is found both in the *Antiquities* and in Acts. This is the information about the famine in the days of Claudius Caesar.[44] This item agrees completely with the story of Josephus, that a famine occurred in Judea in the days of the procurator Tiberius Alexander, the years of whose rule (about 46–48) correspond to the years of the rule of Claudius Caesar (41–54). But here there is no necessity of concluding that Luke drew this information from the book of Josephus. This famine (or drought) occurred during the childhood of Luke (even if he was much younger than Paul), and he could have remembered it or have heard about it from Paul and Barnabas and their disciples.

6. It cannot be denied that in the three principal historical items which are shared by Luke and Josephus there are appreciable differences. Therefore, various scholars, led by Harnack, have concluded that the time of the composition of

[41] Acts 21:38.

[42] *Jewish War* II xiii 5; *Antiq.* XX viii 6.

[43] I erroneously wrote "four thousand" in place of "four hundred" in *Historia*, IV, 23 and in *Yeshu*, p. 11 [Eng. ed., p. 21].

[44] *Antiq.* XX ii 5 (§§ 51–3) and XX v 2 (§ 101); Acts 11:28.

the Acts of the Apostles does not depend upon the publication of the *Antiquities of the Jews* by Josephus (about 94 C.E.); so they put back the composition of the former to the years 63–64 or 70 C.E. If the only evidence of the late date of Acts were its dependence upon the *Antiquities*, it would be possible for these scholars to maintain their opinion. But in the last analysis it is nearer to the truth, that Luke drew his historical items from the *Antiquities*, but did with this book what he was accustomed to do with the Epistles of Paul; that is to say, he made use of it from memory without the exactness characteristic of scholars. But this is not the only reason for bringing down the composition of Acts to the last ten years of the first Christian century. The most weighty reason which forces us to date it late is that all the contents and characteristics of Acts bear witness to a time when the first events of the rise of Christianity appeared to the author as the happenings of a more or less remote period—a period which had already come to an end, and around which had been formed legends and miracle stories, while historical events which had occurred in it were dim and obscure. In short, the whole spirit of the Acts of the Apostles is not that of a book written immediately after the occurrence of events which are still fresh in the mind of the author. We have already seen that in relating even the latest events, the author was obliged to quote from the diary, because he did not any longer remember them well.

Now I come to the author's attitude to Peter and Paul. Evidently, the author of Acts has an inclination to Paul and to Paul's ideas, and he sets great store by Paul's deeds. Nevertheless, he does not refrain from praising Peter, and pointing out that Peter was, if not the first, at least one of the first who attempted to spread Christianity among the pagans. There is in his words hardly a sign of the sharp conflict between Paul and the early church at Jerusalem led by James the brother of Jesus—the conflict which shook the very fiber of the soul of Paul even many years later as he wrote the Epistle to the Galatians. The author pictures the beginning of dissemination of Christianity among the Gentiles not as the great and revolutionary accomplishment of Paul alone, but as the work of the heads of the Jerusalem church, who were scattered far and wide after the death of Stephen. The author does not feel—and does not wish to emphasize—the *internal* conflict between the first Christians; he lays great emphasis only upon their conflict with *outsiders*. Within, dissension is arbitrated and mediated, bitterness is removed, and everything becomes more or less smooth; both sides are good, both are right. This is trustworthy evidence that the Acts of the Apostles was *not* written during the years 63–70. It *was* written during the years 94–96. Thirty years before this the conflicts leading to these compromises and concessions had not yet been settled.

There is still further trustworthy evidence.

Luke was, of course, a Greek Christian; nevertheless, to a man writing in the year 63 or even in the year 70, that is to say, before the destruction of the Second Temple or in its time, it would be impossible to take such an attitude as Luke does toward the Jews and the Romans. For the whole book is saturated with one "ruling idea," the beginning of which is already to be found even in the Gospel according to Mark, although it does not come to extreme expression until in Acts. This idea is that *the Jews are the source of evil*. They persecute the Christians and slander them before the Roman authorities; and these authorities are charitably inclined toward the Christians and do not inhibit Christianity except under pressure from the Jews. Emphatic hate like this would not have been possible in 63–70, when Palestinian Jewry was still a great power in the land and when primitive Jewish Christianity still had a decisive influence. This hate could have found such sharp expression only in the years 94–96, when Judaism had to a great extent lost its importance in the Roman Empire, when Domitian had begun to persecute Judaism and Christianity alike and there was need to emphasize the difference between them, and when primitive Jewish Christianity had passed away and given place to Gentile Christianity, the face of which was of course turned toward Rome, which was both pagan and powerful. . . .

Out of these circumstances many scholars explain the abrupt ending of the Acts of the Apostles.

The book ends with the coming of Paul as a prisoner to Rome. He lived there two years in a private house which he hired for himself, and a Roman soldier guarded him. In spite of this supervision he "received all that went in unto him, preaching the kingdom of God, and teaching the things concerning the Lord Jesus Christ with all boldness, none forbidding him" (end of book). This is not a natural ending for a book in which Paul is the principal character; we should expect the book to tell what finally happened to him. This deficiency of Acts is explained by some thus: Paul was killed, according to tradition, in the persecution of Christians in the time of Nero, or, possibly, the sentence of death was imposed when his appeal was heard by the emperor; this fact did not suit the purpose of Luke, who intended to show that the Romans took a tolerant attitude toward the Christians and only the Jews persecuted them; therefore he did not finish his history of Paul, which really came to an end with his unnatural death at the hands of the Romans.

There is still another opinion. Perhaps Luke, who intended to relate the successes of the "good news"—the rapid spread of Christianity in the whole expanse of the Roman Empire— did not wish to close with a failure—with the martyrdom of Paul in a time of severe persecution of the Christians in the principal city of that very empire.

Some think that because the author wrote, according to those favoring an early date, in the year 63 while Paul was still alive, Luke had no reason to close his book otherwise than with the coming of Paul to Rome and the first years of his stay there. But against this latter opinion stands the statement that Paul "abode *two whole years* in his own hired dwelling, and received all that went in unto him." [45] If Luke mentioned *exactly* the number of years Paul lived in Rome, it is an indication that he also knew what came after these two years. Therefore I am inclined to suppose, with the Dutch scholar de Zwaan,[46] that the Acts of the Apostles was published after the death of its author as a book which the author began but never finished. Indeed, if Luke is the author of Acts and was the companion of Paul from Alexandria Troas and Philippi on—and afterwards to Jerusalem and Rome, and if he wrote Acts not before the years 94–96 C.E., as I have tried to prove above, then he was already a very old man, and perhaps was not able to finish his book, it being stopped short by his death.[47] To be sure, the book gives an impression of having been revised in most of its parts; but it is possible that whoever published it also edited it more or less. By means of this hypothesis it is also possible to explain the inconsistencies in different parts of the book: the author was not able to revise and finish all parts to an equal degree. By this means it is also possible to explain the introduction of fragments from the diary in order to complete what was lacking without any special revision, and even without the change from the first person to the third.

At any rate, with all the defects in the Acts of the Apostles

[45] Acts 28:30.

[46] See J. de Zwaan, "Was the Book of Acts a Posthumous Edition?" *Harvard Theol. Rev.*, XVII (1924), 95–153.

[47] Why H. von Soden, *Urchristliche Literaturgeschichte*, S. 117, thinks such a hypothesis "a vain phantasy" I do not know. Are there not numerous cases of important books which have not been finished by their authors owing to circumstances beyond their authors' control?

and with all the caution which it is necessary to observe with this book, as with any book which has a distinctly religious purpose when we attempt to use it for historical needs, there is yet in it very important material for the history of the rise of Christianity; without this material we should be groping in darkness with regard to the short period between the crucifixion of Jesus and the time when Paul came into prominence, and with regard to the longer period in which the lifework of Paul was realized and established.

CHAPTER II

The Epistles of Paul

[See on this: E. Renan, Saint-Paul, XIIIème éd., Paris 1893, pp. III–
LXXVII (Introduction); H. von Soden, Urchristliche Literaturgeschichte,
Berlin 1905, SS. 11–60, 145–68; P. Wendland, Die hellenistisch-römische
Kultur, SS. 342–67; M. Dibelius, Die Briefe des Apostels Paulus an die
Kolosser, Epheser, an Philemon, Tübingen 1912; D. A. Hayes, Paul and His
Epistles, New York-Cincinnati, 1915, pp. 69–482; A. Schweitzer, Geschichte
der paulinischen Forschung, 1933; H. Lietzmann, Zur Würdigung des Ches-
ter Beatty-Papyrus der Paulusbriefe, Berlin 1934 (Sitzungsberichte der
Preussischen Akademie der Wissenschaften, Phil.-hist. Klasse, 1934, XXV,
11); Ed. Meyer, Ursprung und Anfänge des Christentums, III, 116–500;
Aimé Puech, Histoire de la littérature grecque chrétienne, I, 175–328; H.
Delafosse, Les ècrits de Saint-Paul, I–IV, Paris, 1928; A. Omodeo, Prolego-
meni alla Storia dell' Età Apostolica, pp. 121–370; G. H. Gilbert, Greek
Thought in the New Testament, pp. 62–100; G. L. Hurst, The Literary
Background of the New Testament, New York 1928, pp. 64–70; M. van
Rhyn, Treasures of the Dust, Eng. Tr., London 1929, pp. 109–16.]

1. In the New Testament are found thirteen Epistles
(letters) attributed to Paul: to the Romans, to the Corinthians
I and II, to the Galatians, to the Ephesians, to the Philippians,
to the Colossians, to the Thessalonians I and II, to Timothy
I and II, to Titus, and to Philemon. The two addressed to
Timothy with the one addressed to Titus are called "Pastoral
Epistles" because they contain much advice as to how the
"pastors" are to lead the churches. The early Alexandrian
church (Clement, Origen, et al.) and the Western church
from the fourth century onward attributed to Paul also the
Epistle to the Hebrews, but without good reason. The author
of this Epistle includes in it many of the ideas of Philo of
Alexandria, and in its views and manner of expressing them
there is not much similarity to the ideas of Paul. The thirteen
Pauline Epistles have the general name "Apostolic."

Paul himself, in one of his letters,[1] requests the readers that "after this epistle hath been read" by them, they "cause that it be read also in the church of the Laodiceans," and that they, the first readers of the letter, shall "also read the epistle from Laodicea." In an Epistle attributed to Peter [2] "all the epistles" of Paul are already mentioned. Clement of Rome (of the time of Domitian), Ignatius of Syria (Antioch), and Polycarp —all of them of the second generation of Gentile Christianity —know the Epistles of Paul and mention them. Marcion, who rejected the Old Testament and recognized only the Pauline conception of Christianity, arranged in order the first (or the first known to us) Christian "Canon" a short time after 140 C.E. In this there is the *Apostolicon*, which includes only *ten* Epistles of Paul, as follows: Galatians, I and II Corinthians, Romans, I and II Thessalonians, Laodiceans, Colossians, Philippians, and Philemon. The Pastoral Epistles (I and II Timothy and Titus) are lacking here; and in place of the Epistle to the Ephesians there is an Epistle "to the Laodiceans." [3] In contrast to this, the apologist Tatian published [3a] all thirteen Epistles of Paul about 160–170. In the Muratorian Fragment [4] thirteen Epistles of Paul are mentioned—nine to churches and four to individuals.

It may be remarked first of all, that the Epistles of Paul are undoubtedly actual letters. That is to say, they are not mere essays and treatises written in the *form* of letters and intended for publication from the beginning (like, for example, the letters at the beginning of II Maccabees, or most of the letters of Seneca); instead, they are actual letters in form and in spirit. This fact is shown by the concern with numerous personal details in each letter, the greetings to disciples, helpers, and friends at the end of almost every letter, and the like.

[1] Col. 4:16. [2] II Pet. 3:15, 16.
[3] See Tertullian, *Contra Marcionem* V 11 and 17.
[3a] [Or attempted to revise; see Eusebius, *Hist. Eccl.* IV 29 6. Tr.]
[4] See on this fragment above, p. 209.

But we have already seen that Paul requested the Colossians to read the letter to the Laodiceans and to transmit for reading to the latter the letter addressed to them, the Colossians.[5] Thus we see that Paul intended to make his letters more or less public—at least in the Christian churches. And indeed the deep investigations and the important religious discussions in all his Epistles do lift these Epistles above the level of private letters and enhance their value as religio-philosophical treatises that are high in quality and sometimes (as, *e.g.*, in Romans) not inconsiderable in quantity. Even in the smallest and most personal letter of Paul which we have, the Epistle to Philemon, there are religious ideas which have general value. Because of these facts, not only were the letters of Paul to churches and to individuals kept, but they were circulated, perhaps even in the lifetime of Paul, and at any rate shortly after his death, in all the Christian congregations, especially in those of the Gentile Christians; and by the year 200 they were the common heritage of the whole Christian Church.

2. Until the beginning of the nineteenth century, when F. Schleiermacher published his book *On the So-called First Epistle of Paul to Timothy*,[6] no scholar had dared deny to Paul as a whole any Epistle which had been attributed to him by the tradition of the Christian Church.[7] Only after the "Tübingen School," led by Ferdinand Christian Baur, had come and taught that in almost the whole Christian "Canon" are to be sought traces of the great conflict between primitive

[5] See above, p. 234.

[6] See F. E. D. Schleiermacher, *Ueber den sogenannten ersten Brief des Paulus an Timotheus* (Berlin 1807).

[7] J. H. Semler (*Abhandlung von freier Untersuchung des Canons*, 4 Bände, 1771–75) dared only to conclude that certain chapters and verses in the Epistles of Paul are not in their proper places, and that the Epistles are not in the form in which they left the hands of Paul; the Church reworked them in order to make them more suitable for liturgical reading. See A. Schweitzer, *Geschichte der Paulinischen Forschung* (1933), SS. 3–5.

Jewish Christianity and Gentile Christianity, and hence that only the first four Epistles attributed to Paul in the New Testament are to be considered absolutely authentic [8]—only then arose the German Bruno Bauer, the Swiss Rudolf Steck, and particularly the "Dutch School" (Allard Pierson, W. C. Van Manen, A. D. Loman) to deny the genuineness of all "Pauline Epistles." All the Epistles of Paul are, in their opinion, nothing more than compositions from the beginning of the second century C.E., near the time of Marcion, written by members of *the Gnostic sects*. In order to gain toleration and support for the new ideas of the Gnostics, these sectaries forged letters of an anti-Nazarene character (that is, opposed to primitive Jewish Christianity). These letters were addressed to churches and individuals, and were attributed to "Paul the Apostle," *who perhaps never existed at all*, and if he did, the picture of him found in the Epistles should not be accepted, but rather, that found in Acts.[9]

This completely negative attitude toward all the Pauline Epistles has not been accepted by the vast majority of Christian scholars. A great and unique personality speaks from such Epistles as Romans, Galatians, and I and II Corinthians, and they corroborate much of what we know of Paul from Acts. Hence too extreme is the claim that letters like these, with all their greatness and originality, with all the fine and powerful emotion which is revealed in them, and with all the biographical details which are found in them, are mere forgeries. The biographical details have in them no trace of falseness, and there is no satisfactory explanation of how or why they could have been forged at such a late date.

But although almost all scholars reject the claim that all the Pauline Epistles are spurious, that does not prevent many

[8] See Schweitzer, *op. cit.*, SS. 10–7; Paul Feine, *Der Apostel Paulus* (Gütersloh 1927), SS. 13–20.

[9] See Schweitzer, *op. cit.*, SS. 92–111; P. Feine, *op. cit.*, SS. 25–30; A. Omodeo, *Prolegomeni alla Storia dell' Età Apostolica*, pp. 121–37.

from casting doubt upon the authenticity of certain Epistles. We have already seen that *Baur* himself (who must be distinguished from *Bauer*, who rejected all), when he came to describe the life and teaching of Paul, relied upon the four principal Epistles only: Romans, I and II Corinthians, and Galatians. He considered the Pastorals spurious. The rest of the Epistles he left "in need of examination." [10] But the scholars following the Tübingen School removed from any suspicion both Philippians and I Thessalonians, and left II Thessalonians, Colossians, and Ephesians "in need of examination," while in the opinion of the majority of these scholars the Pastorals were undoubtedly spurious. [11] More recently, thanks particularly to the detailed researches of Adolf Harnack, [12] who is sometimes perhaps too conservative, an affirmative attitude has been taken toward some of the Epistles which were formerly regarded as spurious, or at least doubtful. But even the scholars who are less conservative and more daring than Harnack have removed Colossians from any suspicion, and have left as doubtful II Thessalonians, while considering both the Pastorals and Ephesians as spurious. [13]

On what grounds do the doubters and deniers base their doubts and denials?

3. With regard to II Thessalonians, doubt as to its authenticity has been expressed for two reasons: *first*, it repeats what is written in I Thessalonians, but without the warmth of feeling found in I Thessalonians; *second*, in II Thessalonians 2:1-12 the Day of the Lord and the coming of the Messiah are mentioned in connexion with "he that opposeth" and "the

[10] See above, p. 236.
[11] See for details on this P. Wendland, *op. cit.*, SS. 358–67.
[12] See *e.g.*, A. Harnack, "Das Problem des Zweiten Thessalonicherbriefes" (*Sitzungsberichte der Berliner Akademie*, 1910).
[13] So thinks, *e.g.*, Ed. Meyer, *Ursprung und Anfänge des Christentums*, III, 132–4; 368–75; 482–9; 587–91.

lawless one," that is, the Antichrist, while in I Thessalonians
5:2 it is said that the end "will come as a thief in the night"—
hence very suddenly.[14]

In my opinion, there is no need of the hypothesis of Harnack, that the second letter was written to a congregation of
Jewish Christians that existed in Thessalonica, while the first
was addressed to the Gentile Christian congregation there, this
latter congregation being nearer to the heart of Paul.[15] The
matter seems to me much simpler. If a person writes two letters one after the other in the space of a short time, because
some problem which formerly appeared not so pressing (in
this case, the coming of the Messiah and the resurrection of
the dead) has become meanwhile a "burning" issue, then of
course he will repeat part of what he wrote before and repeat
it without the warmth of feeling which was present in the
first writing. This is common in any collection of letters in
which there are two letters on one subject separated by only
a short space of time.[16]

As regards the difference in the view of "the End" in the
two letters, verily the time has arrived when we must cease
to regard Paul, and also the ancients in general, whether
prophets of Israel or sages of Greece, as professors of philosophy or research scholars. Paul was a man of unusual temperament—intense and emotional and acrid. It is inevitable that
a man like this, in a time of excitement, in anger, or in a
flight of imagination, should experience changes of opinion
that would flash into his mind in a moment of intense
thought. And in general, who knows what changes may
come about in the mind of a man in one day or even in one
hour?

Here is one example out of a thousand, which occurs to me

[14] See W. Wrede, *Die Echtheit des* II. *Thessaloniker-Briefes* (*Texte und Untersuchungen*, XXIV, 2, Leipzig 1903).

[15] See A. Harnack, *op. cit.*

[16] See Ed. Meyer, *op. cit.*, III, 370, Anm. 1.

by chance at this moment: The great Theodor Herzl, founder of the Zionist movement, which has renewed the strength and spirit of the Jewish people and brought about the National Home in Palestine, wrote a letter on August 1, 1896 to David Wolffsohn, in which he speaks about the calling together of a *general* Zionist conference ("Einberufung eines allgemeinen Zionistentages"), in which the masses should participate and which should be the result of democratic organization; but on the next day, August 2, same year, he wrote to the Parisian rabbi, Zadok Kahn, that he agreed to a "secret conference" of notables, which is the reverse of any democratic gathering.[17] This is an open and outstanding contradiction in the course of two days; and if it were not for the fact that we can recognize Herzl's handwriting, and if Herzl had lived not in our time but two thousand years ago, then undoubtedly scholars and researchers would come to the conclusion that whoever wrote to Wolffsohn did not write to Zadok Kahn or that someone forged the letters of Herzl. And so, can we not say that Paul, in spite of his greatness, or even because of his greatness, was a tempestuous and emotional man, whose thinking was subject to conflict and change?—

"II Thessalonians does not have the warmheartedness of I Thessalonians"—and what of it? Is a great man always in one frame of mind, and do his literary creations always stand on the same level? If we did not know for certain that the great Goethe, the classicist, the Homerid, the superb artist, wrote both the very romantic and impassioned composition entitled *Die Leiden des jungen Werthers* and also something of lesser artistic value called *Der Grosskophtha*—it would not occur to any scholar or investigator to attribute two works so different from the rest of the works of Goethe to the great master himself.

Can there be such absolute unity in the soul of any man?

[17] See *Theodor Herzls Tagebücher* (Berlin 1922), I, 513-4.

The poetry of the great Sephardic Hebrew poet, R. Solomon ben Gabirol (Avicebron), and particularly the splendid poem *Royal Crown*—is full of religious fervor and divine mysteries, because it is based almost entirely on the Old Testament, the Talmud, and the *Book of Creation*; and his book *The Improvement of the Moral Qualities* is replete with Biblical verses and quotations from all Hebrew literature before him. Yet that same Solomon ben Gabirol wrote a philosophical book called *Fountain of Life (Fons Vitae)*, which contains in all five of its lengthy "divisions" hardly a single poetical expression, not one verse from the Scriptures, nor is there mentioned in it the name of a prophet or Tanna; and in spite of the pantheistic-poetic character of its contents, there is in it not a trace of anything written by any one of the great Hebrew poets of previous times.

An example of a different kind is provided by Emile Zola, the extreme "naturalist," author of *Le Ventre de Paris*. He arose one bright morning and wrote the novel *Le Rêve*, which is all imagination and romance; and he wrote this novel not in his youth, "while a young man uttering words of song," but in the year 1889, when he was almost fifty years old; moreover, he did this in the midst of his completely naturalistic writing, in the period when he was composing the Rougon-Macquart series, *La Bête humaine*, *L'Argent*, and the like. . . . Is the mind of a man really so simple and always so thoroughly in accord with itself?—

Human beings can vary from time to time, as well as manifest conflicting tendencies at the same time. Who could have supposed, for instance, that the great Hebrew storyteller Shalom Jacob Abramovitz, having written in his youth *Fathers and Sons*, *Natural History*, and *Luaḥ ha-Soḥarim*, would be prepared to write in his old age, under the pseudonym Mendelé Mocher Sefarim (Mendelé the Bookseller), the novel *The Vale of Weeping*, which is separated by a chasm in both content and form from the earlier compositions?—

I do not mean by this to deny the great importance of scholarly investigation of sources and meticulous critical analysis. Undoubtedly, critical and analytical study often finds evidence that writings which tradition puts much earlier are in fact comparatively late. But much caution is needed here. It must always be remembered that a man, and especially a great man, is not such a simple and easily understandable organism. He is not always unified and constant, nor do his occasional outward expressions always correspond to the *totality* of his nature, which we learn by continuous and more general observations. Man experiences changes and variations in different periods of his life, and even in one period of life he is not a perfect unity.

Therefore, far be it from us to doubt the authenticity of a Pauline Epistle and to deny it to Paul, whose general views and usual attitudes we know, simply because it has a different tone, or because it is written in a different style, or even because it reveals an unusual view or a different degree of talent from that found in the rest of the Epistles of Paul. If there were not other reasons to deny, for example, the "Second Epistle of Peter" to the well-known apostle Simon Cephas, I would not deny it to him merely because there is mentioned in it "our beloved brother Paul" and "all his epistles," [18] although we know that there was a sharp conflict between Peter and Paul. More than once it has happened in our own times and according to our own observation, that two notables who had quarreled over religious matters afterwards made peace, and in the course of time the one opponent came to admire and praise the other. The first antagonist may have experienced a radical change of opinion, or—if his opinion remained the same—the intensity of his feeling abated, and

[18] II Pet. 3:15, 16.

he saw that there was some ground for another opinion. Time brings together those who were far apart, just as it separates those who had been close.

From this point of view, just as it is difficult for me to agree to the late dating of certain sections of the Old Testament, so it is difficult for me to accept the late dating of various Greek and Latin works and Pauline Epistles. In my opinion, not only does II Thessalonians belong to Paul, but even the Epistle to the Ephesians, which very many scholars consider absolutely spurious.[19] This denial of the Epistle to Paul is based on the following fundamental claims:

(a) From certain verses in the Epistle,[20] it would appear that Paul did not know personally the people for whom the letter was intended, in spite of the fact that we learn definitely from Acts that Paul spent much time in Ephesus and knew the Ephesian congregation. I myself have already mentioned above [21] that Marcion's Canon substitutes an "Epistle to the Laodiceans" for Ephesians.

(b) In the Epistle it is mentioned that the Church was "built upon the foundation of the apostles and prophets"; and in general there is an excessive emphasis on the importance of the Church,[22] which is an idea too advanced for Paul.

(c) The style of the Epistle is heavier and more involved than is usual in the rest of the Pauline Epistles.

(d) There is a number of similarities between the Epistle to the Colossians and the Epistle to the Ephesians.[23]

All these arguments are important and worthy of consideration, but they are not decisive. For, in the last analysis, Ephe-

[19] See H. von Soden, *op. cit.*, SS. 145–55; P. Wendland, *op. cit.*, SS. 361–64; A. Omodeo, *op. cit.*, pp. 323–36; M. Dibelius, *Die Briefe des Apostels Paulus an die Kolosser* (Handkommentar zum Neuen Testament, herausg. v. H. Lietzmann, Band III, 2, Tübingen 1912), SS. 96–7, 113–4; Van Rhyn, *Treasures of the Dust*, pp. 112–4.

[20] Eph. I:15; 3:2; 4:21.

[21] See above, p. 234.   [22] **Eph.** 2:20; see also 3:5.

[23] *Cf.*, *e.g.*, Col. 3:18–4:1 with Eph. 5:21–6:9.

sians contains genuine Pauline ideas.[24] Perhaps the Epistle received in the course of time an incorrect address ("Ephesians" instead of "Laodiceans"); or it may have been a "circular letter" to various churches whose members Paul did not know personally; the Ephesians may have somehow received the letter, and may have copied it, so that by chance their name became attached to it. These possibilities are no harder to imagine than it is to suppose that some forger, a disciple of Paul, so immersed himself in the study of the Epistle to the Colossians that he learned to write in the idiom of Paul and found occasion to forge (for what purpose is not clear) the following words:

But that ye may also know my affairs, how I do, Tychicus, the beloved brother and faithful minister in the Lord, shall make known to you all things: whom I have sent unto you for this very purpose, that ye may know our state, and that he may comfort your hearts.[25]

As regards the mention of "the apostles and prophets" and the emphasis on the importance of the Church, is it not possible that Paul, the prisoner in Rome [26] toward the end of his life, knew how to appreciate the apostles and the Church better than did the young and pugnacious Paul or even the middle-aged Paul whom we find in the rest of his Epistles?

And as regards style and repetitions, I have already remarked that nobody writes letters that are always equal in originality and literary quality, and that different letters of

[24] See Ed. Meyer *Ursprung u. Anfänge*, III, 482–3. A. Omodeo (*op. cit.*, pp. 323–36), who considers Ephesians spurious, is forced to confess that "if we examine one point after another, we shall hardly find an idea of which one can say with certainty that it is not Pauline" (p. 334). Aimé Puech (*op. cit.*, I, 262–8) doubts the authenticity of Ephesians, although he presents refutations of all arguments against it. See also A. Harnack, "Die Addresse des Epheserbriefes des Paulus" (*Berichte der Berliner Akademie*, 1910, SS. 696 ff.).

[25] Eph. 6:21, 22.   [26] Eph. 4:1; 6:9.

the same man reveal his skill and style to a different degree. Even repetitions are inevitable when a man having one all-important idea writes to *different* churches, many of which are in need of the *same* instructions.

Therefore, I cannot see sufficient reason why we are forced to consider the Epistle to the Ephesians unauthentic.

This is not to say that all the Pauline Epistles which have been handed down and received as such have come to us exactly as they went forth from the pen of Paul. Undoubtedly they contain words, phrases, verses, and perhaps even certain sections which have been changed or added by disciples and copyists. But in deciding about additions and partial falsifications extreme caution is necessary. It must always be remembered that Paul was not a philosopher of religion or a rationalistic theologian who had a system that was reasoned through and homogeneous in all its parts. Like any person of deeply religious and mystical nature, who is an enigma not only to others but above all to himself, Paul was strange and unusual in his thinking, possessed of strong emotions, and given to sudden flashes of intuition and mystical experiences, for which it was difficult to find clear and logical means of expression. At the same time, he was constantly striving for systematization and clarification in order to hold his influence over all the members of the young churches which he had founded.

In dealing with a man like this, we must be very cautious about denying the authenticity of any letter with regard to which we have ancient witness that it belongs to him, merely because it is not like the rest of his letters or does not agree with what is related about him in the Acts of the Apostles.

4. It is different with the "Pastoral Epistles": I and II Timothy, and Titus.

First of all, these three Epistles are not included in the Canon of Marcion although all the rest of the Pauline Epistles are included.[27] This is, in my opinion, weighty "negative evidence" against the Pastorals. Of course, it is possible to explain this lack of the Pastoral Epistles in the Canon of Marcion on the grounds that they are opposed to Gnosticism, to which Marcion adhered.[28] Nevertheless, if Marcion had thought these three Epistles to be Pauline, we should find in the fragments of his works or the works of his fellow sectaries arguments against them—something which is not to be found in any book concerned with the refutation of Marcion and the Marcionites which quotes their writings.

But, apart from this, there are in the two Epistles to Timothy and the Epistle to Titus a number of "facts," which are disturbing to our minds because they do not agree with what we know of the life and works of Paul. Thus, for example, it is mentioned in one of these Epistles that Paul left Titus in Crete and that Paul, having afterwards decided to spend the winter in Nicopolis, requested Titus to make haste and join him there.[29] But from Acts and from the rest of the Epistles of Paul we cannot find time or opportunity for visits in Crete and Nicopolis.

According to another letter, Paul requested Timothy to remain at Ephesus while he, Paul himself, went to Macedonia.[30] But according to Acts, when Paul left Ephesus to go to Macedonia, Timothy accompanied him on his way; and we do not hear that Timothy remained in Ephesus to serve the Christian church there.[31]

In one letter Paul speaks of his journey to Rome "that through me the message might be fully proclaimed, and that all the Gentiles might hear: and I was delivered out of the mouth of the lion";[32] and in the same passage he says, "but Trophimus I left at Miletus sick."[33] But we know from an-

[27] See above, p. 234.
[28] I Tim. 6:20, ". . . the knowledge which is falsely so called."
[29] Titus 1:5 and 3:12.
[30] I Tim. 1:3.
[31] Acts 20:1–4.
[32] II Tim. 4:17.
[33] II Tim. 4:20.

other source that Paul accompanied by Trophimus visited Miletus on the way to Jerusalem and not to Rome. Moreover, all the troubles which Paul had in Jerusalem came about because the Jews of Asia saw the uncircumcised "Trophimus the Ephesian" associating with Paul in Jerusalem, and "supposed that Paul had brought (him) into the temple."[34] Erastus, who in Acts is sent with Timothy from Corinth [Ephesus?] to Macedonia,[35] here is left behind at Corinth;[36] and Tychicus, who in Colossians is sent with Onesimus to Colossae,[37] here is sent to Ephesus.[38]

To explain all these inconsistencies, certain scholars have proposed the "hypothesis of the second imprisonment," of which there are already hints in some of the Church Fathers.[39] This hypothesis is that Paul was released from the imprisonment in Rome known to us from Acts and went "to the utmost bounds of the West," that is, fulfilled the desire of his heart to go to Spain and spread Christianity there;[40] afterwards, he was again in the East and there he wrote the *First* Epistle to Timothy and the Epistle to Titus; then he was taken a second time as a prisoner to Rome, and during this second imprisonment he indited the *Second* Epistle to Timothy; finally, he was killed in Rome along with Peter during the persecution of Christians by Nero.

All this is only an imaginative hypothesis without any real foundation whatever. The desire of Paul to go to Spain[41] was taken by the Church Fathers to mean that Paul actually went to Spain. No trustworthy source tells us that Paul was imprisoned twice, having been released the first time. And his being killed along with Peter at the time of the Neronic persecution

---

[34] Acts 20:4 and 21:29.　　　[35] Acts 19:22.
[36] II Tim. 4:20.　　　[37] Col. 4:7-9.
[38] II Tim. 4:12. See for further details on this H. von Soden, *op. cit.*, SS. 159-60.
[39] See Eusebius, *Hist. Eccl.*, II, 22, §§ 162-4 (journey to Spain not mentioned here); I Clem. ad Cor. 5:5, 6.
[40] Rom. 15:24, 28.　　　[41] *Loc. cit.*

is at most a plausible hypothesis.[42] Yet without the "hypothesis of the second imprisonment" it is impossible to reconcile all these contradictions between what we find in Acts and the rest of the Pauline Epistles, on the one hand, and what is told in the Pastorals, on the other. Does not all this cast a shadow of doubt upon these three Epistles?—

Also, the content and style are different in these Epistles from what they are in the rest of the Pauline Epistles. First of all—the *style*. It lacks the depth and power of expression found in the rest of the Epistles. Moreover, the Pastorals contain scores of words which are not found in the other Epistles (74 in I Timothy, 46 in II Timothy, and 48 in Titus). Thus, for example, we find ἐπιφάνεια ("epiphany") instead of παρουσία ("parousia"). Here are found for the first time the word νεόφυτος ("neophyte"), and the expression Σωτὴρ ἡμῶν Θεός ("God our Saviour"), which is repeated six times in these Epistles. There are other instances like these.[43] Hence an expert in Hellenistic Greek testifies that the whole vocabulary of the Pastoral Epistles is "un-Pauline." [44]

I have already pointed out above that a writer or thinker in his old age can hold ideas and use expressions different from those of his youth. For this reason, no decision can be made on the basis of ideas and style alone. But the *basic content* of the Pastoral Epistles indicates a time later than the sixties of the first century.

The three Epistles before us are noteworthy for two special characteristics. *First*, they are greatly concerned with fixed forms in the Church. The impression is that we now have before us a Church in which an end has already come to the first excitement of enthusiastic people, who dreamed dreams, saw visions, "spoke with tongues" hysterically, and prophesied—their influence upon the surrounding pagans

[42] See Ed. Meyer, *Ursprung u. Anfänge*, III, 131–2.
[43] See on this in detail D. A. Hayes, *Paul and His Epistles*, pp. 451–2.
[44] See Wendland, *op. cit.*, SS. 364–5; also A. Omodeo, *op. cit.*, pp. 359–60.

coming from hearts burning with zeal for the new religion. Here we have officials who serve in the sanctuary, "elders" (πρεσβύτεροι) and "bishops" (ἐπίσκοποι), who stand at the head of the congregations and in a proper and understanding spirit direct the affairs of the congregation, at the same time acting as teachers of the doctrines of the new religion (δι-δάκτικοι). The fervid new faith and the spiritual revolution are not here the main things, as they are in the rest of the Pauline Epistles; instead, the emphasis is on piety and good works. The new must has fermented and become old wine.

To be sure, Paul was an excellent organizer, and it is not to be wondered at that he was concerned with the external organization of the congregations. It is possible that by the time of his old age the congregations were already more or less organized and firmly established, and that Paul was concerned with the fixing of their external organization and with their officials both high and low. Already at the beginning of the Epistle to the Philippians "bishops and deacons" (ἐπίσκοποι καὶ διάκονοι) are mentioned;[45] and it is difficult to believe that even there the appointment is on a voluntary basis only.[46] But we have other Epistles of Paul from the time of his Roman imprisonment, and thus from the time of his old age or near it; why do we not find in them this new spirit of rationality and orderliness? Of course, even this is not decisive proof, since, as I have already pointed out, a writer is not always the same in his feeling and thinking, and he does not always exhibit the best of his talents; nor are the ideas and concerns of a young religious zealot the same as those of an elderly lover of order. Nevertheless, a certain basis for considering the Pastoral Epistles late is to be found here.

More important is *another aspect* of the Pastorals. In them, verses and phrases from the Old Testament have no place, and

[45] Philipp. 1:1.
[46] See the compendious article of Beyer on ἐπίσκοπος (*Theologisches Wörterbuch zum Neuen Testament*, II, 612-3).

do not influence content and style as they influence the content and style of the rest of the Epistles of Paul the "Pharisee, a son of Pharisees." Instead, the Pastoral Epistles are filled with polemics against wrong doctrines—against Jewish-Nazarene, ascetic, and Gnostic heresy. These Epistles contend against "men that speak lies," who forbid marriage, certain kinds of food, and even the drinking of wine.[47] At the same time they contend against strange doctrines—against "fables and endless genealogies,[48] which bring about questionings."[49] Nothing of this fits the end of Paul's lifetime, that is, 62–64 C.E. All this fits better the beginning of the second century, when the enthusiasm and excitement of the young Church had died down and formal organization of the congregations had firmly established itself on the one hand, and on the other hand, all kinds of heretical Gnostic and Judaeo-Christian sects had sprung up, such as the early Church Fathers fought against with all their might.[50]

There is no mathematical certainty even about this conclusion, since in the last analysis we do not know with certainty what was the condition of the Christian Church at the end of Paul's lifetime; at the same time, we now know that Gnosticism, antinomianism, and religious syncretism existed even before Christianity appeared.[51] Nevertheless, one senses in the Pastoral Epistles a time later than the time of Paul and recognizes the writing of a man less "spiritual" and less fervent

[47] I Tim. 4:1–5. Paul also says that it is permissible for Timothy to drink "a little wine for thy stomach's sake and thine often infirmities."

[48] This is perhaps a reference to the discrepancies between the Gospels of Matthew and Luke in the matter of the genealogies tracing the Davidic descent of Jesus.

[49] I Tim. 1:3, 4.

[50] See on this Ed. Meyer, op. cit., III, 585–6.

[51] See the answers to all the arguments against the attribution of the Pastoral Epistles to Paul in the book of D. A. Hayes, op. cit., pp. 365–7. See also B. Weiss, Die Briefe an Timotheus und Titus (Göttingen 1902). H. Windisch, "Zur Christologie der Pastoralbriefe" (ZNW, XXXIV [1935], 213–38), concludes that the Pastoral Epistles contain a primitive Messianic viewpoint.

than Paul. With all of Paul's practicality and organizing ability, it is difficult to suppose that even in his old age his enthusiasm waned and his mystical inclination was entirely lost. It is impossible to nail the matter down; but it is close to certain that in the Pastorals we have a later time and another author.

It is proper to point out one thing more. From the first of these Epistles it is to be seen that Paul was in Ephesus a short time before he wrote this Epistle, and in it he promised to return to Ephesus again after a short time.[52] So why did Paul have to write these two letters to Timothy at all?—

We may then, with a considerable degree of confidence, attribute the Pastoral Epistles to a disciple of Paul.

But the abundance of detailed information and the greetings to people called by name in these Epistles—why were they fabricated and how were they fabricated? For what possible reason or purpose could a verse like this, for example, have been fabricated: "The cloak that I left at Troas with Carpus, bring when thou comest, and the books, especially the parchments"?[53] It has been asked, Why did Paul refrain from seeking the cloak and the books and parchments for so many years after he left Troas? (He remained two years in prison in Caesarea, and besides that the journey to Rome and the spending of the winter in Malta and the greater part of his imprisonment in Rome would require a considerable length of time.) But a much greater question is this: Who had any need of or interest in or benefit from the fabrication of this simple, human request? In the opinion of many, it is to be concluded from this that into these later Epistles the fabricator introduced sections from genuine letters of Paul.[54] To me, it appears more probable to suppose that genuine Pauline letters

[52] I Tim. 1:3 and 3:14.   [53] II Tim. 4:13.
[54] See on this hypothesis H. von Soden, op. cit., SS. 160-1. Against this possibility, see A. Omodeo, op. cit., pp. 365-7.

were changed—that is to say, unintentionally falsified—by later copyists, who introduced corrections and additions in language and in content; but many of the ideas of the real Paul were retained, and along with these the intimate personal details which were in his genuine letters and which there was no reason for changing at a later time.

At any rate, it is impossible to use the Pastoral Epistles for a correct description of the beliefs and opinions of Paul, and caution must be observed in using them for the events of his life. For as soon as Epistles which have suffered alterations are partly suspect, they become wholly suspect.

Fifth Book

JEWISH CHRISTIANITY AND GENTILE CHRISTIANITY

CHAPTER I

Jesus of Nazareth in the Conception of His Disciples

1. Jesus claimed to be Messiah, he was arrested, condemned, and crucified. Many Messiahs arose in Israel in the last days of the Second Temple—and were slain and forgotten. Jesus was slain—but he was not forgotten.

Why was only he not forgotten? How was he different from all the rest of the Messiahs who did not succeed, and therefore were considered false Messiahs?

We shall obtain the answer to this question only if we note first of all the fact that his memory was preserved from the beginning by three women, among them Mary Magdalene, "from whom seven demons had gone out," [1] that is to say, a woman hysterical to the point of madness. Apparently, she was the one who reported that she had seen Jesus after his crucifixion, and hence that he had risen from the dead. Ernest Renan says, not without good reason:

> The glory of the Resurrection is accordingly due to Mary Magdalen. Next after Jesus, hers was the most essential part in the founding of Christianity. The image created by her vivid susceptibility still hovers before the world. She, as chief and princess among visionaries, has better than any other made the vision of her impassioned soul a real thing to the world's conviction. That grand cry from her woman's heart, "He is risen!" has become the mainspring of faith to mankind. Hence, feeble Reason! Test not by cold analysis this masterpiece of ideality and love! If wisdom despairs of consolation to the unhappy race of man, abandoned by

[1] Luke 8:2 (and in the addition to Mark, Mark 16:9).

destiny, let unreason attempt the venture! Where is the wise man who has bestowed upon the world so exalted joy as this visionary Mary Magdalen? [2]

The answer is, therefore, that the memory of Jesus was not blotted out, as was the memory of the other false Messiahs, because of the story of his resurrection.

But within this answer a new question is embodied: Why about *Jesus specifically* did a story like this arise—a story in which its creators, Mary Magdalene and her companions, believed so absolutely? Afterwards, Jesus appeared in a vision also to a number of his disciples—to Peter, Thomas, his (Jesus') brother James, and even to Paul. There can be no doubt that we have this story without fabrication or conscious deception, since a faith that embraces millions of men and endures for thousands of years cannot be based on fabrication and conscious deception. The women and disciples actually saw Jesus after his crucifixion—in a vision which appeared to them, enthusiastic to the point of madness and credulous to the point of blindness, as a complete reality. So the question returns, What brought it about that Jesus specifically, and not some other false Messiah near the end of the Second Temple, made such a strong impression upon his disciples, both male and female, that they believed in the resurrection of one crucified and saw him in their imagination as one who was alive?

The answer to this question is possible only after one important matter is clarified:

—How much remained in the minds of the principal disciples of Jesus of his life, his acts, and his teaching?

For, truly, only if we clarify this matter, can we obtain an answer to the question, Why was the memory of Jesus pre-

[2] See E. Renan, *Les Apôtres* (Histoire des Origines du Christianisme, livre 2-ème, Paris 1866), p. 13 [translation by J. H. Allen, Boston 1898, p. 49]. pp 58 - 62

served, and not that of the rest of the Messiahs of the time of the Second Temple, and preserved in such measure as to bring into being a sect of Nazarenes believing in the messiahship of Jesus in spite of the fact that his life came to an end in complete frustration—in the shameful death of crucifixion?—

2. In my opinion, ten things were fixed and preserved in the minds of the disciples; these were:

(a) That Jesus was baptized in the Jordan by John the Baptist for repentance and spiritual purification, which were to serve as preparation for the coming of the Messiah. Thus, John the Baptist was the herald of the Messiah, Elijah the Prophet, and Jesus himself is the expected Messiah, in spite of the fact that he came from small and lowly Nazareth and from a humble family, and in spite of the fact that he died a shameful death.

(b) That Jesus associated with the common people and did not despise publicans and sinners.

(c) That Jesus healed the sick in a marvellous manner.

(d) That Jesus regarded the ethical requirements—righteousness and good works—as more important than the ritual requirements—for example, washing of the hands; that he healed on the Sabbath even ailments which did not involve danger to life, and that he even permitted the plucking of ears of grain on the Sabbath under stress of hunger; and on account of this he came into conflict with the Pharisees.

(e) That Jesus formulated a brief prayer, "The Lord's Prayer," in which there is a petition that the Kingdom of Heaven may come, and along with this requests for man's "daily bread" and for his deliverance from evil.

(f) That Jesus had twelve disciples, whom he sent forth to preach repentance in anticipation of the coming of the Messiah—and to preach it *among the Jews only*.

(g) That Jesus believed that he would come "with the clouds of heaven" on the Day of Judgment to judge, together with his twelve disciples, the twelve tribes of Israel.

(h) That Jesus celebrated with his disciples the "Seder" of Passover before his arrest and commanded that they institute a fellowship meal in his memory.

(i) That Jesus was crucified by the Romans because he persisted in the belief that he was Messiah and would appear as Messiah "at the right hand of Power" (the "Parousia").

(j) That Jesus, after he was crucified, rose from the dead and ascended to heaven, having been seen in a vision by Mary Magdalene and her companions, and afterwards by Simon Cephas (Peter) and his companions.

This is what the disciples of Jesus who still believed in him after his crucifixion knew of his life, his acts, and his teaching. Of course, they knew many more incidents and "sayings" bound together in the form of short anecdotes; but these did not include that large part of the stories and sayings found in our Gospels which are myths formed by the Oriental imagination of the disciples and their followers, or precepts and homilies created by the primitive Nazarene Church for the needs of preaching and missionary propaganda.

3. There are those who deny the early date of these ten concepts which, in my opinion, remained in the minds of the disciples of Jesus after his crucifixion. Some believe that most of them or even all of them, or almost all, were formed in a time later than Jesus himself.[3] The *Formgeschichtliche Schule*,

[3] Extremely skeptical and negative is the important book of the French scholar Ch. Guignebert, *Jésus* (L'Evolution de l'humanité, XXIX, Paris 1933, Eng. ed., London 1935). By contrast, the analytical book of another French scholar, M. Goguel, *La Vie de Jésus* (Paris 1932, Eng. ed., New York 1933), is conservative; yet Goguel also takes a sharply critical attitude toward all Gospel data that is at all open to suspicion. A sharply critical attitude toward Gospel data is also to be found in the important book of the American scholar, S. J. Case, *Jesus* (Chicago 1927).

founded by Dibelius, Bultmann, Bertram, K. L. Schmidt, *et al.*, has reached the point of almost complete skepticism with regard to everything which the Gospels—even the earliest parts of them—tell of Jesus and his teaching. Thus, there is left to this school of the entire life of Jesus almost nothing except the mere fact of his existence. Even his existence is denied by Bruno Bauer, W. B. Smith, Arthur Drews, J. M. Robertson, *et al.* One of the heads of the *Formgeschichtliche Schule* comes to the conclusion that "we can now know almost nothing concerning the life and personality of Jesus," and that "for no single word of Jesus is it possible to produce positive evidence of its authenticity." [4]

But I have shown in another place,[5] that these denials, which come from *Hyperkritik* and a sophistical skepticism, do not succeed in disproving the data in the early parts of the Gospels. Later tendencies do not justify the fabrication of these data by the first primitive Christians; on the contrary, these data are opposed to the general tendencies of the first forty years after Jesus, during which the first Gospels were formed. After all, the Gospel according to Mark was in existence in almost its present form by the end of the sixties of the Christian era, from thirty-five to forty years after the crucifixion, while the younger disciples of Jesus were still alive; and even the Gospels according to Matthew and Luke were composed between 80 and 100 C.E., that is to say, from fifty to seventy years after the crucifixion; and the "Sayings-Source" in these two latter Gospels ($Q = Quelle$) is even earlier than this, having been formed not later than 70 C.E. on the basis of recollections of the first disciples, particularly the apostles Peter

---

[4] See R. Bultmann, *Jesus* (Berlin 1926), S. 12 [Eng. ed., *Jesus and the Word*, New York 1934, p. 8]. See also by the same author, *Erforschung der synoptischen Evangelien* (Giessen 1925), S. 33 [Eng. translation in F. C. Grant, *Form Criticism* (Chicago 1934), p. 61].

[5] See Klausner, *Yeshu*, pp. 105–8 [4th Heb. ed.; not in Eng. ed., which was made from 1st Heb. ed.].

and Matthew.[6] How could those living in this period of the early Church gainsay the testimony of eyewitnesses who were still alive?

If we had ancient sources like those in the Gospels for the history of Alexander the Great or Julius Caesar for example, we should not cast any doubt upon them whatsoever. It is true that the Evangelists were influenced by religious views and religious propaganda; but do the political views and political propaganda by which ancient historians were influenced, consciously or unconsciously, render invalid or blur historical data any less than do religious opinions and inclinations? If skeptical and hairsplitting criticism like this were applied to the historical sources for the life and views of Charlemagne or Mohammed, we should not have left of them anything of even relative historical validity except their mere existence.[7]

In the end, I return to my first fundamental claim: that many Messiahs arose in Israel in the time of the Second Temple, and that all of them, after they failed in their attempt and were killed or fled were almost completely forgotten, no record of them being preserved save in the works of Josephus and in the Talmud ("Ben Stada"). Why did Jesus alone achieve the honor of having a whole sect attribute its existence to him, and of having connected with him a new religion which in the course of time conquered the world?

[6] Ibid., pp. 131-4 [Eng. ed., pp. 125-7].

[7] Also, I wish to point out this: my book Yeshu ha-Notsri (Jesus of Nazareth) appeared in its first edition in 1922; in spite of the fact that I have revised it through successive editions (particularly numerous are the revisions in the fourth Hebrew edition of 1933, and in the second edition of the German translation, 1934; and fairly numerous also the revisions in the French translation of 1933)—in spite of this, it is possible that there remain in this book details of the life and teaching of Jesus, according to my presentation, upon which doubt can be cast; this I confess to-day, after eighteen years of unceasing new research. But the main points of my presentation still appear to me to be correct. The reason for this may be that I have attempted to describe the life and teaching of Jesus—and also the life and teaching of Paul—not as a Jewish or Christian theologian, but, above all, as a historian, to whom theology is only an auxiliary subject.

If Jesus had not been a remarkable personality, who did remarkable deeds and spoke remarkable words, he would have faded from the memory of his disciples after his shameful death on the cross as faded the memory of the rest of the "false Messiahs," that is to say, the saviors who did not succeed in saving. The very fact that his disciples, both male and female, cherished his memory even after the crucifixion, reaching the point where they saw him in their imagination as risen and alive—this very fact proves that the influence of Jesus upon the little group brought about wonderment and adoration. And without certain deeds of healing the sick, the distressed, and the hysterical, without the formulation of a new prayer, without a distinctive attitude toward the ritual requirements as over against the ethical, without opposition toward the Pharisees and Sadducees, without the choosing of disciples and the sending out of apostles (preachers), without incisive moral aphorisms—without all these things it is impossible to imagine such adoration lasting after the crucifixion and beyond the time of burial. However, Jesus himself did not deliver a single word with intent to found a new religion or a new religious community;[8] he laid down a number of precepts for his disciples only, and it was they alone who made of these precepts ritual requirements in commemoration of him, or by imitation of his deeds and words. Thus they built up ritual requirements for a new church which was in process of formation.

Because of all these considerations, I still hold to my former opinion,[9] that Jesus left with his disciples after his crucifixion, without any organizational intention whatever, these

[8] See W. Michaelis, *Täufer, Jesus, Urgemeinde* (Neutestamentliche Forschungen herausg. v. O. Schmitz, II, 3, Gütersloh 1928), S. 112.

[9] This opinion was put forth in my book *Yeshu ha-Notsri* (*Jesus of Nazareth*). Detailed arguments and discussions on this subject are to be found particularly in the fourth Hebrew edition (Jerusalem 1933) and in the second edition of the German translation (Berlin 1934).

ten concepts, out of all those things mentioned in the Gospels; these concepts pertained partly to his own individual life and character and partly to his own characteristic teaching. Of course, there are in the Gospels many things which are nothing more than the creations of credulous imagination; of course, even the Gospel stories which I consider to be historic fact are tinged with imaginative and religious coloring; of course, Jesus did not intend by his "ordinances" and suggestions what his disciples and their followers read into them, as said above. But the ten things listed above are historical, at least *in substance*. *Ex nihilo nihil fit*. But for these, the earliest primitive Christianity would have had nothing upon which to base itself, and Pauline Christianity nothing upon which to depend or be supported.

CHAPTER II

The Beginning of Primitive Christianity: Simon Cephas-Peter

1. The crucifixion of Jesus made a deep impression upon his disciples far and near. The Messiah, who was supposed to save his people, was not able to save himself and died a shameful death at the hands of the uncircumcised. He died a "death of slaves" (*supplicium servile*), according to the idea of the Romans.[1] Even more shameful was his death in the eyes of the Jews, to whom the sentence of crucifixion was foreign.[2] For since all who are crucified are hanged, they applied to the crucified Jesus the Biblical verse, "for he that is hanged is the curse of God."[3] Hence it was that "Christ crucified" was "unto Jews a stumblingblock, and unto Gentiles foolishness."[4] Against this doubly unfavorable view the apostles were forced to fight continually—and first of all to fight with the Jews, for whom the idea of a defeated and hanged ("crucified") Messiah could not fit into any of their conceptions of the promise and function of the saving and liberating—and hence victorious—Messiah. Therefore, the crucified Jesus was a disappointment to most of those who followed him in life— all those who were not very close to him, who were merely "dragged along" after the new Messiah.

The disciples closest to him (the "Twelve," minus Judas

[1] See Tacitus, *Hist.* IV 3 11.
[2] See *Midrasch Tannaim* (to Deut.) ed. by D. Hoffmann (Berlin 1908–9), p. 132, 1. 8. See also Klausner, *Yeshu*, p. 395, n. 6 [Eng. ed., p. 349].
[3] Deut. 21:23. [4] I Cor. 1:23.

Iscariot) scattered widely, fearing persecution. They also were disappointed; moreover it was harder for them to reconcile themselves to the idea that their righteous Messiah, to whom they had been so devoted, had died a criminal's death. Here again comes in the vision of Mary Magdalene, who saw in her imagination Jesus risen from the dead; [5] for the resurrection of the dead was in the time of the Second Temple a belief accepted among all groups in the nation except the Sadducees. Hence, the disciples carried in their minds not only disappointment and fear, but also a belief that the fate of Jesus would not be like the fate of all false Messiahs. After the Days of the Messiah there would come, according to Jewish belief, the resurrection of the dead; [6] and who was worthy to experience this resurrection first, if not the maltreated Messiah himself?—

The disciples fled to Galilee, with Simon bar Jonah Cephas (Peter) at their head, although Peter had previously denied out of great fear his Lord Messiah at the time of the arrest. Galilee was the place of origin of the Messianic movement that grew up around Jesus; the news of what had happened in

[5] Some think that the vision of Mary Magdalene by the tomb of Jesus in Jerusalem is a conscious literary fabrication, since it is not mentioned in the list of appearances of Jesus reported by Paul (I Cor. 15:3–8), and that the first vision of the appearance of Jesus after the crucifixion was experienced by Peter in Galilee (Ed. Meyer, *op. cit.*, III, 210–4). But it is difficult to explain why the Evangelists fabricated this. Paul's failure to mention Mary Magdalene is understandable: *first*, he did not wish to depend upon the support of a hysterical woman; *second*, the main thing for him was to show that he, Paul, was equal to the rest of the apostles—just as Jesus appeared after the crucifixion to Cephas and James and the Twelve, so also he appeared to Paul. Moreover, it is possible that had it not been for the first visionary appearance to Mary Magdalene in *Jerusalem*, the disciples would not have made such haste to return to Jerusalem from *Galilee*.

[6] In the Sabbath morning prayer *Hakkol Yodúkha* ("All shall thank Thee") we say: "There is none but Thee, O our Redeemer, for the Days of the Messiah; neither is there any like unto Thee, O our Saviour, for the resurrection of the dead" [S. Singer, *The Standard Prayer Book*, N. Y. 1915, pp. 186–7]. See for details Klausner, *Ha-Ra'yon*, pp. 261–8, particularly p. 266, n. 1.

Jerusalem had not yet reached there; moreover, in these little provincial towns there were no prying official eyes, as in Jerusalem. There in Galilee, upon a mountain,[7] Peter also saw Jesus in a vision as Mary Magdalene had "seen" him in Jerusalem. He also was incurably emotional and visionary, and had already seen strange visions in Caesarea Philippi.[8] After this imaginative experience by means of which Peter achieved a conviction that Jesus would shortly be revealed in all his glory as "the Son of Man . . . coming with the clouds of heaven," Peter hastened to return to Jerusalem; for where would the Messiah appear if not in Jerusalem?— And along with him there returned to Jerusalem almost all the disciples who had fled to Galilee. All this can be clearly inferred from the "command" of Jesus to Peter to go to Galilee, where Jesus would appear to him.[9]

2. Gradually all eleven of the disciples (Judas Iscariot was missing, of course) gathered themselves together in an upper chamber in Jerusalem, in an obscure corner of the great city; this upper chamber became the meeting place of the disciples of Jesus. Thither came afterwards also the female disciples, and some time later the mother of Jesus, Mary the widow of Joseph of Nazareth, and at least two of the brothers

[7] Does not "the mountain" designated by Jesus, upon which he appeared to his disciples (Matt. 28:16), have some relation to "one of the mountains which I will tell thee of" in the story of the attempted sacrifice of Isaac? In a way, the sacrificial death of Jesus in Christianity takes the place of the intended sacrifice of Isaac: God sacrificed "his only-begotten son," just as Abraham had agreed to sacrifice his son Isaac (see M. Rabinsohn, " 'Aqedat-Yitshaq," Ha-Shiloah, XXV, 312–4).

[8] On this see Klausner, Yeshu, pp. 337–8 [Eng. ed., pp. 302–3]; and in more detail A. Harnack, "Die Verklärungsgeschichte Jesu, der Bericht des Paulus und die beiden Christusvisionen des Petrus," Berichte der Berliner Akademie (1922), SS. 62–75.

[9] Mark 14:28 and 16:7; Matt. 28:7, 10 and 16:17. In Luke and Acts this matter is not mentioned, because apparently their Pauline author did not wish to record that the very first appearance of Jesus to his disciples was experienced by Peter.

of Jesus, James and Judas. While he was alive, his mother and brothers had not believed in him, and had even attempted "to lay hold on him"—probably to take him back home, "for they said, He is beside himself"; Jesus rebuffed them and was not even willing to go out to see them, since only "whosoever shall do the will of God . . . is my brother, and sister, and mother." [10] But after the great tragedy of the crucifixion, and after his mother and brothers saw that in spite of his untimely death there was still a group believing in Jesus, it was inevitable that they should join this company of believers; for whom did they have except this company?— James, the eldest brother of Jesus, himself once saw his dead brother in a vision of his imagination—although after Peter and "the twelve" and many "brethren" had already "seen" him.[11] Jesus at that time was not yet considered to be "Son of God," "Logos," or "heavenly man," but he was regarded as the Messiah born of a man and a woman; thus his mother and brothers were "holy seed" and "of noble descent"; naturally, after a certain time, James the brother of Jesus became the head of the Nazarene sect and remained so for many years.[12] Therefore, his mother and brothers came back with the Eleven from Galilee to Jerusalem. (His father apparently had died before Jesus came into prominence.)

From this we see how strong was the influence of the personality of Jesus upon his disciples during his lifetime, and also how great was the impression left by his terrible agony and death. After his death, the Eleven and those with them could persuade even his mother and brothers to change their attitude toward him. The memory of the deceased, his beautiful parables, his lofty ethical precepts, and also the frightful tortures which he suffered as a political revolutionary (which he was not)—all these still lived in their minds and hearts.

---

[10] Mark 3:31–5. See on this Klausner, *Yeshu*, p. 311 [Eng. ed., p. 280].
[11] I Cor. 15:5–7.   [12] See below, pp. 278–80 *et passim*.

And enthusiasts and visionaries that they were, they also saw him in their visions—at least those of them who possessed the strongest imaginations—just as the women had seen him on the third day after the crucifixion and as Peter had seen him in Galilee.[13] Is it an unusual thing for tender-hearted men under stress of grief to see in imagination their beloved wives or children who have died before their time, as though they were still alive?——

Gradually their doubts, occasioned by the shameful death of the Messiah who was innocent of the crime of rebellion, passed away. They began—of course not immediately, but after a short time—to apply Isaiah 53 ("Who hath believed our report?") to the Messiah who had been abused and unjustly put to death. He was "as a lamb that is led to the slaughter, and as a sheep before its shearers"; "surely he hath borne our griefs, and carried our sorrows"; "he was wounded for our transgressions, he was bruised for our iniquities," "and with his stripes we are healed"; "the Lord hath laid on him the iniquity of us all," and "made his grave with the wicked," "although he had done no violence, neither was any deceit in his mouth"; "he was numbered with the transgressors—yet he bore the sin of many, and made intercession for the transgressors." These verses, so difficult of interpretation, it was easy to apply to the crucified Messiah. This was possible even if in the days of the Second Temple these verses had been interpreted as applying only to the nation Israel, which had suffered innocently on behalf of the Gentiles, whose well-being Israel desired; yet the verses may also have been applied on occasion to a slain Messiah [not Jesus], as was done later.[14]

But there was in the messiahship of Jesus also a political side, even if this side was not so fundamental in it as Robert

[13] I Cor. 15:5–7. Matthew (28:16, 17) also records this vision of the Eleven, adding however, ". . . but some doubted."

[14] See A. Neubauer, *Jewish Interpretations of the Fifty-third Chapter of Isaiah* (London 1876).

Eisler, for example, thinks.[15] Even Jesus gave consideration
to the emancipation of the Jewish nation from subjection to
earthly kingdoms by means of repentance and good works,
and by the establishment of the Kingdom "not made with
hands" through the agency of a supernatural power which
God would give to the ethico-spiritual Messiah.[16]

The first verse after the introduction of the Acts of the
Apostles indicates this clearly:

> They therefore, when they were come together, asked him,
> saying, "Lord, dost thou at this time restore the kingdom to
> Israel?" [17]

This verse comes suddenly, without any connexion with what
precedes, and it seems strange as the beginning of the story of
Christianity. If the author of Acts begins his history of the
rise of the new religion with such a question, this cannot be
explained except by the fact that this question, the question
of the restoration of the kingdom to Israel, forced itself upon
the disciples of Jesus from the very first day on which they
came together after the crucifixion. They were in a state of
spiritual and intellectual crisis, for the crucifixion had been a
fearful frustration of the hope of redemption . . .

The answer which they received was:

> "It is not for you to know times or seasons, which the Father
> hath set within his own authority." [18]

That is to say, the crucified Messiah has been forced to become for your sakes not a victorious and conquering Messiah,
but the abused and suffering Messiah of Isaiah 53. The kingdom of Israel will of course be restored by him, but—"in the

---

[15] See R. Eisler, Ἰησοῦς βασιλεύς, etc., 2 vols. (Heidelberg 1928–9); see
also J. Spencer Kennard, Jr., *Politique et religion chez les Juifs au temps
de Jésus et dans l'Eglise primitive* (édition revisée, Paris 1927).

[16] See for details Klausner, *Yeshu*, pp. 352–3, 452 [Eng. ed., pp. 312–3,
402].

[17] Acts 1:6.   [18] Acts 1:7; *cf.* Mark 13:32.

last days," in the time "which the Father hath set within his own authority," and quite unexpectedly. The kingdom will come like the sudden lightning, "as a thief in the night," and "as were the days of Noah," which no one saw at the beginning.[19] By means of this change of viewpoint, which was necessary if the young movement wished to survive and develop, the disciples of Jesus gained a twofold advantage: *First*, their ethico-religious movement would have no taint of rebellion, and thus there would be no cause for the Romans to persecute them; this was an essential thing for the new and young movement which had gone forth in the name of a *Messiah*. *Second*, Jesus would not be a false Messiah like all the rest of the rebellious Messiahs, since he had not intended to restore the "kingdom" to Israel "in this time"; and thus there would be no reason for disillusionment if he died without redeeming his people . . .

So their enthusiasm and power of imagination coupled with their new interpretation of the Biblical verses attracted other enthusiasts and imaginative people like themselves. Gradually there joined them—or returned to them—more believers, either new ones or some of those who had formerly been attached to Jesus but had dispersed after the crucifixion, until their number reached about 120 persons.[20] These were, at the beginning, undoubtedly all Galileans, who had come with Jesus to Jerusalem. The number is symbolic in Israel: ten times twelve; even "the men of the Great Synagogue" numbered 120.[21] But the number "Twelve" of the disciples (or "apostles") is also symbolic—of the tribes of Israel. Thus it could not be diminished. Yet it was diminished by Judas Iscariot, who died (an unnatural death, of course) after his betrayal of his Master. It was necessary, therefore,

[19] Luke 17:24; Matt. 24:37-9 and 42-4; I Thess. 5:2, 3.
[20] Acts 1:15.
[21] This was already pointed out by Isaac M. Wise, *The Origin of Christianity* (Cincinnati 1868), p. 19.

to choose another to fill his place. The choice was between
Joseph Barsabbas surnamed Justus, and Matthias. The lot fell
upon Matthias. Thus the number of the "Twelve" was kept
intact.

3. At the head of the little company of about 120 persons
stood Simon Cephas-Peter, the first and foremost of the disciples of Jesus.[22] The Christian Church, and especially the
Catholic Church, whose Pope sits upon the "throne of Peter,"
adored him greatly and accorded him a place greater than
Paul, or at least equal with Paul. Protestantism, which revolted
against Catholicism and the Popes, attempted to minimize his
importance for Christianity in favor of Paul; it therefore laid
stress upon the Gospel story that Peter denied Jesus at the
time of the latter's arrest, and upon the harsh words of Paul
about Peter in the Epistle to the Galatians. In recent years
respect for Peter has in large measure been restored.[23]

To be sure, without Paul Christianity would not have become a world religion with a distinctive theology and a highly
developed ecclesiastical organization; but without Peter there
would not have sprung up a special sect believing in a crucified Messiah. Peter was not a man of broad culture and
profound knowledge like Paul,[24] nor did he have the tena-
cious and obstinate nature of Paul; but he did have very sensitive feelings and a very strong imagination—and feeling and
imagination were two things which the new religious movement were in great need of *at the beginning*. No inquiring
and speculative theologian could have given impetus to an
irrational religious movement based on the belief that a cruci-

[22] On the place of Peter in the career of Jesus, see Klausner, *Yeshu*,
pp. 288, 315, 390 *et passim* [pp. 260, 284, 344 in the Eng. ed.].
[23] Thanks particularly to Ed. Meyer (*Ursprung u. Anfänge*, III, 152–3,
228–9, and many other places). See also J. A. Findlay, *A Portrait of Peter*
(New York 1935).
[24] Acts 4:13: ". . . unlearned and ignorant men."

fied Messiah not of the house of David had risen from the dead and after a little would come to judge the tribes of Israel. This had to be done by an enthusiastic believer with a warm heart **and a lively and powerful imagination.** Such a person was Simon Cephas, and such he remained to the end of his days. An emotional and imaginative man like this would be somewhat fickle in his opinions and conduct at times, or inconsistent in his words and deeds, and could even deny his own beliefs in a moment of sudden danger.

But complete faith in and unquestioning loyalty to the adored "rabbi" were much more important in the *first days* of a movement founded upon a supernatural belief, than any sort of systematizing, consistency, or profundity. Thus, not only Mary Magdalene of "the seven demons" laid the foundation for Christianity as a new religious movement, but also Simon **Cephas the "fickle." For he, the unstable,** was in a certain sense the "rock" upon which was founded, if not the new Church, at least the new Nazarene sect, in spite of the fact that he was not "solid as a rock" in his opinions, and perhaps *because of that very fact.* His ideological flexibility, his lack of consistency, made it possible for Christianity to adapt itself to the needs of the hour, to absorb various elements to which a logical and consistent man would not have given a place in the new movement.

Simon Peter stood at the head of the sect during the first years of its growth, which are the critical years for any new sect. Only after some time, during which Stephen was stoned, James the son of Zebedee put to death, and Peter forced to flee,[25] was the place of Peter taken by James the brother of Jesus; with the latter was associated John the son of Zebedee, brother of the slain James and one of the first disciples. These three—Simon, James, and John—were called the "pillars" of the sect.[26] The whole group was called the "fellowship" of

[25] See on this below, in the next chapter, pp. 280–6.   [26] Gal. 2:9.

the "disciples of Jesus," or the "Nazarenes," after Jesus the
Nazarene (from the city of Nazareth). Among themselves
they were called "companions" or "brethren," "disciples" or
"believers." The "Church" (ἡ ἐκκλησία) in the technical sense
came some time later. Meanwhile, they had a "synagogue" (or
place of assembly for the Nazarenes), like the synagogues of
the Libertines, the Cyrenians, the Alexandrians, and the
Cilicians, which existed in Jerusalem at that time.[27] From this
weak little "congregation" or "synagogue" of Nazarenes there
afterward branched out the Christian Church in Jerusalem
and in all Judea, and later—in the whole Roman Empire, and
finally—in the entire world.

[27] Acts 6:9. Eduard Meyer (*Ursprung und Anfänge*, III, 230–1) thinks
that for the first Christians the Temple sufficed as a place of worship, even
though their gatherings were held in a private house. But if the rest of the
Jews who had come to Jerusalem from elsewhere had need of special synagogues, why did not this new sect from the beginning have the same need?

The "Speaking with Tongues"; Possessions in Common; James the Brother of Jesus; The First Persecutions

1. Jesus was crucified on the eve of Passover. Seven weeks after Passover came Pentecost (the Feast of Weeks). In the course of these few weeks there had joined themselves to the believers in Jesus, besides the simple Galileans, also some *non-Palestinian* Jews lacking in proper Jewish training but eager for miracles. These Jews from the Diaspora of Israel were rootless exiles who had come to Jerusalem for the festival of Unleavened Bread and had remained for the Feast of Weeks; or they may even have been residing in Jerusalem for some time. They were from Egypt, Parthia, Cappadocia, Pontus, Phrygia, and Rome; and while the Galileans and the rest of the Palestinian-Jewish disciples of Jesus spoke Aramaic—and also a little Hebrew [1]—these Jews of the Diaspora spoke Greek and also the vernacular languages which then still existed in their native lands. [2]

Now, since it is related that on "the day of Pentecost" the disciples "began to speak with other tongues," and that of the Jews who had come to Jerusalem from other lands "every

[1] See E. Ben-Yehudah, *'Ad Ematai Dibberu 'Ivrit?* (New York 5679–1919), pp. 60–124; G. Dalman, *Jesus-Jeschua* (Leipzig 1922), SS. 6–34 [Eng. ed. (1929), pp. 27–37].

[2] See K. Holl, "Das Fortleben der Volkssprachen in Kleinasien in nachchristlicher Zeit" (*Hermes*, 1908, SS. 240 ff.).

man heard them speaking in his own language," [3] the opinion has been advanced,[4] that the "miracle" of the "speaking with tongues" ("glossolalia") was as follows:

Different Jews spoke in one place, the place of assembly of the believers in Jesus, in different languages, until the assemblage of believers seemed like the Tower of Babel—yet all of them were of one mind.

It would also be possible to suppose that this was the *Bath-Qol* (heavenly echo) of the Talmudic Haggadah, of which it is said: "Every single word that went forth from the Omnipotent was split up into seventy languages." [5] (This refers to the Ten Commandments, which according to tradition were given at the Feast of Weeks; the Feast of Weeks is therefore known as "the time when our Law was given.")

But it is more likely that "speaking with tongues" was the breaking forth of disconnected and unintelligible utterances from the mouths of highly emotional people at a time when they were greatly excited and their imaginations were stirred to the point of ecstasy. These were cries of excitement and ecstasy which their hearers interpreted as divine revelations and words of prophecy; and since they were disconnected and inarticulate, it seemed to each one of the hearers as though he heard within them a word or words of his own language.[6] This explanation of glossolalia—a phenomenon known to psychopathologists [7]—comes clearly forth from the pointed

[3] Acts 2:4-6.

[4] See H. Graetz, *Geschichte der Juden*, III, 2[5], 409.

[5] Shabbath 88b.

[6] See K. L. Schmidt, *Die Pfingsterzählung und das Pfingstereigniss* (Arbeiten zur Religionsgeschichte des Urchristentums, I, 2—Leipzig 1919), S. 19–35; G. A. Barton, *The Apostolic Age and the New Testament* (Philadelphia 1936), pp. 9–14.

[7] See what K. L. Schmidt, *op. cit.*, SS. 29–30, quotes from E. Lombard, *De la Glossolalie, etc.* (1910); E. Mosiman, *Das Zungreden, etc.* (1911); further bibliography in the article γλῶσσα by Behm in *Theologisches Wörterbuch zum N.T.*, I, 719–26.

words of Paul on the subject of vague and unintelligible "speaking with tongues" as compared with clear and sensible "prophecy." [8] Even the author of Acts relates, with regard to those speaking in tongues: "But others mocking said, 'They are filled with new wine.'" [9] Paul also says:

If therefore the whole church be assembled together and all speak with tongues, and there come in men unlearned or unbelieving, will they not say that ye are mad? [10]

Thus we do not have here a real speaking in foreign languages,[11] but rather the shouts and hysterical cries of enthusiastic ecstatics, what the Russians call *klikushestvo*. Nevertheless, this psychopathological phenomenon communicated itself to others, so that by means of it there were added to the believers in Jesus about five hundred persons.[12]

Among these "converts" were Hellenistic Jews of the Diaspora. These Jews it was who provided the basis for Christianity as a religion. If it had not been for them, Christianity would have remained a Jewish sect like the Essenes. Detached Jews, not rooted in the soil and traditions of Palestine, spiritually rent asunder and suspended between Judaism and Hellenism, they were the very best material for a new religion the first tendencies of which were: a definite depreciation of the ritual requirements in favor of the ethical; a definite exaltation of blind belief in a personality and in miraculous deeds at the expense of the study of Torah; and along with this, an indifferent attitude toward political life and the polit-

---

[8] I Cor. 14:1–25.   [9] Acts 2:13.   [10] I Cor. 14:23.

[11] According to Foakes-Jackson and Lake, *The Beginnings of Christianity*, I, 1, 323–4, the editor of Acts already did not know the real nature of glossolalia, and thought that it was "a miraculous gift of speaking foreign languages."

[12] I Cor. 15:6 against Acts 2:41, where occurs the exaggeration "about three thousand souls."

ical future of the nation, and a covert inclination to put a higher evaluation upon the individual than upon the nation and a stronger emphasis upon humanity than upon Jewish nationality. Only a non-Palestinian Jew, a Jew of the Diaspora, half Jew and half Greek, could have created a religion like this, in which Judaism and paganism were mixed together in confusion as soon as it went forth from Jerusalem to Tarsus and Antioch.

But I shall return to this matter in later chapters. In the meantime, we need to consider the small group of Jesus' disciples, which was composed of Palestinian Jews (Galileans, and of course also in part Jerusalemites) and Hellenistic Jews from the numerous lands of the Diaspora of the Roman Empire.

What were the beliefs and opinions and "ceremonial laws" of this "fellowship of Jesus"?—

First, all its members believed that Jesus was the suffering Messiah of Isaiah 53, who had been crucified and had risen from the dead, and after a certain time, not longer than the life of the first generation after Jesus, would appear on the Day of Judgment at the right hand of Power to judge the tribes of Israel (and all nations) and to restore the kingdom to Israel—and in general to reform the world by the establishment of the Kingdom of God (Kingdom of Heaven). This was the essential point of their faith.

Second, the first disciples (the "apostles") would repeat to the new believers the ethical teaching of Jesus just as it had been retained in their memories: ethical maxims and incisive parables which had been spoken in connexion with the events of his life.

Third, they would pray together (in my opinion, "The Lord's Prayer" in addition to ancient Hebrew prayers).[13]

Fourth, they would baptize in the name of Jesus the Messiah

[13] See Klausner, *Yeshu*, pp. 435-7 [Eng. ed., pp. 386-9].

(although Jesus himself did not institute baptism) as a sign of confession and remission of sins.[14]

Fifth, they would eat a meal "in fellowship"—an ancient Jewish custom [15]—and at the time of the meal they would recall the practices and words of Jesus (although Jesus himself did not institute the "meal").

Sixth, and finally, their life was a life of economic sharing; not, indeed, as a result of communistic theory, but out of an actual necessity for the "brethren" to be equal in everything and for the poor Nazarenes to share in the possessions and incomes of the more well-to-do (there were as yet no really wealthy among them). Hence the first primitive Christians would sell everything which they had and put the proceeds into a common fund, so that anything which any one of them had was "parted to them all, according as any man had need." [16] This practice not only suited the condition of the small, poverty-stricken "fellowship" and tended to attract members to the "fellowship," but it was also most natural, in view of their way of thinking. In the near future Jesus the Messiah would appear, and then the old world would be destroyed and a "new world" would take its place—so what advantage was there in mammon and private property? [17]

---

[14] Christian baptism, in my opinion, was instituted some time after Jesus, when the Nazarenes had begun to receive proselytes—and proselytes were required to be baptized, according to Jewish law; there is no need to conclude that the Nazarenes took the practice of baptism from the disciples of John the Baptist specifically.

[15] See W. O. E. Oesterley, *The Jewish Background of the Christian Liturgy* (Oxford 1925), pp. 156–9.

[16] Acts 2:42–6; 4:34–5:11.

[17] Some deny altogether the existence of communism in primitive Christianity, on the ground that not even one of the ancient critics of Christianity accused it of this practice (see A. Ranovitch, *Antitchnye Kritiki Khristianstva,* Moscow 1935, pp. XIV, XV). To this it may be replied: *first,* neither did the communism of the Essenes arouse any antagonism in the ancient world; on the contrary, Pliny praises it; *second,* the communistic life of the first Christians did not derive from socialist doctrine; moreover, it did not last long, and was therefore quickly forgotten, so that by the

All six of these ideas and practices (or five of them, if we except baptism as coming a little later) served to unify the believers; and the sharing of possessions, their non-theoretical spiritual communism, brought their hearts together in unity and caused an increase in the number of believers, by reason of the novelty which was in the thing for all, and by reason of the distinct advantage of the thing for those who were rather poor or absolutely penniless.

2. It is worthy of special attention that all six of these things belonged to the fundamental beliefs and practices of the Essenes. The Essenes believed in a more spiritual Messiah,[18] and the belief in the resurrection of the dead was very close to their hearts. In the eyes of the Essenes there was special value in prayer together. The Essenes held baptism to be of great importance. They had meals in common. And lastly, they lived a life of economic sharing.

It is almost certain that all these things came into primitive Christianity through the influence of "James the brother of the Lord," whom the Church Fathers picture as an ascetic living a life very much like that of the Essenes. It is said of him that he drank no wine or strong drink, ate no meat, did not go to the baths and anoint himself with oil, did not touch his head with a razor, and had only a single garment of linen, never wearing wool. Hence he was called "the Just" (ὁ δίκαιος) and was credited with "excessive righteousness" (ὑπερβολὴ δικαιοσύνη). He was also called ὠβλίας ὅ ἐστιν Ἑλληνιστὶ περιοχὴ τοῦ λαοῦ ("Oblias that is in Greek, 'Rampart of the people' "), which may stand for "Strong tower of the

---

time the critics of Christianity arose, the memory of this life no longer existed.

[18] This is not stated specifically in the works of Josephus and Philo, who refrained—especially the former—from speaking of the Messianic belief, for political reasons; but the *excessive* spirituality of the Essenes necessitated a more spiritual conception of the Messiah.

people" (עם עופל, if we read ὠβλίαμ) or "Strength of the people" (עם לעם, if we read ὠζλίαμ).[19] Moreover, it is said of him that he alone (of the Nazarenes?) was allowed to enter the Temple, and that

. . . he used to enter alone into the Temple and be found kneeling and praying for forgiveness for the people, so that his knees grew hard like a camel's because of his constant worship of God, kneeling and asking forgiveness for the people.

This is told by Eusebius, quoting the Jewish Christian writer Hegesippus, who lived about 180 C.E.[20]

Such was the brother of Jesus, who stood at the head of the sect of believers in Jesus after Peter (about 44–66 C.E.). It can be said almost with certainty that from this ascetic Nazarene Jew, who was so loyal to the ceremonial laws, and whom we shall see again below fighting against Paul for abrogating the ceremonial laws, branched off the ascetic and communistic (holding to "spiritual communism," if it is possible to speak thus) sect of the Ebionites, in whose eyes Jesus was only a man born of Joseph and Mary. (How could the actual brother of Jesus—and not a mere "relative," as conservative Christians have wished to interpret the word ἀδελφός—have thought otherwise?) But the Ebionites did think that Jesus was "the Savior" who would "come to reward each according to his deeds." [21]

It is also worthy of mention that the New Testament Epistle of James, which was certainly not written in its pres-

[19] It is possible that ōbliam-ōblias is to be interpreted as Heb. ab la'am ("father of the people") in the sense of "father and patron," i.e. a defender and protector of the people, which would fit the translation "rampart of the people."

[20] Eusebius, Hist. Eccl. II 23, §§ 166–8 (ed. Schwartz, minor, 3te Aufl., Leipzig 1922, pp. 68–9).

[21] Of this there are hints elsewhere in the extract from Hegesippus partially quoted above (Eusebius, op. cit., § 168, ed. Schwartz, p. 69). See on this also Klausner, Yeshu, pp. 31–5 [Eng. ed., pp. 40–4]; Graetz, Geschichte der Juden, III, 1⁵, 311–2.

ent form by James the brother of Jesus although it is composed in the spirit of this James, contains nothing specifically Christian except mention of Jesus as Messiah. *Everything else is Jewish.*[22] Therefore, Eusebius reckons this Epistle among the "Disputed Books" (ἀντιλεγόμενα).[23] Luther called it *eine recht strohene Epistel* ("a right strawy Epistle"), and supposed that it at first was a completely Jewish work, which found its way into the New Testament only by means of Christian additions.[24] But because of this very thing it suits the spirit of James the brother of Jesus—this Ebionite observer of the Law, who was still completely Jewish (a Pharisee with Essenic inclinations), who as the brother of Jesus could not consider him (Jesus) as "heavenly" and "son of God" even after he recognized him as the Messiah, or even after he had seen him once after the crucifixion in a vision.[25] James did not recognize Jesus as Messiah during his lifetime, but only after some time, not even immediately after the crucifixion. He recognized Jesus as Messiah because of the ethical doctrine which Jesus preached and because of the cruel sufferings which Jesus innocently bore.

3. Since by means of the common fund the first Christians (Jewish Nazarenes) were freed from concern about livelihood, and since they were still devout Jews, except that they

[22] See Joseph Halévy, "Lettre d'un rabbin de Palestine égarée dans l'Evangile," *Revue Sémitique*, XXII (1914), 197–201.

[23] Eusebius, *op. cit.* III 25, §§ 250–2, ed. Schwartz, p. 104.

[24] See Fr. Spitta, *Der Brief des Jakobus* (Göttingen 1896); K. Kohler, *Jewish Encyclopedia*, VII, 68–70. Luther thought this, of course, because he considered faith superior to works, and not the opposite, which is the position of the Epistle of James.

[25] I Cor. 15–7. In the same passage, vss. 5–7, Paul says that Jesus appeared to Cephas, then to the Twelve, then to "above five hundred brethren," and only then to James—which proves that James was late in joining the sect; if it had not been so, Jesus would not have appeared to him only after the "brethren" numbered five hundred. See further on James, P. G. Kunst, *Joodsche Invloeden bij Paulus* (Amsterdam 1936), pp. 144–9.

added to the Jewish Messianic faith, according to which the Messiah was *still* to come, the belief that he had *already* come (and after being crucified had risen and would appear soon for the Day of Judgment)—the situation being thus, the disciples of Jesus would frequently visit the Temple without being disturbed. There they preached the fundamentals of their new faith, and found among the multitudes of Jerusalem attentive ears eager for signs and wonders; but to an even greater extent they attracted the lower classes of Hellenistic Jews, who had acquired from their Gentile neighbors in Asia Minor and elsewhere a taste for miracles. Simon Cephas-Peter and John the son of Zebedee even tried to heal the sick in the name of Jesus. James the brother of Jesus is not mentioned in Acts as a healer of the sick in the name of Jesus. In the first days after he joined the sect, the "messiahship" of his brother was still a new thing for him; perhaps he did not dare transgress the injunctions of the Sages that it is forbidden to heal the sick in the name of anyone, this being in their eyes like the practice of magic. For them, the man who did this was as "he that utters charms over a wound," and hence had "no share in the world to come." [26] But at a later time, during the youth of R. Eliezer ben Hyrcanus, we find in the Talmud, as a healer of the sick in the name of Jesus, one called Jacob (James) of Kefar Sekanya or Jacob of Kefar Sama; it may be that he was James the brother of Jesus.[27]

This effrontery of "uttering charms over a wound" in the name of a false Messiah, together with an unconscious contempt for the ceremonial laws which began to manifest itself in the new sect, particularly among the "fickle" Hellenistic Jews who had fallen under pagan influence, angered the Sad-

[26] Mishnah, Sanhedrin X 1; Tosephta, Hullin II 22–3; Babli, 'Abodah Zarah 27b; Yerushalmi, Shabbath, end of XIV (14d); Yer., 'Abodah Zarah II 2 (40d and 41a).

[27] I have tried to adduce convincing evidence for this view in my book *Yeshu*, pp. 27–35 [Eng. ed., pp. 37–42].

ducean priests and their "captain," who was chief of the Temple police.[28] The latter, being conservative by nature and not believing in the resurrection of the dead, could not endure hearing the resurrection story that was so ludicrous in their eyes, nor could they countenance a new sect which was based entirely upon a foolish belief in the resurrection of a crucified person, and even showed contempt for the ceremonial laws because the ethical sayings of a false Messiah were much more important in the eyes of its members than the commandments written in the Torah.

Thus persecutions of the "sect" began at the hands of the Temple authorities. Simon Cephas-Peter and John the son of Zebedee were arrested.[29] James the brother of Jesus was not molested, either because he was not yet a member of the sect, or because he was an observing Jew and a keeper of the ceremonial laws. At any rate, he did not yet stand at the head of the sect; Peter still occupied that position.

Peter and John remained in custody overnight. The next day, when their case was heard, Peter and John defended themselves and proved that they were guilty of no wrong. They believed what the Pharisees believed—in the resurrection of the dead; and on the basis of this belief they affirmed that a man named Jesus had thus risen. This belief and its specific application appeared to the highborn and "enlightened" priests more ludicrous than dangerous. In particular, it appeared that Simon and John "were unlearned and ignorant men." [30] Hence they were set free. What could be done with these "ignoramuses"? What danger could there be from such boors and idiots?—They were set free with a warning that they should never again mention the name of Jesus.

This was the first mistake which the Jewish leaders made with regard to the new sect. And this mistake was fatal. There

---

[28] Here (Acts 4:1) the Pharisees are not mentioned at all.
[29] Acts 4:3.   [30] Acts 4:13. See also above, p. 270, n. 24.

was probably no need to arrest the Nazarenes, thus calling attention to them and making them "martyrs." But once arrested, they should not have been freed so quickly. The arrest and release increased the number of believers; for these events showed on the one hand that the new sect was a power which the authorities feared enough to persecute, and on the other hand they proved that there was no danger in being a disciple of Jesus (he, of course, being the one who had saved them from the hand of their persecutors!).

It is the way of simple people, when they see a new movement being persecuted, yet standing firm, to follow after the movement as long as there is no very great danger involved in belonging to it. And because of the "miraculous" deliverance of the two disciples, they began to see in them, as in Jesus before them, doers of miracles, who could heal nervous and partly deranged ("vexed with unclean spirits") people of all sorts in the name of Jesus. It is reported that the number of believers in Jesus quickly grew to about five thousand persons.[31] This is an exaggeration, of course; but there can be no doubt that the number of adherents to the sect increased rapidly. The converts came especially from Hellenistic Jews and proselytes, who were numerous in Jerusalem at that time. Love of miracles, desire for the healing of manifold diseases by means of charms and appeals to the dead, laxity with regard to the ceremonial laws, the effort to bring into the sect the 'amme-ha-arets, and particularly the common sharing of worldly goods—all these brought about such an increase in the number of believers in Jesus as would have been difficult to imagine at the beginning.

4. So the disciples of Jesus, who had been close to him in his lifetime, continued to make speeches of persuasion or propaganda in the precincts of the Temple; and in these

[31] Acts 4:4.

speeches, they made use—especially an unstable man like
Simon Cephas and a hotheaded man like John the son of
Zebedee, one of the "sons of thunder" [32]—of harsh expressions
against the established Judaism of their time. They were particularly violent against the Sadducees and the religious leadership of the priests in the Temple, where Simon and John
were frequent visitors, pointing out the defects in its services
and spurning its blood sacrifices. As this continued, "Annas
the high priest, and all they that were with him, that is, the
sect of the Sadducees" (thus it is written plainly in the book
of Acts) became angry and again arrested Simon and John.[33]
But the latter had friends who enabled them to escape from
the prison by secret ways.

Then the Sadducean high priest sent the "captain" and his
police with orders to arrest them once again—but to arrest
them without violence, without stirring up a tumult among
the "fellowship." They were arrested and brought before the
Sanhedrin for judgment. The "apostles" were not willing or
able to deny what many had heard. Some of the members of
the Sanhedrin sought to impose the death sentence and turn
the prisoners over afterwards to the Roman procurator, as
they had done to Jesus. Then, "there stood up one in the
council, a Pharisee, named Gamaliel, a doctor of the law, had
in honor of all the people." This was no doubt Rabban
Gamaliel the Elder, grandson (son?) of Hillel the Elder.[34]
Gamaliel said that it was not proper to persecute these dreamers for this reason:—If the new movement has no substance
(and Rabban Gamaliel, the pious Pharisee and Tanna, was
sure that it had no substance), it will fail of its own weakness,

---

[32] See Klausner, *Yeshu*, p. 288, n. 5 [Eng. ed., p. 260, n. 6] and also in the
Additions and Corrections, p. 467, lines 11 and 12.

[33] Acts 5:17, 18. In place of Ἀναστάς ("rose up") in vs. 17, Blass rightly
reads Ἅννας (Annas)—the name of Hanan the high priest. Perhaps the two
arrests are only one; they may have been incorporated into Acts from *different* sources that told of *one* event. But it is difficult to make a decision
on this matter.

[34] See on him Klausner, *Historia*, III, 251-4.

just as the rest of the false Messianic movements have failed. And the proof:—Neither the false Messiah Theudas (who actually appeared a considerable time *after* the events we are now considering), nor "after him" Judas of Galilee (who arose in the time of the census of Quirinius, and hence lived a long time *before* Theudas) succeeded in the Messianic movements which they stirred up.[35]

This gross historical error, by which Theudas is reckoned as coming before Judas of Galilee, has caused many scholars to look upon the whole story of the intervention of Rabban Gamaliel in the case of Peter and John as a deliberate fabrication. It appears to me that there is no reason for this negative attitude.[36] There was no need for the author of Acts, who was a Gentile Paulinist and not favorably inclined toward the Jews in general or the Pharisees in particular, to fabricate this favorable story about the Pharisaic Tanna, Rabban Gamaliel. Nor does the gross historical error invalidate the whole story. This historical error, as I have already said in the chapter on the Acts of the Apostles,[37] was not an error of Rabban Gamaliel, but of the author of Acts, growing out of the latter's tendency toward a "historical" method. That is to say, he loved to connect events in the development of Christianity with general historical events without regard for exact chronology.[38] Therefore, this error does not require the invalidation of this unintentional testimony to the character of Rabban Gamaliel; for from all we know of him, he strove for "the glory of the Law," [39] but he was not one who fought for the love of it, and therefore he did not leave a deep impression on Judaism. In this he was like all the pious Sages who were

[35] Acts 5:36, 37.
[36] See also what I have quoted above, p. 226, from the words of Dessau, *Geschichte der römischen Kaiserzeit*, II, 2, 785, Anm. 1.
[37] See above, p. 226.
[38] As is revealed also in Luke's Gospel, *e.g.*, in the connexion of the census of Quirinius with the birth of Jesus.
[39] Mishnah (Baraitha), Sotah IX 15.

not innovators ("makers of history") because they were not
fighters.[40] Further on, I shall attempt to prove that the statement that Paul learned Torah from Rabban Gamaliel ("sat at
his feet") is also not intentional fabrication.[41]

From these considerations, I think that there is reason to
believe that the naturally patient Rabban Gamaliel did advise
that Simon Cephas and John should not receive the extreme
penalty and that innocent blood should not be shed; for according to the rules of the Pharisees, at whose head Rabban
Gamaliel stood, Simon and John did not deserve death, just
as Jesus had not deserved death in his time. It is also possible
that, because as a Pharisee Rabban Gamaliel was in favor of
the belief in the resurrection of the dead, as opposed to the
Sadducees, who denied it, he was not so provoked against the
two believers in the miraculous resurrection of Jesus, they
being in his eyes only *exaggerating* and *extremist* believers in
the resurrection of the dead—and nothing more.

The Sanhedrin listened to Rabban Gamaliel and did not
impose the death penalty on Simon and John. It merely
ordered them to be beaten with forty stripes, lacking one
[Deut. 25:3], as was the custom with transgressors, and then
to be set free. They "departed from the presence of the council, rejoicing that they were counted worthy to suffer dishonor[42] for the Name" (of Jesus).[43] In the last analysis, there
was, apparently, nothing more than "dishonor" in this flogging. And it stands to reason that they rejoiced particularly
over the fact that they were only flogged and not sentenced
to death—nor turned over to the Romans for the latter to
"do justice" to them, as was done to Jesus.

[40] See Klausner, *Historia*, III, 251-2.
[41] See below, Sixth Book, Chap. I.
[42] This expression reminds one of the phrase in Deut. 25:3, ". . . then
thy brother should be dishonored before thine eyes," also said in reference
to flogging.
[43] Acts 5:41.

The Controversy Between "Hebrew" and "Hellenistic" Christians; The Stoning of Stephen

1. We have already seen [1] that Jews of the Diaspora (Hellenists) joined the disciples of Jesus shortly after the original group made up of Palestinian (mostly Galilean) Jews came into existence. These two Jewish elements were very different from one another. They were different not only in language —one spoke Jewish Aramaic (and in part also Hebrew), while the other spoke Greek and other foreign languages— but also in their culture and in religious and ethical ideas. The original, the Palestinian, the Hebrew Judaism did not countenance the half, the one-third, the quarter Judaism of the Jews of the Diaspora—the "exiled" Jews, as we say to-day. Hence it was inevitable that this great difference between two kinds of Jews should be felt in the little Nazarene fraternity also.

Therefore, when the "disciples" from among the "Greek Jews" increased in number, there arose opposition between them and the "Hebrew" disciples, that is to say, those from among the Palestinian Jews. The Greek-speaking Jews, who were more or less foreigners in the Holy City, began to murmur and complain against the native Jews that the latter were not giving the widows belonging to the former group a fair share "in the daily ministration," that is to say, in the preparation of the meals, which were paid for from the common fund of the Nazarene "community." We have here a case of dis-

[1] See above, pp. 273, 275.

crimination against the "foreigners" on the part of the "original" members. There was an urgent necessity of setting the
matter right in order to silence the complainants, who undoubtedly had some justice on their side; for apparently, the
"Hebrews" had not recognized the "ritual cleanness" of the
Hellenistic widows in respect to the dietary laws.[2]

Hence, the "fellowship," which by that time had become a
sizable congregation (but it was still an essentially *Jewish* congregation), chose seven "ministers" (*ḥazzanim*, who in earlier
Jewish practice had not been leaders of public prayers only),[3]
or "deacons" (διάκονοι).[4] These seven "ministers" or "deacons" correspond in some measure to "the seven 'good men' of
the town" in the Talmud,[5] who are also mentioned in the
works of Josephus.[6] Upon these seven "ministers" the Twelve
laid their hands, and the "minister-deacons" assumed charge
of all the business affairs of the congregation, particularly the
administration of the common meals,[7] while the Twelve were
to occupy themselves solely with preaching and the propagation of the new gospel ("the ministry of the word").[8]

But the "ministers" were not at that time "deacons" or
administrators alone; they also read the Scriptures and taught
the children.[9] Therefore, the Seven did not have an economic

[2] What was in question here was the right to "serve tables" (Acts 6:2).
See also below, n. 7.

[3] *Cf.* "minister (*ḥazzan*) of the synagogue" (Mishnah, Yoma VII 1);
". . . the *ḥazzan* may see where the children read" (Shabb. 11a). [See the
note on this functionary in the Soncino Talmud, Shabbath I, p. 41, n. 7, Tr.]

[4] *Cf.* the clear statement of Epiphanius: ". . . the 'Azanites,' who among
them are interpreted as ministers or assistants" (*Haereses* XXX 11; ed.
Dindorf, II, 102).

[5] Megillah 26a (end).   [6] *Antiq.* IV v 14; *Jewish War* II xx 5.

[7] This inference can be drawn from the expression of the Twelve, "serve
tables" (Acts 6:2).

[8] Acts 6:1–7. With this latter expression, compare "the service of Torah"
(Berakoth 7b, near end), which of course has a somewhat different meaning,
to wit, recognition of the practical side of religious instruction by giving
diligent attention to the teacher.

[9] See above, n. 3.

function alone—to "serve tables." They quickly became also preachers, expositors of Scripture, and "ministers of the word" like the Twelve; [10] but they did oversee, apparently, both the material and spiritual affairs (administration of meals and preaching alike) of the Hellenistic Jews, who understood only the language of the Seven but not that of the Twelve, the latter being all Galileans and Palestinians. For all the Seven had Greek names, and among them there was even one called "Nicolaus a proselyte of Antioch." [11]

Apparently, the controversy was not about the matter of "tables" and the common fund alone, but also about the matters of leadership and preaching, which the "Hebrews" had arrogated to themselves as being closer to Jesus.[12] Finally, they arrived at a compromise: since all the Twelve were best fitted to preach the gospel to "Hebrews," being Palestinian Jews themselves, the seven Greek-speaking "ministers" were to supervise the common fund and also preach the new gospel to the Hellenistic Jews.

But the "life in common" was not a success and hence did not last long. Money became scarcer and scarcer; also, some of the members failed to put what they had into the common fund. This is the meaning of the story about Ananias and his wife Sapphira. These two sold some land, but handed over to the "apostles" only a part of the price received; the rest they hid. Thereupon Peter became angry at them and rebuked them; and when they died shortly thereafter, of course their death was attributed to this rebuke by the chief and first apostle.[13] The "spiritual communism" was soon given up after

[10] On the grounds that we afterwards see Stephen and Philip of the Seven engaged in preaching, certain scholars wish to conclude that the Seven were not originally assigned to economic duties (see W. Brandt, *Dienst und Dienen im Neuen Testament*, 1931); but this claim obviously cannot be sustained.

[11] Acts 6:5.

[12] See Ed. Meyer, *Ursprung und Anfänge*, III, 154-7, 250-1, 270-1.

[13] Acts 5:1-11. At the beginning of Tammuz 5683 (June 1923), during

Jesus failed to appear quickly "at the right hand of Power"
and bring about a "new world." Then the Seven became
mainly preachers of the gospel.

2. Among the Seven was found one named Stephanos
(Stephen). According to Basil of Seleucia (of the fifth century C.E.), his Jewish name was Kelila ("crown").[14] Perhaps
he called himself this as an equivalent of his Greek name
Stephanos ("wreath," "crown of glory"). But it appears that
he was a Hellenistic and not a Palestinian Jew, or at least, he
had lived a long time outside of Palestine among the Greeks.
This is proved by the fact that it is related of him that he,
being "full of grace and power" (that is, a man of strong faith
and great influence over people), was "disputing" with "certain of them that were of the synagogue called the synagogue
of the Libertines, and of the Cyrenians, and of the Alexandrians, and of them of Cilicia and Asia."[15] Thus he was talking fluently with Greek-speaking Jews, who had their own
synagogues in Jerusalem, as has been proved by the Greek
inscription found at the beginning of 1914, which tells of
"Theodotos, son of Vettenos,[16] priest and ruler of the synagogue."[17]

---

excavations for the building of a house in the Yemenite quarter near Bezalel
in Jerusalem, there was found a beautifully decorated ossuary, upon which
is inscribed in Hebrew שפירא and in Greek ΣΑΦΕΙΡΑ. Is not this the
Σαπφεῖρα of Acts, the wife of Ananias? In spite of the letter Aleph at the
end of the Hebrew name, it is difficult to suppose that this is the name of
a man; and it is difficult to decide from the bones whether they are those
of a male or a female. I have already proposed this identification in *Historia*
IV, 74, n. 2.

[14] In the sermon of Basil of Seleucia entitled *Oratio de S. Stephano.*

[15] Acts 6:8, 9.

[16] Is this name equivalent to "Abtinus"? *Cf.* "House of Abtinus" (an
order of priests) and "Chamber of Abtinus" (in the Temple), Mishnah,
Yoma I 5 and III 1, Shek. V 1, Tamid I 1; Tosephta, Yom ha-Kippurim II
6–10; and elsewhere. See S. Klein, *Jüdisch-palästinensisches Corpus Inscriptionum* (Wien 1920), Ergänzungen, SS. 101–4; H. Lietzmann, ZNW, XX
(1921), 171 [Barton, *Archaeology and the Bible*, 7th ed. (Phila. 1937), p.
564].

[17] See S. Klein, *op. cit.*, pp. 101–4.

If Stephen debated with Jews in the synagogue of the Cilicians, it is possible that Saul of Tarsus in Cilicia participated in this debate. Saul, a Hellenistic Jew studying in Jerusalem, was still at that time an enthusiastic Pharisee and hence he opposed with all his might the opinions of Stephen with regard to "the crucified Messiah" and "the curse of God that was hanged." At the time of the debate, Stephen had permitted himself to say that "Jesus of Nazareth shall destroy this place,[18] and shall change the customs which Moses delivered unto us." [19] Irked by this, certain Greek-speaking Jews faithful to the Law and to the Temple testified against Stephen before the Sanhedrin; and it is very possible that one of these was the Cilician Jew, Saul of Tarsus, who afterwards participated in the stoning of Stephen, as we shall see below.[20]

Naturally, the Nazarenes called the Greek Jews who testified against Stephen "false witnesses." [21] But Jesus himself had already been accused—and not without good reason—of boasting that he would destroy the Temple and build a new one in its place.[22] There can be no doubt that a similar statement was made by Stephen. He certainly said that the Temple was not all-important, and that Jesus was coming to destroy it in order to build in its place a new sanctuary not founded on sacrifices, but on faith and good deeds; and also that Jesus would set aside the ceremonial laws when he appeared at the right hand of Power, since the ceremonial laws are invalid for the Days of the Messiah.

It was impossible that words like these should be acceptable to the minds of religious Jews of that time, even if they were Hellenistic Jews. Hence Stephen was brought by force

[18] *I.e.*, the Temple, called simply "the place" in II Macc. 2:18, 30 and 5:19, 20; in Philo it is "the holy place" (*De Specialibus Legibus* III 123, M. II, 321; C.-W., § 130 [V, 187, 1. 10]; *Legatio ad Gaium* 40, M., II, 592; C.-R., § 318 [VI, 213, 1. 19]).
[19] Acts 6:14.
[20] See below, Sixth Book, Chap. II.
[21] Acts 6:13.
[22] See Klausner, *Yeshu*, p. 387 [Eng. ed., pp. 341–2].

before the Sanhedrin as a transgressor. At this point the author of Acts inserts a long speech,[23] which of course in the form before us is artificially constructed, like the speeches in the works of Thucydides and Josephus. But nevertheless, there is in this speech a kernel of truth, since Luke, the author of Acts, could have heard all the details of the trial of Stephen from Philip, one of the Seven and an associate of Stephen in the "ministry" (or "diaconate"); Luke could have obtained this information while he and Paul were lodging in the house of Philip in Caesarea.[24]

In this speech of Stephen's there are hard words against the Temple and against Jerusalem and its leaders; and Stephen even claims that Jesus is "the Son of Man," who approached "the Ancient of Days," as stated in the book of Daniel.[25] Heretical words like these enraged the crowds of people who had gathered near the Chamber of Hewn Stone, the meeting-place of the Sanhedrin, and listened from afar to the hard words of Stephen. Among these people were some fanatical persons who decided the case for themselves. They saw in Stephen a "blasphemer" worthy of stoning,[26] although according to the Talmudic rule "the blasphemer is not culpable unless he pronounces the Name itself"[27]—which Stephen had not done. The fanatics did not trouble themselves about the judicial rule; they took Stephen outside the city and stoned him.[28]

The Sanhedrin could not see fit to impose the death sentence on him, although he may have been deserving of that according to the rules of the Sadducees. But in the opinion of the Pharisees there was in his words no actual blasphemy, but only an offense requiring the forty stripes lacking one, which Peter and John had received earlier, and Paul was to receive

[23] Acts 7:1–53.
[25] Acts 7:41–56.
[27] Mish. San. VII 5.

[24] Acts 21:8.
[26] Mishnah, Sanhedrin VII 4.
[28] Acts 7:57–9.

later. The execution of Stephen was accomplished by "lynch law"; it was not according to the rules of the Pharisees, and probably not according to the rules of the Sadducees either. This thing happened about 30 C.E.

It was the first spilling of blood of believers in Jesus at the hands of a hostile and fanatical mob. Stephen was the first martyr of young Christianity; therefore, Christianity calls him the Protomartyr, that is to say, the "first witness" who testified with his own blood to the truth of Christianity as he understood it and believed in it.

The Beginning of Primitive Christian Preaching to the Samaritans and to the "God-Fearers" Among the Gentiles

1. The death of Stephen was an impressive event in the life of the young sect. It showed that the mass of the Jewish people, and not only the Sadducees occupying the place of authority, were opposed to the new views. This brought about great dismay in the ranks of the Christians for, apparently, the affair of Stephen stirred up a general persecution against the sect. And since Stephen was a Hellenistic Jew, the Hellenistic "disciples" suffered a larger share of the persecution. So they fled for their lives from Jerusalem and dispersed themselves in the cities of Judea and Samaria. But the Twelve, who were all "Hebrews" and observers of the ceremonial laws to whom the Hellenist Stephen appeared a complete antinomian, were not touched by the persecution, and they remained in Jerusalem.[1] This is a sign that there was not here a blind fanaticism directed against holders of other opinions in general, but a zeal for the foundations of Judaism as they were understood at that time—foundations which were being weakened among the Hellenistic Nazarenes. The "Hebrew" Nazarenes, with Cephas-Peter at their head, continued to stay in Jerusalem and carry on the affairs of the young sect for about fourteen years (c. 30–44) without being disturbed.

But even this ordeal of blood and the dispersal which followed it benefited the young faith instead of doing it harm. Thus every persecution of opinions.

[1] Acts 8:2.

Philip, one of the Seven and therefore a Hellenistic Jew, was among the fugitives. He fled to Samaria—to the Cutheans, ancient enemies of the Jews. Heedless of the command of Jesus, "Go not into any way of the Gentiles, and enter not into any city of the Samaritans," [2] Philip attempted to proclaim the gospel of the crucified Messiah, who would shortly appear, to these Samaritans, who, if they were not complete Jews, at least were not Gentiles, and even believed in a Messiah named Taëb.[3] Philip came in contact with Simon the Magian (Simon Magus), who apparently had made himself out a savior and divinity and had founded a new Samaritan sect, and prevailed upon Simon to confess faith in Jesus.[4]

James the brother of Jesus, the thoroughly Jewish Nazarene, questioned whether it was permissible to preach the new faith among the Samaritans after the opinion had prevailed among the first disciples that Jesus had opposed this and had sent the "apostles" only to "the lost sheep of the house of Israel." [5] Philip was not scrupulous about this, being a Hellenistic Jew belonging to the Seven, that is to say, one of the first Christians who had not known Jesus personally and who were more lax in their opinions concerning all matters fundamental to Judaism. Therefore, to counteract Philip, James sent to Samaria Simon Peter and John the son of Zebedee, the two outstanding disciples of Jesus, who knew the opposition of Jesus to preaching among the Samaritans. Peter, at least at that time, in the beginning of the growth of Christianity, held to

[2] Matt. 10:5.

[3] See A. Merx, *Ein samaritanisches Fragment über den Taeb oder Messias* (Leiden 1893); *idem, Der Messias oder Taeb der Samaritaner* (Beiheft zur ZAW, XXVII, Giessen 1909).

[4] See for details Ed. Meyer, *Ursprung und Anfänge*, III, 277–302.

[5] Matt. 10:6 and 15:24. I have attempted to show in another place that these words, attributed to Jesus himself, are *not* the mere reflexion of the later views of the Nazarene Jews (*Yeshu*, pp. 316–8 [Eng. ed., pp. 285–6] and particularly p. 317–8, n. 6 [Eng. ed., p. 286, n. 20]). See also Rengstorf's article ἀπόστολος in *Theologisches Wörterbuch zum N.T.*, II, 406–48.

the opinion that the Samaritans were not to be converted; only true Jews were to be converted. This can be inferred from the story of Peter's meeting with Simon the Magian. (Incidentally, this Simon actually lived and was not merely an artificially concocted pseudonym for Paul—"Simon Magus" opposed to "Simon Peter"—as the Tübingen School incorrectly supposed.) Simon wished to bribe Peter to make him an "apostle," but Peter would not agree to this. Simon Cephas could not agree to convert Cutheans, who were only half Jews; only genuine Jews were to be received as Nazarenes. Nevertheless, by means of Philip was made the first breach in the view that Jesus had come only "to the lost sheep of the house of Israel." [6]

2. From Samaria Philip turned toward the south. And on the way from Jerusalem to Gaza he met the Ethiopian eunuch of Candace, queen of Ethiopia.[7] This eunuch was a "God-fearer," but he had not been baptized as a proselyte (some Ethiopians were circumcised). The eunuch was in his chariot reading in a loud voice, as was the custom in reading at that time, from the book of Isaiah, chapter 53 (of course from the translation of the LXX); and he was perplexed to know whom the prophet meant by the Suffering Servant. Philip explained that the one signified was Jesus, who "was led as a sheep to the slaughter" and "bore the sin of many and maketh intercession for transgressors." This interpretation commended itself to the eunuch, and when they came to a stream Philip baptized him in the name of Jesus.

This was the first attempt to convert a man who was not a

[6] Matt. 10:6.

[7] In the kingdom of Meroë in Ethiopia there was a royal lady, the queen-mother, whose title of honor was Κανδάκη (Bion, fragm. 3). See on this Wiedemann, *Muséon*, III, 117 ff.; H. Guthe, *Kurzes Bibelwörterbuch* (Tübingen and Leipzig 1903), S. 110.

Jew by birth, although he was already a Jew by conviction.[8] *And the one who made this beginning was not a Palestinian Jew* (a "Hebrew"), *but a Hellenistic Jew.*

Philip afterwards passed through all the coastal cities of Judea from Ashdod to Caesarea, preaching the gospel—to be sure, not actually to Gentiles, but to Palestinian and Hellenistic Jews, and even—and this was the innovation—to Samaritans and proselytes. If he also preached Christianity to the "God-fearers" it is difficult to tell; but it is clear that if these "God-fearers" were Gentiles who had not become proselytes, Philip demanded of them circumcision, ritual ablution, and observance of the ceremonial laws (even though without undue emphasis on these), and in addition to all this, belief in Jesus as Messiah shortly to appear, and baptism in his name. In short, *in the first years after the crucifixion of Jesus, Christianity* (more correctly Nazarenism) *was nothing more than an adjunct to Pharisaic-Essenic Judaism.* Whoever became a Christian was first a Pharisaic (Essenic) Jew. Did not Jesus say: "Except your righteousness shall exceed the righteousness of the scribes and Pharisees, ye shall in no wise enter into the Kingdom of Heaven"?[9]

3. But it was quickly felt that if the new faith did not wish to remain only a small Jewish sect, it would have to make its righteousness *less* than the righteousness of the scribes and Pharisees, and not *more.*

For it soon became apparent that the Jews in general, for all their sects, would not believe in "the curse of God that was hanged," in a crucified Messiah, whom the Sanhedrin had condemned to death and whom the Roman authorities had

---

[8] Acts 8:26–39. This story of the baptizing of the Ethiopian eunuch would have been difficult to fabricate deliberately. Undoubtedly, Luke heard it from Philip himself while he was in Philip's home in Caesarea.

[9] Matt. 5:2.

executed without stirring up any opposition. The Jewish Messiah had to be both a warrior and a man filled with the spirit of wisdom and understanding; he must redeem his people from political servitude and bring about justice and goodness in a liberated land. Only then "shall all nations flow unto it," and only then shall he redeem by his wisdom and by the spirit of God which is in him the whole world from evil and sin, from idolatry and all the abominations of the Gentiles, and shall bring it about that "nation shall not lift up sword against nation, neither shall they learn war any more." All this is very far from what Jesus actually did—so how could an ordinary Jew believe that one "hanged" had risen from the dead and would appear "at the right hand of Power," and only then would bring about the Kingdom of Heaven on earth?

Even the emphasizing of the ethical requirements at the expense of the ritual requirements which was embodied in the teaching of Jesus, and the extremeness of his ethical demands in regard to social relationships, an extremeness which may be realized only in the Age to Come, when "the righteous will be sitting with their crowns on their heads basking in the bright light of the Shekhinah"—even this emphasis on ethics and this extremeness could not attract the hearts of the Jews to Christianity.

On the other hand, the pagans, whose gods were for the most part only human beings with natures magnified by exaggeration or imagination—these pagans, feeling great need for a "savior" (sōtēr), especially in those days, the days of the first Roman emperors, were already prepared to exaggerate the greatness of the personality of Jesus and to see in him a supernatural savior who had nothing to do with the *national* claims of the people of Israel, but was a preacher of exaggerated ethics and extreme good works valid for every man, whether Jew or Hellenist or completely foreign Gentile. Thus the young and new sect had to turn to the pagans, from whom the Pharisees had already taken a large number of proselytes.[10] But it was still necessary to throw off from the necks of the Gentiles "the yoke of the Law and the ceremonial requirements," to which they were not accustomed, and to put in their place a much easier thing—belief in Jesus and his ethical teaching only. Naturally therefore, and of necessity, the new sect turned itself into a new religion.

To this must be added the fact that we are dealing with the end of the period of the Second Temple, when the political fortunes of the Jews were sinking lower and lower. Gentiles in general and the Romans in particular at that time felt scorn and contempt for the Jews and Judaism. The powerful of the earth were Gentiles and not Jews. To speak of a Jewish Messiah at that time was very dangerous, since there was a political side in such a Messiah, upon which the Romans constantly looked with suspicion. It was necessary, therefore, to depart more and more from the Jewish Messianic idea, to transform the Jewish Messiah into a pagan "savior," to compromise more and more with the Gentiles in general and the Roman Empire in particular, to load the sin of the crucifixion of Jesus upon the shoulders of the weak Jews, to blame them and not the Roman authorities for the persecution of the Christians, and to make all sorts of exemptions and lightening of requirements for Gentiles and Gentilism. These things the general situation of those days required. It was necessary to separate from Judaism as much as possible, to bring the pagans as near as possible, and to become gradually not only a new sect, but also a new religion and a new church—of course in a restricted sense and not in the broad sense of later times.

These things could not be done by a Jewish Palestinian Nazarene—one who lived among his people and felt strongly that without the ceremonial requirements the nation Israel was likely to be assimilated by the Gentiles, and without faith

[10] Matt. 23:15.

in political and territorial salvation the nation Israel was in danger of deterioration. These things had to be done by a non-Palestinian Jew, a Hellenistic Jew, who, although he had received some instruction in Palestine, had also imbibed doctrines and learning from the Gentiles, a Hellenistic Jew who could speak both Hebrew (Jewish Aramaic) and Greek, and who was familiar with the Greek religious and philosophical ideas which had become the common possession of the cultured Gentiles of that time. He had to be sufficiently denationalized so as not to care about the damage to the nation caused by the putting aside of the belief in political redemption; for only if the Roman authorities, in whose eyes a political Messiah might be a danger to the empire, did not persecute him, could this Hellenistic Jew preach the new faith not only among denationalized Jews, but also among the Gentiles of all the more or less Hellenized lands round about.

And a Hellenistic Jew like this was quickly found in the person of *Saul of Tarsus*.

Sixth Book

THE LIFE AND WORK OF SAUL (PAUL) OF TARSUS (C. 10-64 C.E.)

CHAPTER I

The Childhood and Youth of Saul of Tarsus

1. Among those who participated in the stoning of Stephen [1] was a young man by the name of Saul. I have already suggested [2] that this Saul debated with Stephen in the synagogue of the Cilicians, in which Saul, as a native of Tarsus in Cilicia, prayed and preached, and that Saul, out of zealous opposition to the faith in a crucified Messiah, denounced Stephen before the Sanhedrin. This is by no means a mere guess, for it is related that "the witnesses laid down their garments at the feet of a young man named Saul"; [3] it is also plainly said, "And Saul was consenting unto his [Stephen's] death." [4] Saul was, therefore, one of the witnesses who brought about the sentence against Stephen, this fact being implied in the words "the witnesses laid down their garments at the feet of . . . Saul." [5] And perhaps he was among those who urged the stoning of Stephen, this fact being implied by the words placed in the mouth of Paul: "and when they [the believers in Jesus] were put to death I gave my vote against them." [6]

This Saul was the real founder of Christianity as a new reli-

[1] See above, pp. 290–2.
[2] See above, p. 291.
[3] Acts 7:58; 22:20.
[4] Acts 8:1; see also 26:10.
[5] According to the Pentateuch, after the one guilty of incitement to apostasy has been brought "without the camp" (Num. 15:35–6), as was in fact done in the case of Stephen, then "the hand of the witnesses shall be first upon him to put him to death"—by stoning—"and afterwards the hand of all the people" (Deut. 17:5–7, cf. Deut. 13:10, 11).
[6] Acts 26:10.

gion and a new church after it had been in existence for some
years as a Jewish sect and Israelite congregation alone.

2. Saul was born in the city of Tarsus in Cilicia [7] about 5–10
C.E., since at the time of the stoning of Stephen (c. 30 C.E.)
he was still "a young man" (νεανίας); [8] and in one of the later
Epistles which Paul wrote from Rome, and thus at the end of
his life (c. 60–63), he calls himself "Paul the aged." [9]

According to Jerome, the forebears of Saul were from the
city "Gischala of Judea," having fled to Tarsus when the
country was laid waste by the Romans.[10] Because of the
words "of Judea," while Gischala is in upper Galilee, some
have wished to set aside this datum. But *first*, "Judea" is in
Greek and Roman literature a general name for all Palestine,
including Galilee; and *second*, what interest would anyone
have in fabricating a datum like this? For in saying that Paul's
family came from Gischala, no particular honor is paid him.
Gischala was important to the Zealots and the fighters for
freedom because John of Gischala came from there, but it
was not important to Christianity or to any religious or
cultural movement. And the devastation of the country
by the Romans could have been in the time of Pompey or
Varus.[11]

Paul, like Hillel the Elder,[12] identified himself as belonging
to the tribe of Benjamin.[13] But the Benjaminite origin of even
Hillel the Elder is something to be called in question, since
it is difficult to imagine that books of genealogy according to

---

[7] Acts 21:39, *cf*. Acts 9:30 and 11:25.
[8] Acts 7:58.   [9] Philemon, vs. 9.
[10] See Hieronymus, *De Viris Illustribus*, c. 5; *Comment. in Epistolam ad
Philemonem*, vers. 23; Opera, ed. Vallarsi VII, 1, 762.
[11] See on this also A. F. Puuko, *Paulus und das Judentum* (Societas
Orientalis Fennica, Studia Orientalia, II, Helsingforsiae (1928), SS. 2–4.
[12] Yerushalmi, Kilayim IX 4 (39b); Gen. Rab. XXXIII 3 (ed. Th. Albeck, p. 306).
[13] Rom. 11:1; Philippians 3:5.

tribes still existed at the end of the period of the Second Temple; and even if such a pedigree were still possible for a man of illustrious family like Hillel the Elder (his descent was traced from the house of David) in Babylonia, to which the tribes of Judah and Benjamin went into exile, it is difficult to credit it in the case of a man like Paul (even though he was of a worthy family, as we shall see below) in Cilicia of Asia Minor, or even Gischala of Galilee. It is easier to suppose that the name Saul caused Paul to attribute his origin to the tribe of Benjamin, because King Saul came from there and because Paul's name was also Saul. Surely, if Paul could without sufficient grounds assign Jesus to the house of David,[14] why could he not assign himself to the house of Saul?

Saul of Tarsus calls himself "a Hebrew of the Hebrews," [15] meaning a Jew from those speaking Aramaic-Hebrew (which strengthens the possibility that his forebears came from Gischala). Nevertheless, he was a Hellenistic Jew, since he was born and grew up to a certain period in his life in a Hellenistic city. He spoke Greek and Aramaic (perhaps also Hebrew, since he was something of a scholar, as we shall see below). Christian scholars are confident that he learned the Torah in Greek, in the translation of the LXX, since in his Epistles he quotes Old Testament passages in the version of the LXX. But actually, this fact is not very decisive; it is possible that he was making it easy for himself by copying (or having his amanuensis copy) Biblical quotations from the already prepared Greek translation; it is also possible that copyists of his Epistles who had access to the LXX altered his earlier wording to conform to this widely current translation. Hence this does not prove at all that he did not read the Old Testament in the original.[16] And in general, can it be imagined that a Jew who

[14] Rom. 1:3.
[15] Philipp. 3:5.
[16] The case is much like that of Philo (above, pp. 179–80), except that Philo did not live a considerable time in Jerusalem as did Paul.

had studied in Jerusalem (as we shall see below) would not know the Torah in its original language?

But Saul was born in Tarsus of Cilicia, as has been said. And Tarsus was a city filled with Greek culture and Greek philosophers and men of letters, although the Oriental element was rather strong in it. Paul calls it "no mean city." [17] Indeed, in an inscription Tarsus is called, and rightly, "the great and splendid metropolis of Cilicia and Isauria." [18] It was of the nature of a border city between East and West. A trade route led from Tarsus over the Taurus Mountains through the passes of Cilicia (Cilician Gates) to Lycaonia on the west and Galatia on the north. Tarsus was an important commercial city because it was distant only one kilometer from the sea, and maritime traffic would go through Tarsus to Asia Minor, Cyprus, Phoenicia, Egypt, and the lands of the West. Its religion was polytheistic and naturalistic. Its chief deity, Sandon-Heracles (Ba'al Taraz in Aramaic), was similar to Attis in Phrygia, Adonis in Syria, Tammuz in Babylonia, and Osiris in Egypt. Dio Chrysostom (of Prusa) praises the morals of the Tarsians. But Philostratus condemns their love of luxury and folly.[19] At any rate, Tarsus was a city of culture, even though there were in it the shortcomings of all seaport towns. Strabo [20] mentions that it was the seat of a national university which could vie with the universities of Athens and Alexandria. Among well-known Tarsian philosophers was Athenodorus son of Sandon, teacher of Augustus Caesar (74 B.C.E.–7 C.E.). This Athenodorus was an ardent Stoic, pupil of Posidonius. Likewise well known were various Epicurean philosophers, litterateurs, and tragedians of Tarsus.[21]

[17] Acts 21:39.
[18] See G. La Piana, "Foreign Groups in Rome," *etc.*, *Harvard Theol. Rev.*, XX (1927), 260, n. 25.
[19] See Philostratus, *Vita Apollonii* I 7.   [20] See Strabo, XIV 5 13 (673).
[21] On the political and cultural situation in Tarsus (Taraz in Aramaic), see H. Böhlig, *Die Geisteskultur von Tarsus im Augusteischen Zeitalter* (1913); Ed. Meyer, *op. cit.*, III, 308–11; A. F. Puuko, *op. cit.*, SS. 11–6.

Paul, who grew up in these more or less Greek surroundings, no doubt learned Torah in Greek translation or by comparing it with the accepted Greek translation, the Septuagint; and he had acquired a certain amount of Greek culture even if it had not gone very deep. If there are imperfections in the Greek of his Epistles, nevertheless his language is a rich and flexible late Greek; there are even in his Epistles verses of Greek poets.[22] Of course, one must not exaggerate the measure of his knowledge of Greek culture; he had not gone deeply into the Greek philosophy of his time, nor did he deem it very important in comparison with the word of God in the Holy Scriptures or the teaching of Jesus. But it cannot be imagined that a man who wrote and spoke Greek as he did would be lacking in those elements of Greek culture which were common to all the educated people of Asia Minor in those days.[23]

The father of Paul was apparently a well-to-do and honored man in Tarsus; for he was a Roman citizen, a privilege which was attained outside of Rome proper only by people of wealth or influence. Thus Paul was born into Roman citizenship.[24] This was of great use to him during the course of his life, and toward the end of his life even saved him from death. Without this citizenship, which protected him in his numerous journeys and conflicts (although a number of times he received forty stripes lacking one in a Jewish court and did not appeal to the Gentile courts), he would not have been able to preach the new doctrine without endangering his life. As a Roman citizen he had, like the rulers of the

[22] At Athens in the Areopagus speech (Acts 17:28), he quotes from the *Phainomena* of Aratus, or from Cleanthes, who imitated Aratus; and in I Cor. 15:33 he presents a line from Menander (see on this Ed. Meyer, *op. cit.*, III, 100).

[23] Against A. Loisy, *Les mystères païens et le mystère chrétien* (1930), p. 311 [1914 ed., p. 332], according to whom "his [Paul's] literary acquaintance did not go beyond the Scriptures, which is probably the only book that he ever studied."

[24] Acts. 22:28.

Hasmonean line before him (John Hyrcanus, Judas Aristobulus, Alexander Jannaeus, Mattathias Antigonus), a double
name; his Hebrew name was Saul and his Graeco-Roman
name was Paul (Paulus). But it is also possible that he called
himself by this foreign name only after he had administered
Christian baptism to the Roman proconsul, Sergius Paulus, in
Cyprus.[25] Changing of the Hebrew name on the principle of
assonance ("Saul"–"Paul") was not yet at that time customary
among the Jews.

3. In spite of the fact that Saul was the son of a well-to-do
Jew, he learned a trade. For, "the father is obligated to his
son to teach him Torah and to teach him a trade," [26] and "he
who does not teach his son a craft . . . it is as though he
taught him brigandage." [27] Thus Saul also learned a trade; he
was a tentmaker (σκηνοποιός).[28] This trade suited an inhabitant
of Cilicia, since that country was rich in goats' hair, from
which was made felt for blankets, clothing, hats, and saddles.[29]
This trade, at which Paul worked even after he became an
apostle preaching the gospel and organizing Christian congregations, was of great advantage to him; for he was not dependent upon these congregations for his support as were the
rest of the apostles.[30]

When the boy had grown up, but was still in the springtime

[25] See Ed. Meyer, op. cit., III, 196–7.

[26] Tosephta, Kiddushin I 11; Mekhilta, Pisḥa (Bō') XVIII (ed. Friedmann 22b; ed. Horowitz-Rabin, p. 73; [ed. Lauterbach, I, 166]).

[27] Kiddushin 29a; Tosephta, ibid., I 11.

[28] Acts 18:3. There are some who think that Paul was a saddlemaker
(G. A. Barton, The Apostolic Age, 1936, p. 30).

[29] ". . . a Cilician goat-hair cloth [הקילקי], a money-belt, turban, or
curtain" (Mish., Kelim XXIX 1); the same expression ("Cilician" cloth) is
read in Siphra by the Aruch, the Oxford MS, and other authorities, in
place of קילקלים (Siphra, Shemini, VI 8, ed. Weiss 53b; note the accompanying commentary of RABaD). Cilicium (κιλίκιον) was a felt made of
goats' hair, which was used for heavy cloaks, hangings, blankets, saddles,
etc. See also Schürer, Geschichte d. jüd. Volkes, etc., II⁴, 80, Anm. 219.

[30] I Cor. 9:6–15.

of life,[31] his father sent him to learn Torah in the metropolis of Judaism—in Jerusalem. Paul was not an entire stranger in Jerusalem, for he had relatives there. His sister had married in Jerusalem, and she had a son who lived there.[32] Paul testifies of himself, that he was "a Jew, born in Tarsus of Cilicia, but brought up in this city (Jerusalem) and educated at the feet of Gamaliel according to the strict manner of the Law of our fathers." [33]

Graetz, along with many Jewish and some Christian scholars, decides that Paul did not learn Torah from Rabban Gamaliel, the evidence being that Paul was an *'am ha-arets*, since he says of a verse in Isaiah "In the Law [Torah] it is written." [34] This evidence is contradictory and could prove the opposite; just such an expression as this would be fitting and natural in the mouth of a pupil of Rabban Gamaliel; for in the eyes of the Pharisees and Tannaim all is Torah—the Five Books of Torah (Pentateuch), the Prophets, and the Writings (Hagiographa) alike. The verses which Paul quotes by the score in his Epistles show that he had a sufficient knowledge of the Pentateuch; and the manifold interpretations which he gives to these verses are, if not in content, at least in form and method, typically Talmudic interpretations —a fact which irritated both Wellhausen and Eduard Meyer. But there will be further occasion for me to weigh the question of the extent to which Paul actually knew the fundamentals of Judaism.

It seems to me that there is evidence, even if it is not absolutely conclusive, that Paul *was* a pupil of Rabban Gamaliel.

[31] This fact comes forth clearly from Acts 26:4 and Gal. 1:14. See P. Feine, *Der Apostel Paulus*, SS. 416-20.

[32] Acts 23:16.

[33] Acts 22:3

[34] I Cor. 14:21. See Graetz, *Geschichte der Juden*, III, 2⁵, 414, Anm. 1; see similarly C. G. Montefiore, *Judaism and St. Paul* (London 1914), pp. 58-129; A. Loisy, *Les Actes des Apôtres* (Paris 1920), pp. 284-91; *idem, Les mystères païens et le mystère chrétien*, pp. 310-1, n. 1.

The Talmudic Haggadah [35] relates that Rabbi (Rabbi Judah the Prince) would pray thus: "May it be Thy will, O Lord our God, to save me this day from the impudent and from impudence in matters of learning." The question was asked, What is "impudence in matters of learning"? To this the answer came that Rabban Gamaliel would sit and teach, "Woman is destined (in the Days of the Messiah) to bear every day." But "that pupil" scoffed at him, quoting the words of Koheleth (1:9): "There is no new thing under the sun." Then, by way of answer, Rabban Gamaliel showed him a hen which laid an egg every day.

On another occasion, Rabban Gamaliel sat and taught: "Trees are destined (in the Days of the Messiah) to yield fruit every day." Again "that pupil" scoffed in the same words of Koheleth. And in reply, Rabban Gamaliel showed him the caper bush.

Finally Rabban Gamaliel sat and taught: "Palestine is destined (in the Days of the Messiah) to bring forth Lesbian cakes and robes of Melat" (rolls of fine flour, and garments of fine wool which could be obtained only from Miletus). Still again "that pupil" scoffed at him. So Rabban Gamaliel showed him morels and truffles [Palestinian edible fungi which resemble cakes], and the bark of the palm tree [which resembles fine wool].

Who was "that pupil" whose name the authors of the Talmud did not wish to mention, who manifested "impudence in matters of learning," and who provoked Rabban Gamaliel on the subject of the *mundane side* of the Messianic idea?

Jesus is called in ancient Hebrew literature "that man"; and only Paul could have been intended by the words "that pupil"—the pupil of Rabban Gamaliel who "went wrong"

---

[35] Shabbath 30b. See on this W. Bacher, *Agadah der Tanaiten*, II, 96, Anm. 2; Bacher-Rabinowitz, *Aggadot ha-Tannaim*, I, 1, 67-8; Klausner, *Ha-Ra'yon*, pp. 328-9.

and thus could not be mentioned by name. Jesus was considered "impudent," [36] and likewise Paul his "disciple" ("apostle"), who "interpreted Torah in a perverse manner." [37] Jesus was judged "a scoffer against the words of the Sages"; [38] Paul was a "scoffer" against the words of the Sage Rabban Gamaliel, who emphasized the material and terrestrial bliss of the Days of the Messiah, while Paul says, ". . . the kingdom of God is not eating and drinking, but righteousness and peace and joy in the Holy Spirit." [39] Thus there is almost no doubt in my mind that "that pupil" means Paul, who sat "at the feet of Gamaliel." [40]

Saul-Paul emphasized over and over that he was "a Pharisee, a son of Pharisees" and that "after the straitest sect of our religion I lived a Pharisee"; [41] that "I advanced in the Jew's religion beyond many of mine own age among my people, being more exceedingly zealous for the traditions of my fathers"; [42] and that he was "as touching the Law, a Pharisee; as touching zeal, persecuting the church; as touching the righteousness which is in the Law, found blameless." [43] And

[36] Tractate Kallah (*Hamishah Konteresim* ["Five Pamphlets"], ed. N. N. Coronel, 18b). See on this Klausner, *Yeshu*, pp. 20–2 [Eng. ed., pp. 30–3].

[37] See on this below, in the last chapter of the present work.

[38] Gittin 57a. See also on this Klausner, *Yeshu*, pp. 23–4 [Eng. ed., pp. 33–4].

[39] Rom. 14:17.

[40] There is no good basis for the conclusion that the Rabban Gamaliel who discoursed about the Messianic Age was Rabban Gamaliel II (Rabban Gamaliel of Jabneh [or Jamnia]), as claims Bacher against I. S. Bloch (Bacher-Rabinowitz, *Aggadot ha-Tannaim*, I, 1, 68, n. 1). I have now shown that these Messianic portrayals are very similar to those in the Pseudepigrapha of the time of the Second Temple, and also very similar to the chiliastic descriptions handed down from Jesus (see Klausner, *Ha-Ra'yon*, pp. 328–31, where I made the very same error and attributed the discourses about the Age to Come to Rabban Gamaliel II). Hence these discourses are much earlier and are to be attributed to Rabban Gamaliel I and not Rabban Gamaliel II. See also I. S. Bloch, Kobak's *Jeschurun*, deutsche Abteilung, VIII (1871/2), 190–4; 254–6 (this article was called to my attention by my competent pupil, B. Rubinstein).

[41] Acts 23:6 and 26:5.   [42] Gal. 1:14.

[43] Philipp. 3:5, 6.

we have no reason to cast doubt on his words; for persons of this type, exceedingly zealous for one religion, are the very ones who become extremely zealous for another religion, if for any reason they change their beliefs; and changes like these take place very suddenly in the minds and hearts of passionate, emotional, excitable men of zeal. Yet one thing can be said of Paul: in spite of all his zeal and extremeness, he was not completely at home either in his first religion or in his second, after his conversion. His soul was torn between Palestinian Pharisaism, the teachings of which he learned particularly in Jerusalem (although he was "a Pharisee, a son of Pharisees" and thus a Pharisee by family descent), and Jewish Hellenism—and in a certain measure also pagan Hellenism, in the midst of which he was born and educated in his childhood in pagan and half-Hellenistic Tarsus. This two-fold state, or rather, this half-and-half condition was the cause of the complete overthrow of historic Judaism brought about by Paul— Paul, who was much more denationalized and divided in soul than was Jesus—the latter being a Jew of Palestine only, and hence not affected by foreign and conflicting influences.

4. Did Paul know Jesus in the flesh?

As long as it was thought that a considerable number of years intervened between the crucifixion of Jesus and the conversion of Saul into Paul, most scholars were convinced that Paul never saw Jesus in the flesh, since Paul hardly mentions the actual human existence of Jesus at all, but instead emphasizes the sufferings of the crucifixion and the heavenly characteristics of Jesus. But since it has become clear that Paul was converted to faith in Jesus shortly after the crucifixion, it is possible to suppose that Paul knew Jesus in person, even if he was not intimately acquainted with him.

Paul came to Jerusalem as a youth and received much of his education there. He himself says: "My manner of life then from my youth up, which was from the beginning among mine own nation and at Jerusalem, know all the Jews." [44] It was natural that an alert man like Paul, who a short time after the crucifixion was persecuting the disciples of Jesus, should take an interest in the commotion (even if this was not a great commotion) aroused by "the prophet (or Messiah) of Nazareth." In his intense Pharisaic zeal, he of course took a thoroughly antagonistic attitude toward Jesus and approved of the judgment against him; moreover, he foresaw danger for Pharisaic Judaism in the disciples of Jesus and began to persecute them. But a Pharisee of that time, even a very zealous one, would not have permitted himself to persecute people for their opinions, unless he knew the nature of these opinions and who first taught them. For the Pharisees were not only "by nature lenient with regard to punishments" among all the Jewish sects,[45] but this attitude of theirs was the chief point involved in the controversies between certain Tannaim, and between the Tannaitic "schools" (the "school of Shammai" and the "school of Hillel"). Difference of opinion was not, therefore, a sin in the eyes of the Pharisees unless they were convinced that this difference was contrary to the fundamental principles of the Torah. Thus it was inevitable that Paul should take an interest in Jesus and his teaching, since a short time after the crucifixion of Jesus he was already persecuting Jesus' disciples.

Paul says:

Wherefore we henceforth know no man after the flesh: even though we have known Christ after the flesh, yet now we know him so no more.[46]

Of course, these words are somewhat ambiguous. It is possible to say that the meaning of Paul is: Even if I had known Jesus

44 Acts 26:4.
45 Josephus, *Antiq.* XIII x 6 (§ 294).
46 II Cor. 5:16.

during his lifetime, I should not now desire any knowledge whatever of this earthly Jesus. According to this interpreta-. tion, Paul did not know Jesus during his lifetime. But it is also possible to say that the meaning of Paul is: Although I knew the earthly Jesus, I do not now desire any knowledge whatever of this earthly Jesus. According to this interpretation, Paul did know Jesus during his lifetime, *but wished to disregard the fact.*

It seems to me that this last point is fundamental. Paul fought all his life against the idea of his "inferiority," if it is possible to speak thus, as an apostle. The disciples and brethren of Jesus who were intimate with the crucified Messiah during his lifetime and had received instruction, parables, and promises from his own lips, would reproach Paul in effect thus: You are not a true apostle, and in vain do you on your own authority set aside the ceremonial laws; for you did not attend the Messiah, you were not intimate with him, and you cannot know his teaching firsthand. To this Paul would reply, that the important thing is not corporeal knowledge ("after the flesh"), but spiritual knowledge—the revelation by vision whereby Jesus revealed himself to him. The *heavenly* Jesus is of more significance than the *earthly* Jesus. For the earthly Jesus is important only because of his sufferings and death, which were propitiatory sufferings and a ransoming death; the earthly Jesus is not important because of his career as a human being in the midst of his disciples.

For, if this career had been the main thing, it would have been necessary to consider only Simon Cephas, James the brother of Jesus, and the rest of the disciples who shared this human career, as true apostles, since Paul not only did not share this career, but even kept himself distant from it and opposed it. Therefore, Paul does not make any mention of the earthly life of Jesus except with regard to something that concerns Jesus' heavenly messiahship; such as the fact that he was of the seed of David; or that he delivered certain sayings (including some not found in the Gospels) which were of importance to the nascent church; and in particular, that he died a guiltless death and redeemed with his blood all those believing in him.[47] The rest is not important in his eyes; therefore it is not important to Paul that he once knew Jesus "after the flesh." Apart from the fact that according to Paul "the flesh" is not important in the case of Jesus, just as in general "the flesh" is only a disturber of the spiritual life, something else is to be remembered. This is that while Jesus was still alive "after the flesh" Paul was opposed to him; so how could Paul dare to call attention to the fact that he knew Jesus in Jerusalem during the latter's lifetime? [48]

Indeed, it seems to me that the vision on the road to Damascus would not have been possible at all if Paul had not seen Jesus one or more times during the latter's lifetime. It is natural for a person, and especially for a strongly imaginative person, to picture in his imagination—or even to see in a vision—what he once actually saw with his eyes, even if he did not come very near to what he saw, or *because* he did not come near. Of course, sometimes the imagination pictures to a man not what he has actually seen, but what he has often heard of or read about and as a result has meditated much on it; but more frequently a vision reproduces, and reproduces more vividly, what was once actually seen, especially what was seen in a fleeting and uncertain experience, like a dream during waking hours.

Therefore, I think that Paul knew Jesus and his teaching and opposed both while Jesus was in Jerusalem disputing with the Pharisees; and it is possible that Paul was present at the

[47] See Ed. Meyer, *op. cit.*, I, 236; III, 354, Anm. 2; A. D. Hayes, *Paul and the Epistles*, pp. 127–36.

[48] See on this the detailed and to me convincing study of P. Feine, *Der Apostel Paulus*, SS. 413–37.

hour of crucifixion.[49] And this fearful sight, along with the sight of the stoning of Stephen, in which Paul participated—these two fearful sights haunted him, and in conjunction with an involved psychological process brought about the vision on the road to Damascus.

[49] P. Feine (*op. cit.*, SS. 433-4) calls attention to Gal. 3:1: "O foolish Galatians . . . *before whose eyes* Jesus Christ was openly set forth crucified."

CHAPTER II

Saul Becomes Paul

1. About two years passed by after the crucifixion of Jesus
(31–32 c.e.). This reckoning is based upon the imprisonment
of Paul at the hands of the Roman procurators Felix (53–61)
and Festus (61–62), and even more upon the inscription of
Gallio of Corinth, according to which Gallio was proconsul
in the Roman province of Achaea (in Greece) in the year 51–
52 c.e.[1] During the two years which followed the crucifixion,
the Sadducees, and perhaps the more extreme among the
Pharisees, began to persecute the new sect. They began to
persecute it not because it held the beliefs of Jesus, but because it transgressed these beliefs and argued that since the
Messiah had already come, a "new era" had begun, and since
the ceremonial laws had been ordained for "the old era," there
was no obligation to obey them. Had not Jesus himself held
the ethical requirements to be superior to the ceremonial?

This transgression was brought about especially by the
"liberal" Hellenistic Jews, who had attached themselves to
the sect almost from the beginning of its growth. Transgressors are always more numerous among the "uprooted"
and "denationalized."

In the persecution of the sect, Saul of Tarsus, the meticulous Pharisee, had a share. From everything which he himself
relates in all his "speeches" in Acts, and in a number of his
Epistles, about his excessive zeal and about the persecutions

[1] See A. Deissmann, *Paulus* (1911), SS. 159–61; A. Harnack, "Chronolo-
gische Berechnung des Tages von Damaskus" (*Berichte der Berliner Akademie der Wissenschaften*, 1912); E. Barnikol, *Die drei Jerusalemreisen des
Paulus* (Kiel 1929).

which he inflicted upon the young "church," [2] as also from
what is related of him in the reliable source of a thoroughly
Paulinistic writer ("And Saul was consenting unto his death"
—the death of Stephen.—"And there arose on that day a great
persecution against the church which was in Jerusalem."),[3] it
is to be concluded that the hypothesis is correct, that Saul, as
a Cilician Jew understanding Greek, was the one who acted
as informer against Stephen before the Sanhedrin.[4]

At any rate, a reliable Paulinist testifies that Saul was "still
[after the stoning of Stephen] breathing threats and slaughter
against the disciples of the Lord." [5] He persecuted them in
Jerusalem. In one of the "speeches," which of course Paul did
not deliver in the exact form in which we now have them,
but which were undoubtedly composed from reliable information, Paul says:

> I verily thought with myself that I ought to do many things
> contrary to the name of Jesus of Nazareth. And this I also did in
> Jerusalem: and I both shut up many of the saints in prisons, hav-
> ing received authority from the chief priests, and when they were
> put to death I gave my vote against them. And punishing them
> oftentimes in all the synagogues, I strove to make them blaspheme;
> and being exceedingly mad against them, I persecuted them even
> unto foreign cities.[6]

This should occasion no surprise. Eusebius has preserved for
us the information that Paul was a Jewish apostle before he
became a Christian apostle; [7] it was inevitable that "a Pharisee,

---

[2] See above, pp. 291, 311-2.

[3] Acts 8:1.

[4] See, *e.g.*, Graetz, *op. cit.*, III, 2 [5], 410-1.

[5] Acts 9:1.

[6] Acts 26:9-11. Again in Gal. 1:13 Paul says: ". . . beyond measure I
persecuted the church of God, and made havoc of it"; also in I Cor. 15:9:
". . . I persecuted the church of God."

[7] Eusebius, *In Esaiam*, 18, 1. See on this A. Loisy, *Les mystères païens*,
etc., pp. 314-5; A. Omodeo, *Paolo di Tarso*, p. 180; E. Barnikol, *Die vorchristliche und frühchristliche Zeit des Paulus* (Forschungen zur Entstehung
des Urchristentums, I, Kiel 1929), SS. 18-24; *idem, Die Christwerdung des
Paulus* (Forschungen, IX, Halle 1935), S. 13.

a son of Pharisees," possessing an ardent and zealous temperament like Paul's, should persecute in anger and in fury the Hellenistic Nazarenes, although he was closely related to them by birth and language; typical of these Nazarenes was Stephen, who, because of his faith in Jesus, spoke about the setting aside of the ceremonial laws and the destruction of the holy and revered Temple.

2. When the persecutions against the Nazarenes in Jerusalem became severe, a part of them fled to Damascus (or this part may have fled there even before, after Peter and John were imprisoned—because in that city there was a sect called "the sons of Zadok," who were deeply devoted to a faith in the Messiah, as testifies "The Book of the Covenant of Damascus" found in the Genizah of Fustat, Egypt, some years ago).[8] Also in Damascus there were many female proselytes, as we shall see below.

Saul the zealous could not rest. Those disciples of Jesus would corrupt also the Jews of Damascus! So he sought from the high priest letters to the synagogues of the Damascene Jews, who had, like the Jews in all Roman provinces, a certain measure of autonomy in their own internal affairs, although subject in religious matters to the heads of the nation in Jerusalem. These letters authorized Paul to arrest and bring back to Jerusalem the fleeing Nazarenes, "any that were of the Way [of Jesus], whether men or *women*."[9] The question arises, What authority did the high priest in Jerusalem have to arrest Jews in Damascus and bring them back in chains to Jerusalem?[10] For this reason, some reject all this information

---

[8] This "Book of the Covenant of Damascus" was published in Hebrew with introduction and notes by M. Z. Segal in *Ha-Shiloah*, XXVI, 390–406, 483–506.

[9] Acts 9:2.

[10] See H. Lietzmann, *Geschichte der antiken Kirche*, I, 103; J. Juster, *Les Juifs dans l'Empire Romain*, II, 145, n. 5.

found in Acts. It would appear that the answer to this question is to be found if we suppose that the persons referred to were Jewish residents of Palestine who had fled to Damascus, and not being citizens of Syria, were subject to the laws of Palestine; or that they were Damascene Jews who had voluntarily subjected themselves to the supreme ecclesiastical authority of the Jewish metropolis in all matters pertaining to faith and religion. Paul himself, the Roman citizen and native of Tarsus, received a number of times the forty stripes lacking one at the hands of a Jewish court without protesting against this as a foreign subject and freeborn citizen.

I have emphasized the word "women," which occurs in the authorization to make prisoners which Saul took with him as he started for Damascus. For Josephus relates, that when the Gentiles of Damascus decided to fall upon the Jews living in their midst, at the beginning of the war between the Jews and the Romans (66 c.e.), they kept this decision secret from their wives "who, with few exceptions, had all become converts to the Jewish religion." [11] On the way to a city like this, which contained many female proselytes, and no doubt male proselytes also, there inevitably occurred to the mind of a man who thought deeply and was possessed of an unstable temperament like Saul of Tarsus the natural thought: Here are foreigners, both male and female, from among the Gentiles who have given up the beliefs and opinions handed down to them from their forebears, but it is difficult for them to observe the ceremonial requirements, especially the requirement of circumcision. This is the very thing about which Jesus was lax and about the setting aside of which Stephen spoke, and paid with his life. . . .

As a Pharisee of a line of Pharisees, Paul was a devout believer in the Messiah; and as a Pharisee he knew that the Days of the Messiah are bound up with the "Messianic birth-

[11] *Jewish War* II xx 2.

pangs"; and finally, as one well versed in the Holy Scriptures he knew that the prophets were persecuted and put to death, and that Isaiah prophesied of the Servant of the Lord, who "would give his back to the smiters, and his cheeks to them that pluck off the hair." Why should it be impossible, then, for one who had been disgraced and crucified to be Messiah? [12] To be sure, the disciples of the crucified one scorn the ceremonial laws and scoff at the words of the Sages, while they hold as most important the faith in a Messiah; and of course this is not a good thing. But with the coming of Days of the Messiah, in the Kingdom of Heaven, evil shall cease, "the impulse to evil" shall die, and the fire of lust, which was caused by the impulse to evil, shall be quenched, and hence the ceremonial laws shall certainly be set aside along with the coming of the Messiah.[13] Thus, if Jesus really were the Messiah, then it would be proper for those believing in him to disregard the requirements, the need for which had passed away with the coming of Messiah.

Again it must be admitted that the requirement which is most difficult for the pagans to fulfill is that of circumcision. And because circumcision is not required in the case of women, therefore the large number of female proselytes in Damascus. Is it not possible to set aside circumcision, at least

[12] Only by implication does Paul in his Epistles derive support from Isa. 53.

[13] Undoubtedly, the ancient view was that the ceremonial laws are to be set aside in the Messianic Age; there is already a difference of opinion in the Mishnah as to whether "the going forth from Egypt" [third section of the *Shema'*, Num. 15:37-41] is to be recited in the Days of the Messiah (Berakoth I 5; likewise Tosephta, *ibid.* I 12, and Babli, *ibid.* 12b; also Mekhilta, Bō' [Pisḥa] XVI, ed. Friedmann 19a, ed. Lauterbach, I, 135). We also have in the Midrash: "All the fixed festivals shall be abolished" (Midrash Mishle IX 2 on Prov. 9:2, the verse, *She hath prepared her meat, she hath mingled her wine*), although the fixed festivals are ceremonial laws from the Torah. See M. Zuker in the Jubilee Volume in honor of A. Kaminka (Vienna 5697), Hebrew section, p. 48, n. 46; S. Lieberman, *Sheqi'in* (Jerusalem 5699), pp. 80-1. Without good reason is the attack upon me by J. M. Gutmann (see Klausner, *Yeshu*, pp. 465-6).

in the case of Gentiles, and thus increase the number of male proselytes in Israel? Stephen and his companions, the Hellenistic Nazarenes, spoke of the setting aside of the ceremonial requirements—who knows?—perhaps they were right—and if this be true, why should one persecute the disciples of Jesus? —and why should one revile the name of the afflicted Messiah?—

3. Immersed on the long and arduous journey to Damascus in thoughts like these, Paul naturally remembered Stephen, who was killed before his very eyes and because of his own testimony against the legitimacy of Stephen's ideas; thereupon, *Jesus* also stood before him, as he had seen him once in life, and perhaps as he had seen him on the cross . . . for an imaginative and emotional man was Paul. And it is not to be wondered at, that out of thoughts like these he suddenly experienced a vision,[14] as described a number of times in the New Testament.[15]

According to the first description in Acts, "a light out of heaven" suddenly shone round about Saul; he fell upon the earth and heard the voice of Jesus saying to him: "Saul, Saul, why persecutest thou me?" Similar to this is a passage in the speech of Paul before King Agrippa, put into the mouth of Paul by the author of Acts, except that in this speech it is added that Jesus said to him, "it is hard for thee to kick against the

[14] Nor is it to be wondered at, that Paul did not mention even once that "the first impression leading him towards Jesus of Nazareth came from the stoning of Stephen" (E. De Faye, *Saint Paul*, 3-ème éd., Paris 1929, p. 10). The vision came upon Paul suddenly, without any *conscious* connexion in his mind with impressions of or reflexions upon the death of Stephen; these impressions and reflexions acted upon the lower reaches of Paul's mind, or, as we say to-day, they were "below the threshold of consciousness" or "subliminal." See on this K. Holsten, *Die Christusvision des Paulus und die Genesis des paulinischen Evangeliums* (Rostock 1861); W. Olschewski, *Die Wurzeln der paulinischen Christologie* (Dissert., Königsberg i. Pr. 1909), SS. 16–23.

[15] See Acts 9:3–19; 22:6–13; 26:12–19; Gal. 1:12–16; I Cor. 15:8, 9.

goads." [16] This expression is presented by Paul as though it was spoken by Jesus "in the Hebrew language"; but actually, it is a Greek expression found in Pindar, Aeschylus, Euripides (especially in the tragedy *Bacchae*, 794–5), and elsewhere.[17] The persons journeying with him heard the voice, but they saw no one; or they saw a light, but did not hear the voice.[18]

Paul was certain that he had seen Jesus, but in a vision and not in actuality. In his "speech" before Agrippa he calls what he saw a "heavenly vision" (οὐράνιος ὀπτασία).[19] And in one of his Epistles he says that God had seen fit "to reveal his Son *in me*" (ἐν ἐμοί).[20] At another time, when Paul was speaking, apparently about another vision,[21] but a very similar one, he says:

I know a man in Christ, fourteen years ago (whether in the body, I know not; or whether out of the body, I know not; God knoweth), such a one caught up even to the third heaven. And I know such a man (whether in the body, or apart from the body, I know not; God knoweth), how that he was caught up into Paradise,[22] and heard unspeakable words, which it is not lawful for a man to utter.[23]

Here again, we do not have clear words of Jesus, but vague, veiled, and esoteric words, which cannot be told and which it is forbidden to man even to utter. . . .

At any rate, these descriptions, in spite of all their contra-

[16] *Cf.* Acts 9:5 with 26:14 (in some texts and versions this expression is also found in 9:4 or 5, and even in 22:7).

[17] See for details Lothar Schmidt, article κέντρον, *Theologisches Wörterbuch zum N.T.*, III, 662–8.

[18] *Cf.* Acts 9:7 with 22:9.

[19] Acts 26:19.

[20] Gal. 1:16 [Klausner takes this to mean "within me." Tr.].

[21] See Ed. Meyer, *Ursprung u. Anfänge d. Christentums*, III, 204–5.

[22] *Cf.* the mystical Baraitha: "Four men entered *Paradise*. . . . Ben ʿAzzai cast a look and died. . . . Ben Zoma looked and became demented. . . . Aḥer (Elisha ben Abuyah) mutilated the shoots [apostatized, lost his religion]. . . . R. Akiba departed unhurt" (Hagigah 14b; Tos., *ibid.* II 3 and 4).

[23] II Cor. 12:2–4.

dictions, prove that we are here not dealing with fabrication and fraud, but with a psychological phenomenon which is found among dreamers and visionaries, a phenomenon such as we saw in the "resurrection-story" which was woven around the crucified Jesus by Mary Magdalene and the rest of Jesus' disciples,[24] something like the "visions" of the Mormons in our time. An even more understandable recent example is afforded by the remarkable poet and dramatist, the Kabbalist R. Moses Hayyim Luzzatto. He was certainly no fraudulent falsifier, no deceiver; rather, he was a cultured man, well-versed in the Italian literature of his time. Yet he wrote in a private letter to R. Benjamin Cohen, his teacher, on the third day of Hanukkah, 5490 (1730), as follows:

On the first of the month of Sivan of the year 5487 (1727), while keeping in mind a kabbalistic formula, I fell asleep; and upon awaking I heard a voice saying: "I have come down to reveal hidden secrets of the Holy King." [25] I stood trembling a little, then I felt encouraged, and the voice did not stop revealing things mysterious. The next day at the same hour I took the precaution to be left to myself in the room, and the voice came again revealing another secret. Then one day he told me he was a Maggid [messenger] sent from heaven, and gave me certain formulas to keep in mind every day, until he should return. *I saw nothing of him; but I heard his voice* speaking out of my own mouth.[26]

A voice of this nature was heard by Paul. He repeatedly mentions the vision in his Epistles, and hence it is certain that he believed in its genuineness; but he was not able to make

[24] See Klausner, *Yeshu*, pp. 403–6 [Eng. ed., pp. 356–9]; see also above, p. 264.
[25] [The voice spoke in Aramaic; Klausner translates into Hebrew in this note. Tr.]
[26] S. Ginzburg, *R. Mosheh Hayyim Luzzato u-Bene Doro* (Tel-Aviv 5697–1937), part I, p. 39. [See in English, Simon Ginzburg, *The Life and Works of Moses Hayyim Luzzato* (Philadelphia 1931), pp. 34–5].

clear even to himself, whether it was an entirely subjective phenomenon, or whether it corresponded to some external event.

4. In the same Epistle in which Paul describes himself as the "one caught up even to the third heaven" and "he that was caught up into Paradise," he says:

And by reason of the exceeding greatness of the revelations, that I should not be exalted overmuch, there was given to me a thorn [27] in the flesh, a messenger of Satan to buffet me, that I should not be exalted overmuch.[28]

What was this "thorn" or "sting" or "sharp stake" in the flesh of Paul, which was as though "a messenger of Satan" struck him actual blows?

Paul once praises the Galatians because they did not make use of "that which was a temptation to you" (another reading is "to me") "in my flesh" to despise and "spit upon" him.[29] And in Acts it is related that after he had seen the vision of Jesus on the road to Damascus, "he fell upon the earth," and then

. . . arose from the earth; and when his eyes were opened, he saw nothing; and they led him by the hand, and brought him into Damascus. And he was three days without sight, and did neither eat nor drink.[30]

Many have been the attempted explanations of this "thorn" ("sting") or "sharp stake" in the flesh of Paul; it is almost certain that it is the same as the "temptation" in his flesh which caused contempt and "spitting." Nearly all agree that a severe ailment is meant. But what sort of an ailment?

Some have decided that it was a fever of Malta or of the

---

[27] Greek σκόλοψ, meaning "thorn," "sting," or "sharp stake."
[28] II Cor. 12:7.　　　　　　　[29] Gal. 4:14.
[30] Acts 9:4, 8, 9; cf. 22:11-13.

Mediterranean Sea, or malaria (thus think Alexander and Ramsay); others suppose that it was an acute disease of the eyes (thus Farrar, Eduard Meyer, *et al.*); still others think that it was a severe case of neurasthenia (thus Herzog, Lietzmann, *et al.*).[31] But none of these diseases bring contempt or "spitting" [32] upon their victims, nor do any of them cause a "falling to earth" because of a very strong flash of light (a "heavenly vision," "a light from heaven, above the brightness of the sun") or temporary blindness ("three days without sight").

Therefore, I am inclined to believe (with Ewald, Hausrath, Holsten, Schmiedel, Wrede, *et al.*) that Paul was afflicted with "falling sickness," as it is called ordinarily in Hebrew, or epilepsy, as it is called in foreign languages.[33] We know that in ancient times people would spit upon an epileptic in order to protect themselves from being seized by this disease, which they attributed to an unclean spirit—or in order to drive out the "evil spirit" in the epileptic; this naturally involved a certain amount of contempt.[34] Moreover, some epileptics have

---

[31] See for details of all these hypotheses D. A. Hayes, *op. cit.*, pp. 36–46.

[32] There is a widespread opinion that the reference here is to a loathsome disease of the eyes, for the healing of which in ancient times someone would spit upon the eyes of the patient; but if so, how could there be contempt in such spitting in order to heal; and what credit could there be to the Galatians for not spitting upon the eyes of Paul in order to heal him?

[33] See also W. Wrede, *Paulus*, S. 17.

[34] Hans Lietzmann (*Geschichte der antiken Kirche*, I, 112 [Eng. ed. entitled *The Beginnings of the Christian Church*, p. 147]) says: "Some have tried to regard him [Paul] as an epileptic—owing to a once modern whim —but without grounds." Below I shall show that there *are* grounds for the supposition of epilepsy; Ewald, Hausrath, Holsten, *et al.*, who hold to this supposition are not all "modern." Here I merely ask, What about the supposition of Lietzmann which follows in the next sentence after the above? —"However, his nerves were overstrung, and they plagued him with appearances which brought bitter suffering to him and others." Is not this much more of a "modern whim"? To the best of my knowledge, neurasthenia is a more modern disease than epilepsy. A view similar to Lietzmann's is also held by the Muscovite professor, L. O. Dakshevitch, *Apostol Pavel* (in Russian, Berlin 1923).

been great and powerful personalities, who made a name for themselves in world history: Mohammed, Augustine, Saint Bernard, Savonarola, Jakob Boehme, and Swedenborg among great figures of religion and mysticism; Julius Caesar, Peter the Great, and Napoleon I in the political field; and Pascal, Rousseau, and Dostoevsky in the world of thought. Their strange malady, which arouses anxiety at the times of attack, not only did not lessen their greatness, but perhaps was an important factor in this greatness, just as nervousness (to which epilepsy is closely related) sometimes causes a passion for creativity, to which those who are not nervous cannot attain.

Naturally, in the case of a mystical person, a "spiritual man," like Paul, his psychic condition, the fruit of his malady, would be abnormal; and this psychic condition it was which caused, or at least helped to cause, his excessive and unusual spirituality.

If this is the true explanation, the vision on the road to Damascus affords a specific illustration.

According to the Acts of the Apostles, Paul says that he "fell unto the ground" at the time of the vision and was blinded by a sudden great light. This is the state of the last moment before the epileptic "fit" as it is described with marvellous skill by the great Russian novelist, Dostoevsky, who was himself an epileptic. In his distinguished novel, *The Idiot*, he describes this unique moment in these remarkable words:

. . . suddenly in the midst of sadness, spiritual darkness and oppression, there seemed at moments a flash of light in his [the epileptic's] brain, and with extraordinary impetus all his vital forces suddenly began working at their highest tension. The sense of life, the consciousness of self, were multiplied ten times at these moments which passed like a flash of lightning. His mind and his heart were flooded with extraordinary light; all his uneasiness, all his doubts, all his anxieties were relieved at once; they were all merged in a lofty calm, full of serene, harmonious joy and hope.

Dostoevsky adds that "these gleams and flashes of the highest sensation of life and self-consciousness" had in them "the highest form of existence." "For this moment one might give one's whole life" since it is

. . . the acme of harmony and beauty, and gives a feeling, unknown and undivined till then, of completeness, of proportion, of reconciliation, and of *ecstatic devotional* merging in the highest synthesis of life.

Yet "stupefaction, spiritual darkness, idiocy stood before him [the epileptic] conspicuously as the consequence of these 'higher moments'." [35]

Thus Dostoevsky tells out of his own experience of the moment before the "fit" and the moment after it.

And Sophie Kovalevsky, the famous Russian mathematician, relates in her "Memories of Youth" that Dostoevsky talked with her about his epilepsy, telling her about the moment before the fit thus: "I felt as if heaven came down to earth and swallowed me up. I literally received God into myself and was filled with Him." Dostoevsky went on to say:

You healthy persons cannot even imagine the bliss which we epileptics feel in the moment before the attack. Mohammed assures us in the Koran that he had been in Paradise. All overwise fools believe that he was simply a liar and deceiver. But no, he did not lie! He had really been in Paradise during an epileptic attack which he suffered, even as I do.

Whether this bliss continued for seconds, or hours, or months,

[35] See Russian (Niva) edition of *The Idiot* (St. Petersburg 1894), Vol. II, Chap. V, pp. 240–2; [Eng. ed., *The Idiot*, by Fyodor Dostoevsky, translated by Constance Garnett (London 1913), p. 224–5]. In the Hebrew translation of S. Herberg (2 vols., Tel-Aviv 5689–90), see I, 256–7.

I cannot say. But believe me, when I say this: I would not exchange it for all the joys which life can offer.[36]

Here, in these remarkable words, is to be sought the key to the vision of Paul. The "heavenly light," which suddenly shone round about Paul, his "falling to earth," his being "caught up even to the third heaven"—"whether out of the body, I know not; God knoweth"—his entrance into "Paradise," his being "without sight" for three days so that his companions were forced to take him "by the hand" and bring him to Damascus, and only afterwards "there fell from his eyes as it were scales, and he received his sight"[37]—all these things show clearly, in my opinion, that we have here an attack of "falling sickness" or epilepsy. The new idea of Jesus as a suffering Messiah flashed into the brain of Paul a moment before the epileptic attack, when the "heavenly light" shone upon him and engulfed him, just as it shone upon Prince Myshkin, Dostoevsky's "hero" (that is to say, Dostoevsky himself), just as it shone upon Balaam ("the man whose eye is opened," who was "fallen down, yet with opened eyes"), just as it shone upon Julius Caesar, upon Mohammed, and upon Napoleon I. And *after* the marvellous moment of "heavenly light" and the being "caught up into Paradise," came darkness and "blindness of eyes" (the "stupefaction" and "spiritual darkness" of Dostoevsky), just as also *before* the wonderful moment Dostoevsky felt "sadness, spiritual darkness and oppression." All these are consequences of the disease, which

[36] Sonia Kowalewsky, *Kindheitserinnerungen*, I. Teil, Deutsch von M. Kurella (Halle n.d.), S. 118; another translation by L. Flachs and Fock-Schaneanu, *Jugenderinnerungen* (Berlin 1897), SS. 171–2. Mohammed is also mentioned in *The Idiot* thus: ". . . at that moment I seem somehow to understand the extraordinary saying that *there shall be no more time.* Probably," he added smiling, "this is the very second which was not long enough for the water to be spilt out of Mahomet's pitcher, though the epileptic prophet had time to gaze at all the habitations of Allah" (Russian ed., Vol. II, Chap. V, p. 240; Hebrew trans., I, 257 [Eng. tr., p. 225]).

[37] Acts 9:18.

was considered in ancient times to be the "work of Satan"; the epileptic, they thought, was possessed of an "evil spirit"—a devil had entered into him—and therefore everyone who saw an epileptic would spit upon him, in order that the discreditable disease, which was caused by "evil spirits" and "demons," might not communicate itself to the beholder. Naturally, then, Paul was grateful to the Galatians, who had not scorned him because an "evil spirit" had entered into him, and had not spat in his face or in front of him in order to ward off the disease from themselves.

The long list of epileptics, who were great in the political life of their time, like Julius Caesar, Peter the Great or Napoleon; who possessed strong wills and an almost mystical faith in themselves, or distinguished themselves by mystical beliefs and thereby produced many innovations, like Augustine, Mohammed, Savonarola, Jakob Boehme; or who did great things in philosophy and literature, like Pascal, Rousseau, and Dostoevsky—this long list helps us explain—*mutatis mutandis*, of course—the twofold work of Paul: *On the one hand*, Paul was the exponent of a unique mystical faith; *and on the other*, he was the great organizer of a new church, which it would have been impossible to create and administer without the great skill of a politician who took account of actual life and knew that "for everything there is a season" [Ecc. 3:1].

CHAPTER III

The Beginning of the Activity of Paul as a Nazarene

1. The vision on the road to Damascus, which occurred about 31 C.E., made a strong impression on Paul. Nevertheless, he naturally was torn by inner conflict between a heart full of the new vision and the power of endurance of the old views. A man like Paul could not lightheartedly surrender deeply rooted beliefs and opinions.

But one of the disciples of Jesus, Ananias by name, came to visit him during the time of his sickness after the attack of epilepsy, and persuaded him (removed the "scales from his eyes"—helped him to see the new movement with different eyes) not to be *against* the sect, but *for* it. I imagine that Ananias was the one who explained to him that there was hope for the new faith to win converts from the Gentile God-fearers only if they did not have to bear the heavy yoke of the ceremonial laws. There is, he may have said, a multitude of *women* in Damascus who have become proselytes.[1] Why? Because baptism is all that is required of them. Hence, if we do not demand circumcision of the Gentile men either, and in their case also, satisfy ourselves with *baptism alone*, greater and greater will be the number of proselytes who can be Jews and disciples of Jesus at the same time. . . .

But this idea bore fruit only after some time. At first Paul tried to preach faith in Jesus among the Damascene Jews only. Yet he remained "with the disciples that were at Dam-

[1] See above, pp. 319-20.

ascus" only "certain days."[2] For from the beginning the
disciples of Jesus in Damascus did not believe in Paul. It was
hard for them to believe in a man who had been converted so
suddenly from persecuting the new faith to preaching this
faith. Hence he was forced to go away to Arabia.[3] There,
where no one knew his past, he attempted to clarify to himself
the great change which had taken place in his soul; and perhaps he attempted also to preach his new faith among the
Jews of Arabia (or among the Jews of the Hauran), and
among the already circumcised Arab proselytes, who undoubtedly were found here as in all the Jewish Diaspora, it
being especially noteworthy that they did not need to be
circumcised again in order to become proselytes and that
hence baptism alone was sufficient for them.

From Arabia (or the Hauran) Paul returned to Damascus
to remain a longer time.[4] Then he presumed to preach Jesus
as Messiah in the synagogues of the Jews of Damascus (more
probably, to the Hellenistic Jews and their associates), who
were amazed at the fact that the persecutor of the Nazarene
faith had been converted into a devotee of it. Apparently, he
began to spread propaganda on behalf of Jesus not only
among the Jews, that they should be baptized in the name
of Jesus, but also among the circumcised Arab proselytes, for
whom baptism alone was sufficient to make them Jews and
disciples of Jesus, as has been said. By this he aroused the anger
of the "governor" ("ethnarch"), who was, apparently, the
head of the Arab [Nabatean] colony in Damascus, having been
appointed by Aretas IV, "lover of his people" (רחם עמה

---

[2] Acts 9:19.

[3] Gal. 1:17. Graetz (*Geschichte der Juden*, III 2[5], 417) supposes the meaning of "Arabia" to be the Hauran in Transjordania, the population of
which was a mixture of Jews and Arabs.

[4] Gal. 1:17. In Acts the two periods in Damascus are combined into one,
because the first was very short—only "certain days"—while of the second
it is said, ". . . when many days were fulfilled. . . ." *Cf.* Acts 9:19 with
9:23.

according to the Nabatean inscription, in Greek *philodēmos*).[5]
But it is also possible that the ethnarch had heard about the
doings of Paul in Arabia or the Hauran, which had stirred
up the Jews and the Arab proselytes. However that may be,
the ethnarch ordered his arrest and imprisonment, and the
Jews, Paul's opponents, guarded the gates of Damascus in
order that Paul might not escape through one of them. But
the disciples of Jesus in Damascus let him down by night
from upon the wall in a basket [6]—and Paul escaped.

I assume that Damascus and Arabia (Hauran) completed
the spiritual revolution which passed over Saul of Tarsus,
playing a part much greater than might be supposed from the
meager references to his stay in them found in Acts and the
Epistles. For Paul spent in them the first three years after he
was converted to the Nazarene faith (32–35)—and the first
years after a spiritual revolution are always the decisive years,
the years that leave their stamp upon all the rest of life.

2. During the three years while Paul was staying in Damascus, in Arabia, and again in Damascus, he feared to return to
Jerusalem; for there he had persecuted the Nazarenes most
bitterly, and there he was hated most bitterly. Only "after
three years," [7] and thus about 34/35, when the resentment and
hatred had finally subsided, did he return to Jerusalem "to
visit Cephas," that is to say, to get acquainted with Simon
Peter and to hear from him details about Jesus and Jesus'
teaching. Paul "tarried with him (Cephas) fifteen days," during which time he saw no other apostles (disciples) except
Cephas-Peter and "James the Lord's brother." To the truth

[5] The opinion that Aretas IV was then ruler of Damascus (Schürer,
op. cit., I[4], 734, Anm. 16, and 737; II[4], 108 and 153–4) is in error. See Ed.
Schwartz, *Nachrichten der Göttinger Gelehrten Gesellschaft*, 1906, SS.
367–8; Ed. Meyer, *op. cit.*, 346, Anm. 1.
[6] II Cor. 11:32; Acts 9:22–5.
[7] Gal. 1:18.

of this Paul swears as follows: "Now touching the things which I write unto you, behold, before God, I lie not." [8] So when the book of Acts relates that when Paul "was come to Jerusalem, he essayed to join himself to the disciples: and they were all afraid of him, not believing that he was a disciple," [9] that is to say, they feared him as a spy and *provocateur*, not wishing to receive him into their fellowship, and of course not believing in his vision—when this is related in Acts, there is in it no contradiction of what Paul affirms in his oath. Paul actually did not visit, in the two weeks which he spent in Jerusalem for the first time after the vision, any others than these two—one disciple-apostle (Cephas), and the man most closely related to Jesus (his brother James). Even they accepted Paul only thanks to the recommendation of the Hellenistic Nazarene, Joseph (Joses) Barnabas,[10] the Levite of Cyprus.

Joseph Barnabas was a man who played an important rôle in nascent Christianity. Since he was a Levite and the possessor of a name compounded with "Bar," he was a Jew—and a Jew belonging to a family that spoke Hebrew-Aramaic; but he himself was from Cyprus, being thus a Greek-speaking Jew. The author of Acts testifies that "he was a good man, and full of the Holy Spirit and of faith." [11] He was among the first Nazarenes who, "having a field, sold it, and brought the money and laid it at the apostles' feet." [12] We shall meet him

---

[8] Gal. 1:19, 20.   [9] Acts 9:26.

[10] In Acts 4:36 this name is translated into Greek as υἱὸς παρακλήσεως ("son of consolation"); if this is correct, it would be necessary to read Bar-Nuḥama in Aramaic and in Greek Barnamas instead of Barnabas. In the opinion of some, "Barnabas" is "Bar-Nebuah" ("son of prophecy"), or even a name compounded with the name of a pagan deity, Bar-Nebo (Dalman, Deissmann), and the author of Acts took the name out of its real meaning, or else accepted a popular etymology. In my opinion, the conjecture of "Bar-Nebuah" ("son of prophecy") is preferable, Luke the Gentile Christian having confused *nebuah* with *neḥamah-nuḥamā* because of inexact knowledge of Hebrew and Aramaic.

[11] Acts 11:24.   [12] Acts 4:36, 37.

again many times as we follow the work of Paul. Here we have already seen him coming to the aid of Paul at the difficult juncture when the disciples-apostles, fearing their former persecutor and slanderer, did not wish to receive him.

Joseph Barnabas, a goodhearted man, and, as we shall see below, one not very rigid in his opinions (like Peter in this respect), but devoted to the Nazarene movement, presented Paul to the two heads of the new movement, Simon Cephas and James the brother of Jesus, and recommended him to them.[13] Barnabas testified before them that Paul had experienced a sincere repentance and had courageously preached in Damascus his faith in Jesus. This testimony swayed both of the leaders. Simon Cephas, the "fickle," was not much concerned about what had happened in the past, and he received Paul, who remained with him fifteen days, as has been said; and during these two weeks Paul certainly heard from Simon much about the life and teaching of Jesus. And James the brother of Jesus, this Jewish Ebionite who was "not of this world," did not understand the character of Saul, nor did he know his chief ambition, which no doubt had not yet fully matured in Paul's own mind; therefore James accepted Paul with entire good will. The rest of the "apostles" Paul did not see, perhaps because *they* did not wish to see *him*, or perhaps because he did not consider them sufficiently important.

At any rate, on the authority of Simon and James, Saul began to work among the Greek Jews, who were close to him linguistically—and to a certain degree spiritually also. But Saul, possessed of a stormy temperament, uttered in his controversies anti-Jewish opinions which even the Hellenistic Jews could not accept; even they rebelled against his extremeness and sought to kill him. The thing became known to the

[13] In Acts 9:27 it is said that Barnabas brought Saul "to the apostles." This is partly true, since Cephas was an actual apostle and even James, along with the rest of Jesus' brothers, was an apostle for a time (I Cor. 9:5).

Nazarene "brethren" among his admirers—and they removed him to half-pagan Caesarea, where the power of the Jews was not great; and from there, a principal seaport of that time, he returned to the city of his birth—to Tarsus in Cilicia.

CHAPTER IV

The First Flowering of Gentile Christianity

1. Paul remained in Tarsus about eight or nine years (c. 35–43 C.E.). Meanwhile important changes had taken place in the young religious movement.

After the persecution which culminated in the death of Stephen and the flight of the Hellenistic "deacons," came years of peace and expansion:

So the church throughout all Judea and Galilee and Samaria had peace, being builded up; and, walking in the fear of the Lord and in the comfort of the Holy Spirit, was multiplied.[1]

From this we learn that the Jewish authorities did not anywhere persecute the "Hebrew" Nazarenes, who obeyed the ceremonial laws and were not "antinomians" like their Hellenistic Nazarene brethren. And we also learn from this that the apostles carried on much propaganda on behalf of their doctrines in all three provinces of Western Palestine.

Who were the propagandists? Most of the apostles, and the brothers of Jesus; but above all, Simon Cephas-Peter.[2] It is said of Peter that he "went throughout all parts"; and as miracle stories are told of his master, so also are they told of Peter. He heals one sick of the palsy (Aeneas), and raises from the dead a woman called Tabitha (in Greek Dorcas, meaning "gazelle"). These were, of course, a pronounced neurasthenic (neuropath) and a morbid woman, who were healed by an enthusiastic faith (it is unwarranted to suspect fabrication in

[1] Acts 9:31.
[2] Cf. I Cor. 9:5 with Acts 9:32–11:18.

337

the case of reports giving the names of those healed and the places of healing). But Peter did a more significant thing than this.

In Joppa he was staying in the house of Simon the tanner.[3] And from there he came by sea to Caesarea. Here he met a "centurion of the Italian Cohort," Cornelius by name, and dined with him. By this act he disregarded the laws of cleanness and uncleanness, and perhaps also those of forbidden foods (if he ate things forbidden to the Jews). We are further told that Peter baptized Cornelius and his family and friends in the name of Jesus—thus administering Christian baptism to Gentiles.[4] This act at that time is difficult to imagine even if we take into consideration the "fickleness" of Peter. Therefore it has been suggested that the baptism of Cornelius took place only after the persecution of Agrippa (see the next chapter), in the spring of 44, when Peter was forced to leave Jerusalem. The evidence for this view is as follows: Cornelius was, according to the Acts of the Apostles, a centurion of the "Italian Cohort" (*Cohors Italica*); but it is known to us from inscriptions that the *Cohors II Italica Civium Romanorum* was stationed in Syria in the time of Nero; perhaps it was there even before that, but not before the death of Agrippa I in 44 C.E.[5]

But the correctness of this hypothesis is to be doubted. *First*, the author of Acts is careful about his chronology; *second*, the author of Acts, who is thoroughly Pauline, would not have given Peter precedence over Paul in a fundamental matter like baptism of Gentiles if the matter had not been in fact that way; and he certainly would not have related this baptism *in extenso*, nor have given it the central place which he did. Therefore, I think that Cornelius actually had this experience about the year 35; also then, when there was no

[3] Acts 9:43 (end) and 10:32.
[4] Acts 10:45-8.
[5] See for details on this Ed. Meyer, *op. cit.*, III, 146-50.

king or native prince in Judea and Samaria (after Archelaus was banished), an Italian cohort could have been stationed in the country. But I think that only then could Peter have permitted himself to eat and drink with Cornelius the Gentile God-fearer without investigating carefully whether Cornelius had been baptized and circumcised, or only baptized without being circumcised.[6] It was against this eating with a Gentile who had not been circumcised that the "Hebrew" Nazarenes of the type of James the brother of Jesus complained; Peter defended himself on the grounds that he had been accorded a special revelation from heaven on the subject.[7] But the baptism of Gentiles in general came about at a later time; the author of Acts has combined it with the end of the story of Cornelius.[8] Part of the evidence for this is the fact that, in connexion with the baptism of the Gentiles by Peter, it is not mentioned *specifically* that Cornelius was baptized with them.[9]

At any rate, close association with Gentiles to the point of eating with them was something which the "Hebrew" Nazarenes, being observers of the ceremonial laws, could not endure. They saw that this would lead gradually to a breaking down of the fence of Judaism. But it was hard to contend with Peter, the first of the disciples, when he leaned for support upon his revelation in a dream.

Yet even the Hellenistic Jews among the Nazarenes still did not dare to preach the doctrine of Jesus among outright Gentiles:

[6] See on this point Yebamoth 46a and b (difference of opinion between R. Eliezer and R. Joshua). See also above, pp. 39, 40.

[7] Acts 10:9–11:18. From this passage it is to be concluded that the essence of the complaint of "the apostles and the brethren that were in Judaea" against Peter was not that he administered Christian baptism to Gentiles, but that he ate with them: "And when Peter was come to Jerusalem, they that were of the circumcision contended with him, saying, 'Thou wentest in to men uncircumcised, and didst eat with them'" (Acts 11:2, 3).

[8] Acts 10:44–8.

[9] Acts 10:48.

They therefore that were scattered abroad upon the tribulation that arose about Stephen travelled as far as Phoenicia, and Cyprus, and Antioch, speaking the word to none save only to Jews.[10]

2. But "there were some of them, men of Cyprus and Cyrene, who, when they were come to Antioch, spake unto the Greeks also." [11] This was natural and this was bound to come. From the beginning, Philip had preached faith in Jesus to the Samaritans, who were half Jews, and afterwards to the Ethiopian eunuch of Queen Candace—the eunuch being, apparently, a proselyte from paganism. Later on, Peter approached Cornelius the Roman, who was only a "God-fearer," and ate with him at the same table. Now it was necessary to take one more step; it was necessary to administer Christian baptism to outright pagans, who had not taken upon themselves any part of Judaism whatsoever. Peter had done this; but he did not do it because of any systematic process of reasoning. Rather, he defended what he had done on the grounds of what he had seen in a "vision." And he quickly "repented" and decided thus: Continue to preach faith in Jesus *to Jews only* and to avoid forbidden foods—as we shall see below.

Now arrived the time for the growth of the fruits of the germ of negation of the ceremonial laws, which was embodied in embryonic form in the teaching of Jesus.

It would appear that Joseph Barnabas was the first to clarify for Paul an idea of which Paul had been dimly aware even before: namely, that circumcision and the observance of the rest of the ceremonial laws should not be demanded of Gentiles believing in Jesus. As in Hebrew-Syrian Damascus, so also in Antioch, the capital city of Syria in those days, there were many proselytes from among the pagans. At first the

[10] Acts 11:19.   [11] Acts 11:20.

Hellenistic Nazarenes who had fled from persecution in connexion with the stoning of Stephen proclaimed the "gospel" to Jews only even in Antioch.[12] But after a time the "men of Cyprus and Cyrene" began to preach in Antioch also to uncircumcised Greeks. The names of these men have been preserved: Barnabas, Symeon who was called Niger (the Black), Lucius of Cyrene, Manaen (Menahem) who was brought up (σύντροφος) with Herod (Antipas) the tetrarch, and Saul.[13]

Thus, apart from Saul-Paul and Barnabas, we have three men otherwise unknown. And since their names are preserved here, it is a sign that they fulfilled a certain function at a certain time, but were afterwards forgotten because their work was insignificant in comparison with that of Barnabas and Saul. And it is worthy of note that in this list Barnabas comes first, and Saul only at the end.

All these were Hellenists who had lived for a longer or shorter time in Jerusalem. Barnabas was from Cyprus and Lucius from Cyrene; it is almost certain that they were the "men of Cyprus and Cyrene, who, when they were come to Antioch, spake unto the Greeks also." [14] They saw the Pharisees preaching Judaism to Gentiles and making proselytes of them—why should not the disciples of Jesus do likewise? To be sure, Barnabas and Lucius themselves required of the Gentiles, besides baptism, also circumcision and observance of all the rest of the ceremonial laws, or at least the most essential of these laws. Nevertheless, the Nazarene congregation in Jerusalem, headed by James the brother of Jesus, the strict observer of all points of Pharisaic-Essenic Judaism, complained against them, just as it complained against Peter and against his attitude toward Cornelius. The basis of this complaint was that *true* believers in Jesus can be only those who

---

[12] This appears clearly from Acts 11:19, where Antioch is specifically mentioned.

[13] Acts 13:1.

[14] Acts 11:20.

have been Jews from the beginning, according to the words
of Jesus to his disciple-apostles: "Go not into any way of the
Gentiles . . . but go rather to the lost sheep of the house of
Israel." [15]

The congregation in Jerusalem had sent Barnabas, a good
and devoted man, who had not yet approved in principle the
idea of relaxing the ceremonial laws for the benefit of Gentiles,
but thought it worth while to convert the Gentiles and make
them immediately Nazarene Jews, even if they had not first
been proselytes to Judaism—this Barnabas the congregation in
Jerusalem sent to Antioch to rebuke the innovators. No doubt
the report had reached Jerusalem that the Gentiles who had
been converted in Antioch were not observing the ceremonial
laws. But Barnabas, the "good man," found that these Gentiles
had become good Nazarenes; however, "he exhorted them all,
that with purpose of heart they would cleave unto the Lord"
("the Lord" here may refer to either Jesus or God).[16] It may
be inferred from this that not all of them believed with all
their hearts in Jesus as Messiah (or perhaps, in the God of
Israel). But Barnabas, being, like Peter, "fickle" and "tolerant," was satisfied with little. He also, like Symeon the Black,
like Lucius of Cyrene, and like Manaen, received proselytes
and God-fearers from among the Gentiles in Antioch, and
even outright pagans, allowing them to accept Nazarene Judaism directly; and of course he did not investigate them closely
with regard to strict observance of the ceremonial laws, even
if he had not yet agreed to throw off from them the yoke of
Torah and ceremonial laws completely.

3. Then occurred in Antioch an important event.

In Palestine the adherents of the new faith were called
"disciples of Jesus" or "Nazarenes"—after Nazareth, the native
city of Jesus. The latter name has been preserved in Hebrew

[15] Matt. 10:5, 6.   [16] Acts 11:23.

and Arabic to this day, because the Semites—Jews and Arabs —had to do mostly with Nazarenes (Jewish Christians). But since in Antioch there was a large number of believers in Jesus from among pagan Greeks, to whom the city of Nazareth was not known, and in whose eyes the actual life of Jesus the Jew was not particularly important, and who were inclined to disregard this life because the important thing to them was the messiahship of Jesus in their own sense, that is, his appearance as a "savior" (σωτήρ)—because of this they began in Antioch to call the believers in Jesus by a new name, "Christians" ("Messianists"); [17] that is to say, people distinguished from both Jews and pagans by the fact that they believed that the Messiah had already come, and that the essential thing was belief in this Messiah.

But neither the unknown men mentioned above, nor even Barnabas, succeeded in converting at Antioch Hellenistic Jews, proselytes, or pagans in great numbers. None of these "apostles" were capable of swaying masses of seekers after God and organizing them as a great new force. Barnabas, the greatest of them, recognized clearly that for this task just one man had been created. To be sure, not this man, but Peter and Barnabas and their fellows, had been the first to receive pagans directly into Christianity; nevertheless, he was the only one fitted to transform Christianity from a Jewish sect into a world religion.

This man was Saul-Paul of Tarsus.

[17] Acts 11:26.

The Execution of James the Son of Zebedee and the First Missionary Journey of Paul (C. 43–47)

1. Paul having fled from Jerusalem and returned by way of Caesarea to his native city Tarsus, remained there a comparatively long time.[1] During the course of these years matured all that new interpretation of Christianity, the first signs of which had already appeared in his preaching in Jerusalem (if it had not been so, he would not have been forced to flee; James the brother of Jesus never had to flee) and which we shall soon see again in his Epistles.

But it is impossible for a man of an enthusiastic and emotional temperament like Paul to sit for any number of years with folded hands. To be sure, during these eight or nine years (c. 35–43 C.E.) he was being influenced by the religious and cultural life of Asia Minor in general and of Tarsus—the cultural center of Cilicia—in particular.

Of course, it cannot be determined definitely that Paul at that time first began to study deliberately the mystery religions of Asia Minor, in a number of which there are such close likenesses to a dying and rising Messiah (in these religions there is a dying and rising god), to the Savior-Messiah (in these religions the god is the savior), and to the strange pneumatology (doctrine of "spirit"), upon which the faith of Paul is in general founded. The root and stem of this faith are Jewish, but its branches incline toward the paganism of the period.[2]

[1] See above, pp. 336-7.
[2] See on these religions, above, pp. 112-19.

Nor can it be definitely proved that Paul then for the first time purposely studied the Greek philosophy of the period, especially the Stoic philosophy, the ethics of which bears a certain resemblance—though somewhat remote—to the ethical teaching of Paul. Saul the Jew abhorred paganism and hated pagan philosophy like any zealous Pharisee in those days. But without his knowing it, by daily contact with the cultural life of a city steeped in this paganism and this philosophy—the latter having been popularized by orators and Sophists, who would preach it at the head of every street—it was impossible for him to escape being influenced by both of them either favorably or unfavorably. Thus Paul formed for himself during those years in Tarsus a religious and ethical world-view, which afterwards amazes us so much in his Epistles.

But a man who was energetic and an active organizer by nature like Paul could not be satisfied for eight or nine years with speculative activity alone. Undoubtedly, he preached faith in Jesus to congregations round about Tarsus. He himself writes, after he has related that he had been in Jerusalem meeting with Cephas and James:

Then I came into the regions of Syria and Cilicia. And I was still unknown by face unto the churches of Judaea which were in Christ: but they only heard say, He that once persecuted us now preacheth the faith of which he once made havoc.[3]

It follows from this that Saul preached Christianity to the *Jewish* congregations (for concerning "the churches of Judaea" he adds that they were "in Christ") of Syria and Cilicia immediately after he had fled from Jerusalem. Evidently, he made a success of his preaching and distinguished himself in it; if it had not been so, Barnabas would not have called him to Antioch. Yet the Nazarene congregation in Jerusalem, the mother-church of primitive Christianity, still

[3] Gal. 1:21–3.

was not willing to recognize him and his work, because it felt that he was as extreme in his Nazarenism as he had been in his Judaism. But Joses Barnabas, who had presented him before Cephas and James, and who knew the sincere repentance of Paul and had heard of his success in Syria and Cilicia, went from Antioch to Tarsus for the express purpose of seeking out Saul to make use of the latter's talents for the propagation of the new faith. And when he found him, he brought him, Paul, to Antioch to help him, Barnabas, in his missionary work among Hellenistic Jews, Greek proselytes, and even pagans. For "a whole year" (43–44 c.e.) Barnabas and Paul stayed with the Christian congregation in Antioch and "taught much people." [4]

Since Barnabas and Saul had been so successful in their work at Antioch, the mixed "Messianistic" congregation of Antioch decided to send the two of them on a preaching tour to nearby countries.

This was the first official missionary journey of Paul (43–47). What he had done before this had been more or less haphazard and without authorization from an important Christian congregation.

2. Meanwhile, there occurred a significant event for the Nazarene mother-church in Jerusalem.

In the year 41 c.e. Agrippa I became king of all Palestine, after having been king of a part of it since the year 37. Upon becoming a "great king" ($\beta\alpha\sigma\iota\lambda\epsilon\grave{\upsilon}\varsigma$ $\mu\acute{\epsilon}\gamma\alpha\varsigma$, according to certain Greek inscriptions), he hastened to return from Rome to Jerusalem. Thereupon he manifested evidences of that change for the better which had come about after his "years of folly" had passed, and particularly after the humiliation which he had experienced in Alexandria as a Jew. As far as it was possible for a king enslaved to Rome and forced to show defer-

[4] Acts 11:25, 26.

ence to the Greeks, he became devoted to the teaching of the
Pharisees and was minded to sacrifice himself for the sanctity
of the Temple (in the dangerous matter of the image in the
Temple in the time of Gaius Caligula), conducting himself as
a native king thoroughly loyal to his people. Josephus, Philo,
and the Talmud—all three speak well of him, particularly
after he became king in Judea.[5] And as one endeavoring to
find favor in the eyes of the Pharisees, and careful about the
observance of the ceremonial laws, it was impossible for him
not to give attention to complaints against the Nazarenes,
among whom transgressors of the laws had become numerous
even in Jerusalem. He executed James the son of Zebedee,[6] one
of the two brothers who were called Boanerges (בְּנֵי־רְגֵשׁ—
"sons of fiery zeal"). In his excitability this James had no
doubt committed some grievous religious transgression or had
spoken very harsh words about the traditional and accepted
Judaism.

It has been held that Agrippa also executed the second
"son of fiery zeal"—John the son of Zebedee, brother of
James.[7] But it seems to me that if the author of Acts does not
mention specifically the execution of John when he is mentioning the execution of his brother, we are not justified in
believing any later testimony. And to offer as evidence the
fact that John (the son of Zebedee, of course) is mentioned in
connexion with the Apostolic Council, and because of this—
on the grounds that he was executed along with his brother
James—to make the date of this council earlier, as do Wellhausen, Eduard Schwartz, and Eduard Meyer[8]—this is to

---

[5] See Klausner, *Historia*, III, 227–51; *idem*, "Ha-Pogrom ha-Rishon ve-ha-
Tselem ba-Hekhal" (*Ke-she-Ummah Nilhemet 'al Herutah*, 2nd ed., Tel-
Aviv 5699, pp. 91–124).

[6] Acts 12:1–3.

[7] See Ed. Schwartz, *Göttinger Gelehrte Nachrichten* (1907), S. 267,
Anm. 2; ZNW (1900), S. 109; H. Dessau, *Geschichte der römischen Kaiserzeit*, II, 2, 791, Anm. 5; Ed. Meyer, *op. cit.*, III, 174–7 and 420.

[8] See below, p. 365, n. 12.

commit the fallacy called in logic *petitio principii* ("begging the question"), of which the Talmud says that "the argument itself implies its refutation."

Then Agrippa put Peter in prison, because he also was considered among the transgressors—to be sure, not among the grievous transgressors, since he was only imprisoned and not executed like Stephen and James the son of Zebedee. But Peter escaped from the prison by means of some stratagem; and when he appeared suddenly in the night before the Nazarenes of Jerusalem, who had gathered in the house of Mary the mother of John Mark, he seemed to them to have been miraculously delivered.[9]

These acts of Agrippa I of course aroused the anger of the Nazarenes, so that they saw in the sudden and unnatural death of Agrippa the punishment of heaven for the killing of James the son of Zebedee and the seizure of Peter.[10] Not only the author of Acts and the Church Fathers, but even Christian scholars of our own times cannot take an objective attitude toward Agrippa I; they think that all his good deeds for his land and nation, and even his zeal for Pharisaic religion, were only for the sake of appearance.[11] Actually, Agrippa I did not persecute the Nazarenes for their peculiar Messianic ideas, but because they had disregarded the ceremonial requirements, which were in his time and in his kingdom *the law of the state*, and because they had failed to do honor to the Temple, which was at that time a *politico-religious institution*. The evidence for this is that Agrippa did not touch James the brother of Jesus because this James was punctilious about observing the ritual requirements and honoring the Temple.

[9] Acts 12:2–19.
[10] See above, p. 226. Therefore most scholars think that the execution of James the son of Zebedee took place near the end of the reign of Agrippa I, in 44 C.E. But actually, this assumption is not necessary
[11] Thus thinks even the best among them, Emil Schürer (*Geschichte*, I⁴, 560–2).

Peter, having been "miraculously" delivered, was forced to flee from Jerusalem, and James the brother of Jesus took his place as the head of the Nazarene congregation (C. 43-44 C.E.). Thereafter, the authorities in Judea did not disturb the Nazarenes for about twenty years, until 62 C.E., when the high priest Ananus son of Ananus (Hanan ben Hanan) condemned to be stoned James the brother of Jesus, at a session of the Sanhedrin which he convened on his own authority. This Sadducean sentence displeased "those who seemed the most moderate of the citizens, and strict in the observance of the laws," that is to say, the Pharisees. They lodged a complaint against Ananus before Agrippa II, and some of them even went so far as to go to Alexandria to meet Albinus, who in the meantime had been appointed procurator of Judea; these men represented to Albinus "that it was not lawful for Ananus to assemble the Sanhedrin without his [Albinus'] consent." So Albinus wrote an angry letter to Ananus, and because of this illegal act Agrippa II promptly deposed Ananus after the latter had exercised the high priesthood only three months.[12]

Here indeed we have one of the fundamental reasons, or perhaps *the* reason, for the rapid spread of Christianity: only the Sadducees opposed it. The Pharisees saw in it until the later years of Paul only a Jewish sect like the rest of the sects —indeed, a good sect believing in the Messiah, the resurrection of the dead, and the observance of the ceremonial laws. This difference of opinion between Sadducees and Pharisees with regard to the new sect saved the young Christianity more than once. Undoubtedly this was the "miracle" which happened to Peter. The guards of the prison or the judges were Pharisees, and they did not see any grievous sin in the beliefs of Peter, who at that time was still in favor of the cere-

[12] *Antiq.* XX ix 1 (§§ 200-3). For proofs that this passage is not forged, see Klausner, *Yeshu*, pp. 51-3 [Eng. ed., pp. 58-60]; *idem, Historia*, IV, 26.

monial laws; so they freed him. Up to the destruction of the
Temple we hear of only three serious persecutions of Christianity by the Jews in Judea: the stoning of Stephen, the execution of James the son of Zebedee, and the stoning of James
the brother of Jesus. Of these, the first represented a yielding
to the demands of an angry crowd, the last was perpetrated
by the Sadducees against the will of the Pharisees; and all
three were brought about by infractions of the laws either
in deed or word. Apart from these isolated incidents, the
Nazarene community, during the forty years from the crucifixion of Jesus to the Destruction (30–70 C.E.), remained
at peace and unmolested both in Jerusalem and all Palestine; it therefore was able to develop with amazing rapidity.[13]

We see the little "congregation" continually growing and
becoming an important community or church. It had a leader
at its head—James the brother of Jesus—it had "elders,"
"bishops," and "deacons"; and there were also "prophets" and
"teachers." All these constituted the governing body of the
"holy church" in all material and organizational, as well as
spiritual affairs, since both were closely connected with each
other. Every important decision was made with the consent
of the "prophets and teachers" (in the form of the laying on
of hands),[14] while matters having to do with organization,
administration, and the satisfaction of material needs in the
congregation were decided upon by the "elders" and carried
out by the "deacons" and "bishops." The secret idea shared
by all brought the members of the group close to each other.
And since they lived their real inner lives in a closed and
secluded circle, they did not attract the attention of the
Jewish authorities in Jerusalem, and only occasionally did they
come into conflict with these authorities. The most severe
conflicts took place outside of Palestine, between Jewish

[13] See Acts 9:31.   [14] Acts 13:3.

Nazarenes and Gentile Christians; and almost all these conflicts were brought about by Paul and his partisans.

3. On the first missionary journey (43–47 C.E.), Barnabas and Paul set out accompanied by John Mark, the son of Barnabas' sister Mary. We have already seen this Mary providing a place in her house for the gatherings of the Nazarenes,[15] to whom John Mark was devoted. This is the same Mark of whom Papias says that he was "the interpreter of Peter," and that for this reason the "Gospel according to Mark" was attributed to him.[16] From this it is apparent that the first missionary journey was undertaken with the approval of Peter and not against his will. And of course, Barnabas and Paul were sent off by the "prophets and teachers" of the Antiochene congregation after special prayers and fasting, and after these prophets and teachers had laid their hands on them.[17]

Barnabas and Paul went down to Seleucia in Syria. The first part of their sea voyage took them—as was natural—to the island of Cyprus, the birthplace of Barnabas. Arriving at the city of Salamis in Cyprus, they preached in the synagogues of the Jews; apparently, John Mark served them there as interpreter.[18] But it is doubtful if they had any success in their preaching; if they had made any converts, the author of Acts would have emphasized the fact as the first success. They crossed the island to its chief city, Paphos, where, in the presence of the proconsul, Sergius Paulus,[19] they came into conflict with a Jewish miracle-worker ("false prophet"), Bar-

[15] See above, p. 348. See also on her and John Mark Acts 12:12 and 25; 13:5; Col. 4:10.
[16] See Eusebius, *Hist. Eccl.* III 39 (§§ 290–2); Klausner, *Yeshu*, p. 71 [Eng. ed., pp. 74–5].
[17] Acts 13:2, 3.   [18] Acts 13:4, 5.
[19] This man is known to us with practical certainty from a Greek inscription. See W. M. Ramsay, *St. Paul the Traveller and the Roman Citizen*, 16th ed. (London 1927), p. 74.

Jesus Elymas the Magian ("sorcerer"), who opposed the teaching of Paul and Barnabas. But Paul won the argument with him, and the doctrine of Jesus found favor in the eyes of the proconsul, Sergius Paulus. There are some who suppose that it was at this time that Saul of Tarsus took the name Paul, after the name of the proconsul, and no longer called himself by his Jewish name, except when he spoke "Hebrew" (Jewish Aramaic).[20]

From Cyprus the three of them—Joses Barnabas, Saul-Paul, and John Mark—went on to the city of Perga in Pamphylia, Asia Minor. Thus they passed to the broad Greek world. And then Mark came to the realization that his way, the way of a "Hebrew" Jew and a disciple of Simon Cephas, was different from the way of the two Hellenistic Jews. John Mark held fast to the view of Jesus—"go rather to the lost sheep of the house of Israel"; but they—Saul and Barnabas—their chief aims were to convert pagans, to weaken the authority of the ceremonial laws, and consequently to minimize the peculiar significance of the Jewish nation. So when John Mark recognized this basic difference between himself on the one hand, and Saul and Barnabas on the other, he parted company with them and returned to Jerusalem.[21] Afterwards, we find him accompanying his uncle Barnabas, still later he is found in Peter's company,[22] and finally he returns to Paul, apparently becoming reconciled to Paul's opinions.[23] But at the beginning of the first missionary journey he was still "Petrine" in spirit,

[20] Some have concluded that Paul, as a Jew with a Greek education, had from the beginning two names, as had the Hasmoneans (John Hyrcanus, Judas Aristobulus, Alexander Jannaeus, Antigonus Mattathias), and as have the Jews of western Europe to-day (see on this A. Deissmann, *Paulus*, 2. Aufl., Tübingen 1925, S. 72). But the two names of this sort were in ancient times very dissimilar in sound (*cf.* John Mark), while "Saul" and "Paul" are very similar in sound; this makes the impression that the foreign name was artificial and an afterthought. See also H. Dessau, "Der Name des Apostels Paulus," *Hermes*, XLV (1905), SS. 347 ff. and above, p. 308.

[21] Acts 13:13.   [22] I Pet. 5:13.
[23] Col. 4:10; II Tim. 4:11.

that is, he was a Jewish Nazarene, who could not reconcile himself to the new way, so dangerous to Judaism, in which Paul and Barnabas were beginning to travel—the way of preference for Gentiles over Jews and the way of abrogation of the ceremonial laws.

From Perga of Pamphylia Paul and Barnabas went on alone, without John Mark, to Antioch in Pisidia.[24] In all these places, through which Paul and Barnabas passed, there were, along with the half-primitive native population, a Greek or Hellenized population possessing a considerable degree of culture, and also a more or less Hellenized Jewish population, which occupied an important place in the locality by reason of numbers, culture, and influence upon the rest of the inhabitants. The secret of Paul's success in all these places was that he found the ground already prepared for him by previous religious propaganda, or sometimes actual missionary effort, which the Jews had been carrying on among the pagans, particularly those who were Greeks or had been Hellenized. Paul found in these places true proselytes and "God-fearers," particularly *women*, to whom the law of circumcision did not apply and for whom baptism alone was sufficient to make them proselytes. Thus Paul almost always built his new structure upon the foundations of the old structure of Judaism.

And this was the manner of his work: he first turned to the Jews, and attempted to make among them converts to his teaching. There is nothing easier than to preach to Jews;

For Moses from generations of old hath in every city them that preach him, being read in the synagogues every Sabbath.[25]

When Paul succeeded among the Jews, he was delighted; then he attempted to preach faith in Jesus also to the "God-fearers"

[24] W. M. Ramsay, St. Paul the Traveller and the Roman Citizen is still the best book on the route of Paul's journeys, in spite of the corrections that have to be made here and there.

[25] Acts 15:21.

among the Gentiles. But for the most part he did *not* succeed among the Jews, so he turned to the pagans, and among them he had more success. For he came to them with a message about things which were more acceptable to their opinions than to the opinions of the Jews, since the essence of his preaching was approximately as follows: The Messiah, who was crucified and rose from the dead, is the sinless son of God (in the sense of being very closely related to God) who died of his own good will in order to atone by his blood for the sins of the world. By this means the world was redeemed from sin, so that there is no longer any need to observe the ceremonial laws for the purpose of making oneself worthy for earthly life; it is sufficient only to believe in this Messiah, who will shortly appear at the right hand of God to judge all peoples and to gain the privileges of eternal life and the Kingdom of Heaven for those believing in him.

A world-view like this was completely foreign to Palestinian Jews. It was more understandable to a portion of the Hellenized Jews, into whom without their knowing it had penetrated half-pagan ideas from their pagan neighbors with the effect of weakening their fundamental Judaism. But this world-view was even more agreeable to Greek or Hellenized pagans, especially to those who had come into contact with Jewish neighbors and had been more or less influenced by them. We have seen that the religious pagans of that time were filled with longings for a "savior" who would redeem them from sin and death. Paul made full use of this religious situation then existing in Asia Minor. Whenever and wherever he found Hellenistic Jews with their Judaism weakened, or more especially, pagans who were inclined toward Judaism, he made them "Messianists," that is to say, believers in the fundamental of fundamentals—that Jesus was the Savior-Messiah, who had risen from the dead after being crucified, and would shortly appear, with the coming of the "Kingdom of Heaven," to judge the world in righteousness on the Day of Judgment. In Palestine it was difficult for Paul to succeed in his new teaching; *for there the Jews had not been uprooted from their historic soil.* A peasant rooted in the soil is naturally conservative. But even those who were not peasants were attached to the traditions of the Fathers—traditions which had come into being in Palestine and which had been developing in that historic land from the days of Moses to those of Hillel and Shammai. In the Diaspora there were no national soil, no continuous traditions, and no complete and consolidated Judaism; therefore it was easy for Paul to alienate further the already alienated.

Nevertheless, even the Hellenized Jews were for the most part angered by the innovations in the teaching of Paul; sometimes their leaders also laid upon him the forty stripes lacking one, or were even minded to have him stoned.[26] But Paul was not only an excellent theologian, an influential preacher, and a talented organizer; he was also a diplomatic politician who knew how to adapt himself to any situation. Of course not always, but for the most part he was cautious in his words and deeds. He says of himself: ". . . to the Jews I became as a Jew, that I might gain Jews; to them that are under the Law, as under the Law";[27] he knew how to "rejoice with them that rejoice," and "weep with them that weep";[28] and he strove to "please all men in all things." [29] When, in the city of Lystra in Lycaonia (Asia Minor), he found the disciple Timothy, "the son of a Jewess that believed, but his father a Greek," and wished to take Timothy with him in order to train him for preaching, "he took and circumcised him because of the Jews that were in those parts: for they all knew that his father was a Greek." [30]

[26] Acts 14:19; II Cor. 11:23-5.
[27] I Cor. 9:20.
[28] Rom. 12:15.
[29] I Cor. 10:33.
[30] Acts 16:1, 3.

But sometimes Paul did not succeed in all his clever schemes and in all the concessions which he made, and things would reach the point where crowds of Jews would collect themselves together and attack him. Thus because of him there would occur tumults and conflicts in Greek cities possessing a considerable Jewish population. Under such circumstances, Paul knew how to explain to the foreign Graeco-Roman authority of these places that the controversy was about a purely Jewish matter which did not touch the security of the country or the religion prevailing there. In other words, Paul would say that the controversy had nothing to do with politics, but was an internal Jewish dispute regarding belief in the resurrection of the dead. Then he would endeavor to disparage and make people forget the political aspect of the word "Messiah," whereas in the eyes of the Jews the political significance was fundamental. Because of the danger in the political aspect of the Jewish Messianic idea, the first Nazarenes had already endeavored—perhaps not intentionally at first, but only from an instinctive feeling of urgent necessity— to emphasize the purely religious and abstractly ethical side of Jesus' messiahship.[31] Indeed, Paul, being forced to work in lands which lay under the harsh servitude and close surveillance of the Roman government, put aside the political aspect of the Messianic idea, and thus freed himself to a considerable extent from interference with his preaching. When he came into conflict with the Roman authority, he would explain to it that in the controversy between himself and the Jews the main issue was whether a certain "son of man" or "son of God" by the name of Jesus had risen from the dead or not; and what concern was this to the Roman authority or to the native Greek administration?[32] When the danger be-

[31] See above, pp. 268-9.
[32] This comes forth clearly from Paul's behavior before the Roman proconsul in Corinth and the Roman procurator in Jerusalem (Acts 18:14-6; 25:19).

came greater, Paul would take refuge in the fact that he was a Roman citizen by birth, upon whom therefore it was not lawful to impose overhasty penalties; for he had the right to "appeal to Caesar," that is, to demand that he be sent to Rome to be judged by the emperor. Jesus, who was a subject of Palestine, was not able to avail himself of this important privilege.

4. In the manner in which Paul had delivered his homilies everywhere in Asia Minor, so also he did in Antioch of Pisidia. He preached on the Sabbath in the synagogue a sermon based upon an exposition of Scripture, after the manner of a good Pharisee; and on the basis of a review of the history of Israel in a biased Nazarene spirit, he attempted to persuade the Jews gathered in the synagogue that Jesus was the Messiah, that he rose from the dead, and that the Jews could obtain remission of sins only by faith in the messiahship of Jesus and not by observance of the Mosaic Law.[33] These arguments found favor in the eyes of "many of the Jews and of the devout proselytes," and they begged him to preach in the synagogue again the next Sabbath. Of course, this request was made by uprooted Jews, and Gentiles superficially influenced by Judaism.

But on the second Sabbath, there came to the synagogue also Jews of another kind—crowds of Jews attached to their religion, who did not yield to Paul. They showed open opposition to every idea which he expressed, and flatly contradicted all his words. Thereupon, Paul and Barnabas said that, since the Jews had rejected "the word of God" as delivered by Paul and had thus shown that they were "unworthy of eternal life," they (Paul and Barnabas) perforce had to "turn to the Gentiles." And indeed, they met with much more success among the Gentiles. But the Jews were not content with

[33] Acts 13:14-41.

their opposition to the Nazarene preachers in the synagogue, so they "stirred up a persecution against Paul and Barnabas" by inciting against them "the devout women of honorable estate, and the chief men of the city"—and they "cast them out of their borders." [34]

Paul and Barnabas now proceeded to Iconium in Lycaonia, between the western coast of Asia Minor and the passes of the Taurus Mountains. There they remained for some time.[35] Also there they preached in the Jewish synagogue, and also there they made a few converts among the Jews and more among the Gentiles. But this time the Jews opposed to Paul and Barnabas aroused the Gentiles who had not been influenced by the two preachers against the Gentiles who believed in Jesus, so that a serious division arose in the city; one party was inclined toward the Jews, and the other toward Paul and Barnabas. It would appear that the party favoring the Jews was more numerous even among the Gentiles, since it is related that "there was an onset both of the Gentiles and of the Jews with their rulers" upon Paul and Barnabas "to treat them shamefully and to stone them." [36]

The author of Acts, like the Evangelists and like Paul himself, always endeavors to make out that the Gentiles in general and the Roman officials in particular were friendly to Christianity, and only the Jews persecuted it. But we have already seen that all this came about because it was more convenient for the Nazarenes to lay the blame for persecution upon the weak Jews than to hold guilty the powerful Romans and Greeks. To this may be added another good reason: namely, that there was even at that time more actual hope for Christianity from the Gentiles. For it was easier to persuade *them* to adopt a mystical and irrational faith in a dying and rising "savior" than to persuade the Jews. Therefore it was not proper to accuse them of persecution.

[34] Acts 13:42-50.   [35] Acts 14:3.   [36] Acts 14:5.

But something else must also be considered. This matter of the Messiah, as an important Jewish conception, touched the hearts of the Jews much more than it touched the hearts of the Gentiles who opposed the Nazarene messianism. These opposing Gentiles merely mocked at this "superstition," whereas to the Jews it was a denial of political redemption, a belief in "the curse of God that was hanged," and an abrogation of the Torah and the ritual laws. Therefore, the opposition of the Jews was more bitter. This fact lay in the nature of things. The matter caused the Jews keener feeling, and therefore they persecuted the more those who falsified and distorted this important conception; but the whole matter did not greatly concern the Romans, and therefore their persecutions were less severe and less frequent so long as Christianity did not conflict with the political institutions of the Roman Empire, such as emperor worship or service in the Roman army.

Nevertheless, the Romans also persecuted Paul not a little. He says: "Of the Jews five times received I forty stripes save one." Here he emphasizes that he received the stripes "of the Jews"; but when he immediately adds, "Thrice was I beaten with rods," he does not mention at all that this was done to him by the Roman lictors by order of the Roman or Greek rulers.[37] This would have been more dangerous to point out; therefore Paul passes over it in silence.

5. After persecution had been stirred up against Paul and Barnabas in Iconium, they fled to the cities of Derbe and Lystra, also in the province of Lycaonia. They attempted to preach in these two cities and their environs. Apparently, they succeeded in Lystra in some sort of healing of a neurasthenic, of whom Paul saw that "he had faith to be made

[37] II Cor. 11:24, 25. See on this Th. Mommsen, *Gesammelte Schriften*, III, 439.

whole." [38] This made a great impression on the crowds of simple pagans, who began to cry out: "The gods are come down to us in the likeness of men!" Because Barnabas was, apparently, handsomer and stronger than Paul, they called him *Zeus*; Paul, being "the chief speaker," they called *Hermes*; and they even wished to offer sacrifices to them. Paul and Barnabas very carefully explained that they were ordinary human beings, and that gods do not come down to earth in the form of men; [39] yet the Christians themselves afterwards taught that Jesus became an actual "son of God," one part of the Holy Trinity . . .

Truly, there is much to be learned from this tragicomic incident about the spiritual state of the pagans among whom Paul preached his new faith . . .

Not so the Jews. They were not impressed by the "miraculous" healing, or by the preaching of Paul and Barnabas. Jews who had already opposed the Nazarene preachers came from Antioch and Iconium, and they "persuaded the multitudes" (Jews or Gentiles?) that Paul had uttered unlawful sentiments. The crowds reached such a pitch of anger that they began to stone Paul, [40] and then dragged him out of the city to finish executing the sentence of stoning. But the "disciples" (Gentiles, of course) whom he had acquired in Lystra surrounded the attackers and saved him. Nevertheless, he was forced to flee with Barnabas from Lystra to Derbe.

In Derbe, Paul and Barnabas gained many believers. Then they returned to Lystra, Iconium, and Pisidian Antioch in order to strengthen the believers in their faith, which apparently had weakened after Paul and Barnabas left these three cities on account of the persecutions by both Jews and unbelieving Gentiles. Paul and Barnabas tried to persuade the

---

[38] *Acts* 14:9.   [39] *Acts* 14:11-8.
[40] *Acts* 14:19. Undoubtedly, the words "once was I stoned" in II Cor. 11:25 refer to this incident.

believers that their courage should not fail on account of the persecutions, because "through many tribulations we must enter into the Kingdom of God." [41] But Paul was not concerned in these places only with the bolstering of courage; he concerned himself also with the organization of the churches. He and Barnabas laid their hands upon "elders" in every church, in order that these elders might become the spiritual leaders of the congregations. Thus was the continuance of the Christian congregations provided for.

From Pisidian Antioch the two of them passed to Pamphylia, which they had already visited at the beginning of this missionary journey,[42] and they again preached the "good news" in Perga. From there they passed on to Attalia (modern Adalia). Then they turned back and came by ship to Antioch in Syria—the point from which they set out on this first missionary journey. There they gave a report of their labors to the Christian congregation which had sent them out on the missionary journey, and they stressed the fact that they had had especial success in preaching to the Gentiles. The church at Antioch, which was itself predominantly Gentile, was much pleased "that God . . . had opened a door of faith unto the Gentiles." Paul and Barnabas now remained in Antioch "no little time" [43]—about the years 46–47 C.E.

And here took place during that time an important event in the history of Christianity.

[41] Acts 14:22.   [42] See above, pp. 352–3.   [43] Acts 14:23–8.

CHAPTER VI

The Controversy Between Peter and Paul in Antioch and the "Apostolic Council"

1. When Paul and Barnabas returned to Syrian Antioch they found Peter, who apparently had been preaching there during the time when Paul and Barnabas were absent. At first there was peace between them. But the peace did not last long.

The Christian church of Antioch, like most of the churches outside of Palestine, was made up of Nazarene Jews and Christianized pagans. Gradually the Christians of pagan origin, owing to their numbers, had gained ascendancy over the Nazarenes of Jewish origin. Their meals were in common, so of course they did not observe carefully the law of forbidden foods; and at the special meals of the Gentile Christians this was the case all the more. At first, Peter "ate with the Gentiles." [1] But James the brother of Jesus, being a Nazarene loyal to Jewish law, could not reconcile himself to practices like these. He sent emissaries to Antioch, to demand that the Gentiles believing in Jesus should also be circumcised and observe the rest of the ceremonial laws; and if they did not, the Christians should be separated from the Jews. [2]

Peter became perturbed immediately, and "fearing them that were of the circumcision," he "drew back and separated himself" from the table of forbidden foods of the Gentiles; all the rest of the Jewish Nazarenes followed him, and "even Barnabas was carried away with their dissimulation." [3] Bitterly

[1] Gal. 2:12.
[2] Cf. Gal. 2:14 with Acts 15:1 and 5.
[3] Gal. 2:12, 13.

362

Paul spoke even after some years about "the false brethren privily brought in, who came in privily to spy out our liberty which we have in Christ Jesus, that they might bring us into bondage." [4] He means the Jewish Nazarenes and those who held to their way of thinking, or, as Christian scholars of our time call them, the "Judaizers," who came and saw that in Antioch the Torah and the ceremonial laws were being radically violated. They did not argue that it was forbidden to receive Gentiles into Christianity; in the years 46–48 all were agreed that Christians were to be received from the Gentiles. But the "Judaizers" did demand that the Gentiles become complete Jews even in their Christianity; and all the more so the Nazarene Jews, in view of their origin.[5] So Peter and Barnabas, the "fickle" ones, who had not thought the matter through and were still devoted to traditional Judaism, were perturbed by the messengers of James and agreed to these demands, which still appeared to them entirely natural.

But this was hard for the many Gentiles. They were not accustomed to the observance of the ceremonial laws, and in particular a difficult requirement like circumcision at a mature age. Even within Judaism there was an opinion that "one who has performed the ritual ablution but has not been circumcised is a proper proselyte." [6] Hence Paul thought that baptism and faith in the Messiah (Christ) were sufficient, and that circumcision should not be demanded of converted Gentiles. This opinion was not acceptable to the minds of the Jewish Nazarenes, in spite of the fact that previously there had been isolated cases in which Gentiles had been received into Christianity without circumcision. They considered cases like these as exceptions to the rule, and not as establishing a fixed prin-

[4] Gal. 2:4.
[5] See on this W. M. Ramsay, op. cit., pp. 155–66.
[6] This opinion of R. Joshua in the Baraitha, Yebamoth, 46a, is based on the argument "that the mothers had performed ritual ablution but had not been circumcised." Also see above, pp. 38–40.

ciple. Strong opposition to the view of Paul was aroused, and the Nazarene congregation in Antioch became a seething cauldron of dissension.

It was decided that Paul and Barnabas should go to Jerusalem, to the mother-church, where were to be found the best authorities, the apostles who had been the immediate disciples of Jesus, with James his brother at their head, to clarify the matter.

In the meantime, the material prosperity of the Jerusalem church had declined. While the renegade Jew, Tiberius Alexander, was Roman procurator, a drought occurred in Judea, leading to a famine, which afterwards spread to almost the whole Roman world.[7] Helena, queen of Adiabene, according to Josephus,[8] and Monobazus, her son, according to the Talmud,[9] expended great wealth in buying food in Egypt and feeding the hungry people. We do not know to what extent the Nazarenes in Palestine benefited from this. We know only the fact that after "early Christian communism" failed to endure, it was necessary during the famine to procure aid from outside for "the brethren that dwelt in Judea," "the poor," or "the saints in Jerusalem." This was proclaimed, apparently, by a certain "prophet" named Agabus—the proclamation being interpreted as a prediction ("prophecy").[10] There was need, therefore, of a *Halukkah* (distribution of charity), in the language of the Jerusalemite Jews of to-day.

So Saul-Paul and Barnabas were chosen as "apostles of Zion" (*Shelihe-Tsiyon*) to carry collections of money for "the holy church at Jerusalem," at the head of which stood the brothers of Jesus and the Nazarenes who had seen Jesus with their own eyes. Thus Paul and Barnabas became actual *apostles* [in a

---

[7] Ed. Meyer (*op. cit.*, II, 165–7) without good reason fixes the famine in Judea in the year 48/9; after 48 Tiberius Alexander was no longer procurator in Judea.

[8] *Antiq.* XX ii 5 (§ 51); *ibid.* XX v 2 (§ 101); see also *ibid.* III xv 3.

[9] Baba Bathra 11a. See Klausner, *Historia*, IV, 4.

[10] Acts 11:27–30. Also see Gal. 2:10 and I Cor. 16:1–4.

Jewish sense]. We still had in Jewry "apostles of Zion" in
the time of the emperor Julian ("Julian the Apostate"), who
attempted in 363 C.E. to suppress this institution, and in the
time of Honorius, who attempted in 404 to forbid the sending of "apostles of Zion"; only by the authority of Theo-
dosius II was the sending of these "apostles" stopped, in the
year 429.[11]

Paul and Barnabas came to Jerusalem, bringing to the destitute "brethren" the "relief money" which had been sent to
them by the richer "brethren," especially the "believing"
Gentiles of Asia Minor. This fact alone was sufficient to incline the hearts of the leaders of "the holy church at Jerusalem" *unconsciously* toward Paul and Barnabas and their
opinions, and toward those Gentiles and their customs. Men
are weak—even men who observe Jewish ritual law . . .

2. In order to clarify the attitude of the original and authentic disciple-apostles in Jerusalem to the difficult question
of the reception of converts by baptism alone, without requiring the observance of circumcision and the rest of the
ceremonial laws, particularly those of forbidden foods, a small
conference was called, which has been given a much too re-
sounding name: the "Apostolic Council" (in German, *Apos-
telkonzil* or *Apostelkonvent*). It took place about the year 47,
a short time after the persecutions of the Nazarenes had come
to an end with the death of Agrippa I in 44, and the apostles
who had fled from Jerusalem had returned.[12]

[11] The expression *Sheliaḥ-Tsiyon* ("apostle of Zion," "messenger to
Zion") served of course to designate not only one sent from Babylonia
to Palestine, but, more specifically, one sent to carry monetary donations.
See Betsah 25b; also Yerushalmi, Horayoth III 7 (47a); *ibid.*, Pesahim IV 9
(near the end of the chapter, 31b).

[12] According to Julius Wellhausen (*Kritische Analyse der Apostelgeschichte*, S. 29), Eduard Schwartz (*Göttinger Gelehrte Nachrichten*,
1907, SS. 271–3), and Eduard Meyer (*Ursprung u. Anfänge d. Christentums*,
III, 169–73, 178–84, 414–20), the Apostolic Council preceded the first missionary journey, which was accomplished in their opinion in the years 44–6.
They believe that the author of Acts made a mistake in chronology and

Our information about this decisive conference comes from two sources, with much contradiction between them.[13] As would appear from the words of Paul in the Epistle to the Galatians, this was a small meeting between Paul and Barnabas, who for their part defended the right of receiving Gentiles without requiring the observance of circumcision and the rest of the ceremonial laws, and the three "apostles," "who were reputed to be pillars," as Paul says with veiled irony;[14] these latter, James (brother of Jesus), Cephas (Simon Peter), and John (son of Zebedee) defended the practice of preaching to Jews only, or to Gentiles also on condition that they be circumcised and observe all the requirements. But according to Acts, this was a great gathering including the "apostles," the "elders," and the entire congregation. Of course, Paul is more to be believed. Naturally, just as Luke was prone to magnify the importance of the conference, so Paul was prone to minimize its importance, because the whole purpose of the Epistle to the Galatians is to show that Paul was not dependent upon "the very chiefest apostles," [15] as he in irony calls James, Peter, and their associates; and that he was an "apostle" on the same footing as they were, and therefore was not bound by the decision which had been arrived at privately by the agreement of five men, three on one side and two on the other. But it was even more natural that, with the passage of time, the

---

that the Apostolic Council was convened in the winter of 43/4, before the persecution by Agrippa, which occurred, according to them, a short time before his sudden death in 44. But *first*, it is difficult to attribute a gross chronological error like this to the author of Acts, who was careful about the order of events. *Second*—and this is the important thing—all the development of the Pauline point of view took place, according to this opinion, very quickly; therefore, those holding this opinion have to make many unnecessary and unjustified chronological changes in the events recorded in the book of Acts (in *e.g.*, the story of Cornelius, see above, pp. 338–9, or the work of Peter in Antioch, which would have no meaning at all after the decision of the Council, above, pp. 362–3—and so on).

[13] *Cf. Gal.* 2:1–10 with Acts 15:1–29.
[14] Gal. 2:9.   [15] II Cor. 12:11.

"Apostolic Council" should assume larger proportions in the eyes of second-generation Christians, so that it appeared to the author of Acts as a great council, largely attended by apostles, elders, and the whole community; while as a matter of fact it was as Paul describes it, a small gathering of five apostles, three veterans and two novices.

On the other hand, we should believe the author of Acts when he says that Simon Cephas the "fickle" experienced a sudden change of heart at this conference and was the first to demand a yielding to the Gentiles in the matter of the ceremonial laws. This sort of thing fits his character and his conduct with regard to Cornelius. Scholars of the Tübingen School were wrong when they made Peter the strongest and the most consistent opponent of Paul. He was merely doubtful and hesitant, and sometimes perverse; yet he was among the first to agree to yield to the converted Gentiles on the ceremonial laws. The complete antithesis to Paul was not Peter, but James the brother of Jesus, the Essene-Ebionitic keeper of the ceremonial laws.

But this time, at the "Apostolic Council," even James weakened, in spite of all his zeal for the ceremonial laws, and agreed to yield to the Gentiles who had confessed Jesus as Messiah— *to the Christian Gentiles but not to the Nazarene Jews!*—in the matters of circumcision and forbidden foods. He was influenced, apparently, by two considerations. *First*, the Jerusalem church was under deep obligation for the aid which Paul and Barnabas had brought from the Gentile Christians in particular. *Second*, time had weakened even him; he also became convinced in the course of time that there was no hope for Christianity from the Jews, but much hope from the Gentiles. Even in Judaism, according to the opinion of R. Joshua, ritual ablution could take the place of circumcision, as was pointed out above.[16] Thus James concluded that Gentiles

[16] See above, p. 363, n. 6.

baptized into Christianity should observe something like the "seven rules of the sons of Noah" [San. 56a]: they should avoid idolatry, adultery, and murder, the three offenses which according to Jewish law come under the rule of "let him suffer death or not transgress." [17] In addition to these three rules, which were self-evident to anyone who had forsaken paganism, Gentiles who had accepted Christianity were required to do three other things not so understandable to Gentiles: they were to abstain from the meat of animals not slaughtered according to ritual rules (πνικτός, literally "strangled"), from blood as a food, and from the meat of animals that had been sacrificed to idols.[18]

According to Acts,[19] this "apostolic decree" was a compromise agreement between the apostles of Jerusalem and Paul, which was effected a comparatively short time after the begin-

[17] R. Johanan said in the name of R. Simeon b. Jehozadak: By a majority vote, it was resolved in the upper chambers of the house of Nithza in Lydda that in every [other] law of the Torah, if a man is commanded: 'Transgress and suffer not death' he may transgress and not suffer death, excepting idolatry, incest [which includes adultery], and murder" (Babli, Sanhedrin 74a; Yerushalmi, *ibid.* III 6 [21b]). See also Babli, 'Arakhin 15b.'

[18] Here I use the wording of Acts 15:20 (see also the repetition in 21:25) according to the *Eastern* text [as found in the ordinary English Bibles], and not according to the *Western* text, which expunges the three latter things and substitutes the "Golden Rule" of Jesus. It was natural that Christianity at a later time should *omit* Jewish rules, such as those against eating meat not ritually slaughtered ("strangled") and blood; but it was not natural that it should *add* them later. See also Ed. Meyer, *op. cit.*, III, 178–96; L. Venetianer ,"Die Beschlüsse zu Lydda und das Apostel-Konzil zu Jerusalem" (A. Schwarz-Festschrift, Wien 1917, SS. 417–23). Hans Lietzmann (*Geschichte der antiken Kirche*, I, 107–8 [Eng. ed., pp. 141–3]) affirms that the meaning of "what is strangled" and "blood" (Acts 15:20) is *"kosher* meat," and that Paul afterwards became angry at the demand that Gentiles should observe such rules; for Paul had not agreed to any such demand when he made his compromise with James, Cephas, and John. But it is clear to me that a Jew of the period of the Second Temple, or even the author of Acts, would not call this (abstention from "what is strangled" and "blood" only) observance of the food laws. James yielded to the Gentiles in the matter of *Terephah* [animals ritually unfit even before slaughter], but not in the matters of *Nebelah* [animals that met their death not according to ritual rules] and the eating of blood, both of which were abominable to an Essene and observing Jew like James.

[19] Acts 16:4; 21:25.

ning of Paul's apostleship, and immediately after his first missionary journey. In no passage in the Epistles of Paul are there any clear statements about this, and when we look at the Epistles as a whole,[20] it even appears that no such "decree" based upon a compromise ever existed. On the contrary, Paul relates,[21] that when he came to Jerusalem with Barnabas to confer with James, Cephas, and John, "not even Titus who was with me, being a Greek, was compelled to be circumcised." That is to say, the "pillar-apostles" did not at first demand that a Gentile who had received Christian baptism should also be circumcised. According to the words of Paul here, the compromise was not an "apostolic decree" requiring observance of the ceremonial requirements laid down in the book of Acts, but an agreement as follows: Cephas was intrusted with "the gospel of the circumcision," and Paul with "the gospel of the uncircumcision"; and for this latter, James, Cephas, and John gave their right hands to Paul and Barnabas, that is, they ratified the agreement by shaking hands. Then Paul was asked to "remember the poor" in the Jerusalem church, that is, to gather contributions for the "relief" of the Nazarenes in Jerusalem.[22] Many impartial Christian scholars think, therefore, that the testimony of Paul is the more weighty.

But it is difficult to suppose that the "apostolic decree" is entirely a deliberate fabrication.[23] There is good reason for Paul's not mentioning this "decree," in that it yielded to the *Gentiles* on most of the ceremonial requirements, *but not on all*; and to *Jews* who had become believers in Jesus, it yielded *nothing*.[24] But Paul began immediately after the Apostolic

[20] Gal. 2:15-21; 3:23-9; 5:2-6; I Cor. chs. 8-10; Rom. ch. 14.

[21] Gal. 2:3-10.

[22] Gal. 2:9, 10.

[23] See also the opinion of Eduard Meyer (*op. cit.*, III, 185-96).

[24] See Gal. 5:3 ("Yea, I testify again to every man that receiveth circumcision, that he is a debtor to do the whole Law"). J. de Zwaan ("Was the Book of Acts a Posthumous Edition?" *Harvard Theol. Rev.*, XVII [1924], 110-24) sees even less than this in the Apostolic Decree.

Council to set aside *all* the ceremonial requirements, from circumcision on down, for both Gentiles and Jews. So why should he, in an Epistle like Galatians, which is a polemic against the "Judaizers," mention a decree which was for him a token of iniquity, inasmuch as he in a certain sense nullified the essential part of it? This, in my opinion, is the key to the understanding of all the subsequent acts of Paul and to the understanding of the whole battle which Peter and James and all the observing Jewish Nazarenes fought with Paul, demanding thenceforth obedience to the Torah on the part of Nazarenes of Jewish origin, at least.

3. The "apostolic decree" was prepared by the "pillar-apostles" in the form of a letter, into which was introduced, besides the decisions with regard to the Gentiles and their obligations to Christianity, a rebuke to the Judaizers for "subverting" "the brethren who are of the Gentiles." Then they chose two worthy "brethren," Judas Barsabbas and Silas,[25] to take the "decree" to Antioch and confirm by word of mouth that it had actually been formulated by the apostles.

Judas Barsabbas and Silas came to Antioch with Paul and Barnabas, called the "brethren" together, and read the letter to them. The Christianized Gentiles, and even some of the Jewish Nazarenes, "rejoiced for the consolation," that is rejoiced at the lightening of the yoke of the ceremonial requirements. Judas and Silas returned after a few days to Jerusalem, while Paul and Barnabas continued to preach and expound the gospel in Antioch for some time.[26]

All this took place about 47–48 C.E.

[25] It appears to me that the Hebrew-Aramaic name of Silas was Shilā (שילא, and not an abbreviation of Silvanus). Some say that his Hebrew-Aramaic name was She'il (שאיל).

[26] Acts 15:22–36.

CHAPTER VII

The Second Missionary Journey of Paul
(C. 48–52)

1. About the year 48, it occurred to Paul that the time had come to visit the churches which he had founded during his first missionary journey, and to see how they were faring. For he knew that they were not yet thoroughly established in an organizational sense, and not sufficiently firm in their new faith.

Paul asked Barnabas to go with him again. Barnabas advised taking with them once more his nephew John Mark, who had left Paul and Barnabas during the first missionary journey.[1] Apparently, not even Barnabas was completely in agreement with Paul—for we saw him inclining toward Peter in Antioch,[2] in the matter of setting aside all the ceremonial requirements for Gentiles and for Jews believing in Jesus. Therefore he wanted Mark, "the interpreter of Peter" and a man whose opinions were close to his own, to serve as a counterbalance to the extreme antinomian opinions of Paul.

But to this suggestion Paul was not at all agreeable. He would not take with him the man who had forsaken them at Pamphylia after having refused to help them in the task of preaching (to be sure, preaching according to the ideas of Paul . . .). A dispute flared up between Paul and Barnabas— and Barnabas also forsook Paul. He took his nephew Mark with him, and they returned to Cyprus, the birthplace of Barnabas. From then on we lose all sight of him. All that which

[1] See above, pp. 352–3.   [2] Above, p. 362.

Christian tradition attributes to him (the "Epistle to the Hebrews," the "Epistle of Barnabas") has no solid foundation.

In place of Barnabas, Paul took with him as companion Silas,
one of the two men whom James and Peter had sent from
Jerusalem with the "apostolic decree." [3] Silas was, apparently,
in perfect agreement with Paul, and they did not again separate one from the other. It has been proposed that this Silas
wrote the book of Acts, or at least the We-Source.[4]

Paul and Silas paid new visits to the cities of Syria and
Cilicia, and visited all central Asia Minor, where Paul and
Barnabas had labored on the first missionary journey. In all
the cities where he had founded Christian churches, Paul used
the "apostolic decree" as his authorization to relieve the
converted Gentiles of "Judaizing" demands. Naturally, this
worked in his favor, for this easy way of becoming a Christian increased greatly the number of conversions from among
the pagans.[5]

Again Paul came—this time with Silas—to Derbe and
Lystra, in which places he had founded churches on the first
missionary journey. At Lystra they were joined by the half-
pagan half-Jewish Timothy.[6] From there the three of them
proceeded not to the west (to the Roman province of Asia)
but to the north—to Phrygia and Galatia. The names of districts in Acts are almost always not those of Roman provinces,
but those which were used by the inhabitants of these districts.
Thus "Galatia" in Acts cannot be the province of Galatia,
which included part of Lycaonia (with Lystra and Derbe),
part of Phrygia (with Iconium), and also Pisidia and Isauria;
perhaps the Galatia of Acts was only the northern part of
Roman Galatia, the part near Pessinus and Ancyra, where

[3] Above, p. 370.
[4] See A. Omodeo, *Prolegomeni alla Storia dell' Età Apostolica* (Messina
1920), p. 66.
[5] This is the logical connexion between the two verses Acts 16:4 and 5.
[6] Acts 16:1-3.

lived the Galatians, a half-wild pagan people. But judging by order of itinerary, it is difficult to think that Paul was in the vicinity of Pessinus and Ancyra; it is more reasonable to suppose that "Galatians" and "Galatia" in the Epistles refer to Lycaonia and Pisidia.[7] In Galatia Paul remained a fairly long time on account of an illness.[8]

From there Paul, accompanied by Silas, proceeded to Mysia, and was desirous of going on to Bithynia; but for some unknown reason he could not reach Bithynia. So he went down to Troas (more correctly, Alexandria Troas) and from there he decided to cross to Macedonia. The fact that Paul did not go to the Roman province of Asia nor to Bithynia, but turned to Macedonia, is explained by the author of Acts by means of mysterious influences. The "Holy Spirit," he says, prevented Paul from preaching Christianity in Asia and Bithynia; and it was in response to a vision (a Macedonian appeared to Paul in a dream by night and asked him to cross over to Macedonia)[9] that Paul went from Alexandria Troas to Macedonia. Of course, the true reason was that information reached Paul that his opponents among the Jews or Gentiles of Asia and Bithynia were very numerous and powerful.

As regards his crossing to Macedonia, it appears that Paul at this time felt an inner urge to get away from the small and uncultured provinces to the broad world of culture which had its centers in Greece and Rome. First of all, he hoped to win to his new faith the Greek world of the Aegean Sea; only after that would come the capital of the world, Rome. This was the "vision" which he saw in his dream: *Paul—and Christianity with him—crossing from Asia to Europe.* This crossing was a mighty event in the life of young Christianity, and it was inevitable that it should have stirred the imagination of a

[7] See W. M. Ramsay, *op. cit.*, pp. 104–51; Ed. Meyer, *op. cit.*, III, 78–80, 198–205.

[8] Gal. 4:13–5. [9] Acts 16:6–10.

religious historian such as the author of Acts—and perhaps the imagination of Paul himself—to the point of conjuring up a vision.

At Alexandria Troas, an important commercial city of Mysia, a little south of Tenedos, Paul was joined by Luke the physician; and from there on we have in Acts a narrative in which is incorporated the We-Source (*Wir-Quelle*).[10] From Troas, they went down by ship by a "straight course" to Samothrace, thence to Neapolis, and soon reached "Philippi, which is a city of Macedonia, the first of the district, a Roman colony." [11] There they spent some days. On the Sabbath, Paul and Luke (who remained a longer time in Philippi) "went forth without the gate by a river side, where was wont to be a place of prayer." [12] There Paul and his companions attempted to influence *the women*, as they had done in a number of other places, since the law of circumcision did not apply to women. Naturally, they succeeded in enticing "a certain woman named Lydia, a seller of purple, of the city of Thyatira," who took them into her house as guests.

But opposition to them also came about because of a woman, a girl who was a soothsayer. She served a master in Philippi, bringing him a large income from her divinations. Being persuaded to become a Christian, she was no longer able to practice magic—or bring in money. Her master laid accusations against Paul and his companions, that they were Jews who preached a faith strange and inimical to the Romans. The Roman rulers sentenced them to be beaten with rods (by the Roman lictors), put their feet in the stocks, and cast them into prison. But the keeper of the prison being, apparently, a Greek "God-fearer," attempted to free them. Paul called the atten-

[10] See on this source above, pp. 216–7.

[11] Acts 16:12.

[12] Acts 16:13. On these places of prayer beside rivers, see for particulars S. Krauss, *Synagogale Altertümer* (Berlin-Wien 1922), SS. 281–6; E. Schürer, *Geschichte d. jüd. Volkes*, II[4], 519.

tion of the rulers to the fact that he, Silas, and Luke were "men that are Romans," whom it was forbidden to beat with rods without a proper trial. Upon learning this fact, the rulers were perturbed, and "besought" them to leave quickly both the prison and the city.[13]

Through Amphipolis and Apollonia, by the *Via Egnatia*, they passed on to Thessalonica in Macedonia. Here, there was a Jewish population with a synagogue; and on three successive Sabbaths Paul argued with the Jews in the synagogue, claiming on the basis of the Scriptures (of course, Isaiah 53 or Hosea 6:2) that the Messiah would be afflicted and then rise from the dead. Only a part of the Jews, but more of the "God-fearers" from among the Greeks, "and of the chief women not a few," believed the words of Paul and Silas. On the other hand, the Jews who did not believe, being greatly in the majority, attacked the house of a certain Jason, where Paul and his companions were staying. They wished to drag them before the rulers of the city, but when they did not find them, they dragged Jason, the owner of the house, before the rulers and accused him of harboring men who did not obey the decrees of Caesar, "saying that there is another king, one Jesus." The heads of the city demanded a pledge of Jason, that he would not continue to act as host to these transgressors. So Paul and Silas fled by night from Thessalonica to Beroea (in Macedonia, not far from Thessalonica).

In Beroea there was also a Jewish synagogue, and the Jews there were more patient; but also there only a small part of the Jews "believed," while the main part of the believers were "of the Greek women of honorable estate, and of men, not a

[13] Acts 16:14-40. In this passage (vss. 25-34) it is related that, while Paul and Silas were confined in the prison, an earthquake occurred and the doors of the prison were shaken loose, so that the prisoners could have escaped; but since they did not make use of their opportunity, the jailor was so affected that he—became a Christian then and there! To be sure, an earthquake is not an impossible thing in those regions; but all the details bear a legendary stamp.

few." The Jews of Thessalonica heard what had happened in Beroea, and they hastened to Beroea and incited its inhabitants against the Christians. The "brethren" were forced to send Paul away from Beroea, so they conducted him to Athens. Silas and Timothy remained behind, the former in Beroea and the latter in Thessalonica.[14]

2. Paul brought with him from Judaism the belief that Israel would be "for a light of the Gentiles," and that "the mountain of the Lord's house shall be established . . . and all nations shall flow unto it." But as he saw the matter, *not* Pharisaic Judaism, which had placed a heavy yoke of ceremonial laws upon the necks of men, and *certainly not* Sadducean Judaism, which was foreign to one who based his faith upon the resurrection of the dead, would be a light to the Gentiles. Instead, a new religion would be this light, a religion which, on the one hand, would bring to the Gentiles faith in a single God hidden from the eyes of all living; and on the other hand, would bring them faith in a "savior" redeeming mankind by his blood, the *Soter* for whom the pagans of that period of transition were yearning so eagerly, yet whom paganism was failing to provide for the religious people of the Graeco-Roman world; and in the third place, would free those accepting it from circumcision and the rest of the ceremonial laws. Naturally, the great dream of Paul could not have been to bring under the wings of his new religion merely the Jews and Gentiles in the small and out-of-the-way provinces of Asia Minor. He dreamed of spreading the doctrine of Jesus ("preaching the gospel") *in the great centers of culture*, which were, at that time, above all, Greece and Rome.

For this purpose, Paul suddenly went over to Macedonia. In Philippi, in Thessalonica, and perhaps also in Beroea, he had succeeded in founding Christian churches; but he had also

[14] Acts 17:1–15.

aroused dangerous opposition. Yet he did not slacken his efforts. He went to Athens, the capital city of Greece (the province of Achaea in the Roman Empire), which to be sure no longer had the splendor of the days of Plato and Aristotle, yet still contained "Epicurean and Stoic philosophers." [15] It was worth while to attempt to gain influence in this city over both Jews and Gentiles. And to aid him would come Silas and Timothy, the first of whom he had left in Beroea and the second in Thessalonica, with the injunction that they should quickly come to him. [16]

So Paul came to Athens, and found it full of idols—something which angered greatly the Jew in him. [17] As usual, he attempted to gain influence in the synagogue over Jews and God-fearers, and in the market place (Agora) over any and all who would gather there. Whether his efforts bore much fruit is very doubtful, since such success is not mentioned at all in Acts, whose author loves to emphasize every slightest success of Paul's. The Christian preacher tried to explain to "the Epicurean and Stoic philosophers" the faith in Jesus and Jesus' resurrection after the crucifixion. Naturally, his ideas were ludicrous in the eyes of the philosophers. For educated Greeks, nothing was more outlandish than the bodily resurrection of the dead, in spite of the fact that most of them believed in the immortality of the soul apart from the body. So they ridiculed Paul. Some of them asked, "What would this babbler [18] say?" Others said, "He seemeth to be a setter forth of strange gods," very much as Socrates was accused in his time.

They brought him to the Athenian Areopagus, where from time to time orators, Sophists, and various curiosity seekers were wont to assemble. Now, they said, let him expound his

[15] Acts 17:18.   [16] Acts 17:10-5.   [17] Acts 17:16.
[18] In Greek σπερμόλογος, "scatterer of talk," "dispenser of nonsense." See for details on this Greek word Ed. Meyer, *op. cit.*, III, 91, Anm. 1.

"new doctrine" before a large assemblage. And the author of
Acts explains that "all the Athenians and the strangers so-
journing there spent their time in nothing else but either to
tell or to hear some new thing." [19] Paul made use of this
opportunity and delivered a whole speech, which he began
by flattering the Athenians—Paul was a diplomat—saying that
they were "very religious" and that he had seen in Athens an
altar inscribed To An Unknown God; [20] now, he said, he
could tell them the nature of this "Unknown God": He is the
God who created the world; he is the Lord of heaven and
earth, who does not dwell in temples, and has no need of anything, since "he himself giveth to all life, and breath, and all
things"; and he is not far from men, "for in him we live, and
move, and have our being." Certain Greek poets [21] have
already said that "we are also his offspring." And if we are
the offspring of God, it is impossible for us to think that "the
divine" resembles gold, silver, or stone as formed by the art
of man. "The times of ignorance" have now passed. Men in
all the world must return to him, to the God of all, "inasmuch
as he hath appointed a day in which he will judge the world
in righteousness" by means of a man whom he has raised
from the dead.[22]

The Athenians were flattered by the beginning of the
speech, their curiosity was aroused by the middle of it, but
when they heard at the end of it about a dead man who had
risen and would become the judge of the world, they began
to ridicule Paul and would not listen to him any longer.
Mockingly they said to him, "We will hear thee concerning

[19] Acts 17:19–21.

[20] Acts 17:22, 23. Actually, the inscription was in the plural number,
To Unknown Gods. For the literature on this see E. von Dobschütz, Der
Apostel Paulus, I (Halle 1926), SS. 51–2, Anm. 27–9; E. Norden, Agnostos
Theos (Berlin 1923), SS. 31–124.

[21] The poet Aratus in the hymn to Zeus in the introduction to his
Phainomena. See above, p. 307, n. 22.

[22] Acts 17:22–31.

this yet again." Only Dionysius "the Areopagite" (one of the judges of the Areopagus), a woman named Damaris, and a few others, adhered to the teaching about Jesus.[23] Paul departed from Athens having accomplished almost nothing.

The Areopagus (or Mars Hill) speech is considered by almost all students of early Christianity and Hellenism (Wellhausen, Norden, Wilamowitz-Möllendorff, *et al.*) to have been written by the author of Acts long after the event, since it does not agree in spirit with the Pauline Epistles known to us. But there are also defenders of the authenticity of at least the substance of the speech; and Eduard Meyer even thinks that "with regard to the Areopagus speech, the very conciseness of the wording is an indication that there lay before him [Luke, the author of Acts] a brief report [*Referat*] of the words of Paul, as well as the rest of the events in Athens." [24] It is very difficult to suppose that there actually was before the author of Acts a report of the speech and the events in Athens. At that time, all sorts of speeches were composed by historians to suit the events and the individuals who figured in the events. But it must be confessed that the general content and basic thought of the speech suit the occasion and the place, and hence it is possible that Paul actually delivered a speech of this nature in Athens, and that the gist of his words was preserved in the memory of Paul or someone else, who transmitted it to Luke.

3. After his poor success in Athens, Paul went to Corinth "in weakness, and in fear, and in much trembling." [25] There he found Aquila and his wife Priscilla (or Prisca), of Pontus. They had lived in Rome, having been driven out of Italy at the time of the expulsion of Jews from Rome by order of

---

[23] Acts 17:32-4.

[24] See Ed. Meyer's detailed treatment in the section "Paulus in Athen— Die Areopagrede" (*op. cit.*, III, 89-108, especially p. 93).

[25] *Cf.* Acts 18:1 with I Cor. 2:1-3.

Claudius Caesar in 49 C.E. on the grounds that they had "made a great tumult because of Chrestus" (*impulsore Chresto*).[26] The Romans still did not distinguish between Jews in general and Jewish Nazarenes; and it is very possible that Aquila and Priscilla had already become Nazarenes in Rome. Apparently, there had been a sharp controversy in Rome between observing Jews, on the one hand, and Nazarene Jews, in conjunction with Christianized pagans, on the other; and this controversy, in which Aquila and Priscilla (Prisca) took part, brought about the expulsion of the Jews from Rome for slander, or because in the controversy it was revealed that even pure Romans had become Christians.

Aquila and Priscilla were of the same trade as Paul: tentmakers (saddlemakers?). Paul worked with them at their common trade. By this work he gained his living, and not by gifts from the churches, which was the method by which the rest of the apostles and the brothers of Jesus were supported. He boasts to the Corinthians thus: "For we are not as the many, making merchandise of the word of God"; "I preached to you the gospel of God for nought"; "is it only Barnabas and I that have no right to give up working for a living?"[27] But he did not always maintain this practice; for he says, immediately after telling of preaching "the gospel of God for nought," the following:

I robbed other churches, taking wages of them that I might minister unto you; and when I was present with you and was in want, I was not a burden on any man; for the brethren, when they came from Macedonia, supplied the measure of my want.[28]

Nevertheless, in Corinth Paul supported himself by work and did not fall as a burden upon the "brethren."

In Corinth Paul went on Sabbaths, according to his custom,

[26] See for details on this Klausner, *Yeshu*, pp. 54–5 [Eng. ed., pp. 60–1].
[27] II Cor. 2:17 (end of the chapter) and 11:7; I Cor. 9:6.
[28] II Cor. 11:8, 9.

to the synagogues, and preached to the Jews and God-fearing Greeks, since the latter would also attend Jewish synagogues to hear the word of God. Apparently, as long as Paul was alone in Corinth, he did not dare to reveal to the Jews all his ideas. Only after Silas and Timothy arrived from Macedonia, did he lay before the Corinthian Jews his doctrines in all their extremeness—and he immediately roused the Jews to anger.[29] They reproached and reviled him—until he decided definitely: "I will go unto the Gentiles."

He went to stay at the house of a Greek "God-fearer," Titus Justus by name. This house was near the synagogue, and Paul prevailed upon Crispus, the head of the synagogue, along with many Corinthians from among the poor, the simple, and the uneducated,[30] to accept Christian baptism. The Jews were enraged at this, and appealed to the proconsul, Annaeus Gallio (brother of Seneca), governor of the province of Achaea. From an inscription found at Delphi near the end of the last century and published in 1905, the time of the incumbency of Gallio can be fixed as the years 51-52; because of this, the whole chronology of the life and work of Paul has been changed.[31]

The Jews dragged Paul to the place of judgment and complained against him before Gallio that he "persuadeth men to worship God contrary to the law." Gallio answered that he did not see here any act of trespass against men or the emperor; and that there were only "questions about words and names and your own law," and that therefore he was "not minded to be a judge of these matters"—then he drove them from the place of judgment. The Greeks, seeing that the Jews were in bad odor with the proconsul, made use of the opportunity to beat without any cause, in the very judgment hall

[29] This can be seen from Acts 18:4-6.

[30] See I Cor. 1:26-8.

[31] See above, p. 317. See also G. Baglio, *Gesù e re Erode* (Napoli 1938), pp. 153-90.

itself, Sosthenes, the head of the synagogue, who apparently had been appointed to this post after Crispus became a Christian—and Gallio did nothing to hinder them.[32] Thus Roman "justice"!—but the author of Acts does not utter any protest; even "Christian" justice was not concerned about this . . .

Paul stayed in Corinth a year and a half.[33] Most of his stay preceded the trial before Gallio. But even after the trial he remained "many days." [34] Thus it is to be supposed, that he was in Corinth during the years 50–51/52—which suits both the banishment of Gallio from Rome by Claudius Caesar and his proconsulate in Achaea.

From Corinth, where he had succeeded measurably well in comparison with what happened in Athens, Paul set out for Syria with Aquila and Priscilla. He was still enough of an observing Jew that he had his head shorn in Cenchreae, the eastern harbor of Corinth,[35] after having fulfilled a vow that he would not be shorn for a certain period of time.[36] The Nazirite sacrificial offering he of course postponed until he should reach Jerusalem; but it was permissible for him to be shorn outside of Jerusalem after he had fulfilled "the days of his Naziriteship." [37] Therefore, Paul permitted himself to be shorn outside of Palestine; it is possible that such was the custom at that time among the Jews of the Diaspora.[38]

From Cenchreae Paul went to Ephesus, where he left Aquila and Priscilla. As was his custom, he went to the Jewish syna-

---

[32] Acts 18:12–7.   [33] Acts 18:11.

[34] Acts 18:18.

[35] See on this place W. M. Ramsay, *op. cit.*, p. 263.

[36] Acts 18:18.

[37] Mishnah, Nazir VI 8: "But if he cut off his hair (outside the Temple) in the City [some translate "in the province"], he does not cast it under the cauldron." See also Gemara Babli, *ibid.* 45b and Yer., *ibid.* VI 9 (55c); and particularly Tosephta, Neziruth I 5: "Naziriteship is practised in Palestine and outside Palestine." See J. N. Epstein, "Lilshon Nezirut," *Sepher-Magnes* (Jerusalem 5698), p. 15, n. 21.

[38] See Strack-Billerbeck, *Kommentar zum Neuen Testament aus Talmud und Midrasch*, II, 749.

gogue and preached there. But he now remained in Ephesus only a short time. He was anxious to make the pilgrimage to Jerusalem and to deliver there the collections for the "saints" who were "poor." He did not wish to break the ties with the mother-church of Christianity in the hour of the budding growth of the new religion. In the last analysis, the Jerusalem church was the natural seat of authority; in it were to be found the brothers of Jesus and the disciple-apostles who had attended Jesus during his lifetime.

About the year 52, Paul came through Caesarea—after a sea voyage—to Jerusalem. This time he did not meet with great opposition on the part of James and the apostles (part of whom had no doubt gone on preaching journeys, and part, perhaps, were already dead). *First*, he still conducted himself as a Jew; he had fulfilled his Nazirite vow; "Gentiles may not vow the Nazirite vow." [39] *Second*, in Thessalonica, Corinth, Ephesus, and elsewhere he had preached for the most part only to Gentiles, and had succeeded among them; thus he had not violated to any extent the agreement between himself and James, along with the apostles, according to which he was designated for preaching among the "sons of the uncircumcision" (he of course also preached to the "sons of the circumcision," but had no success among them). *Third*—and this is of fundamental importance—during these years of scarcity he had provided for the poor and destitute church by collections of money. Considering the state of the Jerusalem church at that time, it was entirely natural that this fact should have made an impression. [40] All these factors together

[39] Mishnah, Nazir IX 1 (beginning of the chapter). See also below, Chap. IX.

[40] How important to Paul was the matter of the collection of money as a means of effecting compromises with the Judaizing Nazarenes in Jerusalem we see from the large number of passages in his Epistles in which he mentions such collection (Rom. 15:25-7; I Cor. 16:1-3; II Cor. 8:1-14; Gal. 2:10).

brought it about, that this time opposition to the acts of Paul was not expressed by James and the rest of the "Judaizing" Nazarenes, and certainly not by Simon Cephas, the "apostle to the Jews."

CHAPTER VIII

The Third Missionary Journey (54-59)

1. From Jerusalem Paul went to Antioch (53 C.E.). There he remained only a short time, after which he began his third missionary journey (c. 54).

He again passed through Galatia and Phrygia, strengthening the churches which he had founded in these districts on the first and second missionary journeys; and to places which he was not able to visit in person, he wrote letters of instruction and reproof, as well as encouragement. These letters ("Epistles") are the principal source for a knowledge of his teaching and his peculiar "gospel"; for this reason I shall give them due consideration below. Here it is sufficient to point out only that in most of his letters he contends with the "Judaizing" Nazarenes, who had offered two severe criticisms of him: *First*, Paul is not a true apostle, since he was not an actual disciple of Jesus, there having indeed been a time when he even persecuted Jesus' disciples; *second*, he adulterates the teaching of Jesus, who was Jewish in every respect, conforming to the ceremonial laws and laying down that the good news of the Kingdom of Heaven was to be brought to Jews alone or else also only to those Gentiles willing to take upon themselves the yoke of Torah and ceremonial laws and thus become as Jews in every respect.

The "Judaizers" did not recognize his mystical teachings, which involved a negation of Judaism; they did not recognize baptism of Gentiles into Christianity without their having first become Jews; they did not recognize the apostleship of Paul; and they did not recognize annulment of the ceremonial laws, particularly annulment of circumcision—that

symbol of a holy covenant which God impressed in the flesh
of the race of Israel and the flesh of those proselytes who
joined themselves with Israel. And when the "Judaizers," by
way of compromise, though with great reluctance, agreed to
exempt the baptized Gentiles from circumcision and the rest
of the ceremonial requirements (the "apostolic decree"), they
did not intend by any means to exempt from all these requirements baptized Jews and their children. To this were
added, apparently, certain personal criticisms: This Paul is not
consistent and sincere ("his heart is not like his face"); sometimes he piously conducts himself like a genuine Pharisaic Jew,
and sometimes like an outright Gentile; sometimes he is
humble and modest, and sometimes he is arrogant and speaks
sarcastically of the rest of the apostles; sometimes he is timid
and suppliant, and sometimes he is harsh and profane.[1]

In his letters, Paul lays bare to the churches which he
founded (with the aid of a number of assistants—Barnabas,
Silas, Timothy, Tychicus, Erastus, *et al.*) his own peculiar
gospel, striving with all his might against the ideas of the
Jewish Nazarenes who wished to make of the new faith only
a Jewish sect, arguing that he is no less an apostle than James
or the Twelve, and telling of his own integrity, his labors,
and his many burdens. Besides all this, he admonishes and reproves the members of his churches for the evil deeds they
are doing, rebuking them because they break the laws of
morality, quarrel with one another and then take their cases
before the courts of strangers, and persecute those of different
customs. Finally, he sets forth what attitude they must take
toward the state, toward marriage, and toward divorce; also
what must be the relation of husband to wife, of master to
slave, and the like.[2] These letters, which of course have been

[1] To all this I shall be obliged to return below, when I speak of "The
Personality of Paul," pp. 422–32.

[2] I shall treat these matters in detail below, in the chapters on "The
Teaching of Paul."

preserved only in part, are written in language that is far from simple; yet there is in them a pent-up fire along with loving tenderness, strong and violent outbreaks along with soft and endearing words, mysterious expressions that tax the imagination by their lack of clarity along with strongly polemical phrases which are so plain that they stir up animosity by the very heat that reveals itself in them, a deeply abstract religiousness along with very practical instructions, words of sharp cleverness and nicely balanced diplomacy along with simple and kindly greetings. Naturally therefore, these letters exercised a strong influence upon all the churches, so that the churches had them copied and preserved them for future generations.

2. Paul came a second time to Ephesus (c. 54–55 c. e.), one of the most cultured cities of Asia Minor. In this city was an Alexandrian Jew by the name of Apollos, who was "mighty in the Scriptures." He possessed an enthusiastic nature and a great talent for speaking, and knew how to expound Biblical passages. According to Acts, "he spake and taught accurately the things concerning Jesus," but knew "only the baptism of John." [3] Undoubtedly, there is some confusion here; for if Apollos knew "only the baptism of John," he could not have "taught accurately the things concerning Jesus." [4] It is difficult to suppose that the followers of Apollos thought that Jesus had not been baptized by John; if this had been the case, Jesus would not have been important enough in their eyes for them to teach "accurately" things concerning him. No doubt, Apollos and the twelve men who had not even heard "whether the Holy Spirit was given," who had been baptized only "into John's baptism," and whom Paul found in Ephesus

[3] Acts 18:25.
[4] The words "instructed in the way of the Lord," also found in Acts 18:25, do not necessarily mean that Apollos had been instructed concerning Jesus; "the Lord" *could* refer to God.

while Apollos was in Corinth—all these were disciples of John the Baptist; at first they did not recognize Jesus at all, and only after some time, when the report had been spread that Jesus saw in John the prophet Elijah, the forerunner of the Messiah (since if Elijah did not come, it was impossible, according to the Jewish view in the time of the Second Temple, to expect the Messiah)—only then did they join the Nazarenes and become assimilated to them.[5]

Aquila and Priscilla, who had remained in Ephesus since the first time Paul was there, found out about Apollos and persuaded him to join the sect of Christians founded by Paul. For an Alexandrian—and Hellenistic—Jew, this was not a difficult thing. At their request, Apollos went to Achaea (that is, to Greece) and strengthened the faith of the Christian churches there, since "he powerfully confuted the Jews, and that publicly, showing by the Scriptures that Jesus was the Christ";[6] that is to say, he interpreted Scripture by the Alexandrian allegorical method.[7] To this Apollos has been attributed the conception that Jesus is the Logos—the conception with which the Gospel of John begins and with which this whole Gospel is filled. Also, Luther supposed that Apollos was the author of the Epistle to the Hebrews, which others attribute to Barnabas. Both of these hypotheses with regard to Apollos are possible, but we do not have convincing proof of either.

After Aquila and Priscilla had won Apollos to Christianity, Paul himself won the twelve disciples of John (corresponding in number to the twelve tribes of Israel, as corresponded also

[5] See for details Klausner, *Yeshu*, pp. 275–6 [Eng. ed., pp. 249–50]. See also G. Hölscher, *Urgemeinde und Spätjudentum* (Oslo 1929), SS. 11–27 (Avhadlingen utgift av det Norske Videnskap-Akademi i Oslo, Hist.-Filos. Klasse, No. 4).

[6] Acts 18:28.

[7] On this see for details E. Stein, *Die allegorische Exegese des Philo aus Alexandreia* (Giessen 1929); *idem, Philo und der Midrasch* (Giessen 1931, Beihefte zur ZAW, 51 und 57).

the disciples of Jesus during his lifetime), of whom, apparently, Apollos was the leader.[8]

Why did not Apollos himself win them to Christianity after he was converted to faith in Jesus and his baptism? If we believe the author of Acts,[9] Apollos did not, simply because Paul arrived in Ephesus, where he found the disciples of John, while Apollos was absent in Corinth; thus Apollos had no opportunity, after his own conversion, to see the twelve "Johannines" until Paul had converted them. But the matter is not so simple. Apollos played a much more important rôle in Christianity than would appear from the statements about him by the author of Acts. On this we have testimony from the pen of Paul himself. In one of his Epistles he rebukes the Christians of Corinth for quarreling among themselves, various ones saying, "I am of Paul; and I of Apollos; and I of Cephas," etc.[10] Of this he says further:

For when one saith, I am of Paul; and another, I am of Apollos; are ye not men? What then is Apollos? and what is Paul? Ministers through whom ye believed; and each as the Lord gave to him. I planted, Apollos watered; but God gave the increase. So then neither is he that planteth anything, neither he that watereth; but God that giveth the increase. Now he that planteth and he that watereth are one: but each shall receive his own reward according to his own labor.[11]

And again Paul mentions Apollos, Cephas, and himself, as equals in importance.[12] He also speaks of "Apollos the brother," and urges him to come to Corinth "with the

---

[8] Paul himself did not win Apollos the Alexandrian to Christianity; moreover Paul preached Christianity in almost the entire Roman Empire even to remote Illyria, and yet did not preach it in nearby Egypt. Could it have been that Apollos the Egyptian was responsible for this by his continued opposition to Paul's Christian teaching—an opposition that was overcome only by Aquila and Priscilla and not by Paul himself?

[9] Acts 19:1.

[10] I Cor. 1:12.

[11] I Cor. 3:4–8.

[12] I Cor. 3:22 and 4:6.

brethren" (probably the twelve "Johannines").[13] From this
we learn that this Apollos played an important rôle in Christianity. Alas, that we do not know clearly the nature of that
rôle!

3. In Ephesus Paul remained this time about three years
(54/5–57), out of which he devoted three months to special
work in the Jewish synagogue.[14] But the Jews had no faith
in his preachments, and expelled him from their congregation.
He was, therefore, forced to preach to his believing disciples
(from among the Greek "God-fearers") in the school of
Tyrannus (doubtless a well-known orator or Sophist). There
were also Jews who imitated him in performing miracles, "and
there were seven sons of one Sceva, a Jew, a chief priest, who
did this"; but they did not succeed, of course! Only Paul succeeded. And the books of sorcerers, who were numerous
among the followers of Paul, were by his advice burned because he saw in them signs of idolatry.[15]

Paul had measurable success, therefore, in Ephesus among
the Gentiles. But opposition against him soon arose also from
among the idolatrous pagans.

In Ephesus there were a number of craftsmen who made
images; their business was damaged by Paul's preaching
against idols and in favor of one God, who cannot be seen or
perceived by the senses, and has no bodily form. Accordingly,
these craftsmen rose against him under the leadership of the
silversmith Demetrius, who was something of a contractor or
proprietor of an establishment making silver miniatures for
the temple of the goddess Artemis (Diana); in this establishment were many workmen engaged in the manufacture of

---

[13] I Cor. 16:12.   [14] Acts 19:8.
[15] Acts 19:9–20. Why there was a Jewish "chief priest" (or "high priest")
in Ephesus (vs. 14) cannot be known. As a matter of fact, this whole story
of "the seven sons of Sceva" is strange and surprising, and it is difficult to
believe that there is a kernel of truth in it.

these miniatures.[16] Demetrius and the workmen organized a great demonstration in the theater of Ephesus, seizing and taking with them Gaius, who afterwards accompanied Paul to Rome, and Aristarchus, who also accompanied Paul from Greece to Palestine and thence to Rome. These two were "Paul's companions in travel," that is to say, the representatives which the Christian congregations sent along with Paul to assist him particularly in monetary affairs.[17] Paul himself was prevented by the disciples and certain of his followers among government officials [18] from going to the demonstration or to the theater, or else they would not permit the crowd to drag him along as it did Gaius and Aristarchus.[19] The slogan of the demonstration was: "Great is Artemis (Diana) of the Ephesians!" To be sure, the demonstration was directed, above all, against the Jews in Ephesus, who did not acknowledge Artemis or any "gods made with hands"; Paul appeared in the eyes of the demonstrating image-makers merely as a Jew of a special kind.

The tumult and uproar were great, "and the more part knew not wherefore they were come together." They knew only one thing, namely, that they were acting against the Jews, who would not acknowledge their idols. The Jew Alexander wished to speak in order to placate the mob, but the Jews feared the outcome of his words—and pushed him outside; then he fell into the hands of the mob on the outside, who at first thought he was a pagan; but when he attempted to defend himself, the crowd recognized that he was a Jew, and began to cry out afresh, "Great is Artemis of the Ephe-

---

[16] Acts 19:24. From this verse it does not appear at all that Demetrius was the head of the association of silversmiths, as think a number of scholars (so Ed. Meyer, op. cit., III, 119).

[17] See Acts 19:29; 20:4; 27:2; Col. 4:10; Philemon vs. 24.

[18] The "Asiarchs." See on them Th. Mommsen, Römische Geschichte, V[8], 318–22; Ed. Meyer, op. cit., III, 121.

[19] Acts 19:30, 31.

sians"—so that he could not speak; according to Acts, the
crowd shouted for "about the space of two hours" (an exaggeration, no doubt).

The town clerk, who had taken charge of the demonstration in the theater, quieted the shouters and proposed to them
that they could bring their complaints at the proper time for
judgment before the proconsuls or the popular assembly, provided that they did not make too much commotion over the
greatness of Artemis and Ephesus, the city of Artemis, since
this greatness was already known to the whole world without
further proclamation. Whereas, if they continued to demonstrate and shout, they might make themselves guilty of riot or
even rebellion. The assemblage heeded the advice of the town
clerk, and dispersed.[20]

But Paul was no longer able to remain in Ephesus. Even
though the demonstration was concluded peacefully as far as
Paul was concerned, and Gaius and Aristarchus were released,
yet resentment against him and against the Christians in general was strong on the part of both Gentiles and Jews; and we
shall see below that Ephesian Jews went to Jerusalem and laid
charges against Paul, thus bringing about his imprisonment.[21]
It has been conjectured also that Paul was imprisoned for a
time in Ephesus,[22] and would therefore have been forced to
leave Ephesus hurriedly, even if he had not been planning to
go by way of Macedonia and Greece to Jerusalem—and
thence to Rome.[23]

That the situation in Ephesus was much more serious than

---

[20] Acts 19:33-41. Eduard Meyer (op. cit., II, 118-30), who treats this
occurrence at length and with understanding, finds here occasion for criticism of the Jews of Asia Minor, a criticism which reveals a trace of anti-
Semitism.

[21] Acts 21:27-9. See below, pp. 399, 400.

[22] On the basis of Rom. 16:7 and Philipp. 1:12-6. See W. Michaelis,
Gefangenschaft des Paulus in Ephesus, 1925 (not accessible to me); A. Deissmann, Licht vom Osten, SS. 201-2.

[23] Cf. Acts 19:21 with 20:1.

it is pictured by the author of Acts is to be seen from the words, "If after the manner of men I fought with beasts at Ephesus . . ." [24] It seems clear to me that this refers to the violent human antagonists, both Gentile and Jewish, about whom Paul speaks farther on in the same Epistle,[25] and not to a fight with actual wild beasts; for if such a fearful and extraordinary thing as the latter had actually happened to a man like Paul, the author of Acts would have heard of it from any number of sources and have recorded it in his book.

In those days the number of Paul's antagonists was increasing—and no wonder! The Gentiles saw in him a dangerous iconoclast, and the Jews saw in him an even more dangerous heretic. And to these were added the Jewish Nazarenes, who still considered observance of the ceremonial laws quite as necessary as belief in Jesus as Messiah. But Paul began teaching in those days *that even the Jews believing in Jesus were exempt from all the ritual requirements, and that the Torah was only a heavy yoke that itself caused sin and was not worthy to be observed at all.* With this bait he did succeed in enticing a few disloyal Jews; but most Jews—and even the Nazarenes in general—saw in him a transgressor and a renegade. We must understand that, for a Jew, the Torah always and in all times is inseparable from the ceremonial laws; and that includes the time of the Second Temple. Hence, to any number of places where Paul had established Christian churches on the basis of abrogation of the Torah of Israel, there came after him disciples of Peter and James and the rest of the "Judaizers" and taught another doctrine: namely, that Christianity is the Torah (or religion) of Israel, including its ritual requirements, with certain Nazarene additions—and no more. These "Judaizers" also minimized the importance of Paul as an apostle. They saw in him "a ruler by his own authority" [a usurper], since he had not ministered to Jesus as a

[24] I Cor. 15:32. [25] I Cor. 16:8, 9.

disciple; and they likewise accused him of any number of shortcomings and evil deeds. Hence, as I have already said,[26] his Epistles are filled with strong and bitter contention against the views of the Jews and Nazarenes about himself and his teaching.

4. From Ephesus, Paul went forth—or, more correctly, fled—to Macedonia.[27] From there he went to Greece, where he stayed this time three months. From there he wished to go to Syria and reach Jerusalem quickly, but he heard that the Jews were lying in wait for him in Syria; so he returned to Macedonia (spring of 59), and from there went by land to Alexandria Troas, and from Troas departed by sea for Palestine. In Macedonia he was joined by many to help him in spreading the antinomian and soteriological kind of Christianity. These helpers were from Beroea, Thessalonica, Derbe, and Ephesus; among them were Aristarchus, Gaius, Timothy and Tychicus, already known to us, and also Trophimus, whom we shall meet again with Paul in Jerusalem. Most of these went ahead and waited for Paul at Alexandria Troas. Paul came again to Philippi of Macedonia for the Feast of Unleavened Bread. Here he was for the second time joined by Luke the physician, who had separated from Paul about ten years before, having remained, apparently, all that time in Philippi.[28]

Paul went on to Miletus without stopping at Ephesus, be-

[26] See above, pp. 385-6.

[27] There is a hypothesis that at this time Paul stayed a longer time in Macedonia than would appear from Acts, and extended his preaching from Macedonia into Illyricum (Rom. 15:19). He went to Macedonia because he had heard about the tumults in the Christian church at Corinth; to quiet these he sent his disciple Timothy to Corinth. But after both Timothy and Paul's First Epistle to the Corinthians failed to achieve their purpose, Paul himself went by sea from Ephesus to Corinth, stayed there during the winter of 57-8, wrote there the Epistle to the Romans, and afterwards left the establishment of peace in the Corinthian congregation in the hands of his disciple Titus (see E. von Dobschütz, *op. cit.*, S. 13).

[28] See above, p. 374.

cause, according to the author of Acts, he was in haste to make the pilgrimage to Jerusalem for the Feast of Weeks.[29] It would be more correct to suppose that he feared to visit Ephesus again, after all that had happened there. Therefore, he summoned the elders of the Christian church of Ephesus to Miletus. He spoke to them of the danger awaiting him in Jerusalem—he had, like Jesus at Caesarea Philippi, a foreboding of evils destined to come upon him, without of course knowing precisely what to expect in Jerusalem. So he recounted before the Christian elders of Ephesus his suffering and afflictions, reminding them that he had not taken anything from even one of them, and had taken pains to work for his own support; and he admonished them to guard the "flock" in Ephesus against the "grievous wolves" from without—Jews and Gentiles not believing in Jesus—and against those "speaking perverse things" from within—"Judaizing" Nazarenes. For, he said, he could no longer hope that he would again see them in person. This latter statement saddened the elders of Ephesus greatly. Paul prayed with them, and they fell upon his neck, kissing him and weeping profusely.[30] This was a parting saddened by the consciousness of imminent death—unnatural death, death at the hands of men . . .

Journeying by the islands of Cos and Rhodes, Paul and his helpers reached Tyre in Phoenicia. The "disciples" in Tyre also had the feeling that it would be dangerous for Paul to go to Jerusalem; but Paul refused to listen to their pleas that he should change his plans, and continued on his way, after the "disciples" with their wives and children had escorted him and his helpers to the ship. When they came, by way of Acco (Ptolemais), to Caesarea, they lodged there in the house of Philip "the evangelist," father of "four virgin daughters who prophesied." (Philip was, of course, one of the seven Hellen-

[29] Acts 20:16.   [30] Acts 20:17–38.

istic "deacons," who became "evangelists" after the death of Stephen, but were not among the "apostles" who had been disciples of Jesus.) They remained in Caesarea "some days," and thither came from Judea the "prophet" Agabus.[31] He also attempted—by imitating the symbolic acts of the ancient prophets—to dissuade Paul from going to Jerusalem. The whole group in Caesarea knew how great was the opposition in Jerusalem and elsewhere to Paul's antinomianism. But again Paul refused to listen, this time to Agabus; and he said that he was ready for anything, if only he could be once more in the mother-city of Christianity.[32] Apparently it was particularly important in his eyes, in those difficult days when he was being persecuted by Jews and Nazarenes alike, to receive the approval of the elder Jerusalemite apostles headed by James the brother of Jesus. He believed that this approval would placate his opponents and persecutors. And because of an inner conviction of his own righteousness, he was confident that he would find exculpation and justification in the presence of James and the apostles; moreover, the "relief" offering which he was bringing with him from Greece and Asia Minor would subdue anger,[33] especially since he was bringing along also representatives of the new churches which he had founded, who no doubt would champion his cause.

Thus were completed the three missionary journeys of Paul. There still remained the one great event in his life which brought him from Jerusalem to Rome, not of his own free will as he had dreamed of it, but as a prisoner to stand judgment before the emperor.

The foreboding of tribulations, sufferings, and unnatural death did not deceive him.

[31] See on him above, p. 364. [32] Acts 21:1-14.
[33] Acts 24:17.

CHAPTER IX

The Arrest in Jerusalem and the Imprisonment in Caesarea (59–61)

1. Paul and his party came to Jerusalem (59 C.E.), and certain disciples from Caesarea, who had accompanied them, found lodging for them in the house of "an early disciple," Mnason (Manasseh)[1] of Cyprus. Most of the "brethren" in Jerusalem gave Paul and his helpers a hearty welcome. The passage of time had to some degree dulled the sharpness of their mutual antagonisms; and the "relief" which Paul brought with him was also most opportune.

The next day Paul and his companions called on the head of the Jerusalem church, James the brother of Jesus, in whose house all the "elders" had gathered. Paul handed over the collected money, and told them what he had done in the way of bringing in believers from among the Gentiles by surrendering circumcision and most of the ceremonial laws. James and the rest of those assembled gave their approval; for, according to the "Apostolic Council," Paul was appointed to be "the apostle of the Gentiles," and according to the "apostolic decree," most of the ceremonial requirements were relaxed for the Gentiles. But James and his colleagues did not conceal from Paul the fact that his procedure with regard to Jewish believers was dangerous. Thus they described the situation:

[1] Of course, Mnason is also a pure Greek name; a disciple of Aristotle by that name is known to us. According to the Western text of Acts, it appears that the house of Mnason (or Mnasos of Cyprus) was not in Jerusalem, but at a stopping place some distance from Jerusalem; perhaps it was at Antipatris (Acts 23:31), on the road from Caesarea to Jerusalem (see E. von Dobschütz, op. cit., S. 18; SS. 52–3, Anm. 37).

Thou seest, brother, how many thousands there are among the Jews of them that have believed; *and they are all zealous for the Law*: and they have been informed concerning thee, that thou teachest all the Jews who are among the Gentiles to forsake Moses, telling them not to circumcise their children, neither to walk after the customs.[2]

By this they meant to say: There is in the practice of Paul open violation of the "apostolic decree," according to which Paul was not to preach to the Jews at all—that was the business of Peter—nor was he to release *the Jews* from circumcision and the rest of the ceremonial laws.

In order to counteract this bad impression, they advised Paul to pay the "charges" for four Nazarene Nazirites "that they may shave their heads," and even to "purify thyself with them"—no doubt because he also had been "a Nazirite the like of Samson," having had his head shorn in Cenchreae, but not yet having offered the *Asham-Nazir* ("Nazirite guilt-offering")[3]—

"and all shall know that there is no truth in the things whereof they have been informed concerning thee; but that thou thyself also walkest orderly, keeping the Law."[4]

As to "the Gentiles that have believed," it had been agreed that they should abstain only from idolatry (sacrifices to idols), from blood (murder, or actual eating of blood?), from fornication (adultery), and from animals not ritually slaughtered ("what is strangled")—all according to the "apostolic decree."[5]

Now Paul, the man who had accused Peter of hypocrisy and called the Judaizers "false brethren," was himself acting hypocritically. So Paul purified and sanctified himself with the four Nazarene Nazirites, and offered a sacrifice for each one

---

[2] Acts 21:17-21.   [3] See on this above, p. 382.
[4] Acts 21:24.
[5] Acts 21:25. See above, pp. 367-8, and P. G. Kunst, *Joodsche Invloeden bij Paulus*, pp. 65-8.

of them [6]—very much after the manner of Agrippa I, the Pharisaic persecutor of the Christians.[7]

But the Jews of Asia Minor, particularly those from Ephesus, who had made the pilgrimage to Jerusalem, recognized Paul in the Temple as the man who had enticed Jews in the localities of Asia Minor to put aside Torah and ceremonial requirements; they also accused him of bringing into the Temple an uncircumcised Greek, Trophimus of Ephesus, who was seen face to face and recognized by Ephesian Jews. This was an offense punishable by death, according to the famous Greek inscription found by Clermont-Ganneau in 1871, which reads as follows:

Let no foreigner enter within the balustrade and embankment about the sanctuary. Whoever is caught makes himself responsible for his death which will follow.[8]

This interdict is based upon Jewish law;[9] but apparently the Roman government had concurred in the interdict, and had put up this inscription in Greek for the benefit of Gentiles, to save them from transgressing in this weighty matter and thus incurring the death penalty.[10]

[6] Acts 21:26. Apparently, Naziriteship was at that time a convincing symbol of piety. Queen Helena was a Nazirite for fourteen or twenty-one years (Mishnah, Nazir III 6); Queen Bernice also was a Nazirite (*Jewish War* II xv 1); King Agrippa I bore the cost of Nazirites' having their heads shorn (*Antiq.* XIX vi 1); also James the brother of Jesus was a Nazirite who refrained from having his head shorn and did not drink wine (see above, pp. 278–9.)

[7] Cf. Acts 21:26 with *Antiq.* XIX vi 1 (§ 294).

[8] See Dittenberger, *Orientis Graeci Inscriptiones Selectae*, II, No. 598 (p. 127); Schürer, *op. cit.*, II[4], 329–30; Deissmann, *Licht vom Osten*, 4. Aufl., SS. 62–3; [Bailey and Kent, *History of the Hebrew Commonwealth* (New York 1935), p. 341].

[9] Kelim I 8: "The Rampart is still more holy, for no Gentiles and none that have contracted uncleanness from a corpse may enter therein."

[10] Cf. Mommsen, *Römische Geschichte*, V[5], 513; Dittenberger, *op. cit.*, II, 295; Graetz, *Geschichte*, III, 1[6], 224, Anm. 2. In the opinion of Graetz, this was only a threat of death at the hands of heaven. But both Philo and Josephus saw in it the death penalty at the hands of man (Philo, *Legatio ad Caium* § 31, M., II, 577, C.-R., VI, § 212, p. 195; *Antiq.* XV xi 5, § 417; *Jewish War* V v 2, § 193; *ibid.* VI ii 4, § 124).

The impression made by the words of the author of Acts is that Paul kept company in Jerusalem with Trophimus, the uncircumcised Gentile, and that therefore he was suspected of bringing Trophimus into the Temple—something which he had not done, according to the implication of the text of Acts. However, it is possible that Paul may actually have brought Trophimus into the Temple, since Paul would not have seen any harm in an act like this, after he had put aside the differences between Jew and Greek in all matters pertaining to religion: but no Jew could agree that he had the right to do any such thing.

At any rate, a great disturbance arose, and the crowd of Jews, which was always large in the Temple, was desirous of dealing with Paul by lynch law, as had been done in the case of Stephen.[11] They had already dragged him outside the Temple, and were beating him,[12] when the report came to the chief (chiliarch) of the Roman cohort then stationed in Jerusalem that a disturbance had broken out in the city. This officer quickly took soldiers and centurions, arrested Paul, and put him in chains to prevent his escape; then the chiliarch began to inquire and investigate who the man was and what he had done. In answer to the question of the chiliarch, the crowd responded with such an uproar that it was impossible to hear anything clearly. The soldiers had to intervene in the affair in order to save Paul from the wrath of the crowd, which continued to shout and demand, "Away with him." The chiliarch decided to imprison him in "the castle" ($\pi\alpha\varrho\epsilon\mu\beta o\lambda\dot{\eta}$), apparently the fortress of Antonio, which was near the Temple. Since the Roman officer had heard the people arguing with Paul about a certain Messiah who had died and risen again, he concluded that Paul himself was the Egyptian Messiah (or "prophet") who had escaped from the hands of the procurator

[11] See above, p. 293.
[12] Acts 21:27-32.

Felix.[13] Paul, who could, of course, speak Greek, being a Jew of the Diaspora, explained to the chiliarch that he was a Jew of Tarsus and a Roman citizen there, and he requested that he be given permission to address the people in their own language, "the Hebrew dialect," that is, Jewish Aramaic (or perhaps, even actual Hebrew, which had not yet ceased to be spoken in Jerusalem) in order to quiet the crowd. The officer permitted him to speak.

Taking his stand on the stairway of the fortress, Paul beckoned for silence to the milling crowd, which was quite willing to quiet down after it heard Paul speaking in its own language. Paul told the crowd how he had come from Tarsus, his native city, to Jerusalem, where he had sat "at the feet of Gamaliel" in order to learn the Law in all its details and subtleties; how he had persecuted "this Way," that is, belief in Jesus; how he had gone to Damascus for this purpose—to persecute also there the disciples of Jesus—and how on the way Jesus had revealed himself to him in his true nature; how in Damascus itself he had been influenced by "one Ananias, a devout man according to the Law"; and finally, how, when he had returned to Jerusalem and was praying in the Temple, he "fell into a trance" (ἐν ἐκστάσει) and had a vision that he should be sent forth "far hence unto the Gentiles." [14] By this Paul hoped to quiet and pacify the Jewish crowd, on the grounds that he was initiating into the covenant of Jesus only Gentiles, and not Jews—and of what concern was this to the crowd of Jews which had gathered here and was threatening him?

But this defense did not move the crowd, which began to shout as before: "Away with such a fellow from the earth; for it is not fit that he should live!" The chiliarch saw that he had a serious affair on his hands, so in order to pacify the people he commanded Paul to be taken to "the castle" and

[13] Klausner, *Historia*, IV, 23–4. See also above, pp. 226–7.
[14] Acts 21:33–22:21.

beaten with scourges. Then Paul pointed out that he was a Roman citizen and that it was unlawful to scourge him without a proper trial. The chiliarch was particularly embarrassed when Paul told him that he had not obtained Roman citizenship with money, as had the chiliarch, but had been born into it. The officer loosed Paul's chains, and, by way of facilitating the investigation, took him to the Jewish Sanhedrin, in order to clarify whether Paul was accused of religious transgression or a civil offense. In the former case, it would be proper to remand him to the Jewish judicial body, *i.e.*, the Sanhedrin, for final judgment; but in the latter case, he could be tried only by the Roman procurator, and if—as in the present case —the defendant was a Roman citizen, only by the emperor himself or the emperor's special representative.[15]

Paul knew that among the members of the Sanhedrin were both Sadducees and Pharisees. And Paul was not only a visionary, but also a clever politician and astute diplomat. Hence he realized that, in order to save himself, it was first of all necessary to bring about a division of opinion and conflict between the members of the Sanhedrin itself.[16] Therefore, he called himself "a Pharisee, a son of Pharisees" and gave the impression that his sole offense was that he believed in the resurrection of the dead (*i.e.*, that he considered it possible that Jesus had risen from the dead). By this device he accomplished his purpose. The Sadducean scribes and the Pharisaic scribes began to argue heatedly among themselves about the resurrection of the dead and the existence of angels and spirits.

[15] See for details on this E. Springer, "Der Prozess des Apostels Paulus" (*Preussische Jahrbücher*, B. 218 [1929], SS. 182–96).

[16] The story in Acts 23:1–5 that Ananias (Hananiah) the high priest (son of Nedebaeus) ordered Paul to be struck on the mouth, whereupon Paul said, "God shall smite thee, thou whited wall; and sittest thou to judge me according to the Law, and commandest me to be smitten contrary to the Law?" and when it was pointed out to Paul that he had reviled the high priest, Paul defended himself on the grounds that he had not known that it was the high priest—this whole story is out of accord with the rules of procedure in the Sanhedrin.

According to the Pharisees, it was not impossible that Paul had been visited on the Damascus road by "a spirit . . . or an angel"—but of course not by Jesus; this latter not even the Pharisees could believe.

The chiliarch concluded, from everything which he had heard, that this affair was more religious than political, but feared that the Jews would execute judgment for themselves upon a Roman citizen; so he took Paul away from them and placed him in protective custody (to use a modern expression) in the "castle." The assemblage of Jews saw that the chiliarch was on the side of Paul, and they were enraged because the officer had not allowed them to finish the trial of Paul for a religious offense which was within the authority of the Jewish tribunal to adjudicate. And Paul had a suspicion—probably groundless—that there were fanatics among the Jewish group who wished to fall upon him and kill him or beat him when he should be brought before the Sanhedrin for a continuation of his trial. Paul had a nephew (sister's son) in Jerusalem, who was concerned for his uncle Paul, and undertook to let him know about the danger that was impending. Paul requested that the chiliarch hear from his nephew in person the story that the Jews were lying in wait for him (Paul). Then the chiliarch decided that he would not again turn the case of Paul over to the Sanhedrin, but would send him by night under a choice guard of foot soldiers and horsemen to the procurator Felix (53–61),[17] whose official residence was in Caesarea. The chiliarch sent along a written opinion that Paul had been accused by the Jews not of a political crime, but "about questions of their Law"; and he stated that he was also sending the accusers to Felix at Caesarea, in order that they might clarify their charges against Paul.

2. On the way from Jerusalem to Caesarea they came to the fortified town Antipatris, where Paul was left for the

[17] See on him Klausner, *Historia*, IV, 18–25.

night. The next day, the horsemen alone took him to the procurator Felix at Caesarea; for the danger of attack by the Jews no longer existed—or it may have been only imaginary anyhow—and hence the foot soldiers returned to Jerusalem. To Caesarea came after five days the high priest Ananias (Hananiah) son of Nedebaeus [or Nebedaeus] and certain elders;[18] they had also hired an orator named Tertullus to act as interpreter and attorney for them. He was told to argue that Paul was a transgressor against the Jewish religion, and therefore was to be tried in the Jewish religious court and not in the secular tribunal of the Roman procurator. Tertullus said, after words of flattery for the procurator, that Paul had gone like a "pestilence" among the people, being "a mover of insurrections among all the Jews throughout the world, and a ringleader of the sect of the Nazarenes: who moreover assayed to profane the Temple: on whom we also laid hold." The Jews confirmed the allegations of their advocate.[19] The accusations were fundamentally religious: Paul is stirring up tumults among the Jews specifically, spreading a Nazarene heresy, and is ready to profane the Temple. Only to the first accusation is there a political side; the other two accusations are purely religious. Therefore, the Jews must judge Paul "according to their Law."

Felix permitted Paul to defend himself. Paul denied the charge of profaning the Temple, and according to his words, he did not stir up controversies or tumults either in synagogues or anywhere in Jerusalem; but he frankly confessed that he had a special "Way" of serving "the God of our fathers"—the way of the sect which the Jews had mentioned

[18] Did the high priest in person actually go with the elders to Caesarea and appear before the Roman procurator for such a relatively unimportant matter as the affair of Paul must have seemed at the time (Acts 24:1)? It is hard to believe this. Perhaps the author of Acts confused the high priest with some ordinary priest whose name he did not know, and therefore he (Luke) called the priest by a name that was familiar to him.

[19] Acts 24:3-9.

by name, a way which reveals itself by belief in "a resurrection both of the just and unjust," something for which the Pharisees also look. He had come to Jerusalem to deliver monetary contributions to his "nation" and to offer sacrifices —and "certain Jews from Asia" had found him while he was purifying himself in the Temple "with no crowd, nor yet with tumult"; for no sin was found in him when he was brought for judgment before the Sanhedrin purely on the question of the resurrection of the dead.[20] Paul did not mention the matter of the "messiahship" of Jesus. "Messiahship" was a dangerous subject, since the Messiah was to be King-Messiah, and therefore a competitor for the authority of the Roman emperor. Not so the resurrection of the dead. To be sure, Greek and Roman intellectuals scoff at this faith, and consider it a superstition; but in the last analysis it is only a religious matter peculiar to the Jews—so what does a Roman ruler have to do with it? Why should one punish a man who believes in it, merely because the Jews consider it an improper belief? . . .

Felix, whose wife was a Jewess (see below), understood the matter before him better than did the chiliarch.[21] And he recognized that it was not a political affair. Therefore, he postponed the final decision on the question of this controversy between Paul and the rest of the Jews; for he did not wish to anger the Jews by deciding that Paul must be judged by the Roman tribunal. Meanwhile, he placed Paul under guard (protective custody), but commanded that his confinement be made easy and that his friends be allowed to visit him and minister to him. After some days, Paul was summoned to make his defense in the presence of Drusilla, wife of Felix and sister of Agrippa II, and thus a Jewess, although an apostate

[20] Acts 24:10–21.

[21] Thus I understand the phrase "having more exact knowledge concerning the Way" (Acts 24:22). If he had known "concerning the Way" (Christianity) with absolute clarity, it would not have been necessary to turn for information to Drusilla, his Jewish wife.

Jewess, since she had married a Roman who was not a prose-lyte.[22] Paul discoursed before Felix and Drusilla in his place of confinement about "faith in Christ" (the Messiah)—not, however, on the political side, but on the spiritual side—"of righteousness, and *self-control*, and the judgment to come." It is difficult to believe that even Drusilla understood this abstract discussion, which was so remote from the Judaism current in her half-assimilated circle of acquaintance.

Paul remained in confinement in Caesarea two full years (c. 59–61). This long imprisonment without standing trial the author of Acts wishes to explain on the grounds that Felix hoped to receive a bribe from Paul or his associates; for Felix had heard Paul say, "I came to bring alms to my nation."[23] Felix was one of the worst of the Roman procurators. Tacitus said of him: "Indulging in every kind of barbarity and lust," he "exercised the power of king in the spirit of a slave."[24] Hence the conjecture of the author of Acts that Felix expected a bribe is not impossible. But it is not absolutely necessary to explain the length of this imprisonment by Felix' hope of a bribe. The cause may simply have been that Felix could not decide what to do about this unusual and perplexing question. The Jews and their leaders were accusing a man of deeds dangerous both to the state and to religion; yet the man himself claimed that the controversy involved only something that was in the eyes of the Romans a superstition—the resurrection of the dead. How could he, a pagan Roman, decide the matter? It was for this reason, and not in the hope of receiving a bribe, that Felix "sent for him [Paul] the oftener, and communed with him."[25] Felix hoped to clarify, by these

[22] On her see Klausner, *Historia*, IV, 10 and 18.

[23] Acts 24:26.

[24] Tacitus, *Historiae* V 9 [Eng. translation by Church and Brodribb (London 1894), p. 198]. See for details on Felix and his evil deeds Klausner, *Historia*, II, 18–23.

[25] Acts 24:26 (second half of the verse).

interviews, whether the case belonged under Jewish or Roman jurisdiction. This explanation is much more plausible.[26]

3. Meanwhile, Nero removed Felix from the procuratorship of Judea, and Porcius Festus (61–62) took his place. I have already shown in another place,[27] that there is no reason to believe that Festus was a better or more just procurator than those who preceded him. As soon as Festus reached Jerusalem, "the chief priests and the principal men of the Jews" demanded of the new procurator that Paul be handed over to them for judgment in Jerusalem. Festus also was of the opinion that this was a religious and not a political matter—and in religious matters the Sanhedrin in Jerusalem still had full authority, near the end of the period of the Second Temple, even to impose the death sentence.[28] The author of Acts decides that the Jews made this demand because they were "laying a plot to kill him [Paul] on the way" from Caesarea to Jerusalem.[29] This is only a conjecture; nevertheless, Paul feared this and strove not to be sent to Jerusalem.

Festus, as soon as he had gone from Jerusalem to Caesarea, the city of permanent residence of the Roman procurators and Paul's place of confinement, ordered the trial of Paul to be held. Representatives of the Jews came from Jerusalem to Caesarea and accused Paul, "bringing against him many and grievous charges which they could not prove." [30] To be sure, the Jews could not bring evidence of the truth of all the charges; but concerning a great part of them they certainly could . . . Yet Paul insisted: "Neither against the Law of the Jews, nor against the Temple, nor against Caesar, have I

[26] See on this also E. Springer, *Preussische Jahrbücher*, B. 218, S. 193.
[27] Klausner, *Historia*, IV, 25–6.
[28] See my clarification of this matter, with correction of the opinion of Juster (*Les Juifs dans l'Empire Romain*, II, 139–49), in my book *Yeshu*, pp. 378–9 [Eng. ed., pp. 333–4].
[29] Acts 25:3.   [30] Acts 25:7.

sinned at all." [31] Thus he argued that there was no offense, either religious or political. But Festus finally decided that it was a religious matter only, and therefore that Paul ought to be judged in Jerusalem by the Sanhedrin. When he made known this decision to Paul, Paul announced: "I appeal to Caesar!" That is to say, Paul demanded that he be sent to Rome for judgment. As a Roman citizen, Paul had the right of *provocatio*, which originally was an appeal to a *tribunus plebis*; but after the prerogatives of the "tribunes of the people" passed to the emperors, the emperor took the place of the "tribune of the people" in such cases. So Festus took counsel with his advisers and said: "Thou hast appealed unto Caesar: unto Caesar shalt thou go." [32]

Meanwhile, before Festus had sent Paul to Rome, King Agrippa II and Queen Berenice (Bernice) his sister came to visit Festus in Caesarea—in order, no doubt, to congratulate him on his appointment. Festus, who did not know how he should formulate the letter of accusation against Paul when he should send the latter to Rome,[33] told the Jewish royal pair that he had before him the case of one Paul, involving "certain questions against him of their own religion," *i.e.*, Judaism, and also something about "one Jesus, who was dead, whom Paul affirmed to be alive." [34] Such was the idea of the Roman ruler of Judea about Christianity more than thirty years after the crucifixion of Jesus! How much an utterance like this can teach us, even if it did not actually come from the mouth of Festus,[35] is difficult even to explain . . .

Agrippa and Bernice requested that Paul be brought before them. Festus granted their request. Paul was happy to speak

[31] Acts 25:8.   [32] Acts 25:9–12.
[33] Acts 25:26, 27.   [34] Acts 25:19.
[35] Even if the author of Acts himself coined this expression, it shows how the author of this book pictured to himself the idea of Jesus and Jesus' teaching held by the Romans in his time; and of course, this was on the basis of actual facts and interviews.

this time before Jews well-versed in the customs of Israel. He began to flatter Agrippa. He was confident, he intimated, that the Jewish king believed in the prophets;[36] then he told the king and his sister, in the presence of Festus, the chiliarch [chiliarchs], and the heads of the city of Caesarea, everything which had happened to him and everything which he had done. He emphasized that he had lived "after the straitest sect of our religion . . . a Pharisee," and pointed out that he had formerly despised the name of Jesus of Nazareth and persecuted his disciples in Jerusalem and elsewhere; he told of the "heavenly vision" which he had seen on the road to Damascus, and pointed out the possibility of seeing a dead man who had risen, since the larger part of the Jews (the Pharisees) believed in the resurrection of the dead, and even "the prophets and Moses" had foretold "how that the Christ must suffer, and how that he first by the resurrection of the dead should proclaim light both to the people [the Jews] and to the Gentiles."[37] Here, in the presence of the Jews Agrippa and Bernice, Paul mentions the people of Israel first, and afterwards the Gentiles; but this he does regularly also in his Epistles.

To Festus the Gentile, the words of Paul appeared so strange and confused that he said "with a loud voice": "Paul, thou art mad! Thy much learning turneth thee to madness."[38]

Then Paul appealed to Agrippa the Jew on the grounds that the latter knew that these were not words of madness, but words which any Jew believing in the prophets would recognize. And Agrippa said to Paul in jest: "With but little persuasion thou wouldest fain make me a Christian!"[39]

Festus, Agrippa, Bernice, and the advisers of Festus withdrew to a special room and took counsel about the matter.

---

[36] Acts 26:2, 3, also 27.
[37] Acts 26:22, 23—the last words after Isa. chs. 49 and 53.
[38] Acts 26:24.   [39] Acts 26:28.

All of them were of the opinion that there was nothing dangerous to the state in either the words or deeds of Paul, and that he deserved neither death nor imprisonment. Agrippa II, who was not a particularly deep sort of person, yet was not unkind by nature either, expressed the opinion that it would have been possible to free Paul, except that since the latter had "appealed unto Caesar" it was necessary to send him to Rome.[40] It may also have been felt that an outright release would anger the Jews still more.

Paul was taken from Palestine, his second homeland—this time, forever.

---

[40] Acts 26:29-32.

CHAPTER X

The Voyage to Rome and Paul's Last Years
(61–64)

1. In the autumn of 61, Paul and some other prisoners, among them Aristarchus of Thessalonica, were delivered over to a centurion of the Augustan cohort (*cohors Augusta*) with orders that he should take them to Italy.

They departed by ship from Caesarea on the sea and the next day arrived at Sidon. The attitude of the centurion toward Paul was kindly; he even allowed Paul to visit his friends in Sidon. From there the prisoners came to Cyprus, borne by contrary winds, and from there they passed by Cilicia and Pamphylia, reaching the city of Myra in the province of Lycia. There the centurion found an Alexandrian ship bound for Italy, and he took Paul and his fellow-prisoners aboard her. The winds were not favorable; the ship went along with difficulty, suffering both from "storm" and from "calm." [1]

Winter was approaching, "and the voyage was now dangerous, because the Fast [*Yom Kippur*—Day of Atonement], was now already gone by." (Paul evidently reckoned the seasons according to the Jewish festivals). Hence Paul warned

[1] In the "Prayer of the Sea," which is appended to the "Prayer of the Road" in a number of the old prayer books (likewise also in the Pentateuch with commentaries of Rashi and Rashbam, ed. Romm, Vilna 5657–1897), we find this: ". . . and may He not delay us either by a *calm* (משבית) or a *storm* (מבריח). I have already called attention to this in my article "Ginze-ha-Lashon shel Ben-Sira ha-'Ivri" (*Sephatenu*, II [5683], 35, n. 20). I have not found these two important [Hebrew] technical terms in the new book of R. Patai, *Ha-Sappanut ha-'Ivrit* (Jerusalem 5698). [See now in English, R. Patai, "Jewish Seafaring in Ancient Times," *Jewish Quar. Rev.*, XXXII (1941), 1–26. Tr.]

the officers of the ship and the centurion not to continue the
voyage. But the place where the ship had stopped was not a
suitable one in which to winter, and therefore the master of
the ship attempted to reach one of the harbors of Crete which
would be more suitable for spending winter days—days of
rains and storms. But a severe gale or tempest "called Eura-
quilo" or "Euroclydon" (Εὐρακύλων or Εὐροκλύδων) [2] broke
upon them and the ship began to be tossed about in the sea,
whereupon the voyagers lost almost all hope of being saved.
Then Paul encouraged crew and passengers alike, advising
them to partake of food in order to keep up their strength
and thus be able to do the work necessary for their being
saved. Paul was a man of courage who found himself in a
moment of danger. Finally, the ship was broken up, but all
the voyagers were saved. Some of them reached land by
swimming and some floated to the shore upon planks or other
parts of the wreckage of the ship.[3]

The shore which the voyagers reached, after being cast up
by the sea, was that of the island of Malta (called in ancient
times Melita or Melitene). There they were forced to remain
three months—the main part of the period of rain (the Mediterranean winter being merely a rainy season). This was in

[2] This word is also found, in the forms Arkolaon (ארקולאון), Arke-
lin (ארקלין), and Alkolaon (אלקולאון), in the Midrash (Song of Songs
Rabbah I 2, on the passage Let him kiss me, and I 11, on the passage
Circlets of gold) and in Targum II to Esther (see J. Levy, Wörterbuch
über die Talmudim und Midraschim, I, 174; Jacob Reifmann, "Ha-Sharon,"
the scientific section of Ha-Karmel (weekly of Rabbi S. J. Fuenn), yr. VI,
folio 276; D. Kahana, Ha-Shiloah, XIV, 93–4).

[3] Acts 27:1–44. Eduard Meyer (op. cit., III, 32) thinks that the "planks"
and the "other things from the ship" ("other" is not in the Greek) would
be the same thing, and therefore he interprets the latter phrase to mean
"the backs of the sailors" (since the gender may be neuter or masculine).
But a ship has other parts besides planks. See also Ed. Meyer, op. cit., III,
27–36 for refutation of the hypothesis of Wellhausen (Kritische Analyse
der Apostelgeschichte, 1914, SS. 53–5) that the whole story of the tempest
and the foundering of the ship is only a borrowing from an unknown story
of travel, and has no real relation to the journey of Paul.

the winter of 61/62. The "miracles" which Paul exhibited here are not outside the bounds of the natural. A serpent or viper (ἔχιδνα) fastened on the hand of Paul but did him no harm—not all snakes are poisonous. Fever has always been common in Malta (being found there even to-day); Paul cured the fever of the father of Publius, "chief man of the island," [4] who entertained Paul and his companions for three days; other fever patients are also reported to have been cured by Paul—but "Luke, the beloved physician" was among the companions of Paul in Malta, and of course the fever patients could not have been healed solely by the prayers of Paul.

From Malta, Paul and his companions sailed in another Alexandrian ship to Syracuse, and from there they came quickly through Rhegium to Puteoli, the principal seaport of Italy in those days for ships coming from lands of the East to Rome. In Puteoli, Paul and his company found "brethren," so they stayed there with them seven days, and then went on to Rome. The "brethren" of Rome came out and met Paul and his companions at "The Market of Appius" (*Forum Appii*) and at the inn of "The Three Taverns." Paul was over-joyed at this, of course, and it gave him fresh courage.[5] At the end of April, year 62, he reached Rome itself.

2. The centurion, in whose charge Paul had been placed as a prisoner, took an attitude of respect and clemency toward Paul. The officer perceived that Paul was a man worthy of honor. Paul knew how to adapt himself to all conditions of existence—and a man like this always finds favor in the eyes of authority. Paul was, of course, chained to a soldier to pre-vent his escape, as was the custom with prisoners of Rome; yet at the same time he had a certain freedom. Thus he was

[4] We actually have two inscriptions from Malta mentioning the "chief man of the Maltese" (Ed. Meyer, *op. cit.*, III, 31).

[5] Acts 28:1-15.

allowed "to abide by himself with the soldier that guarded him," to live "two whole years in his own hired dwelling," [6] and to receive vistors in this dwelling.[7] In this way he received Epaphroditus of Philippi, who brought him a contribution of money,[8] and Onesiphorus of Lystra [Ephesus], who had difficulty in finding him (Paul) in Rome.[9]

In Rome there was a Jewish community of long standing, which even in the year 59 B.C.E., when Cicero delivered his speech defending Flaccus, was large and not unimportant.[10] And we know that by the year 49 C.E. (in the reign of Claudius) there were enough Nazarenes in Rome to cause controversy and bring about expulsion of the Jews.[11] It is difficult to determine who founded this Nazarene community. It has been proposed that two Jewish Nazarenes, Andronicus and Junias, who had been with Paul in Ephesus and had shared one of his imprisonments there, and whom Paul greets as residents of Rome, saying that they are his "kinsmen" and "fellow-prisoners," that they are "of note among the apostles," and that they were "before" him "in Christ" [12]—it has been proposed that these two founded the Jewish-Nazarene community in Rome.[13] At any rate, as appears from the entire Epistle of Paul to the Romans, the "Christian" community of Rome was Jewish-Nazarene and not Gentile-Christian, having been found by "missionaries" sent out by Peter and James the brother of Jesus; for this reason the Paulinistic author of Acts does not mention the founding of this "church." [14] Because of the great importance of this com-

---

[6] This is the usual translation of the phrase ἐν ἰδίῳ μισθώματι; but some translate it "on his own earnings," "at his own expense" (see G. A. Barton, *The Apostolic Age*, 1936, p. 88).

[7] Acts 28:16, 17, and 30.

[8] Philipp. 2:25–30. See E. von Dobschütz, *op. cit.*, S. 17.

[9] II Tim. 1:15–8.   [10] Cicero, *Pro Flacco*, 28.

[11] See above, pp. 379–80.   [12] Rom. 16:7.

[13] G. A. Barton, *op. cit.*, pp. 82–4.

[14] This point has, in my opinion, been convincingly proved by Ed. Meyer (*op. cit.*, III, 463–500).

munity, existing as it did in the midst of the cultural metropolis of the world, Paul dedicates to the battle against the Jewish-Nazarene views prevailing in it the Epistle that is greatest in extent and most important in content of all those which have been preserved—the Epistle to the Romans. In this Epistle he fights his fundamental battle with Judaism. In it he argues that faith is more important than the ceremonial laws; nevertheless, the Gentile Christians are not entitled to exalt themselves above the Jewish Nazarenes, and there is an obligation upon both to support with their contributions the church in Jerusalem.

But when it came to the matter of preaching in Rome, Paul here, as everywhere else, turned first of all to the true Jewish community. He wished, if possible, to convert actual Jews. After he was imprisoned in Rome, he was not able, even though his imprisonment was an easy one, to go in person to the leaders of the Jews; therefore, he invited some of them (perhaps not the actual heads) to come to him. Before them he defended himself on the grounds that he "had done nothing against the [Jewish] people, or the customs of our fathers"; nevertheless, the Jews had arrested him in Jerusalem and turned him over to the Gentiles, the Romans, who wished to set him free because they could not find in him any crime worthy of death; but because the Jews opposed his being released, he was forced "to appeal unto Caesar"—"not that I had ought whereof to accuse my nation." "For," he said, "because of the hope of Israel I am bound with this chain," [15] meaning to imply that he was suffering for the Messianic idea, for the hope of the redemption of Israel. He spoke, therefore, even at the very end of his days, like a thorough Jew. He did not feel at all that, by the negation of the importance of Israel's Torah which he had taught and preached for years, he had cut himself off from the people of Israel. Hence it is clear that he observed "the customs of the fathers" to the very end.

[15] Acts 28:17-20.

He himself obeyed the ceremonial laws;[16] but he would not impose the obligation upon *others* who had been baptized into Christianity, whether Gentiles or Jews. He was strict with himself and lenient with others.

The leaders of the Jews replied to Paul that they had not received any letters from Judea concerning him, "nor did any of the brethren [Jews] come hither and report or speak harm of thee." But they knew about "this sect" (or heresy), since "everywhere it is spoken against"; therefore they desired to hear an exposition of it from the mouth of Paul, the "authority" on the subject. Paul fixed a time for the exposition, and many came to hear his words. For a whole day, "from morning till evening," he expounded to them the nature of the Kingdom of Heaven and the teaching about Jesus "both from the Law of Moses and from the Prophets"—of course, according to the strange interpretation of Scriptural texts which we find in his Epistles. The author of Acts confesses that "some believed the things which were spoken, and some disbelieved." It would appear that the number of those believing was very small, while the great majority did not believe and even disputed with the handful of believers. Finally, all of them turned and went off, each his own way. Thereupon Paul spoke bitterly against them, and concluded that "this salvation of God is sent unto the Gentiles—and they will hear." [17]

And he abode two whole years in his own hired dwelling [or "on his own earnings"], and received all that went in unto him, preaching the Kingdom of God, and teaching the things concerning the Lord Jesus Christ with all boldness, none forbidding him.

With these lines closes the book of the Acts of the Apostles.

3. Clear historical information about the last acts of Paul and what his end was is not available to us. From his authentic

[16] Also on his voyage to Rome, at the time of the storm at sea before Malta, he said grace over the bread and broke it like a thorough Jew (Acts 27:35).

[17] Acts 28:21-8.

Epistles it is to be seen that he succeeded in his propaganda among the Gentiles in Rome, and reached the point where he made converts to Christianity even among the officials or the family of the Emperor Nero; for he plainly writes in one of his Epistles: "All the saints salute you (Christians in the city of Philippi), especially they that are of Caesar's household." [18] It is to be supposed that until matters reached the point of extensive preaching among the pagans in Rome, Paul remained in his easy confinement, and that only after his preaching had penetrated into the household of the emperor was he sentenced to death.

But concerning the actual end of Paul, three opinions are current in the world of scholarship:

(a) Paul was set free by Nero, who found no fault in him, and then visited Crete, came a second time to Asia, and there wrote the Epistles to Timothy and Titus (the "Pastoral Epistles"); afterwards he went to Spain, planted Christianity there, and only after a time, upon his return to Rome, was he executed by Nero. This opinion attempts to save the authenticity of the Epistles to Timothy and Titus; but we have already seen [19] that these Epistles, in their present form, do not come from Paul. The hypothesis of the journey of Paul to Spain comes from the expression of his desire to go there; [20] but this does not prove that his desire was actually fulfilled. The words of Clement of Rome from the year 96 C.E., that Paul "preached the gospel to the uttermost bounds of the west," [21] are only an exaggeration of which not even Eusebius knows anything. There are no signs of Pauline activities in Spain; Christianity did not penetrate to that country before the end of the second century C.E.[22]

[18] Philipp. 4:22.
[19] See above, pp. 244–51.
[20] Rom. 15:24 and 28.
[21] Clemens Romanus, *Ad Corinth.* 5:7.
[22] See on this Ed. Meyer, *op. cit.*, III, 131–2.

(b) Clement of Rome,[23] followed by Eusebius,[24] relates, about the year 96 C.E., that Peter and Paul were both killed together in the persecution of Christians by Nero Caesar in the year 64. The opinion that Peter and Paul were together in Rome during the last days of Paul is supported by the fact that Paul mentions, in a letter from Rome, "Mark the nephew of Barnabas" as one of three "of the circumcision" who assisted him in preaching "the Kingdom of God";[25] Mark was "the interpreter of Peter";[26] hence it is natural to suppose that where Mark was, Peter was there also. The fact that Paul does not mention Peter in his letter from Rome does not prove that Peter was not in Rome; for the opposition between them had been very strong, and their reconciliation was not complete. On the other hand, Mark, like his uncle Barnabas, had again recognized that Paul was justified in his work among the Gentiles and in his relaxation of the ceremonial laws, after the Jews, except for a small minority, had refused to accept the new teaching and the Gentiles offered the only hope for its success. We know that in the course of thirty years opinions can change and conflicts can be smoothed out. Therefore, it is not to be wondered at that even Peter was no longer in Rome what he had been in Jerusalem and Antioch decades before; yet the battle between Peter and Paul for the top place in Christianity did not permit either of them to make complete peace with the other during their lifetimes. But it is very possible that the unnatural death shared by both at the hands of Nero brought peace between them—in the eyes of the generation of Christians coming after them. This generation saw what was common to them and not what divided them one from the other, just as Nero, perhaps, also saw only

[23] Clemens Romanus, *loc. cit.*
[24] Eusebius, *Chronicorum Libri Duo*, ed. Schöne (Berlin 1876), II, 156.
[25] Col. 4:10, 11.
[26] See above, p. 351.

what was common to them, and thus killed both of them together. . . .[27]

(c) But there is also a third opinion. Professor Cadbury investigated the practice of the Romans in cases like that of Paul, in which the accusers failed to come to Rome to follow up the prosecution of a Roman citizen who had "appealed to Caesar." He concluded that in such cases the accused was released in the course of a year or two after he came as a prisoner to Rome. I called attention above to the statement of the Jews in Rome to Paul, that no one had come from Judea to accuse him.[28] According to this view, the author of Acts meant by the words "two whole years" the two years during which Paul expected to stand trial in case accusers should come from Judea; but when these two years had passed and no one came, since the whole affair had ceased to be of any concern to those in Judea because of the distance, Paul was released and went about the business of preaching in Rome "with all boldness, none forbidding him." [29] Thus the ending of the book of Acts is not necessarily abrupt or "mutilated." And it is possible to suppose that Paul was executed by Nero because it was revealed that Paul enticed into Christianity important pagan Romans "of Caesar's household," without any connexion with the accusation of the Jerusalemite Jews or the burning of the city of Rome.[30]

My mind inclines to picture the course of events thus: In the spring of 62 Paul came to Rome. Until the spring of 64 he was held there in easy confinement, he wrote various letters to the churches, setting forth in them his peculiar teaching,

[27] See H. Lietzmann, Petrus und Paulus in Rom (Berlin 1905); Ed. Meyer, op. cit., III, 480–509.

[28] See above, p. 416.

[29] See what Cadbury has written in the great work of Foakes-Jackson and Lake, The Beginnings of Christianity, V, 319–38.

[30] See Barton, op. cit., pp. 98–103.

he fought against Peter and the Jewish Nazarenes in Rome, and insofar as his confinement allowed, he even preached Gentile Christianity in Rome—and succeeded in this preaching.

The two years of his confinement (spring 62–spring 64) passed, and Paul was set free for lack of a clear charge against him, since there was no one to accuse him—his opponents in Jerusalem were no longer interested in him. He was not particularly important in their eyes after he had been arrested and removed from Palestine.

From the spring of 64 to July of that year, Paul was at liberty in Rome and continued to preach the new Christianity, as he understood it, among the pagans and to quarrel with the Jewish Nazarenes. In July of 64, the great fire broke out in Rome. The story that Nero himself started the fearful conflagration in order to enjoy the "glorious" spectacle of the burning of a great city is only a fable. When the fire began, Nero was at Antium, outside of Rome; and when the news of the fire reached him, he hastened to Rome and endeavored to have it extinguished, although he did not succeed readily in this. Then he began to seek those who were to blame for this frightful occurrence—and it is natural that suspicion should fall upon the Christians, whom both Suetonius [31] and Tacitus [32] denounce in very bitter terms. "The Christians" (*Christiani*) were, according to their words, "a sort of people who held a new and impious superstition" (Suetonius); and Christianity was a "detestable superstition" (*exitiabilis superstitio*), being a part of all the "horrible and shameful iniquity" which flowed into Rome "from every quarter of the world"; moreover, the Christians were "detested for their abominations" (*flagitia*), and it would have been for the "public good" to eradicate the "hatred of the human race" which was embodied in Christianity (Tacitus).

Thus, it is not to be wondered at, that in Rome there

[31] Suetonius, *Nero* 16.   [32] Tacitus, *Annals* XV 44.

should be imputed to this hated sect, out of both ignorance and hatred of foreigners (xenophobia), all sorts of evil deeds, and even the most frightful thing of all, the burning of Rome —just as all sorts of lies and false charges were heaped upon the Jews in the Middle Ages or in our own times in Germany and Italy (and as Tacitus more or less also heaped charges upon the Jews). And since suspected Christians were being punished, it is not to be wondered at that the leaders of the Christians at that time, Paul and Peter, were seized and both of them put to death (Peter was then apparently in Rome along with Mark, as has been said). Peter, being a Palestinian subject, was crucified in Rome just as Jesus was crucified in Jerusalem; but Paul, being a Roman citizen, could not be crucified; he was beheaded with a sword, as is related in a Christian apocryphal book of about the year 160.[33]

The authenticity of this story is not absolutely certain.[34] Yet all the many painstaking investigations of sources lead us inevitably to the almost certain conclusion, that thus was the end of Saul of Tarsus, who became Saint Paul and transformed a little Jewish sect into an anti-Jewish religion—or more correctly, a half-Jewish, half-Christian religion—that spread over the whole world.

[33] Acts of Paul X 5 (M. R. James, *The Apocryphal New Testament*, Oxford 1924, pp. 295-6).

[34] Another opinion—that Paul was killed in the year 63 and Peter in 64 —is expressed by E. von Dobschütz, *op. cit.*, SS. 17, 18.

CHAPTER XI

The Personality of Paul

[See on this: E. Renan, *Les Apôtres*, Paris 1866, pp. 163–90; A. Haus-rath, *Die Zeit der Apostel* (Neutestamentliche Zeitgeschichte, III. Teil, II², 38–47); W. Wrede, *Paulus*, 2. Aufl., Tübingen 1908, SS. 5–27 (Religions-geschichtliche Volksbücher, I, 5/6); O. Schmitz, *Das Lebensgefühl des Paulus*, München 1922; A. Deissmann, *Paulus*, 2. Aufl., 1925, SS. 44–66; E. v. Dobschütz, *op. cit.*, SS. 19–32; P. Feine, *Der Apostel Paulus*, Gütersloh 1927, SS. 517–617; A. Schweitzer, *Geschichte der Paulinischen Forschung*, 2. Aufl., 1933, SS. 185–94; H. Lietzmann, *Paulus* (aus "Geschichte der antiken Kirche, I"), Berlin u. Leipzig 1934; Ed. Meyer, *Ursprung und Anfänge des Christen-tums*, III, 411–4; D. A. Hayes, *Paul and His Epistles*, 5th ed., 1924, pp. 34–66; C. A. Anderson Scott, *Saint Paul the Man and the Teacher*, Cambridge 1939, pp. 14–9; J. Edman, *The Mind of Paul*, New York 1935, pp. 41–50; A. Omodeo, *Paolo di Tarso* (Studi Filosofici, diretti da Giovanni Gentile, XIII), Messina 1922, pp. 103–8, 427–39; E. Buonaiuti, *Il Messaggio di Paolo*, Roma 1933, pp. XVI–XXVI; E. De Faye, *Saint Paul*, 3-ème. éd., 1929, pp. 118–38.]

1. In regard to the physical appearance of Paul, the follow-ing description is preserved in a Christian apocryphal docu-ment of the years 160–70—a description which gives the impression of an ancient tradition and not mere imagination:

. . . a man little of stature, thin-haired upon the head, crooked in the legs, of good state of body, with eyebrows joining, and nose somewhat hooked, full of grace: for sometimes he appeared like a man, and sometimes he had the face of an angel.[1]

There would appear to be an internal contradiction in this description. On the one hand, here was a man of Jewish type, ugly in external appearance ("an ugly little Jew," says Eduard Meyer): little of stature, crooked in the legs, with a hooked nose, partly bald, and with close-set eyebrows—nevertheless,

[1] Acts of Paul and Thecla, 3 (Lipsius, *Acta Apostolorum Apocr.*, I, 237; James, *Apocryphal New Testament*, p. 273).

he was "full of grace" and "sometimes had the face of an angel." Actually, this contradiction is only superficial. In the case of a man of the spirit like Paul—inner emotions, reflected in his face, would beautify him in certain moments, so that he would then in truth have "the face of an angel"; and the light in his eyes, which are not described here (truly, the essential thing is missing from the book!), would make him sometimes "full of grace." Well says one of the few historians of Christianity who are not entangled in the web of theology:

At any rate, we make out almost the same picture of him from his own writings: a little Jew, filled with bodily afflictions, but possessing all the talent for activity of his race, always heatedly arguing and gesticulating, defending his own views and forcing them upon others with untiring perseverance.[2]

2. Saul-Paul was a man of polarity, that is to say, a man possessed of two extremes, and not one-sided or greatly inclined to one extreme only. His great influence came from a combination of extremely diverse qualities. The one-sided extremist is much more limited, and cannot accomplish things that are great either in depth or in breadth. Only the man compounded of good and evil, of lofty ideals and base passions, yet fighting against the latter, can attain true greatness.

Saul-Paul was a complex personality of this sort. On the one hand, he was a man passionate and inclined to sin, and no mere rhetorical exaggeration is this declaration of his: "Wretched man that I am! Who shall deliver me out of this body of death?" For, he said, "I see a different law in my members" (different from "the law of God after the inward man"), "warring against the law of my mind, and bringing me into captivity under the law of sin which is in my members." [3] But he fought with himself and sometimes overcame his

[2] Ed. Meyer, *op. cit.*, III, 413.   [3] Rom. 7:23, 24.

passions.[4] When he persecuted the Christians before the Damascus vision, he persecuted them with anger, fury, and extreme fanaticism, even assisting in the murder of Stephen; but afterwards, when he had been converted to Christianity, he became extremely zealous for the new faith, and antagonized by his extremeness both Jews and Jewish Nazarenes. This is, in fact, the real explanation of the Damascus vision. Religious zealots of the type of Paul are converted into extreme zealots for a new religion opposed to their former faith if for any reason they change their opinions; and changes like this take place very suddenly in the souls of such fiery and emotional zealots.

Saul-Paul was lacking in humility, exceedingly confident of himself, and boastfully condescending.[5] But he knew his own shortcomings, fought against them, and sometimes conquered them.

He had great energy and courage, he never retreated, he was even willing to suffer martyrdom for his opinions. I have already mentioned [6] his account of how he five times, by decree of Jewish courts, received forty stripes lacking one as a religious transgressor, and three times was beaten with rods by the Roman lictors as an instigator of public disorders. Once he was stoned by a Jewish (or even Nazarene-Jewish) mob, and barely escaped death. Even if in those days of the Roman Empire travel was more or less well organized,[7] yet nevertheless the numerous journeys of Paul were attended with dangers of the road, with cold and rain, with danger from robbers, with storms at sea, with hunger and thirst, with difficult riding in the desert, and with difficult voyaging by sea.[8] Yet Paul, a sickly man, withstood all these hardships and dangers, and let nothing keep him from his preaching journeys or from

---

[4] On the shortcomings of Paul alongside of his virtues see W. Wrede, *Paulus*, SS. 20–7.

[5] I Cor. 4:4; II Cor. 1:14; 7:8; 11:21–30.   [6] See above, p. 359.

[7] See above, pp. 55–6.   [8] II Cor. 11:23–8.

ceaseless activity both in writing and in speaking up to the end of his days. Herein is revealed the great energy of his great people, of whom it is written, "No weapon that is formed against thee shall prosper" [Isa. 54:17].

But alongside of this we find in him also the characteristics of a thorough melancholiac. The lack of success in Athens or in Ephesus crushed his spirit to the ground.[9] Always he saw before him woes and distresses, imminent world catastrophe; and in the envisioning of his spirit all creation was writhing and groaning and longing for salvation.[10] Thus he saw everywhere sighs and pains, weaknesses and failures—yet at the very same time he could send up a shout of victory over death and angels, over present and future, over height and depth.[11]

Saul-Paul was in his personal desires satisfied with little.[12] We have already seen [13] that he could earn his own living as a tentmaker, and that for a considerable time he labored in the workshop of Aquila and Priscilla; and like all Pharisaic scholars of that time, he derived no income from his teaching as did the rest of the apostles.[14] Nevertheless, he did receive help from various churches,[15] perhaps for his assistants, or even for himself in time of need. He had no wife, while Cephas-Peter and the rest of the apostles and the brothers of Jesus took their wives ("sisters") with them.[16] Thus Paul did his difficult and dangerous work—of course with the aid of a number of assistants (Timothy, Titus, Silas, Luke, Tychicus, Epaphroditus, Aristarchus, *et al.*, and for a time Barnabas and John Mark also), but he was isolated and lonely in his private life, hated and persecuted, without family life, without a fixed abode or dependable place of rest.

[9] I Cor. 2:3; 4:11; 6:4, 5; I Thess. 3:3–7; and elsewhere.
[10] Rom. 8:19–26.
[11] Rom. 8:35–9.
[12] Philipp. 4:11–3.
[13] Above, p. 380.
[14] I Cor. 9:6–18.
[15] II Cor. 11:9; Philipp. 4:14–9.
[16] I Cor. 7:7; 9:5.

3. Paul was small of stature and sickly, yet he was a man who loved authority and insisted on having his own way. From his own letters and from what is related in Acts about his relations with Barnabas and John Mark, nephew of Barnabas, we may conclude that it was hard to work with him. He could not bear having around him persons with any authority of their own, and his opponents complained against him, not without justification, that he imposed his will upon them in a tyrannical fashion.[17] He belongs among those "spiritual tyrants" to whom their own individuality and their work have become one and the same thing, and in the name of the work they permit themselves to do what egotism whispers to them without their knowing or recognizing it, namely that their personal satisfaction, and not the success of their work, demands acts of tyranny in relation to others. . . .

So, of course, the attacks of Paul upon his opponents among the "Judaizers" knew no bound or limit. Not even once does he say a good word for them, or consider that they too had opinions of their own and could speak and act only in accordance with these opinions. He says of them to the Gentile Christians of Philippi: "Beware of *the dogs*, beware of the *evil workers*, beware of the *amputation-party*."[18] There is almost no abusive name which Paul does not give to his opponents. They are "false brethren," "false apostles," "hypocrites," and "dissemblers." They are "enemies of the cross of Christ: whose end is perdition, whose god is the belly."[19] In the last expression he is of course hinting at the dietary

[17] II Cor. 1:34.

[18] Philipp. 3:2. "Amputation-party" is a free translation of *katatomē*, a term which is a mocking play on words with *peritomē* (circumcision). Is not Paul here referring to "removal of the membrane of the corona" (*peri'ah*) which follows circumcision, since according to the Talmud, "If one circumcises *but does not uncover the circumcision*, it is as though he has not circumcised" ([Freedman in the Soncino Talmud,] Shabbath 137b, beginning) [or, "If one is circumcised *without having the inner lining torn*, it is as though he had not been circumcised," Mish., Shabb. XIX 6, Danby's translation]?

[19] Philipp. 3:18, 19.

laws kept by the "Judaizers," or at the observance of the Sabbath and the celebration of the festivals, which the Jews enjoy with eating and drinking.

But he could also be tender and kind and even sentimental. Toward the churches which he had founded he took the attitude of a father to his daughters or even of a mother to her sons and daughters. He also knew how "to change his tone";[20] and when he attempted to make peace between a runaway slave and his master, he did this with proper tact and ingratiating words.[21]

Not in this way alone are the contrasting tendencies in his personality revealed. His opponents charged against him, that he was bold and resolute from a distance and in his Epistles, but that when he attempted to wield influence by personal persuasion, face to face, he was weak and feeble and "his speech of no account."[22] They charged him with "fickleness" in giving advice, and with frequently changing his mind, one time saying "yea yea" and another time "nay nay";[23] that he was guilty of "seeking the favor of men" and "striving to please" them.[24] On the one hand, they said of him that he was mad—no doubt, thus they explained his strange opinions and extreme demands;[25] and on the other hand, they accused him of cunning and deceit—even in matters of money.[26] But he knew how to defend himself and appease wrath and even subdue his own anger. He knew how to elucidate and explain his ideas and his deeds so as to avert all blame and all trouble. Yet when angry he could also excommunicate and expel from the Church, and even threaten with the rod.[27]

4. The polarity in the soul of Paul is revealed still further by two other extremes of his personality: namely, his mysticism and his practicality.

[20] Gal. 4:20.
[21] Philemon vss. 9–21.
[22] II Cor. 10:1; 10:10.
[23] II Cor. 1:17.
[24] Gal. 1:10.
[25] II Cor. 5:13.
[26] II Cor. 12:16–8.
[27] I Cor. 4:21.

On the one hand, the whole "apostleship" of Paul is based on the "heavenly vision" which he saw on the road to Damascus. He was such a visionary and mystic that he could say that he had been "caught up into Paradise, and heard unspeakable words, which it is not lawful for a man to utter." [28] He boasts that he knows how to "speak with tongues" more than others.[29] Not "the wisdom of this world" is important in his eyes, but "God's wisdom in a mystery, even the wisdom that hath been hidden";[30] that is to say, he has esoteric knowledge. So of course, all his teaching is full of mysteries, marvels, and secrets. And in the book of Acts, we hear that many of his decisions were made as the result of visions and revelations which he experienced in his imagination.[31]

On the other hand, Paul had outstanding talent as a preacher, controversialist, and debater. His sermons, controversies, and debates are far removed from mysticism, and very closely related to the "sound logic" of the preachers, controversialists, and debaters among the Jewish Tannaim and the Greek orators and Sophists. Even more important than this is the fact that Paul had *a sense of reality, a practical common sense*, which enabled him to become *an organizer and administrator of the first rank*. He it was who organized and administered—of course, with the help of a number of assistants—the numerous Christian churches which had been founded thanks to his effective preaching; and he it was who brought about order and peace among the quarreling mem-

[28] See above, p. 323.   [29] I Cor. 14:17.   [30] I Cor. 2:5-15.

[31] See, *e.g.*, Acts 16:9, 10; 27:23, 24, *et passim*, against von Dobschütz, *op. cit.*, SS. 42-3. To be sure, Paul was not a "mystic" in the sense of "mere emotional religiosity" and "abandonment of the ethical-active." But there was in him a longing "to be one with deity," "to be freed from the self," and also an "intoxication with the love of God"—all of which even in the opinion of von Dobschütz (*op. cit.*, S. 42) are distinguishing characteristics of a mystic (however, in the case of Paul, one must say "Jesus" or "Christ" instead of "deity" or "God"). Moreover, without this mysticism it is impossible to explain Paul's acceptance by the Gentiles and his rejection by the Jews, as will be shown in the following chapters.

bers of these churches by his oral rebukes and by the Epistles which he wrote.

For, truly, Paul had one important talent which brought about his great success, although it cannot be considered an actual ethical virtue; this was the talent of *adaptability*. Paul, in spite of the fact that he was an inveterate fighter, in spite of the fact that in essential matters he would insist upon his own opinion with all his might, nevertheless taught that it was proper to "rejoice with them that rejoice" and to "weep with them that weep." [32] He describes his own procedure thus:

And to the Jews I became as a Jew, that I might gain Jews; to them that are under the Law, as under the Law, *not being myself under the Law* . . . ; to them that are without Law, as without Law, *not being without the Law of God* . . . To the weak I became weak . . . [33]

And in general he points out that he had become "all things to all men." [34] Thus, he was a thoroughgoing opportunist. [35] He circumcised Timothy because the Jews knew that Timothy's father was a Greek and his mother a Jewess. He kept the vows of "a Nazarite like Samson," and had his head shorn in Cenchreae only after "the days of his Naziriteship" had passed. He paid the expenses of haircutting for four Nazirites in Jerusalem, in order that the Jews might see that he also was a keeper of the Law. He boasted of his Jewish origin at the time of his conflict with the "Judaizers," while in his Epistles to

[32] Rom. 12:15. Thus Paul accepted the saying of Hillel the Elder (Tosephta, Berakoth II 21 end). See also below, n. 35.

[33] I Cor. 9:20-2.

[34] I Cor. 9:22; *cf*. 9:23 and 10:23.

[35] Hillel the Elder also taught: "Keep not aloof from the congregation" (Aboth II 5; see above, n. 32). But Hillel was not in general a belligerent person, and he introduced his "reforms" into the life of the people without strife or violent change (see for details Klausner, *Historia*, IV, 101-21, especially p. 109, n. 1).

Gentile Christians he minimized the importance of origin and race. He expressed surprising loyalty to Judaism before the Sanhedrin, before King Agrippa and his queen-sister Bernice, and before the Jews of Rome, while in a number of his Epistles he spoke harshly of the people of Israel, and emphasized that the birthright of being the Chosen People had been taken from the unbelieving Jews and given to the believing Gentiles. And there were not a few other contradictions and contrasts of this sort, resulting from adaptation, compromise, and opportunism.

It must be said immediately that without adaptation and compromise Paul could not have succeeded as well as he actually did during his own lifetime. The prophets, who were not "practical" and did not know how to compromise and adapt themselves, succeeded only in influencing future generations. Jesus was able to produce but a few disciples. Only complex personalities like Paul, in whom are combined delusion and rationality, mysticism and practicality, can create something that is not only a new religious faith and ideology, but also a church, that is to say, a religion existing in the world of practical affairs.

5. The talent of adaptability was useful to Paul in his work also from another angle. Paul was obedient to the government and advocated the paying of taxes. He also demanded of wives and slaves (here, wives are compared with slaves as they are in the Talmud in relation to the ceremonial laws) that they should be obedient to their husbands and masters, even as they were obedient to Jesus himself.[36] Moreover, women must "keep silent in the churches: for it is not permitted unto them to speak; but let them be in subjection, as also saith the Law";[37] and again, "let the wife see that she fear her hus-

[36] Rom. 13:1-7; I Cor. 7:1-24; Eph. 5:22-33 and 6:5-9; Col. 3:18-25.
[37] I Cor. 14:34, 35; Eph. 5:22-4; Col. 3:18. On the question of whether this decree is Pauline, see below, in Chap. XI, sect. 3 of the Seventh Book ("The Teaching of Paul").

band." [38] In regard to the government, Paul decreed that "every soul be in subjection to the higher powers: for there is no power but of God; and the powers that be are ordained of God." [39] In regard to the eating of forbidden food or of flesh sacrificed to idols, Paul thought, to be sure, that since all food is created by God it is permissible to eat all; but if the Christian "brother" should see in the eating of such food a stumbling block, he ought not to eat it, lest he disturb the "brethren." [40] Also, Paul allows for marriage and family life, although with reluctance; and he advises continuance of the marriage relation, even if one of the partners remains a pagan after the other has become a Christian. [41]

Here we have a whole series of concessions and compromises, whereby Paul succeeded in finding favor with the Roman government, with strong-minded slave owners, with domineering husbands, and with compromisers and appeasers of the usual sort. Who knows, if all this did not bring about not only the rapid acceptance of Christianity, but also its rapid degeneration? How remote is all this from the sayings of Jesus, that he had come not "to give peace in the earth . . . but rather division," and that he had come "to cast fire upon the earth" and how he wished "that it were already kindled!" [42] Ethical extremism is an outstanding characteristic of the teaching of Jesus; in the Epistles of Paul, ethical compromise and adaptation to reality go hand in hand with extremism in religious belief, as will appear in detail below, in the chapters on "The Teaching of Paul."

Paul was, therefore, a "clever politician," and he was far from being a saint, particularly in the Christian sense of that word. [43] Actual saints frequent places of prayer and live in

---

[38] Eph. 5:33.   [39] Rom. 13:1.

[40] Rom. 14:19–23; I Cor. 8:1–13 and 10:25–32.

[41] Rom. 7:1–16.

[42] Luke 12:51 and 49; Matt. 10:34.

[43] This has also been pointed out with special emphasis by the Christian Eduard Meyer (*op. cit.*, III, 61, 71, 411–4 and a number of other passages).

monasteries, but they do not organize and administer sects and congregations and churches. . . . Along with all his sharp fighting against everybody whose opinion was different from his own, Paul was a compromiser, a yielder, and an appeaser. This compromising attitude toward troublesome facts softened opposition to the new faith and to its propagation in circles remote from its world-view, which was Jewish-prophetic in essence. This was an important factor in the spread of Christianity, but there was here no great ethical loftiness. . . .

Truly, the man who "makes history," yet is forced to be also a warrior for his cause, distinguishes himself not only by his excellencies but also by his shortcomings. Napoleon I would not have become what he did if even one of his virtues had been lacking; but he also would not have been Napoleon if he had lacked a single one of his shortcomings. . . .

CHAPTER I

The Personal and Cultural Factors in the Teaching of Paul

The special factors in the teaching of Paul were four; two personal and two cultural. The personal factors were, *first*, the peculiar status of Paul as an apostle, and *second*, his peculiar psychological make-up. The cultural factors were, *first*, the religious universalism of Judaism, and *second*, the yearning for salvation felt by enlightened Gentiles in the days of the first Roman emperors.

1. Paul as an apostle felt himself in a peculiar position; he was different from all the rest of the "apostles." All these were disciples or brothers of Jesus, they had received instruction from his own lips, they had ministered to him, they had come into personal contact with him, all of them were Galileans, or at least Palestinians. But he, Paul, was a foreigner and outsider among the apostles. Even if he had seen Jesus (and this I believe absolutely), Paul was not in the lifetime of Jesus his disciple, but his enemy. Paul had not received instruction from his lips, nor had Paul been chosen by him as a "disciple" or "apostle." (If we take the view, as do many scholars, that Jesus did not choose apostles at all, at least he did choose disciples—and Paul was never one of them.) So what authority did Paul have to consider himself one of the Twelve or to be equal to them in importance?—And indeed, Cephas and the brothers of Jesus received their wages as "apostles" or "evangelists" from the common Christian fund

or from the Christian churches in which they preached (according to the saying of Jesus "that those who proclaim the gospel are to get their living by the gospel," I Cor. 9:14), and they had the authority to take with them their wives ("sisters")—something which Paul was not permitted to do.[1] To the end of his days, Paul was not recognized by the mother-church in Jerusalem as an apostle equal to the rest of the apostles, and all his life he was fighting for this recognition.[2] And in this battle it is impossible to overlook Paul's *feeling of inferiority*, which he was endeavoring to overcome.

This significant fact strongly influenced the view of Jesus held by Paul.

For indeed, if there was any great significance in Jesus "after the flesh," in the earthly, actual, historical Jesus, then Paul was not as high in importance as any one of the disciples, evangelists, or apostles who had lived in the company of the earthly, historical Jesus; for this Jesus, while he lived, had had nothing to do with Paul. Therefore Paul, against his own will, was obliged to emphasize not the actual historical Jesus, but the visionary, the spiritual Jesus, that is to say, not the living and working Jesus of Nazareth, but Jesus the dying and rising Messiah, the Jesus seen in the vision on the road to Damascus. And "even though we [Paul] have known Christ after the flesh, yet now we know him so no more."[3] From this followed a number of peculiar phenomena in the thinking of Paul:

Since the true Jesus was not he of flesh and blood, but he of the vision, it was easy to exalt him to the supreme rank of the spiritual "heavenly man," the spiritual Messiah, who was raised on high by the Deity after the unnatural and

[1] I Cor. 9:1–18. Also see above, p. 425.
[2] I Cor. 9:1–18; 15:8–10; II Cor. 12:11; Gal. 1:1; 1:11, 12; Eph. 3:7, 8—and elsewhere.
[3] II Cor. 5:16.

shameful death of the cross. If the Jesus of vision is the essential Jesus, then the imagination can have full sway to enhance his greatness and significance and to make him "Savior of the World," "Lord" (lord of the living and the dead), judge on the Day of Judgment, and abrogator of the Torah, redeeming mankind with his own blood. Then it can be said that Jesus lives within Paul and that Paul is "in Christ." Then there is no limit to the secret mysteries which can be attached to him who shall sit "on the right hand of Power" in the Day of Judgment to judge men and nations alike. And then—then is Paul an apostle no less, and perhaps even more, than Peter; and he is no less important, but perhaps more, than James the brother of Jesus. All these, of course, knew the earthly Jesus, Jesus "after the flesh"; but of what significance is this earthly Jesus, whom God made in his earthly life an example of servitude, of poverty, of humiliation, and of subjection to the Law,[4] giving him over to be crucified with harsh cruelty— what is such a Jesus in comparison to the heavenly Jesus, who appeared to Paul in the road to Damascus and made him an apostle to proclaim the new faith to all the Gentiles?——

To be sure, the beginning of the exaltation of Jesus to this high estate was made by the Twelve. For there can be no doubt of the fact that though Jesus was not actually a revolutionary, as very many scholars have wished from time to time to prove [5]—I have already made it clear [6] that if this had been the case, Jesus would have been forgotten after his ill success like all the false Messiahs—yet there was in his messiahship also *a genuinely political element*, as testifies his having as a

[4] II Cor. 8:9; Gal. 4:4; Philipp. 2:5-8.

[5] Well known is the large work of R. Eisler, Ἰησοῦς βασιλεύς, etc., 2 vols. (Heidelberg 1928-9). Less well known is the book of J. Spencer Kennard, Jr., *Politique et religion chez les Juifs au temps de Jésus et dans l'église primitive*, éd. revisée (Paris 1927). Kennard considers Jesus a political rebel only.

[6] See on this Klausner, *Historia*, III, 225-6; idem, *Yeshu*, p. 463, n. 2 [Eng. ed., pp. 413-4].

disciple the "Zealot," and as testifies also one of the first verses of Acts.[7] In the last analysis any Messiah is *King*-Messiah, that is to say, he is to free the people from subjection to foreign powers, being therefore also a "son of David" from the liberated and liberating royal house of Israel.

But such an idea was dangerous for two reasons. *First*, the crucifixion had put an end to all political hopes; *second*, to speak of the *King*-Messiah, of a *political* Messiah, was very dangerous in those days of Roman rule in Judea and indeed in most of the then known world. Hence, if the first disciples and the primitive Jerusalem congregation had held on to the political, the earthly, messiahship of Jesus, they would have, on the one hand, ended in complete disillusionment, just as after the downfall of any false Messiah; and on the other hand, it would have been difficult, and almost impossible, to preach Christianity in any country under Roman rule, and particularly in Palestine. For Jesus had been crucified as a political Messiah, and hence as a rebel against the Roman Empire.

Therefore, both the Twelve and the early Jerusalem church were forced to seize upon the other side of the preaching of Jesus—*the extremist ethical side*, the ethic "not of this world," which Jesus had left them as an inheritance in his "Sayings" ("Logia"). Here there was no room for disillusionment, nor any danger from the Roman government. And because of the latter consideration—the danger from the Roman government—we find in the Gospels and later books an attempt to exonerate the Romans from blame for the crucifixion and to heap this blame upon the Jews. During the years immediately preceding and following the incident of the crucifixion, the Jews stood in a difficult and lowly political position, subservient to Rome, struggling for their freedom, near to de-

[7] Acts 1:6, 7. See for details on this Klausner, *Yeshu*, pp. 279–80, 315–6, 352–3 [Eng. ed., pp. 253–4, 283–4, 312–3].

struction. Hence, of course, there was no danger in attributing to them the principal guilt in connexion with the crucifixion, and in making out Pontius Pilate as justified in washing his hands of the matter. . . .[8]

Thus Jesus became an ethical Messiah *only*, and not a political Messiah at all. It was only *by mistake* that the Romans crucified him, seeing in him "The King of the Jews," *i.e.*, a political revolutionary. . . . In this view there is *much* truth, but not the whole truth.

But, in the last analysis, Jesus died an unnatural death, and in his last moments cried out: "My God, my God, why hast thou forsaken me?" God did not answer this prayer, nor deliver his Messiah from going down to the grave after such an unnatural and shameful death—so how could faith in a Messiah like this be perpetuated?——

To the rescue of the disciples from such disillusionment came *the belief in the resurrection of the dead*.

The first disciples came from the Pharisees, not the Sadducees; moreover they were from those circles from which came the authors of the Jewish apocalypses (Book of Enoch, Book of Baruch, Fourth Ezra, *etc.*)—books literally filled with faith in miracles ("signs") which will take place in "the last days," and with all sorts of mystical beliefs in a Messiah whose actual person or whose name [I Enoch 48:2, 3] preceded the creation of the world, and in a Messiah who will stand at the right hand of God and judge peoples in the Day of Judgment, in the time of the "Messianic birth pangs."[9] Thus, it was not difficult for them to believe the story of Mary Magdalene that Jesus the Messiah had risen from the dead. With this belief in the resurrection of Jesus—for in the Days of the Messiah there would be a *general* resurrection of the dead, and it was natural that the Messiah should be the *first* of those to rise—the whole outlook of the Nazarene com-

[8] See above, pp. 268-9.   [9] See Wrede, *Paulus*, SS. 84-7.

munity was transformed. By means of the resurrection it was proved to them that God had *exalted* his Messiah after the latter had been *degraded* by the crucifixion. It was possible for them to believe that Jesus had not denied his messiahship at the time of his trial before the Sanhedrin, but had said that "the Son of Man" would come "with the clouds of heaven" and sit "at the right hand of Power." [10] As to the fact that the Messiah had suffered scourging and the agonies of crucifixion —behold, they quickly found justification and support for this in Isaiah 53, a chapter in which they saw a "suffering Messiah" and "vicarious atonement." And the Messiah is not so much a "son of David" as he is "son of God"—not in the later corporeal sense, but in the sense of an *exceptional* nearness to God, since Jesus repeatedly spoke of "*my* Father in heaven" instead of "*our* Father in heaven," and as in the verse in the Psalms (2:7) which speaks of the *King*-Messiah: "Thou art *My son*, this day have I begotten thee" (verse 6 says, "I have set *My king* upon My holy hill of Zion").

Thus the primitive community was saved from disillusionment and Jesus as Messiah was saved from oblivion—the oblivion of all the false Messiahs whom the Romans put to death and whose followers were scattered far and wide after the death of their champions. For the entire Messianic movement which had been aroused by the executed Messiahs vanished in smoke.

All this Paul took from the first disciples and from the primitive Jerusalem community.[11] But what he took he greatly developed and broadened and deepened.

Simon Cephas, James the brother of Jesus, and their asso-

---

[10] Mark 14:62; Matt. 26:64; Luke 22:69.

[11] Paul Feine (*Der Apostel Paulus*, Gütersloh 1927) has already pointed out that the primitive community (*Urgemeinde*) prepared the way for Paul in a number of its viewpoints, and thus that the "apostle of the Gentiles" did not start everything from the beginning nor create everything by his own efforts and genius.

ciates were not able to conceive Jesus as *entirely* spiritual and heavenly; after all, they had known him and seen him face to face as flesh and blood. As much as they had worshipped and exalted and honored him, it was not psychologically possible for them to make him a "heavenly man." Along with the citizens of Nazareth, they were forced to say of him: "Is not this the carpenter [or "the carpenter's son"], the son of Mary [or "Joseph's son"], and brother of James, and Joses, and Judas, and Simon? And are not his sisters here with us?" [12] And since they knew his father and mother and brothers and sisters, and also the humble profession of himself and his father, how could they consider him a "heavenly man" who was "Lord of all," in whose name "every knee should bow, of things in heaven and things on earth and things under the earth," in whom "were all things created, in the heavens and upon the earth, things visible and things invisible," and who "is before all things, and in him all things consist"? [13]—And they, who had seen him following the same religious practices as did all Jews: observing the ceremonial laws, regarding his Jewish coreligionists as a favored group, and comparing the Gentiles to "publicans" and "little dogs"—how could they suppose that Jesus had set aside the Torah and the ceremonial laws and made Gentiles the equal of Jews in every respect?— Only Paul, who had seen Jesus only from afar and who based his apostleship on an imaginative vision of Jesus as one risen from the dead; only Paul, who was a Jew of the Diaspora, a Jew accustomed to living among a multitude of Gentiles; only this Paul could have gone so far in the adoration of Jesus as to pass beyond the bounds of the human, to make Jesus "but a little lower than God," and to bring it about that after a time even this "little" should be obliterated and Jesus should become the equal of God, one of the persons of the Trinity

[12] Mark 6:3; Matt. 13:54; Luke 4:22.
[13] Philipp. 2:9–11; Col. 1:13–9—and elsewhere.

—something which Paul could not possibly have done as a Pharisaic Jew, the son of Pharisees. . . .

For the more that Jesus became spiritual and heavenly, and the less he became earthly, actual, historical, the more it was possible for Paul to claim "apostleship" for himself on the basis of the vision which he had seen on the road to Damascus.

But another and a more objective reason—more correctly, a reason subjective and objective at the same time—caused Paul to be the one to make over the Jewish teaching of Jesus into an un-Jewish and anti-Jewish teaching.

Paul, "the apostle of the Gentiles," like Balaam the prophet of the Gentiles, one "fallen down, yet with opened eyes," was an epileptic, and in the moments preceding an attack he would see divine visions, according to his own descriptions—descriptions which, as we have seen, correspond with surprising exactness to those of Dostoevsky.[14] Of course, Peter and James and the rest of the members of the primitive community were also dreamers and visionaries. To them also Jesus appeared in a vision, as Paul himself bears witness.[15] Moreover, many of the members of the primitive community frequently "spoke with tongues" and "prophesied."[16] But Paul was outstanding even among these. He was marvelously compounded of mysticism and practicality, as has been said. He was a visionary and ecstatic, who boasted of the signs and miracles which he performed, and saw in them proof that he was a true apostle;[17] he also took pride in the fact that he could "speak with tongues,"[18] see visions,[19] and keep watch from a distance.[20] But he was also the great organizer and administrator of Christian churches everywhere. He was ready to receive lashing, scourging, and stoning for his opinions, yet he represented to the Roman rulers and King Agrippa that the

---

[14] See above, pp. 326–9.
[15] I Cor. 15:5–7.
[16] Acts 2:1–13; I Cor. all of ch. 14.
[17] II Cor. 12:12; Rom. 15:19.
[18] I Cor. 14:18.
[19] II Cor. 12:1–6.
[20] I Cor. 5:3, 4.

whole controversy between himself and the rest of the Jews was about nothing but the resurrection of the dead, and a dead man who, according to his opinion, had risen. This representation saved the young Christianity from persecution on the part of the Romans.

But this representation also saved it from persecution by the Jews. The Sadducees, who did not believe in the resurrection of the dead, hated the Nazarenes mostly because the latter made belief in the resurrection of the dead the cornerstone of their faith; sometimes they persecuted the Nazarenes, but for the most part they despised and scorned them. Not so the Pharisees, who constituted the majority among students of the Law and had the largest following among the Jewish masses. They could tolerate the Nazarenes as believers in the resurrection of the dead, in spite of all their opposition to the Nazarenes' strange Messiah who rose from the dead after being crucified. And it is entirely possible that in the first days of primitive Christianity Pharisees too joined the movement.[21] Paul, as we have seen, took advantage of this controversy between Pharisees and Sadducees, not only when he stood trial before the Jewish judicial body, but also when being tried before the Roman authorities. Here again is revealed his eminent practicality existing alongside of his strong mystical tendencies. If we add to this the fact that after all Paul was a Jew of the Diaspora, a Jew from a Hellenized city, a Jew speaking and writing Greek, a Jew influenced by a Greek environment and a Greek atmosphere, we come to the conclusion that nobody was more fitted to develop, from the small lements of non-Judaism already present in the teaching of Jesus, a whole new doctrine which was not Judaism, which was in fact anti-Judaism, the complete antithesis of Judaism.

These were the *personal* factors in the teaching of Paul.

[21] The "great company of the priests" who "were obedient to the faith" (Acts 6:7) were of course Pharisaic and not Sadducean priests.

2. But *cultural* factors also impelled Paul to create the new teaching out of which and by means of which a new religion was formed.

In Judaism from the beginning of its growth there has been a latent conflict between *nationalism* and *universalism*.

The monotheistic faith that was created within Judaism was not an accident. "A people that dwelleth alone" in a monotonous wilderness and "not reckoned among the nations," moreover an exceedingly subjective and sensitive people—it was inevitable that such a people should set apart for itself a single national God devoted to the special interests of the one nation.[22] But this *henotheism* necessarily spread and broadened and became *monotheism*—the God of the nation became the God of the world. Nor was this an accident either. The situation of Palestine between two powerful states—Egypt on the one side and Assyria-Babylonia on the other—and among the three greatest and most ancient civilizations: the Egyptian, the Assyro-Babylonian, and the Canaanite, all three of which in turn influenced Greece and gave the Greek nation breadth of view and vast aspirations—this peculiar situation made the Israelite faith necessarily a universalistic faith, and the God of Israel a God of the whole world. Not without reason did our great prophets lift up the burden of their prophecies over all peoples and all kingdoms. One of the greatest of them said, "My heart crieth out for Moab," and "moaneth for Moab like a harp";[23] another prophet could not forgive Moab "because he burned the bones of the king of Edom into lime." [24] A prophet of the days of the Restoration of Zion, whom we call the Second Isaiah, while others

---

[22] See in particular Klausner, *Yahadut ve-Enoshiyut*, 3rd ed. (Tel-Aviv 5701–1941), pp. 131–76. I am in opposition to a great part of the viewpoint of Ezekiel Kaufmann (*Toledot ha-Emunah ha-Yisreelit*, vol. I, books I–III, Tel-Aviv 5697–8) even though there are many correct ideas in this important book of his.

[23] Isa. 15:5 and 16:11.   [24] Amos 2:1.

attribute some of the chapters of his prophecy to a Third Isaiah [25]—this prophet is filled with the subject of the restoration of the nation, and prophesies of national greatness, both material and spiritual; yet at the same time he voices remarkable universalistic aspirations, which are unique in world literature.

In the Jewish Messianic conception throughout its history, the national and universal elements are so combined and fused together that they cannot be separated. There was, to be sure, a time not long after that of Paul, the time following the downfall of Bar Cochba, when Jewish Messianic speculation was forced to create for the purely politico-national Messiah who fights and falls in battle a special designation, and to split the Messiah-Redeemer into two individuals— *Messiah ben David* and *Messiah ben Joseph*, the spiritual and universalistic Messiah and the fighting politico-national Messiah.[26] But these two aspects of the Jewish Messiah have always existed side by side, except that sometimes the politico-national aspect received more emphasis, and at other times the universalistic-spiritual aspect. Even in the Messianic ideas of Philo the two aspects are found together.[27]

Nevertheless, it cannot be denied that the universalistic element *in general* stands out more in the writings of Philo than it does in the Palestinian literature of the days of the Second Temple and after. This is natural; for Jews who lived among divers Gentiles, in the days of the intermingling of nations during the period after Alexander the Great, and in the days of the religious and cultural syncretism of imperial Rome, were necessarily not only more universalistic, but were to a certain extent even cosmopolitan.

[25] Isa. chs. 40–56.
[26] See for details on this Klausner, *Ha-Ra'yon*, pp. 313–25; idem, *Die messianischen Vorstellungen des jüdischen Volkes im Zeitalter der Tannaiten* (Berlin 1904), SS. 80–103.
[27] See above, pp. 197–8.

But even Pharisaic-Palestinian Judaism did not turn its back
upon the great universalistic ideals of Isaiah and Amos. In the
apocalypses which were written in Palestine (Ethiopic Enoch,
Syriac Baruch, Fourth Ezra, *etc.*), the Messianic idea is connected with the brotherhood of all peoples and the recognition
of one God by all of them. Indeed, one of the Gospels testifies
of the "scribes and Pharisees" that they "compass sea and
land to make one proselyte." [28] And not only did the Pharisees
strive to win proselytes; a great part of them was willing to
recognize also the "God-fearers"—those persons who accepted
the beliefs and opinions of Judaism, but had not been circumcised and had not undertaken to observe all of the ceremonial
laws.[29]

Saul-Paul of Tarsus was after all, in spite of all his "Pharisaism" and "Hebraism," a Jew of the Diaspora; and the
politico-national side of the Jewish Messiah could only bring
about disillusionment with regard to the crucified Jesus, as
has been said. Hence Paul took from the Jewish Messianic idea
its universalistic side, and ignored—consciously or unconsciously—its politico-national side, which might appear dangerous in the eyes of the Roman authorities, as has been explained. And naturally there was strengthened in his mind the
idea that the essential thing was to win converts to belief in
Jesus from among the Gentiles; particularly since, without
much thinking, Barnabas and his associates, and even Peter,
had already actually attempted to do this; also particularly
since the proclamation of the faith in Jesus among the Jews
had met with so little success. Gentiles it would be easy to win
to the new faith if he did not demand of them more than
that which a part of the Pharisees demanded of the "God-
fearers"—a new faith without new ritual requirements. The

[28] Matt. 23:15.
[29] See especially in the chapter on "The Proselytes and the 'God-fearers',"
above, pp. 39-49.

Judaism of the period—Palestinian Judaism to some extent and Hellenistic Judaism to a much greater extent—had already prepared the way for this attitude toward the reception of proselytes from the Gentiles, and Paul only drew further and more extreme conclusions—that the believing Gentiles had become "the true Israel," and that even the Jewish Nazarenes were not under obligation to observe the ceremonial laws, since faith had taken the place of Law.

This was the first *cultural* factor in the teaching of Paul— the *Jewish* factor. Now we pass to the second cultural factor— the *pagan* factor.

Among the Gentiles—especially among educated Gentiles —there was a great religious ferment in those days. The general feeling of the more enlightened Gentiles was that the pagan religion had served its time. They endeavored to interpret the pagan mythology "symbolically," and they introduced into it ethical and philosophical meanings—but this is the beginning of the end of any direct and simple faith. The new philosophy, in spite of its flowering in the teaching of the Stoics led by Posidonius, was converted in the mouths of the "popular philosophers" of the period into sophistry and rhetoric.[30] And in spite of the economic prosperity and the political security of the "Augustan age" and of the period of the emperors following Augustus, there was felt throughout the whole Roman Empire a psychological dejection that cried out for spiritual salvation.

One apocalypse—although a Palestinian apocalypse—gives an idea of the general spiritual state in the days of Paul:

> For the youth of the world is past,
> And the strength of the creation already exhausted,
> And the advent of the times is very short,
> Yea, they have passed by;

[30] See above, pp. 79, 80.

And the pitcher is near to the cistern,[31]
And the ship to the port,
And the course of the journey to the city,
And life to (its) consummation.[32]

It would be hard to describe in more vivid, yet somber, colors the fearful expectation of "the end of the world" which had seized upon the people of that generation. Paul himself gives a figurative description of this depressed spiritual condition: "For we know that the whole creation groaneth and travaileth in pain together until now," hoping to "be delivered from the bondage of corruption," and from "the sufferings of this present time." [33] Everything—man and all creation—was standing, as it were, on the verge of world catastrophe. And there was no escape and no one to deliver. Darkness and decay were round about; "the youth of the world" had passed and its old age had come—that old age which is described in such somber colors at the end of the book of Koheleth.[34]

The only way out was by faith in a savior. All creation—and man within it—was looking for salvation—for one to save it from dejection and spiritual distress, from the world catastrophe which had aroused a haunting fear in restless hearts. Hence came about the rapid success of the mystery religions at that time. Hence came about the widespread belief in a dying and rising god, and in the possibility that men could be transformed by sanctification into gods and thus die and rise again like the gods themselves.[35] The educated people of all nations were crying out at that time for salvation—and whence would come the savior if not from the East? Belief in a savior from the East was widely current, and Josephus,[36] Tacitus,[37] and Suetonius [38] all give this as a cause of the out-

[31] See Koheleth (Eccl.) 12:6: "And the pitcher is broken at the fountain."
[32] Syriac Baruch 85:10 [Forbes *apud* Charles].
[33] Rom. 8:18–26.
[34] Koheleth (Eccl.) 12:1–7.
[35] See above, pp. 103–19.
[36] *Jewish War* VI v 4.
[37] *Hist.* V 13.
[38] *Vespasianus* ch. 4.

break of the great rebellion leading to the Second Destruction; Josephus tells of the vogue of "an ambiguous oracle, likewise found in their [the Jews'] sacred scriptures, to the effect that at that time one from their country [Palestine or the East in general] would become ruler of the world." [39]

Paul, a Jew living among Gentiles, and a man exceedingly sensitive to everything going on in the world, was aware of the longings for salvation which were filling the pagan world of his time. So, being a believer mystical to the point of hallucination, yet at the same time a talented organizer of amazing practicality, Paul came to those yearning for salvation and preached an attenuated Judaism, from which had been taken the sharp edge of the Torah and the difficulties in the observance of the ceremonial laws; and in place of a dying and rising *god*, such as was common in the various pagan religions of that time, he added to this attenuated Judaism a dying and rising *Messiah*.

Is it any wonder that he succeeded in his preaching, and created, consciously or unconsciously, a new religion based upon elements of the ancient faith, along with concessions to the current religions?——

[39] See on this "ambiguous oracle" Ed. Norden, "Josephus und Tacitus über Jesus Christ und eine messianische Prophetie," *Neue Jahrbücher für das Klassische Altertum*, XXXI, 637-60.

CHAPTER II

Paul, the Hellenistic Jew

[See on this in particular (there is no book on Paul that does not treat this problem): A. Deissmann, *Paulus* (1925), SS. 67-89; H. Weinel, *Paulus*, 2. Aufl. (1915), SS. 1-48; O. Schmitz, *Das Lebensgefühl des Paulus* (München 1922), SS. 15-29; F. Philippi, *Paulus und das Judentum* (Leipzig 1916); W. Bousset, *Kyrios Christos*, 3. Aufl. (1925), SS. 104-54; G. Kittel, *Rabbinica* (Leipzig 1920), SS. 1-16; A. F. Puuko, *Paulus und das Judentum* (Studia Orientalia, II, Helsingforsiae 1927, SS. 1-87); H. Windisch, *Paulus und das Judentum* (Tübingen 1936); A. Schweitzer, *Die Mystik des Apostel Paulus* (Tübingen 1930); *idem, Geschichte der Paulinischen Forschung* (1933); C. G. Montefiore, *Judaism and St. Paul* (London 1914); M. S. Enslin, *The Ethics of Paul* (New York and London 1930), pp. 1-16; M. E. Andrews, *The Ethical Teaching of Paul* (Chapel Hill 1934), pp. 135-75; J. Edman, *The Mind of Paul* (New York 1935), pp. 51-84; P. G. Kunst, *Joodsche Invloeden bij Paulus* (Amsterdam 1936).]

1. Paul boasted of his Jewish origin. With regard to his opponents he says: "Are they Hebrews? So am I. Are they Israelites? So am I. Are they of the seed of Abraham? So am I." [1] He says emphatically: "For I also am an Israelite, of the seed of Abraham, of the tribe of Benjamin." [2] Again he says in debate with his opponents:

. . . if any other man thinketh to have confidence in the flesh, I yet more: circumcised the eighth day, of the stock of Israel, of the tribe of Benjamin, a Hebrew of the Hebrews; as touching the Law, a Pharisee.[3]

In his speech before the Sanhedrin in Jerusalem he is recorded as saying: "I am a Pharisee, a son of Pharisees" [4]—not "a Pharisee, the son of a Pharisee," but "a Pharisee, a son of *Pharisees*," that is to say, a Pharisee from a family of Pharisees, a

[1] II Cor. 11:22.
[3] Philipp. 3:4, 5.
[2] Rom. 11:1.
[4] Acts 23:6.

450

family that had been Pharisaic for generations. Also in the speech "on the stairs," which Paul delivered to the people of Jerusalem at the time of his arrest, he pointed out:

I am a Jew, born in Tarsus of Cilicia, but brought up in this city, at the feet of Gamaliel, instructed according to the strict manner of the Law of our fathers, being zealous for God, even as ye all are this day.[5]

Words very similar to these he spoke also before Agrippa and Bernice.[6]

Nor was the idea of "Thou hast chosen us" (the Chosen People) ever given up by Paul, just as it was never given up by Jesus. Once he cries out in vexation: "We . . . [are] Jews by nature, and not sinners of the Gentiles!" [7] With all his universalism, he says emphatically three times in succession: ". . . to the Jew first, and also to the Greek." [8] And in his great love for his people he declares:

For I could wish that I myself were anathema from Christ for my brethren's sake, my kinsmen according to the flesh: who are Israelites, whose is the *sonship*,[9] and the glory, and the covenants, and giving of the Law, and the service,[10] and the promises; whose are the fathers, and of whom is Christ according to the flesh.[11]

When the pagans in the Christian congregations began to manifest racial hatred toward the Jewish Nazarenes who were among them, Paul came out against them in stinging words: Israel is "a good olive tree" and the pagans are "a wild olive tree," which has been grafted upon the "good olive tree." [12]

---

[5] Acts 22:3.
[6] Acts 26:4, 5.
[7] Gal. 2:15.
[8] Rom. 1:16; 2:9, 10.
[9] *Cf.* the saying of Jesus: ". . . it is not meet to take the *children's* bread and cast it to the little dogs" (Mark 7:27; Matt. 15:26).
[10] The Temple, or prayer.
[11] Rom. 9:3-5.
[12] It is to be seen here that Paul, unlike Jesus, is a city man and not a man of the country; he does not know that the "good olive" is grafted upon the "wild olive" and not the reverse. This was already noted by Origen. See on the matter of Columella, *De Re Rustica* V 9 16 the commentary of Lietzmann on Rom. 11:17 (*Handbuch zum Neuen Testament*, 8⁴, 105).

Israel is the root (or trunk) and the pagans are branches which
have grown out from the trunk; the branches do not support
the trunk, but the trunk supports the branches. Thus the chief
element is the believing Israel and not the believing pagans;
therefore the pagan Christians have no right to despise the
Jewish Nazarenes. For in the end God will fulfill his promise
delivered by the prophets, and the sons of Israel will be saved.[13]
From the heart of a Jew gone astray, yet loving his people,
he cries:

Brethren, my heart's desire and my supplication to God is for
them, that they may be saved. *For I bear them witness that they
have a zeal for God, but not according to knowledge.*[14]

Even at the end of his life, after he had had many sharp conflicts with the Jews, and they had punished him a number of
times with forty lashes lacking one and even attempted to
stone him to death; and after he had been taken a prisoner to
Rome with the accusation of the Jews of Jerusalem upon him
—after all this, he called to his place of confinement *first of
all* the Jews of Rome, and assured them that he had nothing
"whereof to accuse" his people ("my nation").[15]

Paul never felt himself a non-Jew, in spite of the fact that in
moments of bitterness, when he was being persecuted by
Jews or Nazarenes, he would forget the "Christian love" to
which he sang such a glorious hymn of praise,[16] and would
speak harshly about the Jews, or even curse them with violent
curses.[17] On such occasions he would say the opposite of his
statement given above that the Jews had "the covenants . . .
and the promises," and would declare that the Jews who did
not believe in Jesus as Messiah were no longer God's first-born
son, Israel, but that the birthright had been taken from them
and given to the believing Gentiles.[18]

[13] Rom. 11:16–31.   [14] Rom. 10:1, 2.   [15] Acts 28:19.
[16] I Cor. 13:1–8.   [17] I Thess. 2:14–6.
[18] Rom. 2:28, 29; Gal. 3:14; 3:28, 29; Eph. 2:11–22; Col. 3:9–11—and elsewhere.

Yet we feel that even in his moments of anger he speaks of Israel as he does out of a consciousness of the primogeniture of Israel, and out of a desire that the "first-born" of God should accept the faith in Jesus. If someone had suggested to Paul that he cease being a Jew, he not only would not have agreed to this, *but he would not even have understood such a suggestion.* He always saw Christianity according to his own conception of it, namely, that it was the true Judaism; and he considered that he was *bringing the Gentiles into this Judaism,* and *not taking the Jews out of Judaism* at all. Paul was mistaken in thinking this. Actually, he led the Jews believing in Jesus out of Judaism, and after a time he easily inducted them into a kind of compromising half-paganism, a mixture of Judaism and paganism; but he was not aware of this, he did not intend to do it, and he never imagined that this would be the outcome. For him Christianity was a new and improved kind of Judaism, like Essenism, for example; except that in this new Judaism it was possible and necessary to include Gentiles, and therefore it was proper for this Judaism to be distinguished from the old and unbelieving Judaism by a special type of congregation made up of both believing Jews and believing Gentiles. But he did not see or understand that this distinction would of necessity bring into being *an essentially new religion,* which would have in it *only a part* of Judaism—and thus would not be true Judaism at all.

How could a disciple of Rabban Gamaliel the Elder, even though a disciple who had gone astray, have thought otherwise? Truly, Paul was a Jew not only in his physical appearance, but he was also a typical Jew in his thinking and in his entire inner life.

For Saul-Paul was not only "a Pharisee, a son of Pharisees," but also one of those disciples of the Tannaim who were brought up on the exegesis of the Torah, and did not cease to cherish it to the end of their days. It would be difficult to find more typically Talmudic expositions of Scripture than those in the Epistles of Paul. Here are some examples:

First Example

But the righteousness which is of faith saith thus, "Say not in thy heart, 'Who shall ascend into heaven?' (that is, to bring Christ down:) or, 'Who shall descend into the abyss?' (that is, to bring Christ up from the dead.)" But what saith it? "The word is nigh thee, in thy mouth, and in thy heart": that is, the word of faith, which we preach: because if thou shalt confess with thy mouth Jesus as Lord, and shalt believe in thy heart that God raised him from the dead, thou shalt be saved: for with the heart man believeth unto righteousness; and with the mouth confession is made unto salvation. For the Scripture saith, "Whosoever believeth on him shall not be put to shame." [19]

Paul here changes one part of a passage from the Pentateuch [20] to suit his needs, and in place of "Who shall go over the sea for us?" he substitutes another Scriptural phrase, "Who shall descend into the abyss?"; [21] then he interprets this garbled passage arbitrarily, drawing from it conclusions desired and needed by him, although there is no hint of them in the passage itself; continuing, he supports his interpretation with a supposed verse from the Prophets, [22] although even in the Septuagint this verse lacks the words "on him," while in place of the reading "shall not be put to shame" of the Septuagint, the Hebrew has "shall not make haste."

Second Example

It is related in the Pentateuch that the skin of Moses' face "shone" (or "was radiant") when God had spoken with him,

[19] Rom. 10:6–11.   [20] Deut. 30:12–4.

[21] Or "into Sheol." More correctly "to the deep," according to the verse "They mount up to the heavens, they go down to the deeps" (Ps. 107:26). See Ed. Böhl, *Die alttestamentliche Citate im Neuen Testament* (Wien 1878), SS. 181–5; A. F. Puuko, *Paulus und das Judentum* (Studia Orientalia, II), pp. 49, 50.

[22] Isa. 28:16.

and therefore Aaron and all the children of Israel were afraid to go near him; whereupon, Moses put a veil over his face whenever he spoke with the people.[23] But Paul, like a true Tannaitic exegete, could not take the story literally. According to Paul, Moses put the veil over his face "that the children of Israel should not look stedfastly on the end of that which was passing away." [Here Paul interprets the "glory" on Moses' face as a symbol of the old Judaism which, according to Paul's view, was destined to pass away in favor of Christianity.] But the hearts of the children of Israel were hardened, and "until this very day at the reading of the old covenant the same veil remaineth"; "unto this day, whensoever Moses is read, a veil lieth upon their heart" and the true meaning (according to Paul) is hidden from them.[24] This interpretation is typically Midrashic in its form, and is changed from a Jewish to a Christian interpretation only by its deliberately altered content.

THIRD EXAMPLE

Now to Abraham were the promises spoken, and to his *seed*.[25] He saith not, "And to seeds," as of many; but as of one, "And to thy seed," which is Christ.[26]

As though Paul did not know that "seed" is a collective noun, the plural number of which does not, and probably could not, occur in this sense ("descendants") in the entire Old Testament! (Only in the Mishnah is there זרעיות as plural of זרעית in this sense.)[27] Is not this typically Talmudic exegesis (of which, to be sure, there are also examples in the

[23] Ex. 34:29-35.   [24] II Cor. 3:3-18.
[25] Gen. 12:7; 13:15; 17:7; 22:18; 24:7.
[26] Gal. 3:16.
[27] Cf. ". . . the blood of him [that is wrongfully condemned] and the blood of his descendants" (זרעיותיו, Mish., San. IV 5). In our texts the word is זרעותיו, but see Jacob Levy, *Wörterbuch über die Talmudim und Midraschim*, I, 555 (art. זרעית).

writings of Philo), like all those interpretations in Talmud and Midrash which are based on the presence or absence of the letter Waw? [In this case a distinction between the singular and plural numbers is implied.]

FOURTH EXAMPLE

Abraham had two sons, one the son of the "handmaid" Hagar, and the other the son of the "freewoman" Sarah; the son of the handmaid was born "after the flesh," but the son of the freewoman was born "through promise." The two women with their sons are only an "allegory" signifying "two covenants," which God made with Israel. The first covenant is that of Mount Sinai, a covenant which brought about slavery; for "Hagar is Mount Sinai in Arabia." [28] The second covenant is that of "the Jerusalem on high," signified by the freewoman; the Christians, since they believe in the second covenant, the "new covenant," are the sons of the freewoman Sarah, being thus, like Isaac, "children of promise." And "as he that was born after the flesh (Ishmael) persecuted him that was born after the Spirit (Isaac), so also" now do the sons of the covenant of Sinai, the sons of the handmaid Hagar, persecute the "children of promise," the sons of the freewoman Sarah. Hence, says Paul, thus "saith the Scripture (Gen. 21:10): 'Cast out the handmaid and her son; for the son of the handmaid shall not inherit with the son of the freewoman.' " [29] Is this not typical casuistry after the manner of both Philo and the Midrash?

[28] Some say that Paul, having stayed in Arabia after the vision on the road to Damascus and having learned Arabic, identified "Hagar" with ḥajar, the Arabic for Sela (rock); but since Mount Sinai is not Sela (or a rock), it is more correct to suppose that Paul the Hebrew identified the name Hagar with the word Ha-Har ("The Mountain"); The Mountain (with the definite article) is Mount Sinai. See Puuko, op. cit. (Studia Orientalia, II), p. 7.

[29] Gal. 4:22–31.

FIFTH AND FINAL EXAMPLE

For it is written in the Law of Moses, "Thou shalt not muzzle the ox when he treadeth out the corn." Is it for the oxen that God careth, or saith he it altogether for our sake? Yea, for our sake it was written; because he that ploweth ought to plow in hope, and he that thresheth, to thresh in hope of partaking [of some of the products of the plowing and the threshing]. If we sowed unto you [Christians] spiritual things, is it a great matter if we shall reap your carnal things? [30]

In other words, the real meaning of the command, "Thou shalt not muzzle the ox when he treadeth out the corn," is not its simple, literal sense, that it is cruelty to animals if the threshing ox is not allowed to eat some of the grain which he has threshed. God forbid that the matter should be that simple! "Is it for the oxen that God careth?" No, rather the ox is the preacher of the gospel, who sows "spiritual things" among the Christians; and the interpretation of the verse, "Thou shalt not muzzle the ox," *etc.*, is that it is forbidden to deny the sower of "spiritual things" the right of obtaining "carnal things" (financial support) from the converts, since even Jesus himself "did . . . ordain that they that proclaim the gospel should live from the gospel." [31] Here again we have Jewish exegesis of the usual kind.

Paul uses this thoroughly Talmudic casuistry in order to prove the essential, fundamental truth of his teachings. For example, in order to prove that the death of Jesus on the cross ended the obligation to obey the injunctions of the Torah, Paul adduces this strange proof: A woman during the lifetime of her husband is forbidden to another man unless she has received a bill of divorce from her husband; but if her husband dies, she is free to marry another man without a bill of divorce. Hence death sets aside the commandments of the

[30] I Cor. 9:9-11.   [31] I Cor. 9:14.

Torah. Therefore Jesus, by dying a shameful death on the cross, set aside by this death the Torah and the ceremonial laws.[32] Could there be a more unnatural interpretation than this? Truly, only Paul the Jew could have based his entire teaching on radical reinterpretations of Torah like these, which the Polish Jews call *pshet'lakh*.

Paul lived by Jewish law like a proper Jew; also, he knew the Old Testament in its Hebrew original and meditated much upon it. Those who sat "at the feet of Gamaliel" of course learned the Old Testament in its Hebrew original, and also studied Oral Law in the language of Mishnah, the later Hebrew which afterwards became "the language of the Sages." Hence there are Semitisms and Hebraisms in the language of the Epistles, in spite of the richness of their Greek.[33] If Paul was "a Hebrew of the Hebrews" and "a Pharisee, a son of Pharisees," educated in Jerusalem and able to make speeches in Hebrew (or Aramaic), obviously he was not a "Septuagint Jew" (*Septuaginta-Jude*) only, as various Christian scholars have been accustomed to picture him.[34] I have already shown [35] that it is not proper to draw this conclusion merely because Paul quotes Scriptural passages according to the Septuagint. This practice in quotation was natural when a man was writing Greek for Gentiles and Greek-speaking Jews in churches outside of Palestine. But actually he does not always quote according to the Septuagint. Sometimes he quotes from memory, making mistakes in certain words; and sometimes he changes what stands written in Scripture to suit the needs of his own interpretation.[36] But sometimes he quotes precisely according to the Hebrew text.[37] It is also possible that the copyists of the New Testament, being accustomed to the

[32] Rom. 7:1-6.
[33] Puuko, *op. cit.*, pp. 4-11 has recently reaffirmed this in detail.
[34] Thus Deissmann (*Paulus*, S. 79) calls him.
[35] See above, p. 305.   [36] Above, p. 454.
[37] See for details Puuko, *op. cit.*, SS. 34-63.

Septuagint, found it proper to "harmonize" from time to time the text of Paul with the version familiar to them, even if they did not do this throughout in a systematic manner.

Paul arranged his itinerary according to the dates of the Jewish festivals.[38] Even after he became "the apostle of the Gentiles" he still lived in accordance with Jewish practices, observing for himself the ceremonial laws while relaxing them for others. He circumcised the half-Jew Timothy,[39] he observed the Nazirite vow,[40] he offered sacrifices for four Nazirites and apparently for himself also,[41] he returned thanks and broke bread before eating,[42] he visited the Temple; and in general he conducted himself like a Jew in every respect, except that where there were Jewish Nazarenes and Gentile Christians he ate with all of them, in order not to cause division in the young churches which he had founded. Moreover, at the height of his fight for unity between the Jewish Nazarenes and the Gentile Christians, at the height of his opposition to the unequal attitude of Peter and James toward believing Jews on the one hand and believing Gentiles on the other, and at the very moment of his compromise on circumcision, he yet says: "Yea, I testify again to every man that receiveth circumcision, that he is a debtor to do the whole Law." [43]

All these facts have brought it about that a whole series of Christian scholars see in Paul a thorough Jew, a typically Pharisaic Jew, speaking Aramaic (or even late Hebrew) and observing the ceremonial laws, a Jew devoted to his people, who was willing to accept without recourse to his Roman citizenship the lashes imposed by Jewish courts of law; and only because he desired the good of his nation as he understood that "good," did he endeavor to induct his Jewish

[38] I Cor. 16:8: "But I will tarry at Ephesus until Pentecost." See also Acts 27:9: ". . . the voyage was now dangerous, because the Fast [Yom Kippur] was now already gone by" (see above, p. 411).
[39] Acts 16:3.   [40] Acts 18:18.   [41] Acts 21:26.
[42] Acts 27:35.   [43] Gal. 5:3.

brethren into the company of believers in the crucified Messiah. Some of these scholars insist that even the things foreign to Judaism at first sight, such as the elevation of Jesus to the rank of "heavenly man," the "being in Christ," and the distinction between "the natural" (ψυχικός) and "the spiritual" (πνευματικός)—things which we shall discuss farther on—even these things, they insist, do not come from foreign, pagan sources, but from Judaism itself, which at the end of the period of the Second Temple had within itself a number of mystical currents,[44] as is shown by the existence of the sect of the Essenes and the mystical and "ultraspiritual" apocalypses, such as the Ethiopic and Slavonic books of Enoch, the Syriac and Greek books of Baruch, Fourth Ezra, and the like.[45] There are also those who argue that the mysticism of the time, the mysticism of the pagan religions, is not a part of the mind of Paul at all, and that what we think is mysticism is only deep religious piety.[46] Likewise, there are interpreters who say that the whole unique religious teaching of Paul was brought about by the Jewish "doctrine of the last days" (eschatology), which Paul seized upon and entered into more deeply than did others; and that his special ethical doctrines were due to the influence of the Hebrew Old Testament only.[47] Thus these scholars come to the conclusion that there are not to be found in the teaching of Paul any foreign, non-Jewish influences at all.[48]

[44] In the opinion of Rudolf Kittel (Die hellenistische Mysterienreligion und das Alte Testament, Stuttgart 1924) there were such mystical currents long before this.

[45] See on all these in the works of the following authors as cited above: Puuko, Windisch, Omodeo, Schweitzer.

[46] See K. Deissner, Paulus und die Mystik seiner Zeit (Leipzig-Erlangen 1921); E. von Dobschütz, op. cit., SS. 42-3. See what has been said against this above, p. 428, n. 31.

[47] See on this especially M. S. Enslin, The Ethics of Paul (New York 1930).

[48] See A. Schweitzer, Die Mystik des Apostels Paul (Tübingen 1930); idem, Geschichte der Paulinischen Forschung (1933), SS. 171-94.

2. But in opposition to all these important scholars stand scholars no less important who see many foreign influences in the teaching of Paul. They present numerous convincing arguments for the opinion that in various ideas of Paul and in many expressions in his Epistles are to be seen the beliefs and opinions of his time as found in the literature of the period. In other words, the views of Paul are stamped with the religious syncretism which prevailed at that time, when a flood of Oriental religions came into the West, and a mixture of Occidental—Greek and Roman—religions penetrated into the East; and various expressions in the Epistles of Paul are already found in the Greek or Hellenized Oriental literature of the last centuries before the Christian Era and the first centuries of that era. Matters have reached such a point as to give rise to a new method of scholarly research called the "History of Religions" explanation (*Religionsgeschichtliche Erklärung*) of Christianity.[49] From much intensive research in the history of ancient Oriental religions, it has transpired that there is hardly an idea or expression in the Epistles of Paul and in what is related of Paul in Acts the like of which is not to be found in the ancient Oriental religions or in the obscure, mystical corners of Greek religion. Matters had also earlier reached the point where, as in the "Dutch School," [50] many concluded that Paul never lived, and that his Epistles are only late fabrications, the creations of a Greek-Jewish-Hellenistic influence.

[49] See on all this the two books of A. Deissmann, *Licht vom Osten* (1923); *Paulus* (1925). See also P. Wendland, *Die hellenistisch-römische Kultur* (1912); C. Clemen, *Religionsgeschichtliche Erklärung des Neuen Testaments*, 2. Aufl. (Giessen 1924)—Clemen gives a history of this question on pp. 1–18; the history of the view connecting Paul with the Greek or Oriental mysteries is to be found in K. Deissner, *op. cit.*, pp. 1–17. See further W. Bousset, *Kyrios Christos* (1926); R. Reitzenstein, *Die hellenistichen Mysterienreligionen* (1927); Gerhard Kittel, *Die Religionsgeschichte und das Urchristentum* (Gütersloh 1933); A. Loisy, *Les mystères païens et le mystère chrétien* (1930), pp. 223–324; also the bibliography at the beginning of Chap. III of the Second Book, above, p. 95.

[50] See on this above, p. 236.

Likewise, many conclude to-day that the whole story of the work of Paul and the entire contents of his Epistles come almost entirely from mystical Oriental and Hellenistic religions, thus leaving almost no traces of Paul's personality or of his own particular teachings.

What is the truth of the matter?

Anyone who takes proper account of the Judaism of the period at the end of the Second Temple, and reads the data about Paul in the book of Acts and in his Epistles, will see in this man a Jew by custom and by conviction, who never intentionally went so far as to deny Judaism. But along with this the student will feel that we have here a Jew who went astray, a Jew who deviated from the path of Palestinian Judaism as it was understood at that time.

How could he have been otherwise? He was "a Hebrew of the Hebrews," yet nevertheless he was born in Tarsus, a Hellenized city of the Diaspora. He grew up partly in Jerusalem —but we do not know at what age he went to Jerusalem. He sat at the feet of Rabban Gamaliel—yet "that disciple" mocked at everything which Rabban Gamaliel taught. Paul could speak Hebrew or Jewish Aramaic—yet all his writings are in Greek, which in spite of all the Hebraisms and Aramaisms in it is an adequate and rich Greek. He lived in Jerusalem a number of years and visited Jerusalem many times; yet he returned to Tarsus in the prime of his life and stayed there eight years (c. 35–43). Could it have been possible for a talented and perceptive man like Paul *not* to have been influenced by the splendid pagan culture of Tarsus, his native city? For thirty years or more (32–64) he carried out his journeys in foreign states, passing through nearly all the great and extensive Roman Empire (except Egypt and most of the countries of Europe), which was inhabited chiefly by pagan Gentiles—so can it be supposed that he would not be influenced during all these years by all the beliefs and opinions which were then current in the Roman Empire? Nor was it a mere accident that Paul specifically, and no other, was chosen to be "the apostle of the Gentiles"; he was the one who was best fitted among the "apostles" to sway the Gentiles; and this would have been the case only if Paul knew not alone the language of the Gentiles, but also their religions, their culture, and their customs. The question is, how could it have been possible for an adherent of a Judaism that was quite uncontaminated by foreign influences to create a religion (or give the impetus to and assist in the creation of a religion) which was to a considerable extent non-Judaism and which after no very long time became a half-Jewish, half-pagan faith? At this point we can have recourse to a well-known generalization: *Ex nihilo nihil fit*. If there had not been in Paul something external to Judaism, he could not have created a creed which the great majority in Judaism could not accept, but which pagans in particular could and did accept!

To be sure, Paul the apostle did not formally study "Greek learning," in spite of the verses from Aratus, Epimenides, and Menander which he is said to have quoted or which he actually did quote. Like all the Sages of Israel, Paul despised that learning; for it was not religious and devout but pagan and profane; and even the best of it, the Platonic philosophy, was full of examples and fables from Greek mythology. I doubt very much if he had any knowledge of the current philosophy of the period, the Stoic and Cynic (to say nothing of the Epicurean) philosophy, from Greek books or from formal lectures in the schools of Sophists and rhetoricians. Nevertheless, it is clear that a man who spoke and wrote excellent Greek, and frequented Greek and Hellenized cities, would naturally hold, even if he were not conscious of the fact and did not mean to do so, any number of religious opinions which a purely Palestinian Jew like Jesus could not have held, since Jesus never went beyond the borders of his own land. Here the chief factor was not the acquisition of "Greek learning," not a conscious interest in the mysteries of Isis and Osiris, of Mithras or of Attis and the like, but the *general atmosphere* which then surrounded every cultured man who moved about in the lands of Asia Minor, Macedonia, and Greece, breathing in the very air of the time as it could be felt in the whole reach of the Roman Empire. However much a man may oppose the views of his time, he nevertheless unknowingly falls under their power. For, as I have said elsewhere,[51] we learn *consciously only from those we like*, but *unconsciously from those we dislike*. It is not necessary to suppose that Paul attended the schools of the Greek Sophists and read their books or the books of various Oriental cult leaders in order to learn their teachings. Rather, pagan teachings, both Greek and Oriental, were then in the very air; hence it was *inevitable* that Paul should have been *unconsciously* influenced by them. The clearest example of this is, to my mind, the book of Koheleth in the Old Testament. This book contains no systematic Greek philosophy at all; but there is already felt in it that atmosphere which was created by the later period of Greek philosophy, an atmosphere which surrounded in the times of the author of Koheleth all thinkers in the [Near] East in such a manner that it was impossible for a Jew who thought deeply about universal questions to be entirely free from it.

Thus, according to my view of the matter, it is necessary to realize that such names as "complete Hebrew," "Hellenistic Jew," "Jew of the Diaspora," "Septuagint Jew," and the like do not mean much by themselves, without proper explanation. All the influences playing upon Paul, which scholars seek to find in Greek literature and in the philosophy of Plato and the Stoics on the one hand, and on the other hand in the Hellenistic literature: in Philo, in the Wisdom of Solomon, and the like—all these are uncertain, even if it is difficult to doubt

[51] See Klausner, *Yeshu*, p. 434, n. 9 [not in Eng. ed.].

them absolutely.[52] What is absolutely certain is that Paul lived most of his life—except for a few years which he spent in Jerusalem—in a pagan-Gentile, a Greek or Hellenized, environment; and that it was inevitable that he should absorb influences from the total intellectual, religious, and cultural life then prevailing in the many states which were held together by two strong forces, namely, the political power of Rome and the cultural power of Greece.

For, with all his "Hebraism," Paul was a Jew of the Diaspora, a Jew of the "exile" of Israel in Asia Minor. And in this sense he was detached from the *authentic, living Judaism* which was rooted in its own cultural soil. Only by reason of this could he have created such an ideology as he did, thus founding a new religion which was Judaism and non-Judaism at the same time. Such a religion could not have been created or founded by Jesus, who, with all the strange, un-Jewish elements that came to him, perhaps from the schismatic Jewish sects founded by apocalyptists, or more correctly, from a very vivid expectation of "the end of days," was nevertheless a Jew rooted in the soil of Palestine. Neither could a religion like this have been created by a completely detached Jew, who did not know Judaism at its source at all, who had never lived in Palestine, and who had never been a disciple of Palestinian sages. A religion like this could have been formed only by a man like Paul, who on the one hand had his origin from Hebrew-speaking Palestinian Jews ("a Hebrew of the Hebrews") and was "a Pharisee, a son of Pharisees," and on the other hand was a Jew of the Diaspora, a detached Jew—a native of Cilicia and a wanderer in Asia Minor, Macedonia, and Greece for many years, knowing Greek thoroughly and

---

[52] Puuko, *op. cit.*, SS. 34–52, denies the influence of the latter (Philo, Wisdom of Solomon, *etc.*); Deissner, *op. cit.*, SS. 18–147 denies the influence of the former [Greek literature and philosophy]. We shall see below that the influence of the Wisdom of Solomon is almost certain.

writing down in that language his basic thoughts. Only a Jew like this—a joint product of Palestine and Asia Minor, of an attenuated Judaism and a systematized Hellenism—was capable of forming Christianity as a special religion (yet to the end of his days, he undoubtedly saw in it actual Judaism, which was given to the pagans only in a new form), after he had found a supreme authority—namely Jesus as he had seen him in the vision of his imagination.

Finally, one general remark which derives from everything said above:

Intensive research over many years has brought the writer of the present book to a deep conviction that there is nothing in the teaching of Paul—not even the most mystical elements in it—that did not come to him from authentic Judaism.[53] For all the theories and hypotheses that Paul drew his opinions *directly* from the Greek philosophical literature or the mystery religions of his time have no sufficient foundation. But it *is* a fact that most of the elements in his teaching which came from Judaism received unconsciously at his hands a *non-Jewish coloring* from the influence of the Hellenistic-Jewish and pagan atmosphere with which Paul of Tarsus was surrounded during nearly all of his life, except for the few years which he spent in Jerusalem.

This proposition I shall attempt to prove in the following chapters.

[53] To this opinion, which I presented in a detailed letter some years ago, the great expert in both Talmudic and early Christian literature, Prof. George Foot Moore, agreed. During the last two years of his life, he wrote me important letters on this question. These letters should be published, and at the first opportunity I shall endeavor to have them printed.

CHAPTER III

God and Satan — and Christ

1. With regard to belief in a one and only God, Paul was still a Jew and not a Christian; belief in the Trinity still did not exist for him. There is only one God in the world, the God of Israel, whose children call him "Abba, Father";[1] there is "one God and Father of all, who is over all, and through all, and in all."[2] Paul says definitely, "God is one."[3] And still more definitely, ". . . the same God . . . worketh all things in all."[4] Yet he also says with Jewish absolutism:

. . . we know that no idol is anything in the world, and that there is no God but one. For though there be that are called gods, whether in heaven or on earth; as there are gods many, and lords many; yet to us there is one God, the Father, from whom are all things, and we (belong) unto him; and one Lord, Jesus Christ, through whom are all things (made), and we through him.[5]

But in another place he says of God: "For of him, and through him, and unto him, are all things. To him be the glory forever."[6] Here is lacking the conclusion that through (or by) Jesus everything was made, including ourselves.

We have in all this a thorough monotheism; yet it is not pure monotheism. The addition with regard to Jesus, that through him "are all things, and we through him," although this matter is not emphasized in every passage—this addition, to be sure, does not completely nullify the fundamental as-

[1] Rom. 8:15; Gal. 4:6.
[2] Eph. 4:6.
[3] Gal. 3:20.
[4] I Cor. 12:6.
[5] I Cor. 8:4-6.
[6] Rom. 11:36.

sumption that there is only one God, through whom and unto whom "are all things"; but it does weaken it. If we use Biblical language we can say that this addition makes the "brightness to cease" [Ps. 89:44/45] and disturbs the fundamental assumption of the unity of God.

Of course, when "the end" comes, when all arise from the dead and acknowledge Jesus as Messiah, Jesus will turn the rulership over to God the Father:

> Then cometh the end, when he shall deliver up the kingdom to God, even the Father; when he shall have abolished all rule and all authority and power.

Then he shall abolish death, which is "the last enemy," and all things shall be put "in subjection under his feet." [7]

> And when all things have been subjected unto him, then shall the Son also himself be subjected to him that did subject all things unto him, that God may be all in all.[8]

In other words, Christ is subject to God the Father of all, who controls everything, and at the end of time God will be "all in all"; yet God himself has subjected everything to Christ ("He put all things in subjection under his feet"), who is not subject to anything except to God alone—to the Father, whose son Christ is.

Jesus is, therefore, second to God—not actual deity, yet everything which God did in the world he did through (or by means of) Christ. To be sure, "the head of Christ is God"; yet "the head of every man is Christ," just as a man is "the head of the woman." [9] Paul says to the members of a church which he had founded: ". . . ye are Christ's; and Christ is God's." [10] Thus Christ is the head of mankind, like God himself, except that God is also the head of Christ. Of course, a man is "the

---

[7] Ps. 8:6/7.
[9] I Cor. 11:3.

[8] I Cor. 15:24-8.
[10] I Cor. 3:23.

image and glory of God" (the glory of the Shekhinah), and "all things [both man and woman] are of God." [11] Nevertheless, Christ is the head of all humanity, and God has made everything through him and by means of him. Hence it comes about that Paul in one of his Epistles uses the phrase "the God and Father of our Lord Jesus Christ" in place of "the God of Abraham, Isaac, and Jacob" of Judaism.[12]

Even here we still have the Jewish belief in the unity of the Godhead, but it is blurred and made uncertain by the special function of the Pauline Messiah ("Christ")—a function which in Judaism is carried out by the one and only God himself. Belief in the Trinity is not yet present; but the first step toward such a belief has been taken.

The Jewish Messiah is *a political savior* of his enslaved nation, which is depressed and afflicted in an exile among peoples who hate and persecute it; the Jewish Messiah is also *a spiritual redeemer* of all mankind, who by the spirit of God which "shall rest upon him," and by the righteousness which "shall be the girdle of his loins" in such a manner that "he shall smite the land [or "the tyrant"] with the rod of his mouth" alone, "and with the breath of his lips (alone) shall he slay the wicked" [Isa. 11:2–5]—by means of these "gifts of the Holy Spirit" he shall conquer heathenism. Then shall all peoples call upon the name of the one God, "all nations shall flow unto . . . the mountain of the Lord's house" [Isa. 2:2], they shall cease to make war upon one another, and "they shall all become one band [a band of peoples or League of Nations] to do the will of God with their whole hearts"; then "shall all wickedness disappear like smoke," "the rule of arrogance shall pass from the earth," and the "Kingdom of Heaven" shall be established upon earth forever.[13]

[11] I Cor. 11:7, 12.
[12] Rom. 15:6; II Cor. 1:3 *et passim*.
[13] The prayer *Shemoneh 'Esreh* for "Solemn Days" and the prayer *'Alenu*.

But it was never said in the old, original Judaism, that of the prophets and of the Tannaim, that the world was created by (or through) the Messiah, and that the one and only God had given up one of his most important functions and turned over to his Messiah his own essential prerogatives, such as the creation of the world and the supreme headship over all mankind. To be sure, even Judaism sees the Messiah as greater and higher than all the rest of mortal men; and as a symbol of righteousness, faithfulness, and goodness he is the head of mankind according to the view of Judaism also. But this headship is entirely apart from that of the Deity. The Jewish Messiah is the head of humanity by reason of his ethical standards, but not because God has turned over to him his (God's) own headship, as Paul would have it. Indeed, Paul goes so far in this opinion that he dares to place God and Jesus on the same footing: "Grace to you and peace from God our Father and the Lord Jesus Christ." [14] Here we have the essential and basic difference in Messianic belief as between Jews and Christians—even Pauline Christians. [15]

2. How did Paul acquire this new Messianic belief?

It would seem that it came to him *because of his fear of spirits.*

Cosmic existence is, according to Paul, as we shall see in the next chapter, dualistic: there are in it *flesh* and *spirit.* The supreme spirit is the Spirit of God. Yet the spirit of Christ (the Messiah) is by nature closely related to it. There are in addition *good spirits:* ministering angels and angels of the presence—"Seraphim" and "Ophannim" and "Holy Living Creatures"; but there are also many *evil spirits*—devils and demons and angels of destruction, at the head of whom stands

[14] I Cor. 1:3; II Cor. 1:2.
[15] See Klausner, "Ha-Mashiaḥ ha-Yehudi ve-ha-Mashiaḥ ha-Notsri," *Sepher-Magnes* (Jerusalem 5698), pp. 207-15.

Satan, the leader of all evil spirits.[16] Satan is "the god of this world." [17] He—as in the book of Job and in Talmud and Midrash—is the one who seduces men, leading them astray and driving them into temptation;[18] and he is the deceiver who takes advantage of men, being a master of trickery,[19] disguising himself as the angel of light.[20] Also, he is the one who hinders Paul from doing the right things.[21] Obviously, Satan is for Paul "the prince of the powers of the air," [22] to whom are subject all kinds of evil spirits and powers of darkness. These spirits and powers Paul calls "elements" (or "rudiments," στοιχεῖα).[23] He says to the members of a church which he had founded:

For our wrestling is not against flesh and blood, but against the principalities, against the powers, against the world-rulers of this darkness, against the spiritual hosts of wickedness in the heavenly places.[24]

Paul also thinks of the idols of the Gentiles as evil spirits;[25] Satan is, to be sure, the head of all of them. When there was found in the Corinthian church a man who had married his father's wife, Paul commanded the church members "to deliver such a one unto Satan for the destruction of the flesh, that the spirit may be saved." [26] And Paul can offer no better prayer for the "brethren" in Rome than this: "And the God of peace shall bruise Satan under your feet shortly." [27]

This fear of Satan and his household—the evil spirits—was

[16] Paul knows only the term "Satan." The passages in the Epistles attributed to Paul in which we find the term "the devil" (diabolos) are suspected of being later. The Talmud calls Satan "Sammael," and the Midrash says of him that he is "the chief of all the accusing angels" (literally "Satans," Deut. Rabbah XI 10). See on all this Klausner, Yeshu, pp. 214-5 [Eng. ed., pp. 198-9].

[17] II Cor. 4:4.
[18] I Thess. 3:5; I Cor. 7:5.
[19] II Cor. 2:11.
[20] II Cor. 2:11, 14.
[21] I Thess. 2:18.
[22] Eph. 2:2.
[23] Gal. 4:9.
[24] Eph. 6:12.
[25] I Cor. 10:19-21.
[26] I Cor. 5:5.
[27] Rom. 16:20. See on all this M. Goguel, Jésus de Nazareth: Mythe ou Histoire? (Paris 1925), pp. 137-45 [Eng. ed., pp. 136-44].

at least one of the fundamental causes of the alteration of
the function of the Jewish Messiah.[27a]

We must be careful about modernizing Paul—a matter in
which Christian scholars, even the best of them, have stumbled.
It is always to be remembered that what seems to us a superstition could have been considered in the later Hellenistic
period a perfectly legitimate belief, even by a profound and
realistic, yet visionary and mystical, man like Paul. Both
Judaism and Hellenism each contributed its part to this
superstition.

The God of Israel is called in the Old Testament "the
God of the spirits of all flesh." [28] Here there is a distinction
between spirit and flesh, although Judaism did not emphasize
this distinction very much; it was emphasized much more by
later Greek philosophy and the mystery religions in the time
of Paul. Of the God of Israel it is also said in the Old Testament: "Who makest *spirits* ["winds" is the usual English
translation in this verse] Thy messengers," [29] and "the Lord
weigheth the spirits." [30] In the Ethiopic Enoch (37:1–38:6)
God is called "the Lord of Spirits" (which can also be translated "the *God* of Spirits," since the Ethiopic word *Egzi'e*
means "Lord," but also "God," like the Hebrew *Adonai*).[31]
There is evil in the world—this is a fact which cannot be
denied; but it was impossible, according to the purified religious consciousness of Judaism in the period of the Second
Temple, to attribute the evil to God, who is the source of
good only.[32] Out of necessity, then, it was concluded that evil

---

[27a] On "God and Satan" see now W. O. E. Oesterley, "The Belief in
Angels and Demons," *Judaism and Christianity*, I (London 1937), 191–209.
[28] Num. 27:16.   [29] Ps. 104:4.   [30] Prov. 16:2.
[31] See Klausner, *Ha-Ra'yon*, p. 181, n. 2.
[32] Whence it came about that the interpreters were forced to interpret
the unclear verse, "Out of the mouth of the Most High proceedeth not evil
and good" (Lam. 3:38), as a question thus: Is not God the one who makes
final decision as to what is evil and what is good? See *Ekhah* (Lamentations), as interpreted by F. Perles in the Old Testament with critical commentary edited by A. Kahana (Tel-Aviv 5690), p. 113.

comes about by the incitements of Satan, as in the book of Job, or by means of "evil spirits" which "were created on the eve of Sabbath between the suns," even in the Mishnah, which in general is far from any superstition.[33] Indeed, in the opinion of an early Amora (the opinion itself is undoubtedly much earlier than the period of the Amoraim), "He is called Satan. . . . He is called the evil prompter. . . . The same is also the Angel of Death";[34] and a Baraitha says of Satan, "He comes down to earth and seduces, then ascends to heaven and awakens wrath; permission is granted to him and he takes away the soul." [35] Also, "Satan accuses" is a regular expression in Talmud and Midrash.[36]

God himself could overcome the strong and crafty Satan, as shown above.[37] But with the subjugation and destruction of this mysterious potentate Satan, who is almost *anti-God*, and at any rate is *anti-Messiah* (Antichrist), and with the subjugation and destruction of his satellites the demons and evil spirits, God—"the God of Spirits"—must not concern himself, for he is too high and holy and exalted. The conquest of these spirits must be accomplished by *one who is also a spirit*, but a spirit of holiness, not a spirit of uncleanness. Paul's times and Paul's environment were full of beliefs in evil spirits and in ways of combatting them.[38] So, for Paul, the holy spirit which fights against the evil spirits is the Messiah ("the Lord"):

Now *the Lord is the Spirit*; and where the Spirit of the Lord is, there is liberty. And we all, who with unveiled face behold as in

[33] Aboth V 6 ("Some say also: The evil spirits . . .").

[34] Baba Bathra 16a.   [35] *Loc. cit.*

[36] Yer., Shabbath II 3 (5b, beginning); Gen. Rabbah XCI 9 (ed. Th. Albeck, p. 1133 [Soncino edition, II, 846]); Eccl. Rabbah III 2 on the text *A time to be born* [Soncino ed., p. 75]; Tanhuma ha-Qadum (A) XVИ, ed. Buber III, 27.

[37] From Rom. 16:20.

[38] Every book on the intellectual life of the Imperial period of Rome gives an idea of the attitude toward *spirits* at that time. See *e.g.*, Deissmann, *Licht vom Osten*, SS. 214-8.

a mirror the glory of the Lord, are transformed into the same image from glory to glory as though by *the Lord of the Spirit*.[39]

"The Spirit of the Lord" (Christ) and "the Spirit of God" (who is "the Lord of Spirits") are for Paul almost the same thing, and he uses the two expressions more or less interchangeably.[40] And the Spirit of Christ, which is in a certain sense the Spirit of God, will conquer the spirit of uncleanness —Satan and the evil Spirits.

This is the great importance of Christ in particular and of the Spirit in general. On the basis of the Scriptural verse (which Paul changes to suit his needs)—"For from of old men have not heard, nor perceived by the ear, neither hath the eye seen a God beside Thee, who worketh for him that waiteth for Him" [41]—Paul says that the bliss in store for the righteous will be revealed to him and to the believers by the Spirit of God:

. . . for the Spirit searcheth all things, yea, the deep things of God. For who among men knoweth the things of a man, save the spirit of the man, which is in him? Even so the things of God none knoweth, save the Spirit of God. But we received, not the spirit of the world, but the spirit which is from God; that we might know the things that were freely given to us of God. Which things also we speak, not in words which man's wisdom teacheth, but which the Spirit teacheth; and thus we interpret spiritual things with spiritual words.[42]

Apparently Paul is speaking here of the human mind as the spirit of the man; but actually the spirit is the antithesis of

[39] II Cor. 3:17, 18. Vs. 18 as given in the *Apostolicon* of Marcion reads as follows: "Already we, who with unveiled face contemplate Christ, are transformed into the same image, from the glory of the Lord to a glory as though from *the Lord of Spirits*" (see P. L. Couchoud, "Première édition de Saint-Paul," *Revue de l'Histoire des Religions*, 1926, p. 261).

[40] Rom. 8:9–11. See H. Weinel, *Paulus*, 2. Aufl. (Tübingen 1915), SS. 69, 70.

[41] Isa. 64:3. See on the Hebrew and Greek versions E. Böhl, *Die alttestamentlichen Citate im Neuen Testament* (1878), SS. 211–3.

[42] I Cor. 2:9–13.

"man's wisdom," since it is the Spirit of God—the mystical-intuitive insight which is the basis of Paul's faith.

3. Also, Jesus as Messiah is spirit and not flesh. To be sure, Paul speaks of him as "his [God's] Son, who was born of the seed of David according to the flesh," [43] and says that God sent "his own Son in the likeness of sinful flesh." [44] And he makes it clear that Jesus is not only flesh, but also flesh and blood.[45] Moreover,

. . . Christ Jesus, although existing in the form of God, counted not the being on an equality with God a thing to be grasped, but emptied himself, taking the form of a slave, being made in the likeness of men; and being found in fashion as a man, he humbled himself, becoming obedient even unto death, yea, the death of the cross.[46]

And Paul specifically says: "God sent forth his Son, born of a woman, born under the Law." [47] Yet *this* Jesus had no real existence for Paul, as I have already explained a number of times, for three reasons:

First, the Jesus of flesh and blood, Jesus the Jewish Messiah (and the Jews never pictured the Messiah except in the form of flesh and blood, in spite of all his superiority to the rest of the sons of flesh and blood), strove to re-establish the

---

[43] Rom. 1:3.   [44] Rom. 8:3.
[45] See Rom. 3:25; I Cor. 10:16; Col. 1:20.
[46] Philipp. 2:5–8. It is difficult to know whether the words "taking the form of a slave" mean that before his baptism he was actually someone's slave (perhaps thus arose the famous story that Jesus was a slave in Egypt), or whether they mean that Jesus was a slave to the Torah and ceremonial laws. See on this C. A. Anderson Scott, *Saint Paul* (1936), p. 92. See also Bornhäuser, *Neue kirchliche Zeitschrift*, XLIV (1933), 428–34; 453–62. Bornhäuser connects this idea of Paul's with the Second Isaiah's "Servant of the Lord," on the one hand, and emperor worship, on the other. Likewise ambiguous is the expression in II Cor. 8:9 ". . . though he was rich, yet for your sakes he became poor, that ye through his poverty might become rich." No doubt, the idea here is *spiritually* rich. See M. Dibelius, *Handbuch zum Neuen Testament*, 11², 60–3; Lietzmann, *ibid.*, 9³, 132–4.
[47] Gal. 4:4.

kingdom of the house of David, although not by actual deeds of rebellion, not by the power of an army of revolutionaries, but by an army of penitents led by their Messiah. God was to take his stand by this Messiah and this army, and destroy from before them the rule of Rome (to be identified with the rule of Satan), then to restore to penitent Israel its land and its kingdom, and teach the Gentiles the ways of God—the ways of peace and love. Nothing of this entered into the calculations of Paul. If the Twelve, and Paul with them, had conceived of Jesus in this fashion, *i.e.*, as a Jewish Messiah political and spiritual at the same time, the Romans would have persecuted them from the very first, and there would have been no possibility for them to have propagated a Messianic-revolutionary doctrine like this (in spite of all its spirituality) among either the Jews or the Gentiles—as I have already pointed out a number of times.[48]

Second, if the first disciples of Jesus, and Paul with them, had held to a Jewish Messiah like this, a Messiah who retained some measure of political function, everyone would have said to them that they were following a false Messiah, since he had failed to "restore the kingdom to Israel," [49] just as the other false Messiahs had failed.

Third, and finally, Paul relied above all upon the vision on the road to Damascus, wherein he had seen not the earthly Jesus, but the Jesus who had already ascended to heaven and then descended again and appeared to him in a "heavenly vision." So how could he hold to a Messiah like that pictured in the minds of the Jews of his time, or even like that pictured in the minds of the first Nazarenes, headed by near relatives of Jesus, who knew so much about Jesus' earthliness and humanness?

From these three considerations, Paul was *forced* to ignore

[48] See above, p. 356 *et passim*.
[49] Acts 1:6.

Jesus the Jewish Messiah, the Jesus of flesh and blood, even if he knew that in his earthly life Jesus was a simple man, "slave" and not "Lord," flesh and blood. This ignoring of the earthly Jesus meant *the setting aside of the political aspects of the Jewish Messianic conception*—a setting aside that was very agreeable and very necessary to primitive Christianity at that time from many standpoints. This attitude was quickly taken up by the Twelve, by James the brother of Jesus, and by Paul. Especially by Paul. For only by such means could Paul become equal as an apostle to the rest of the apostles. Otherwise, they had a great advantage over him; for they had gone about with Jesus on earth and had received instruction from his very lips, while Paul had to rely in his apostleship on the fact that he had seen the crucified Jesus in a vision.

Thus, Paul was forced to preach not the Jesus of the flesh, but the Jesus of the spirit, the heavenly Jesus. Therefore, the essential things for Paul became not the life of Jesus, nor even his ethical teaching, but *his death and resurrection, and his appearance on the road to Damascus*. Thus the crucifixion and the cross became for Paul not "a stumblingblock to the Jews and foolishness to the Gentiles," [50] but things *of extreme importance*, which entered into the plan for the salvation of the whole world—a plan which God had determined to carry out by means of the Messiah his son. The resurrection of Jesus was also a part of this plan, since according to Jewish belief the resurrection of the dead would take place in the Days of the Messiah. The Messiah could be afflicted and put to death, as the Twelve and Paul had learned from Isaiah 53; but if he were a true Messiah, he could not remain in affliction and death—he must rise to life again. And if, as the Twelve already believed on the testimony of Mary Magdalene and as a result of their own visions, the Messiah had been *the first* to rise from the dead, then, they said, this is a wonderful sign that the

[50] I Cor. 1:23.

Days of the Messiah are really approaching, and also that Jesus is the true Messiah and not a false Messiah, and that God has not forsaken him ("My God, my God, why hast thou forsaken me?"!) even after the crucifixion, but that God in his supreme wisdom had decreed that in the person of their Messiah should be fulfilled the verse:

> Because he bared his soul unto death,
> And was numbered with the transgressors;
> Yet he bore the sin of many,
> And made intercession for the transgressors.[51]

4. Thus Jesus became for Paul more and more spiritual, and more and more heavenly. Even in Judaism, the Messiah is "son of God" ("Thou art My son, this day have I begotten thee")[52] to a greater extent than the rest of the children of Israel, although they too "are the children of the Lord," their God.[53] And in Judaism the *name* of Messiah existed before the creation of the world,[54] even if not the Messiah himself.[55] To Paul, Jesus became "Christ Jesus" (the Messiah Jesus; this is Paul's usual expression instead of the "Jesus Christ" of later times, when "Christ" had become a standard surname affixed to Jesus), the Son of God in a metaphysical sense, "the image of the invisible God,"[56] "the mystery of God,"[57] "the power of God and the wisdom of God,"[58] also the "heavenly" (last) man (or Adam)[59] as opposed to "the first" or "earthy" man (Adam).[60] This idea is much like that of the prototype of

---

[51] Isa. 53:12. Paul does not expressly derive support from this passage, but it is hinted at in his various discussions.

[52] Ps. 2:7.   [53] Deut. 14:1.

[54] Ethiopic Enoch 48:3 (the "Similitudes"); Pesahim 54a; Nedarim 39b; Gen. Rabbah I 4; Targum of Pseudo-Jonathan to Zech. 4:7.

[55] The meaning of the phrase "the name of Messiah" is the Messianic *idea*, the concept of redemption. See for particulars Klausner, *Ha-Ra'yon*, pp. 297–8.

[56] Col. 1:15. See also II Cor. 4:4.   [57] Col. 2:2.

[58] I Cor. 1:24.   [59] I Cor. 15:49.

[60] Rom. 5:12–9; I Cor. 15:21, 22, 45–9.

man in Philo (πρωτόγονος ἀσώματος ἄνθρωπος),[61] also called the "Logos," "Primordial Man," and "Incorporeal Man"—as well as the "Word" of God.[62] And of course, like the Philonic "Logos," Jesus is also "the firstborn of all creation," [63] "the beginning, the firstborn from the dead." [64] Not once does Paul call Jesus "son of man," as Jesus called himself according to the Gospels; the reason being that for Paul "Jesus Christ" is not a man even in the most exalted sense, but is a heavenly figure, the antithesis of the "son of man" in Ezekiel, or even in Daniel. Thus it is but a step from this spiritual and heavenly Messiah to complete equality with deity, as in the later doctrine of the Trinity.[65]

As a matter of fact, although for the most part God ranks ahead of Jesus in the Epistles of Paul, as was shown above,[66] things reached such a point that twice in these Epistles Jesus precedes God! [67] Not only so, but Paul makes bold to say instead of "unto Me [God] every knee shall bow, every tongue shall swear" [68] this:

that in the name of Jesus every knee should bow, of those in heaven and on earth and under the earth, and that every tongue

[61] See Philo, *De Confusione Linguarum* XIV (M., I, 414; C.-W., II, 241, §§ 61–2).

[62] *Ibid.* XXVIII (M., I, 427; C.-W., II, 257, §§ 146–7). See also the note of Edmund (Menahem) Stein to the German translation of the "Confusion of Tongues," *Philo's Werke*, V, 138, Anm. 4.

[63] Col. 1:15.   [64] Col. 1:18.

[65] Contrary to the view of Ernst Barnikol, *Mensch und Messias* (Kiel 1932). See E. Lohmeyer, "Vom Problem paulinischer Christologie," *Theologische Blätter*, XIII (1934), 43–53.

[66] See above, pp. 467–8.

[67] "Now our Lord Jesus Christ himself, and God our Father . . ." (II Thess. 2:16); ". . . the kingdom of Christ and God (Eph. 5:5).

[68] Isa. 45:23. And in the prayer '*Alenu*, which we, the Jews, say three times daily to this day, we find this: "Let all the inhabitants of the world perceive and know that unto Thee every knee must bow, every tongue must swear. Before Thee, O Lord our God, let them bow and fall; and unto Thy glorious name let them give honor; let them all accept the yoke of Thy kingdom, and do Thou reign over them speedily, and for ever and ever" [Singer, *Standard Prayer Book*, p. 94].

should confess that Jesus Christ is Lord, to the glory of God the Father.[69]

In spite of the last words, "to the glory of God the Father," expressing a certain limitation according to which in the last analysis everything is for the glory of the one and only God, Paul does actually transfer to Jesus as Messiah the kneeling and bowing before God of the Prophet Isaiah—whereas the Jews think so much of these wonderful words of the prophet that they have introduced them into their cherished prayer *'Alenu.*[70]

So, of course, Paul prays not to God to remove his "thorn in the flesh," [71] but to Jesus "the Lord";[72] for he preached "Christ Jesus as Lord," [73] whereas the Jews apply the name "Lord" to the one and only God. The verse, "but let him that glorieth glory in this, that he understandeth, and knoweth Me," [74] *i.e.*, God, is applied by Paul to Jesus.[75]

In "the Day of the Lord" of the Prophets, and "the Day of Judgment" of the Talmud and the Pseudepigraphical books (the two books of Enoch, the two books of Baruch, IV Ezra, the Assumption of Moses, *etc.*), the Messiah of course has a share. So it is in all those books which interpret Daniel's "son of man" coming "with the clouds of heaven" as the Messiah. But in Daniel God is the predominant figure. Likewise, in all the rest of the Old Testament and in all the ancient Tannaitic parts of the Talmud, God alone is the judge on the Day of Judgment. Yet in spite of this and in contrast to it, we have in the Epistles of Paul a number of times "the day of Christ." [76] "Christ"—and not God—is the one who will over-

---

[69] Philipp. 2:10, 11.   [70] See n. 68 just above.
[71] See on this "thorn" above, p. 325.   [72] II Cor. 12:8.
[73] II Cor. 4:5.   [74] Jer. 9:23.
[75] I Cor. 1:29-31; *cf.* II Cor. 10:16-8.

[76] ". . . the day of our Lord Jesus Christ" (I Cor. 1:8); so also ". . . in the day of the Lord Jesus" (I Cor. 5:5). That the judging of all mankind, and even all creation, will on the Day of Judgment be handed over to Jesus exclusively—this idea is found in Rom. 2:16, I Cor. 5:5, I Thess. 1:10, II Thess. 1:7-10, and elsewhere.

throw Satan, put an end to sin, and abolish death.[77] In spite of the fact that all this is to be done in the name of and for the glory of God, Paul does not leave any active function to God himself, but turns over *everything* to Jesus—the fate of mankind and the fate of all creation.[78] God is like an old father, who, having passed the age of competence, turns over everything to his only son to inherit and administer even while the father is still alive. . . .

The conception of Jesus as "Logos" or the "Word" was taught, apparently, by the Alexandrian Jew, Apollos, who was influenced by his fellow Alexandrian, Philo. Paul met him in Ephesus, and he is mentioned by Paul in the First Epistle to the Corinthians as a person of great influence, whose reasonings were followed by a group in the Corinthian church.[79] This conception, that the Messiah is identical with the Logos, brought it about after a time that Jesus became one of the three members of the Trinity. Paul, who saw Greek philosophy ("the tradition of men") as something opposed to "the mystery of God," [80] did not accept this idea in its philosophic form. Nevertheless, the excessive and exaggerated adoration, going beyond all natural bounds, which Paul bestowed upon the crucified and risen Jesus, the heavenly and spiritual Jesus, who as a spirit would overcome Satan and the evil spirits, made Jesus equal to God in importance and superior to God in significant activities.

5. Whence came this new idea of Paul about the Messiah? We have seen above,[81] that there were three factors, which are essentially only two: *first*, the need to minimize the political side of the new messiahship; *second*, the need to put the crucified and risen Jesus, the Jesus who appeared on the road

---

[77] I Cor. 15:22-8.
[78] See for details on this W. Bousset, *Kyrios Christos*, 3. Aufl. (Göttingen 1926), SS. 104-54.
[79] See above, pp. 387-90.   [80] Col. 2:2, 8 and elsewhere.
[81] Above, pp. 475-7.

to Damascus, in place of the Jesus who had lived and taught a new doctrine to his disciples, and had intended to "restore the kingdom to Israel." But these two reasons are not sufficient to explain why a Pharisaic Jew and a disciple of Rabban Gamaliel should come so near deifying the Messiah who preceded the creation of the world.

Of course, Paul did not study in the schools of the Greek philosophers, and it cannot be possible that he *consciously* accepted the doctrines of the pagan mystery religions. Moreover, *there is nothing in all the teaching of Paul, as there is nothing in the teaching of Jesus, which is not grounded in the Old Testament, or in the Apocryphal, Pseudepigraphical, and Tannaitic literature of his time.* For the writer of these words, this is an axiom arrived at after decades of intensive study of the teachings of Jesus and of Paul. Now Jesus, who did not go outside the borders of Palestine, and almost certainly knew no Greek at all, only carried certain conceptions of Judaism to extremes out of which easily arose a non-Judaism, as I have explained in another place.[82] But Paul, who came from a Hellenized city—Tarsus in Asia Minor—and spent about eight years among Gentiles before he became "the apostle of the Gentiles," then was "the apostle of the Gentiles" for about twenty years, journeying in almost all the lands of Hellenistic culture—this Paul was influenced, although for the most part unconsciously and against his will, by the Stoic philosophy as the orators and Sophists taught it in the market place, and by the mystery religions insofar as he had heard about them from the Greeks and Hellenized Orientals among whom he carried on Christian propaganda.[83] Thus the entire Pauline point of view rests upon the foundations of Judaism. But the structure built upon these founda-

[82] See Klausner, *Yeshu*, pp. 423–4 [Eng. ed., pp. 375–6].
[83] See above, pp. 461–6. On the state of the problem of extra-Jewish influences on Paul, see also H. Weinel, *Biblische Theologie des Neuen Testaments*, 4. Aufl. (Tübingen 1928), SS. 337–41.

tions, or at least the upper story of this structure, came from pagan influence, for the most part unsuspected by Paul; and to some extent it came from a strong desire on the part of Paul to make himself understood by Hellenized Jews (Jews following the authentic tradition accepted his teaching only in limited numbers, and even among the Hellenized Jews many were opposed to him) and by the natives of Asia Minor, whose mystical beliefs had been affected alike by Persian influences, by Judaism, and by Hellenism.

The Jewish Messiah, even as he is pictured in Isaiah 11, the Psalms of Solomon, and IV Ezra, is only a human being, albeit one exalted above all the rest of mortal men and endowed with extraordinary powers. The verses

The Lord said unto me: "Thou art My son,
This day have I begotten thee," [84]

and

. . . behold, there came with the clouds of heaven
One like unto a son of man,
And he came even to the Ancient of Days,
And he was brought near before Him.
And there was given him dominion,
And glory, and a kingdom,
That all the peoples, nations, and languages
Should serve him;
His dominion is an everlasting dominion, which shall not pass away,
And his kingdom that which shall not be destroyed [85]

—these verses actually speak of the people Israel and not of a Messianic individual; but already in Hasmonean times, a hundred years and more before Paul, they were interpreted as applying to the Messiah, as we find in one of the earliest of the Pseudepigraphical books (Ethiopic Enoch). If this interpretation is accepted, then both in the Psalms and in Daniel

[84] Ps. 2:7.   [85] Dan. 7:13, 14.

the Messiah is a supernatural person. Paul of course held to the interpretation of these verses whereby they apply to the Messiah. If we add to this the fact that Isaiah 53 was interpreted—or could be interpreted, according to the method of the Pharisees, to whom Paul belonged in his youth and boasted of the fact all his life [86]—as applying to the suffering and afflicted Messiah, then it seems there should be no surprise at the exaggerated homage which Paul paid to Jesus as Messiah. And since the Jewish Messiah is *King*-Messiah, he could be called "Lord" (Κύριος or *Dominus*), as were the Greek kings of the Hellenistic period or the Roman emperors in the time of Paul himself. These kings were men who made themselves divine; surely the Messiah is a greater king than these from every point of view.

Nevertheless, it is difficult to explain the adoration, amounting almost to deification, with which Paul regarded Jesus merely as an intensification of the Jewish Messianic idea. It is clear to me, that if people in the Persian and Hellenistic periods, and in the Imperial period of Rome, had not been accustomed to calling their kings and emperors *Kyrios* ("Lord") in Greek or *Dominus* in Latin, Paul would not have called Jesus *Kyrios*, nor would Christian copyists have introduced into the Septuagint Χριστὸς Κύριος ("Christ the Lord") in place of Χριστὸς Κυρίου as a translation of the phrase "the anointed of the Lord." [87] Even Christian scholars admit that in the early Palestinian Christian Church it would have been impossible to ascribe completely divine attributes and functions to Jesus as Messiah.[88] To be sure, this primitive Church, believing in the resurrection of Jesus, believed also in his greatness and his exalted position after the crucifixion; but although

---

[86] It is an interesting fact that, contrary to what is the case with Jesus, we do not hear of any specific controversies between Paul and the Pharisees as such.

[87] Lam. 4:20.

[88] See, *e.g.*, W. Bousset, *op. cit.*, SS. 91–101.

this belief had departed from its purely Jewish framework, it had not yet entered into the pagan framework of the time. But in the ideas of Paul, along with an extension of Jewish notions of the Messiah to the utmost possible limits, there is also a Graeco-Persian pagan influence, even though it is clear to me that Paul did not study in any school of the Stoics or receive instruction from any priests of the mystery religions. There was a mixture of pagan-philosophic beliefs and opinions, which *hovered in the air* in the Hellenized cities in which Paul lived and preached, with Pharisaic-Jewish religious thinking, after the syncretistic fashion of that time. It was by such means that Jewish beliefs and opinions attained an exaggerated and unnatural intensification, so that the Judaism of that time sensed the presence of an extraneous shoot grafted upon itself for no good, and hence refused to accept these beliefs and opinions because it could not assimilate them without becoming half Judaism and half paganism.

Of the treatment of Jesus by Paul it might well be said, "Thou hast made him but little lower than God";[89] and this "little" that was lacking was quickly supplied—it *had* to be supplied quickly—by Matthew and Luke, the latter being the assistant and travelling companion of Paul. So Matthew and Luke soon spoke of Jesus' being born of a virgin and the Holy Spirit; and before long they were followed by the Evangelist John, a writer seeing in Jesus the "Logos" who existed at the beginning of all creation, and was with God, and was himself —God. . . .

What could Judaism have to do with such views as these?———

[89] Ps. 8:6.

CHAPTER IV

Flesh and Spirit; The "Life in Christ"

1. Even Old Testament Judaism knows the distinction between *flesh* and *spirit*. I have already mentioned above the Pentateuchal verse containing the phrase "the God of the spirits of all flesh," from which is derived the expression "the Lord [or 'God'] of Spirits" in the Ethiopic Enoch.[1] Worthy of notice are the passages, "Now the Egyptians are *men* and not *God*, and their horses *flesh* and not *spirit*," [2] and "My [*i.e.*, God's] *spirit* shall not abide in man forever, for that he also is *flesh*." [3] There is also in the Old Testament a contrast between "flesh" and "soul": "both soul and body" (literally "flesh").[4] There is also a contrast between "spirit" and "soul": "For the *spirit* that enwrappeth itself is from Me, and the *souls* which I have made." [5] But there is one verse in which all three things are contrasted: "In whose [God's] hand is the *soul* of every living thing, and the *spirit* [English translations 'breath'] of all human *flesh* [English translations 'mankind']." [6] Here we have in one verse "soul," "spirit," and "flesh" distinguished from each other.[7]

It is clear, therefore, that Paul, when he placed in the center of his teaching the contrast between flesh and spirit, did not necessarily take this antithesis from Greek philosophy alone. Many consider as typically Pauline and un-Jewish the pro-

---

[1] See above, p. 472. See on this whole matter also Ahad Ha-Am, "Basar ve-Ruaḥ," *'Al Parashat Derakhim*, III, 222–32.

[2] Isa. 31:3.   [3] Gen. 6:3.

[4] Isa. 10:18.   [5] Isa. 57:16.

[6] Job. 12:10.

[7] All this contradicts the opinion of W. Bousset, *Kyrios Christos*, SS. 134–5, Anm. 1.

found and original conception in the following passage from one of the Epistles:

. . . it is sown a natural body [literally, a body of the *soul*, or a *psychic* body]; it is raised a *spiritual* body. If there is a natural body, there is also a spiritual body. So also it is written, "The first 'man'—Adam—'became a living soul'." [8] The last Adam became a life-giving spirit. Howbeit that is not first which is spiritual, but that which is natural [or, of the soul]; then that which is spiritual.[9]

But it is my deep conviction that even this profound conception, which appears to be absolutely original, and actually has in it much originality, has its roots in the Scriptural passages which I have just quoted. In these passages Judaism also makes a distinction between "flesh" and "soul," and between "soul" and "spirit." Paul's originality is that he insisted upon these distinctions and contrasts as did no other Pharisee of his time. And I think that Paul, and no other Pharisee, insisted upon these contrasts and distinctions not only because Paul was a mystic and a man of profound religious insight, but also because he was born in a Hellenized city and lived and worked for about thirty years among Hellenized pagans. This is why Paul strongly emphasized the value of the spirit and abhorred the flesh more than any other Pharisaic Jew, so that starting from a Jewish point of view he came to a non-Jewish, and almost an anti-Jewish, point of view.

To be sure, the very essence of Judaism is the struggle of the spirit with the flesh. Nevertheless, neither the prophets, who in spite of all their great spirituality had an unsurpassed sense of realism, nor the authors of the Talmud, who taught: " 'He shall live by them,' [10] but he shall not die because of

---

[8] Gen. 2:7.   [9] I Cor. 15:44-6.

[10] It is written in the Pentateuch: "Ye shall therefore keep My statutes, and Mine ordinances, which if a man do, *he shall live by them*" (Lev. 18:5). Cf. Neh. 9:29: ". . . they hearkened not unto Thy commandments, but sinned against Thine ordinances, which if a man do, *he shall live by them*."

them" (*i.e.*, the laws of God);[11] "the Torah was not given to the ministering angels";[12] "the Holy One, blessed be He, does not deal imperiously with His creatures,"[13] or "the Holy One, blessed be He, does not lay burdensome laws upon Israel";[14] and "we should not impose a restriction upon the community unless the majority of the community will be able to stand it"[15]—neither the prophets nor the authors of the Talmud put undue emphasis on this antithesis, nor did they seek to mortify the flesh and make man entirely spiritual.[16] But in this respect —as in many others—Paul followed in the footsteps of Jesus, who also carried Jewish spirituality to extremes, wherefore the Jews could not accept his teaching. Jesus reached these extremes only because of his concern with "the end of days" and his conclusion that the life of "this world" no longer had any significance.[17] In regard to this matter of placing "spirituality" over against "carnality," Paul was even more extreme than Jesus, although by personal endowment he was also a practical man—an administrator and a man of affairs—who did not have to be so abstractly spiritual. The reason for Paul's attitude was rather that the atmosphere of the Jewish Diaspora and of paganism, which surrounded him from the time of his conversion from a Pharisaic persecutor of the Christians to a preacher of Christianity, was saturated with the ideas of Plato and the Stoa about the defectiveness of the flesh—ideas which were hovering, so to speak, in the air, and were widespread even among non-philosophers. In the philosophical world of that time—except among the Epicureans—the sharp antagonism between flesh and spirit was strongly emphasized, and people were taught to despise, mortify, and castigate the flesh

[11] Yoma 85b.   [12] Berakoth 25b.

[13] 'Abodah Zarah 3a.

[14] Pesikta de-Rab Kahana, Shekalim (Piska II), Siman 166, ed. Buber 20b; Pesikta Rabbathi XVI end, ed. Friedmann 84b; Exodus Rabbah XXXIV beginning.

[15] Baba Kamma 79b; Baba Bathra 60b.

[16] See Ahad Ha-Am, *op. cit.*, pp. 222–32.

[17] See Klausner, *Yeshu*, pp. 416–56 [Eng. ed., pp. 369–407].

for the good of the spirit. This widespread point of view affected Paul in spite of himself and without his knowing it.

In numberless passages Paul speaks with scorn and contempt about the inferiority of the flesh to the spirit. The flesh, he argues, arouses sinful desires.[18] For instance, the following:

For what the Law could not do, in that it was weak through the flesh, God, sending his own Son in the likeness of sinful flesh and as an offering for sin, condemned sin in the flesh: that the requirement of the Law might be fulfilled in us, who walk not after the flesh, but after the Spirit. For they that are after the flesh mind the things of the flesh; but they that are after the Spirit the things of the Spirit. For the mind of the flesh is death; but the mind of the Spirit is life and peace: because the mind of the flesh is enmity against God; for it is not subject to the law of God, neither indeed can it be: [19] and they that are in the flesh cannot please God. But ye are not in the flesh but in the Spirit, if so be that the Spirit of God dwelleth in you. But if any man hath not the Spirit of Christ, he is none of his. And if Christ is in you, the body is dead because of sin; but the spirit is life because of righteousness.[20]

"Flesh" and "sin" are here identical, while "spirit" and "righteousness" are also identical. Thus, a completely negative attitude toward the flesh is taken in a number of passages: *e.g.*, "For I know that in me, that is, in my flesh, dwelleth no good thing";[21] or, "So then I of myself with the mind, indeed, serve the law of God; but with the flesh the law of sin." [22] For the flesh can corrupt even the freedom of the spirit and convert it into licentiousness.[23]

2. The flesh is not merely "weak" in contrast to the spirit, as Jesus is quoted as saying in the Gospels,[24] but altogether evil, altogether unclean, altogether corrupting and productive

---

[18] Rom. 7:5.
[19] That is to say, the carnal mind cannot be obedient to the law of God even if it wishes to be.
[20] Rom. 8:3–10.
[21] Rom. 7:18.
[22] Rom. 7:25.
[23] Gal. 5:13.
[24] Mark 14:38; Matt. 26:41.

of wickedness. Christ the extraordinary, the "heavenly man," the "son of God" (not actually, but in the sense of being far above all men in nearness to God), was without sin, and hence his "sinful flesh" (flesh in general is sinful, therefore even the flesh of Christ, who was without sin, is "sinful flesh") was crucified, not for his own sin, which did not exist, but for the sins of the rest of mankind, which to the extent that it is flesh is evil and sinful. And only by means of the crucified "sinful flesh" of the sinless Christ can the followers of this Christ be freed from sin. This is true in spite of the fact that they must continue for a while—until the Parousia—in the flesh. In order to attain this sinless state they must "be in Christ" or "in the Lord"; for

. . . they that are of Christ Jesus have crucified the flesh with the passions and lusts thereof.

If we live by the Spirit [and "Christ is spirit," as has been said], by the Spirit let us also walk.[25]

Paul says to the "brethren":

But I say, Walk by the Spirit, and ye shall not fulfil the lust of the flesh. For the flesh lusteth against the Spirit, and the Spirit against the flesh; for these are contrary the one to the other; that ye may not do the things that ye would. But if ye are led by the Spirit, ye are not under the Law.

Moreover, the flesh brings about all kinds of transgressions and immoralities, sins of man against God, and of man against his fellow. Paul lists these *in extenso* one by one as opposed to the spirit, which for its part brings about all sorts of good deeds and qualities without recourse to the Law.[26] The spirit also performs miracles; it enables the man "living in Jesus" or in his spirit to speak with tongues, to prophesy, to reveal secrets, to heal the sick, to drive out evil spirits, and so on.[27]

[25] Gal. 5:24, 25.
[26] Gal. 5:16-23. On the list of good and evil qualities in this passage see K. Weidinger, *Die Haustafeln* (Leipzig 1928), S. 76.
[27] See Bousset, *op. cit.*, SS. 110-7.

Paul himself, from the day that Jesus appeared to him near Damascus, lived not in the flesh but in the spirit; he became spiritual or "pneumatic." For Paul could speak with tongues even more than the other Christians;[28] he saw visions,[29] and also wrought signs and wonders.[30] Hence many scholars wish to see here the influence of pagan mystery religions upon Paul.[31] But as a matter of fact, there is a fundamental difference between the "spiritual man" (the "pneumatic") of the mystery religions and the "spiritual man" of Paul. The pagan "spiritual man" departs from common humanity, while the Pauline "spiritual man" remains within the bounds of humanity.[32] To this extent Paul is still a Jew.

Nevertheless, Paul's conception of the "spiritual man" stands on the border between Pharisaic Judaism, or even Essenism, and the pagan mysteries. Paul created this conception of the state of "being in [or with] Christ" (or "in the Lord"), and the expression occurs 164 times in the Epistles.[33] He says also:

I have been crucified with Christ; and *it is no longer I that live, but Christ liveth in me*: and that life which I now live in the flesh I live in faith, the faith which is in the Son of God, who loved me, and gave himself up for me.[34]

Of course, it cannot be inferred from this, as think Reitzenstein, Bousset, Deissmann, Clemen, *et al.*, that we have here "duality of personality," *i.e.*, twofold mystical life: one personality that of an ordinary man, the other that of a super-

[28] I Cor. 14:18.
[29] Gal. 1:15, 16; II Cor. 12:1–7.
[30] Rom. 15:19; II Cor. 12:12.
[31] See, *e.g.*, Bousset, *op. cit.*, SS. 129–34.
[32] See K. Deissner, *op. cit.*, SS. 18–100.
[33] See on this A. Deissmann, *Die neutestamentliche Formel "In Christo Jesu"* (Marburg 1892); *idem, Paulus* (1925), SS. 111–24 (the literature on this question in note to S. 112); E. Lohmeyer, *Grundlagen paulinischer Theologie* (Tübingen 1929), SS. 139–46.
[34] Gal. 2:20.

human, mystical-divine being.[35] But even in the Jewish mysteries of the Essenes, the Therapeutae, and the rest of the Jewish mystery cults up to that of the Gaonic period, we do not find any Jewish view whereby it is possible for a man "to be in the Messiah" or "to be in God." The Jew says: "My soul shall be joyful in my God";[36] "I will be glad and exult in Thee."[37] The Jew also says:

> Whom have I in heaven but Thee?
> And beside Thee I desire none upon earth.
> My flesh and my heart faileth;
> But God is the rock of my heart and my portion for ever.
> For, lo, they that go far from Thee shall perish;
> Thou dost destroy all them that go astray from Thee.
> But as for me, the nearness of God is my good;
> I have made the Lord God my refuge,
> That I may tell of all Thy works.[38]

This is the only great spiritual approach to God which Judaism considers possible. Scriptural Judaism says: "But ye that did cleave unto the Lord your God are alive every one of you this day";[39] and it teaches its adherents "to love the Lord thy God, to hearken to His voice, and to cleave unto Him, for that is thy life."[40] On this, the Talmudic Haggadah asks: "Is it possible for a human being to 'cleave' unto the divine presence?"[41] The answer is that it is possible only "to cleave unto the *attributes* of the Holy One, blessed be He"; "be thou like Him: just as He is gracious and compassionate, so be thou gracious and compassionate."[42] This is what Judaism pictures to itself as possible in the relations between God and man. "To be in God" is not an ancient or authentic Jewish idea; "to be in the Messiah" is even less so. It is rather the "mystic union" (*Unio Mystica*), or at least the "mystic com-

---

[35] For weighty considerations against this view see Deissner, *op. cit.*, SS. 79–100.

[36] Isa. 61:10.

[37] Ps. 9:3.

[38] Ps. 73:25–8.

[39] Deut. 4:4.

[40] Deut. 30:20.

[41] Kethuboth 111b.

[42] Shabbath 133b; Yer., Peah I 1 (15b).

munion" (*Communio Mystica*), which is known from the mystery cults of that period.[43] This pagan belief in being swallowed up in God, a belief then existing in the circles with which Paul came into contact through his preaching, became fused in the soul of "the apostle of the Gentiles" with the Jewish belief in the possibility of cleaving to God in the sense just described. And since "Christ" had become the center of Paul's entire existence, this *Jewish belief with a pagan coloring* attached itself in the thought and sentiment of Paul the mystic, Paul the sensitive religionist, to the personality of Jesus as Messiah—and he conceived the new, Jewish-pagan idea: "being in Christ [or the Lord]" or the "life in Christ."

3. "Life in Christ" is possible, according to Paul, because the crucified Messiah is alive. This whole new belief was founded upon the dogma of the resurrection of Jesus, who was "the firstfruits of them that are asleep," "the firstborn from the dead." Twice Paul repeats this idea and emphasizes it:

. . . and if Christ hath not been raised, then is our preaching vain, your faith also is vain. . . . and if Christ hath not been raised, your faith is vain; ye are yet in your sins.[44]

Although he was crucified, Jesus is not dead; the cross, which appeared "unto Jews a stumblingblock, and unto Gentiles foolishness," is the foundation stone of the new faith. Through the sufferings of the cross, which were laid upon him although he was without sin, Jesus obtained everlasting life for himself, since he arose from the dead; moreover, by this means he obtained everlasting life for all his followers also, and indeed for all the children of Adam and Eve. *The first Adam,* he alone, brought death upon all mankind from the beginning of time up to Jesus. Jesus Christ, who is "the last Adam," because as Messiah he is the son of God (in the sense explained

[43] See Bousset, *op. cit.,* SS. 114–5, 138–40, 280.
[44] I Cor. 15:14, 17.

above), and thus is the highest conception that can be attained by man—"the last Adam," and he alone, can redeem all mankind from Satan, from death, and from sin. "For as in Adam all die, so also in Christ shall all be made alive." [45] The first Adam listened to the voice of the serpent—meaning Satan and the impulse to evil—and sinned, bringing death upon mankind; "the last Adam" did not listen to the voice of Satan, he did not sin, and by his death he saved mankind from Satan, from death and from sin. Therefore, whoever believes in Jesus will "put away . . . the old man, that waxeth corrupt after the lusts of deceit" and "put on the new man, that after God hath been created in righteousness and holiness of truth"; [46] for with Jesus "our old man was crucified." [47] And all believers are "always bearing about in the body the dying of Jesus, that the life also of Jesus may be manifested in our body." [48]

Thus Jesus lives even after being crucified. After the resurrection, Jesus again has a "body"; yet it is not a body of flesh, but a spiritual body, [49] a heavenly body, [50] which has a supreme radiance like the brightness of deity or the glow of the Shekhinah ("the body of his glory"). [51] Thus Jesus continues in a heavenly existence, with a body of celestial brightness and splendor, until the time of his "Parousia" shall arrive.

And whoever believes in Jesus is no longer a citizen of earth but a citizen of heaven. He dies to earthly life and to sin along with Jesus, and rises to a heavenly life without death and without sin; finally, he becomes like Jesus even in his body. This is the proper interpretation of the following verses:

For our citizenship is in heaven; whence also we wait for a Saviour, the Lord Jesus Christ: who shall fashion anew the body of our humiliation, that it may be conformed to the body of his glory. [52]

[45] I Cor. 15:22. See also I Cor. 15:45-9 and Rom. 5:14-9.
[46] Eph. 4:22-4; so also Col. 3:9, 10.
[47] Rom. 6:6.
[48] II Cor. 4:10.
[49] I Cor. 15:44-6.
[50] I Cor. 15:47-9.
[51] Philipp. 3:21.
[52] Philipp. 3:20, 21.

This is the basis and this the essence of the "spiritual" faith of Paul the "pneumatic." One delusion is founded upon another delusion. The crucified Jesus rose from the dead and lives in his glorious heavenly body, and Paul and the believing "brethren" live within this dead-alive heavenly Jesus, who is so near to God and has been so exalted as the Son of God that one cannot tell which is more important, God or Jesus! To be sure, God preceded Jesus. But God does not do anything; everything is done by "his Son" the Messiah. Not only so but men "are" or "live" not "in God" (although even this would not be imagined by thorough believers in monotheism), but in "Christ" his son. . . .

Could the Jews, thorough monotheists then and now, have accepted this strange faith based upon such unnatural beliefs?——

CHAPTER V

Abrogation of Torah and Ceremonial Laws

1. *Death provides release from the ceremonial laws.* A woman during the lifetime of her husband is forbidden to another man unless she has received a bill of divorce from her husband; but after the death of her husband she is permitted to marry again without a bill of divorce. *Death also annuls the requirements of the Torah.* Thus the death of Jesus on the cross annulled both Torah and ceremonial laws.[1] This conclusion is decidedly forced, and resembles Talmudic casuistry.[2] But the idea itself, that death releases from the ceremonial laws (releases the dead, of course, and not the living), is found in the Talmud. The words of the verse, "Set apart among the dead" (literally, "free among the dead"),[3] are interpreted by the Talmud thus: "When a man is dead, he is *free* from the ceremonial laws." [4] On the basis of this the Talmud concludes: "The ceremonial laws shall be abrogated in the time to come";[5] and, at least according to the Amora Rab Joseph, the meaning of "the time to come" is the time after death.[6]

Paul drew still another new conclusion from this idea of the abrogation of the ceremonial laws through death: with Jesus "the old man" is crucified and dies, and with him "the new man" rises to life.[7] For those believing in Jesus "are not under law, but under grace." [8] Thus Paul teaches that "Christ

---

[1] Rom. 7:1–6.
[2] See above, p. 457.
[3] Ps. 88:6.
[4] Niddah 61b.
[5] *Loc. cit.*
[6] See Klausner, *Yeshu*, p. 305 [Eng. ed., p. 275]; also *ibid.*, "Additions and Corrections," pp. 465–6 [not in English ed.], against J. M. Gutmann; also above, p. 321, n. 13.
[7] See above, p. 494.
[8] Rom. 5:20, 21; 6:1.

is the end of the Law." [9] That is to say, with the coming of the Messiah was fulfilled what was foretold by the prophets about the time to come, on the one hand; and on the other hand, sin was done away with by this Messiah, and with the disappearance of sin the Torah was also done away with. Thus did Paul reach a conclusion that was necessarily very offensive to the Jews.[10]

It is difficult to observe the whole Law. The Scripture says: "For there is not a righteous man upon earth, that doeth good, and sinneth not";[11] and "there is none that doeth good, no, not one." [12] In another place it is written:

Behold, He putteth no trust in His servants,
And His angels He chargeth with folly.[13]

Also:

What is man, that he should be clean?
And he that is born of a woman, that he should be righteous?
Behold, He putteth no trust in His holy ones;
Yea, the heavens are not clean in His sight.[14]

And in one of his most important Epistles, Paul gives a moving description of the battle of a man against sin, and of his attempts to observe all the requirements of the Law in order to be completely righteous—but without avail:

For we know that the Law is spiritual: but I am carnal, sold under sin. For that which I do I know not: for not what I would, that do I practise; but what I hate, that I do. But if what I would not, that I do, I consent unto the Law that it is good. So now it is

---

[9] Rom. 10:4.

[10] See R. Travers Herford, *Pharisaism* (London 1912), pp. 173–225; *idem, The Pharisees* (1924), pp. 215–24; *Talmud and Apocrypha* (1933), pp. 297–305.

[11] Eccl. 7:20.

[12] Ps. 14:3. And see Rom. 3:10–8, which is a whole series of Old Testament quotations that aim to show how numerous are the sinners in the world.

[13] Job. 4:18.   [14] Job. 15:14, 15. See also 25:4–6.

no more I that do it, but sin which dwelleth in me. For I know that in me, that is, in my flesh, dwelleth no good thing: for to will is present with me, but to do that which is good is not.[15] For the good which I would I do not: but the evil which I would not, that I practise. But if what I would not, that I do, it is no more I that do it, but sin which dwelleth in me. I find then the law,[16] that, to me who would do good, evil is present. For I delight in the law of God after the inward man: but I see a different law [17] in my members, warring against the law of my mind, and bringing me into captivity under the law of sin which is in my members. Wretched man that I am! who shall deliver me out of this body of death? [18]

In this whole passage—and particularly in the last entreaty —we sense the severe distress, agitation, and searchings of soul that accompany the wrestling of the body with the spirit. There is a controversy among scholars as to whether this is a general and impersonal description of men in Israel who strove to fulfill all the requirements but could not, or whether it applies to Paul himself, who waged this hard battle to keep all the ceremonial laws, but did not succeed.[19] I am inclined to apply these words to the psychological state of Paul himself. *First*, because he was, on his own admission, a Pharisee very zealous for the Law before the Damascus-road incident.[20] *Second*, the words seem to come from the heart of a man for

[15] That is to say, it is in my nature to will the good, but I do not have the power to do it.

[16] Here the word *nomos* is used, apparently, in a different sense, meaning "generalization" or "conclusion." Franz Delitzsch [in his Hebrew translation of the New Testament] used in this place the word *ḥoq* ("rule"); and this is not incorrect, according to the meaning. However, by thus taking account of the meaning, we are forced to use two different words to translate the same Greek word in the same passage.

[17] Or "another rule"; see the preceding note.

[18] Rom. 7:14–24.

[19] Thus the opinion of Deissmann, *Paulus*, SS. 53–4, 73–4. Against this opinion see Ed. Meyer, *Ursprung und Anfänge d. Christentums*, III, 387–8; Enslin, *The Ethics of Paul*, pp. 12, 13. Deissmann was anticipated in this opinion by Friedrich Nietzsche (*Morgenröthe*, I, 68; ed. Leipzig 1917, I, 4, SS. 64–8).

[20] See above, pp. 311–2, also 318–9.

whom their significance is not a mere matter of doctrine alone, but also of personal experience. And *third*, they are preceded by words which, because of the "I" in them, are difficult to construe impersonally:

. . . I was alive apart from the Law once; but when the commandment came, sin revived and I died. Thus the commandment, which was given for life, I found to be for death; for sin, finding occasion through the commandment, beguiled me, and through it slew me.[21]

Thus can write only a man who has himself been torn between desire to fulfill the ceremonial requirements and his inability to do so—a man who out of deep personal distress has arrived at new convictions which he regards as generalizations applicable to all.

2. The Talmud distinguishes "seven types of Pharisees," condemning almost all of them; among these is the Pharisee who says "What is my duty that I may perform it?" and the Pharisee "out of fear." [22] From Romans, ch. 7, much of which I have quoted, it is to be supposed that Paul, who was "zealous for the Law" before his conversion, would have belonged to one of these two types of Pharisees so thoroughly condemned by the Talmud. For there is no religion like Judaism in allowing for human weakness and imperfection, and there is no book like the Talmud in modifying its stringent demand for observance of the ritual requirements, when it sees the impossibility of observing all of them. I have already quoted above the expression, "the Torah was not given to the ministering angels," and the great principle—*the Golden Rule of the Halakhah*—"we should not impose a restriction upon the community unless the majority of the community will be able

[21] Rom. 7:9–11.
[22] Sotah 22b; Yer., *ibid.* II 2 and Ber. IX 7; Aboth de-Rabbi Nathan XXXVII (51) and beginning of XLV (52), ed. Schechter 55a and p. 124. See for particulars Klausner, *Yeshu*, pp. 232–3 [Eng. ed., pp. 213–5].

to stand it." [23] To be sure, whoever reads all the Sabbath laws in the Mishnah or Tosephta can easily come to the point of despair because of the multiplicity of restrictions in them. Yet it is well known that the Jews *enjoyed* the Sabbath and were not *pained* by it; also to-day there is no more common expression among the Jews—even among the simplest of them—than the phrase "enjoyment of the Sabbath." This is the case to such an extent that Ahad Ha-Am, one of the most liberal-minded of Jews, yet with all his liberalism a defender of historic Judaism, could express the following sentiment: "To a greater extent than Israel has kept the Sabbath has the Sabbath kept Israel." [24]

This fact about Judaism had not been grasped by Paul while he was a zealous Pharisee, and still less was it understood by him after he became zealous for the faith in Jesus.[25] It is actually possible that the fear of sin felt by this "Pharisee out of fear" brought about the radical change which occurred in him on the Damascus road; for Stephen, who according to all signs was an antinomian, had been put to death on the accusation of Paul, or at least as a result of Paul's testimony. At any rate, Paul thought that anyone who acknowledged obligation to the Law and wished to observe it was necessarily bound to acknowledge also that he was a sinner, since it was utterly *impossible* for him to observe *all of it*—"in all its details and fine points, and the 613 commandments which depend upon it," according to the Hebrew expression which is late, yet characterizes the minds of those devoted to Torah and ceremonial requirements and zealous for the whole Law. But to return to Paul—when a man reaches a conviction like this, it is inevitable that he should go far afield to a place from which there is no returning. . . .

---

[23] See above, p. 488.   [24] Ahad Ha-Am, *op. cit.*, p. 79.
[25] For the Christians whom he had converted, Paul grasped this fact and said: ". . . but God is faithful, who will not suffer you to be tempted above that we are able" (I Cor. 10:13).

Paul says, "for through the Law cometh the knowledge of sin." [26] Moreover, *the very idea of sin arises because there is an idea of law.* The natural man, who has no law, like the animals and like babes without understanding, does not sin: "where there is no law, neither is there transgression." [27] Before the giving of the Law, sin was not considered sin, although it existed even then.[28] Hence "the power of sin is the Law." [29] Paul explains this idea in phrases that are exquisite, yet sophistical:

Howbeit, I had not known sin, except through the Law: for I had not known coveting, except the Law had said, "Thou shalt not covet": but sin, finding occasion, wrought in me through the commandment all manner of coveting: for apart from the Law sin is dead.[30]

And Paul arrives at this strange paradox: ". . . the Law came in besides, that the trespass might abound"; all this is said in order to conclude thus: "but where sin abounded, grace did abound more exceedingly." [31] That is to say: by the Law, sin and trespass were increased, since every commandment calls attention to a transgression which is forbidden; but the death of the sinless Messiah abolished what had been increased by the Law, namely sins and trespasses. Thus now, after Christ has come and by his death has abolished sin, there is no longer any need of a Law which increases sin!

Lest someone should say, "The Law is from God; how is it possible to abolish something divine and hence very important?"—Paul is ready with this answer: the Law was not given by God at all; it was given by the angels and by a "mediator" (μεσίτης).[32] And lest someone should say, "The Law is the

---

[26] Rom. 3:20.

[27] Rom. 4:15.

[28] Rom. 5:13.

[29] I Cor. 15:56.

[30] Rom. 7:7, 8.

[31] Rom. 5:20.

[32] Gal. 3:19. *Cf.* Acts 7:53; Col. 2:18; see also Heb. 2:2. In Talmud and Midrash the angels are present at the time of the giving of the Law, but it is not given by them. See Shabbath 88b; Siphre 102 (on the text *And the Lord came down in a pillar of cloud*), ed. Horowitz, p. 100, lines 17–8

guide of life for individual and nation," Paul has this reply:
the Law was a "nurse" or "tutor" to Israel only up to the time
of the Messiah; but now that he has come, died, and risen,
there is no longer any need of it.[33] Now there is no longer
any need of circumcision, of avoiding forbidden foods, of
keeping Sabbaths, feasts, or new moons.[34] "For if righteousness is through the Law, then Christ died for nought." [35] Men
can be "justified" only "by faith in Christ, and not by the
works of the Law; because by the works of the Law shall no
flesh be justified." [36]

But the Pharisaic Jew in Paul also demanded his share. Thus
we see Paul, whom Nietzsche called the "destroyer of the
Law" (*Vernichter des Gesetzes*),[37] refraining from speaking
against the Torah with absolute finality. And in the *very same*
passage in which he accuses the Law and the commandments
of being the cause of sinning, he also says: "the Law is holy,
and the commandment holy, and righteous, and good." [38]
Whenever he appears to attack the Law, he excuses himself
with the expression "God forbid!" (μὴ γένοιτο).[39] Not only
so, but he attempts to prove by forced interpretations of the
words of the Torah itself that it has been set aside. Hence he
can say: "For I through the Law died unto the Law." [40]

Such a view of the Torah was not, of course, acceptable to
the minds of Jews faithful to Judaism, nor even to the minds
of the Jews of the Diaspora. For, they felt, the Torah is from
God, the will of God is expressed in it, it is the tradition of

---

[translation of Levertoff (London 1926), p. 82]; Mekhilta, Tractate
Baḥodesh IX (on the text *And stood afar off*), ed. Friedmann 71b, ed.
Horowitz-Rabin, p. 236, lines 15–6 [ed. Lauterbach, II, 269]; Pesikta Rabbathi
XXI, ed. Friedmann 44a. See also Bousset, *Kyrios Christos*, S. 194.

[33] Gal. 3:24.
[34] I Cor. 10:23; Gal. 5:6; Col. 2:16—and elsewhere.
[35] Gal. 2:21.   [36] Gal. 2:16.
[37] Friedrich Nietzsche, *Morgenröthe*, I, 68, ed. Leipzig 1917, I, 4, S. 67.
[38] Rom. 7:12.
[39] Rom. 7:7; see also 7:13 and many other passages.
[40] Gal. 2:19.

the Fathers from of old, and divine wisdom is contained in every word of it, and even in every letter and tittle of it. So how could those believing in all these things accept the annulment of the Torah because of a strange superstition, which claimed that the Torah, the source of life and light, brought about sin and death? Hence came about the persecutions which Paul suffered at the hands of the Jews in Jerusalem and in the Diaspora—persecutions which are related in the book of Acts and in a number of Epistles of Paul, and which culminated in his arrest in Jerusalem followed by his being taken as a prisoner to Rome.

3. But we have already seen more than once that it was not only the Jews disbelieving in Jesus who opposed Paul. All the Twelve also, and almost the whole Jerusalem church, along with James the brother of Jesus (and apparently the rest of his brothers also, since they had joined the movement), were utterly opposed to this interpretation of Christianity. For they, the kinsmen and associates of Jesus, his brothers and disciples, had seen Jesus conducting himself as a Jew in every particular (even though they had also heard him opposing himself to certain restrictions of the Pharisees), and they had heard from his own lips the following trenchant words:

Think not that I came to destroy the Law or the Prophets; I came not to destroy, but to fulfill. For verily I say unto you, Till heaven and earth pass away, one jot or one tittle shall in no wise pass away from the Law, till all things be accomplished.[41]

They had also heard from his lips these clear words: "Go not into any way of the Gentiles, and enter not into any city of the Samaritans; but go rather to the lost sheep of the house of Israel." [42] Again, they had heard him deliver this extremely nationalistic saying: "It is not meet to take the children's bread

[41] Matt. 5:17, 18.   [42] Matt. 10:5, 6.

and cast it to the little dogs"—"I was not sent but unto the lost sheep of the house of Israel." [43]

All these are words which cannot be supposed to have been deliberately fabricated at a later time, in spite of the claims of the new school of "Form Criticism." And how could all these disciples of Jesus have reconciled themselves to the fact that there came a man who was a stranger to Jesus, who had even for a time persecuted the followers of the Galilean Messiah, and that this man should set aside the Torah and the ceremonial laws, and particularly circumcision, for which the Jews had suffered martyrdom in the days of the harsh enactments of Antiochus Epiphanes, it being the sign of the Holy Covenant between Israel and its God?

It is not to be woundered at, therefore, that Paul stirred up the anger also—and perhaps in particular—of the most intimate disciples of Jesus, and that they preached, in opposition to his peculiar gospel, another gospel, a Jewish-Nazarene gospel, [44] in which they demanded observance of the law of circumcision, the keeping of Sabbaths and feasts, and the avoidance of forbidden foods. The whole Epistle to the Galatians, and a great part of the Epistles to the Romans, [45] the Corinthians, [46] and the Colossians [47] are concerned with these questions. In Galatians, Paul comes forth with harsh words against those proclaiming "a different gospel" and says:

> But though we, or an angel from heaven, should preach unto you any gospel other than that which we preached unto you, let him be anathema. As we have said before, so say I now again, If any man preacheth unto you any gospel other than that which ye received, let him be anathema. [48]

He argues in this Epistle that to demand circumcision of the believer in Jesus is to pervert the whole faith in Jesus; and

[43] Matt. 15:24–6; Mark 7:27.   [44] Gal. 1:6–12.
[45] Rom. 14 (the whole chapter).
[46] I Cor. 8 (the whole chapter); 10:18–33.
[47] Col. 2:16–23.   [48] Gal. 1:8, 9.

he emphasizes over and over that "in Christ Jesus neither circumcision availeth anything, nor uncircumcision; but faith working through love." [49]

But Paul is not entirely consistent, as appears in the stinging rebukes which he administers to his opponents. For instance, he exclaims thus: "Behold, I Paul say unto you, that if ye receive circumcision, Christ will profit you nothing"; [50] but he immediately adds: "Yea, I testify again to every man that receiveth circumcision, that he is a debtor to do the whole Law." [51] This is the case not only with regard to circumcision. It is the case also with regard to forbidden foods, prayers and blessings, Sabbaths and festivals. He says, for instance: "Whatever is sold in the shambles, eat, asking no question for conscience' sake"; [52] but he straightway adds: "If I pronounce a blessing over my food, why should I be denounced for what I have blessed?" [53] Of course, one must eat, drink, and do everything "to the glory of God"; but one must "give no occasion of stumbling, either to Jews, or to Greeks, or to the church of God" (i.e., the Nazarene church), "even as I also please all men in all things." [54]

Compromise reaches the height of extremity in the Epistle to the Romans, which is apparently addressed to a Nazarene congregation in Rome, and not to a Gentile congregation. [55] In this letter Paul says that some consider it permissible to eat everything, while to others only vegetables are permissible; [56] that is to say, there were Nazarenes who became vegetarians in order to avoid eating forbidden foods with Gentile Chris-

[49] Gal. 5:6. Cf.: "For neither is circumcision anything, nor uncircumcision, but a new creature" (Gal. 6:16); again, "Circumcision is nothing, and uncircumcision is nothing; but the keeping of the commandments of God" (I Cor. 7:19).
[50] Gal. 5:2.
[51] Gal. 5:3.
[52] I Cor. 10:25.   [53] I Cor. 10:30.
[54] I Cor. 10:31-3.
[55] See important arguments for this in Ed. Meyer, op. cit., III, 490-500.
[56] Rom. 14:2.

tians. There are those who "esteem one day above another,"
that is, they keep Sabbaths and festivals; and there are those
who "esteem every day alike." [57] Although Paul says:

I know, and am persuaded in the Lord Jesus, that nothing is
unclean of itself; save that to him who accounteth anything to be
unclean, to him it is unclean,[58]

nevertheless, his advice is not to be strict with the one eating
or not eating forbidden foods, or the one keeping or not keeping Sabbaths and festivals, and he recommends to all the general rule not "to do anything whereby thy brother stum-
bleth." [59] And we have already seen above that Paul boasted
of the fact that "to the Jews I became as a Jew, that I might
gain Jews; to them that are under the Law, as under the Law,
though not being myself under the Law." [60] For him, the end
that was good in his eyes justified the means, if they were
not too bad. . . .

Thus, it is not to be wondered at, that even at the end of
his life, when he had come to Jerusalem for the last time, and
was informed by James the brother of Jesus and some of the
Twelve that there was need of appeasing the wrath of the
pilgrims from Asia Minor resulting from his negatory attitude
toward the observance of the ceremonial laws—it is not to be
wondered at, that Paul bore the expenses of the sacrifices
of four Nazirites, and even came in person to the Temple to
"purify himself"—deeds which availed him little.[61]

Thus the "freedom"—freedom from Torah and ceremonial
laws—which Paul preached,[62] even if not with entire consistency. This is in direct contrast to the Talmud, which interprets the Biblical phrase "and the writing was the writing of
God, graven upon the tables" [63] as follows:

[57] Rom. 14:5.   [58] Rom. 14:14.
[59] Rom. 14:21.   [60] I Cor. 9:20. See above, p. 429.
[61] See above, p. 398.   [62] Gal. 2:4; 5:13, *et passim*.
[63] Ex. 32:16.

Read not *haruth* (graven) but *heruth* (freedom), for thou findest no freeman excepting one that occupies himself in the study of the Law.[64]

But Paul's special gospel, the new law which he offered, taught that the old Law was abolished and put aside, since it was the cause of sin and death, representing not freedom but slavery.[64a]

The Jewish Nazarenes were not willing to accept this doctrine of Paul, their companion in Messiah-worship. So how could it be accepted by the rest of the Jews, for whom Torah and ceremonial laws were their inmost soul, their life, and their very existence as a separate nation and as a religion? For they put into the mouth of their God this remarkable saying: "Would that they had forsaken Me but kept My Law!" [65]

[64] Aboth VI (chapter called "Kinyan Torah") 2; 'Erubin 54a.

[64a] On the abrogation of Torah and ceremonial laws by Paul, see now also T. W. Manson, "Jesus, Paul, and the Law" (*Judaism and Christianity*, III, 123-41).

[65] Yer., Hagigah I 7; Lam. Rab., Proem II [Soncino ed., p. 2, bottom].

CHAPTER VI

New Ceremonial Laws in Place of the Old

Paul pursued "freedom in Christ"—he wished to be free of the ceremonial laws. But man cannot dispense with ceremonial laws. When the Social Democrats denied the importance of the religious festivals, they established their own festival—the First of May; and when Soviet Russia abolished the religious holidays, it added to the First of May various holidays commemorating the Revolution.

Paul, in setting aside the old ceremonial laws of Judaism, accepted and strengthened two ritual practices which apparently had already been seized upon by the "brethren" of the church in Jerusalem. These two practices were *baptism* and the *fellowship* meal.

1. Ablution was an ancient custom in Israel. All ancient peoples were wont to practise ablution for bodily and spiritual cleanness. Jewish ablution was based, no doubt, on these verses:

And I will sprinkle clean water upon you, and ye shall be clean; from all your uncleannesses, and from all your idols, will I cleanse you. A new heart also will I give you, and a new spirit will I put within you; and I will take away the stony heart out of your flesh, and I will give you a heart of flesh.[1]

Thus was ablution for both male and female proselytes cus-

[1] Ezek. 36:25, 26.

tomary in Israel.[2] By means of the ablution they were, so to speak, cleansed from all their pagan "uncleannesses," while receiving "a new heart" and "a new spirit." Indeed, the male proselyte, who was circumcised and baptized, and the female proselyte, who was only baptized, became "as newborn children."[3] And baptism was so important in the eyes of the Tannaim that an early Tanna thought baptism more important than circumcision.[4]

The Essenes made much of ablutions,[5] and for this reason a number of scholars have wished to identify them with the "morning bathers" [or "bathers at dawn"] of the Talmud.[6] John the Baptist, who was much like the Essenes in his ways, although apparently he was not an actual member of the sect, made baptism in the Jordan an essential thing. This was for him a "baptism of repentance unto remission of sins," wherefore those receiving baptism could be heard "confessing their sins."[7] Josephus says of John's baptism that it was "for the purification of the body, supposing still that the soul was thoroughly purified beforehand by righteousness."[8] All this shows clearly that baptism was a Jewish practice which was accepted and followed in Israel even before its adoption by the "Jerusalem church." It is hardly necessary to say that it

[2] For female proselytes this was the *only* religious ceremony necessary for reception into Judaism. The Talmud understood this and said: "Whence does R. Joshua infer that the mothers performed ritual ablution?—It is a logical conclusion, for, otherwise, whereby did they enter under the wings of the Shekhinah!" (Yebamoth 46b). Therefore there is no basis for believing that baptism of proselytes arose after the period of Jesus and Paul, as does S. Zeitlin, *Hebrew Union College Annual*, I (1924), 356–63. See above, p. 40, n. 35. [See now H. H. Rowley, "Jewish Proselyte Baptism and the Baptism of John," HUCA, XV (1940), 313–34, for a view more like Klausner's. Tr.]

[3] Yebamoth 22a.

[4] See Yebamoth 46ab.

[5] Josephus, *Jewish War* II viii 5.

[6] Tosephta, Yadayim II 20 (near end); Berakoth 22a; Yer., *ibid.* III 4 (6c). [See *Jesus of Nazareth*, Eng. ed., p. 245].

[7] Mark 1:4, 5. See also Acts 19:4.

[8] *Antiq.* XVIII v 2, § 117.

preceded the time of Paul, since it was of such great importance in Pharisaic and Essenic Judaism.[9]

In spite of all the doubts of various scholars, it is to be
thought that Jesus was baptized by John the Baptist; for the
Evangelist attempts to explain away the amazing fact that
Jesus the greater than John was baptized by John, who was
lesser that Jesus.[10] There is even a theory that Jesus himself
administered baptism for a time.[11] We do know that a number
of years after the crucifixion, when Paul was in Ephesus, he
found Apollos and his group still baptizing in the name of
John.[12] And Paul himself was so convinced that baptism was
ancient in Israel that he says that our fathers in the Wilderness, after they had passed into the midst of the sea on dry
ground, proceeding "under the cloud," [13] "were all baptized
unto Moses in the cloud and in the sea." [14] That is to say, they
were baptized in the name of Moses (or into the spiritual
company of Moses), the baptism being accomplished by the
moisture from the water of the cloud and the sea. Thus it can
be seen that in the eyes of Paul baptism was a very ancient
institution.

Paul himself relates that he administered baptism only three
times: to Crispus, to Gaius, and to the household of Stephanas;
he thus refrained from baptizing lest it be said that he baptized
in his own name.[15] But he deemed baptism in the name of Jesus

[9] All this against C. A. Anderson Scott, *Saint Paul* (Cambridge 1936),
pp. 122–3. And see W. Brandt, *Jüdische Baptismen* (Giessen 1910, Beihefte
zur ZAW, XVIII); J. Scheftelowitz, "Die Sündenvergebung durch Wasser"
(*Archiv für Religionswissenschaft*, XVII, 353 ff.); G. Hölscher, *Urgemeinde
und Spätjudentum* (Oslo 1929), SS. 11–27 (mentioned more specifically
above, p. 388, n. 5).

[10] Matt. 3:13–5.

[11] See M. Goguel, *La vie de Jésus* (Paris 1932), pp. 246–61 [Eng. ed.,
pp. 272–9].

[12] See above, p. 387.

[13] That is to say, under the "pillar of cloud" which accompanied the
children of Israel on their exodus from Egypt (Ex. 13:21, 22 and 14:19).

[14] I Cor. 10:1, 2.

[15] I Cor. 1:14–6.

very important.[16] Yet even here Paul introduced extraneous elements into what was a purely Jewish precept or practice. First of all, he taught that by means of such baptism, people would receive the Holy Spirit, the spirit of prophecy, and the ability to speak with tongues.[17] But this is not all. Paul says besides:

Or are ye ignorant that all we who were baptized into Christ Jesus were baptized into his death? We were buried therefore with him through baptism into death: that like as Christ was raised from the dead through the glory of the Father, so we also might walk in newness of life.[18]

And by way of further explanation, this:

[Ye have] been buried with him [Christ] in baptism, wherein ye were also raised with him through faith in the working of God, who raised him from the dead.[19]

Finally, we begin to hear mystical words in the manner of the pagan mystery religions, in which the initiate became like that deity to whom he had dedicated himself by symbolic acts: "For as many of you as were baptized into Christ did *put on* Christ." [20] Matters reached such a point, that in the Gentile-Christian church in Corinth members were "baptized for the dead," and Paul approved of this—provided that it (this "baptism of the dead") should serve as an additional proof to the converted pagans that there is a resurrection of the body (in which the pagans did not believe), and thus that Jesus too rose from the dead.[21]

It is doubtful if such strange baptism as this, based upon superstitious and half-pagan foundations, could be accepted

[16] Acts 19:3–6.
[17] Acts 19:6.
[18] Rom. 6:3, 4.
[19] Col. 2:12.
[20] Gal. 3:27. On the likenesses and differences between the pagan mysteries and Pauline mysteries, see A. Omodeo, *Paolo di Tarso* (Messina 1932), pp. 172–82.
[21] I Cor. 15:29.

even by the Nazarene Jews, who saw in every practice received from Jesus a sacred thing; it would be even less likely
to be accepted by the Pharisees and Essenes, to say nothing of
the Sadducees! Certainly a new "commandment" of this sort
could not be accepted in such an amazing form. Yet Paul
reached such a point that he regarded baptism as absolutely
fundamental, and placed it in the same category with faith in
Christ: "one Lord, one faith, one baptism." [22]

Could Judaism have accepted such a strange point of view?

2. The second precept was that of the *fellowship meal*.

The "religious repast" had existed in Israel for a long time.[23]
Such were the Sabbath and holiday repasts, betrothal and marriage feasts, the repast of the covenant of circumcision, and
the like. There were also the *fellowship meals*, or *meals in
common*, which the Essenes raised to the rank of ceremonial
occasions;[24] but meals like these were also celebrated by other
religious groups.[25] Jesus and his disciples undoubtedly were
accustomed to partake of a fellowship meal together; and the
"Last Supper" of Jesus and his disciples was, in my opinion,
the most solemn meal of Judaism—the Passover meal or
"Seder." [26] But it is hard to believe that at the time of this
"Last Supper" Jesus said of the bread, "This is my body," and
of the wine, "This is my blood"; and of course he did not say
that his blood was "unto the remission of sins" (which is only
in Matthew and not in Mark and Luke); nor did he say, "This

[22] Eph. 4:5.   [23] See *e.g.*, Pesahim 49a.

[24] See the notable description of these ceremonial meals in *Jewish War*
II viii 5.

[25] See W. O. E. Oesterley, *The Jewish Background of the Christian
Liturgy* (Oxford 1925), pp. 166-9.

[26] In spite of all the arguments that have been lodged against this view
of mine since my book *Yeshu ha-Notsri* (*Jesus of Nazareth*) was first published (1922), I still hold firmly to this opinion. Not only so, but I have
even been strengthened in my opinion by later researches. See the fourth
[Hebrew] edition of *Yeshu* (1933), pp. 366-70, and particularly n. 5 to
pp. 366-7 and n. 1 to p. 369.

do in remembrance of me" (which is only in Luke and not in Mark and Matthew).[27]

Now Paul says of this "Lord's Supper" as follows:

> For I received of the Lord that which also I delivered unto you, that the Lord Jesus in the night in which he was betrayed took bread; and when he had given thanks, he brake it, and said: "(Take, eat;) [28] this is my body, which is (broken) [29] for you; this do in remembrance of me." In like manner also (he took) the cup, after supper,[30] saying: "This cup is the new covenant in my blood; this do as often as ye drink it, in remembrance of me." For as often as ye eat this bread, and drink the cup, ye proclaim the Lord's death till he come.[31]

Apparently, the tradition was already widespread in the time of Paul that these were the words of Jesus at the Last Supper —a tradition stemming from the account of the very solemn occasion in the book of Exodus:

> Then went up Moses, and Aaron, Nadab, and Abihu, and seventy of the elders of Israel; and they saw the God of Israel; and there was under His feet the like of a paved work of sapphire stone, and the like of the very heaven for clearness.[32]

Preceding this account, it is written that over the blood of the peace offerings which Moses sprinkled on the people he said: "Behold the blood of the covenant, which the Lord hath made with you in agreement with all these words." [33] *Then* the blood of the sacrifices was "the blood of the covenant"—the Old Covenant—and *now* the wine is the blood of Jesus, and also the blood of a covenant—the New Covenant.

---

[27] Klausner, *Yeshu*, p. 368 [Eng. ed., pp. 328–9].

[28] In most texts these two words are lacking; they were introduced here into some texts from the Gospels.

[29] This word is lacking in most texts.

[30] "The cup of blessing" (Sotah 38b), over which a blessing was said preceding the benediction over the food [but after the meal]. See I Cor. 10:16 for the very same phrase, "the cup of blessing."

[31] I Cor. 11:23–6.   [32] Ex. 24:9, 10.

[33] Ex. 24:5–8.

But even the fellowship meal, the meal in common, which was already revered by the Jerusalem church, was converted by Paul into a mystery. Paul admonishes and reproves the members of the Gentile-Christian church in Corinth because they eat and drink at "the Lord's Supper" in an unseemly manner: the rich and powerful among them get their meals first, and even become intoxicated with the wine, while the poor remain hungry,[34] which shows clearly that there were no mystical features in this common meal. But Paul had already converted this meal into a "sacrament" and a mystery; and he went so far as to conclude that, since the Corinthians had not conducted the occasion properly, "many among you are weak and sickly, and a number even dead." [35] And indeed in the same Epistle to the Corinthians, he actually says:

The cup of blessing which we bless, is it not a participation in the blood of Christ? the bread which we break, is it not a participation in the body of Christ? seeing that we, who are many, are one bread, one body: for we all partake of the one bread.

Then Paul compares the participants in the Lord's Supper to "Israel after the flesh," wherein "they that eat the sacrifices have communion with the altar." [36] The "meal of fellowship," therefore, begins to be not only a sacred act, taking the place of sacrifice, but it brings those eating it into communion with the flesh and blood of the Messiah—something which greatly resembles the ideas of the devotees of the pagan mysteries with regard to the communion between the initiate and the body of the god to whom the initiate was consecrated.[37]

It is possible that Jesus himself spoke vaguely during his last meal of the sufferings which would come upon him, since he

---

[34] I Cor. 11:20-2.   [35] I Cor. 11:30.

[36] I Cor. 10:16-8.

[37] See above, pp. 113-4. That we have here a foreign element introduced by Paul is admitted also by Weinel, *Biblische Theologie des Neuen Testaments*, 4. Aufl. (Tübingen 1928), S. 248. See also W. R. Halliday, *The Pagan Background of Early Christianity*, pp. 312-7.

knew the fate of all the Messiahs that had preceded him, and had seen the hostility which he himself had aroused.[38] Nevertheless, not he but Paul made the "sacred meal" what it became in Christianity. Through the words of Paul quoted above, there was introduced into it the mystery of "transubstantiation" (the changing of the bread into the flesh of the Messiah, and the wine into his blood), which undoubtedly—in spite of the opposition to this opinion on the part of various scholars—brought in its wake the mistaken belief of the heathen all the way from ancient Rome to modern China, that Christians use human blood for their "Passover." And afterwards, when the heathen became Christians, they themselves accused the Jews, on the basis of this very Christian belief, of using in their Passover the blood of Christians. This false and disgraceful blood accusation has cost the Jews myriads of human sacrifices from the Middle Ages up to the present. In the Middle Ages there was added a second accusation—that the Jews profaned the "consecrated bread" (or the "host") by piercing it, thus causing blood to come forth . . . and this absurd accusation also cost the Jews thousands of lives. . . .

These were the principal "ceremonial laws" which Paul established, or more correctly "deepened," and "elevated" to the rank of sacraments and mysteries—thereby unintentionally bringing affliction through the ages upon his people Israel. . . .

Could the Jewish people have taken upon itself the yoke of these new "commandments" in place of the commandments of the Torah—commandments that were very ancient and rooted in the national life?——

[38] See on this Klausner, *Yeshu*, p. 372 [Eng. ed., pp. 330–1].

CHAPTER VII

Faith in Christ, the Sin of the First Adam, and Salvation by Grace

1. The Torah of Israel, with all its regulations, was null and void. What came to take its place, besides the two ceremonial practices just mentioned (baptism and the "Lord's Supper")?—

The answer to this question is brief: *faith in Christ.*

From now on man shall be justified not by the law of *works,* but by the law of *faith:* "a man is justified by faith apart from the works of the Law."[1] The proof is that Abraham was justified even before he was commanded to undergo circumcision and before that rite existed merely because he "*believed* God, and it was reckoned unto him for righteousness";[2] and also before he was commanded to observe circumcision as a ceremonial law, God promised him: "In thee shall all the families of the earth be blessed."[3] Moreover, King David said:

> Blessed are they whose iniquities are forgiven,
> And whose sins are covered.
> Blessed is the man to whom the Lord will not reckon sin.[4]

Paul concludes from all this that the essential thing is not obedience to the Law as a means whereby the iniquities of man are pardoned, but divine grace—the willingness of God to pardon transgressions, to forgive sins, without holding man

[1] Rom. 3:27, 28.   [2] Gen. 15:6; Rom. 4:1–24.
[3] Gen. 12:3; Gal. 3:6–9.   [4] Ps. 32:1, 2; Rom. 4:6–8.

accountable for his iniquities. Verily the prophet said, "The righteous shall live by his *faith*." [5]

Obviously, continues Paul's reasoning, it is to be concluded from all these verses that the essential thing is faith in God. The Jews believe in God, yet they do not find salvation and divine grace except by observance of Torah and ceremonial laws. But these two things do not save them. One necessarily says, they are wrong, and the essential thing is—*faith in Christ*.[6] Christ as the spiritual son of God was without sin; yet he bore severe sufferings, was crucified, and died a shameful death. His sufferings were, therefore, *vicarious sufferings*, and his death was an *atoning death*. He who had in him no sin was crucified as a sacrifice for *all mankind*, in whom sin had lodged since the days of the first Adam. Death came upon man through the first "Adam's transgression." [7] Until Jesus, all died by this sin, even Moses; only Jesus, who also died, and a shameful death with much suffering on the cross, rose. Since he died a death of punishment, although he was without sin, behold his afflictions and resurrection provide redemption from death and inherited sin alike—that is to say, from "Original Sin" (*culpa originalis, péché original, Erbsünde*).[8]

Judaism also thought that death was a penalty laid upon mankind because of "the first Adam," [9] as set forth already in the Pentateuch.[10] There is reason to believe that the idea of "the sin of the first Adam" or "original sin" in the Pauline sense is already present in the Hellenistic "Psalms of Solo-

---

[5] Hab. 2:4; Rom. 1:17; Gal. 3:11.

[6] See on this A. Schlatter, *Der Glaube im Neuen Testament* (Leiden 1885), SS. 305–93; E. Lohmeyer, *Grundlagen paulinischer Theologie* (Tübingen 1929), SS. 115–46.

[7] Rom. 5:14.

[8] The fine distinction which Weinel (*Biblische Theologie des Neuen Testaments*, S. 224) makes between *Erbsünde* [inherited sin] and *Erbschuldlehre* [inherited guilt] does not much change the essence of the matter.

[9] IV Ezra 7:116–8; Syriac Baruch 17:2, 3 and 23:4; Siphre Deut. 323, ed. Friedmann 138b.

[10] Gen. 2:17 and 3:19.

mon." [11] But the original Palestinian Judaism, which also knows a death without sin, not however of the Messiah, but of the thoroughly righteous, called this "death through the machinations [12] of the serpent." [13] Judaism also knows redemption from death—but *only by the Torah*:

For when the serpent came upon Eve he injected lust into her: as for the Israelites who stood at Mount Sinai [*i.e.* who received the Torah], their lustfulness departed; as for the idolatrous nations of the world [who did not receive the Torah], their lustfulness did not depart.[14]

Since according to the view of Paul the Torah was rendered void at the coming of Jesus Christ, and since he longed in particular to convert the idolatrous nations of the world, he could not think that the Torah by any means erased "the lustfulness of the serpent," "original sin," or "the sin of the first Adam." According to his view, Jesus redeemed from death and from inherited sin, not the observers of the Law, but those believing in Jesus as the crucified and risen Messiah. *Faith took the place of the Law.* Faith in Jesus redeems from both death and sin, since it offers salvation on the Day of Judgment when Jesus shall appear "at the right hand of Power" (the Parousia) and shall sit in judgment upon the world and nations; then will he save those believing on him, not permitting them to taste death even if they have no Torah or ceremonial laws.[15]

2. But this is not all that Paul thought.

Judaism also teaches that there is atonement for the sin of

[11] See E. Gärtner, *Komposition und Wortwahl des Buches Weisheit* (Berlin 1912), SS. 68-9.

[12] בעטיו, similar to בחטיו or בחטאו. See J. Levy, *Wörterbuch, etc.*, III, 634a, article עט II. According to A. Kohut, *Aruch Completum*, VI, 186, article עט, this word is from the Greek αἰτία, "cause."

[13] Shabbath 55b; Baba Bathra 17a.

[14] Shabb. 145b and 146a; Yebamoth 103b; 'Abodah Zarah 22b.

[15] Rom. 2:16; 3:5, 6, *et passim*.

the individual (it is otherwise with regard to the sin of the community or the nation) apart from punishment in this world or after death, in the world to come. There is atonement by means of *repentance*: "Repentance and good works are a shield against retribution." [16] The ceremonial laws are not the important thing, but repentance; on days when the Jewish community fasted, it would be said by way of admonition to the fasters:

"Brethren, it is not written of the men of Nineveh that 'God saw their sackcloth and their fasting,' but *'And God saw their works that they turned from their evil way'*." [17]

By way of clarification the matter is put thus: ". . . neither sackcloth nor fastings are effective but only penitence and good deeds." [18] The Talmud draws this conclusion: "Nothing will rise up against all those who repent." [19] Famous is the saying: "The place occupied by repentant sinners cannot be attained even by the completely righteous." [20] Well known is the charming haggadah that Manasseh son of Hezekiah, king of Israel, had committed such great sins that when he came to repent, after having been bound with fetters and carried off to Babylon,[21] the angels closed the windows of the firmament in order that the prayers of this thoroughly evil man, who had spilled so much blood, might not reach the Throne of Glory, since Manasseh had turned to repentance only in the hour of his humiliation and distress. So what did the Holy One, blessed be He, do?—"He made him a kind of opening in the heavens, in order to accept him [Manasseh] with his repentance";[22] or, "He dug for himself a hole under the Throne of Glory and thus heard his [Manasseh's] petition." [23]

[16] Mish., Aboth IV 11.
[17] Mish., Ta'anith II 1; Jonah 3:10.
[18] Ta'anith 16a.
[19] Yer., Peah I 1 (16b middle).
[20] Sanhedrin 99a; Berakoth 34b.
[21] See II Chron. 33:12–9.
[22] Sanhedrin 103a.
[23] Yer., *ibid.*, VI 2 (28c).

And indeed, the proclamation of John the Baptist and Jesus was first of all, "Repent!" [24]

Paul thinks that the sinner has no need of either Torah or repentance. All sin died with the death of the sinless Jesus; therefore, all believing on him have "died to sin." [25] From the day that Jesus rose from the dead, *grace* (χάρις, also χάρισμα) has ruled: ". . . much more did the grace of God, and the gift by the grace of the one man, Jesus Christ, abound unto the many"; for if the judgment which was pronounced upon the one sin (of the first man) caused mankind to be under condemnation, grace acted to clear mankind of many transgressions. Thus

as one man's trespass issued in doom for all,[26]
so one man's act of redress issues in acquittal and life for all.[27]

Matters reached such a point with Paul that he introduced into Scriptural verses strange and unlikely meanings in order to draw from them conclusions agreeing with his new teaching. In this he was much like the casuists of the Talmud. For example:

For as many as are of the works of the Law are under a curse: for it is written, "Cursed is every one who continueth not in all things that are written in the book of the Law, to do them." [28] Now that no man is justified by the Law before God, is evident: for, "The righteous shall live by faith"; [29] and the Law is not of faith; but, "He that doeth them shall live in them." [30] Christ redeemed us from the curse of the Law, having become a curse for us; for it is written, "Cursed is (every) one that hangeth (on a tree)": [31] that upon the Gentiles might come the blessing of

---

[24] See Klausner, *Yeshu*, pp. 271-2 [Eng. ed., pp. 245-6].
[25] Rom. 6:2.
[26] They were found worthy of death, and death assumed power over all the children of Adam and Eve.
[27] Rom. 5:15-9 [Moffatt].
[28] Deut. 27:26.
[29] Hab. 2:4.
[30] Lev. 18:5.
[31] Deut. 21:23.

Abraham in Christ Jesus; that we might receive the promise of the Spirit through faith.[32]

To such a point as this did homiletic casuistry reach: since it is written, "Cursed is every one who continueth not in *all* things that are written in the book of the Law, to do them," and since it is difficult to *do* all the things written in the Law, the Law has been changed from a blessing into a curse . . . thus there is no need of Torah, or ceremonial laws, or repentance; faith in Christ and "his grace" alone is sufficient [33]—and immediately the righteous man and the sinner, the Jew and the foreigner, are on the same level——

3. What is the nature of this sin, which brought death upon the race of men, and from which Jesus saves them?——

Sin is for Paul, like death, an inexhaustible heritage of the human race. Sin enfolds all of us, without exception, from the womb to the grave. Paul says, ". . . for we before laid to the charge both of Jews and Greeks, that they are all under sin"; and immediately follows a long series of Scriptural verses, which go to show that "there is none righteous, no, not one." and "there is none that doeth good, no, not so much as one." [34] For Paul, sins are "works of the flesh"; sin is implanted by nature in the body and the parts thereof.[35] There is, to be sure, an impression left by Paul that for the most part (not always, of course) sins come from the persuasions and enticements of those "powers of darkness," those evil spirits with Satan at their head, which it is so hard for man to conquer—sin rules in man and has dominion over him, and man does not have the power to oppose these evil powers of darkness except with the help of the "grace" of Jesus.[36] But sin is also connected with "the nature of the flesh" of man, which is the reason

[32] Gal. 3:10-4.
[33] Rom. 11:6.
[34] Rom. 3:9-17.
[35] Rom. 5:12; 6:12-4.
[36] See on this C. A. Anderson Scott, *Saint Paul*, pp. 79-81.

why the powers of darkness can prevail over him. Man was punished with death because of sin. Thus the two of them—both sin and death—are the lot of man—of all mankind, without exception, save only Jesus.[37] This is the most dreadful thing about the teaching of Paul, that for him the flesh and sin are identical. And since man is "flesh and blood," then also man and sin are identical. Hence the abysmal pessimism of Paul: if sin is closely joined to the flesh, then there is no deliverance for man, "for that he also is flesh." [38] That is to say, there is no salvation for man except "freely by . . . grace through the redemption" which God gives him by means of the blood of Christ.[39] Paul emphasizes again and again to the members of the churches which he founded:

. . . for by *grace* have ye been saved through *faith*; and that not of yourselves, it is the gift of God; not of works, that no man should glory.[40]

That was enough for Paul.

4. Will all men be saved by means of this "free grace"?——No. Not all. "We [the believers in Jesus] are not under the Law, but under grace." [41] Hence not all men will be saved —although it would be possible for all men to be saved by faith in Jesus. Whoever does not believe will not be saved. Whoever remains "under the Law" will not be "under grace."

But—is it just or equitable to divide men into "saved" and "unsaved" like this?——

The "apostle of the Gentiles" has scruples about this, but there is no other way out. In order to justify this unnatural, unjust, and inequitable idea of two kinds of men, Paul adduces proof for his opinion from the Pentateuch and the Prophets. From the womb of their mother before they had done any-

[37] Rom. 5:12.
[38] Gen. 6:3.
[39] Rom. 3:24, 25.
[40] Eph. 2:8, 9.
[41] Rom. 6:15.

thing either good or bad, there was a distinction between Jacob and Esau, sons of the same father and mother. God determined his choice not according to deeds. Even before Esau sinned, he was chosen to be the bearer of sin, and even before Jacob did good deeds, the choice fell upon him, and he received the eternal promise, even as it is written:

> Was not Esau Jacob's brother?
> Saith the Lord;
> Yet I loved Jacob,
> But Esau I hated.[42]

God "hardened the heart of Pharaoh" to show his divine power;[43] wherein was Pharaoh at fault, if God gave him a "hard heart" and if God had a will to show his power? "So then he [God] hath mercy on whom he will, and whom he will he hardeneth." [44] The Prophet Isaiah rebuked "him that striveth with his Maker," trying to show God what to do.[45]

Now, there is also in the Old Testament the idea that there is inequality among men:

And many of them that sleep in the dust of the earth shall awake, some to everlasting life, and some to reproaches and everlasting abhorrence.[46]

Consequently one might think that in their *lifetime* there were distinctions among "them that sleep in the dust of the earth," *i.e.*, that those who "shall awake . . . to everlasting life" did good deeds, and those who "shall awake . . . to reproaches and everlasting abhorrence" did evil deeds. Yet Paul comes out against this point of view, and with all the eloquence at his command insists that those who are saved and put under grace—the recipients of "eternal life"—have no particular

---

[42] Rom. 9:10–3; Mal. 1:2, 3.   [43] Ex. 9:12–6.
[44] Rom. 9:18.
[45] Rom. 9:19–23; Isa. 45:9 and 29:15.
[46] Dan. 12:2.

merit because of the deeds which they have done, but are protected only by the "gift of God" and the "grace of Jesus," and only from these will they become "vessels of mercy"; whereas the rest of humanity, being completely sinful, since God did not put faith in Jesus into their hearts, will be chastised as "vessels of wrath fitted for destruction." [47]

From this hate-filled doctrine came later the belief in the "dual predestination" (*praedestinatio duplex*) of Saint Augustine. A part of humanity was created *from the beginning* for damnation—and repentance will avail this part nothing, since their condemnation to hell was not brought about by sin.

And thus Torah and ceremonial laws have no significance.

5. The idea that "predestination" determines the fate of man brought about a deep cleavage in Christianity, beginning with the Middle Ages and continuing up to the time of Luther and his followers. But the abrogation of the Torah and the substitution of faith in Jesus for it likewise caused a cleavage very early in primitive Christianity. In the name of James the brother of Jesus, a Nazarene who observed Jewish law, an Epistle was composed,[48] in which we find these words:

What doth it profit, my brethren, if a man say he hath faith, but have not works? Can that faith save him?—Even so faith, if it have not works, is dead in itself.[49]

And in another place it says: "For whosoever shall keep the whole Law, and yet stumble in one point, he is become guilty of all." [50] If the Nazarene Jews felt this way, how could Judaism proper have accepted mystico-pessimistic beliefs like Paul's, which through a mystico-religious determinism rob man of free choice and appoint him in advance "to wrath or

[47] Rom. 9:22, 23.
[48] See on him and on the Epistle attributed to him, above, pp. 278-80.
[49] James 2:14-7.   [50] James 2:10.

to mercy," without giving him a chance to determine his own fate? For in authentic Judaism there is such faith in life and such strong optimism that all the hate of Schopenhauer for Judaism and the Jews perpetuating it arose largely from the fact that he could not forgive Judaism for its affirmation of life.——

Judaism also knows *vicarious suffering*. Even if we do not interpret Isaiah 53 messianically, but apply it to Zerubbabel, to the prophet himself, or even to the people Israel, there is in any case vicarious suffering in this passage:

Surely our diseases he did bear, and our pains he carried;
. . . .
But he was wounded because of our transgressions,
He was crushed because of our iniquities:
The chastisement of our welfare was upon him,
And with his stripes we were healed.
. . . .
And the Lord hath made to light on him
The iniquity of us all.
. . . .
And they made his grave with the wicked,
. . . .
Although he had done no violence,
Neither was any deceit in his mouth.
. . . .
Of the travail of his soul he shall see to the full, even My servant,
Who by his knowledge did justify the Righteous One to the
    many,
And their iniquities he did bear.
. . . .
Because he bared his soul unto death,
And was numbered with the transgressors;
Yet he bore the sin of many,
And made intercession for the transgressors.[51]

[51] Isa. 53:4–12. See for a detailed discussion of this chapter Klausner, *Ha-Ra'yon*, pp. 101–3.

Vicarious suffering is also found in the extracanonical books.[52] In the Talmud we find, ". . . so does the death of the righteous afford atonement [for the living they have left behind]," [53] and "the righteous are seized [by death] for the [sins of the] generation." [54] Well known is the stock expression of R. Ishmael: "The Children of Israel—may I make atonement for them!" [55] And the Messiah is a redeemer and savior according to the view of Judaism also.

But *first*, the Jewish Messiah is above all a redeemer of his nation from subservience to foreign rulers. *Second*, sin shall cease in the Days of the Messiah,[56] among the Jews first, and afterwards among the Gentiles also, when they have all acknowledged the One God, the God of Israel, and his Torah, the Torah of the prophets. *Third*, the Jewish Messiah redeems not "by his blood," but by the spirit of God, the spirit of righteousness, which is in him. The view of Paul, that the death of Jesus is an atonement for the whole world, not only for all mankind, but even for *the world of nature*, which has been "groaning and travailing," waiting "with earnest expectation" for its redeemer [57]—such a view is pleasing to the fancy, having in it something poetic and sublime. But in its essence, although it is built on Jewish foundations, it is pagan, and there is an odor of the mystery religions of the Greeks, the Egyptians, the Persians, and the pagan peoples of Asia Minor —of Dionysus, Isis and Osiris, Attis, and Mithras—emanating from it. For this reason Judaism could not accept it. And to-day this view, with its hard-and-fast conclusions which

[52] IV Macc. 6:29 and 17:21, 22.
[53] Mo'ed Katan, 28a.
[54] Shabb. 33b.
[55] Mish., Nega'im II 1 and elsewhere. See above, pp. 139–40.
[56] Psalms of Solomon 17:21–44.
[57] Rom. 8:19–22. On the quaking of nature and its hope for salvation, see G. Schläger, "Das ängstliche Harren der Kreatur," *Niew Theologisch Tijdschrift*, XIX (1930/1), 352–60. In the opinion of this author, "nature" is here the world of pagan nations.

fetter the spirit, and stifle the joy in living and the potent energies of man aspiring to greatness and performing miracles in our time, in spite of all the errors, the cruelties, and the wanton deeds for which he and no power outside of him is responsible—can such a view find acceptance to-day in the minds of those holding a modern world outlook?——

CHAPTER VIII

Paul's Universalism and the Abrogation of Jewish Nationalism

1. The Hebrew Old Testament is full of universalistic ideas alongside of nationalistic ideas.

Of course the people Israel is in the eyes of all the prophets the chosen people of God, the one and only people which by appointment is properly adapted to carry the standard of faith in the one and only God, the people which shall triumph in the end of days over all its persecutors and detractors and then dwell in honor and greatness in the land of its Fathers. But along with the emphasis on the national side of Israel's Messianic promise, there is constant stress also on the hope for all humanity.

In the book of Kings we read:

Moreover concerning the stranger that is not of Thy people Israel, when he shall come out of a far country for Thy name's sake . . . when he shall come and pray toward this house; hear Thou in heaven Thy dwelling-place, and do according to all that the stranger calleth to Thee for.[1]

The First Isaiah and Micah the Morashtite prophesy of the brotherhood of peoples, of a day when wars between nations shall cease, and "all nations shall flow" unto "the mountain of the Lord's house,"

> And they shall beat their swords into plowshares,
> And their spears into pruning-hooks;
> Nation shall not lift up sword against nation,
> Neither shall they learn war any more.[2]

[1] I Kings 8:41–3.   [2] Isa. 2:2–4; Micah 4:1–4.

The Second Isaiah is full of prophetic words about the spread of the idea of the One God and his prophetic morality among all peoples; particularly saturated with this idea are the Servant of the Lord passages.[3] The book of Jonah, in spite of the restrictive interpretations which Jewish and Christian exegetes wish to force upon it, is a book of the greatest and most sublime universalism, showing an incomparable attitude of broad humanitarianism even to Nineveh, the destroyer of the Kingdom of Israel. Zechariah says: "And many nations shall join themselves to the Lord in that day, and shall be Mv people." [4] Malachi says also:

For from the rising of the sun even unto the going down of the same
My name is great among the nations;
And in every place offerings are presented unto My name,
Even pure oblations;
For My name is great among the nations,
Saith the Lord of hosts.[5]

And like the Prophets, thus also the Writings. The book of Psalms is full of hope and faith that all nations will acknowledge the God of Israel and enter under the wings of the Shekhinah. The book of Job presents as the embodiment of humanity's deepest problem "a man . . . perfect and upright" from the land of Uz *in Edom*; even those who remonstrate with him are not from Israel or even Palestine. The book of Daniel is primarily a philosophy of history, which ponders the fate of *all mankind*. And the books of Enoch, Ethiopic and Slavonic, the books of Baruch, Syriac and Greek, IV Ezra, the Wisdom of Solomon, IV Maccabees, also the writings of Philo of Alexandria, are full of universalistic conceptions and expectations as well as purely Jewish-nationalistic promises.

[3] Isa. 42:1–13; 44:1–5; 49:1–8; 56:6–8.
[4] Zech. 2:15.   [5] Mal. 1:11.

Paul said nothing new, therefore, when he came and asked: "Or is God the God of Jews only? Is he not the God of Gentiles also?"—and then answered, "Yea, of Gentiles also." [6] Even the most nationalistic Jew in our time would answer likewise. And we have already seen the great effort to win proselytes, which was made with considerable success by the Jews toward the end of the period of the Second Temple.[7]

But Paul came to the proselyting (or Christianizing) of pagans not from an attitude of affirmation, but from an attitude of negation—the abrogation of Torah and ceremonial laws. Yet Jewish nationalism, insofar as it is connected with religion, is bound up with the ceremonial laws. *First*, they are in the eyes of Jewish nationalism the expression of the will of God through Moses, the spiritual father of the prophets. *Second*, they are a defense against assimilation by the heathen peoples which surround the Jews on every side. And finally, *third*, they sanctify secular life and make even it holy by the habits of restraint and frugality, and by a self-control which is expressed in the saying, "Sanctify yourself by that which is permitted to you." [8]

But all this Paul did not wish to understand. He saw only one thing—that the ceremonial laws were exceedingly numerous and difficult to observe—which cannot be denied—and hence that it was impossible for any man to become completely righteous by virtue of observing all of them; and since they cannot bring about "sanctification"—better to abrogate them all and substitute for them *faith*. This is the course of the reasoning of the zealous Pharisee, who had passed from one extreme to another. His second extreme—abrogation of

[6] Rom. 3:29.
[7] See above, pp. 31–49. On the whole question of nationalism and universalism in Judaism and Christianity, see also Ezekiel Kaufmann, *Golah ve-Nekhar*, I, 2, 395–432; M. H. Amishai, *Mahashavah ve-Emet* (Tel-Aviv 5699), II, 271–94.
[8] Yebamoth 20a.

the ceremonial laws—had one great advantage for him: through this abrogation he was able to offer faith in Christ to the pagans, who would never have agreed to take upon themselves *en masse* the 613 commandments (which are difficult for even born Jews to observe), particularly circumcision, observance of the dietary laws, and keeping of the Sabbath and the fixed festivals. If *faith* could take the place of these, it would be very easy to make converts to the new religion among the Gentiles. For if faith is the primary thing, and, as Paul attempted to prove, even Abraham was justified by God thanks to his faith ("Abraham believed in God, and it was reckoned unto him for righteousness"),[9] then are the Gentiles believing in Jesus sons of Abraham also, while the Jews not believing in Jesus have ceased to be sons of Abraham —or they are not sons of Isaac but sons of Ishmael—and not by them will come fulfillment of the promise to Abraham: ". . . in thee shall all the families of the earth be blessed."[10]

Here begins the attempt of Paul to put aside all distinctions between Israel and the other nations. He says: ". . . he is a Jew who is one *inwardly*; and circumcision is that of the heart, in the spirit, not in the letter."[11] All—both Jews and Greeks—are dependent upon "redemption" by Jesus.[12] Thus from now on, since Jesus was crucified to achieve this "redemption" of the world and all humanity, and then rose from the dead, it may be said:

There can be neither Jew nor Greek, there can be neither bond nor free, there can be no male and female; for ye all are one in Christ Jesus.[13]

Or in other words, when one puts off "the old man" and puts on "the new man," he reaches a state

[9] See above, pp. 516-7.   [10] Rom. 4:11-25; Gal. 4:21-31.
[11] Rom. 2:25-9; *cf.* "Circumcise therefore the foreskin of your heart" (Deut. 10:16).
[12] Rom. 3:23-5.   [13] Gal. 3:28.

where there cannot be Greek and Jew, circumcision and uncircumcision, barbarian, Scythian, bondman, freeman; but Christ is
all, and in all.[14]

Since this is so, all the advantage of Israel over the Gentiles,
which came to it from its ethical-monotheistic Torah, has
passed away: "And if ye are Christ's, then are ye Abraham's
seed, heirs according to promise." [15] Thus "there is no distinction between Jew and Greek; for the same Lord is Lord of
all." [16]

2. In the relations between Israel and its God, Paul sees
three stages, corresponding to three historical periods. The
first period was from Abraham to Moses, the period before
the giving of the Law, in which there was sin in the world,
but it was not considered sin, since there was not yet a
Law: ". . . sin is not imputed when there is no law." [17] Abraham received the promise that in his seed "all the families of
the earth [should] be blessed" without fulfilling the Law,
merely by *believing*. Here we have the reverse of the Talmudic view of Abraham in relation to Torah and ritual laws:
"Abraham our father kept the whole Torah . . . even the
law concerning the *'erub* [pooling] of dishes." [18] Also according to the Pseudepigrapha, Abraham observed the ceremonial
laws: he tithed, he offered sacrifices, he kept Sabbaths and
festivals, and so on.[19] But the Talmud also knows the distinction between the time before the giving of the Law and the
time after in relation to the obligation to observe ritual requirements.[20]

The *second* period began with Moses, in whose days the
Law was given. This second period extended from Moses to
Jesus. It is the period of the Law. But the Law did not suc-

---

[14] Col. 3:11.
[15] Gal. 3:29.
[16] Rom. 10:12.
[17] Rom. 5:13. And see above, p. 501.
[18] Yoma 28b.
[19] Book of Jubilees 13:26–7; 15:1, 2; 16:31, *et passim*.
[20] See, *e.g.*, 'Abodah Zarah 24a; Gen. Rabbah XXII, XXXIV, *et passim*.

ceed in making men righteous and good: the Law lacked power, "in that it was weak through the flesh"; [21] therefore it was able to bring only "sin and death." [22] Again Paul goes to an unnatural extreme: "And the Law came in besides, that the trespass might abound; but where sin abounded, grace did abound more exceedingly." [23] Thus there is no salvation or redemption in the Law because it has no power to "make alive." [24] Observance of the ceremonial laws is only "worshipping of angels" [25] and not worship of God. As for the Torah, the Jews do not understand it: Moses put a veil over his face,[26] and the children of Israel do not remove the veil from the face of the words, when they read the "Old Covenant"; only by Christ can the veil be removed.[27] That is to say, true understanding of the Torah becomes possible only through Jesus, who according to Paul opposed everything in it having to do with the ceremonial laws and interpreted the Messianic passages in a new way (or else by the death of Jesus these passages were explained in a new way). Therefore, salvation can come only by faith in Jesus. Until Jesus came, mankind was dependent on a "nurse" or "tutor"—the "Old Covenant"; but "the fulness of time came," and "God sent forth his Son, born of a woman, born under the Law, that he might redeem them that were under the Law." [28] One might assume that only the children of Israel properly participate in this redemption, since they are the ones "under the Law." But since faith in Jesus is the essential thing, there is no distinction between Jew and Greek, as has been explained.[28a]

Thus we have not only *abrogation of the Torah of Israel*, but also *abrogation of Jewish nationalism*.

[21] Rom. 8:3.
[22] Rom. 8:2.
[23] Rom. 5:20. See also above, p. 501.
[24] Gal. 3:21.
[25] Col. 2:18.
[26] See Ex. 34:29-35.
[27] II Cor. 3:13-8.
[28] Gal. 3:23-6 and 4:1-5.
[28a] The *third* period, omitted here by the author, is no doubt the period of redemption and salvation through Christ. See also the next chapter. Tr.

3. It was inevitable that this should arouse strong opposition on the part of Judaism—Palestinian and that of the Diaspora alike—to Paul and his "special gospel." Here he abandoned not only the *political* side of the Messianic faith, but also the idea of the *election*, or—more correctly—the *adoption* of the people Israel, although he himself had professed this very idea.[29] This idea is not the result of a mere chauvinistic and foolish pride. The idea of adoption means to Judaism that it stands in "splendid isolation" as the one and only mono-theistic nation among all the great and numerous polytheistic nations. So it was clear to the Jews that if all "the seventy nations" of the pagans should accept the teaching of Paul, monotheism would be assimilated by polytheism, and not the reverse; a drop of wine cannot flavor a bucket of water. Yet of course, the Jews have always expected, and they continue to expect even to-day, that a time will come when all the Gentiles will become proselytes and mankind "will be made one band" [30] of fraternal peoples holding fast to ethical mono-theism; but of course at that time the Gentiles will accept the teaching of Judaism as it is found in the Torah and in the Prophets.

But Paul comes and argues that the Torah is a curse, that the Torah brings about sin and death, and that there is no need for the Gentiles to take upon themselves the historic, traditional, and accepted Judaism, since by means of the mystical "grace" of a crucified Messiah, a grace flowing out of faith in this Messiah, who miraculously rose from the dead, all have become alike and hence there is no longer any need to "reform the world by the rule of the Almighty" [the 'Alenu prayer]. So, could Judaism have done otherwise than oppose such a method of receiving converts?

Judaism in the days of the Second Temple, and after, made

---

[29] Rom. 2:9, 10; 9:4, 5; 11:16–24, and so on.

[30] The prayer *Shemoneh 'Esreh* for "Solemn Days" (Rosh ha-Shanah and Yom Kippur). See also above, p. 469.

Gentile proselytes "sons of the Covenant" in such a manner that they were absorbed into *the Jewish national community;* Paul, on the contrary, caused the Christianized Jews—intentionally or unintentionally—to be absorbed into *the pagan community*, which was incomparably greater in size than the Jewish national community. By this means he obliterated the marks of Jewish nationality from his Jewish converts, while from the nationality of the pagans nothing was taken away; for Judaism is different, in that in it religion and nationality are entwined and intermingled: there are no Catholic Jews, Protestant Jews, or Moslem Jews.

The healthy instinct of the Jewish nation, which wished to keep its Judaism, which yearned to live and to work as a distinct nation for a unique religio-cultural ideal, which is the bearer of the idea of a prophetic-monotheistic Kingdom of Heaven, free from all kinds of strange superstitions and independent of the fate of one man, even though he be the Messiah himself—this healthy religio-nationalistic instinct stirred the Jews into opposition to Paul and his teaching.

There was one other deep-seated and important cause of this opposition.

Paul in the last analysis *was concerned only for the individual,* for the salvation of his soul, for his redemption from sin and death. In this he was a loyal disciple of Jesus. Authentic Judaism also has been concerned from the time of Ezekiel the Prophet on for the individual and the salvation of his soul; but in the last analysis the chief concern of the Jewish Messianic idea is the nation, and also human society and all mankind as an aggregate of nations and societies. This Jewish Messianism cannot be entirely dependent upon any one person, nor can it concern itself exclusively with the soul of the individual. Therefore its "Kingdom of Heaven" is in *this world*, and this "Kingdom" will be realized gradually through "reform of the world by the rule of the Almighty," as a result of the cultivation of the good impulses and war against the bad impulses. The hope of this Judaism is not visionary and not mystical. Its basic principle is *nationality for the sake of universality*. For the aspiration to strengthen and develop the Jewish nation in its own land goes along with the aspiration to "reform the world"—to set right all humanity. And for this reason it can be said without any assumption of national superiority that Judaism is the seed of progress in the world.[31]

Could Judaism have exchanged this bright hope for the hope of Paul and his followers?——

[31] See Klausner, "Ha-Mashiaḥ ha-Yehudi ve-ha-Mashiaḥ, ha-Notsri," *Sepher-Magnes*, pp. 207–15.

CHAPTER IX

The Age to Come and the Parousia of Jesus

1. In Paul's view of "the Age to Come" ("the Time to Come") or the Days of the Messiah, which are distinguished by Judaism from "the World to Come" or the life after death,[1] there is a Jewish element, in which there is much of mysticism; but Paul added to the Jewish element a strange element, which changed the mysticism to delusion.

Jesus since the crucifixion has lived in a radiant body in heaven, and from there he will appear again. Hence the eyes of those believing in him are lifted toward heaven. Paul says:

For our citizenship is in heaven; whence also we wait for a Saviour, the Lord Jesus Christ: who shall fashion anew the body of our humiliation, that it may be conformed to the body of his glory.[2]

Jesus will also see to it that those believing in him are preserved until the Day of Judgment and then go forth vindicated from the judgment:

[Ye shall be] waiting for the revelation of our Lord Jesus Christ; who shall also confirm you unto the end,[3] that ye be unreprovable in the day of our Lord Jesus Christ.[4]

Paul believes with complete confidence that Jesus will appear in the world "even speedily and at a near time"—still within

---

[1] See for details Klausner, *Ha-Ra'yon*, pp. 261–8; idem, *Die messianischen Vorstellungen*, SS. 17–26.

[2] Philipp. 3:20, 21.

[3] "The end of the days" (Dan. 12:13), or "the Messianic end" (Megillah 3a).

[4] I Cor. 1:7, 8.

Paul's lifetime.[5] It is possible that there is a connexion between this "Messianic" belief, as it was transferred from a Jewish to a Christian setting, and the Aramaic *Kaddish*, which contains these typical words: "May He establish His Kingdom"—the Kingdom of Heaven in the Days of the Messiah—"*during your life* and *during your days*, and during the life of all the house of Israel, *even speedily and at a near time*." [6] At any rate, Paul says plainly that "the time is shortened," [7] "for the fashion [shape] of this world passeth away." [8] With great solemnity, Paul says:

Behold, I tell you a mystery: We shall not all sleep [die],[9] but we shall all be changed, in a moment, in the twinkling of an eye, at the last trump: for the trumpet shall sound, and the dead shall be raised incorruptible, and we shall be changed.[10]

Here we have "the trumpet of Messiah" of the Talmud, where the expression refers not to a trumpet blown by the Messiah himself but to a trumpet heralding the *Days* of the Messiah; likewise "the birth pangs of Messiah" means not sufferings of the Messiah himself, but the sufferings in the *Days* of the Messiah.[11] According to the prayer *Shemoneh 'Esreh*,[12] God himself will "sound the great horn for *our freedom*"; this blast is to announce the ingathering of the exiles and not specifically the resurrection of the dead.[13] But Judaism also knows the connexion of the trumpet blast, "the last trumpet" —since there is also a trumpet which is not the last [14]—with

[5] Although from the Epistle to the Philippians (1:20–3) it appears that Paul is also prepared to die and to be joined with Christ after death.

[6] See Klausner, *Historia*, IV, 99, n. 1.

[7] I Cor. 7:29. [8] I Cor. 7:31. [9] See Ps. 13:4.

[10] I Cor. 15:51, 52. [11] See Klausner, *Ha-Ra'yon*, p. 304.

[12] The prayer *Shemoneh 'Esreh* in the Babylonian and Palestinian recensions, Benediction X.

[13] See Megillah 17b and 18a; see also M. Friedmann, *Seder Eliyahu Rabbah* (Vienna 5662), Introduction, pp. 140–1.

[14] See P. Volz, *Die Eschatologie der jüdischen Gemeinde im neutestamentlichen Zeitalter* (2. Aufl. der *Jüdischen Eschatologie von Daniel bis Akiba*, Tübingen 1934), SS. 162–3.

the resurrection of the dead.[15] And although this idea of the blowing of the trumpet for the resurrection of the dead is found principally in Hebrew literature later than the period of Paul, it is not to be thought that it was borrowed from Christianity. Undoubtedly, such an idea already existed in the time of Paul, and he borrowed it from his environment; it is only by chance that it is not mentioned in the earlier Hebrew literature. If the blowing of the trumpet for the liberation of the exiles were not mentioned in the *Shemoneh 'Esreh*, we should be prone to think this idea later also.

Thus Paul believed that he and all those believing in Jesus would not die, but would be transformed at the blowing of "the last trumpet." But what actually happened was otherwise. Many of the faithful began to die—yet the Messiah still did not come; "the Coming" (Parousia) was delayed. So when the members of the Christian congregation in Thessalonica were perturbed, and even began to despair, Paul comforted them with these puzzling words:

For this we say unto you by the word of the Lord [Jesus or God?], that we that are alive, that are left unto the coming of the Lord, shall in no wise precede them that are fallen asleep.[16] For the Lord himself shall descend from heaven, with a shout, with the voice of the archangel, and with the trump of God: and the dead in Christ shall rise first; then we that are alive, that are left, shall together with them be caught up in the clouds, to meet the Lord in the air: and so shall we ever be with the Lord.[17]

Here we have "the clouds of heaven" of the book of Daniel, in which the "son of man" was interpreted as the Messiah even

---

[15] *Othiyoth de-R. Akiba* ("The Alphabet of R. Akiba"), Letter Teth (*Midrash Othiyoth de-Rabbi Akiba ha-Shalem*, ed. S. A. Wertheimer (Jerusalem 5674), pp. 31, 32.

[16] *I.e.*, we shall not die, but shall go out to meet and greet those arising from the dead.

[17] I Thess. 4:13–8. See for particulars M. Dibelius in his commentary on these verses, *Handbuch zum Neuen Testament*, 11² (Tübingen 1925), SS. 20–4.

in ancient times (actually the expression refers to Israel); the Messiah, according to this interpretation, would come "with the clouds of heaven" to "the Ancient of Days," who would give the Messiah "dominion, and glory, and a kingdom, that all the peoples, nations, and tongues should serve him." [18] But it was impossible to know exactly the time when "the Lord" (Jesus) would "descend from heaven," since "the day of the Lord [Jesus or God?] so cometh as a thief in the night," [19] that is to say, it would come very suddenly. The Talmud also says that the Messiah is one of those things that will come "when the mind is diverted"—i.e., unexpectedly.[20] Jesus will be revealed "from heaven with the angels of his power in flaming fire, rendering vengeance to them that know not God, and to them that obey not the gospel of our Lord Jesus"; and "in that day," on the Day of Judgment, will go forth the condemnation of all these to "eternal destruction." [21] This is a most severe and bitter punishment upon all who are not Christians. Here there is no measure of "Christian love" whatever.[22]

The first Christians awaited this "Parousia" of Jesus, and their watchword was *Marana Tha*, "Our Lord, come!" (and not *Maran Atha*, "Our Lord has come," as has been mistakenly believed).[23]

2. On the Day of Judgment, which Paul calls "the day of the Lord" (of course, to be interpreted as "the day of Jesus"

[18] Dan. 7:13, 14. And see above, p. 483.
[19] I Thess. 5:1–3; *cf*. Matt. 24:34–44.
[20] Sanhedrin 97a.   [21] II Thess. 1:7–10.
[22] Not valid is the defense of C. A. Anderson Scott (*op. cit.*, pp. 139-40), that the reference is not to actual extinction, but to exclusion from the privileges of the life in God. According to Scott, Paul would not have known how to answer the question whether the wicked would also arise from the dead. But the unmistakable words of Paul about "eternal destruction" prove that to this question Paul would have answered with an absolute negative.
[23] I Cor. 16:22; to this testifies also the Revelation (Apocalypse) of John 22:20. See Ed. Meyer, *Ursprung u. Anfänge*, III, 232, Anm. 1.

and not "the Day of Yahweh"),[24] "God shall judge the secrets of men, according to my [Paul's] gospel, by Jesus Christ."[25] Or, "the Lord" will come, "who will both bring to light the hidden things of darkness, and make manifest the counsels of the hearts; and then shall each man have his praise from God."[26] "God" and "Christ" are here often confused. For instance, at one time Paul says, ". . . we shall all stand before the judgment-seat of God," and "each one of us shall give account of himself to God";[27] yet at another time he says:

For we must all be made manifest before the judgment-seat of Christ: that each one may receive the things done in the body, according to what he hath done, whether it be good or bad.[28]

Yet in spite of the confusion, there is no contradiction here, since, according to Paul, God does everything through Christ —Christ "his Son," who sits "at the right hand of Power" (beside "the Ancient of Days")—and God himself, if the truth must be told, does not do anything at all. . . .

We have already seen that Jesus will render "vengeance to them that know not God, and to them that obey not the gospel of our Lord Jesus," and that their punishment will be "eternal destruction from the face of the Lord and from the glory of his might."[29] Paul is not far, therefore, from the prophetic-Israelitic view. He believes in the vengeance of God upon the wicked; but he adds to the wicked also those who do not obey the gospel of Jesus; upon them too Jesus will take vengeance for affronts to his "gospel."[30]

We have already seen also that the righteous, i.e., those

[24] I Cor. 1:8; 4:5; 5:5; II Cor. 1:14; Philipp. 1:6, 10; II Thess. 1:7–10; 2:2 (another reading, "day of Christ").

[25] Rom. 2:16.   [26] I Cor. 4:5.   [27] Rom. 14:10, 12.

[28] II Cor. 5:10.   [29] II Thess. 1:7–9.

[30] Without good reason, Weinel decides (Biblische Theologie des Neuen Testaments, S. 254) that these hard words were said by Paul because of the "criticism of opponents" (Einrede der Gegner).

believing in God and Jesus, shall not taste death before they shall "be caught up in the clouds, to meet the Lord in the air; and so shall we ever be with the Lord." [31] Not only so, "but we shall all be changed, in a moment, in the twinkling of an eye"; [32] Jesus "shall fashion anew the body of our humiliation, that it may be conformed to the body of his glory." [33] We have already seen that Jesus has a "body," but a "spiritual," "heavenly" body,[34] that is to say, a body of superb brightness, somewhat like the angels, who also have bodies, since they are not deities, although their bodies are of a very fine substance resembling that described by R. Solomon ben Gabirol and taken over from him by the Scholastics of the Middle Ages.[35]

Paul knows the question, How shall the dead arise, and what sort of bodies will they have when they arise? To this question he gives an interesting answer:—The seed dies in the ground and from it grows an ear of grain unlike the seed that was sown. For the sower does not sow what grows up, but he sows "a bare grain, it may chance of wheat, or of some other kind," and to the dead grain in the darkness of the ground "God giveth . . . a body even as it pleased him"— of corn or fruit, different from the grain that was sown, as was said—"and to each seed a body of its own." [36] At any rate, the believers "shall not be found naked," since they shall be clothed in their "habitation which is from heaven," and "what is mortal" shall be swallowed up by eternal life.[37] For every species in nature has a special body, so man has a body different from the bodies of the beasts, the birds, and the fishes; there are earthly bodies and heavenly bodies; there is

[31] I Thess. 4:17, 18. See above, p. 539.
[32] I Cor. 15:51, 52. And see above, p. 538.
[33] Philipp. 3:20, 21. See above, p. 537 and below, p. 543.
[34] I Cor. 15:44-9. See above, pp. 494-5.
[35] See Klausner, *Philosophim*, I, 148-9, 165-6.
[36] I Cor. 15:35-8.   [37] II Cor. 5:2-4.

also a "natural" body (body belonging to the soul, "psychic" body) and a "spiritual" ("pneumatic") body—thus "it is sown a natural body; it is raised a spiritual body." [38] The first Adam was "of the earth, earthy"; but the last Adam—Jesus Christ—is spiritual and heavenly.[39] The righteous who believe in Jesus shall also receive "the image of the heavenly"; [40] or, as I have already mentioned twice, they shall have their "body of . . . humiliation" changed to conform to the glorious body of Jesus.[41] That the dead should arise as they were in life, *i.e.*, in their earthly bodies of flesh—this is an impossible thing in the eyes of Paul. He insists:

Now this I say, brethren, that flesh and blood cannot inherit the kingdom of God; neither doth corruption inherit incorruption.[42]

". . . for the kingdom of God is not eating and drinking, but righteousness and peace and joy in the Holy Spirit." [43]

According to the Talmud, which made the resurrection of the dead a fundamental of Judaism, not only he who denies this doctrine, but even "he that says that there is no resurrection of the dead prescribed in the Law" has "no share in the world to come." [44] Sometimes the Talmudic Haggadoth (popular stories) describe "the Age to Come" (which includes both the Days of the Messiah and life after death), "the World to Come" (which is to be distinguished from the Days of the Messiah, as I have explained in another place),[45] and the resurrection of the dead in material and corporeal terms. For example, there is the opinion that the Holy One, blessed be He, raises the dead from the grave "with their blemishes." [46]

[38] I Cor. 15:39–46.   [39] I Cor. 15:47, 48.   [40] I Cor. 15:49.
[41] Philipp. 3:20, 21. See above, pp. 494–5, 542.   [42] I Cor. 15:50.
[43] Rom. 14:17. And see the answer of Jesus to the Sadducees, Mark 12:25.
[44] Mish., San. X 1.
[45] See Klausner, *Ha-Ra'yon*, pp. 261–8.
[46] Eccl. Rabbah I 4 on the text *One generation passeth away, and another generation cometh*. See also Gen. Rabbah XIV 5 (ed. Th. Albeck, pp. 128–9), and Lev. Rabbah XIV 4 (in Lev. Rabbah XIV we have "the Time to Come" instead of "the World to Come").

But it must always be remembered, as I have pointed out a number of times, that words spoken of "the Age to Come" and "the World to Come" sometimes refer to *the Days of the Messiah*, in which the nature of the world and the nature of men suffer no radical change. It is to be noted that the example of the "bare [naked] . . . grain of wheat" is found also in the Talmud, except that there it serves in a more materialistic description: R. Meir (a Tanna of the second century c.e.) said, ". . . if a grain of wheat, which is buried naked, sprouteth forth in many robes, how much more so the righteous, who are buried in their raiment." [47] Here we have both the wheat and the sowing of the "naked" grain, followed by a springing forth "in many robes" (as Paul says, ". . . we shall not be found naked," but shall be "clothed with our habitation which is from heaven"). Attention must also be called to the words of the early Amora, R. Johanan, who followed close upon the period of the Tannaim:

All of the prophets prophesied exclusively of the Days of the Messiah; but what will be in the World to Come, "No eye hath seen, O God, but Thee." [48]

This same verse, but with certain changes, [49] was also used by Paul when he came to discuss what God had determined upon for believers. [50] And there is a Talmudic Baraitha on the World to Come, a Baraitha which is repeated many times in Talmud and Midrash, being, apparently, from early times:

In the world to come there is neither eating nor drinking; no procreation of children or business transactions; no envy or hatred

[47] San. 90b.
[48] Berakoth 34b; Isa. 64:3/4.
[49] On the changes, see in detail A. F. Puuko, *Paulus und das Judentum* (Helsingfors, 1928), SS. 45–7; E. Böhl, *Die alttestamentliche Citate im Neuen Testament* (Wien 1878), SS. 211–3.
[50] I Cor. 2:7–9.

or rivalry; but the righteous sit enthroned, their crowns on their heads, and enjoy the lustre of the Shekhinah.[51]

This picture is much like Paul's words about the Kingdom of Heaven, quoted above from Romans 14:17, except that here the Messiah takes no special place.

3. There have been great figures in Judaism, according to whose opinion everything would be done by God alone, without a Messiah.[52] But for the most part, Judaism, like Paul, cannot imagine the great changes which are to take place in the Jewish world, and the world of the rest of humanity, without a Messiah. Yet, according to Biblical and Talmudic Judaism, the Messiah only frees Israel from political bondage, makes proselytes of the Gentiles, and judges the nations in righteousness and equity; the rest is done by God alone. And there will be only *one appearance* of the Messiah; after he has come once—and in this world—everything will again be in the hands of God. Not so Paul and the Christianity which he fashioned. According to them, the Messiah who appeared in the world and was crucified, rose from the dead, is sitting in heaven with a radiant spiritual body, and expects to appear on earth at a given time,[53] at which time everything will be done by him. To be sure, it is to be done on behalf of God, but not by God himself, since in Pauline Christianity God retains almost no function at all, as has been said. The Parousia, the great "coming," must take place "even speedily and at a near time," before Paul and the believers who are alive in Paul's time die.

[51] Ber. 17a; Kallah Rabbathi II; Aboth de-Rabbi Nathan, Recension A, ch. I (ed. Schechter, folio 3, end). See for details on this Klausner, *Ha-Ra'yon*, pp. 263-4; *idem, Die messianischen Vorstellungen*, SS. 20-2.

[52] On redemption without a redeemer, see Klausner, *Ha-Ra'yon*, p. 8; J. Drummond, *The Jewish Messiah* (London 1877), pp. 226-7.

[53] The term "Parousia" does not mean essentially the *Second* Coming, but the *great* "appearance" "at the right hand of Power"; for the first time he came, Jesus did not "appear" in a supernatural way.

But when the hope—that "this generation shall not pass away until the Messiah come" and that "he will not allow his saints to see corruption" or "taste death"—was disappointed, there came to take the place of the immediate expectation a more remote anticipation, the belief in the thousand-year period (millennium) or *chiliasm*. The reasoning behind this was that the Parousia would bring with it "the Day of Yahweh" or "the day of the Lord" [Jesus]—"and the day of the Holy One, blessed be He, is one of a thousand years, as it is said, 'For a thousand years in Thy sight are but as yesterday, when it is past.' " [54] And when the first millennium of the Christian Era came to a close, and this hope was also disappointed, Christians continued to expect the coming of Jesus as soon as the people of Israel should be "saved," that is to say, should accept the gospel of Jesus and disappear from the world both as a nation and as a religion. Hence the stubborn opposition of orthodox Christianity to the revival of Israel in its own land; for the realization of Zionism, strengthening Jewry as a nation possessing its own cultural-religious life serves to frustrate the faith in the "Parousia." Hence also the hope of the Christianity that is more friendly to the Jews, particularly Anglican Christianity, that the return of the dispersed Jews to Palestine, the realization of the Jewish Messianic promise, of which all the prophets, accepted also by the Christians, prophesied—that this movement will lead the Jews to the acceptance of "Christian truth"; and that when all the Jews, gathered in their own land, believe in Jesus, then will the "coming" of Jesus be possible. It is still difficult to decide which is more dangerous to Judaism—the stubborn opposition to the restoration of Israel or the aspiration to slay Israel with a deadly kiss. . . .

But the people Israel is an eternal people, an everlasting people, which can neither die nor be transformed. Therefore

[54] Lev. Rabbah XIX beginning; Ps. 90:4.

it refused to modify or change the politico-spiritual, national-universal, earthly-heavenly Jewish Messianic idea which Paul, no doubt unconsciously, attempted to take over by introducing into it elements foreign to Judaism and close in spirit to the pagan peoples of his time.

CHAPTER X

The Ethical Teaching of Paul

[See on this: M. S. Enslin, *The Ethics of Paul*, New York and London 1930 (bibliography in the Introduction, pp. xv-xvii); Mary E. Andrews, *The Ethical Teaching of Paul*, Chapel Hill 1934; C. A. Anderson Scott, *Saint Paul*, Cambridge 1936, pp. 127–36; K. Weidinger, *Die Haustafeln*, Leipzig 1928; P. Feine, *Der Apostel Paulus*, SS. 319–31; H. Weinel, *Paulus*, 2. Aufl. Tübingen 1915, SS. 252–63; *idem, Biblische Theologie des Neuen Testaments*, 4. Aufl. 1928, SS. 290–304.]

1. Paul's ethical and social teachings contain the same contradiction which was necessarily present also in Jesus' ethical teaching and social views. For both Jesus and Paul expected the speedy establishment of the Kingdom of Heaven on earth through the mediation of the Messiah. Jesus, however, thought up to the moment of his crucifixion that he was the Messiah who would establish this Kingdom of Heaven, while Paul thought that Jesus was the Messiah, who was crucified, rose from the dead, was sitting on the right hand of God, and would *soon* reappear in the world to establish the Kingdom of Heaven. Hence the ethics of both of them could not have been other than an "interim ethics" (*Interims-Ethik*), that is to say a morality which is not fixed and permanent for all time, but is intended for a temporary and transient period—until the Kingdom of Heaven is revealed or until Jesus reappears. Yet for Jesus at least, morality is indispensable, since according to him without repentance there is no salvation ("Repent ye, for the Kingdom of Heaven is at hand!"); and repentance consists in forsaking evil deeds and doing good deeds.[1] Paul, however, does not make repentance a condition for salvation. Actually, for Paul salvation has already come; it came at the

[1] See Klausner, *Yeshu*, pp. 453–6 [Eng. ed., pp. 403–7].

moment when the sinless Jesus redeemed with his blood all sinners. When Paul speaks of the abolition of sin, he speaks also of the abolition of the Torah: every believer in Jesus has died to sin just as he has died to the Law; he was crucified with Christ and he arose to life with Christ.[2] Thus, what need has Paul for a special and fixed ethical teaching, especially a system of social ethics?[3]

Nevertheless, there is not an Epistle of Paul's which does not contain a section devoted to ethics—and for the most part, even to social ethics. This is understandable; those who remained to await the Second Coming of Christ, the Parousia, must live properly; otherwise, how could the new churches and the believers constituting them properly meet the Messiah? And how could the new Church attract believers if it could not show an example of morality and uprightness both in its individual members and in itself as an organization?——

The doctrine of the abolition of the Torah which Paul was forced to preach in order to win *many Gentiles* to faith in the Jewish Messiah and in order to prevent the new religion from being confined to the small circle of Nazarene Jews of the type of James the brother of Jesus—this doctrine carried with it the danger that the new believers from among the Gentiles would, along with their nullification of the ceremonial laws, also nullify the ethical laws. Indeed, "if any man . . . in Christ . . . is a new creature" and "the old things are passed away; behold. they are become new"[4]—then there is no longer any significance in what was forbidden or permitted in the "old creation" even on the ethical side. The "old" standards have been abolished, and what was forbidden in the old order is not necessarily forbidden at all in the new order.—There is good reason to believe that even during the

[2] See above, p. 491.
[3] Thus should be set at rest the perplexity of Enslin (*op. cit.*, Intro., p. xi) over the relative paucity of books devoted *specifically* to the ethics of Paul.
[4] II Cor. 5:17.

lifetime of Paul such ideas as these were disseminated among the Christian congregations, particularly the Gentile congregations. For *antinomians*, those opposing both the ceremonial and the ethical laws, existed in Judaism even before this, being known by the epithets "sons of Belial," "fools," [5] and "the impious"; [6] their influence increased and they became more and more extreme particularly as a result of the preaching of abolition of the obligations of the Torah.

Apprehensions about these matters forced Paul to include in each of his Epistles a special section addressed to questions of morality, or to rebuke for definite infractions. He felt that danger to morality was to be expected from his teaching, and that he was more or less responsible for the new views about the setting aside of even the *ethical* laws which were beginning to find lodgment in the Gentile Christian churches founded by him. He had reference, of course, only to an individual and social "interim ethics"; for we have seen [7] that he was thoroughly convinced that before long "the fashion of this world passeth away," and that perhaps even he would not taste death but have the privilege of greeting the Messiah so shortly to appear. [8]

I have already pointed out a number of times that there was in Paul a dualism amounting to polarity. On the one hand, he was a dreamer and ecstatic, seeing visions, "speaking with tongues," given to mysticism; but, on the other hand, he was a man of action and a master of logic, an excellent leader and a talented agitator, a wonderful administrator and diplomat who knew "the time for everything" [Eccl. 3:1]. [9] Naturally it was impossible for a man like this to live only for the dream of the Parousia. The *practical* man in him was aroused—one might almost say, the *practical Jew* in him

[5] "The *fool* hath said in his heart: 'There is no God'" (Ps. 14:1).
[6] See Klausner, *Philosophim*, I, 76; also above, pp. 248–9.
[7] See above, pp. 537–40.
[8] I Cor. 7:31; I Thess. 4:15.   [9] See above, pp. 422–32.

(since there has been almost no really great Jew who concerned himself wholly with the world to come, without caring at all for the life of this world). And as a practical man and a practical Jew, Paul fully realized that the new churches would have no chance of survival, no public esteem, and no power of attraction if there did not exist in them an orderly moral life—even if the time before the end was short. The community would not endure them, the state would not endure them, if they did not conduct themselves lawfully and virtuously, and if they did not conform to the established usages of the existing social and political order. Hence is explained the presence of ethical and social teaching in all the authentic Epistles of Paul.

2. The ethical teaching of Paul, taking into consideration the individual and the community (apart from the state and its institutions), is founded almost entirely on the morality of Judaism—to such a degree that there is little or no intrusion upon this on the part of the characteristically Pauline mysticism. Strange as it may seem, the ethical teaching of Paul is less different from that of Pharisaic Judaism than is the teaching of Jesus. Perhaps this is because Jesus actually felt himself organically connected with the Messianic Age, while as for Paul—he merely awaited the era that would arrive with the second coming of Jesus. It is a remarkable fact that only rarely did Paul depend in his ethical teaching on Jesus. Even the "Golden Rule" of "Love thy neighbor as thyself" was not mentioned by Paul as coming from Jesus, although Paul, like Hillel the Elder before Jesus and like Jesus before Paul, saw in it "the whole Law," the epitome of all human morality, and repeated it twice in his Epistles.[10] Perhaps, as a disciple of Rabban Gamaliel, Paul knew that this "rule" belonged to Hillel, Gamaliel's grandfather (or father, if the first "Simeon"

[10] Rom. 13:8–10; Gal. 5:13, 14.

in the expression "Hillel and *Simeon*, Gamaliel and Simeon" is only an error for "Hillel and *Shammai*").[11]

But in the ethical teaching of Paul there are also non-Jewish influences from the ethics of the Stoa, and even from the ethics of the Oriental mystery cults.[12] For instance, in the "catalogue" of good and evil qualities which we find in a number of Paul's Epistles, there is a marked similarity to the *Haustafeln* [lists of household virtues and duties] of Hellenistic Judaism and Hellenistic philosophy.[13]

First of all, then, what, according to Paul, are *the bad and unethical things?*

The bad and unethical things are, first of all, those which characterize the idolatrous pagans of that time: fornication and adultery, exchange of wives, sodomy, and "women committing lewdness with each other" ("Lesbian love"). Some of these vices had already been attacked by Plato,[14] and the Sibylline Oracles had also warned against some of them.[15] To these pagan abominations, against which the soul of a Pharisaic Jew naturally revolted, Paul dedicates the introduction to the Epistle to the Romans. In this introduction he connects these vices with idolatrous paganism in general, and then ties up with this paganism and these vices all other kinds of evil practices, such as "wickedness, covetousness, maliciousness; . . . envy, murder, strife, deceit, malignity"; gossip, slander, godlessness, insolence, haughtiness, boastfulness, trickery, disobedience to parents, ignorance, treachery, bearing of grudges, cruelty, hate, and lack of mercy.[16]

In almost every list of evils (what the Germans call a *Las-*

[11] See Klausner, *Historia*, III, 102, 104, 251 [also Shabb. 15a, end].

[12] See Enslin, *op. cit.*, pp. 17–59; 90–129 (*in general*, Enslin inclines more toward Judaistic influences).

[13] See K. Weidinger, *Die Haustafeln*, SS. 23–62.

[14] See my introduction to Plato's *Symposium* (*Philosophim*, I, 50–63); also the translation of Plato, edited by J. Klausner (Jerusalem 5689), I, 3–16.

[15] See above, pp. 142, 159.   [16] Rom. 1:18–31.

terkatalog) presented by Paul, there is to be found a warning against sexual immorality and riotousness.[17] Matters reached such a point that when there was found in Corinth a "brother" supposed to be a believer in Jesus, yet who had married his father's wife (his stepmother), Paul agreed "to deliver such a one unto Satan for the destruction of the flesh, that the spirit may be saved in the day of the Lord Jesus," [18] that is to say, Paul agreed to the death sentence.[19] Other evils discussed by Paul are about the same as those just quoted from the first chapter of Romans, with certain additions: "revelling and drunkenness . . . chambering and wantonness." [20] Paul reprimands in another place the fornicators and adulterers, also the catamites and sodomites among the "brethren" along with the covetous, the idolaters, the revilers, the gluttons, the drunkards, and the extortioners.[21] And he warns that "the body is not for fornication, but for the Lord" (Christ); ". . . shall I then take away the members of Christ, and make them members of a harlot? God forbid!" For the body of a believer "is a temple of the Holy Spirit which is in you, which ye have from God; and ye are not your own, for ye were bought with a price," that is to say, with the price of the body of Jesus, who was crucified for you; "glorify God therefore in your body." [22] This is one of the finest passages in the ethical teaching of Paul. It resembles what is told of Hillel the Elder in the Midrash:—Whenever he would go to the bathhouse to bathe he would say that he was going "to perform a religious

[17] See Rom. 13:13; I Cor. 5:1–5; 6:13–20; II Cor. 12:21; Eph. 5:18, *etc.*
[18] I Cor. 5:1–5.
[19] According to H. Lietzmann, Kommentar zu "An die Korinther I–II" (*Handbuch zum Neuen Testament*, 9), 3. Aufl., S. 23, the reference here is to the curse of the congregation, which would bring as a consequence death at the hands of heaven. But I am not convinced. Paul in his zeal would have been prepared to go farther than this. In the last analysis, we have here to do with a man of ancient times, who is not to be measured by the standards of modern morality.
[20] Rom. 13:13.   [21] I Cor. 5:9–11; 6:9, 10.
[22] I Cor. 6:13–20.

duty," since man was created "in the image of God" and hence his body is like "the statues of kings" entrusted to keepers to guard and keep clean.[23]

When Paul, addressing a *second* letter to the Corinthians, expresses the fear that if he visits them again he will find among them "strife, jealousy, wraths, factions, backbitings, whisperings, swellings [pride], and tumults," he adds again that he fears that he will have to "mourn for many . . . that have repented not of the uncleanness and fornication and lasciviousness which they committed." [24] To the Christian church in Ephesus (or Laodicea) he writes:

But fornication, and all uncleanness, or covetousness, let it not even be named among you, as becometh saints; nor filthiness, nor foolish talking, or jesting, which are not befitting: but rather giving of thanks. For this ye know of a surety, that no fornicator, nor unclean person, nor covetous man, who is an idolater,[25] hath any inheritance in the kingdom of Christ and God.[26]

In a similar vein he writes also in the Epistle to the Colossians, where he expressly equates covetousness with idolatry and numbers among the vices also anger, wrath, and all evil desire.[27] In the First Epistle to the Thessalonians he attributes "the passion of lust" to "the Gentiles who know not God"; and along with the injunction to refrain from fornication and uncleanness comes the demand "that no man transgress, and wrong his brother in the matter, because the Lord [28] is an avenger in all these things." [29]

These are the vices. There is not much new in them. Oppo-

---

[23] Lev. Rabbah XXXIV 3. See also Klausner, *Historia*, III, 113.

[24] II Cor. 12:20, 21.

[25] Adultery, uncleanness, and covetousness are as idols in the eyes of Paul, and whoever devotes himself to them makes himself the same as an idolater.

[26] Eph. 5:3-5.   [27] Col. 3:5-9.

[28] Here "the Lord" is of course God and not Christ.

[29] I Thess. 4:3-6.

sition to all these things Paul found in Judaism, which advocates purity and holiness, and warns against uncleanness and licentiousness and all the rest of the evil and disgusting practices which Paul detailed in his Epistles, and which were found much more among the Gentile Christians than they were among the Jewish Nazarenes.[30]

3. What are the *virtues* according to Paul's view?

For the most part they are the virtues of Pharisaic Judaism. According to the well-known Talmudic expression, a righteous man must be among "those who are insulted but do not insult, who hear themselves reviled without answering"; [31] so says Paul, "Why not rather take wrong, why not rather be defrauded?" [32] It is forbidden to repay evil instead of good, and one must "abstain from all appearance of evil" (εἶδος πονηροῦ).[33] The Talmud and Midrash go even farther than this; they not only demand that one abstain from the "appearance of evil," but they decree even more pointedly: "Keep aloof from hideousness and whatever resembles it"; [34] or in another version, "Keep aloof from everything hideous and from whatever seems hideous." [35]

In the moral duties which Paul details in the Epistle to the Romans,[36] there are to be distinguished, on the one hand, those standards which are common to every ethical religion, as when it is said: "Abhor that which is evil, cleave to that which is good"; "in love of the brethren be tenderly affectioned one to another, in honor preferring one another . . . pursuing hos-

---

[30] On the moral conditions in the Pauline churches see S. J. Case, *The Social Origins of Christianity* (Chicago 1923), pp. 117–60.

[31] Shabb. 88b; Gittin 36b.

[32] I Cor. 6:7.   [33] I Thess. 5:14–22.

[34] Hullin 44b; Aboth de-Rabbi Nathan, Recension B, ch. II beginning, ed. Schechter, p. 8.

[35] Numbers Rabbah XIII; Aboth de-R. Nathan, Rec. A, ch. II, ed. Schechter 5b.

[36] Rom. 12:9–21.

pitality," and the like. On the other hand, there are the qualities of ethical opportunism: "Rejoice with them that rejoice; weep with them that weep"—something which is included in the saying of Hillel the Elder, "Keep not aloof from the congregation." [37] To the same Hillel the Elder is attributed also the saying so similar to one in the Gospels: "Do not appear laughing, do not appear weeping" [for your own concerns].[38] Of course, it is possible to see in this saying of Hillel another meaning, namely, Do not pretend to be something you are not.[39] But such a meaning cannot be read into the words of Paul, for he indicates clearly and unmistakably that he sought to "please all men in all things." [40]

A saying of Paul recalls the teaching of Jesus (although he does not attribute it to Jesus): "Bless them that persecute you; bless, and curse not." [41] And indeed, Paul says of himself and the rest of the apostles: ". . . being reviled, we bless." [42] But immediately afterwards, in the passage from Romans, we find the ethical viewpoint of the Old Testament and not that of Jesus:

Avenge not yourselves, beloved, but give place unto wrath; [43] for it is written, "Vengeance belongeth unto me; I will recompense," [44] saith the Lord. But "if thine enemy hunger, feed him; if he thirst, give him to drink; for in so doing thou shalt heap

[37] Mish., Aboth II 5.

[38] Tosephta, Ber. II 21 end. If Paul was a pupil of Rabban Gamaliel, as appears almost certain in my eyes, it would have been natural that he should have learned from the son (or grandson) of Hillel any number of Hillel's ethical maxims.

[39] See Klausner, *Historia*, III, 109.

[40] I Cor. 10:33.   [41] Rom. 12:14.   [42] I Cor. 4:12.

[43] *I.e.*, to the wrath of God. On the wrath of God as conceived by Paul in general, see G. Bornkamm, "Die Offenbarung des Zornes Gottes," ZNW, XXXIV (1935), 239–62.

[44] In the LXX the reading is, "In the day of vengeance, I will recompense," in place of "Vengeance is Mine, and recompense" (Deut. 32:35). Incidentally, Tolstoy, the great advocate of "nonresistance to evil," made this Old Testament saying as given by Paul the motto of his great novel *Anna Karenina*.

coals of fire upon his head." [45] Be not overcome of evil, but overcome evil with good.[46]

On the one hand, we have here "Thou shalt not take vengeance, nor bear any grudge," as found in the Pentateuch—a command that comes in the same verse that has in the second half "Thou shalt love thy neighbor as thyself." [47] But on the other hand, in spite of the injunction to "bless them that persecute you," Paul leaves a place for the wrath and vengeance of God. And in the famous verse from Proverbs,

> If thine enemy be hungry, give him bread to eat,
> And if he be thirsty, give him water to drink,

even Paul does not find it possible to leave out the conclusion of the verse,

For thou wilt heap coals of fire upon his head,—a conclusion which weakens so much the purely ethical drift of the first part of the verse. . . .

Among the good qualities which Paul recounts, he lays great emphasis on *patience* and the *endurance of ill-treatment with a spirit of love toward the wrongdoers* ["longsuffering"]. Of course, Paul himself and the rest of the apostles, and even all the "brethren," as long as they were a small minority among either Jews or Gentiles, actually showed great patience under persecutions and oppressions, although Paul was inclined to speak harshly against his opponents, and even to revile them and curse them.[48] Thus we find in his Epistles exhortations to endure injustices charitably—injustices inflicted by Jews and Romans, and even by Nazarene brethren opposed to the Gentile Christianity which Paul had established.[49] This is a virtue which was *indispensable* to the first Christians because of their lowly status. But as soon as the Christians attained worldly

[45] Prov. 25:21, 22. These verses are quoted by Paul in the exact wording of the LXX.
[46] Rom. 12:19-21.   [47] Lev. 19:18.   [48] See above, pp. 426-7.
[49] I Cor. 4:11-3; II Cor. 6:4; 11:23-8; Eph. 4:2, and elsewhere.

power, this virtue ceased to be Christian, and became—a Jewish "virtue"!

4. I have already mentioned above that Paul quotes twice the Pentateuchal saying "Thou shalt love thy neighbor as thyself" as a rule that summarizes the whole Law; I also mentioned that Paul did not attribute this idea to Jesus, and said that perhaps as a disciple of Hillel the Elder Paul knew that this was Hillel's idea.[50] But Paul goes further: he takes this "Love thy neighbor as thyself," the "Love the Lord thy God" which is found twice in the Pentateuch,[51] and the "Love the Lord your God" which occurs with slight changes ten times in the Old Testament,[52] and, having translated the word *ahavah* ("love") in accordance with the Septuagint as *agapē*, he makes *love* a great ethical principle—*the supreme ethical principle.*

Not correct is the view, which I among others formerly accepted,[53] that this *agapē* is neither the love of God nor the love of one's neighbor as found in the Pentateuch, but is the mystical love of the Greek religious associations (θίασοι). To be sure, the word *agapē* is indeed found outside the Septuagint, and outside the translations of Aquila and Theodotion, the Letter of Aristeas, and the works of Philo, all of which took it from the Septuagint. It is also found in a number of non-Christian inscriptions; even the Egyptian Isis has the appellation *agapē* or *agapē theōn* ["love of the gods," perhaps "beloved among the gods"].[54] Nevertheless, there is no essential difference between ἀγάπη (*agapē*), which Paul took from the Septuagint, and the ordinary Greek ἔρως (*erōs*), or even between *agapē* and *philia* (φιλία).[55]

[50] See above, p. 556, n. 38.   [51] Deut. 6:5 and 11:1.
[52] Deut. 10:12; 11:13, 22; 19:9; 30:6, 16, 20; Josh. 22:5; 23:11; Isa. 56:6.
[53] Klausner, *Historia*, IV, 102.
[54] See for details Lietzmann, Kommentar zu I Korinther 13:13 (3. Aufl., S. 68).
[55] Against A. Deissmann, *Licht vom Osten*, S. 59; Anm. 3, see the cogent words of Ed. Meyer, *Ursprung u. Anfänge*, II, 437, Anm. 5; III, 362-3.

This "love" is a thoroughly Jewish idea, which Paul, like Jesus, made use of along with all other Jewish ethical ideas. Both men emphasized and enlarged upon these ideas—Paul perhaps added something from the foreign influence which he absorbed from his pagan environment—and thus they carried them to such extremes that they almost ceased to be Jewish ideas. Experts in optics know that light can be increased so *excessively* that it turns into darkness. A small dose of medicine is lifegiving, but too large a dose of the same medicine is a deadly poison. Exaggerated resoluteness is impudence and excessive humility is servility.[56] Thus also the Pauline concept of love: Paul spoke so much of Christian love, which in truth is only Jewish love with a mystical coloring,[57] that he forgot to emphasize *righteousness*, apart from which love may be a strong support for *individual life*, but not for *social and national life*. Thus love operates as a characteristic of the God of the individual, but not of the God of the *nation* or the God of *history*.[58]

Beautiful and sublime is the poem which Paul composed to love in the thirteenth chapter of I Corinthians. Christians rightly call it Love's Song of Songs (or the Hymn to Love) and humanity will never forget it. In it Paul reaches the highest pinnacle of preacher and poet alike. It is very possible that there is Greek influence in this poem;[59] but its basis is Scriptural and Jewish, a basis which was intensified in the passionate soul of Paul the Jew until it reached the point of "sublimation" and was exalted beyond any other ethical con-

---

[56] See on this Klausner, *Yeshu*, pp. 423-4 [Eng. ed., pp. 374-5].

[57] Lietzmann (*op. cit.*, S. 57) speaks of "a spiritual fluid which sinks deeply into us and becomes a constituent ingredient of the Christian personality."

[58] See Klausner, *Yeshu*, pp. 427-9 [Eng. ed., pp. 378-80].

[59] See in particular C. Clemen, *Religionsgeschichtliche Erklärung des Neuen Testaments*, 2. Aufl. (Giessen 1924), SS. 326-30. A. Friedrichsen, *Theol. Studien u. Kritiken* (1922), SS. 55 ff., has pointed to the rhetorical hymn to Eros of the Platonist, Maximus of Tyre. See E. von Dobschütz, *Der Apostel Paulus*, I, 56-7, Anm. 23.

cept. Yet in spite of all the mysticism in this lofty poem and in spite of all its ecstasy, its love is not the mystical love of the Greek religious "associations," but the truly Jewish love of God and one's neighbor. It is fitting, therefore, to conclude the discussion of Paul's ethical teaching with this wonderful poem in translation:

Though I speak with the tongues of men and of angels
    And have not love
I am become as clanging brass or a tinkling cymbal.
And though I have prophecy and understand all mysteries and all
   knowledge
    And have not love
I am nothing.
And though I bestow all my goods to feed the poor,
And though I give my body to be burned
    And have not love
It profits me nothing.

Love is long-suffering and kind,
Love envies not, love boasts not, is not arrogant,
Does not act rudely, is not self-seeking, is not ill-tempered, thinks
  no evil,
Rejoices not in wrongdoing but rejoices in the truth,[60]
Covers [pardons] [61] all things, believes all things, hopes all things,
  endures all things.

Love never fails;
But whether there be prophecies they shall fail,
Whether there be tongues [62] they shall cease;
Whether there be knowledge it shall vanish away.
For we know in part and we prophesy in part; [63]
But when that which is perfect is come [64]
Then that which is in part shall be done away.

    [60] Συγχαίρει τῇ ἀληθείᾳ.
    [61] "But love covereth all transgressions" (Prov. 10:12).
    [62] The speaking with tongues (glossolalia).
    [63] *I.e.*, our knowledge and our prophecies are fragmentary, defective, and incomplete.
    [64] At the time of the Parousia our knowledge and perceptions will become complete and perfect.

When I was a child
I spoke as a child, I understood as a child, I thought as a child;
But when I became a man
I put away childish things.
For now we see in a mirror darkly
But then face to face.
Now I know in part
But then shall I know even as also I am known.
And now abideth faith, hope, love, these three;
But the greatest of these is love.[65]

All this is splendid, combining a Jewish-Biblical content with a Greek-Stoic manner of expression. Of course, the wonderful "triad"—"faith, hope, love"—comes from a Greek source; or at any rate Paul here sets forth this religious triad in contrast to the Platonic-Stoic "tetrad"—wisdom, self-control, courage, and justice.[66] But *truth* and *righteousness* (or justice) are lacking in this triad. For if "prophecies . . . shall fail" and "knowledge . . . shall vanish away," there will be no place for righteousness and justice, for which prophecy strives, and no place for truth, for which knowledge strives.

The prophets and sages of Israel were not prophets of love, even though a strong love burned in their hearts for everything high and holy, for their own people and for all mankind. We call them "prophets of truth and justice"; for in the total history of men and nations truth and justice precede faith, hope, and love, whether we as "flesh and blood" and as individuals like it or not. . . .

[65] I Cor. 13:1–13. [The English translation and arrangement given here follow, with slight changes, those of E. F. Scott in *The Literature of the New Testament* (New York 1932), pp. 134–5; Scott's poetical arrangement is very similar to that of Klausner's Hebrew rendering. Tr.]

[66] See Reitzenstein, "Die Formel 'Glaube, Liebe, Hoffnung' bei Paulus," *Nachr. d. Gesellsch. d. Wissensch. zu Göttingen*, Phil.-hist. Klasse, 1916, SS. 189–208. Cf. Enslin, *op. cit.*, pp. 250–2.

CHAPTER XI

The Social Teaching of Paul

1. The Jewish Messianic idea was revolutionary. It had an aspect of *national liberation*—from political servitude and from dispersion in foreign lands; and another aspect of *liberation of all mankind*—of equality among men, the cessation of wars, fraternity of nations, and the acceptance of ethical monotheism by all humanity.

The Jewish Messianic idea gave rise in Judea to two kinds of revolutionaries, which Josephus[1] calls γόητες καὶ λῃστρικοί, *i.e.*, "imposters" and "assassins." There were "false Messiahs" and also "false prophets."[2] Both groups, according to the accusation of Titus, "never ceased from revolution."[3] And when affairs fell into disorder in the time of Nero, these restless people expected to win "the inheritance of the East";[4] for with one accord Josephus,[5] Tacitus,[6] and Suetonius[7] testify that the belief was widespread in Israel (according to Suetonius in the entire [Near] East) that from the [Near] East would come forth a ruler who would hold sway over the entire world. It was, of course, the idea of the Messianic King that was meant. The frequent rebellions of the false Messiahs were connected with this belief and with a two-fold aspiration—*political* and *social*. Naturally, the Romans opposed this

---

[1] See *Antiq.* XX viii 6; *Jewish War* II xiii 4 and 6.
[2] On these latter see *Jewish War* VI v 2.
[3] *Ibid.* VI vi 2.
[4] Preface to the *Jewish War*, sect. 2.
[5] *Jewish War* VI v 4.
[6] Tacitus, *Hist.* V 13.
[7] Suetonius, *Vespasianus*, ch. 4.

belief with all their might, since they saw in it a danger to their authority and to public order in the Empire; hence Josephus guards against speaking plainly about it, and mere hints about it are to be found in his works. Any Messiah was considered by the Romans a rebel—and rightly. The Romans did not investigate closely whether the Messiah in question was a rebel against political authority only, or along with this wished to change the order of nature and "set right the world in the pattern of the Kingdom of the Almighty." They simply persecuted every Messianic movement as a movement to rebellion.

Jesus of Nazareth was crucified as "The King of the Jews" —as a political rebel. If Christianity wished to survive, it had to remove from itself this "stigma." Above all, it had to do this within its own ranks, in order to save itself from disillusionment (for political servitude did not cease with Jesus nor did the "ingathering of the exiles" come to pass); but it also had to do it in the eyes of the outside world, in order that the new sect might not be persecuted by Jewish authority in Palestine and Roman authority everywhere.

Therefore, after the report of the miraculous resurrection of Jesus spread, Jesus suddenly ceased to be a Messiah to "restore the kingdom to Israel," [8] and began to be considered a *spiritual Messiah only*—the "Servant of the Lord," the suffering Messiah as pictured in Isaiah 53. In this way was removed the assumption of political rebellion from Jesus and his disciples.

There still remained the matter of arranging the relations between the believers in Jesus and the state. Naturally, this arranging had to be done in a spirit of thorough prudence, in order to remove from the weak young church the suspicion of revolution.

This task was accomplished by Paul in his Epistles.

[8] Acts 1:6.

2. In the days of Paul, the time of the great clash between loyalty to Christ and loyalty to Caesar had not yet arrived.[9] But Paul laid the groundwork for this clash by describing Jesus as "Lord" (*Kyrios* or *Dominus*), a title which had been bestowed at coronation upon the Ptolemaic and Seleucid kings and upon the Roman emperors from the time of Augustus Caesar on.[10] And since the Hebrew surrogate for God is *Adonai* ("the Lord"), Paul applied to Christ a title similar to that of the Jewish deity as well as titles similar to those of the Roman emperor and his sons (*divus, divi filius*).

But Paul had a pressing problem in connexion with his teaching about the state:

Sacrifices to local divinities, and afterwards to the Roman emperor, were offered in the Greek and Roman cities as "worship" in the sacral sense, being a part of the λειτουργία [11] (whence comes the word "liturgy" for the Christian worship service) which was incumbent upon all citizens. These sacrifices were a perpetual stumbling block to the Jews outside of Palestine; because the Jews did not participate in them on account of religious scruples, hatred of the Jews increased among the Gentiles.[12] Yet Paul had brought into Christianity great numbers of pagans who had been accustomed in their paganism to eating food sacrificed to idols. Hence arose the problem: What attitude should the Gentile Christians take toward these sacrifices?

Paul wavered between two opinions. On the one hand, a pagan divinity has no existence whatever, and hence it is useless to offer sacrifices to him. On the other hand, there is

---

[9] See on this W. Bousset, *Kyrios Christos*, SS. 77–101; A. Deissmann, *Licht vom Osten*, SS. 287–324; C. Clemen, *Religionsgeschichtliche Erklärung des Neuen Testaments*, SS. 29–31; E. Guimet, "Les Chrétiens et l'Empire Romain," *La Nouvelle Revue*, 1909, pp. 1–42.

[10] See above, pp. 108–12.

[11] See Deissmann, *op. cit.*, S. 86.

[12] See in detail on this A. Tscherikower, *Ha-Yehudim ve-ha-Yevanim ba-Tequphah ha-Hellenistit* (Tel-Aviv 5691), pp. 358–80.

no significance in what a man eats or does not eat: ". . . food will not commend us to God; neither, if we eat not, are we the worse; nor, if we eat, are we the better." Nevertheless, Paul comes to the conclusion that it is improper to eat food sacrificed to idols, lest a stumbling block be put in the path of the weak among the believers: "Wherefore, if meat causeth my brother to stumble, I will eat no flesh for evermore, that I cause not my brother to stumble." [13] Thus a more or less opportunistic argument for vegetarianism is derived from the evasion of the dietary laws.

We find a complete opportunism also with regard to *the state and its authority*.

> Let every soul be in subjection to the higher powers: for there is no power but of God; and the powers that be are ordained of God. Therefore he that resisteth the power, withstandeth the ordinance of God: and they that withstand shall receive to themselves judgment.[14]

The good have nothing to fear from the civil authorities ("powers that be"); only evildoers need fear these "powers." If a man is good, he will receive praise from the rulers. The government is the "minister" (servant) of God, and only if a man does evil will he have reason to fear it: ". . . it beareth not the sword in vain; for it is a minister of God, an avenger for wrath to him that doeth evil." [15] This is the view of Paul about the government of his time.

When one considers all the shameful deeds of oppression, the murders and extortions, of the Roman government in every place where the hand of its authority reached, and particularly in the provinces where Paul lived and traveled, one cannot escape a feeling of resentment and protest against this recital of praise for the tyranny of Caligula and Nero, or of Gessius Florus. One is forced to see in it flattery of the rulers,

[13] I Cor. 8:4-13; see also 10:28 and 14:13-7.
[14] Rom. 13:1, 2.   [15] Rom. 13, 3, 4.

on the one hand, and yielding to force, on the other hand—
all in order that "the powers . . . ordained of God" might
not persecute the new sect.[16] This feeling of resentment is
strengthened as one reads further: "Wherefore ye must needs
be in subjection, not only because of the wrath,[17] but also for
conscience' sake." [18] Therefore Paul decrees for believers, that
they should pay taxes and tribute to whomever taxes and
tribute belong, and respect and honor to whomever these two
belong.[19] It is difficult to decide whether this last advice is a
reflexion of Jesus' idea, "Render unto Caesar the things that
are Caesar's, and unto God the things that are God's," [20] or
whether "respect" and "honor" belong to rulers because one
must "submit" to them "also for conscience' sake." . . .

Nevertheless Paul, like a thorough Pharisaic Jew, was angry
when the "brethren" brought lawsuits against one another
before the civil courts instead of having such cases decided
among themselves. He reminds them that in the Age to Come
"we shall judge angels"; "how much more," then, are "the
saints" competent "to judge things that pertain to this life?" [21]

3. The same conservatism with regard to the existing order,
which we saw in the words of Paul about civil authority,
expresses itself also in his attitude toward *women*.[22]

---

[16] Of course I know that the scholars of our time also heap praise upon
the Roman government, and that the Romans had some just and humane
administrators, such as Petronius, who jeopardized his own safety by not
heeding the command of Caligula in the matter of "the image in the
Temple." But Paul speaks approvingly of governmental authority in general,
without making any distinction between good and bad.

[17] *I.e.*, because of fear of the wrath of governmental authorities.

[18] Rom. 13:5.   [19] Rom. 13:6,7.

[20] Mark 12:17; Matt. 22:21.   [21] I Cor. 6:1-6.

[22] See on this in particular H. Preisker, *Christentum und Ehe in den
ersten drei Jahrhunderten* (Berlin 1927), SS. 123-43 (an objective survey,
without apologetics); Elfriede Gottlieb, *Die Frau im frühen Christentum*
(Leipzig 1928), SS. 8-11, 18-20, 28, 29; G. Delling, *Paulus' Stellung zu Frau
und Ehe* (Stuttgart 1931, splendid bibliography); Enslin, *op. cit.*, pp. 169-93
(comparisons with the status of women in Greece and Rome).

A woman must submit to her husband. For if the head of the man is Christ, the head of the woman is her husband: ". . . man was not created from woman, but woman from man; neither was the man created for the woman, but the woman for the man." And just as the Church submits to Christ, so must women submit to their husbands. Not only so, but the man "is the image and glory of God; but the woman is the glory of the man." [23] To be sure, "neither is the woman without the man, nor the man without the woman, in the Lord; for as the woman was created from the man, so also is the man born from the woman; but all things are from God." [24] To this lovely saying there is one very similar in the Midrash: ". . . neither man without woman nor woman without man, and neither of them without the Divine Spirit." [25]

Nevertheless, while the man who prays or prophesies must *not* have his head covered, the woman who does these things —thus we see that a woman *is* permitted to pray and prophesy —*must* have her head covered.[26] To be sure, there is a surprising reason for this: "the woman must have an authority (ἐξουσία) [27] on her head, because of the angels" [28]—because the angels Semjaza and Azazel (or Uzah and Aza'el) were lured by the beauty of the daughters of men to come down

[23] I Cor. 11:3–9; Eph. 5:22–4; Col. 3:18.
[24] I Cor. 11:11, 12.
[25] Gen. Rab. VIII 9 end, ed. Albeck, p. 63.
[26] I Cor. 11:4–7 and 11:13–5.
[27] G. Kittel (*Rabbinica*, Leipzig 1920, SS. 17–31) made the ingenious suggestion that the use of the word *exousia* in the sense of veil or shawl comes from the fact that in the Palestinian Talmud, Shabb. VI, fol. 8b, "fillets" (*shevisim*, the word used in Isa. 3:18) are seemingly identified with the word *shiltoniyah* [which may mean "authority" or may be corrupt]. But Kittel had already been anticipated by Herklotz, *Biblische Zeitschrift*, X, 154, as is pointed out by Lietzmann, Kommentar (to I Cor. 11:10), S. 54.
[28] I Cor. 11:10. On the customs of covering the head and uncovering the head on the part of married women and harlots, see Mary E. Andrews, *op. cit.*, pp. 94–5; Delling, *op. cit.*, SS. 96–105.

from their high estate;[29] or perhaps the women had to veil their heads to protect themselves from the angels of destruction.[30] Aside from this, Paul demands, apparently, the covering of the head of the woman to avoid controversy in the Christian congregations, since among the Gentiles at that time it was the custom to distinguish between men and women by their covering or leaving uncovered their heads. This seems to be the purport of this verse from the Epistles: "But if any man seemeth to be contentious, we have no such custom, neither the churches of God." [31] At any rate, we have also here concessions to public opinion, or in other words opportunism, and likewise social conservatism in the midst of religious innovation.

This is also the case with regard to the rôle of women in the Christian Church. Just now we saw that they were permitted to pray and prophesy, except that they had to do these things with heads covered. But there is a prohibition which serves to contradict the permission to pray and prophesy:

Let the women keep silence in the churches: for it is not permitted unto them to speak; but let them be in subjection, as also saith the Law.[32] And if they would learn anything, let them ask

---

[29] On the basis of Gen. 6:2; Ethiopic Enoch, chs. 6 and 7; Book of Jubilees 4:15–5:2; Yoma 67b; Deut. Rab. XI, end; A. Jellinek, ed., *Beth ha-Midrash*, IV, 127–8 (J. D. Eisenstein, ed., *Otsar ha-Midrashim*, II, 549–50).

[30] See Lietzmann, *loc. cit.* According to the opinion of G. Kittel, *op. cit.*, SS. 25–30) they had to cover their heads in order that the ministering angels might not become angry. See also the article ἐξουσία by Foerster in *Theologisches Wörterbuch zum Neuen Testament*, II, 570–1.

[31] I Cor. 11:16.

[32] Apparently the reference is to the words, ". . . and he shall rule over thee" (Gen. 3:16). This Pentateuchal reference might apply to the words ". . . let them be in subjection." But where in the Pentateuch is it written that women must "keep silence in the churches"? Or perhaps ὁ νόμος is to be translated here not "the Law" (Pentateuch), but "the rule," "the hala-khah," the reference being to the Talmudic halakhah, "A woman should not read in the Torah out of respect for the congregation" (Megillah 23a); or, "A woman should not be brought in to read [Torah] publicly" (Tosephta, *ibid.* IV [III] 11).

their own husbands at home: for it is shameful for a woman to speak in the church.[33]

These two verses, which manifest a low opinion of women, and in any case do away with complete equality of men and women, are considered by various scholars as a later addition, for a number of reasons. *First*, Paul wrote in the same Epistle that it is permissible for women to pray and prophesy if their heads are covered; *second*, these verses seem to break the continuity of thought, and in some manuscripts, come after verse 40; and finally, *third*, Paul himself emphasizes that in Jesus Christ "there can be no male and female." [34]

But none of these three reasons is compelling. To the first reason it may be answered that Paul permitted women to pray and prophesy, but not to preach and express opinions. Prayer (Paul may have argued) is spontaneous worship with the heart and from it comes "prophecy" when "the spirit resteth upon you"; but preaching and the expression of opinion in the churches are things which require deliberate preparation, and things which bring one to public notice and serve to emphasize the personality—privileges of which Paul did not approve for women, like thousands of conservative "intellectuals" in our own time. To the second reason it may be answered that there is here no real interruption. In the same chapter [35] Paul discusses "speaking with tongues" and "prophecy" and the interpretation of the "tongues" and the "prophecy," all of which increased "confusion" in the churches and it was natural that in this chapter he should warn the women against adding to this confusion. And as to the fact that in some manuscripts these verses come after verse 40, surely it is nothing unusual in the New Testament that a verse should appear not in its

[33] I Cor. 14:34, 35.
[34] Gal. 3:28. See H. Weinel, *Paulus*, S. 202; C. A. Anderson Scott, *Saint Paul*, pp. 132-3.
[35] I Cor. 14:1-33.

proper place. And to the third reason it may be answered that of course Paul, like Jesus, attracted many women into the "Messianic" movement, since women are impressionable and emotional; both in Paul's Epistles and in Acts a number of women are praised because they worked for the good of the new faith.[36] Nevertheless Paul, like most of his contemporaries, considered women noisy and frivolous, and for that reason he deemed it proper to distinguish between them and the men in everything having to do with preaching and the expression of opinion.[37] This also was an opportunistic concession to the ideas of the time; it was conservatism in the midst of innovation in order to be "all things to all men." After all, is this the only contradiction in the words of Paul? In any case, we have not found that Jewish women were required to cover their heads specifically in the synagogue [at that time; hence Paul had no precedent from the synagogue].[38] Rightly says a Christian lady scholar: "Paul uses the Law when it is convenient to do so, rejecting it as freely, since [to him] it is not a means of salvation." [39]

4. There is similar ambiguity in Paul's attitude toward *marriage*.

For him, indeed, "It is good for a man not to touch a woman. But, because of fornications, let each man have his own wife, and let each woman have her own husband." *Marriage is a necessary evil;* but if a man and woman are married, they must not be false to one another, and they must fulfill the marital duties to each other "that Satan tempt you not because of your incontinency." But Paul says this "by way of

[36] All the data about these women is collected in the work of E. Gottlieb, *Die Frau im frühen Christentum*, SS. 8–10.

[37] See Mary E. Andrews, *op. cit.*, p. 67.

[38] In general, a married woman did not go out "with her hair unbound" (Mish., Ketuboth VII 6). See also Nedarim 30b: ". . . but women's hair is always covered."

[39] See Mary E. Andrews, *op. cit.*, p. 95.

concession, not of commandment." And he continues: "Yet I would that all men were even as I myself"—*i.e.*, would live without a wife as Paul did, as a bachelor or widower.[40] "Howbeit each man hath his own gift from God, one after this manner, and another after that." "But I say to the unmarried and to widows, It is good for them if they abide even as I"—as bachelors and widowers, maidens and widows.[41] "But if they have not continency, let them marry; for it is better to marry than to burn." [42]

The fact is clear, that Paul has no idea of marriage as a spiritual partnership and a social relationship between man and woman. He does not know "Platonic love," in which (contrary to the understanding of this term in our time) there is both sexual attraction and a spiritual and psychological bond. For Paul, there can exist between man and woman only the sexual relationship. This is admitted even by Christian scholars who are enthusiastic admirers of Paul.[43] For this reason Paul does not have much faith, apparently, in the possibility of the "spiritual marriage" which was practised in his time between ascetic men and pure virgins: he admits that this sort of restraint is good, but advises that if the passions are hard to control, the parties had better marry.[44] According to Paul, marriage brings with it no benefit. He does not know the

[40] According to the opinion of A. F. Puuko (*Paulus und das Judentum*, S. 28, Anm. 1, end), it may be concluded from this that Paul had taken a wife in his youth, like any devout Pharisee, but that during the time of his preaching he remained a widower and did not marry again. The hypothesis seems reasonable to me. Against this see Stauffer, *Theologisches Wörterbuch zum Neuen Testament*, I, 650. According to Clement of Alexandria, Paul was married, like all the apostles (see Enslin, *op. cit.*, p. 138).

[41] See the preceding note.

[42] I Cor. 7:1–9. Incidentally, the expression "to burn" is worthy of note for a number of reasons. The passionate nature of Paul is plainly revealed by it.

[43] Thus says, *e.g.*, H. Weinel (*Paulus*, S. 192): "He [Paul] saw marriage only from the primitive sensual point of view." And see especially H. Preisker, *Christentum und Ehe*, SS. 126–39.

[44] I Cor. 7:35–7. On "spiritual marriage" see for details Lietzmann, *op. cit.*, pp. 36–7.

satisfaction and joy of normal and honorable family life; nor does he know at all the pure love of man and woman, apart from "love in Christ." He permits marriage as a "necessary evil," but he feels sure that the parties will have "tribulation in the flesh" and he feels sorry for them.[45]

For this reason Paul permits a Christian man who has "an unbelieving wife," or a Christian woman who has "an unbelieving husband," to continue the marriage, instead of having a divorce, provided either or both of the parties can be content in spite of the difference in religion.[46] Paul does not expect that one of the pair should necessarily influence the religion of the other: "For how knowest thou, O wife, whether thou shalt save thy husband? Or how knowest thou, O husband, whether thou shalt save thy wife?" Therefore, if one of the mixed pair should wish to separate—let them separate.[47]

But in general, Paul is against divorce. He transmits this command in the name of Jesus:

But unto the married I give charge, yea not I, but the Lord, That the wife depart not from her husband (but should she depart, let her remain unmarried, or else be reconciled to her husband); and that the husband leave not his wife.[48]

Paul says this without any qualification whatever; he makes no special provision in case the husband has found in his wife "some unseemly thing" [Deut. 24:1]. Here we have a *logion* of Jesus, of which, to be sure, we do not know the source of its exact wording, but which closely corresponds to the prohibition of divorce by Jesus as found in the Gospels.[49] And of course, if there is in marriage no spiritual side, and it is to be entered into only to avoid licentiousness, why *should* Paul permit divorce? Will not any woman or any man serve the

---

[45] I Cor. 7:27, 28.   [46] I Cor. 7:12-4.
[47] I Cor. 7:15, 16.   [48] I Cor. 7:10, 11.
[49] Matt. 5:31, 32 (according to the true text, without the addition, ". . . saving for the cause of fornication"); Matt. 19:3-12; Luke 16:18.

purpose of quieting the sex impulse? Nor is it a cause for concern, therefore, if a woman believing in Jesus is married to an unbeliever, or *vice versa;* for spiritual relations between husband and wife, equality in beliefs and opinions, and the like, are not considered of great importance by Paul. Yet Paul places certain restrictions on mixed marriages—of course on religious grounds. The Christian widow whose husband is dead "is free to be married to whom she will," but "only in the Lord"; [50] that is to say, only to one believing in Christ like herself. But it is also possible that the meaning is, only on condition that she remain a believer "in the Lord," her unbelieving prospective husband being agreeable. In any case, Paul concludes: "But she is happier if she abide as she is, after my judgment"; [51] that is to say, if she remains a widow all her life, she will be very much happier.

We see that this ascetic view prevails in all the concessions to the marital state. The authorization of family life is only a concession to the evil impulse in man, coming from the fear that even for the believer it will be hard to subdue the passions. And indeed, how could it be thought otherwise by a man for whom "flesh" is the absolute antithesis of "spirit" and for whom "flesh" and "sin" are synonyms? This is the first reason for Paul's ascetic view of marriage. There is still another and better reason why neither bachelor nor widower, maiden nor widow, should marry. Behold, "the time is shortened" and soon "the fashion of the world" will pass away; [52] and in the world to come there is no need of procreation. In general, marriage only causes trouble and distress. [53] Christian asceticism, the extreme and exaggerated intensification of Jewish morality, is revealed in the social teaching of Paul no less than in that of Jesus. [54] Yet in spite of all his belief in the

[50] I Cor. 7:39. [51] I Cor. 7:40.
[52] I Cor. 7:29-31. [53] I Cor. 7:28.
[54] See Klausner, *Yeshu*, pp. 430-47 [Eng. ed., pp. 381-97].

nearness of the "Parousia" of Jesus, Paul adjusted himself to life as it is; the Christians had somehow to live and keep their affairs in order until Christ should return. This adjustment saved Christianity; the "Parousia" was long delayed, and the *temporary* adjustment became the practice of thousands of years. . . .

Along with the subjection of wife to husband, Paul teaches that "husbands ought to love their own wives as their own bodies; he that loveth his own wife loveth himself." [55] The motive of self-love as given here is not a highly ethical one. As for the rest, the Talmud says the very same thing (the expression "as their own bodies" or "as themselves" or "as himself" being shared by Paul and the Talmud) but in a more beautiful form: "Concerning a man who loves his wife as himself, who honors her more than himself, . . . Scripture says,[56] 'And thou shalt know that thy tent is in peace.' " [57] The Talmud teaches not only that the love of the husband for his wife must be equal to his love for himself, but it teaches also that the husband must honor his wife *even more* than he honors himself. In any case, in his ideas about the love of the husband for his wife, Paul the Pharisaic Jew is close to the opinion of the Talmud, while in the matter of divorce he is far from Talmudic Judaism, even that of the school of Shammai, which permitted the divorce of a wife only if the husband found unchastity in her.[58] Paul does not make even this stipulation, which apparently was interpolated later into the words of Jesus about divorce, by way of compromise with the prevailing opinions.[59] We may note also the verse, "Therefore a man shall leave his father and his mother, and shall cleave unto his wife": Jesus uses it as a support of his pronouncement

---

[55] Eph. 5:25–9; Col. 3:19.   [56] Job. 5:24.

[57] Yeb. 62b, end; San. 76b. *Cf.* ". . . his wife is like part of himself" or ". . . one's wife is as one's own body" (Ber. 24a; Bek. 35b; and with change of language to Aramaic, Keth. 66a; Men. 93b).

[58] Mish., Gittin IX 10.   [59] Matt. 5:32.

against divorce,[60] while Paul applies it to Christ and the Church.[61] Here the homiletic exegete in Paul prevails over the giver of ethical rules for the family and for society.

5. Just as it never occurred to Plato that it would be possible to abolish *slavery*, so it did not occur to Paul. He proclaims:

Let each man abide in that calling [62] wherein he was called. Were you called to be a bondservant? Do not let it trouble you. But even if you can become free, rather make the most of your present opportunity. For he that was called in the Lord to be a bondservant, is the Lord's freedman; likewise he that was called to be free, is Christ's bondservant. You were bought with a price; become not bondservants of men. Brethren, let each man, wherein he was called, therein abide with God.[63]

That is to say, slaves must not rise up and rebel. Far be it from Christianity to foment social revolution! Of course, in order to allay bitterness the words "with God" are added, attention is called to the freedom "in the Lord" (Christ), it is mentioned that Christians "were bought with a price," *i.e.* with the blood of Jesus, and it is said ". . . become not bondservants of men" along with emphasis on the obligation to abide in that state in which the slave was when he was called to be "a bondservant of Christ."

Neither does the Talmud reach the point of demanding the absolute abolition of slavery, nor do the Stoic philosophers, although they emphasize the manhood of the slave, and even teach that the master should take the attitude of a friend to his slave.[64] Rabban Johanan ben Zakkai, a contemporary of

[60] Gen. 2:24; Matt. 19:5, 6. [61] Eph. 5:31, 32.

[62] κλῆσις; in German *Beruf*, from *rufen*, "to call," as in Greek κλῆσις is from καλέω, "to call." In Hebrew there is no word corresponding exactly to this.

[63] I Cor. 7:20-4.

[64] Epictetus, *Dissertationes*, I, 13; Seneca, *Epistolae*, 47. *Cf.* M. E. Andrews, *op. cit.*, pp. 87-8.

Paul, was accustomed to interpret the text, ". . . and his master shall bore his ear through with an awl," [65] symbolically [66] thus:

> Why was the ear to be pierced rather than any other part of the body? Because, although it heard from Mount Sinai the words, "For unto Me the children of Israel are servants, they are My servants," [67] it threw off the yoke of Heaven and took upon itself the yoke of flesh and blood; therefore Scripture commanded that the ear should come and be pierced, because it did not heed what it heard. [68]

These words are more forceful and more humanitarian than the words of Paul.

It is an interesting thing that just as Paul demands of Christians in general that they be faithful to the government not only out of fear but also as a matter of conscience, so he demands also of Christian slaves: "Bondservants, be obedient unto them that according to the flesh are your masters, with fear and trembling, in singleness of your heart, as unto Christ." They are forbidden to be obedient to their masters only "in the way of eye service" or "as man-pleasers," but must obey "as servants of Christ, doing the will of God from the heart." To be sure, Paul endeavors at the same time to persuade the masters not to blame and abuse their slaves unjustly, "knowing that he who is both their Master and yours is in heaven, and there is no respect of persons with him." These words he

[65] Ex. 21:6.

[66] *Ke-min ḥomer* (with Ḥeth) or *ḥomer* (with He). See J. Levy, *Wörterbuch über die Talmud, etc.*, I, 478; S. Krauss, Supplement to *Aruch Completum* (Vienna 5697–1937), p. 160.

[67] Lev. 25:55.

[68] Tos., Baba Kamma VII 5 (ed. Zuckermandel, p. 358). In the Babylonian Talmud (and thus in Rashi on Ex. 21:6) the interpretation is still more striking: "This ear, which heard my Voice on Mount Sinai when I proclaimed, 'For unto me the children of Israel are servants, they are my servants' (Lev. 25:55), *and not servants of servants*, and yet this man went and acquired a master for himself—let it be bored!" (Kiddushin 22b). See also Baba Kamma 116b; Baba Metsi'a 10a.

presents twice, in two different Epistles.[69] And even in the delightful little Epistle to Philemon, in which is revealed the warmheartedness of Paul and his loving attitude toward the converts whom he had received, and in which he implores mercy for a slave, Onesimus by name, who ran away from his master, then became a Christian and returned to his master, while Paul entreated the master, Philemon, to take toward his returned slave the attitude of a companion and brother "both in the flesh and in the Lord"—even in this beautiful Epistle, Paul agrees that Philemon should hold Onesimus as a slave "forever." [70]

In comparison with the Tannaim in Israel and the Stoics of Greece and Rome, there is nothing particularly new in the attitude of Paul toward slaves. It must be remembered that Paul constantly speaks not simply of slaves, but of slaves converted to Christianity, who are therefore freedmen "in Christ" and beloved brethren "both in the flesh and in the Lord" to their masters. The Talmud goes farther in the matter of the equality of a "Hebrew slave" to his master and says: "Whoever buys a Hebrew slave is like one buying a master for himself." [71] What is remarkable in the attitude of Paul toward slavery and slaves is this: the Day of Judgment is near, "the fashion of this world" will shortly pass away, and everything will be changed—but slavery must still continue, and the slave must serve his master as well as Christ, not only "with fear and trembling" but also "in singleness of heart" and "from the heart" (literally "from the soul," Eph. 6:6).

[69] Eph. 6:5–9; Col. 3:24–4:1.   [70] Philemon vss. 10–21.

[71] Kidd. 20a; 'Arakhin 30b. See also Siphra VII 3 (ed. Weiss 109b); and in *ibid.* IX 4 (110a) it is said " 'For unto Me the children of Israel are servants; they are my servants whom I brought forth out of the land of Egypt'—*on condition that they should not enslave each other*; 'I am the Lord your God'—what does this mean? It means that anyone who makes slaves of them here below, *it is to be counted against him as though he made slaves up above*" (in heaven). To a higher degree of condemnation of slavery than this it would be difficult to attain.

Apparently, after the passage of years, the hope of the early Parousia was weakened even in the soul of Paul, and he unconsciously, and as it were instinctively, strove to arrange Christian social life in such a way as not to arouse the anger of the Roman government by revolutionary views with regard to the Messianic *social* order, after he had appeased its anger at the *political* side of Messianism. . . . This was an adjustment—perhaps not clearly conscious—to the demands of practical living. Otherwise the dissemination of Christianity would have faltered and have been rendered impossible in the very first steps of the new faith on account of the severest opposition on the part of the civil authorities.

That there is in the Epistles of Paul a certain weakening of the hope of an immediate Parousia we can see from this interesting fact:

Since the End is near, it might have been asked, and shortly "the fashion of this world" will pass away, when Jesus will appear "at the right hand of Power" and the Kingdom of Heaven will hold sway on earth, why labor and toil in this world whose end is so near? And there actually were found in Thessalonica persons who were wont to "walk . . . disorderly," to "work not at all," and to function as mere "busybodies." So Paul says:

Now them that are such we command and exhort in the Lord Jesus Christ, that with quietness they work, and eat their own bread.

And he precedes this command and warning with the sweeping rule, "If any will not work, neither let them eat." [72] These are fine words, which once served as a slogan for the socialist movement. But they naturally imply that the Parousia is not very near; if it were very near, there would be no occasion to concern oneself with the world that is passing

[72] II Thess. 3:10-2. See also Eph. 4:28; I Thess. 4:11, 12.

away, and those who idle their time away would be right, since their dreams of a "new world" could not then be considered as mere "striving after wind." They could say, "We have not heard that Jesus demanded work; on the contrary, he taught that the flowers of the field do not work, yet they lack nothing. . . ."

All these views about the government, woman, marriage and divorce, slavery, and the importance of work are by no means unethical. Their ethical elevation is more or less equal to that of the views of Judaism in the time of Paul and of the Stoic philosophy in the same period. But in any case, from the standpoint of ethics, Pharisaic Judaism had nothing to learn from Paul. And insofar as these views were connected with an ascetic attitude toward the flesh and with the illusory belief in the Parousia, on the one hand, and with the endeavor to conform to the demands of the Roman government in order to prevent persecution of the young religious movement, on the other hand, it was natural that Judaism should definitely reject these views, or else pay no attention to them at all.

CHAPTER XII

Jesus and Paul

On the subject of "Jesus and Paul" much has been written.[1] Likewise in the course of the present book I have had occasion many times to point out likenesses and differences in the lives and teachings of Jesus and Paul. Therefore I do not see any need for an extensive treatment of this subject here. Only what is most necessary for the evaluation of the originality and the new features in the personality and teaching of Paul, in contrast to the personality and teaching of Jesus, shall I attempt to set forth at this time.

1. There were days in which Paul was considered to be "the inventor of Christianity" (*Erfinder der Christlichkeit*), to use the expression of Nietzsche.[2] At present those holding this opinion are growing fewer. Almost all scholars occupied with Christian origins have come to the conclusion that Paul depended in large measure not only upon the opinions and teaching of Jesus, but also upon the "primitive church" (*Urgemeinde*) of Jerusalem—this "primitive church" being the immediate transmitter of the known facts about the life and teaching of Jesus. If it had not been so, Paul would not

[1] The literature from 1858 to 1925 on the likenesses and differences as between Jesus and Paul is listed by P. Feine, *Der Apostel Paulus* (Gütersloh 1925), SS. 158–60. To this are to be added: certain chapters of Feine himself (*ibid.*, pp. 160–206, 398–439); H. Weinel, *Paulus*, SS. 109–17; H. Windisch, *Paulus und Christus* (Leipzig 1934); J. Leipoldt, *Jesus und Paulus—Jesus oder Paulus?* (Leipzig 1936).

[2] See Friedrich Nietzsche, *Morgenröthe*, I, 68 (ed. Leipzig 1906, V, 68). Against this view of Nietzsche's about Paul, see H. Weinel, *op. cit.*, SS. 101–9.

have attached such great importance to the necessity of his being recognized by "the very chiefest apostles" [3] and the "pillars" [4] of the early church; this in spite of the fact that he speaks of them with suppressed anger and sometimes even deals ironically with them (there is no doubt that in the expressions "very chiefest apostles" and "reputed to be pillars" there is veiled irony).[5] If there had been for Paul no Jesus upon whom to depend, then perhaps Paul would have remained a zealous Pharisee to the end of his days. And if there had been no "primitive church" in which was born the resurrection story, and apparently also the view that the crucified Messiah was the vicariously suffering Messiah of Isaiah 53, then the very foundation stone of Paul's teaching would have been lacking. Likewise, Paul found already established in the primitive church as sectarian practices baptism and the "Lord's Supper"; he also found there a certain opposition to the usual Jewish view that the Torah and ceremonial laws are the absolutely indispensable fundamentals (Stephen), as well as a certain hostility to Judaism in general because it had not recognized Jesus as Messiah but had handed him over to the Romans (Peter). In this sense Paul was connected with Jesus and Jesus' immediate disciples by a very close bond.

Nevertheless, it is permissible to say—of course with certain reservations—that it was not Jesus who created (or more correctly, founded) Christianity, but Paul. Jesus is the source and root of Christianity, its religious ideal, and he became all unconsciously its lawgiving prophet. Jesus did not intend to found a new religion or a new church; he only strove to bring about among his people Israel the Kingdom of Heaven, and to do this as a Messiah preaching the repentance and good works which would result in the politico-spiritual redemption of his

---

[3] II Cor. 12:11.   [4] Gal. 2:9.

[5] Without reason do various scholars (e.g., W. Wrede, *Paulus*, S. 109, Anm. 10) think that these were not "the original apostles" (*Urapostel*).

people, and through them, of all mankind. Not so Paul. He was the clearly self-conscious creator and organizer of Christianity as a new religious community. He made Christianity a religious system different from both Judaism and paganism, a system mediating between Judaism and paganism but with an inclination toward paganism. He was also the great institutionalizer of the Christian Church. Once Paul had welded together Nazarene Jews and Gentile Christians into one body, there was no place for them either in Judaism or in paganism, so they necessarily separated from their respective religious communities and formed a new church.

This contrast between Jesus and Paul derived not only from differences in their personalities, but also from differences in their respective environments and situations.

First, Paul, in spite of all his desire for authority and all the ridicule and hatred which he directed toward those who did not acknowledge his peculiar gospel or his authority as an apostle, did not have what may be called *genuine sovereignty*. Without the Old Testament Scriptures, on the one hand, and without recognition by James the brother of Jesus, by "the very chiefest apostles" and "pillars," and by the entire primitive church in Jerusalem, on the other hand, it would have been impossible for him to find a basis for either his authority or his teaching. With all his masterfulness, he was a pious disciple who stood in fear and trembling before his "Master," Christ, and also had a sense of inferiority before the intimate disciples of "the Master" (even when he was contending with them and speaking harsh words against them, *e.g.*, against Peter) and before the Law accepted by his people (even while he was daring to abrogate it). Jesus too sometimes made use of verses from the Torah, since he of course thought, "Till heaven and earth pass away, one jot or one tittle shall in no wise pass away from the Law"; [6] nevertheless, the essential thing for him

[6] Matt. 5:18.

was not homiletical exposition of Scripture, but the marvellous popular parables and the short and striking aphorisms, which go to their mark like barbed arrows. The theological theories and propositions of which the Epistles of Paul are full were not the weapons of Jesus in his struggle for his way of thinking. In order to illustrate his views, he spoke poetically about the simple life known to all, and took his examples from this simple life. Paul, even if he was not actually a systematic theologian, was none the less quite doctrinaire, quite replete with abstract speculative theories, religious and ethical, philosophical and mystical; and his expositions of Scripture are precisely like those in Talmud and Midrash, except that they are intended to produce an opposite result.[7] Simple and beautiful parables like those of Jesus are hardly to be found at all in Paul. Of Jesus it was said: "And they were astonished at his teaching; for he taught them as (one) having authority,[8] and not as the scribes." [9] Of Paul it would have been impossible to say this. He taught "as the scribes," with Scriptural exegesis, in the first place; like a theologian, in the second place; and like a popular Stoic philosopher, in the third place.

Second, both Jesus and Paul were Jews, and both of them were Pharisees as well. Paul was more "rabbinical" (and thus more Pharisaic) in the information which he possessed, in his way of thinking and in his interpretation of Scripture. But Jesus was entirely a *Palestinian Jew*, who had no acquaintance beyond the Hebrew and Aramaic literature created in Palestine. Not so Paul. He was a *Jew of the Diaspora*, detached from the soil of his proper homeland, even if he did come to Jerusalem in his youth. He had been trained in both the Hebrew-Aramaic and Hellenistic Jewish literatures, and he also knew, at least in part, the Greek literature of his time,

[7] See on these expositions above, pp. 454–8.

[8] Or, "as one speaking parables." See H. P. Chajes, *Markus-Studien* (Berlin 1899, SS. 10–2; see also Klausner, *Yeshu*, pp. 292–4 [Eng. ed., pp. 264–5].

[9] Mark 1:22; Matt. 7:29; Luke 4:32.

or at the very least, he had learned by hearsay a number of the sayings of the famous poets and popular philosophers of his time. To this testify all his Epistles and everything related about him in the book of Acts. Thus we may say that Jesus knew no cleavage in his psychological life, while the soul of Paul was divided between Judaism and Hellenism.

Finally, *third*, Jesus came from the village of Nazareth hidden away among the hills of Galilee, therefore he was nearer the soil, nearer nature, therefore he was more unsophisticated, more immediately in touch with common people such as simple fishermen, taxgatherers in small border towns, and women of the lower classes. Paul came from a city, a city of mixed population and the seat of a university, Tarsus. In his youth he went to the great Jewish city of Jerusalem. Afterwards he traveled and preached throughout his entire life in Hellenistic cities, great and small, such as Corinth, Athens, Ephesus, and Thessalonica. He was so far from being a son of the soil that he did not know how olive trees were grafted —whether the wild olive was grafted upon the good olive or *vice versa*.[10] Jesus was more original, more primitive, more direct, than Paul. His teachings and his sayings welled up from great depths, as it were from the perception of his inmost being, affected very little by knowledge obtained from books or from minute and searching speculations or analyses. For Jesus, *natural understanding* took the place of the heaping up of information. He had an immediate, intuitive insight into the heart of things. Not so Paul. To be sure, mysterious forces worked in him also, breaking forth from the hidden places of his soul, from the depths of his nature; but in the last analysis he was more learned,[11] more cultured, much more given to

[10] Rom. 11:11–9. See for a long and detailed discussion of the "rusticity" of Jesus and the "urbanity" of Paul, J. Leipoldt, *op. cit.*, SS. 29–43 .

[11] Festus, the Roman procurator, when he had heard the sophistical arguments of Paul before Agrippa and Bernice, said to Paul: "Paul, thou art mad; thy much learning is turning thee mad!" (Acts 26:24). And see above, p. 409.

searching speculation than Jesus. Therefore, Jesus gave forth only beautiful parables and flashing aphorisms, which none the less embodied a well-developed doctrine. But Paul created something like a complete theological system—a whole series of religio-philosophic ideas, which can hardly be understood in all their complicated cleverness by anyone.

2. In another place I have attempted to demonstrate that Jesus was not at all the "sacrifice without blemish," the "lamb of God," as imagined by devout Christians and romantic free-thinkers. He knew how to give vent to anger, how to denounce and threaten with "outer darkness" and with "wailing and gnashing of teeth"; he knew how to curse the scribes and Pharisees as "hypocrites," and he could also curse the cities of Capernaum, Chorazin, and Bethsaida for not having accepted him and his teaching; and he even knew how to drive out money-changers from the outer court of the Temple by physical force.[12] Nevertheless, there was a great difference between him and Paul in the matter of revealing the inner emotions. Jesus was, according to my opinion, possessed of marked individuality and great self-confidence, believing in his own supreme authority and rebuking all who did not recognize his messiahship and his teaching. But although he was by nature a man of sensitive and strong feelings, he also knew how to *rise above* the emotions; he knew not only how to quiet them (Paul also knew how to do this), but also how to put them aside and disclaim them, as though they did not exist.

Paul *fought* against his great egoism and his longing for supreme authority and complete spiritual mastery over the apostles and over the Christian churches; but he was not always able to conquer himself. In spite of his idealistic command, in which he followed in the footsteps of Jesus, "Bless

[12] See Klausner, *Yeshu*, pp. 443-4 and 354-5 [Eng. ed., pp. 394-5 and 314-5].

them that persecute you; bless, and curse not," [13] he cursed
and reviled and abused not only his enemies who persecuted
him, but also those who opposed his opinions; [14] and once he
even said, "O that those who are unsettling you would get
themselves emasculated!" [15] Because they were advocating circumcision in opposition to his opinion that circumcision was
annulled, they deserved to be castrated as well as circumcised!
He called his opponents "dogs" [perhaps meaning "male
prostitutes" or "catamites"] and "evildoers"; and Jewish circumcision, which they advocated, he called by the opprobri-
ous name of "amputation" or "lopping off" (in Greek the
opprobrium is expressed by the play on words περιτομή—
κατατομή, in German *Beschneidung-Verschneidung*).[16] Not
only so, but he was "in readiness to avenge all disobedience." [17] In an uncontrolled burst of wrath he commands:

But though we, or an angel from heaven, should preach unto
you any gospel other than that which we preached unto you, let
him be anathema.

And he repeats himself excitedly in the next verse:

As we have said before, so say I now again, If any man preacheth unto you any gospel other than that which ye received, let
him be anathema.[18]

It is hard to imagine Jesus giving vent to words like these,
demanding such an evil thing as the damnation of the opponents of his teaching. Would Jesus have been willing to
condemn to death (even a death at the hands of heaven as a
result of condemnation by the church) [19] a man who had

[13] Rom. 12:14.
[14] See, *e.g.*, Philipp. 3:18, 19; I Thess. 2:14, 15, and elsewhere.
[15] Gal. 5:12.
[16] Philipp. 3:2; but see also above, p. 426, n. 18.
[17] II Cor. 10:6.   [18] Gal. 1:8, 9.
[19] See Lietzmann, Kommentar (on I Cor. 5:5), S. 23.

married (or lived with) his father's wife in Corinth?[20] Paul's ethical teaching is more cautious and conservative, more lacking in revolutionary quality, than the ethical teaching of Jesus, which in spite of its impracticality, charms us by its loftiness and perfectionism.[21] Yet Paul was much the harsher of the two because of the untrammeled passionateness of his nature.

To be sure, all the harsh words that escaped from the pen of Paul, and the severe sentence which he passed upon the man living with his stepmother were delivered at a time of anger, in the heat of controversy, or in connexion with a case of flagrant immorality. But in any case, all this proves that the title of "Saint," by which Christians designate Paul, does not fit him absolutely. Of course, Paul had many outstanding virtues: he suffered much for his opinions, he founded with great toil Christian churches composed of Jews and Gentiles and cared for his churches like a veritable nurse, he won friends and helpers for himself everywhere and gave them much attention in his Epistles, he befriended a runaway slave and arranged to pay out of his own funds what the master had lost by the slave's flight; and what is most important of all, he was absorbed so completely and without stint in his historic undertaking that whatever we may think of it, we must admit that by it he conquered a whole pagan world. Yet he had many human weaknesses, as revealed in his Epistles, without himself being aware of them.[22] These weaknesses Jesus either did not have at all, or else he had them to a much smaller degree than did Paul.

3. But the rule is in history, that a man becomes great not only because of his virtues, but also because of his faults. Take away from great personalities of history such as Mohammed

[20] I Cor. 5:1-5. See also above, p. 553, n. 19.
[21] See the two preceding chapters, above, pp. 548-79.
[22] See on this W. Wrede, *Paulus*, SS. 20-7.

and Luther their faults, and there remain to us respectable people with superior qualities, but somehow limited in imagination and incapable of making history. This was the case also with Paul in relation to Jesus. *Because* Paul had faults which Jesus shared not at all, or to a very slight degree—*for this very reason*, Paul, and not Jesus, was prepared to found a new church consciously and intentionally.

For Jesus only *unwittingly* laid the foundation for a new religion by an *excessive* emphasis upon certain *radical* Jewish ideas—and no more; only by his unnatural death as a suffering Messiah did he become the authoritative source upon which depended a new religion. But the ideological and organizational structure of the Christian faith as a *religion* and as a *church* was built by Paul the Hellenistic Jew, born in Tarsus, educated in Jerusalem, a reader of the Septuagint, a writer of excellent Greek, and—a pupil of Rabban Gamaliel.

There is no doubt of the fact (although the proponents of Form Criticism attribute all this to "the necessities of preaching") that Jesus confined his mission "to the lost sheep of the house of Israel," [23] and said that "it is not proper to take the children's bread and cast it to the little dogs." [24] Nevertheless, because of the emphasis on the part of Jesus upon the higher value of ethics as compared with the ceremonial laws, it was possible for his disciples to find in his words the germ of the equalization of Gentiles with Jews in the Messianic Age (Days of the Messiah). This germ could also be found in Judaism, since according to it all the Gentiles would be saved in the Messianic Age, provided that they became proselytes and took upon themselves the yoke of Torah and ceremonial laws—as far as these laws might remain valid in the Age to Come. But the extreme conclusion that Torah and ceremonial laws must be set aside from the beginning for Gentiles, and afterwards for the Jews also, even before the realization of the

[23] Matt. 10:5, 6 and 15:24.   [24] Mark 7:27; Matt. 15:26.

Kingdom of Heaven (before the "Parousia" of Jesus as chief magistrate on the Day of Judgment)—this bold conclusion could have been reached only by Paul the Jew of the Diaspora, Paul who had lived among Gentiles and had been influenced more or less unconsciously by their doctrines and their mysteries. Without this, the faith in Jesus, retaining observance of the ceremonial laws as demanded by James the brother of Jesus and James' associates, the "Ebionite" Jewish Nazarenes, would have constituted *only a Jewish religious sect*, which after a time would have been absorbed into the main stock of Judaism, or else would have continually grown weaker, like the Samaritans and the Karaites.

So it was with the other matters common to Jesus and Paul. Jesus' belief, that as Messiah he would sit "at the right hand of Power" to judge the world and its peoples, became at the hands of Paul a belief in Jesus "the heavenly man," as opposed to the "earthly man" or the "first Adam." The *excessive* emphasis upon the words *"my* heavenly Father" on the part of Jesus was carried by Paul to the next to the last extreme (the last extreme being the doctrine of the Trinity), wherein God does everything through his "Son" Christ. From the emphasis upon the importance of the Holy Spirit in connexion with the Messiah and the Messianic Age, Paul created the theory of the radical difference between "flesh" and "spirit," and the theory of the spiritual ("pneumatic") man as distinguished from both the fleshly ("carnal") man and the natural ("psychical") man. From the customs of ritual ablution and the fellowship meal as practised by Jesus, Paul made "sacraments," that is to say, mystical acts by which man is joined in union with God or Christ. And from the impractical and pessimistic attitude of Jesus toward marriage and divorce, Paul made fixed rules for the new Church, of which, if he was not the creator, he certainly was the founder and the one who determined its characteristic form.

Thus it can be said with finality: *without Jesus no Paul and no Nazarenes;* but *without Paul no world Christianity.* And in this sense, Jesus was not the founder of Christianity as it was spread among the Gentiles, but Paul "the apostle of the Gentiles," in spite of the fact that Paul based himself on Jesus, and in spite of all that Paul received from the primitive church in Jerusalem.

CHAPTER XIII

The Consequences of Paul's Teaching

1. From everything said up to this point, it is to be seen that at the foundation of Paul's teaching lay Jewish beliefs and opinions, which took on a new, half-pagan complexion from foreign influences, and thus became non-Judaism and anti-Judaism. Paul himself was not aware of this. He considered his teaching as true Judaism, as the fulfillment of the promises and assurances of authentic Judaism. So of course it gave him great pain [1] that his people Israel did not accept his teaching, which he did not consider essentially new since he based it all upon the Scriptures. Hence arises the difficult problem, which every serious scholar who concerns himself with Christianity must face first of all: How is it that Judaism gave birth to Christianity, which, although accepted by half the world from the hands of Judaism, yet was emphatically rejected by Judaism itself?

The answer has been given in what has been said up to this point: In spite of the fact that the *foundations* of all the teachings of Paul are Jewish, his *own* teaching is both the *contradiction of the Jewish religion* and the *rejection of the Jewish nation*.

Paul showed himself in his work as an apostle and in his organization of the churches an eminently practical man, knowing how to adapt himself to varying conditions in everything that was *unessential* in his eyes—provided that he could retain or obtain what he considered *essential*. But in spite of this practicality, his teaching was infused with a spirit of

[1] See his poignant words in Rom. 9:1, 2; 11:1–5; 11:17–32; and elsewhere.

phantasm, which a lucid mind cannot endure. This phantasm was based on a hope of the imminent "Parousia," something which could not be fulfilled. It rested upon three foundations: a crucified Messiah who arose from the dead, an imaginary vision in which this Messiah was revealed to Paul alone in a special way—these things in the past—and a belief in the appearance from heaven ("Parousia") of this Messiah—in the future. Paul himself makes it emphatic that without these beliefs Christianity is mere foolishness and Christians the most "pitiable" people in the world.[2]

In addition to this, there is in the teaching of Paul a pessimistic strain which inevitably leads to a devaluation of normal life and a minimizing of the importance of everything in this world. The teaching of Paul abrogates freedom of the will and exchanges it for "grace" by foreordination; it substitutes blind faith for deeds; it makes the Kingdom of Heaven a mystical affair and not a reconstitution of the world in the spirit of the prophets and their social and national ethics. Thus this teaching, without Paul's knowing it and against his will, degraded the ideal of morality as the prime essential of religion, and introduced into this perverted Messianism (true Messianism teaches the prophetic ethical monotheism and its gradual realization in "the end of days," in the world) half-pagan elements, by which this new Messianism was made easy of reception for the Gentiles, since they saw in it a certain similarity to the pagan mystery religions. Even in Paul's lifetime, he had opponents who claimed—as he himself relates—that he said, "Let us do evil, that good may come";[3] or, they asked, "Shall we continue in sin, that grace may abound?";[4] or, "Shall we sin, because we are not under law, but under grace?";[5] and finally, "Is the Law sin?".[6] Paul was incensed by these questions, and denied that he held any such vicious opin-

[2] I Cor. 15:13-29.   [3] Rom. 3:8.   [4] Rom. 6:1.
[5] Rom. 6:15.   [6] Rom. 7:7.

ions. But it is natural that there were not a few Christians (especially Gentile Christians) who drew conclusions like these from the teaching of Paul—and indulged in all sorts of license, as we shall see below.

The abrogation of the ceremonial laws would necessarily have served to obliterate the distinction between Israel and the nations—and what would have happened then? One drop of wine—even of strong wine—will not give a taste to a great cask of water; and if Judaism had listened to the voice of Paul, it would have disappeared from the world both as a religion and as a nation, without leaving any influence whatever upon the great pagan world. But Judaism wished to endure as a religion, in order that in the course of time the pure ethical monotheism and the ethico-social Messianism of the prophets might prevail; and it wished to endure as a nation, in order that it might again be free upon its own soil to create there politico-national and economico-cultural values as do all other nations. For one simple fact must not be forgotten, although many Jewish scholars with a sense of "mission" and almost all Christian theologians neglect it either intentionally or unintentionally; this fact is that Judaism is *not only a religion, but a nation as well*—a nation and a religion at one and the same time. Hence, if it should surrender its characteristic religious faith, its nationality would also die; likewise, if it should give up its national existence, an end would also come to the particular religion and culture which we call collectively "Judaism." Therefore, only a small minority among the Jews accepted the teaching of Paul, and in the course of time, after a sharp struggle between Jewish Nazarenism and Gentile Christianity, this minority was swallowed up among the Gentiles.

2. In contrast to the Jewish minority, great numbers of pagan Gentiles accepted the new, or renovated, teaching of

Paul. And the consequences were not slow to come: these converted Gentiles straightway drew from this teaching conclusions which had not occurred to its author.

Since the Torah is void, since faith is everything, since Jesus redeemed *all* men with his blood and saved them from *all* sin and iniquity, behold *anything is permissible*. Of course, Paul did not think this. Of course, he intended to abrogate only the *ceremonial* part of the Law, and not the *ethical* part. But pagan "Messianists" understood the words of Paul in such a way that they took from him only the fantastic beliefs, and not the ethical teaching. As has been said, Paul taught and emphasized the ethical element, but it was not fundamental in his teaching as compared with faith. Therefore we see that wherever Paul founded Christian churches, controversies and divisions of opinion and sectarianisms arose between Nazarenes and Ebionites and Gentile Christians; and they divided into Judaizers and antinomians and Gnostics, into disciples of Cephas, disciples of Apollos, and the like. So Paul was forced to fight with all his might against these divisive tendencies, which he himself had brought about by his teaching.[7]

But worse than all these were the *vices* which became rife in young Christianity because of the negation of the value of the Law, and because Gentiles flocked into the new religion in great numbers, bringing with them many crude and foolish individuals.[8] Laziness, idleness, thievery, violence, drunkenness, fornication and adultery, idolatry, scoffing and obscene speech, blasphemy and abusive language, and trafficking in the word of God—these are vices which for the most part are signs of decay and deterioration on account of age, and yet now they appeared in young Christianity, which began to

[7] Rom. 16:17, 18; I Cor. 1:10–3; 15:33, 34; II Cor. 2:17; 6:14–8; 9:5, 6; Gal. 1:6–9; 2:4; 2:11–5; 3:1–4; 4:9–11; 5:12; Eph. 5:6, 7; Philipp. 3:1, 2; 3:18, 19; and elsewhere.

[8] I Cor. 1:26–9.

wither before it had had time to blossom.[9] Unwittingly and unintentionally Paul, by his teaching and his lack of strictness in receiving converts from the pagan Gentiles, even the crude and foolish among them, as has been said (Judaism at that time was also much concerned with the making of proselytes, but was much stricter about receiving them)—for these reasons, Paul himself was responsible for the development of those Christian sects which quickly became antinomian, opposing the God of Israel and the "Old Covenant," and at the same time practising all sorts of licentiousness and immorality. This has to be confessed even by Christian scholars who are favorably inclined toward Paul.[10]

Paul fought against these dangerous sects and the vices of their members with all his might; there is not a Pauline Epistle which does not contain a section devoted to ethical exhortation for the benefit of the Christian churches and to denunciation of the vices of their members. He demanded good morals, he set the churches in order, he enjoined obedience to the empire like any respectable Roman citizen, he was far from the revolutionism of the prophets and even from the extremism of Jesus his Messiah. The essential thing in his eyes was faith in Christ, in the salvation of the world through the Cross. And by way of ceremonial laws, with which he could not dispense entirely, he chose baptism and the fellowship meal —two Jewish practices which were converted by him, aided of course by foreign influences, into acts of mystic symbolism, as has been said.

3. Since the ceremonial laws had ceased to be the national pattern of life for the new Church, it was inevitable that there should come to take their place certain *fundamental doctrines*

[9] Rom. 13:10-4; I Cor. 5:1-5 and 5:9-13; II Cor. 2:17; 12:20, 21; Eph. 4:26-31; 5:3-5; I Thess. 4:3-8; II Thess. 3:10-2; and elsewhere.

[10] "Paul," confesses Eduard Meyer, "is the father not only of the orthodox Church, but of the Gnostic heresy as well" (*Urspr. u. Anfänge*, III, 625).

—"dogmas" of faith. (Basic beliefs [in the form of a creed] were not laid down in any absolute manner [11] by Judaism in ancient times; such tenets were fixed in Judaism at a later time by Maimonides.) Dogmas served to a certain extent as links between the members of the Church in place of the ceremonial laws. Thus Paul freed believers in Jesus from the chains of prescribed rules, but fastened them up again in the chains of even harder dogmas: the dogma of belief in Jesus as Messiah and Son of God in the spiritual sense, the dogma of his resurrection from the dead, the dogma of his Second Coming from heaven, the dogma of predestination in respect to the saved and the unsaved, the dogma of "grace," the dogma of redemption by the blood of Christ, and so on.

The most superb thing of all that we find in Paul's Epistles is the Hymn to Love (agapē).[12] But what came out of this "love"? A few years after Paul, agapē became a fixed name for the "love feast" in the Christian churches, a feast connected with the giving of alms to the poor, and similar to the banquets and commemorative meals of the pagan "associations" (θίασοι).[13] With all his Jewish training, with all his practical common sense and administrative talent, Paul could not overcome the mysticism of his time, because there were mystical depths in his own soul and because he was by nature himself a visionary. It is possible that *he did not even wish* to overcome this foreign mysticism, because by means of it he

---

[11] The Mishnah, Sanhedrin X ("the chapter of the Share") fixes only who shall lose his share in the World to Come by denial of certain beliefs, but does not thereby determine basic principles (a creed) for Judaism. For it would be impossible to say that the prohibition of "uttering charms over a wound" or "reading heretical [uncanonical] books" constitutes religious dogmas like the dogma of the resurrection of Jesus after the crucifixion as affirmed by Paul!—D. Neumark (*Toledot ha-'Ikkarim be-Yisrael*, Odessa 5679–1919, II, 29–89) thinks that these propositions in the Mishnah were laid down for polemical purposes against the dogmas of Christianity.

[12] I Cor. 13:1–14. See above, pp. 558–61.

[13] See on these W. Bousset, *Kyrios Christos*, SS. 277, 280; Ed Meyer, *op. cit.*, III, 235.

could draw into Christianity those among the pagans who had a deep religious yearning. For only those pagans who were not satisfied with their own religion sought out the mystery religions of Isis, Attis, Mithras, *et al.*; and to such pagans, Christianity was as one of these mystery religions. Judaism did not adhere very strongly to mysteries, or at least did not make them basic to its spiritual life. Judaism continued to walk in its own way from the days of the "Scribes" onward; it continued to see in the revealed Torah the revelation of deity in the world, and to see in every new interpretation discovered by a diligent student a sacred thing flowing forth from the Torah, and tending to establish that Torah within the nation and to establish by means of that Torah the nation itself as an effective force in the concourse of nations that makes up mankind. Thus Christianity moved farther and farther away from Judaism.

4. This separation was inevitable. For by means of the exaggerated words of adoration which Paul applied to "Christ Jesus," this Christ became more and more a supernatural figure, and after a little an actual son of God. Luke the physician, who accompanied Paul on his journeys and dedicated the best chapters of the Acts of the Apostles to his "master" the apostle (to-day there is almost no doubt that Luke wrote the book of Acts), began the Gospel bearing his name with the story of the birth of Jesus from a virgin and the Holy Spirit;[14] and Matthew preceded him in this by relating the very same story with certain differences, and supporting it by quoting a verse from Isaiah.[15]

The influence of Paul was so strong that even his antagonists, the Judaizing Nazarenes, unconsciously yielded to him and finally themselves became transgressors of Jewish law. In no other way can be explained the execution of James the

[14] Luke 1:34-7.   [15] Matt. 1:18-25.

brother of Jesus in the year 62 C.E. The Jewish authorities did not touch this ritually correct Ebionite at the time of the stoning of Stephen, or at the time of the slaying of James the son of Zebedee, or even at the time of the persecutions directed against Paul. So why did the high priest Hanan ben Hanan suddenly see fit to bring this James before the Sanhedrin and have the death sentence passed upon him and other Nazarenes like him in the interim between procurators (between Festus and Albinus)? To be sure, the Pharisees were incensed at this act of Hanan ben Hanan and complained against him before Albinus, and as a result Hanan was dismissed from the high-priesthood;[16] but the very act of the Sadducean high priest proves that there were already at that time, even among the cautious Nazarenes of James' group, "transgressors" (παρανομήσαντες in Josephus), whom a Jewish (albeit entirely Sadducean) Sanhedrin could deem worthy of death. And James, as their head, was held responsible (perhaps not rightly) for their deeds.[17]

For, indeed, toward the end of Paul's lifetime (c. the year 64) the break between Judaism and Christianity became complete. Shortly afterwards, within two years or a little more (in 66), the decisive war between the Jews and the Romans broke out. And while even the Essenes, in spite of all their asceticism, joined with the fighters for freedom (John the Essene at the time of the great rebellion was appointed a general and put in charge of such important strategic places as Joppa, Lydda, Thamma [Timnah], and Emmaus; he fell in the battle for Ashkelon),[18] the Christians forsook Jerusalem

---

[16] *Antiq.* XX ix 1 (§§ 200–3). See on this in particular Klausner, *Historia*, IV, 26; *idem*, *Yeshu*, pp. 51–3 [Eng. ed., pp. 58–60]. Now there is to be added H. J. Ebeling, ZNW, XXXV (1936), 290–5. See also above, p. 349.

[17] Perhaps James' agreement to set aside circumcision and the rest of the ceremonial laws for the reception of Christians from among the pagans was a sufficient reason in the eyes of the high priest to condemn to death the head of the new sect, since James had agreed to a radical change like this in Judaism, for which a proselyte was almost "like Israel in every respect."

[18] *Jewish War* II xx 4; *ibid*. III ii 2.

immediately after the outbreak of the rebellion and fled to Pella in Transjordania, a city which was for the most part foreign.[19] In the war of the Jews against the Romans there were both political and religious aspects, as I pointed out years ago.[20] The Christians, and even the Jewish Nazarenes, did not accept the political aspect of Jewish Messianism at all. And the religious and spiritual aspect had for them already been realized in Jesus—so what interest had they in a war between the Jews and the Romans?

In any case, from the end of Paul's lifetime onward Jews and Christians lived in two separate worlds, there being between them no relation except that of kinsmen who have grown apart; hence animosity and conflict between them increased.

Such were the different consequences of Paul's teaching for Judaism, for Jewish Nazarenism, and for Gentile Christianity in his time and in the centuries to follow, even to this day.

[19] See Eusebius, *Hist. Eccl.* III 5, § 196 (ed. Schwarz, minor, p. 81); Epiphanius, *Haer.* XXIX 7; *De Mensuris et Ponderibus* § 15 (ed. Dindorf, II, 87–8; IV, 1, 18). Perhaps Josephus refers to this (*Antiq.* XX xi 1; *Jewish War* II xiv 2) when he relates that because of the fearful deeds of Gessius Florus, many Jews were forced to flee to foreign territories. Pella was one of the cities of the Decapolis, and therefore was foreign territory for the Jewish Nazarenes and in the eyes of Josephus.

[20] See Klausner, *Historia*, IV, *passim*. See also above, pp. 437–8.

CHAPTER XIV

Conclusion: What Is Paul for the Jews?

1. From all that has been said above in the chapters treating the teaching of Paul and its consequences, the fact has become clear that the Jews could not have taken any attitude toward Paul and his teaching except a negative one. So in his time, and so after his time, up to the present day.

The Jews also rejected Jesus; yet he is mentioned a number of times in Talmud and Midrash—and not always unfavorably.[1] But Paul is mentioned clearly not even once in either of the two Talmuds or in any early Midrash. Only hints about him can be found in the Talmud. In this connexion Aaron Jellinek [2] calls attention to the following saying of R. Eleazar of Modi'im, a contemporary of R. Akiba (and thus not much later than Paul):

> If a man profanes the Hallowed things [some texts read "the Sabbaths"] and despises the set feasts and puts his fellow to shame publicly and makes void the covenant of Abraham our father [circumcision], and discloses meanings in the Law which are not according to the *Halakah*, even though a knowledge of the Law and good works are his, he has no share in the world to come.[3]

Jellinek believes that this saying is directed almost entirely against Paul, who abrogated the Sabbaths, the fixed festivals,

---

[1] See for particulars Klausner, *Yeshu*, pp. 8–38 [Eng. ed., pp. 18–47].

[2] See A. Jellinek, "Zur Geschichte der Polemik gegen das Christentum" (*Orient*, X [1847], 413); G. Kittel, "Paulus im Talmud" (*Rabbinica*, Leipzig 1920, SS. 1–16).

[3] Aboth III 11/12. The different versions are to be found in Bacher-Rabinowitz, *Aggadot-ha-Tannaim*, I, 1, 142–3, and in G. Kittel, *op. cit.*, SS. 4–16.

and circumcision, and interpreted the Torah in a perverted manner. Rabbi I. H. Weiss [4] also finds hints in the Talmud and Midrash against Paul, his associates, and his teaching. Likewise, the writer of these lines sees Paul in "that pupil" who scoffed at Rabban Gamaliel and his expositions of the material blessings of the Messianic age, claiming that the blessings would be *only spiritual*. According to his own testimony, Paul sat "at the feet of Gamaliel"; also he said, ". . . the Kingdom of God is not eating and drinking, but righteousness and peace and joy in the Holy Spirit." [5] The Talmudic writer did not wish to specify Paul by name and called him "that pupil," just as afterwards Jesus was called "that man." [6]

If the writers of Talmud and Midrash refused to mention the name of Paul specifically, while they mentioned the name of Jesus many times, and if in the hints about him there is suppressed anger against him, then it is clear that the great majority of Jews in the generation of Paul and in the generations following were strongly opposed to him and his teaching, just as plainly appears from the book of Acts and from the Epistles of Paul himself.

But it was not only the Jews who were opposed to him. Likewise the Jewish Nazarenes, especially the Ebionites, hated him exceedingly and told of him such things as the following:—Paul of Tarsus was a Greek. His father and mother were both Greeks. He went to Jerusalem. Because he ardently desired to marry a daughter of the priest (high priest?— θυγάτηρ τοῦ ἱερέως), he became a proselyte and was circumcised. But because he was not allowed to marry the girl, he became angry and wrote against circumcision, the Sabbath,

---

[4] *Dor Dor ve-Doreshav*, I (reprint 1924, first published 1871), 234-8. Incidentally, Weiss anticipated Gerhard Kittel in pointing out the saying of R. Eleazar of Modi'im as given by Jellinek, although the reference to Jellinek by Weiss (*Dor Dor ve-Doreshav*, I, 237) is confused, apparently because of a typographical error.

[5] Rom. 14:17.   [6] See above, pp. 310-1.

and the Torah.[7]—Of course, all this is mere fabrication.[8] Yet by this fabrication is proved how strong was the animosity of the Nazarenes toward Paul.

2. Can the Jews not accept anything of Paul's?

His teaching in toto absolutely not. Yet there are in his writings certain ideas and expressions which are so lofty and beautiful that no nation and no tongue can do without them. Is this not all the more true of the nation from which Paul came forth and to which he belonged all his life, the nation for which he was ready to be "anathema" and in whose sons he saw his "brethren" and "kinsmen according to the flesh"? [9]

The Hymn to Love, or as it is also called, Love's Song of Songs,[10] cannot be the principal foundation stone of Israel's faith, as has been explained above. But as long as the human heart beats, sublime and beautiful words like these shall never be forgotten:

> Though I speak with the tongues of men and of angels
>> And have not love
> I am become as clanging brass or a tinkling cymbal.[11]

Likewise the expressions "love edifieth," [12] and "love, which is the bond of perfectness." [13] There is no religion like Judaism in holding the *good heart* superior to the rest of human virtues;[14] there is none like it in considering the love that wells

[7] See Epiphanius, *Haer.* XXX 16 (ed. Dindorf, II, 109); *ibid.* XXX 25 (ed. Dindorf, II, 119). That the Ebionites considered Paul a "disbeliever in the Law" is also pointed out by Irenaeus, *Adv. Haer.* I 26 2.

[8] But see what has been written about this by H. Windisch, *Paulus und Christus* (Leipzig 1934), SS. 117–9, 133.

[9] Rom. 9:3. On the Jewish "national consciousness" and the Jewish "patriotism" of Paul, see the proper words of F. Philippi, *Paulus und das Judentum* (Leipzig 1916), SS. 10, 11.

[10] I Cor., ch. 13; given in full above, pp. 560–1.

[11] I Cor. 13:1.   [12] I Cor. 8:1.

[13] Col. 3:14.

[14] See Aboth II 9; there "a good heart" includes all the virtues, according to Rabban Johanan ben Zakkai, a contemporary of Paul.

up from the depths of the soul better than the utmost virtues, better even than knowledge. More than that, Judaism it is that taught

> For into an evil-devising soul Wisdom entereth not,
> Neither doth she dwell in a body enslaved by sin.[15]

To this great and noble conception Paul gave most eloquent and forceful expression. And Judaism cannot do without this, even if it can accept it only with certain reservations.

Likewise, Judaism can accept with certain reservations the beautiful saying, "The letter killeth, but the spirit giveth life." [16] Paul means to convey by this saying, of course, the idea often repeated in his Epistles, that the minute details of the Law bring one, by their many prohibitions, merely to the point of being under sentence of death, while the Christian spirit sets one free from these prohibitions, and thus gives us back our life.[17] To a view like this Judaism can never agree. Judaism honors also the letter, because the letter is the clothing of the spirit. But if the letter becomes petrified and petrifies the spirit, then Judaism rejects the *dead letter*. Judaism recognizes only the *living letter*—that letter which is always prepared to take on a new meaning according to the demands of the time. What is the whole Talmud with its marvellous interpretation of Torah except an adaptation of the letter to the needs of life? Thus it introduces a spirit of life into the letter and makes the letter itself a spiritual force, a living and life-giving letter and not a dead and death-dealing letter.

For example, if it is impossible for a man to exist without going from place to place on the Sabbath, the Talmud comes along and interprets *Let no man go out of his place on the seventh day* [18] thus: Let him not carry objects from a private

---

[15] Wis. Sol. 1:4.   [16] II Cor. 3:6.
[17] See H. Weinel, *Biblische Theologie des Neuen Testaments*, S. 223.
[18] Ex. 16:29.

domain to a public. And even for such carrying, when it is hard to avoid, the Talmud finds permission by means of the *'Erub*.[19] Again, according to the Law, debts are to be cancelled in the year of release; but when this tended "to close the door in the face of borrowers," Hillel the Elder came and instituted, in accordance with the *living letter*, the *prozbol*, which made it possible for both borrower and lender to negotiate loans without fear of the forfeiture of the money.[20] And there has been much more of the same sort. Indeed, the whole history of Jewish religious literature exhibits a continuous adaptation of the dead letter to the living spirit of the individual and the nation through the development of their ideas (*"Eye for eye* means pecuniary compensation")[21] and the fusing of their needs.

And if Paul says to the Christians,

. . . we are a temple of the living God; even as God said, "I will dwell among them and walk among them, and I will be their God and they shall be My people,"[22]

why of course this is a Jewish idea, as is proved by the very verses which Paul uses for support. And when Paul says ". . . know ye not that your body is a temple of the Holy Spirit which is in you?"[23]—this also is a Jewish idea, as is proved by the story mentioned above about Hillel the Elder's saying that the body is in the image of God and thus is a sacred thing.[24] And if the body is such, how much more so the soul!

Judaism will also accept from Paul the lovely saying, "Quench not the spirit."[25] Of course, Judaism does not put

---

[19] See 'Erubin 51a.

[20] See Shebi'ith (Mish. and Yer.) X 4; in Mish., Gittin IV 3, it is said: "Hillel ordained the *prozbol* as a precaution for the general good."

[21] Baba Kamma 84a.

[22] II Cor. 6:16 = Ex. 29:45; Jer. 31:33.

[23] I Cor. 6:19.

[24] See above, pp. 553-4.   [25] I Thess. 5:19.

undue emphasis on the contrast between "flesh" and "spirit."
It does not see them as two domains *absolutely* opposed to
one another, nor does it advocate *complete* repression of the
flesh for the sake of the abstract and ascetic spirit, denying,
for instance, the value of marriage, and sponsoring such things
as convents and monasteries; attitudes and practices of this
kind inevitably dissipate any opportunity for "reforming the
world," and nullify any "precaution for the general good." [26]
To meet actual widespread needs, Judaism greatly modifies
the stricter regulations, which are so difficult to observe in a
world more complex and developed than that which existed in
the early days of the Torah. But Judaism also knows how to
honor the spirit and hold it superior to the flesh; however,
Judaism seeks to uplift the flesh by means of the spirit.[27] Paul
had reference, of course, in his admonition to "quench not the
Spirit" to the "Holy Spirit" which had taken hold of groups
of believers enthusiastic to the point of madness, as is proved
by these words immediately following: "despise not pro-
phesyings." [28] We, the Jews, take the words in their ordinary
sense, knowing how to appreciate them as they are. In like
manner, we know how to appreciate all the lofty ideas and
beautiful sayings of Paul; but we cannot accept his phantasms
or the asceticism and the pessimism in his Epistles.

3. But there is something still greater and more important
than the items which I have enumerated above as being to the
credit of Paul.

There is a very curious fact in the world. It is that Judaism
has survived for thousands of years dispersed among *Christian*
and *Moslem* peoples, but has not survived—at least as a proper
national community fulfilling an important cultural function

[26] Mish., Gittin IV 2–8, and frequently elsewhere.
[27] See Ahad Ha-Am, 'Al Parashat Derakhim, III, 222–32, and above,
pp. 486–95.
[28] I Thess. 5:20.

—either in India, China, or Japan. To be sure, Jewish communities did exist in India and China for hundreds of years, but were finally assimilated by the Indians or Chinese, or else reduced to the point of a "negligible quantity," having no importance either within the total Jewish community, or in the world at large.

What is the reason for this?——

In my opinion, only in a place where the Hebrew Old Testament, in its original form and in translations, is recognized—alongside the New Testament and the Koran—as a great and influential religious book; or in a place where the great Jewish cultural influence of the "Book of Books" is a third part of the total culture alongside the influence of the cultures of Greece and Rome—only in such a place can Judaism survive as a religio-national unit, to develop its internal life and also to influence the outside world. In a place where the Old Testament is not a recognized and influential cultural force, there Judaism is not revealed as a power to itself and to others, and it steadily wastes away or else "vegetates" (*vegetiert*) without revelatory or creative power.

And Paul had this great merit, that in spite of his abrogation of the Torah, he leaned for support in almost every important religious question upon verses from that Torah. To be sure, this constitutes an internal contradiction in his teaching; but it is a fact which cannot be denied. This fact cannot be explained except by supposing that he was firmly rooted in Pharisaic Judaism in spite of himself. In the nine Pauline letters which are considered genuine, there are 84 quotations from the Old Testament, most of them following the Septuagint (according to my hypothesis, Paul incorporated them ready-made into his Greek Epistles, or the copyists of the Epistles, knowing only Greek, changed the quotations to conform to the translation familiar to them) and a few of them following the Hebrew original.[29] And a scholar who endeavors to prove that Paul is fit company even for the "Aryans" is forced to admit that "the sayings of Moses, David, Solomon, and the prophets are more familiar to him (*sind ihm näher zur Hand*) than the sayings of Jesus!" "Indeed," continues this scholar, "one is almost tempted to put it this way: the influence of Gamaliel was stronger in him than the influence of Jesus." [30] And further on this same scholar says: "Paul was well-versed in the Old Testament (*alttestamentlicher Biblizist*).[31] The Old Testament appears to have had a more enduring and stronger influence upon him than the tradition of Jesus." [32] At any rate, explains this Christian scholar, a Christian community which rejects the Old Testament will fail to understand the most and the best of Paul's Epistles, and will be forced to remove them from its Canon.[33] To this it may be added, that Paul interpreted Scripture like a thorough Pharisee—something which incensed so much the "spiritual anti-Semite," Paul de Lagarde.[34] This is what I have called "Talmudic casuistry for an anti-Talmudic purpose." [35]

Of course, there is a strong contradiction between advocating nullification of the Torah, and leaning for support on the

[29] On all this see the detailed and correct treatment of A. F. Puuko, *Paulus und das Judentum*, pp. 52–63; A. Harnack, "Das Alte Testament in den paulinischen Briefen," *etc.* (*Sitzungsberichte der Berliner Akademie der Wissenschaften*, 1928); O. Michel, *Paulus und seine Bibel*, 1929 (this book I could not obtain). Hans Windisch (*Paulus und das Judentum*, SS. 57–76) endeavors to prove, in order to make Paul acceptable to those holding the racial doctrine, that Paul did not make extensive use of Old Testament quotations in *all* the Epistles. This fact may be granted; for *the content* of the Epistles did not always require Scriptural quotations, nor did the addressees of the Epistles always require such quotations by way of proof [some addressees could be convinced without them]; hence there is not in this fact any special intent on the part of Paul, as Windisch himself confesses (*ibid.*, pp. 61, 63, 65, 69, 70, 72, 75).

[30] See Windisch, *op. cit.*, S. 66.

[31] The two words are emphasized by the author himself.

[32] See Windisch, *op. cit.*, S. 72.   [33] *Ibid.*, S. 75.

[34] See Paul de Lagarde, *Deutsche Schriften* (Göttingen 1885), SS. 56–7.

[35] See Klausner, *Historia*, IV, 100.

Torah even to prove that it itself should be set aside. But the
fact remains that Paul, the founder of Christianity as a religion and as a church, based all his new teaching upon the
"Old" Testament. This is one of the fundamental reasons
why the Church Fathers, with all the hate which most of them
had for Jews and Judaism, were *forced* to include the Old
Testament in the Christian Canon, to endow it with the
sacredness of Holy Scripture, and to place it on an equal footing with the writings of the New Testament. This fact is
responsible for the powerful influence of Jewish culture upon
what is called "Christian civilization," although it would be
more correct to call it European-Oriental [or European-Near
Eastern] civilization, since it is based upon Judaism no less
than upon the cultures of Greece and Rome. Hence the feeling of Jews living among Christians (and the weaker, but still
strong feeling of Jews living among Moslems), that the culture
of the dominant people is not something altogether foreign to
them, like the cultures of India, China, and Japan, for example,
and that their share in this culture is large, amounting to a third
part, and more than a third, of the cultural accomplishments
of those countries where dwell the Jews. This inward feeling,
which may not come to the point of open recognition, has
given the Jews a creative power within their own group and
a power to influence the Gentiles among whom they have
been in exile. If most of these Gentiles had not accepted the
Old Testament, this creativity and this influence would not
have been possible even to an imperfect degree (since exile is
naturally an imperfect state!) in the midst of the tribulations,
afflictions, persecutions, and humiliations of an exile lasting
two thousand years.

This is the great merit of Paul for Judaism.

Perhaps he did not intend to do this; but the "Pharisee, a son
of Pharisees," the disciple of Rabban Gamaliel, was so filled
and saturated with the Written Law, and to a certain extent
with the Oral Law (interpretation of the Scriptures) also,

that it was impossible for him *not* to base his teaching on the Holy Scriptures of his people, against whom Paul became angry and spoke harsh words, yet from whom he never to his last days separated himself completely.

4. My deepest conviction is this: Judaism will never become reconciled with Christianity (in the sense of spiritual [religious and intellectual] compromise), nor will it be assimilated by Christianity; for Judaism and Christianity are not only two different religions, but they are also *two different world-views*. Judaism will never allow itself to reach even in theory the ethical extremeness characteristic of Christianity; this extremeness has no place in the world of reality, and therefore is likely in actual fact to be converted into its direct opposite—into brutality such as has been seen in the Middle Ages and in our own time in any number of "Christian" countries. Judaism could say, "What is hateful to you, do not to your neighbor: that is the whole Torah";[36] but it could also say, "Great is vengeance, which is placed between two references to the Divine Name" (Psa. 94:1 says literally, "*God* of vengeance, the *Lord*").[37] It could receive into the Holy Scriptures both the book of Jonah with its love of the enemy, and the book of Esther with its hate of the enemy. This fact comes from two deep causes. *First*, Judaism knows that the nature of man will always be human nature and not angel nature. *Second*, the God of Israel is *the God of history;* and in history there is *justice*. Evil consequences are *inevitably* the recompense of evil deeds:

> Thine own wickedness shall correct thee,
> And thy backsliding shall reprove thee.[38]

Judaism is a more practical faith than Christianity, it is more capable of realization in actual life; that is why it has such great vitality in spite of the severe difficulties attendant upon

[36] Shab. 31a.   [37] Ber. 33a.   [38] Jer. 2:19.

the observance of its numerous and strict ceremonial laws, and in spite of persecutions and humiliations the like of which no other nation or tongue has ever suffered. Therefore, it is not to be supposed that Judaism could accept the teaching of Paul, with its phantasms and mysteries, and with its asceticism and abandonment of life, the results of its loathing of the "flesh" and its deep pessimism.

But we, the Jews, hope and expect that the time shall come when the prayer which we pray three times daily—the *'Alenu* prayer—shall be realized, and the Kingdom of Heaven in the Jewish sense of ethical monotheism shall be established in the world, and the politico-spiritual Messianic ideal of Israel shall also be realized in all its fulness, and the Jewish people shall dwell in their historic national land, and shall speak their historic national tongue, and shall continue to develop their historic national culture in the spirit of their prophets and their sages. Then, of course, much shall be changed in the ceremonial laws of Judaism, although they shall not be altogether abolished, since they serve to protect the existence of the nation. And when in those days the mystical and un-Jewish quality of important parts of Paul's teaching shall be done away with, and Judaism in the form of ethico-prophetic monotheism shall spread over all the world—then shall this refined Judaism know how to appreciate the great merit of Paul: that through him the pagan world accepted, along with many strange and unnatural superstitions, the Jewish Bible as the foundation and basis of a religion for the Gentiles. In this sense—and only in this great and deep sense—was Paul also what Maimonides [39] so beautifully called Jesus:

A preparer of the way for the King-Messiah.

Jerusalem-Talpioth
3rd of Shebat, 5699
(January 23, 1939).

[39] R. Mosheh ben Maimon, *Mishneh Torah* (*Yad ha-Hazakah*), Hilkhot-Melakhim XIV 4, according to the old editions. For the full quotation, see Klausner, *Yeshu* (4th Heb. ed. only), p. 462, n. 2.

Index

[This index is a combination and condensation of the author's two indexes, one an index of names and subjects in Hebrew, and the other an index of names in Latin characters. Tr.]